USING SAP R/3 FI

USING SAP R/3 FI

BEYOND BUSINESS PROCESS REENGINEERING

BEN W. ROCKEFELLER

John Wiley & Sons, Inc.

NEW YORK • CHICHESTER • WEINHEIM • BRISBANE • SINGAPORE • TORONTO

Library of Congress Cataloging in Publication Data:
Rockefeller, Ben W.
   Using SAP R/3 FI : beyond business process reengineering /
Ben W. Rockefeller.
     p.   cm.
   Includes index.
   ISBN 0-471-17996-5 (cloth : alk. paper)
   1. SAP R/3. 2. Client-server computing. 3. Accounting—Computer
programs. 4. Business logistics—Computer programs. 5. Personnel
management—Computer programs. I. Title.
HF5548.4.R2R63   1997
658′.05571376—dc21   97-4236

Printed in the United States of America

10 9 8 7 6 5 4 3 2 1

To Anne-Marie, who encouraged me to finish the manuscript;
to my father, who taught me to see things as they are
and not the way I wished they were;
and to my mother, who taught me to
write in plain English.

Preface

This book is intended for you, the novice user, to reduce your learning time. With a clear table of contents, sample screens, and a plain English style, this book lets you begin to learn the SAP R/3 FI financial accounting module.

You are a financial manager, accountant, or bookkeeper, or even a marketing or IT person. You are trying to learn about SAP, the company and its software products. Your company may be implementing or even thinking of implementing SAP R/3 client-server software. You can use this book as a template or white paper to learn the basic functions of FI, the R/3 module for financial accounting. The book assumes that you have a basic knowledge of double-entry bookkeeping (as well as properly licensed software that has been correctly installed and configured). Designed for international companies, R/3 is a complex, but integrated, client-server business management package. R/3 contains various modules for accounting, logistics, and human resources. Using FI, you can keep a general ledger, accounts receivable, and accounts payable, and do financial reporting.

Using this book, you can begin to unravel the complexities of FI. If you or your company are thinking of implementing SAP R/3, it is advisable to start with FI. The general ledger is the heart of any accounting system, and almost all the other modules record transaction data in general ledger accounts in FI. Based on a clear functional outline, sample screens, and simple, step-by-step instructions, this book can help you get the most out of FI. The highlights of integration of FI with SD (order entry, shipping, and invoicing) and MM (purchasing, receiving, and inventory control) are also covered. With brief descriptions of basic concepts, actual menu sequences, and sample screens to guide you, the book describes the most widely used functions in plain English.

Note that the sample screens in this book will differ from the actual screens on your system, depending on which version you are using and how your system is configured. Whatever system you are using and however your system is configured, you can use this book to reduce your learning time. The book includes details about using FI for international business, such as translating the chart of accounts, keeping accounts in foreign currency, entering transactions in foreign currency, and revaluing accounts and open items in different currencies. There are no country-specific features in this book. Country-specific requirements and features obviously depend on which countries you are using the program in.

The primary country-specific requirements for FI have to do with the following:

- Required (or suppressed) master data about customers and vendors
- Transaction taxes, such as sales tax (United States), value added tax (Europe), and withholding tax
- Payment methods, such as checks, bank transfers, and bills of exchange
- Specific required reports, such as a balance sheet, profit and loss statement, or transaction tax reporting (sales tax or VAT)
- Other requirements, such as EEO reporting of vendors, and so on

This book is intended for beginners everywhere who would like to learn the most common functions of FI. For readers who are thinking of implementing R/3, an overview of a proven project methodology is also included. Last but not least, the book contains a detailed index.

I wrote this book because I noticed that some manuals, while being well-intended, were often written from a technical, instead of a practical business point of view. I thought that the manuals could be more clearly organized and written—in plain English, with a clear outline and a step-by-step approach, including menu sequences and sample screens.

In this book, for readability, text that appears on the screen is printed with the following font—menus. data entry fields. report headings. program messages. and on-line help. Text that you enter is printed in bold, such as names of programs - **RFBILA00** (the program that prepares a balance sheet). Words that represent keys on a keyboard have angle brackets around them, for example, <enter>.

If you have any questions or wish to discuss objective consulting, project management services, or on-site training services adapted to your company, I can be reached via e-mail at: BenRockefeller@compuserve.com.

Contents

CHAPTER 1

Overview

R/3 is a comprehensive business software package designed to run on various client-server platforms. R/3 includes a series of programs with various functions for accounting, logistics, and personnel management. R/3 was ported from a mainframe package (R/2) to client-server platforms and released in 1992. For the user, R/3 differs from R/2 primarily in the following ways:

- It runs on UNIX and Windows NT.
- It requires a relational database, such as Informix or SQL Server.
- It includes a graphical user interface.

Both R/2 and R/3 are based on a table-driven design. They are complex packages. R/3 has the "feel" of having an object-oriented design. Flexibility implies complexity.

This book is divided into five chapters:

1. Overview
2. Using General Ledger
3. Accounts Receivable
4. Accounts Payable
5. Basics of System Administration

FUNCTIONALITY

R/3 is divided into the following groups of modules:

- Accounting
- Logistics
- Personnel

Modules

Specifically, R/3 includes the following modules and primary functions:

Module	Group	Main Functional Areas
FI	Financial/ Accounting	General ledger, accounts receivable, accounts payable, financial reporting, cash management, legal consolidation
SD	Logistics	Order entry, picking/packing/shipping (pick and pack lists), invoicing, inquiries, quotes, sales reporting
MM	Logistics	Purchasing, invoice verification, inventory management, warehouse management
WM	Logistics	Warehouse management, detailed inventory storage, pick lists, block units of stock, such as palettes
CO	Cost Accounting	Cost accounting and internal reporting by cost center, internal order, project, profit center, or other unit
AM	Asset Management	Fixed assets register, depreciation, and reporting
PP	Logistics	MRP; production (most of all discrete) orders, including multilevel bills of materials, work centers, and routing instructions on the factory floor; batch management and process production in 3.0
HR	Personnel	Employee master data, training records, gross/net calculation, payroll, planning, and reporting

SAP enhances these modules and also develops other modules. They also supply certain industry-specific programs (for vertical markets), such as programs for the oil industry, publishers, hospitals, and banks. Contact SAP for details about other modules and vertical market applications.

In addition, R/3 includes a software development system (Development Workbench). This development system includes:

- The ABAP/4 programming language
- An integrated, active data dictionary (to create and format files, records, and fields)
- An integrated screen painter (to create data entry screens with processing logic)
- A menu painter (to create Windows menus with action bars and pull-down menus)

ABAP/4 is an SAP-proprietary, fourth-generation programming language with syntax that vaguely resembles Pascal. You or your programmers can use the ABAP language to develop data interface programs to transfer your data to or from your existing systems and R/3. You can also use ABAP, and possibly the other programming tools, to develop custom reports and even to modify the functions supplied by SAP. All R/3 application modules are developed completely with ABAP. SAP supplies the ABAP source code to these applications. Although it is tempting and comparatively easy to modify this code, beware of modifying the supplied programs. If you modify the source code, you are unlikely to obtain technical support from SAP, since they can never know exactly what you modified and how it altered their code. Furthermore, even if your modifications were clearly and completely documented, which almost never happens, you cannot be sure that you can apply these same modifications to the next release of the software from SAP. In other words, modifications greatly complicate and sometimes prevent upgrading to the next version of the software.

Integration

From a business perspective, the R/3 modules are well integrated. However, the chart of accounts and the main master files are common to all necessary modules. The primary points of integration (shared master data) are as follows:

Shared Master Data	Modules
G/L Accounts	FI/SD/MM/PP/CO/AM/HR
Customer Master Records	FI/SD
Vendor Master Records	FI/MM/PP

Material Master Records   SD/MM/PP/WM
(Products)

This book is concerned with using FI. It also covers briefly the integration of FI with the other modules. For example, a general ledger account (G/L account) in FI is called a cost element in CO. Most of all, FI is designed for legally required external reporting, such as a financial statement (balance sheet and P&L), VAT, and required transaction journals. Sales tax calculation, processing, and reporting, which is required in the United States only, is done with third-party add-on software from either Vertex or AVP.

CO is designed for internal reporting by cost center (department), profit center, or market segment.

Customer master records are common to FI and SD. These records contain screens that you usually maintain in the accounts receivable department and screens that you usually maintain in the order processing, customer service, warehouse, or logistics department. You can have multiple ship-to addresses for one bill-to address. In this way, a central, common customer database is available to all departments. Using SD, you update G/L accounts for all customer shipments and returns in real time. How you maintain customer master records depends on your organization.

Similarly, vendor master records are common to FI and MM. These records contain screens that you usually maintain in the accounts payable department and screens that you usually maintain in the purchasing, receiving, warehouse, or logistics department. In this way, you can keep a central, common vendor database available to all departments. How you maintain vendor master records depends on your organization.

You can use MM to manage both quantities and values of inventory at the same time. In other words, you can use MM to keep track of the count of products in stock, as well as the value of the products in stock. Using MM, you update G/L account balances of all stock movements in real time. How you keep material master records depends on how you organize, or possibly reorganize, your company and on how you keep your physical inventory.

INTERNATIONAL APPLICATION

R/3 was originally developed to test inexpensively the R/2 functionality on personal computers. This design includes menus, screens, reports, error messages, and on-line help in multiple languages, functions to process transactions and accounts in multiple currencies, and functions and reports that comply with accounting regulations (legal requirements) anywhere that SAP does business. If the regulations change, then SAP usually delivers any legally required new or changed report or function promptly. (Call SAP for details.)

You can enter and display numbers and dates according to various local formats, which each user can set and reset. See the section "Setting User Defaults."

Multilingual

If you have licensed and installed the proper language tapes, you can log in in various languages. You then see the menus, data entry screens, error messages, report parameters, report headings, and on-line help in your login language. You can even be logged in twice—in two languages at the same time. This could be useful for technical support, if you have a multilingual company and wish to have a common language for technical support.

For financial reporting in multiple languages, you can translate your chart of accounts and the text of your financial statement without licensing the language tape for the other language.

Depending on the version, module, and language of R/3 being used, the translation is not complete. Since the program was developed in German, missing translations are usually filled in with the German text. Also, the SAP terminology in English does not always correspond to standard accounting terminology in English. As much as practical, this book defines an SAP term the first time that it is used, but uses standard accounting terms.

Multicurrency

Since R/3 is object-oriented software, you can specify the currency of the following business objects in FI:

- Client (for consolidated financial statements in the head office functional currency)
- Group (for financial reporting of related company codes)
- Company code (for financial reporting, usually by a legal entity)
- General ledger account (e.g., a bank account or loan)
- Transaction (e.g., an invoice or a payment)

Note that the currency is not a field in a customer record, nor in a vendor record. One and the same customer could purchase from you in two or more different currencies. FI includes programs to revalue open items, such as invoices posted in foreign currency, and general ledger accounts, such as bank accounts, denominated in foreign currency.

Specifically, you can keep a global chart of accounts, while at the same time permit each local company to keep a legally required chart of accounts. If you have central data storage capacity, possibly requiring a wide-area network, you could also keep a global customer database, for example for order entry, shipping, invoicing, and collection.

Multicompany

You can keep the accounts for multiple companies (and inventory in multiple plants) on the same system. If you record transactions for multiple companies, you should, if possible, use the same machine and the same login client for all companies. In this way, you can readily consolidate the companies later without sending tapes or files to load. A consolidated financial statement eliminates intercompany receivables, intercompany payables, intercompany revenues, intercompany expenses, profits on intercompany transfers of inventory, profits on intercompany transfers of fixed assets, and the investment of the head office in the equity of the subsidiary. You can use either the North American (step-by-step) or the European (simultaneous) method of consolidation.

CLIENT–SERVER-DATA DESIGN

R/3 is commercial application software. It requires an operating system and a database. R/3 runs on popular commercial operating systems, such as various versions of UNIX and Windows NT, and various databases, such as Informix, SQL Server, and Adabas for client-server machines. (Call SAP for the latest details.) After you install the operating system and the database, R/3 runs in three abstract layers:

- Presentation
- Application
- Data

When R/3 is installed, you can have each of these layers run on the same machine, or on a separate machine, or you can combine two layers on one machine. TCP/IP software joins the layers together. Exhibit 1.1 shows the three-level design of R/3. You can run these three separate layers on one and the same machine, on two machines, or on three separate machines. TCP/IP joins the layers together. The RAM and disk requirements are only approxi-

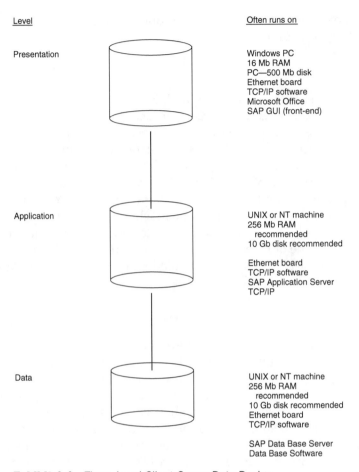

Level

Presentation

Application

Data

Often runs on

Windows PC
16 Mb RAM
PC—500 Mb disk
Ethernet board
TCP/IP software
Microsoft Office
SAP GUI (front-end)

UNIX or NT machine
256 Mb RAM
  recommended
10 Gb disk recommended

Ethernet board
TCP/IP software
SAP Application Server
TCP/IP

UNIX or NT machine
256 Mb RAM
  recommended
10 Gb disk recommended
Ethernet board
TCP/IP software

SAP Data Base Server
Data Base Software

Exhibit 1.1   Three-Level Client-Server-Data Design

mate. Your exact requirements depend on which database you use and on the volume of your transaction data. (Call SAP for details.)

Presentation (GUI)

The presentation layer is also called SAP GUI (for SAP graphical user interface). This layer runs on top of installed graphical user interface, such as various versions of Windows. It can also run on graphical user front-ends of workstations. This layer provides you with a login screen, the menu bars, and the pull-down menus required to use the program interface. Using the presentation layer, you enter data screen-by-screen. After you enter data in a screen, you press <Enter>. R/3 then sends your data to the application layer for validation. Of course, you can have more than one PC running the presentation layer, depending on your license agreement.

Application (R/3)

The application layer is the "engine" of R/3. For example, it contains the program logic that validates the data entry screens. This layer also contains the programs to process your business transactions, such as invoices and payments, and to produce your reports, such as balance sheets and profit and loss statements. When you log in, the application layer receives your login ID and password. It reads the file of valid login IDs and passwords, validates your login ID and password, and then displays a startup menu. You can run the application and the data layer on the same machine, particularly if your load and number of users is low to begin with (in a test system). Alternatively, you can logically attach one or more application servers to one and the same database server. An identical copy of the data dictionary is kept on every application server attached to the same database server.

Data (RDBMS)

The data layer contains the links to whichever of the required SAP-compatible databases that you use. This layer records the data in SAP tables, such as a table of valid login IDs and passwords. These SAP tables are either transparent (in the same format) to the database or compressed (in an SAP-proprietary format). This layer also retrieves the data when you make an inquiry or run a report. In effect, this layer simply reads and writes data in your database. Note that you can mix UNIX and NT systems in the same installation. For example, you could run the application server on an NT machine and the database server on a UNIX machine. However, to mix systems, words (data) must be consistently stored in either little-endian or big-endian format on all machines.

R/3 Application Processes

An R/3 process corresponds to an operating system process. A process is a program running in memory. The three-layer design always includes at least the following processes:

- Dialog (for on-line data entry and validation of screens)
- Update (to record data in tables)
- Enqueue (for record-locking)
- Batch (for batch input and batch jobs)
- Spool (for print jobs)

Some other processes, for internal and external communications, may also be running at the same time. Depending on your system load, you can have more than one of each of these processes running at the same time. For example, depending on your license and the number of active users, you can have several dialog processes, several update processes, and several batch processes running at the same time. If you have many users, you can balance the load by adding one or more machines with application servers (dialog processes). You can then assign each machine to a specific set of users, for example by site or location. For example, in a global company, you could assign each application server machine to a different region or to a different module.

REQUIREMENTS FOR INSTALLATION

Hardware

How much hardware you require depends on the number of active users, which applications you actually use, the load on the system by your data interfaces to other applications, the load on your system by any custom programs you may have developed, and what your actual volume of data is. (See your hardware manufacturer or SAP for details.) Although you might require more and could make do with less, in general, you require at least the following hardware to run R/3 (in a small test system on one machine):

- 200 MHz CPU, at very least
- 256 Mb RAM recommended
- 20 Gb disk recommended
- Tape drive for backup
- Ethernet or other network cards on all machines
- PCs with at least 8 Mb RAM, with 16 Mb RAM recommended, and at least 200 Mb disk for each user

Make sure that the equipment is properly installed and configured.

Software

See your hardware manufacturer, database supplier, and SAP for the latest details of compatible versions required. You require the following software to run R/3:

- An operating system, such as an SAP-approved version of UNIX or Windows NT

- TCP/IP software on all machines
- An SAP-approved database
- Windows on all PCs

Make sure that you order compatible versions of the operating system, database, and R/3. Also make sure that the operating system, TCP/IP, database, and front-end software, such as Windows, are properly installed and configured.

Network

R/3 requires a TCP/IP local area network (LAN). You can also run R/3 in a transcontinental configuration over a wide area network (WAN) with one or more data lines capable of transmitting IP (Internet protocol) packets at least 64 kbps. For example, you could run the application layer and the database layer on one continent, such as North America, while you run the presentation layer, such as Windows PCs, on another continent, such as Europe. Alternatively, you could dial in to an application layer with a 14.4 kbps modem and run R/3 remotely. Due to the volume of data transferred, the application layer and the database layer should always run on the same LAN. The reverse configuration is, of course, also possible. If the network ran reliably and without congestion, then it would appear to your users that they have a local application with local printing. Depending on the number of active users, your pattern of usage, and volume of data, you may require more data transmission capacity (bandwidth) than 64k. Note that Windows NT requires even more bandwidth than UNIX.

Installing R/3

Contact SAP for details. To protect their copyright on the software, SAP tends to control installations carefully and who is allowed to install the software.

STARTING TO USE R/3

Implementing SAP

The keys to finishing your SAP R/3 implementation project are: clear goals, clear roles, and training (with a train-the-trainer approach). In most cases, FI is implemented first or in parallel with the other modules, such as CO (cost accounting), AM (fixed assets), MM (purchasing), and SD (order entry and invoicing). Each software implementation project is different, depending on your company's goals and existing systems. Nevertheless, the following is a proven step-by-step method to set up and start to use SAP R/3:

1. *Analyze your current systems.* Why are you dissatisfied with your current systems? If you are not dissatisfied, why are you thinking of changing one or more of your current systems? What are the *interfaces* (transfer of data between systems) in your current systems? What *financial reports* do you currently prepare regularly? How many companies do you account for? If you do international financial reporting, how do your current systems handle this? What problems do you have with your current accounting system? How could it be improved? Have your organization, markets, or applicable regulations changed since the current system was installed? How? Often, at this stage, it is advisable to receive *training* in SAP R/3 and to compare the functions in your current systems with the functions in R/3. Often, there is a gap. During the project, you can usually resolve most of this gap, either by developing an interface to a current system, by developing a custom report with the ABAP/4 programming language included with R/3, or possibly by modifying your procedures. Sometimes, this stage is called the "As-Is Analysis."

2. *Analyze your business requirements and strategy.* Why are you thinking of changing your system? What is your *business strategy*? What is your *international strategy*? How can your financial reporting support these strategies? What are your legal and internal *financial reporting requirements*? What are your most frequent transactions, besides customer invoices, payments from customers, vendor invoices, and payments to vendors? *How will your organization, markets, or applicable regulations likely change in the future?* At the end of this stage, define clearly any gaps there are between your business requirements and the functionality of the package. Be aware that you have licensed a package and not a piece of custom software that was developed specifically for your company. Develop a plan to resolve any gaps between required functions in your current systems and available functions in SAP. Usually, you can resolve these gaps by developing an interface program or by developing a custom report with the ABAP/4 programming language. As a last resort, you can modify the package, since SAP supplies all ABAP/4 source code with your license. However, beware of modifying the package to add fields or functions. If you modify the source code, then these modifications can be difficult or impossible to repeat when you upgrade the software to the next version. If these gaps are too wide, then stop the project and do not implement the package. Sometimes this stage is called the "To-Be Analysis." It is also known as a feasibility study.

3. Define and configure your *financial organization*—groups (one or more company codes), credit control areas (one or more company codes), company codes (usually legal entities or units of organization that prepare an

independent balance sheet and profit and loss statement), and business areas (any units that prepare an internal balance sheet and profit and loss statement across company codes). If you are setting up SD, define and configure your *sales organization*—sales organizations (usually regional), distribution channels (for example, wholesale, retail, and direct), and divisions (usually by type of product or service). If you are setting up MM, define and configure your purchasing and stockkeeping organization—*plants* (storage or production facilities), storage locations (for example, bonded and non-bonded sections of a warehouse), and purchasing organizations (groups of buyers).

4. Configure your *master data*. In this stage, you determine which fields are required, optional, or suppressed for each account group for each type of master record (general ledger account, customer, or vendor). You also determine how these master records are to be numbered, when they are entered later. Test the entry of all required types of master records.

5. Configure your *transaction data*. In this stage, you determine what types of journals you keep (by the so-called document type) and how the transactions in each journal are to be numbered. Test the entry of all required types of transactions, except payments to vendors.

6. Design, develop, and test any *data interfaces* (programs required to transfer data from existing systems to SAP, and possibly from SAP to your existing systems). This is often the most complicated and time-consuming step in the whole project, since it requires in-depth knowledge of the data (file and record) formats in your current systems, as well as the cooperation of your technical people. The most frequent interfaces to be developed have to do with transferring customer master data, vendor master data, and customer invoices from whatever system you use to enter orders and print invoices. If you will use SD (the SAP module for order entry, shipping, and invoicing), then you can print invoices and post them to FI without an interface. Otherwise, you usually require some programs to transfer your customer invoice data and post it by batch input into FI. SAP can read in customer, vendor, and invoice data from any external system, but you first have to convert your data to the SAP batch input format. To finish your project quickly, it is advisable to develop only the minimal number of interfaces necessary to integrate the new system with your current systems.

7. Design, develop, and test any printed *forms* to be printed by the system, such as checks to vendors, dunning letters to customers, account statements to customers, purchase orders to vendors (MM Purchasing), and invoices to customers (SD). This stage includes setting up and testing the automatic payment program to pay vendors (and employee travel

expenses, if configured properly) based on due dates of invoices. It also includes setting up and testing the dunning program to prepare dunning letters to customers based on overdue invoices.

8. Review the requirements for financial *reporting*. Test the reports supplied with the package based on test data that you enter. Most of all, the supplied reports were intended to meet legal reporting requirements. It is not advisable to develop nor to modify these supplied reports, since it can be difficult or impossible to repeat any modifications, when you upgrade to the next release of the package.

9. *Test* the configuration, data entry, and reporting thoroughly. It is advisable to run the new system in parallel to your current systems for at least one month, if your people will accept this extra workload.

10. *Train your users* thoroughly. Before you train your users, make sure that the trainer is trained.

11. *Document* your specific procedures for entering data and preparing reports. Also document your configuration, so you can repeat it later, if necessary. It is also advisable to document any custom programs that you have developed, so that you and your programmers understand what the purpose of the program is and how to maintain it. Also, document any custom procedures that you have, such as end-of-month closing procedures.

12. *Load your data* and start the new system.

These projects can take 3–12 months, depending on the complexity of your current systems, your requirements, and the interfaces.

Logging in for the First Time

Logging in for the first time can be a trying experience. To simplify your first login, do as follows:

1. Make sure your machine has enough RAM to run the SAP GUI and any other applications that you want to run at the same time. If not, then exit all other applications before you start to log in to R/3.

2. Make sure that the SAP GUI is properly installed for your PC or workstation and your network.

3. Immediately after the SAP GUI is installed, restart your PC and look for the R/3 icon under Windows. (See Exhibit 1.2.)

4. Double-click on this icon to start to log in to R/3. (See Exhibit 1.3 for the login screen.)

Exhibit 1.2
R/3 Icon under Windows

5. In the Client field, enter the client that you are working in. If you are not
    sure what client you are working in, ask your system administrator. If
    you are the system administrator, ask the person who installed R/3
    server what clients are installed. Client 000 is the software delivered by
    SAP. Client 001 is a copy of client 000 for testing. You should use other
    clients for your development, test, and productive systems. If you mod-
    ify any ABAP programs, you should do this on a separate machine with
    a copy of R/3, subject to the terms of your license. Otherwise, if there are
    mistakes in your modifications, these mistakes could disrupt your pro-
    ductive system. The same ABAP programs run in all clients on the same
    machine. Financially, a client is used to consolidate financial statements.
    After you enter the client, press <Tab> to go to the User field.

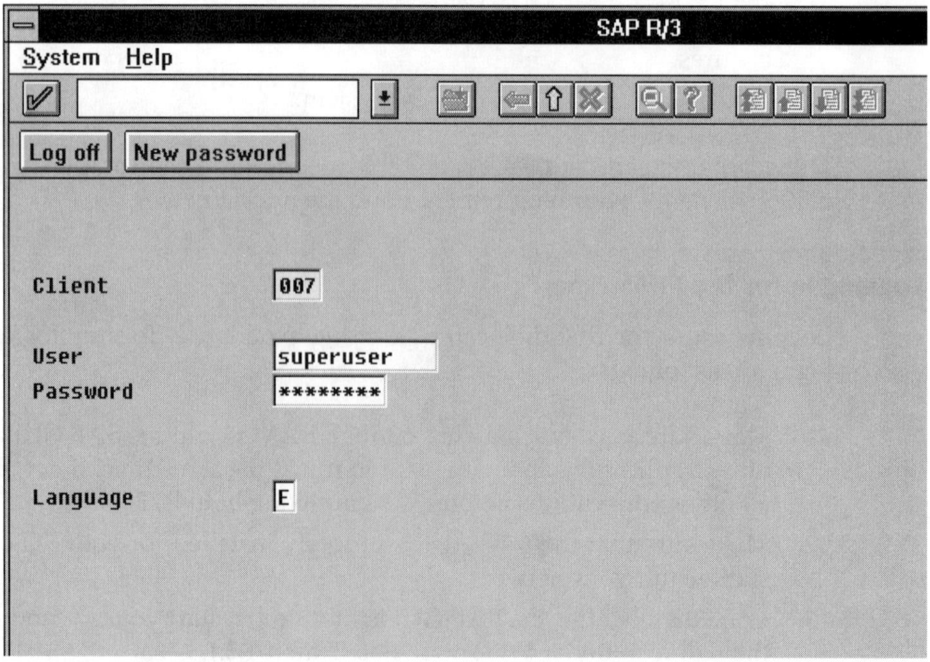

	SAP R/3
System Help	

Log off	New password

Client   007

User   superuser
Password   ********

Language   E

Exhibit 1.3 Login Screen

6. In the User field, enter the **SAP login ID** that your system administrator has assigned to you. This may be the same or it may be different from any login ID that you have in either your operating system or LAN. Technically, the system is simpler to administer if the login IDs and passwords in the application and in the operating system are the same. If you are not sure what your SAP login ID is, ask your system administrator. Enter your login ID letter-for-letter, as your system administrator gave it to you. After you enter your SAP login ID, press <Tab> to go to the Password field.

7. In the Password field, enter the **SAP password** that your system administrator has assigned to you. Similar to your SAP login ID, your SAP password may be the same or it may be different from any login ID that you have in either your operating system or LAN. If you are not sure what your SAP login ID is, ask your system administrator. Enter your password letter-for-letter, as your system administrator gave it to you. After you enter your SAP password, press <Tab> to go to the Language field.

8. In the Language field, enter the one-character code for your **login language.** In any one login session, you can only be logged in in one language. However, depending on the amount of available RAM on your PC, you can be logged in with two or more sessions at the same time— with each login session in a different language. If the translation is complete, you see all menus, data entry screens, text in reports, error messages, and on-line help in your login language. If the translation is not complete, then you see the incomplete text in either German or English. German is usually available as a login language, no matter what language tapes you have licensed and installed. The following languages with their one-character codes are available from SAP, with the latest list also available from SAP:

Language	*Language Code*
English	E
Danish	K
Dutch	N
French	F
German	D
Italian	I
Norwegian	O
Spanish	S
Swedish	V

It is technically possible to combine all of the preceding languages on the same machine. Note that R/3 is also available in other languages, such as Slavic languages and languages that require a 16-bit code to represent each character, such as Chinese, Korean, and Japanese. However, there are sometimes technical limitations on combining a Slavic or Asian language with another language on the same machine. Installing these other, more exotic, languages also tends to be specific to the equipment manufacturer, since there are not yet standard code pages for all languages. (Contact SAP and your equipment manufacturer for the latest details.) In a global installation, you can simplify the internal technical support if you choose a common language among all of your sites. In this way, all of your people are using common terminology, and there is less of a gap in communications due to the use of different terms for the same object. Nevertheless, any legally required reports, such as financial statements, are usually required in the local language.

After you enter the one-character code for the language, press <Enter>.

9. The very first time you log in, you have to re-enter your password or enter another password (see Exhibit 1.4). In this way, if you forget your password, your system administrator could reset your password to a temporary password, such as "INITPASS" or "PASSWORD," that everyone knew. The very first time that you log in with a reset password, you could log in with **INITPASS** or PASSWORD, but then immediately set your password to a password that only you know. In the New password field, enter your new password. Press <Tab> (not <Enter>) to go to the next field. In the Repeat password field, enter the new password again. Then press <Enter>.

10. If all goes well, you will see the default startup screen with the SAP R/3 main menu (see Exhibit 1.5).

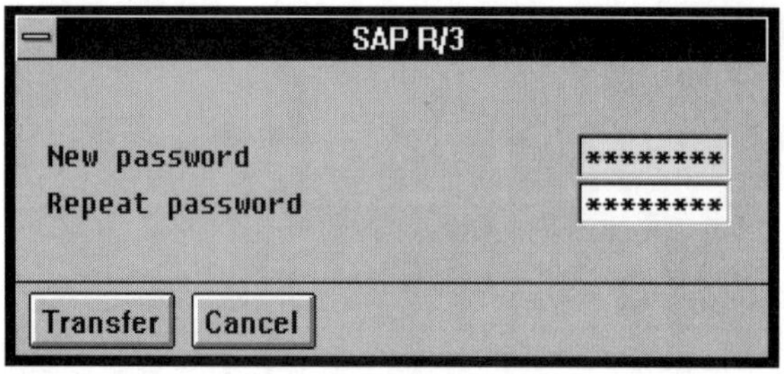

Exhibit 1.4   First Time Login

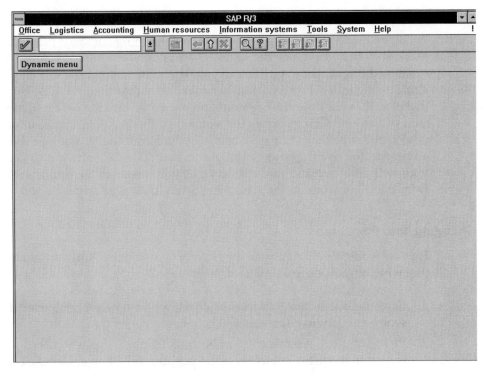

Exhibit 1.5   SAP R/3 Main Menu

Entering Data in R/3 Screens

When you enter data in R/3 screens, to do the following tasks, you have to use the following keys:

To	Use
To	*Use*
Go to the next field in a screen	\<Tab\>
Enter a screen (for validation)	\<Enter\> or ✔
Get on-line help about a field	\<F1\> or ?
Display a list of valid entries	\<F4\> or 🔍

Note that these keys are common to all modules.

If You Cannot Log In

Try again. Make sure you have a valid SAP login ID and SAP password. Also make sure that you enter the login ID and password letter-for-letter, as your system administrator gave them to you. If you still cannot log in, call your system administrator. Have him or her make sure that the SAP GUI is properly installed for your operating system and network. Also make sure that the version of the SAP GUI matches the version of the installed application server. Also make sure that your network is up and running. If you are the system administrator, use the ping command in your TCP/IP software to verify that your network is up and running and that you can reach the application server from the PC or workstation where the SAP GUI is properly installed.

Changing Your Password

It is advisable to change your password occasionally. You can change your password at most once a day. To do this:

1. Double-click on the R/3 icon in Windows. Enter the client, user ID, password, and language as usual.
2. Press the New password pushbutton. To press a pushbutton, use your mouse to move the cursor over the pushbutton. Then click once on the left button of your mouse.
3. In the New password field, enter your new password. (See Exhibit 1.4.) Press the <Tab> key (not the <Enter> key). In the Repeat password field, enter the new password again. Then press <Enter>.

You then see the main menu or your startup menu.

Understanding R/3 Screens

R/3 screens are complicated at first glance. However, if you look at them by their parts, they are comprehensible. For example, look carefully at the R/3 main menu in Exhibit 1.5.

The first line contains the "title bar." (See Exhibit 1.6.)
The second line contains the "menu bar." (See Exhibit 1.7.)
The third line contains the "toolbar" with the R/3 icons. (See Exhibit 1.8.)

SAP R/3

Exhibit 1.6 Title Bar

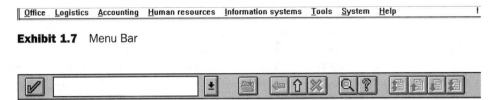

Exhibit 1.7 Menu Bar

Exhibit 1.8 Toolbar

The fourth line contains the "function key bar" with pushbuttons that depend on the function you are using.

The last line on the screen, which is not printed here since it depends completely on your installation, contains the "status bar" with the database instance (the specific database running with a certain startup), the name of the application server, data entry mode (OVR for overtype or INS for insert), and local time.

Understanding R/3 Icons and Meanings

The toolbar contains the SAP icons. (See Exhibit 1.8.) Note that not all icons are available in all screens and functions. The icons that are grayed are not available on this screen. From left to right, this line contains the following icons:

Icon | *Meaning*

 Continue. Clicking once on this icon is the functional equivalent of pressing the <Enter> key.

 Save. Store (save) the master record, transaction, or parameters that you are entering. Note that this icon is only active when you are entering or updating information. Clicking once on this icon is the functional equivalent of pressing the <F11> key.

 Go back (left arrow). Within a function, click on this icon to go to the previous screen. This pushbutton is the functional equivalent of <F3>.

 Exit the function (up arrow). Within a function, click on this icon to exit the function and go back to the menu. Note that the left arrow and the up arrow often do the same thing. You can often use either pushbutton to go back. Any difference depends on how the programmer was feeling that day. This pushbutton is the functional equivalent of <F15> (<shift + F3>).

 Cancel. If you cannot go back by clicking on either the left arrow or the up arrow, then click on this icon to go back. This pushbutton is the functional equivalent of <F12>.

Possible entries. If there is a configured list of possible entries in a field, put the cursor in the field and then click on this icon for the list of possible entries. Note that not all fields have a list of possible entries. This pushbutton is the functional equivalent of <F4>.

Help. For on-line help about any field, put the cursor in the field and then click on this icon. This pushbutton is the functional equivalent of <F1>.

Start of a list (first page). When you are displaying a long list of line items, such as customer invoices, or a long report, such as a detailed financial statement, click on this icon to put the cursor at the beginning of the list or report. This pushbutton is the functional equivalent of <F21> (<shift + F9>).

Scroll up in a list (previous page). When you are displaying a long list of items, and your cursor is after the first screen, click on this icon to go to the previous screen. This pushbutton is the functional equivalent of <F22> (<shift + F10>).

Scroll down in a list (next page). When you are displaying a long list of items, click on this icon to go to the next screen. This pushbutton is the functional equivalent of <F23> (<shift + F11>).

End of a list. When you are displaying a long list of items, click on this icon to go to the last screen. This pushbutton is the functional equivalent of <F24> (<shift + F12>).

Depending on what function you are using, each icon is either active or inactive. In other words, not all icons are active at all times.

Also notice the command box on the toolbar. (See Exhibit 1.9.) The command box makes it possible for you to start a user function or a menu without using the menu bars and pull-down menus. To start a user function or a menu from the command box, you enter the four-character technical name of the user function in the command box and then press <Enter>. The technical name of the user function is, in SAP terminology, the "transaction code."

Do not confuse a transaction code with a business transaction. In SAP terminology, a transaction code is a small *program*. A business transaction is a set of *data* in which the total debits equal the total credits. In SAP terminology, a

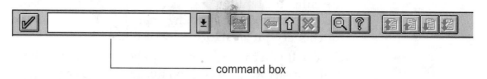

command box

Exhibit 1.9   Toolbar: Command Box

business transaction is often referred to as a "document." This is unfortunate, because it is possible that the business transaction, such as an EDI invoice, has nothing to do with a piece of paper (a document). If you prefer, you do not need to be concerned about transaction codes, and you can ignore the command box and use only the menus.

R/3 was designed to be used by making choices on menu bars and pull-down menus. Almost all software is easier to use via menu bars and pull-down menus than via arcane, technical names of user functions. On the other hand, it is quicker to start up a user function from the command box, if you know the technical name of the user function. If you only use five functions, for example, then you only have to memorize five user function names.

Finding Out Login and User Function Details

R/3 is a complex package. You can find out technical details of your login and what you are doing at any one moment. To find out what client you are logged in to, what application server and data server you are using, and what function you are using, from any menu, select System ➤ Status. (See Exhibit 1.10.)

Notice the key user-oriented fields, from left to right and from top to bottom, on this screen.

Field on Screen	*Explanation*
Client	The client you are logged in to
Date	Date of the login session
User name	SAP user ID of the login session
Time	Time of the login session
License expires on	When the license expires. This depends on your license agreement and installation of R/3.
SAP release	What version of R/3 you are running (on the application server)—required for technical support from SAP along with your SAP customer number.
Language	Language of the login session
Transaction	What user function you are running or user menu you have started. In SAP terminology, a user function is called a "transaction code."

Setting User Defaults (Date, Decimal, and Printer)

Each individual SAP user can set the date and decimal formats, the startup menu, what the default printer is, and certain print control parameters. These

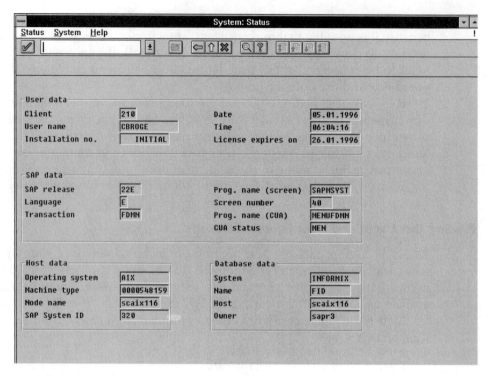

Exhibit 1.10 System: Status

settings are valid after you log off and log in again. They are valid each and every time you log in. To set your user defaults:

1. Log in to R/3 with your SAP user ID.
2. From any menu, select System ➤ User profile ➤ User defaults. (See Exhibit 1.11.)
3. To go from one field to the next on this screen, press the <Tab> key (not the <Enter> key). You can use these fields as follows:

Field	What to Enter
Start menu	This determines which menu, if other than the main menu, starts after you log in. To start up the General Ledger menu, enter **FSMN.** To start up Accounts Receivable, enter **FDMN.** To start up Accounts Payable, enter **FKMN.** To start up the main menu, leave this field blank. To go to the next field, press <Tab>.

```
┌─────────────────────────────────────────────────────────────────────────┐
│ ▭                       Maintain User: Defaults                   ▾│▴│
│  Defaults   Edit   Goto   System   Help                                  !│
│ ┌──┐┌─────────────────┐┌─┐ ┌──┐ ┌─┐┌─┐┌─┐ ┌─┐┌─┐ ┌─┐┌─┐┌─┐┌─┐           │
│ │✔ ││                 ││± │ │ 🗂 │ │⇐││⇧││✖│ │🔍││?│ │ ││ ││ ││ │           │
│ └──┘└─────────────────┘└─┘ └──┘ └─┘└─┘└─┘ └─┘└─┘ └─┘└─┘└─┘└─┘           │
│ ┌────────┐                                                               │
│ │ Choose │                                                               │
│ └────────┘                                                               │
│                                                                          │
│  User              ┌CBROGE─────────┐                                     │
│                                                                          │
│  Start menu        ┌FSMN┐                                                │
│                                                                          │
│  Output device     ┌EY01┐─────────────────────────────────────┐         │
│                                                                          │
│ ┌Print controller────────────────────────────────────────────────────┐ │
│ │  ☒ Print immediately                                                 │ │
│ │  ☒ Delete after printing                                             │ │
│ └──────────────────────────────────────────────────────────────────────┘│
│                                                                          │
│ ┌Date format──────────────────┐ ┌Decimal notation──────────────────┐   │
│ │  ○ DD.MM.YYYY                │ │   ○ Comma                         │   │
│ │  ⊙ MM/DD/YYYY                │ │   ⊙ Period                        │   │
│ │  ○ MM-DD-YYYY                │ │                                   │   │
│ │  ○ YYYY.MM.DD                │ └───────────────────────────────────┘   │
│ │  ○ YYYY/MM/DD                │                                         │
│ └──────────────────────────────┘                                         │
│                                                                          │
└─────────────────────────────────────────────────────────────────────────┘
```

Exhibit 1.11   Maintain User: Defaults

Output device	Enter the four-character name of your printer, as it was installed in R/3.
Print immediately	To print immediately from the spool file, turn this field on by clicking on it, so that a mark appears on your screen just to the left of the text. To hold your print jobs in the spool file, turn this field off. If you are not sure, turn this field on.
Delete after printing	To delete print jobs from the spool file automatically, turn this field on. If you are not sure, turn this field on.
Date format	Using the date format on the screen as an example, select a date format by clicking on it. All dates that you enter or that FI displays or prints will be formatted with this date format.
Decimal notation	Select a decimal format by clicking on it. For example, the comma decimal format makes the

number one thousand two hundred and thirty-four and fifty-six one-hundredths look like 1.234,56. This format is commonly found in continental Europe. The period (full stop) format makes it look like 1,234.56. This format is commonly found in North America and the United Kingdom. You paid your money; you take your choice. You then have to enter all currency amounts with this format. Amounts that R/3 displays or prints will be formatted with this decimal format.

4. To store these parameters, press <F11> or the file folder icon. Note that these parameters are specific to each user. You can change these parameters later at any time. *All of the examples in this course assume that the user default options on this screen are set as shown.*

If you change your user defaults, you have to log out and then log in again to make the change take effect.

Printing for the First Time

Install your printer in the operating system with the maximum settings for row and columns to be printed on each page.

Then, if you use a LAN, install your printer in the LAN.

Lastly, install your printer in R/3.

To print reports on a printer attached to your PC, obtain the saplpd line printer daemon from SAP and install it on your PC. Restart your PC.

Printing a List

R/3 is designed to print or display reports by running ABAP programs. However, if you have displayed a list on your screen, you can print it out also. For example, let us assume that you wish to print out the latest list of currency codes. You can print this list as follows:

1. Put the cursor in the command box.
2. Input **OY03.**
3. Press <Enter>. (See Exhibit 1.12.)
4. To start to print this list, press the Print standard list pushbutton. (See Exhibit 1.13.)
5. From this screen, press the Print pushbutton, or from the menu bar, select System ➤ List ➤ Print. Note that sometimes the Print pushbutton is not

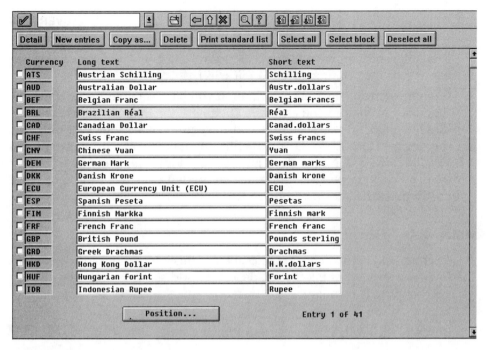

Exhibit 1.12 Printing a List

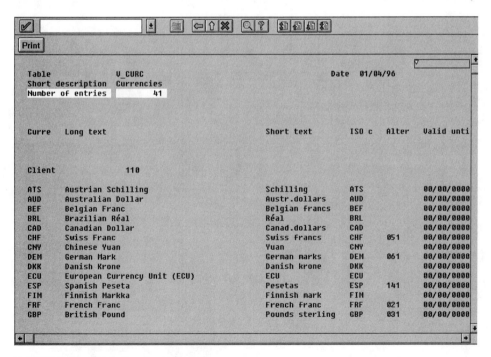

Exhibit 1.13 Print Standard List Screen

available, and you have to select System → List → Print from the menu bar to start the printing. (See Exhibit 1.14.)

6. From this screen, you select a printer. If you have set your user defaults as described in the previous section, "Setting User Defaults", then you see these defaults on this screen. If you have not yet set your user defaults, then in the Output device field, enter the name of the printer, *as it was installed under R/3*. Next, select the options Print immed. and Delete after print by clicking on the button just to the left of each of these options. Lastly, press the Print pushbutton (Exhibit 1.14).

Downloading Data to Excel

R/3 is integrated with Microsoft Office. Due to this integration, you can download most reports to an Excel spreadsheet. First display the report or list on your screen. From any menu, select System → List → Download.

Printing a Screen (with R/3, Windows, and Word)

Using Windows and any word processor, such as Word for Windows, you can capture and then print any R/3 screen as follows:

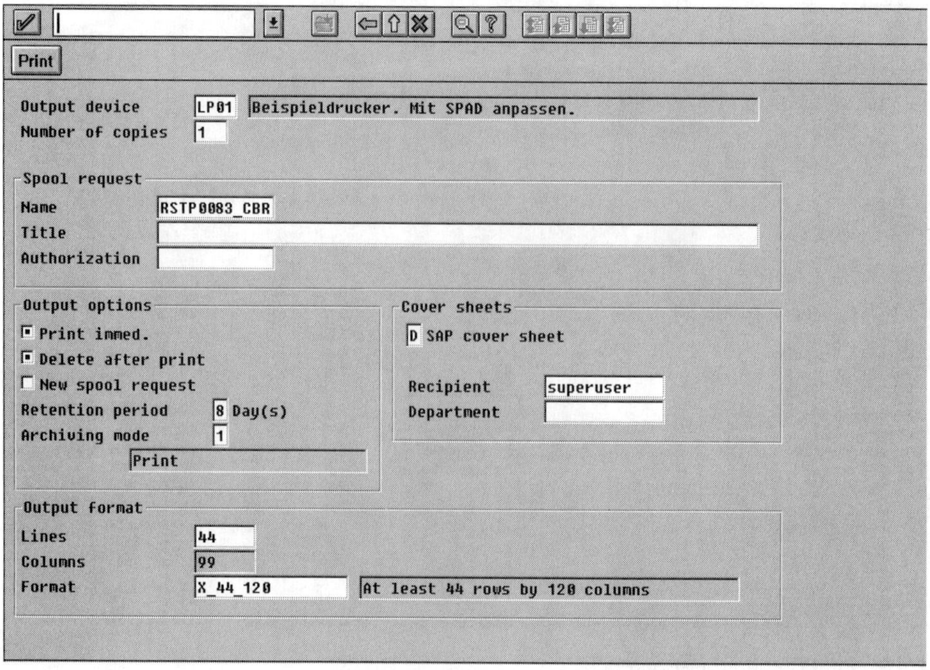

| Print |

| Output device | LP01 | Beispieldrucker. Mit SPAD anpassen. |
| Number of copies | 1 | |

Spool request
Name	RSTP0083_CBR
Title	
Authorization	

Output options
- ☒ Print immed.
- ☒ Delete after print
- ☐ New spool request
- Retention period | 8 Day(s)
- Archiving mode | 1
  | Print |

Cover sheets
- D SAP cover sheet
- Recipient | superuser
- Department | |

Output format
- Lines | 44
- Columns | 99
- Format | X_44_120 | At least 44 rows by 120 columns

Exhibit 1.14   Printing with Output Device Field

1. Display the screen that you wish to print out.

2. To make the window expand to fill the whole screen, press the maximize button in the very upper-right portion of your screen.

3. Press the <Print Screen> key on your keyboard. If you do not have a <Print Screen> key, hold down the <Ctrl> key and then press <C> (for copy). Either way, this step places a copy of the screen into the Windows clipboard.

4. Start up your word processor. Open a new or a previous document, and then place the cursor where you wish to insert the screen.

5. To insert the screen into your document, hold down the <Ctrl> key and then press <V>. Notice a picture of your R/3 screen inside the open document. To print out the screen, simply print out the document.

Opening Another Session

During a login session, you can open another session to use another function. You can open another session without logging in again. For example, you could use another session to look at another record or to run another report. Depending on the amount of RAM installed in your PC, you can have up to nine user sessions open at a time.

To open another session during a login session, select System → Create session.

Note that to open another session in another client, on another machine, or in another language, you have to log in again.

Switching between Sessions

To switch between open sessions in one login session, hold down the <Alt> key and then press the <Tab> key.

Exhibit 1.15   Log Off Screen

Closing a Session

To close a session, from any menu, select System → End session.

Logging Out

To log out at any time, from any menu, select System → Log off. You then see the following message to confirm that you intend to log off, possibly losing any data that you have not yet stored or a transaction that you have not yet posted. (See Exhibit 1.15.)

If you forgot to store a record or post a transaction, click on No. Then complete the record or transaction. To store or post it, press <F11> or the file folder icon and then select System → Log off again.

If you intended to log out, simply click on Yes.

CHAPTER 2

Using General Ledger

This chapter describes how to use SAP General Ledger. The General Ledger (G/L) program lets you keep a chart of accounts, enter and post G/L transactions, inquire on the general ledger, and prepare financial statements. A financial statement always includes all G/L accounts—both the balance sheet accounts and the P&L (profit and loss) accounts. You can use other FI functions to open and close posting periods in FI and to revalue open items or G/L accounts denominated in foreign currency, such as bank accounts or loans in foreign currency.

To go to the G/L menu, from the SAP R/3 main menu, select Accounting ➤ Financial accounting ➤ General ledger. (See Exhibit 2.1.)

FUNDAMENTAL CONCEPTS OF BOOKKEEPING

The two fundamental concepts of accounting are:

- The accounting equation
- The transaction principle

This book assumes that you are vaguely familiar with these two concepts. Users who are not familiar with these concepts, may wish to consult a book about bookkeeping. You can still apply this book to using FI, but it is advisable to learn these fundamental concepts first. A brief explanation of these concepts follows.

```
┌──────────────────────────────────────────────────────────────────┐
│ ▬                              SAP R/3                              │
├──────────────────────────────────────────────────────────────────┤
│ Office   Logistics   Accounting   Human resources   Information systems   Tools   System   Help │
├────────────────────────────┬──────────────────────────────────────┤
│   Financial accounting      │   General ledger                     │
│   Asset management          │   Accounts receivable                │
│   Controlling               │   Accounts payable                   │
│   Treasury                  │   Bill of exch.mgmt.                  │
│   Project management        │   Credit management                  │
│                             │   Extended G/L                       │
│                             │   Consolidation                      │
│                             │   Prep.f.consolidation               │
└────────────────────────────┴──────────────────────────────────────┘
```

Exhibit 2.1 General Ledger Menu

The *accounting equation* states that total assets always equal total liabilities plus equity. In other words, what the company owns, such as bank accounts, cars, and buildings, always equals what the company owes, such as invoices to suppliers, bank loans, and mortgages, plus the owner's capital in the business. The G/L in R/3 supports this concept, since the subledgers (accounts receivable, accounts payable, and fixed assets) are continuously linked to the G/L. When you post a customer invoice, for example, FI immediately updates the account balance of the accounts receivable account assigned to that customer (in SAP terminology, the "reconciliation account").

The *transaction principle* states that in any one transaction, such as an invoice or a payment, the total debits always equal the total credits. For example, if the amount of the goods or services delivered were 100 and the tax rate were 10% on the transaction, then you post the transaction as a debit of 110 to the customer, a credit of 100 to revenue, and a credit of 10 to the tax payable account. The G/L in R/3 supports this concept, since you can only post a transaction if the total debits equal the total credits. If the transaction is not complete, you can hold the transaction, find out the missing detail, and then post it.

OVERVIEW OF R/3 INTEGRATION AND G/L

The G/L is the center of your accounting system. All modules in the accounting group (FI, financial accounting; CO, cost accounting; and AM, fixed assets) post to G/L accounts or are related to G/L accounts. The logistics modules (SD, order entry, shipping, invoicing; MM, invoice verification, goods receiving, inventory control; and PP, production planning and control) also post to G/L accounts, when you record receipts of materials, shipments, or transfers of finished goods or raw materials. The personnel module (HR, human resources) also posts to G/L accounts, but these entries are to only a few G/L accounts for labor and insurance at the end of the pay period. Often, access to the personnel module is tightly restricted.

STARTING TO USE G/L

To start to use the G/L, it is advisable to set certain options that determine how data is entered, processed, and displayed.

Setting User Defaults

User defaults have to do with the date and decimal format, a possible startup menu, and printer control. To set your user defaults:

1. From any menu, select System → User profile → User defaults. (See Exhibit 2.2.)
2. To set it up so that you always start with the General Ledger menu, enter FSMN in the Start menu field. Enter your printer abbreviation in the Out-

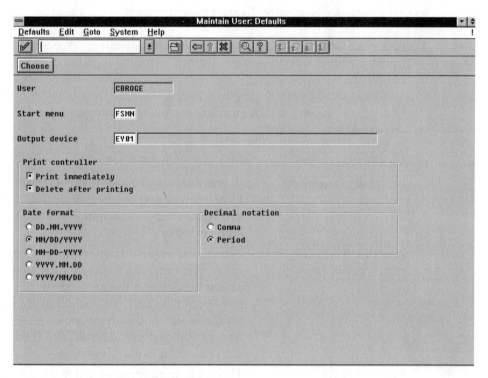

Exhibit 2.2 Maintain User: Defaults

put device field. It is usually advisable to mark Print immediately and Delete after printing. Select the proper Date format and Decimal notation by marking the parameter.

3. To store the parameter for your user defaults, press <F11> or the file folder icon.

Setting Processing Options

You can set various options to process transaction data. These options are specific to each login ID until you change them. There are three sets of processing options:

- Transaction entry and display
- Open item processing (for example, for cash application)
- Line item display

To turn on a processing option, you simply click on the box next to the option, so that a mark appears in the box. To turn off an option, click on the box again, so that the mark disappears. To start to set processing options:

1. From the General Ledger (or Accounts Receivable or Accounts Payable) menu, select Environment ➤ Current options ➤ Editing options. (See Exhibit 2.3.)

    All of the examples in this book assume that the processing options on this screen are set as shown. The primary transaction entry and display options are as follows:

Option	*Meaning if Option is On*
No foreign currency	If you enter and process transactions only in local currency, click on this option. In effect, this option suppresses entry of amounts in foreign currency.
Amount fields only for document currency	When you enter a transaction in foreign currency, you enter the currency code in the transaction header and the amounts in the transaction currency only, in each line item. If the option were off, then you could enter both the transaction currency amount and the local currency amount in each line item.
No special G/L transactions	This option suppresses entry of special G/L transactions, such as down payments, bills of

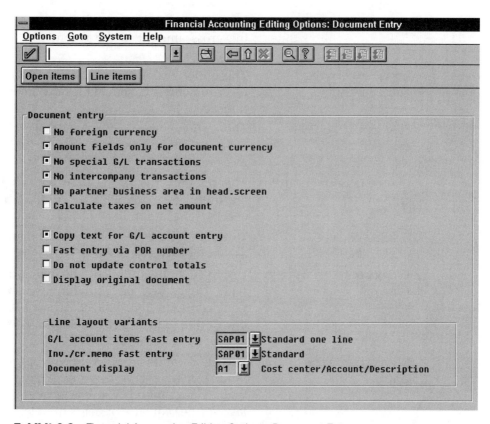

Exhibit 2.3 Financial Accounting Editing Options: Document Entry

	exchange, security deposits, fixed assets invoices in France, and others.
No intercompany transactions	This option suppresses entry of intercompany transactions in which two company codes buy or sell something jointly.
No partner business area in head.screen	This option suppresses the "partner business area" in the transaction header screen. If this option were off and if the transaction involves multiple business areas, then the receivables and payables between business areas are calculated and posted to and from the partner business area and the business areas in the transaction.
Calculate taxes on net amount	This option makes the program calculate transaction taxes based on the net amount in the

	revenue or expense entry. Otherwise, you enter the gross amount in the revenue or expense entry.
Copy text for G/L account entry	This option makes the program duplicate your text from one G/L item to the next (in the same transaction).
Fast entry via POR number	This option is required only in Switzerland to enter vendor invoices based on the Swiss payment number.
Do not update control totals	This option turns off the control totals, which are useful for controlling entry of a batch of checks, for example.
Display original document	Turn this option on if you scan documents such as vendor invoices.
G/L account items fast entry	Use the default (supplied) line layout to begin with. Depending on your requirements and your configuration, you can change the line layout (the sequence of fields from left to right displayed on the screen).
Inv./cr.memo fast entry	Use the default (supplied) line layout to begin with. Depending on your requirements and your configuration, you can change the line layout (the sequence of fields from left to right displayed on the screen).
Document display	Use the default (supplied) line layout to begin with. Depending on your requirements and your configuration, you can change the line layout (the sequence of fields from left to right displayed on the screen). This determines how the overview of the transaction is displayed.

2. To set the open item processing options, press the Open items pushbutton. You will then see the Financial Accounting Editing Options: Open Items screen. (See Exhibit 2.4.)

The following are the primary open item processing options:

Option	*Meaning if Set On*
Process open items with commands	If you set this option on, you can process open items with commands (in the left-most column). Otherwise, you use the mouse and double-click on an item to activate it.

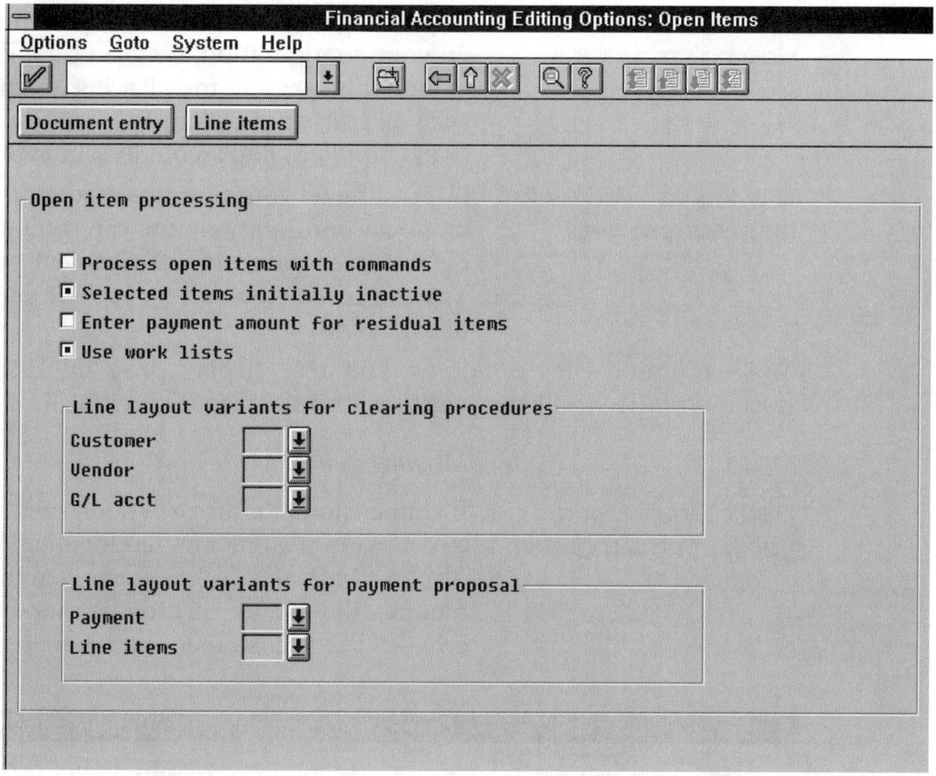

Exhibit 2.4 Financial Accounting Editing Options: Open Items

Selected items initially inactive	If you set this option on, then all open items in the clearing screen (cash application screen) are not active (applied) until you activate them.
Enter payment amount for residual items	If you set this option on, you enter the amount of the payment in the residual item screen when you process a partial payment and close the original invoice. Otherwise, you enter the amount of the residual.
Use work lists	You can combine two or more customers into a work list—to display open items by a work list or to clear open items (apply cash) by a work list. This option turns on work lists when you process (clear) open items.

Line layout variants for clearing procedures	Depending on your business requirements and on your configuration, you can set a different default line layout for clearing open items, such as cash application. You can use the default (supplied) line layout to begin with.
Line layout variants for payment proposal	Depending on your business requirements and on your configuration, you can set a different default line layout for the payment proposal. You can use the default (supplied) line layout to begin with.

3. To set the processing option for line item display, press the Line items pushbutton. This will open the Line Items screen (Exhibit 2.5).

Option	*Meaning if Set On*
Disp.customer and vendor items together	If your customer is also a vendor, such as an intercompany customer or vendor, then this item displays both sets of line items together. This requires the master records be marked properly—with the customer number in the vendor

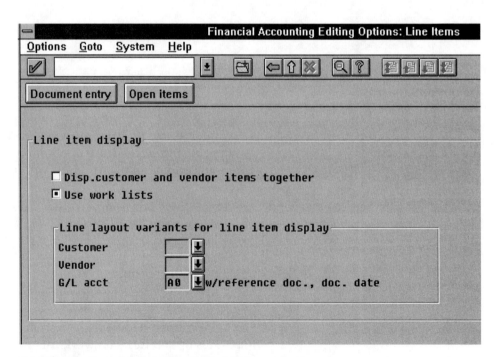

Exhibit 2.5   Financial Accounting Editing Options: Line Items

<table>
<tr><td></td><td>record and the vendor number in the customer record.</td></tr>
<tr><td>Use work lists</td><td>You can combine two or more customers into a work list—to display open items by a work list or to clear open items (apply cash) by a work list. This option turns on work lists when you display open items.</td></tr>
<tr><td>Line layout variants—
Customer</td><td>Depending on your business requirements and on your configuration, you can set a different default line layout to display customer line items. You can use the default (supplied) line layout to begin with.</td></tr>
<tr><td>Line layout variants—
Vendor</td><td>Depending on your business requirements and on your configuration, you can set a different default line layout to display vendor line items. You can use the default (supplied) line layout to begin with.</td></tr>
<tr><td>Line layout variants—
G/L acct</td><td>Depending on your business requirements and on your configuration, you can set a different default line layout to display G/L line items. You can use the default (supplied) line layout to begin with.</td></tr>
</table>

4. To update your user master record with the processing options that you set, press <F11> or the file folder icon.

KEEPING A LIST OF BANKS

Why Keep a List of Banks?

To pay vendors with the automatic payment program, you need a list of your banks (house banks) and bank accounts. To forecast bank balances with the treasury functions, you also need the same list of house banks and bank accounts. Also, many countries, particularly in Europe, use bank transfers as a payment method. This requires a valid bank account number in the vendor master record. The G/L and A/P (Accounts Payable) programs internally validate the bank key (required bank number or sort code) and the bank account numbers, according to the country of the bank. To prepare to pay vendors by bank transfer, you can either enter the list of valid banks, before you enter your vendor master records, or you can enter a valid bank, at the same time that you enter a vendor master record. Some third party-vendors also supply lists on diskette of valid banks in some countries.

Entering a House Bank

The G/L program validates the format of bank numbers (in SAP terminology, called "bank keys") and bank account numbers, depending on country-specific requirements. The program also checks whether the bank is in the list of valid banks (by the bank key). If it is not in the list, then the program prompts you to add the bank number (sort code) and bank address to the list of valid banks. Some countries have specific, required formats for bank keys and account numbers. Others do not.

A house bank is a bank where your company, whose books you are keeping, has a bank account. To enter a bank account, you first have to enter one or more house banks where you keep your account. To enter a house bank:

1. From the General Ledger menu, select Environment ➤ Configuration menu. Then, from the Financial Accounting Configuration menu, select Master records ➤ Banks ➤ House banks.

2. Enter the company code for the company that has the bank account.

3. Press the House banks pushbutton.

4. To add a house bank, press Create bank. (See Exhibit 2.6.)

5. Enter a one- to five-character code name for the house bank. Press <Tab>. Enter the two-character code for the country of the bank. Then press Proceed. (See Exhibit 2.7.)

6. Enter at least a bank number in the Bank key field. Press <Enter>. The G/L program validates these bank keys based on hard-coded country-specific routines. If the bank key is not in the list of valid bank keys, then the program prompts you to add this bank key (and bank address) to the list of valid bank numbers as shown in Exhibit 2.8.

7. Enter at least the name of the bank. To make international payments via this bank-by-bank transfer, enter a SWIFT code number for the bank.

8. To enter the data required for file transfer, select Goto ➤ DME. DME (data medium exchange) is an SAP term for file transfer. Press Continue. This will open the DME Data screen. (See Exhibit 2.9.)

9. To store the bank data, press <F11> or the file folder icon.

Entering a Bank Account

To make payments by bank transfer with the automatic payment program, you have to enter one or more bank accounts in your system. To forecast bank balances by the value date, you also require bank accounts in the system.

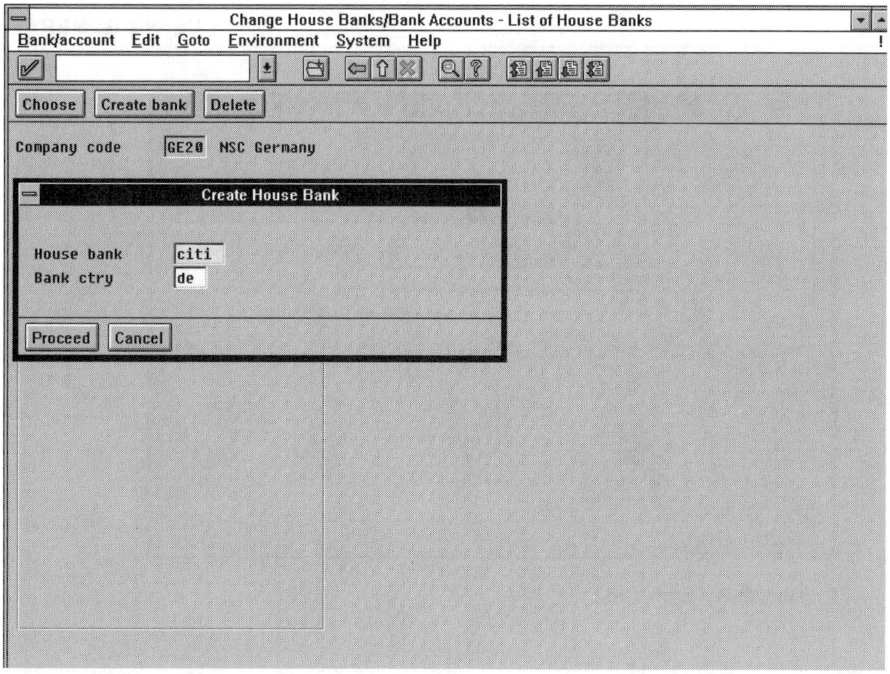

Change House Banks/Bank Accounts - List of House Banks
Bank/account Edit Goto Environment System Help
Choose
Create bank
Delete
Company code GE20 NSC Germany
Create House Bank
House bank citi
Bank ctry de
Proceed
Cancel

Exhibit 2.6 Entering a House Bank Account

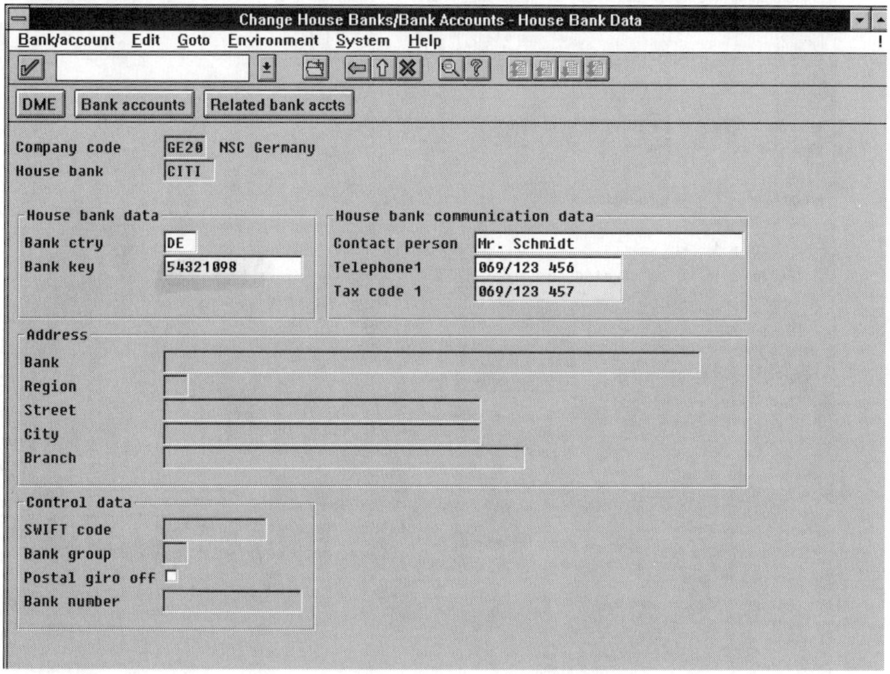

Change House Banks/Bank Accounts - House Bank Data
Bank/account Edit Goto Environment System Help
DME
Bank accounts
Related bank accts
Company code GE20 NSC Germany
House bank CITI
House bank data
Bank ctry DE
Bank key 54321098
House bank communication data
Contact person Mr. Schmidt
Telephone1 069/123 456
Tax code 1 069/123 457
Address
Bank
Region
Street
City
Branch
Control data
SWIFT code
Bank group
Postal giro off
Bank number

Exhibit 2.7 Change House Banks/Bank Accounts—House Bank Data

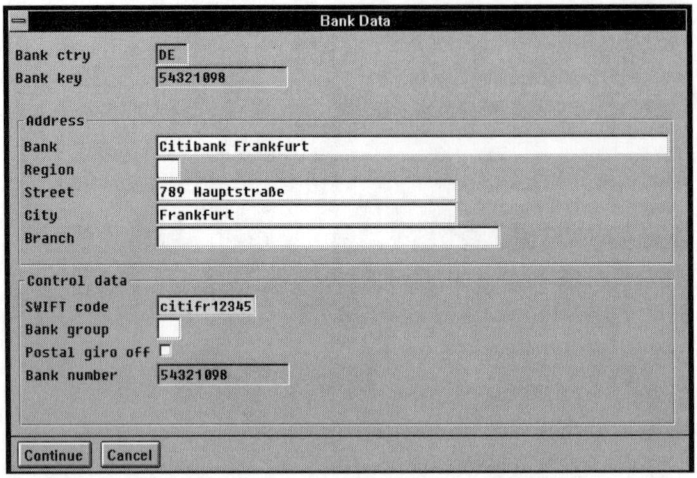

Exhibit 2.8   Bank Data

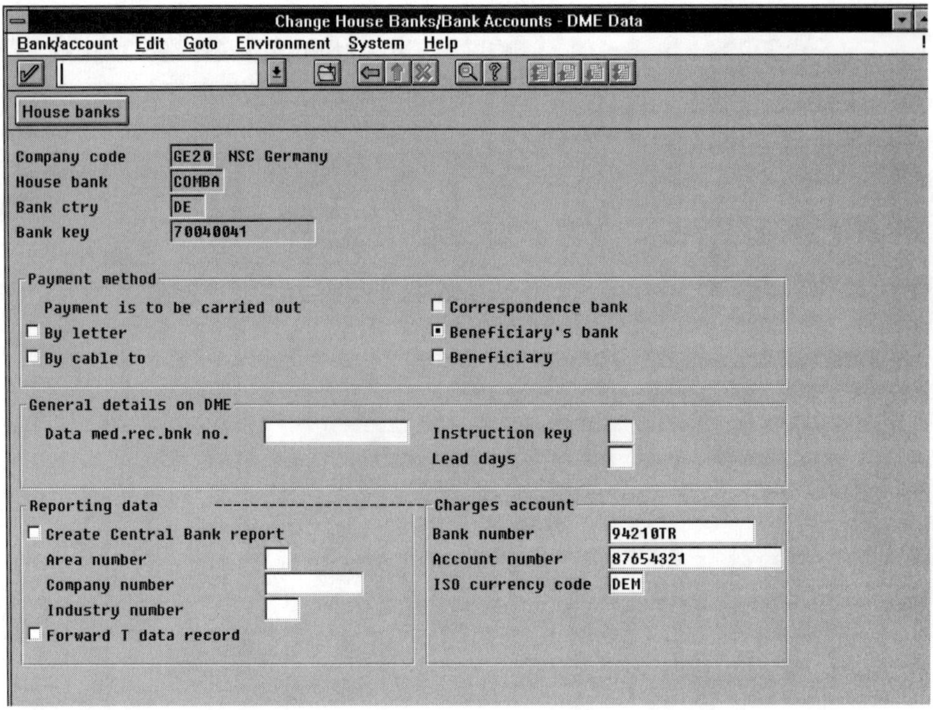

Exhibit 2.9   DME Data

To enter a bank account:

1. From the General Ledger menu, select Environment → Configuration menu. Then, from the Financial Accounting Configuration menu, select Master records → Banks → House banks.
2. Enter the company code of the company that has the bank account.
3. Press the Bank accounts pushbutton.
4. To add a bank, press Create account. (See Exhibit 2.10.)
5. Enter the 1–5 character code name of the house bank in the House bank field, press the <Tab> key, enter a 1–5 character code name for the account in the Acc ID field, press the <Tab> key, and then enter a brief description of the account in the Text field. Then press Proceed. (See Exhibit 2.11.)
6. On the next screen, enter at least the bank account number in the Bank account field, the currency of the account in the Currency field, and G/L account for the bank balance at the bank in the G/L account field.

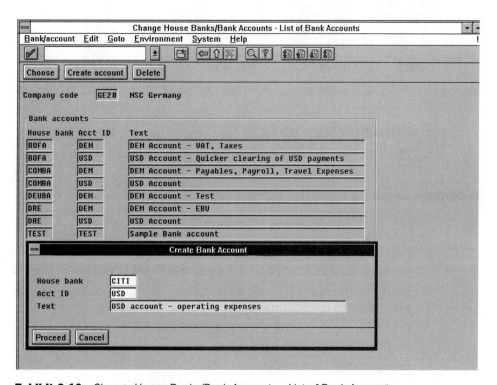

Exhibit 2.10   Change House Banks/Bank Accounts—List of Bank Accounts

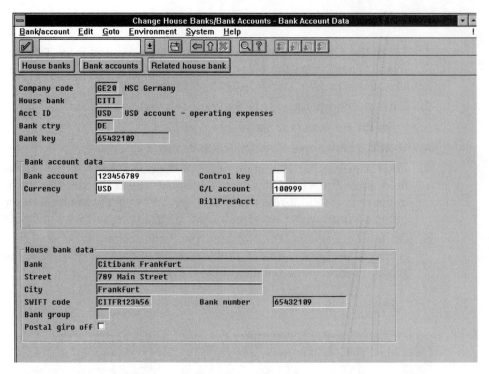

Exhibit 2.11 Change House Banks/Bank Accounts—Bank Account Data

7. Press <F11> or the file folder icon to store the bank account data.

8. Press the <left arrow> three times to go back to the R/3 main menu.

Entering a Vendor's Bank (for Validation)

To enter a bank in the list of valid banks:

1. From the R/3 main menu, select Accounting → Financial accounting → Accounts payable to go to the Accounts Payable menu.

2. From the Accounts Payable menu, select Master records → Banks → Create. You will see the Create Bank: Detail Screen.

3. Enter the country of the bank, the bank key (bank number), and then press <Enter>. (See Exhibit 2.12.)

4. Enter at least the name of the bank.

5. To store the bank, press <F11> or the file folder icon.

```
┌──────────────────────────────────────────────────────────────────────┐
│ ─                        Create Bank : Detail Screen           ▼ ▲     │
│  Bank  Goto  Details  Environment  System  Help                    !  │
│  ┌─┐ ┌─────────────────┐ ┌─┐ ┌─┐┌─┬─┬─┐ ┌─┬─┐ ┌─┬─┬─┬─┐               │
│  │✓│ │                 │ │↓│ │▣││←│↑│✕│ │🔍│?│ │▤│▤│▤│▤│               │
│  └─┘ └─────────────────┘ └─┘ └─┘└─┴─┴─┘ └─┴─┘ └─┴─┴─┴─┘               │
│                                                                        │
│   Bank ctry      │DE│          Germany                                │
│   Bank key       │43210987│                                           │
│                                                                        │
│  ┌─Address────────────────────────────────────────────────────┐      │
│   Bank            │Bank of the Nile                          │        │
│   Region          │ │                                                 │
│   Street          │1 Ancient Boulevard              │                │
│   City            │Alexandria           │                            │
│   Branch          │                                         │        │
│  └────────────────────────────────────────────────────────────┘      │
│                                                                        │
│  ┌─Control data───────────────────────────────────────────────┐      │
│   SWIFT code      │bnknil54321│                                       │
│   Bank group      │ │                                                 │
│   Postal giro off □                                                   │
│   Bank number     │43210987│                                         │
│  └────────────────────────────────────────────────────────────┘      │
│                                                                        │
│                                                    FID (1) scaix116 OVR 12:44PM │
└──────────────────────────────────────────────────────────────────────┘
```

Exhibit 2.12   Create Bank: Detail Screen

KEEPING A CHART OF ACCOUNTS

Understanding the Chart of Accounts in SAP

A chart of accounts is a complete list of all possible general ledger (G/L) accounts. In the chart of accounts in SAP, G/L accounts have two parts:

- A general part
- A company code-specific part

Most of all, the general part of a G/L account contains the following data: the *name* of the G/L account (both a short name for display and a long name for printouts) and the *type of account* (balance sheet or profit and loss). Depending on your configuration, the general part of the chart of accounts (all G/L accounts) is also known as the *global chart of accounts,* since it contains all possible accounts in all company codes. When you enter a G/L account in one step, you always enter the general part of a G/L account first (on the first screen) and then you enter the company code–specific part in the following screens.

Most of all, the company code–specific part of a G/L account master contains the following data: the *currency* of the account, whether the account is a *reconciliation account* (for controlling receivables, payables, fixed assets), the *tax category* (whether the account is subject to VAT or sales tax), whether the account is an *open item* account, and *which fields are required* when entering a line item in this account. When you enter a G/L account, you always enter the company code part of a G/L account on the second, third, and fourth data screens. Note that you can only post a transaction to an account, if you have already entered the G/L account in the specific company code to which you are posting the transaction.

An overview of how G/L accounts are stored and entered is shown in Exhibit 2.13.

Entering a G/L Account

You can enter a G/L account in either one or two steps. If you enter a G/L account in one step (using one function only), then you put the G/L account in the global chart of accounts in the first screen and also in a specific company code in the second through fourth screens.

Entering a G/L Account in One Step

You can enter a G/L account in one step. In other words, you use one function only to add the account both to the global chart of accounts and to a specific company code for posting. To enter a G/L account in one step:

1. From the General Ledger menu, select Master records ➤ Create. You will see the Create G/L Acct: Request Screen (Exhibit 2.14).

2. Enter a G/L account number in the Account number field. Enter a company code in the Company code field. In this way, you start to enter the G/L account in the chart of accounts and in this specific company code. Note that you have the option of entering a reference G/L account in the Account number field in the Reference section and a reference company code in the Company code field, also in the Reference section. FI then copies the data from this reference G/L account. This can make it quicker for you to enter a G/L account. Press <Enter> to go to the Create G/L Account: Control Ch/Accts screen (Exhibit 2.15).

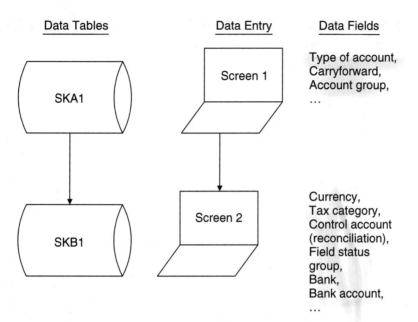

Data Tables   Data Entry   Data Fields

SKA1

Screen 1

Type of account,
Carryforward,
Account group,
…

SKB1

Screen 2

Currency,
Tax category,
Control account
(reconciliation),
Field status
group,
Bank,
Bank account,
…

Exhibit 2.13   Overview of G/L Accounts Stored and Entered

3. Enter the brief name of the account in the Short text field. This account name appears later on the screen, when you enter a line item in this account. Enter a possibly longer account name in the G/L acct long text field. The long text appears later in reports supplied by SAP, such as the chart of accounts. The other fields and what you enter are as follows:

What You See on the Screen What You Enter (Recommended)

Balance sheet account   Click on this field, if the G/L account is a balance sheet account (asset, liability, or capital).

P+L statement acct type   Depending on your configuration, what you enter in this field determines to which G/L account results for this P&L (profit and loss) account are carried forward at the end of the fiscal year (such as retained earnings). If you are entering a P&L account (revenue or

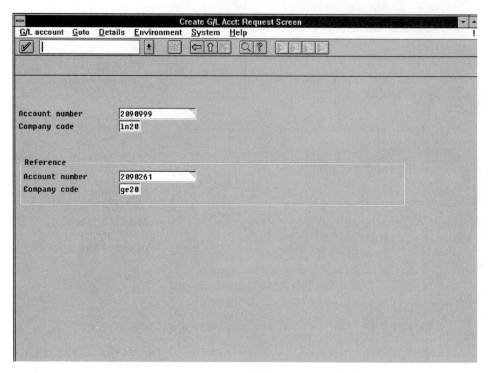

Exhibit 2.14   Create G/L Acct: Request Screen

	expense), you must make an entry in this field. For a list of possible entries, put your cursor in this field and press the down arrow. If you are entering a balance sheet account, leave this field blank.
Account group	The possible entries depend on your configuration. In a standard configuration, enter **BS** for a balance sheet account or **P&L** for a profit and loss account. For a list of possible entries, put your cursor in this field and press the down arrow.
Sample account	The possible entries depend on your configuration. If you use sample accounts to enter your chart of accounts quickly, then enter the sample account number in this field. Using a sample account, you automatically make entries in fields in the next screens.

```
┌──────────────────────────────────────────────────────────────────────────┐
│ ─                    Create G/L Account: Control Ch/Accts          ▼ ▲    │
│  G/L account  Goto  Details  Environment  System  Help                 ! │
│  ┌─┐ ┌──────────────┐ ┌─┐  ┌─┐ ┌─┐┌─┐┌─┐  ┌─┐┌─┐   ┌─┐┌─┐┌─┐┌─┐          │
│  │✔│ │              │ │±│  │🖫│ │⇐││⇧││✖│  │🔍││?│   │🗐││🗐││🗐││🗐│          │
│  └─┘ └──────────────┘ └─┘  └─┘ └─┘└─┘└─┘  └─┘└─┘   └─┘└─┘└─┘└─┘          │
│  ┌───────────────┐                                                         │
│  │ Other account │                                                         │
│  └───────────────┘                                                         │
│  G/L acct          │2090999 │                                              │
│  Chart of accts    │NSC │     NSC Global chart of accounts                 │
│                                                                            │
│   ┌Description──────────────────────────────────────────────────────┐     │
│   Short text              │General Accrual          │                      │
│   G/L acct long text      │General Accrual                          │     │
│                                                                            │
│   ┌Control──────────────────────────────────────────────────────────┐     │
│   Balance sheet account        │▪│                                         │
│   P+L statement acct type      │ │                                         │
│   Account group                │BS │      Balance sheet accounts           │
│   Sample account               │         │                                 │
│                                                                            │
│   ┌Consolidation───────────────────────────────────────────────────┐      │
│   Trading partner              │      │                                    │
│   Group account number         │         ▼│                                │
│                                                                            │
└──────────────────────────────────────────────────────────────────────────┘
```

Exhibit 2.15   Create G/L Account: Control Ch/Accts

Trading partner	If the account is an intercompany account (revenue, expense, receivables, payables, loan, profit or loss from intercompany transfer of inventory, equity, or other), then enter the code for the other company (a one- to six-character code for an organization unit that contains one or more company codes). This prepares for consolidation later. (Read the FI Legal Consolidation Manual from SAP for details.)
Group account number	Depending on your configuration, you can enter a separate group chart of accounts (corporate chart of accounts). If you use a group chart of accounts, you then have to enter a specific G/L account from the group chart of accounts when you enter a G/L account in any other chart of accounts. This field was used in earlier versions for companies with a French chart of

accounts and a corporate chart of accounts. Later releases of R/3 handle the French chart of accounts differently—with a field on a company code–specific screen.

4. To go from one field to the next, press <Enter>. You can also use the mouse to put the cursor in a specific field. At the end of this screen, press <Enter>. The next screen prompts you to start entering the company code–specific part of a G/L account. (See Exhibit 2.16.)

5. Notice that the company code appears at the beginning of this screen. How you enter a G/L account depends on your configuration. Enter the fields as follows:

What You See on the Screen What You Enter (Recommended)

Currency   Currency in which the account is denominated. If you enter local currency as the account currency, then you can post to the account in any currency, but you cannot revalue into group currency. If the account currency is a foreign

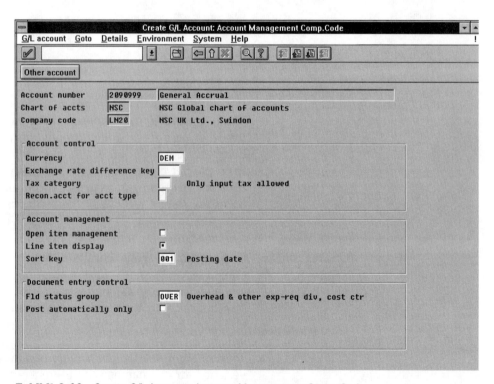

Exhibit 2.16   Create G/L Account: Account Management Comp.Code

	currency, you can only post to the account in that currency. To enter a transaction in any currency and to revalue the G/L account balance later from local currency into group currency, enter *. The limitations on account currencies and transaction currencies also depend on the program version you are using.
Exchange rate difference key	Revaluation key (exchange rate difference key) This depends on your configuration. If the currency of the account is any other than local currency (a foreign currency or *), then enter a revaluation key. This key determines how the G/L account is posted with a gain or loss after revaluing this G/L account.
Tax category	This field determines whether a tax code is required later when entering a line item in this account. This depends on legal requirements and on your configuration. For example, if this account is a revenue account that is subject to sales tax or output VAT, enter + in this field. If the account is an expense account subject to input VAT, enter − in this field. If the account is related to both input and output VAT, such as freight charges billed back to the customer, then enter * in this field. If the account is a tax account, then enter < for input tax (on expenses) and > for sales tax or output tax (on revenues). Make sure FI is properly configured to calculate, post, and report transaction taxes (sales tax or VAT). To process sales tax in the United States, use a third-party package, such as Vertex or AVP.
Recon.acct for acct type	Reconciliation account. This field links the following subledgers to the G/L:

D—Accounts Receivable (customers)

K—Accounts Payable (vendors)

A—Fixed Assets (fixed assets)

If you enter one of these codes, then this account subtotals any transactions posted to accounts (customers, vendors, or fixed assets) that are assigned to this account.

Open item management	To keep open items about the account to be cleared (offset individually), turn this field on by clicking on it. This applies to very few accounts, such as goods received/invoice received, cash in transit, payroll disbursed/cleared, and other clearing (interim) accounts, in which individual line items are cleared. If you are not sure, leave this option off. Clearing accounts are also known as "interim" accounts or "suspense" accounts.
Line item display	To display line item detail in the account later (after posting transactions to the account), turn this option on. If you are not sure, turn this option on. The only accounts that usually have this option off are tax accounts and cash discount accounts.
Sort key	This field determines how line items are automatically sorted later, when you display line items in this account.
Fld status group	What you enter in this field depends on your configuration. The entry in this field determines which fields are required, optional, or suppressed when you enter a line item in this account. In general, you can only have reports as detailed as transactions. In other words, you cannot have a detail in a report without having the same detail required in transactions included in that report. Specifically, make sure FI is properly configured to meet your reporting requirements and transaction data.
Post automatically only	This is required only in the Federal Republic of Germany for VAT accounts.

6. At the end of this screen, press <Enter>. (See Exhibit 2.17.)

7. Depending on your configuration, enter the fields as follows:

What You See on the Screen What You Enter (Recommended)

Planning level	What you enter in this field depends on your configuration. This field is related to cash forecasting. For example, if FI were configured,

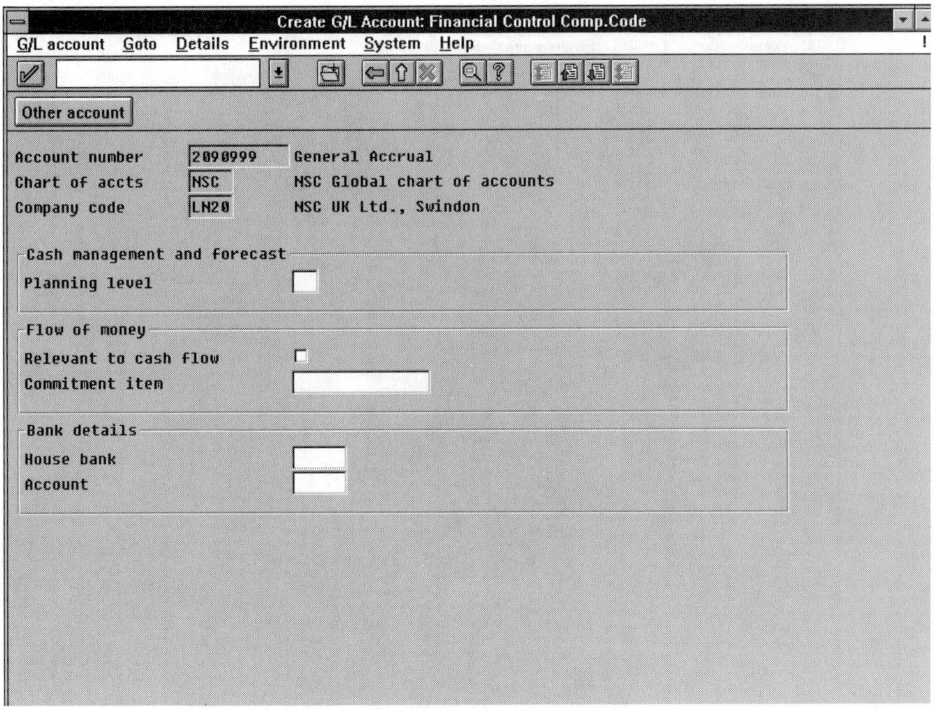

Exhibit 2.17   Create G/L Account: Financial Control Comp.Code

	you could enter **CB** (for cash in the bank) or **CT** (for cash in transit) here.
Relevant to cash flow	If this account is related to payments from customers, turn this field on. The program to print remittance advices then processes these accounts to determine the payment amount.
Commitment item	What you enter in this field depends on your configuration. This field is related to financial budgeting by G/L account.
House bank	If this account is a G/L account for a bank account, you can enter the code of the bank here.
Account	If this account is a G/L account for a bank account, you can enter the code of the bank account here.

8. At the end of this screen, press <Enter>. (See Exhibit 2.18.)

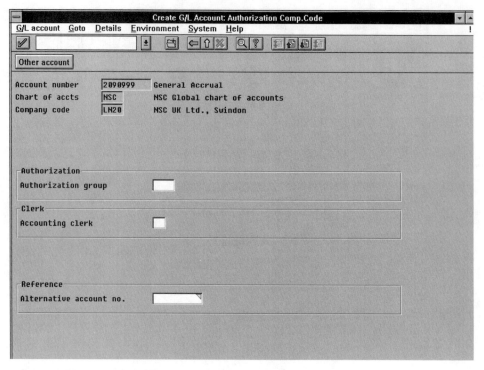

Exhibit 2.18   Create G/L Account: Authorization Comp.Code

9.   Depending on your configuration, enter the fields as follows:

What You See on the Screen What You Enter

Authorization group
The entry in this field depends on your configuration. Using this field, you can restrict or permit access to this account by SAP user ID.

Accounting clerk
The entry in this field depends on your configuration. Enter the two-character code name for an accounting clerk or manager. For example, you could enter a code for the person who entered the account.

Alternative account no.
The entry in this field depends on your configuration. For example, you could use this field to enter a local account number, if you were entering an account in a company code with a global French chart of accounts.* Alternatively, you could put in a French number if

you were using a non-French global chart of accounts.

10. To store the G/L account, press <F11> or the file folder icon.

Entering a G/L Account in a Chart of Accounts (First of Two Steps)

You can enter a complete G/L account in two steps, using two functions. In the first step, you enter the G/L account in the global chart of accounts in the first screen (Exhibit 2.19). In the second step, you enter the G/L account in a specific company code in the second through fourth screens. For example, you could keep a global chart of accounts at your head office (centrally or regionally) while you keep a chart of accounts for each company code locally. In order to enter a new G/L account in a company code, the G/L account must first be entered in the global chart of accounts. To enter a G/L account in the global chart of accounts only (the general data), do as follows:

1. From the General Ledger menu, select Master records → Chart of accounts → Create. (See Exhibit 2.19.)

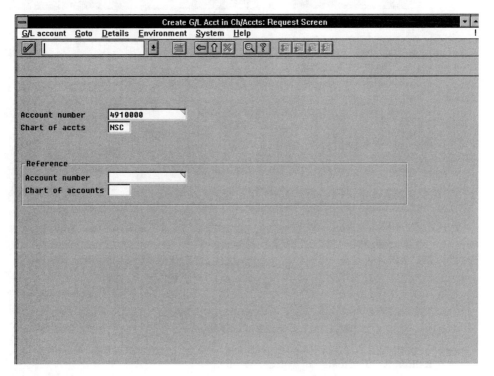

Exhibit 2.19 Create G/L Account in Ch/Accts: Request Screen

2. Enter the new G/L account number in the Account number field. Enter the chart of accounts (global chart of accounts) from your configuration in the Chart of accts field. Press <Enter>. (See Exhibit 2.20.)

3. Enter the first screen in the G/L account in the global chart of accounts in two steps in the same way that you enter the first screen, if you enter the G/L account in one step. See the previous section for details.

4. To store the G/L account, press <F11> or the file folder icon.

Entering a G/L Account in a Company Code (Second of Two Steps)

To post a transaction to a G/L account, you first must enter the G/L account in the company code. However, before you enter a G/L account in a company code, you must first enter the G/L account in the global chart of accounts. You then enter it in a specific company code. If the G/L account is not already in the global chart of accounts, you cannot enter it into a specific company code. How-

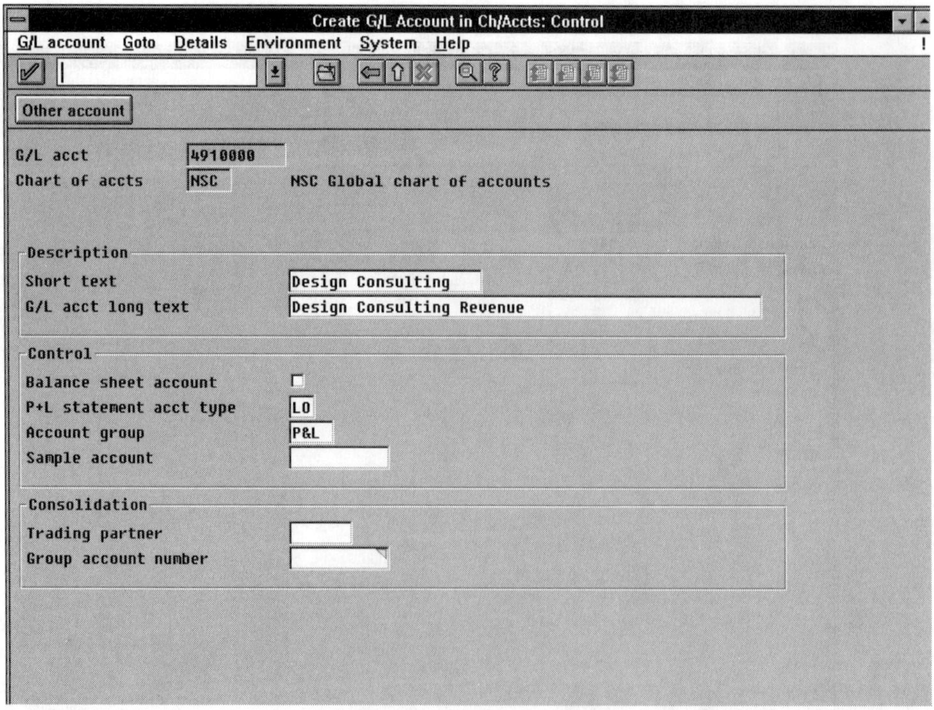

Exhibit 2.20   Create G/L Account: Control

ever, assuming a new G/L account is already in the global chart of accounts, you can create the new G/L account in a specific company code as follows:

1. From the General Ledger menu, select Master records → Company code → Create. (See Exhibit 2.21.)
2. Enter the second, third, and fourth screens in the G/L account in the company code in two steps in the same way that you enter the first screen, if you enter the G/L account in one step. See the section about entering a G/L account in one step for details.
3. To store the G/L account, press <F11> or the file folder icon.

Entering a G/L Account in Foreign Currency

Foreign currency is any currency that differs from the local currency (functional currency) of the company code where you are entering the G/L account.

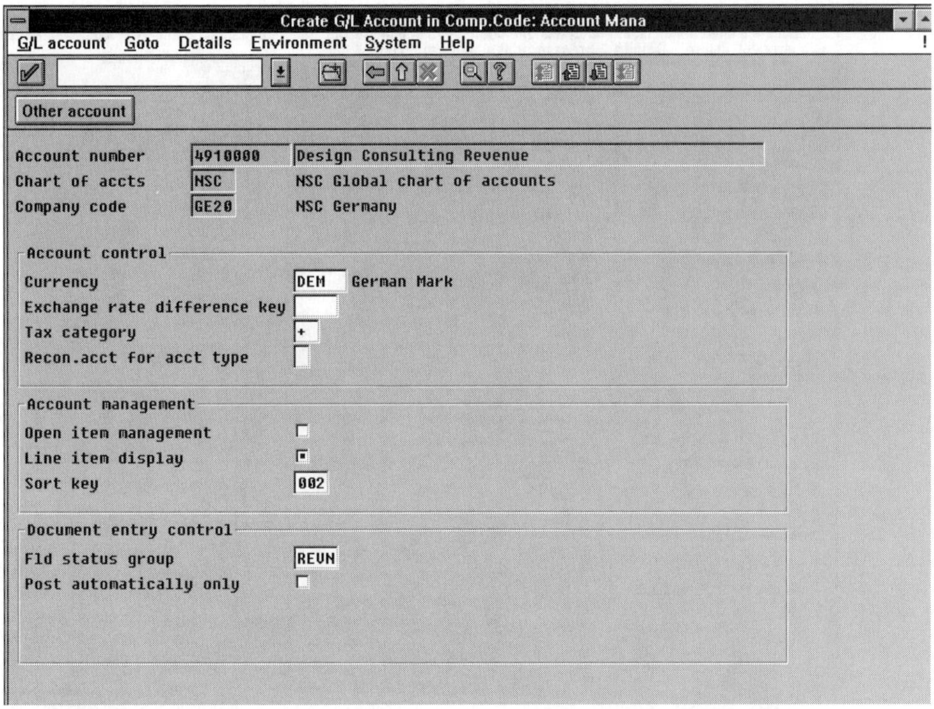

Exhibit 2.21   Create G/L Account in Comp.Code: Account Management

To enter a G/L account in foreign currency, enter the G/L account as usual, either in one step or in two steps. On the second screen, in the Currency field, specify the currency of the account. In Exhibit 2.22, assume the German Mark is a foreign currency.

For example, to enter a G/L account in foreign currency in one step:

1. From the General Ledger menu, select Master records → Create.

2. Enter the G/L account number and the company code, as you would enter a G/L account in local currency. Press <Enter>.

3. On the first screen of the account, enter at least the short and long names of the account, whether the G/L account is a balance sheet or a P&L account, and the account group. Press <Enter>. (See Exhibit 2.22.)

4. On the second screen, enter the currency of the G/L account in the Currency field. If the account is not an open item account, such as a G/L account for cash in the bank, then enter a revaluation key in the Exchange rate difference key field. The revaluation key depends on your specific

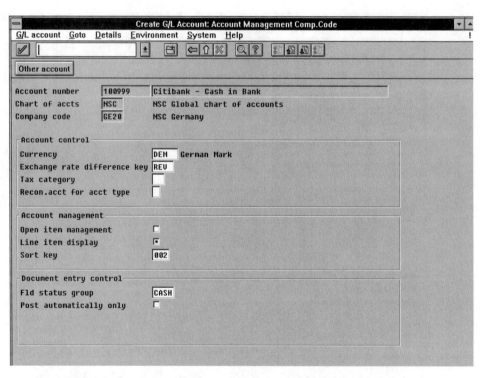

Exhibit 2.22 Create G/L Account: Account Management Comp.Code

configuration, which is not the subject of this book. This key makes it possible to revalue the G/L account balance later.

5. Enter the rest of the G/L account and store it as usual with <F11> or the file folder icon.

Describing a G/L Account (Financial Policy)

You can describe a G/L account with as much text as you require. In this way, you can document your chart of accounts. You can describe a G/L account either on the client level (in the global chart of accounts) or in a specific company code. In this way, you can document how you are going to enter amounts in the opening balance sheet or how you are going to transmit the account balances. Later, you can print out a financial policy manual listing all G/L accounts with the text that you entered. You can describe an account, either when you are entering the account or afterwards. Assume that you have already entered a G/L account and that you wish to document the account in a specific company code. To document a G/L account in a company code:

1. From the General Ledger menu, select Master records ➤ Change.
2. Enter the G/L account number and the company code. Press <Enter>.
3. On the first screen of the G/L account, press <Enter> to go to the second screen, which contains company code data about the G/L account. (See Exhibit 2.23.)
4. As shown in Exhibit 2.23, select Details ➤ Texts. (See Exhibit 2.24.)
5. Double-click on a line with a specific type of text, such as the line with Account description. (See Exhibit 2.25.)
6. To use SAPScript, always press <Enter> at the end of each line. To insert a line before a line, place the cursor at the left end of the line, and then press <F6>. To delete a line, place the cursor at the left end of that line, press Select, and then press Delete. To store the text, press <F11> or the file folder icon. Look for the message Text was saved at the end of the screen. To go back to the previous screen, press the left arrow.
7. To go back to the account, press the Continue pushbutton.
8. To store the G/L account with the text, press <F11> or the file folder icon.

Entering a G/L Account with a Sample Account

A sample account contains company code data about a G/L account. You can enter your chart of accounts more quickly using one or more sample accounts.

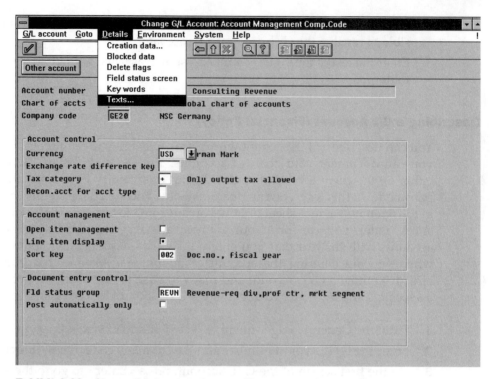

Exhibit 2.23   Change G/L Account: Account Management Comp.Code

If the pattern of entries in a series of accounts, such as overhead or accrual accounts, is the same, then you can make a sample account. To make a sample account:

1. From the General Ledger menu, select Master records ➤ Sample account ➤ Create.

2. Enter a sample account number, depending on your chart of accounts, and the chart of accounts, depending on your specific configuration. Press <Enter>.

3. Enter the details about a sample account as you would enter any other account.

4. To store the sample account, press <F11> or the file folder icon.

Displaying a G/L Account Master Record

From the General Ledger menu, select Master records ➤ Display. To go to the next screen, press <Enter> or select Goto ➤ Next screen. To go to the previous

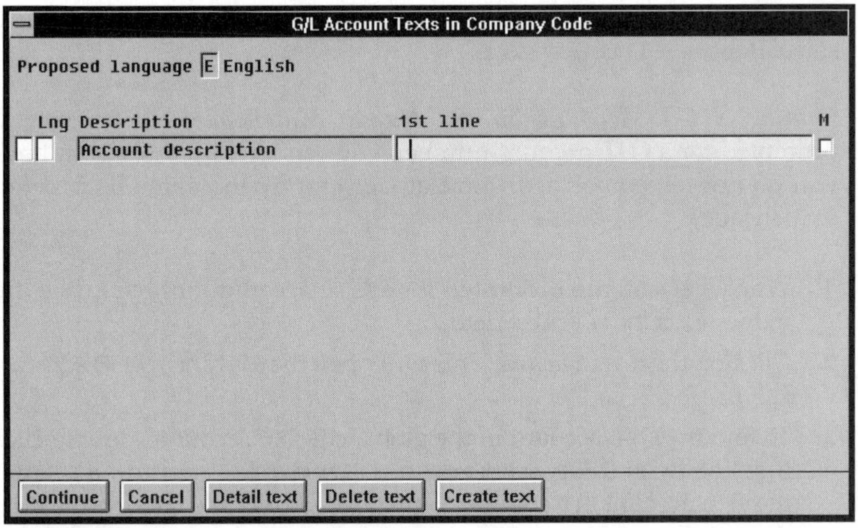

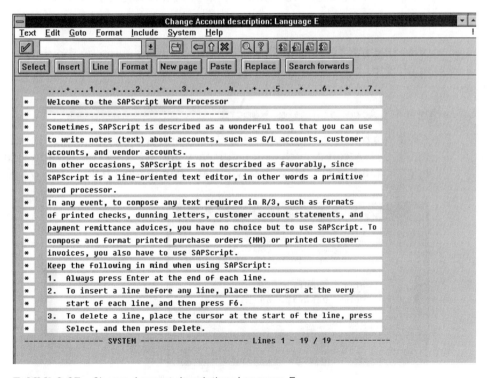

Exhibit 2.24 G/L Account Texts in Company Code

Exhibit 2.25 Change Account description: Language E

screen, select Goto ➤ Previous screen. To see when the account was entered, select Details ➤ Creation data.

Finding a G/L Account by the Name (Matchcode). Whenever you are prompted for a G/L account number, you can look up the account number, if you do not remember it. To find an account by the name or first few digits (matchcode):

1. Whenever you are prompted for a G/L account number, place the cursor in the Account number field.
2. Click on the down arrow. This will open the Matchcode ID screen (Exhibit 2.26).
3. To find the G/L account in the global chart of accounts, double-click on the first line (with C G/L account no. in chart of accounts). For now, to find the G/L account in a specific company code, double-click on the third line of the possible matchcodes (with N G/L account number). (See Exhibit 2.27.)
4. Enter the name or part of the name on the Short text field. Use the * symbol as a wildcard. To continue, press <Enter>. (See Exhibit 2.28.)
5. To select an account from the list, double-click on the line with the account.

Note that this method of looking up accounts by name (without the number) applies to G/L accounts, customer accounts, and vendor accounts.

Updating a G/L Account Master Record

After you post a transaction to a G/L account, you cannot change certain fields in the G/L account, such as the currency and whether the account is an open item account or not. However, you can change most fields in a G/L account,

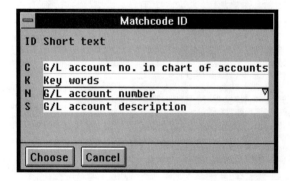

Exhibit 2.26   Matchcode ID

```
┌─────────────────────────────────────────────┐
│ ─            Restrict value ranges           │
├─────────────────────────────────────────────┤
│                                              │
│  G/L account     [          ]                │
│  Company code    GE20                        │
│  Short text      *rent*                       │
│  Language        E                           │
│  G/L acct        [          ]                │
│                                              │
│  ┌──────────┐ ┌────────┐                     │
│  │ Continue │ │ Cancel │                     │
│  └──────────┘ └────────┘                     │
└─────────────────────────────────────────────┘
```

Exhibit 2.27　Restrict Value Ranges

```
┌──────────────────────────────────────────────────────────────┐
│ ─ Matchcode N: Display Data for Search Term 'N..GE20.*RENT*.E.'│
├──────────────────────────────────────────────────────────────┤
│  G/L acct    CoCd Short text                 L G/L acct        │
│                                                                │
│  0100871     GE20 SILVIAS BANK - CURRENT AC  E 100871          │
│  0500050     GE20 PREPAID RENT               E 500050          │
│  2090253     GE20 RENT ACCRUAL               E 2090253         │
│  8000201     GE20 LEASE/RENT - STRUCTURES    E 8000201         │
│  8000203     GE20 LEASE/RENT - OFFICE EQUIP  E 8000203         │
│  8000205     GE20 RENT            ▽          E 8000205         │
│  8000206     GE20 LEASE/RENT - DP EQUIPMENT  E 8000206         │
│                                                                │
│                                                                │
│  ┌────────┐ ┌────────┐ ┌───────────────┐                      │
│  │ Choose │ │ Cancel │ │ New selection │                      │
│  └────────┘ └────────┘ └───────────────┘                      │
└──────────────────────────────────────────────────────────────┘
```

Exhibit 2.28　Selecting an Account from a List

even after you post a transaction to the account. To update a G/L account, changing certain fields such as the account name:

1. From the General Ledger menu, select Master records ➤ Change.
2. Enter the G/L account number and company code. Press <Enter>.
3. Edit the G/L account. To go to the next screen, press <Enter> or select Goto ➤ Next screen. To go to the previous screen, select Goto ➤ Previous screen.
4. You can also enter or edit the notes about the G/L account when you update a G/L account. There are two possible sets of notes about a G/L account, either in the chart of accounts (the first screen) or in the company code (the second through fourth screens).
5. To store the updated G/L account, press <F11> or the file folder icon.

Displaying Changes to G/L Accounts

When you change a G/L account, FI makes a record of the change by field, date, and person. Later, you can trace when and by whom a G/L account was changed. To display changes to a single G/L account master record:

1. From the General Ledger menu, select Master records ➤ Display changes. (See Exhibit 2.29.)
2. Enter the G/L account number and company code, as if you were displaying a G/L account master record. Optionally, enter the most recent date of a change in the From change date field. Also optionally, enter the SAP

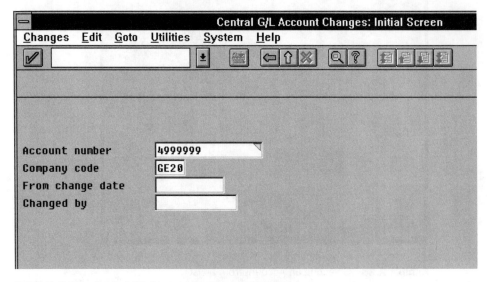

Exhibit 2.29 Central G/L Account Changes: Initial Screen

user ID of the person who made the changes in the Changed by field. Press <Enter>. You will then see the Changed Fields screen. (See Exhibit 2.30.)

3. Double-click on the name of a specific field to see the old and new entries in this field. In this example, double-click on G/L acct long text to bring up the G/L account changes: Overview. (See Exhibit 2.31.)

4. To see the date, time, and user ID (SAP login ID) of the change, double-click on the change to the field. (See Exhibit 2.32.)

5. To go back, press the Back pushbutton and keep pressing the back (left) arrow until you reach the General Ledger menu.

Note that you can also display changes to a G/L account while you are displaying or updating a G/L account by selecting Environment → Change documents → To account.

Blocking a G/L Account from Posting

If a G/L account is inactive or becoming inactive, you can prevent entries from being posted to this account. To block an account:

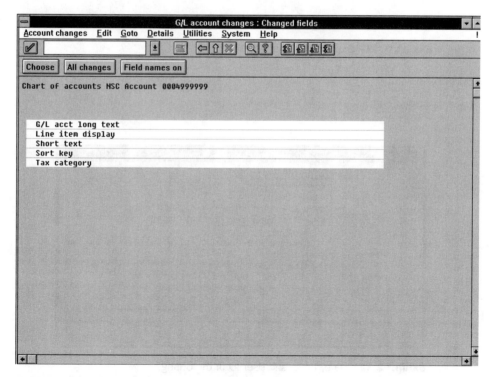

Exhibit 2.30 G/L Account Changes: Changed Fields

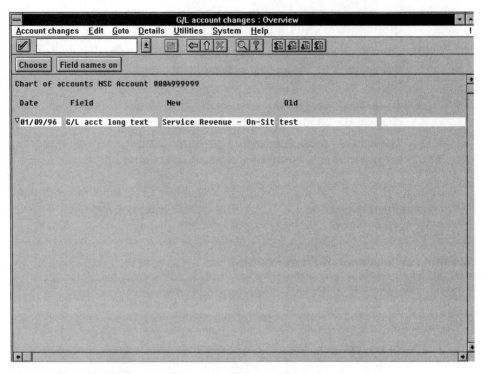

Exhibit 2.31   G/L Account Changes: Overview

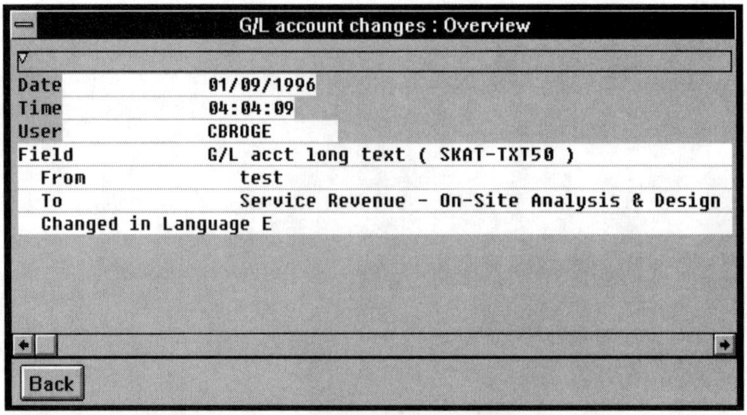

Exhibit 2.32   Date, Time, and User ID of the Change

1. From the General Ledger menu, select Master records → Block/unblock.

2. Enter the account number and the company code. Press <Enter>. (See Exhibit 2.33.)

3. To block the account in all company codes, click on the All company codes box in the Posting block area.

4. To store the block on the account, press <F11> or the file folder icon.

5. Later, to unblock the account, start the same function and click on the All company codes box. If this field is not marked, then the account is not blocked.

Deleting a G/L Account

You can only delete an account (G/L account, customer account, or vendor account) in a test system. Even in a test system, you can only delete an account if there are no transactions posted to the account. In a productive system, you can never delete a G/L account. You can extract and archive a G/L account in

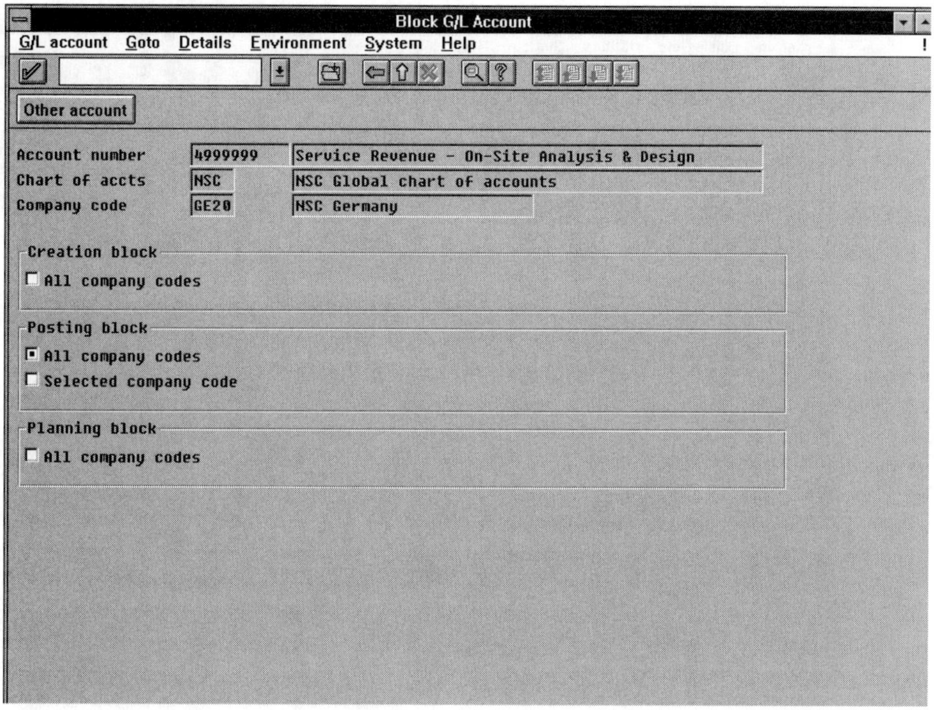

Exhibit 2.33 Block G/L Account

an on-line file. First, you mark the G/L account for deletion. Using an archive program, you then extract and archive the G/L account in a file. Last, using the operating system, you back up the archive file to a removable medium, such as a tape. This section describes deleting a G/L account in a test system. The following section describes marking an account for deletion and archiving a G/L account.

First, assume you have a test system. Further, assume that you have no transactions posted to the G/L account. Delete the G/L account in a test system as follows:

1. From the General Ledger menu, select Environment ➤ Configuration menu.

2. From the Financial Accounting Configuration menu, select Tools ➤ Productive start ➤ Delete master data. (See Exhibit 2.34.)

3. As shown in Exhibit 2.34, to delete one or more G/L accounts, turn on the parameter Delete G/L accounts and specify one or more accounts to delete. If you have entered a G/L account in one specific company code, choose With general master data and then specify the company code. If

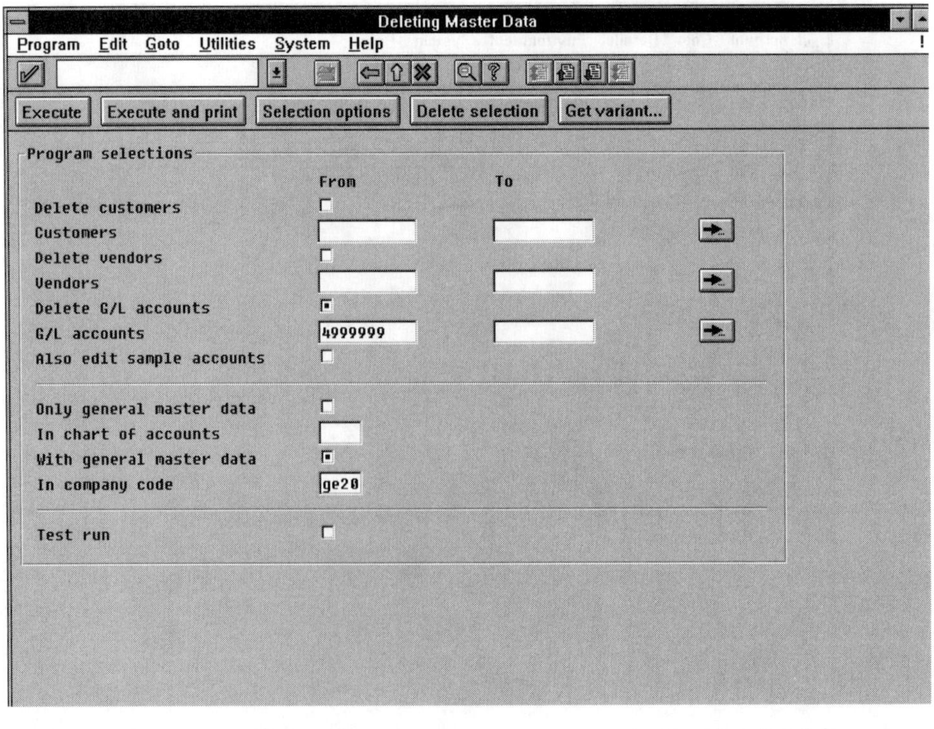

Exhibit 2.34 Deleting Master Data

you have already entered the G/L account in multiple company codes, to delete the G/L account completely, you have to run the program for each company code, leaving With general master data off. When you delete the G/L account for the last company code, mark With general master data. If you have not yet entered the G/L account in a company code, then you can delete the G/L account in the global chart of accounts by turning on Only general master data and then specifying a chart of accounts. To test the deletion, turn on the parameter Test run. To carry out the deletion, turn off the parameter Test run.

4. To start the deletion program, press the Execute pushbutton. If you turn off the Test run option, you then see the message (Exhibit 2.35).

5. Press Continue. The results of the program appear in Exhibit 2.36.

6. Notice the two columns Records read and Records deleted. Entries in these columns confirm that the G/L account was deleted. Almost all report output in SAP is designed for 132-column printers, so you do not see the complete output line on your screen. Use the horizontal scroll bars to move left and right in the report output.

Note that it is only possible to delete a G/L account in a test system, if there are no transactions posted to the G/L account.

Marking a G/L Account for Deletion. In a productive system, to extract and archive a G/L account, you first mark the G/L account for deletion as follows:

1. From the General Ledger menu, select Master records → Mark for deletion.

2. Enter the G/L account number and the company code. Press <Enter>. (See Exhibit 2.37.)

3. Mark one or more options, depending on where you are trying to delete the G/L account—in the specific company code, in the chart of accounts (if it is not entered in a company code), or in both.

4. To store this mark for deletion, press <F11> or the file folder icon.

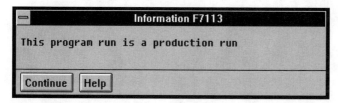

Exhibit 2.35 G/L Account Deletion—Test Run Option Program Message

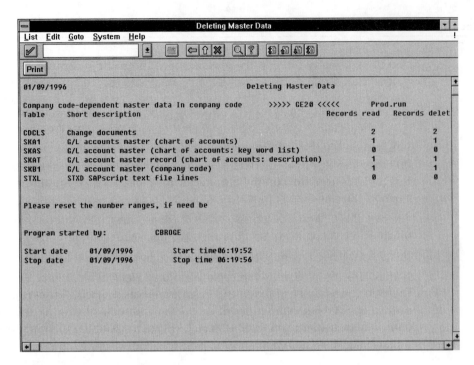

Exhibit 2.36   Deleting Master Data

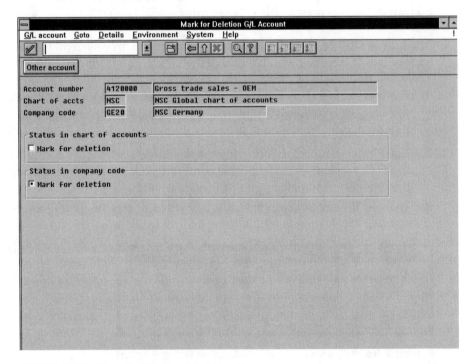

Exhibit 2.37   Mark for Deletion G/L Account

Extracting and Archiving a G/L Account.   Depending on your configuration, all G/L accounts in a productive system will continue to reside in the system for at least two years. In a productive system, you can never delete G/L accounts. You run a program to extract and archive the G/L account into an on-line archive file. You can only extract G/L accounts that are not flagged as cost accounts (primary cost elements) in CO. Furthermore, you can only extract an account if there are no debit and credit balances on the account and no open items.

To extract and archive a G/L account, do as follows:

1. From the General Ledger menu, select Periodic processing → Archiving → G/L accounts. (See Exhibit 2.38.)

2. To specify the G/L accounts to archive, enter the parameters as shown in the Archiving screen (Exhibit 2.38). SAKO refers to G/L accounts. To prevent anyone from logging on and possibly posting a transaction to a G/L account to be deleted, press the Lock logon pushbutton.

3. To start the archiving process, press Start archiving. (See Exhibit 2.38.)

4. To archive all possible G/L accounts (ones marked for deletion), leave the parameter G/L accounts blank. To archive the G/L accounts from the chart of accounts, mark General master records. Otherwise, to archive the G/L account from a company code, mark Financial accounting and then enter the company code. The first time you run the program, test it by selecting the Test run option (Exhibit 2.39).

5. To start the archiving, press Execute. The results of the program appear in Exhibit 2.40.

Exhibit 2.38   Archiving Screen

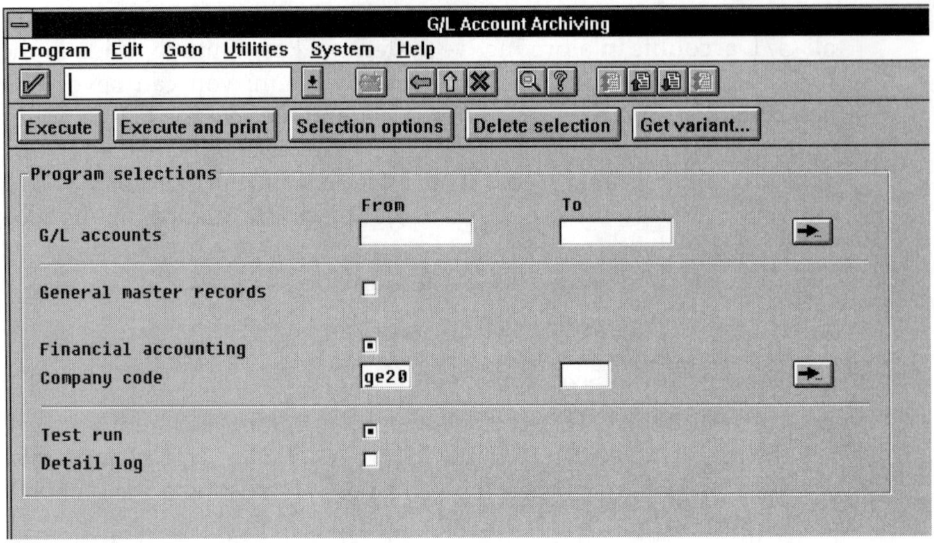

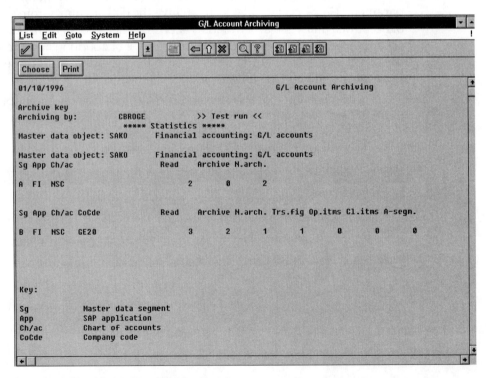

Exhibit 2.39   G/L Account Archiving

Exhibit 2.40   G/L Account Archiving Results

6. Read this report to see which G/L accounts would be deleted if this were not a test run.

Displaying/Printing the Chart of Accounts

It is advisable to develop a specific report to display or print the chart of accounts with each account on one line, including certain posting details. This format is more readable than the one supplied by SAP, which can be a long report without an overview of the key details per account. You should specify to an ABAP programmer that the input be the company code and that the output be the long name of the account, type of account (balance sheet or carry forward key), the currency, tax category, reconciliation account, open item or not, and the field status group.

Using the programs supplied by SAP, you can display or print the chart of accounts on either level—in the (global) chart of accounts or in a specific company code. You can post a transaction only if the G/L account is entered in the company code. To display or print the chart of accounts in a specific company code:

1. From the General Ledger menu, select Periodic processing → Reporting → Accounts list. You will see the first Accounts List parameter screen. (See Exhibit 2.41.)
2. Enter at least the company code in the Company code field and 1 in the Account sorting field. Optionally, click on one or more parameters, such as Status in company code or Account control, to include data for that parameter in the report. To go to the next screen of parameters, press the pushbutton in the lower-right portion of the screen. (See Exhibit 2.42.)
3. For now, leave this screen of parameters blank. Later, you can list the chart of accounts and include more details in the report by selecting a parameter. Using the Opened in company code on parameter, you can list new accounts. Using the Opened in company code by parameter, you can list accounts by the person who opened them. To go to the next screen of parameters, press the + symbol in the lower-right corner of the screen. To go back to the previous screen, press the – symbol. For now, press the + symbol to go to the third and last screen of parameters for this report. (See Exhibit 2.43.)
4. Enter a report heading in the Additional heading field. To run the report, press Execute. (See Exhibit 2.44.)

Finding a String, such as an Account, in the Report. If a report displayed on your screen contains a specific string, you can find lines with that string. For

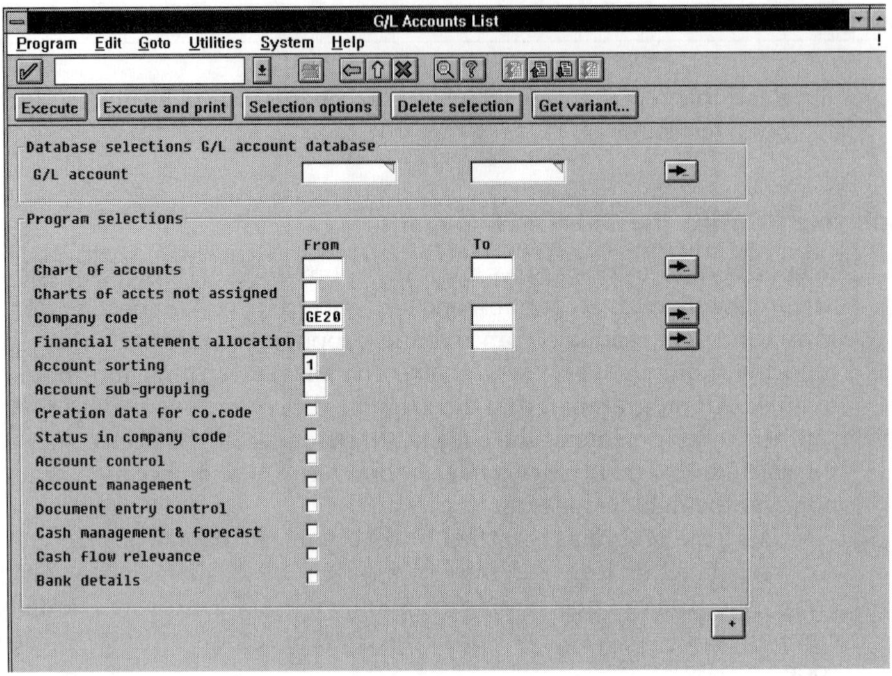

Exhibit 2.41 G/L Accounts List—Parameter Screen 1

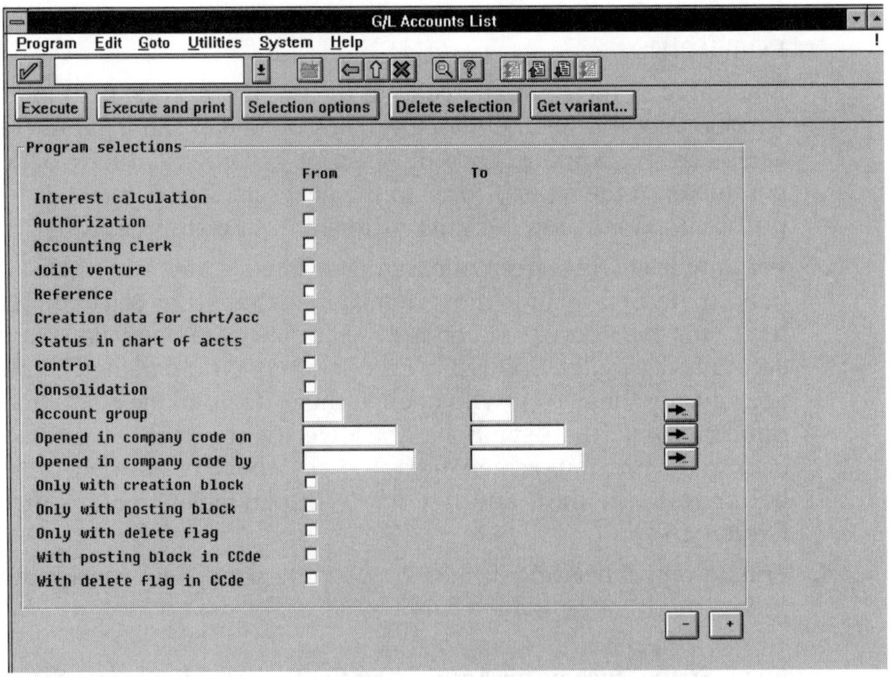

Exhibit 2.42 G/L Accounts List—Parameter Screen 2

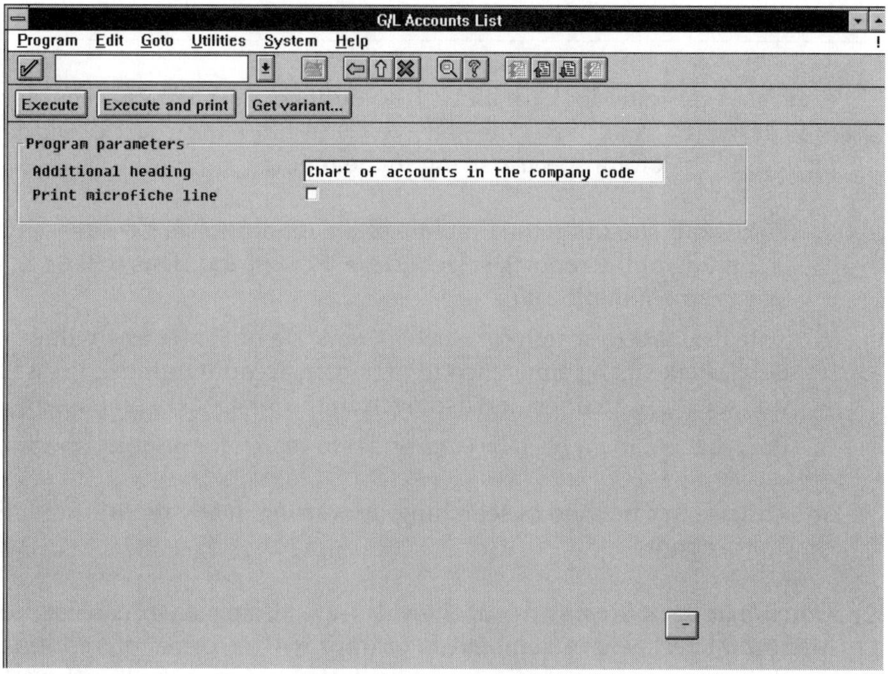

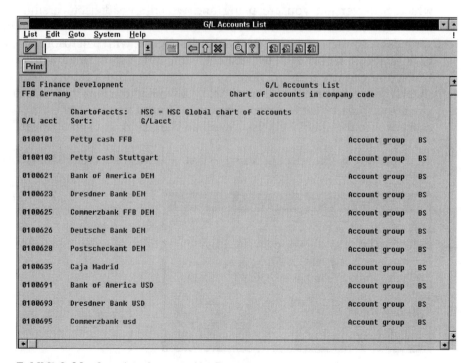

Exhibit 2.43   G/L Accounts List—Parameter Screen 3

Exhibit 2.44   Complete Accounts List Report

example, you could look for all G/L accounts in the chart of accounts containing the word "rent." Assume that you still have the chart of accounts displayed. To look for a specific string in the report:

1. Place your cursor on the first line of the report (to start the search from the beginning of the report), select Edit ➤ Find string. This will open the Find String box (Exhibit 2.45).
2. Enter the text to search for, such as **rent.** Do not enter any wildcard in this field, unlike using a matchcode to find an account number. Press Find. You will see the search results displayed in the Hit List (Exhibit 2.46).
3. Press Cancel to go back or Find again to search for another specific string.

You can use this method of searching for a string in any report (not only in the chart of accounts).

Downloading a Report to a Spreadsheet.   Using a spreadsheet, such as Microsoft Excel, you can embellish, or improve the format of, reports. In other words, with any report displayed on your screen, you can download the report to a spreadsheet. Note that the exact download procedure depends on which SAP version you are using and which spreadsheet version you are using. You can download the report in various formats and open it in various spreadsheet programs, but SAP is closely aligned with Microsoft. The ability to download a report to a spreadsheet is integrated most of all with Microsoft Excel. You can use this function, for example, to print a report via a spreadsheet if your SAP printer is unavailable. Download the report to a spreadsheet. Open the spreadsheet in Excel. Then print from Excel. Assume you have the chart of accounts displayed. To download the report to a spreadsheet:

1. From any menu select System ➤ List ➤ Download. (See Exhibit 2.47.)

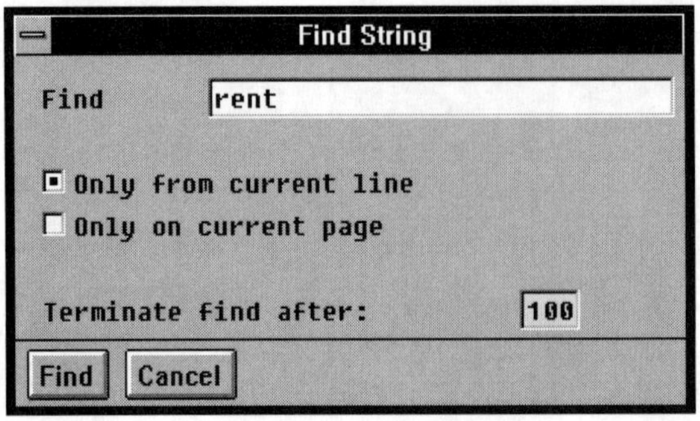

Exhibit 2.45   Find String

```
┌─────────────────────────────────────────────────────────────────┐
│ ─                          Hit List                               │
├─────────────────────────────────────────────────────────────────┤
│ ⌐*** Number of objects found:          10                         │
│                                                                   │
│   0500050    Prepaid rent                                  Accoun │
│   1220001    Deposits-noncur-Lease / Rent                  Accoun │
│   2010001    Current payroll                               Accoun │
│   2090253    Rent accrual                                  Accoun │
│   8000201    Lease/rent - structures                       Accoun │
│   8000203    Lease/rent - office equipment                 Accoun │
│   8000204    Lease rental exo - reproduction equipment     Accoun │
│   8000205    Rent                                          Accoun │
│   8000206    Lease/rent - DP equipment                     Accoun │
│   23GE299    I/L A/P to NSGE - Interdiv. Current           Accoun │
│                                                                   │
│                                                                   │
│ ┌─┬─┐                                                      ┌─┐    │
│ │◄│ │                                                      │►│    │
│ └─┴─┘                                                      └─┘    │
│ ┌───────────────┐ ┌────────────┐ ┌────────┐                      │
│ │Position cursor│ │ Find again │ │ Cancel │                      │
│ └───────────────┘ └────────────┘ └────────┘                      │
└─────────────────────────────────────────────────────────────────┘
```

Exhibit 2.46 Hit List

2. Enter the full MS-DOS path name and filename of the spreadsheet file, such as **c:\msoffice\excel\coa.xls.** Microsoft Office lends itself to use with SAP R/3. If you have Microsoft Office properly installed, the default directory for Excel to open spreadsheets on your C: drive is c:\msoffice\excel. Enter a data format of **ASC** (for ASCII). Then press Send to transfer the report to a spreadsheet.

3. Look for the message at the end of your screen Frontend Multiplexer active. Then look for the message that confirms that your report has been downloaded. (See Exhibit 2.48.)

4. Press Continue. Then start up Excel. Inside Excel, open the spreadsheet file by selecting File → Open. To load the spreadsheet, experiment with the parameters to open the file in Excel. For example, you could specify Fixed width as the original data format. Shift the column lines around to fit your specific report. Specify Text for the column with the account numbers. After you load the spreadsheet, use Excel to adjust the column width and to process the data further.

```
┌─────────────────────────────────────────────────────────────────┐
│ ─                   Send List to a Local File                     │
├─────────────────────────────────────────────────────────────────┤
│ File name        c:\msoffice\excel\coa.xls                        │
│ Data format     │ASC│▼│                                           │
│                                                                   │
│ ┌───────────────────────────────────────────────────────────┐    │
│ │                                                           │    │
│ └───────────────────────────────────────────────────────────┘    │
│ ┌──────┐ ┌────────┐                                               │
│ │ Send │ │ Cancel │                                               │
│ └──────┘ └────────┘                                               │
└─────────────────────────────────────────────────────────────────┘
```

Exhibit 2.47 Send List to a Local File

```
┌─────────────────────────────────────────────────────────────────┐
│ ▬                     Send List to a Local File                   │
├─────────────────────────────────────────────────────────────────┤
│ File name      │c:\msoffice\excel\coa.xls                        │
│ Data format    │ASC                                              │
│                                                                   │
│ 115221  Bytes transferred                                        │
│ ┌──────────┐                                                     │
│ │ Continue │                                                      │
│ └──────────┘                                                     │
└─────────────────────────────────────────────────────────────────┘
```

Exhibit 2.48 Confirmation That a Report Has Been Downloaded

You can download any report to an Excel spreadsheet (not only the chart of accounts).

Printing the Chart of Accounts (Names and Numbers).   First, make sure that your printer is properly installed—first physically, then under the operating system, next under R/3 Basis, lastly in your LAN. To print from your PC printer, you have to obtain and install a piece of software called saplpd (SAP line printer daemon) on your PC. Obtain this software from SAP.

If your printer is installed properly, you can print or display any report. To print any report:

1. First display the report and then select List ➤ Print or press the Print push-button. The Print Screen Output dialog box will open. (See Exhibit 2.49.)
2. Make sure that you specify a printer that is installed correctly. Also mark the parameters Print immed and Delete after print, if they are not already marked.
3. Press Print again.

Checking the Printing in Process.   After you start to print a report, the system places the report in a spool file. FI then prints the report from this spool file. To monitor the spool file (printing in process):

1. From any menu, select System ➤ Services ➤ Output controller. (See Exhibit 2.50.)
2. From the Spool: Request Screen, press <Enter> to see the entry (or entries) in the spool file (Exhibit 2.50).
3. If the report is already printed, then you see a message at the end of the screen No spool requests for the specified selection. Otherwise, you see the entries in the spool file as shown in Exhibit 2.51.
4. Notice the columns with the reference number of the spool file entry (Spool No.); the date and time of the spool file entry (Generation Date and Time); the output status (either Wait for not yet started or In proc for in

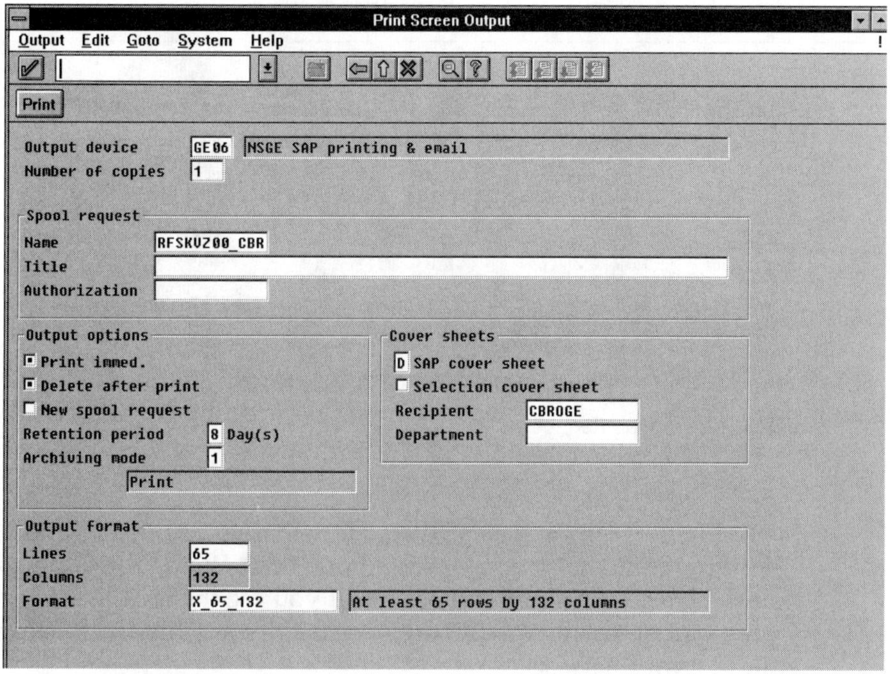

Exhibit 2.49 Print Screen Output

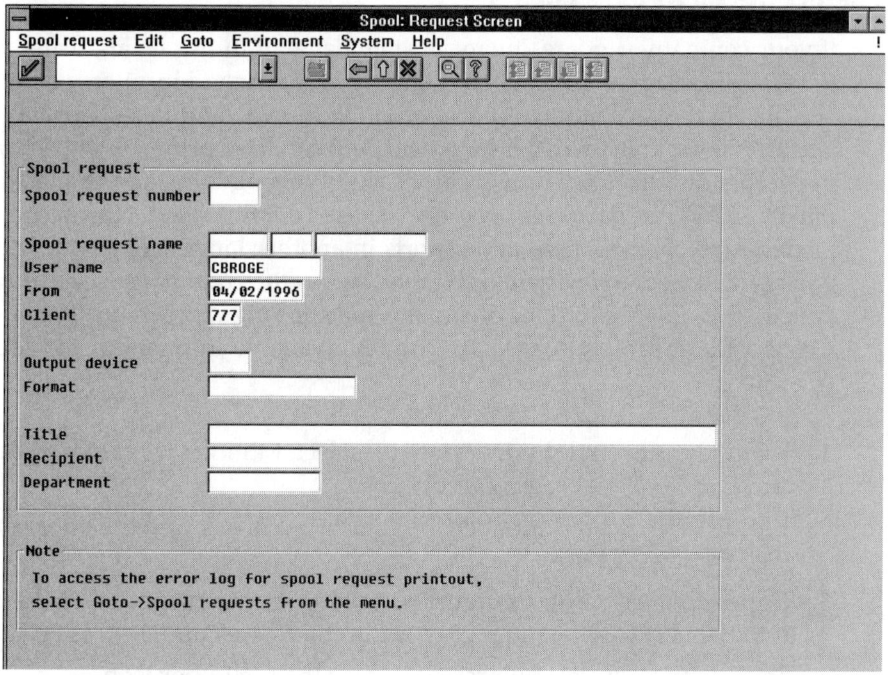

Exhibit 2.50 Spool: Request Screen

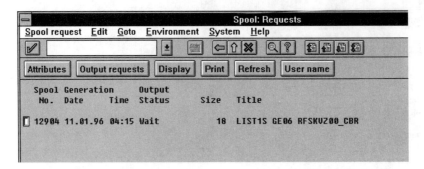

Exhibit 2.51 Spool: Requests

process); the Size (in pages), the printer that you specified, and the name of the program that prepares this report (Title). Press the Refresh button to see the latest status of the spool file. If you see the message There are no more spool jobs, then the report is not in the spool file and is being printed through your network.

Translating the Chart of Accounts

If your company prepares financial statements in multiple languages, you can translate the chart of accounts. Depending on your configuration, you can translate the chart of accounts into any valid alternative language. If you also translate a version of the financial statement, you can later print a financial statement in another language, even without having the language tape (translation supplied by SAP) for that other language licensed and installed. However, to see the menus, screens, messages, and reports in another language, the language tape must be licensed and installed. Depending on the code page in your operating system, there are limitations on mixing specific languages in one system, but all western European languages are usually available in one and the same code page. To translate a G/L account:

1. From the General Ledger menu, select Master records → Chart of accounts → Change account name.
2. Enter a G/L account number, the chart of accounts, and then press <Enter>. (See Exhibit 2.52.)
3. Depending on your configuration, enter the translations of the account into the alternative languages for the chart of accounts.
4. To store the translation, press <F11> or the file folder icon.

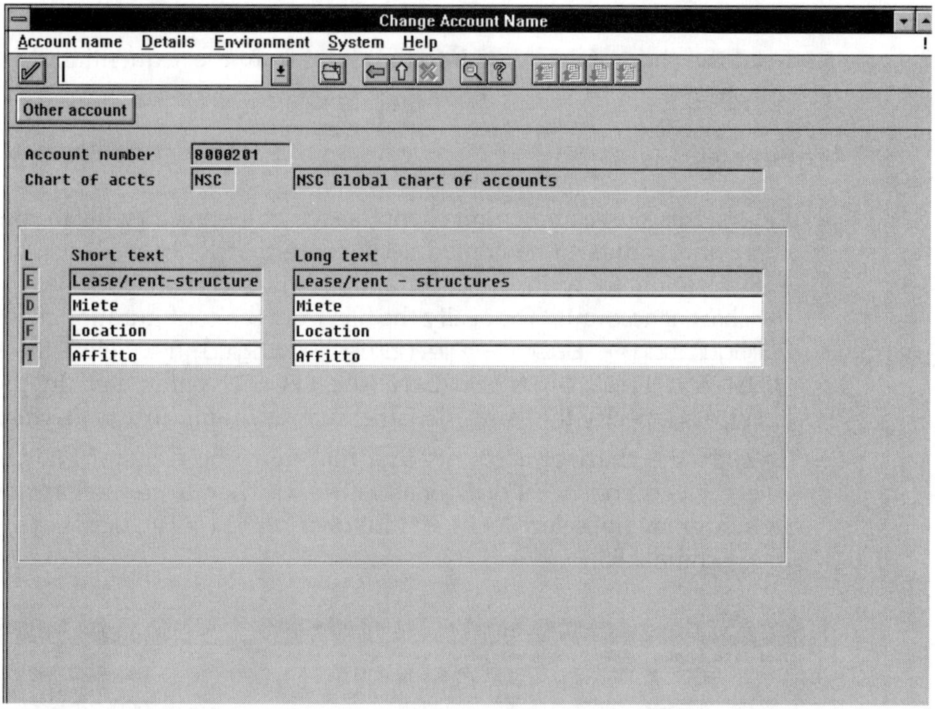

Exhibit 2.52   Translate G/L Account

For details about how to translate the version of the financial statement, see the section called "Translating a Financial Statement" under Financial Reporting from the General Ledger.

Copying the Chart of Accounts

You can copy the chart of accounts from one client to another for a specific company code, for example, from the test client in 210 to the production client in 010. If the clients are on separate machines, you should configure the directory and filename to be the same on both machines—to read and write the chart of accounts. (See Exhibit 2.53.) In summary:

1. Configure both the source and target clients.
2. Copy the chart of accounts to a UNIX file (with a specific directory and file name in the configuration, and a sequential filename in the program).
3. Transfer the UNIX file to another machine, using ftp, possibly copying the file to an intermediate PC.

4. Initialize the sequential file in the target client.
5. Load the chart of accounts into the client from the sequential file that you transferred.

Step-by-step:

1. In both the source and target clients, specify the directory file to contain the chart of accounts to be copied. Make sure that R/3 (or all users) has the authorization to write to a certain file in a certain path that contains the chart of accounts. To specify the file, from the configuration menu, select Configuration ➤ Basis ➤ File names ➤ Logical file. Select the FI_COPY _COMPANY_CODE_DATA_FOR_GENERAL_LEDGER parameter. In the target client, also specify the same filename, such as **/home/fipftp/iftest/coa.**
2. To copy the chart of accounts to a file, from the General Ledger menu, select Environment ➤ Configuration menu. Then from the Financial Configuration menu, select Tools ➤ Data distribution ➤ G/L accounts ➤ Send. (See Exhibit 2.53.)

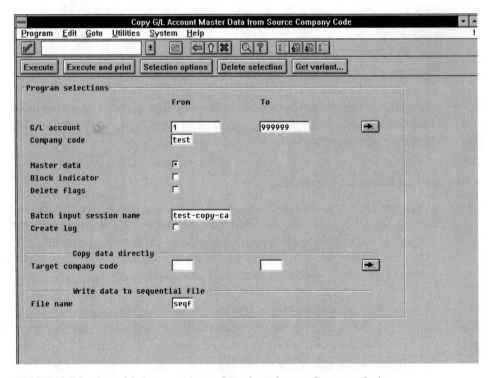

Exhibit 2.53 Copy G/L Account Master Data from Source Company Code

3. If the clients are on separate machines, transfer the file from one machine to the other. First, using your operating system, such as UNIX, log in to the source machine. Next, using your network software (TCP/IP and ftp), transfer the file from the source machine to your PC (or directly to the other machine).

4. Log in to the target client. The first time only, initialize the sequential file on the target machine by writing the same sequential file name in the same company code. To do this, repeat step 2, but in the target client.

5. To load the chart of accounts, from the Financial Configuration menu, select Tools ➤ Data distribution ➤ G/L accounts ➤ Receive. (See Exhibit 2.54.)

If you cannot upload the file, make sure that the file on the target client has the same directory and file name specified in the Basis configuration as in the source client. Also, make sure under UNIX that you can write to the file, although you are only reading the file. Use the UNIX command **chmod** to change file permissions, if required. (See Exhibit 2.54.)

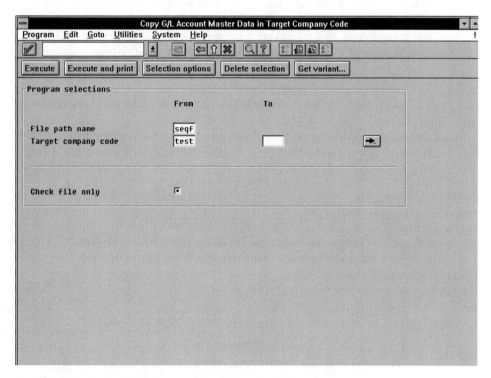

Exhibit 2.54 Copy G/L Account Master Data in Target Company Code

ENTERING AND POSTING G/L TRANSACTIONS

Using the G/L program, you can enter and process various types of general ledger transactions, such as petty cash, expense accruals, revenue deferrals, periodic adjusting entries, transactions in foreign currency, and entries in the bank statement. A transaction can never be deleted. If a mistake is made and you have already posted the transaction, it can be reversed quickly and easily. You then have to re-enter the transaction. Using the G/L program, you usually enter each line in the bank statement as a separate transaction. To reconcile the bank statement, compare the bank balance in the system with the bank balance according to the bank.

Posting a G/L Transaction, Such as Petty Cash

A G/L transaction always contains a transaction header and two or more line items posted to G/L accounts. In any one posted transaction, the total amount of the debit entries always equals the total amount of the credit entries. Otherwise, you cannot post the transaction. In other words, an out-of-balance transaction cannot be posted. Up to 999 line items can be entered in a transaction, with each line item on a separate screen. You can then display an overview of the transaction. If a mistaken amount is entered, select the line item from the overview and then change the amount, but only before posting the transaction. After you post the transaction, you can only correct a mistake by reversing the transaction and entering it again.

You can also enter a long transaction quickly, line-by-line, instead of screen-by-screen.

Assume you wish to enter and post a G/L transaction to record a disbursement of petty cash for taxi fare. Further assume that you enter this transaction in a journal called GJ (general journal). To enter and post this transaction:

1. From the General Ledger menu, select Document entry ➤ G/L account posting. The first screen appears in Exhibit 2.55.
2. The top half of the screen contains the transaction header. The following five fields are always required in a transaction header:

Field	Note
Document date	This is usually today's date, but could be different, for example, when you are entering a bank statement from yesterday.
Doc.type	This is an SAP term for a transaction journal. The valid entries depend on your configuration. For example, the most frequently used journals (in English) are GJ

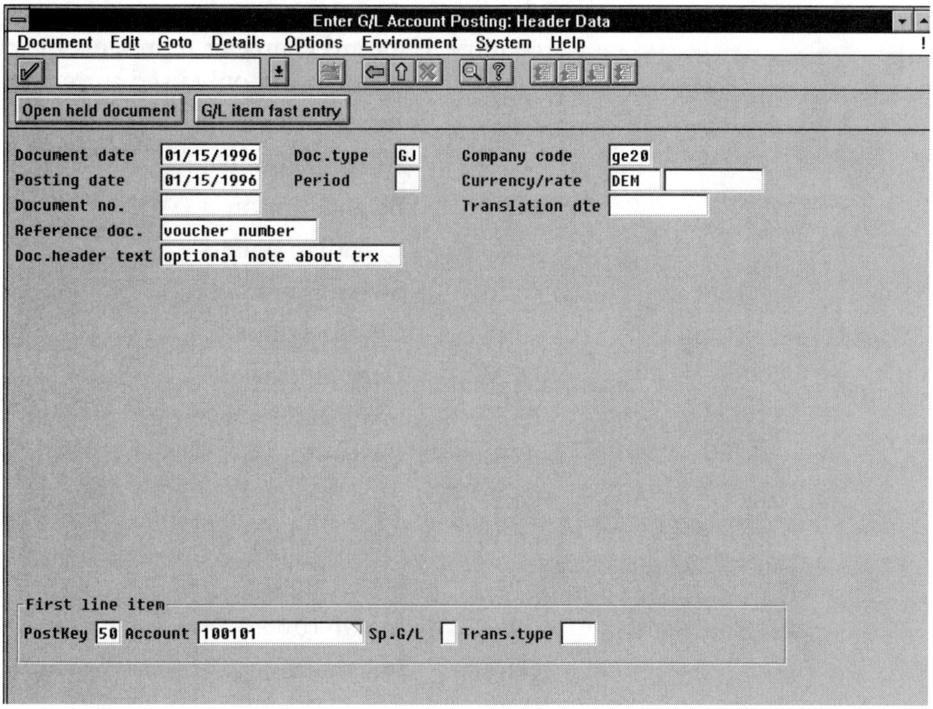

Exhibit 2.55 Entering a General Journal Transaction: First Screen

(general journal), BJ (bank journal), CI (customer invoices), CP (customer payments), VI (vendor invoices), and VP (vendor payments). With your cursor in this field, press the down arrow for a list of available journals (i.e., document types) in your configuration.

Company code | The valid entries depend on your configuration. Enter the four-character code for the company whose books you are keeping. A company code usually refers to a legal entity (single entity subject to income, VAT or sales tax) in your organization.

Posting date | This is also usually today's date, but could be different. The posting date determines the posting period, the period in which FI updates the account balances, immediately after you post the transaction.

Currency/rate | Enter a code for the currency of the transaction. Use the ISO code for the currency, which always has three characters. The first two characters represent the country. The third character represents the currency. The following are commonly used currency codes:

ATS	Austrian shillings
AUD	Australian dollars
BEF	Belgian francs
CAD	Canadian dollars
CHF	Swiss francs
CNY	Chinese yuan
DEM	German marks
ESP	Spanish pesetas
FRF	French francs
GBP	British pounds
HKD	Hong Kong dollars
ILS	Israeli shekels
INR	Indian rupees
ITL	Italian lire
JPY	Japanese yen
KPW	Korean won
MXN	Mexican new pesos
NLG	Dutch guilders
NZD	New Zealand dollars
SGD	Singapore dollars
TWD	Taiwan dollars
USD	US dollars

For a complete list of the currency codes, put your cursor in this field, and then click on the down arrow just to the right of this field. If you enter a code for a currency that is a foreign currency (different from the local reporting currency of the company code), then you can also enter an exchange rate in the field immediately to the right of the Currency/rate field.

Ignore the Period field. FI automatically determines the posting period based on the posting date and your fiscal year as configured. Assuming that your configuration has a "document type" GJ and that these transactions are set up to be numbered internally (automatically by FI when you post), then leave the Document no. field (transaction number) blank. Optionally, depending on your configuration, enter a reference number, such as an external **voucher number** or bank statement number, in the Reference doc. field. Optionally, you can describe the transaction briefly, using the Doc.header text field.

3. At the end of this screen, enter the posting key in the PostKey field. To credit a G/L account, enter a posting key of **50.** To debit a G/L account, enter a posting key of **40.** To see a complete list of available posting keys, place the cursor on the PostKey field and then press the <F4> key or the down-arrow just to the right of the field. (See Exhibit 2.56.)

   PK (in the first column) means posting key. AcTyp means account type, which is hard-coded in the program as follows: S—G/L account; K—vendor account; D—customer account, and A—asset account. D/C means debit or credit, which is hard-coded in the program as follows: S—debit; H—credit. When you enter a posting key, you specify whether the valid account type in the next field at the end of this screen and whether the amount *on the next screen* is a debit or a credit. Depending on the configuration, you can define your own posting keys, but you can almost always use the ones supplied and pre-configured by SAP. Use the

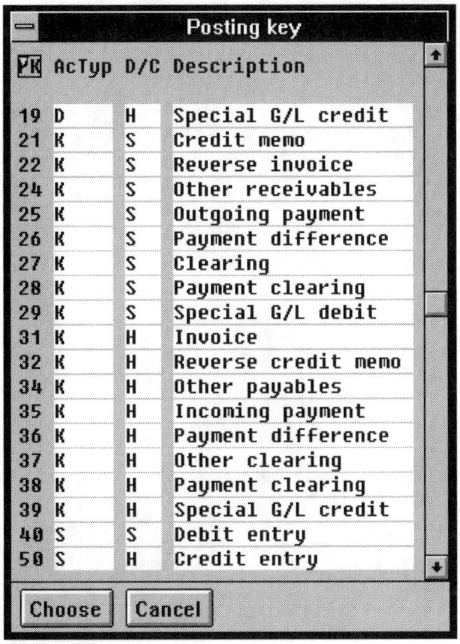

PK	AcTyp	D/C	Description
Posting key			
19	D	H	Special G/L credit
21	K	S	Credit memo
22	K	S	Reverse invoice
24	K	S	Other receivables
25	K	S	Outgoing payment
26	K	S	Payment difference
27	K	S	Clearing
28	K	S	Payment clearing
29	K	S	Special G/L debit
31	K	H	Invoice
32	K	H	Reverse credit memo
34	K	H	Other payables
35	K	H	Incoming payment
36	K	H	Payment difference
37	K	H	Other clearing
38	K	H	Payment clearing
39	K	H	Special G/L credit
40	S	S	Debit entry
50	S	H	Credit entry

Choose   Cancel

Exhibit 2.56   Posting Key

scroll bar to scroll through the list of posting keys. To select a posting key from the list, put the cursor on the line and then press Choose. To go back to the first screen, press Cancel.

To record a disbursement of petty cash, select or enter directly a posting key of 50. In the Account field, enter the G/L account number for petty cash, such as 0100101 - Petty Cash. Then press <Enter>. If you do not remember the G/L account number, then use a matchcode to find it. Put the cursor in the Account field, press <F4>, and then double-click on the line for the G/L account in the company code.

4. The program then validates the data on the first screen and determines the posting period. Among other validations, F1 verifies that you have entered the dates correctly (according to your user defaults). The program also verifies that the "document type" exists and is valid for G/L accounts (the valid account type for this posting key), that the posting period is open, that the company code and currency code exist, and that the posting key and G/L account exist. Assuming that all of these and other conditions are true, then you see the screen in Exhibit 2.57.

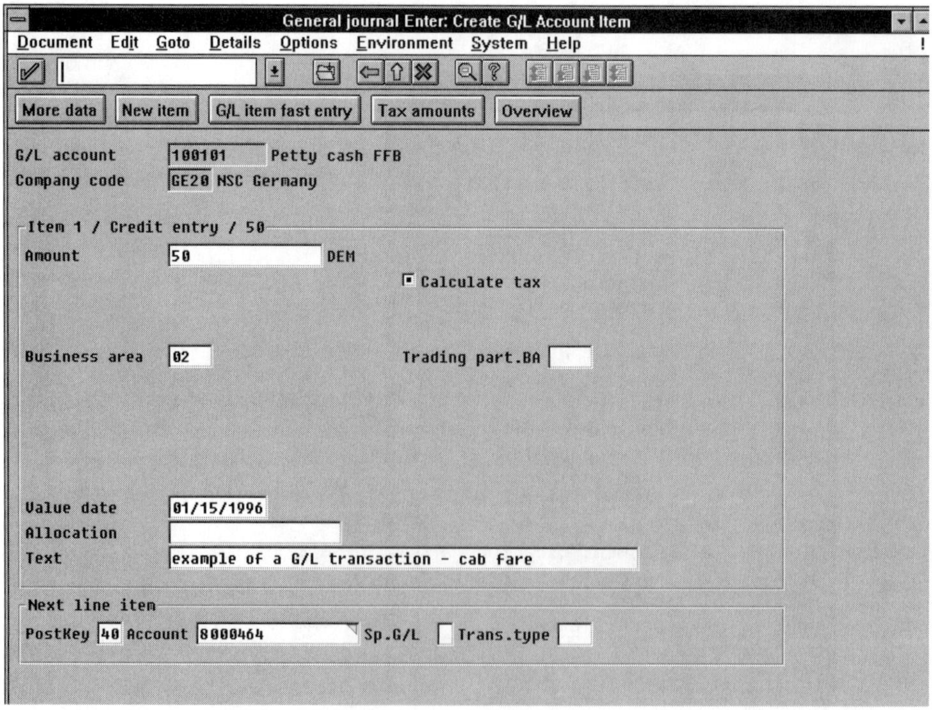

Exhibit 2.57 General Journal Enter: Create G/L Account Item

5. On this screen, the second screen to enter a transaction, enter the amount in the Amount field. If you see the Calculate tax field, mark it. Although VAT does not apply to entries in balance sheet accounts, this prompts the program to calculate tax on other entries in this transaction. Calculating, posting, and reporting VAT depends completely on your configuration. To calculate, post, and report sales tax, install and set up a third-party package, such as AVP or Vertex. Note that *at the end of the previous screen,* you have already specified whether this amount is a debit or a credit and in which account you are entering this amount. These details are displayed at the beginning of this data entry screen and labeled G/L account and Item 1 / Credit entry / 50. To have a balance sheet by division, if you are organized internally into divisions within company codes, enter the Business area (division). Optionally, enter a description of this line item in the Text field. The exact fields that you see on this screen depend on your configuration. Besides an amount, which is always required, fields with a question mark (not shown, but on other screens) require an entry, also depending on your configuration. In general, you can only have reports that are as detailed as the transactions that you have entered. In other words, if the field is required for any report, you should always enter a transaction that is to be included in the report. At the end of this screen, enter the posting key and account of the second line item. For example, to enter a debit to an account for taxi fare, enter **40** in the PostKey field and enter a G/L account number **8000464** in the Account field.

6. After you enter the data on this screen, press <Enter>. The program validates the data entered on this screen and then displays the next screen (Exhibit 2.58).

7. On this screen, the third screen to enter a G/L transaction, you enter the second line item in a G/L transaction. In this example of a G/L transaction, you enter an expense item with the following fields:

Field	*What You Enter*
Amount	Amount of the expense
Tax code	Depending on your configuration, enter the tax code for input VAT. In this example, v1 is the regular rate.
Business area	Enter the division, such as 02. Later, you can prepare an internal balance sheet and P&L by business area.
Cost center	Enter the department, such as **ge5400.**

To see an overview of the transaction, press the pushbutton (on the fourth row of the window) marked Overview. Exhibit 2.59 shows the Display Overview.

```
┌────────────────────────────────────────────────────────────────────────────┐
│ ═              General journal Enter: Create G/L Account Item        ▼ ▲     │
│ Document  Edit  Goto  Details  Options  Environment  System  Help         ! │
│ ┌─────┐ ┌──────────────┐ ± ┌──┐ ⇦⇧✖ ┌───┐ ┌──────────┐                       │
│ │  ✔  │ │              │   │📅│      │🔍❓│ │🗎🗎🗎│                          │
│ ┌──────────┐ ┌──────────┐ ┌────────────────┐ ┌────────────┐ ┌──────────┐     │
│ │More data │ │New item  │ │G/L item fast entry│ │Tax amounts│ │Overview  │     │
│                                                                              │
│ G/L account       8000464   Travel & Local Transport                        │
│ Company code      GE20 NSC Germany                                           │
│                                                                              │
│  ┌Item 2 / Debit entry / 40──────────────────────────────────────────────┐  │
│  │ Amount          50             DEM                                      │  │
│  │ Tax code        v1                                                      │  │
│  │                                                                         │  │
│  │                                                                         │  │
│  │ Business area   02             Trading part.BA                          │  │
│  │ Cost center     ge5400         Order                                    │  │
│  │                                                                         │  │
│  │                                                          □ More         │  │
│  │                                                                         │  │
│  │ Allocation                                                              │  │
│  │ Text                                                                    │  │
│  └─────────────────────────────────────────────────────────────────────────┘│
│  ┌Next line item───────────────────────────────────────────────────────────┐│
│  │ PostKey     Account                     Sp.G/L     Trans.type            ││
│  └─────────────────────────────────────────────────────────────────────────┘│
└────────────────────────────────────────────────────────────────────────────┘
```

Exhibit 2.58   General Journal Enter: Create G/L Account Item

```
┌────────────────────────────────────────────────────────────────────────────┐
│ ═              General journal Enter: Display Overview               ▼ ▲     │
│ Document  Edit  Goto  Details  Options  Environment  System  Help         ! │
│ ┌─────┐ ┌──────────────┐ ± ┌──┐ ⇦⇧✖ ┌───┐ ┌────────┐                         │
│ │  ✔  │ │              │   │📅│      │🔍❓│ │🗎🗎🗎🗎│                        │
│ ┌────────────┐ ┌────────────────┐ ┌─────────────┐ ┌──────────────────┐       │
│ │Display item│ │Display currency│ │Hold document│ │G/L item fast entry│      │
│                                                                              │
│ Document date  01/15/1996   Doc.type   GJ    Company code  GE20              │
│ Posting date   01/15/1996   Period     8     Currency      DEM              │
│ Document no.   Internal      Fiscal year 1996  Translation dte 01/15/1996    │
│ Reference doc. VOUCHER NUMBER                                                │
│ Doc.header text optional note about trx                                      │
│ ┌Items in document currency───────────────────────────────────────────────┐ │
│ │  PK  BusA Acct                        DEM  Amount      Tax amt           │ │
│ │ 001 50  02   0000100101 Petty cash FFB       50,00-                      │ │
│ │ 002 40  02   0008000464 Travel & Local       50,00            V1         │ │
│ │                                                                          │ │
│ │                                                                          │ │
│ │ D 50,00          C 50,00                   0,00  *   2 Line items        │ │
│ └──────────────────────────────────────────────────────────────────────────┘│
│ ┌Other line item──────────────────────────────────────────────────────────┐ │
│ │ PostKey     Account                     Sp.G/L     Trans.type            │ │
│ └──────────────────────────────────────────────────────────────────────────┘│
└────────────────────────────────────────────────────────────────────────────┘
```

Exhibit 2.59   General Journal Enter: Display Overview

8. Note that the total debits in the transaction appear near the lower left corner of the screen just to the right of the letter *D*. The total credits appear just to the right of the letter *C*. *You can post a transaction only if the total debits equal the total credits.* In other words, the program complies with the transaction principle of accounting. If the debits equal the credits, then the balance of the transaction is zero and "0" appears on the same line to the right.

    Start to enter another line item by entering a posting key and an account number *at the bottom of this screen.*

    To correct a line item, for example if you enter a mistaken amount, double-click on the item in the overview and then re-enter the amount on the next screen, the line item detail screen.

    To delete a line, double-click on the line in the overview and then enter zero in the amount on the next screen, the line item detail screen. If you have entered a mistaken posting date in the transaction header, you cannot change it after you enter the first screen. You must then exit this function without posting the transaction by pressing the up arrow and then enter the transaction again with the correct posting date. This is due to the fact that the program always validates the posting date and determines the posting period from the transaction header that you enter on the first screen.

9. To post the transaction, either press <F11> or press the file folder icon.

    The program then validates the transaction. Most of all, the program verifies that the total debits equal the total credits. It also checks whether the tax code is valid and then calculates the tax and posts the tax item. Calculation, posting, and reporting transaction taxes (VAT or sales tax) depend on country-specific legal requirements and also on the configuration. Third-party routines to calculate, post, and report sales tax in the United States are available from AVP and Vertex. Lastly, the program assigns a number to the transaction and updates the G/L account balances in the posting period.

10. Notice the message Document 9999999 was posted. The exact transaction number depends on your configuration.

Displaying the Last Posted G/L Transaction

To verify that the transaction is properly posted, you can display the last posted transaction. From the Enter G/L Account Posting screen (Exhibit 2.55) select Document → Display. The overview of the transaction can be seen in Exhibit 2.60.

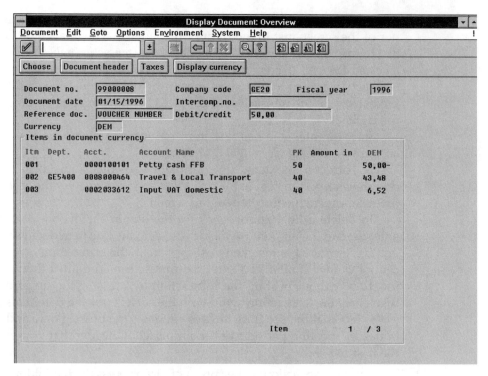

Exhibit 2.60   Display Document: Overview

Setting Entry of Transaction Currency Only

You can set the package so that the screens contain fields for you to enter amounts in transaction currency only when you enter transactions in foreign currency. This makes the screens easier to read and the program easier to use. Otherwise, you see two fields to enter amounts in each line item—an amount in the transaction currency and an amount in local currency. In effect, by entering both amounts, you enter an exchange rate in each line item. This is rarely required, such as for credit card invoices in foreign currency, with all transactions in the same foreign currency. To set entry of amounts in transaction currency only:

1. From the General Ledger menu, select Environment → Current options → Editing options. (See Exhibit 2.61.)
2. Make sure that the parameter Amount fields only for document currency is set on.
3. To store the settings, press <F11> or the file folder icon.

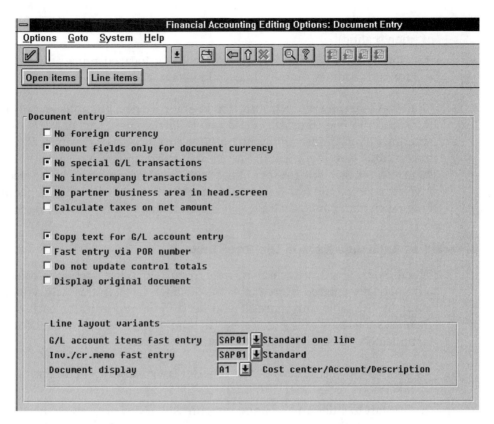

Exhibit 2.61   Financial Accounting Editing Options: Document Entry

Posting a G/L Transaction in Foreign Currency

Foreign currency is any currency that is different from local currency. Local currency is the functional (reporting) currency of the company code where you are posting the transaction. To enter a transaction in foreign currency, you first have to enter the currency of the transaction in the header. You can enter the exchange rate in a transaction in one of three ways:

1. *In the table of exchange rates* by validity dates. FI then automatically transfers the most recent exchange rate valid *on or before the posting date* in the transaction header. You can also override the transfer on the posting date by entering a translation date in the header of the invoice. FI then transfers the most recent exchange rate on or before the translation date.

2. *Directly in the header of the transaction* by entering the number of units of foreign currency per unit of local currency (with the same factor/multiple

as the most recent entry in the table of exchange rates, including the relation scaling).

3. *Directly in each line item* by entering both the local currency amount and the foreign currency amount in each line item.

Note that you can enter a transaction in any currency, but you can only enter a transaction in one transaction and one local currency. This restricts you from entering a single transaction with multiple currencies. For example, assume you have a credit card invoice with line items in various foreign currencies. You then have to enter each line (or set of lines with the same currency) in the credit card invoice as a separate transaction. This does not happen often, but depending on how much your company travels, it is a limitation of this software package.

Entering an Exchange Rate in the Rate Table

When entering a transaction in foreign currency, the exchange rate can be automatically entered from a table of exchange rates. In this way, you need to maintain the table only once. If you keep the table centrally, each company then uses the same exchange rates. This can make eventual consolidation less complicated. To enter an exchange rate in the table:

1. From the General Ledger menu, select Environment → Current options → Exchange rates. (See Exhibit 2.62.)

2. To start to enter an exchange rate, press the New entries pushbutton. (See Exhibit 2.63.)
   On this screen (Exhibit 2.63), you enter the details of the exchange rate as follows:

Field	*What You Enter*
ExRt	Enter the type of the exchange rate. To enter average exchange rates, which are the only ones that are entered automatically in transactions, enter **M** (for middle).
From	Enter the currency that the company would be buying as a result of the transaction. Usually, this is the transaction currency.
To	Enter the currency that the company would be selling as a result of the transaction. Usually, this is the local currency of the company code where the transaction is posted.
Valid from	Enter the date on or before which the exchange rate is valid. The program automatically transfers the most recent rate on or before the posting date of the transaction. If you

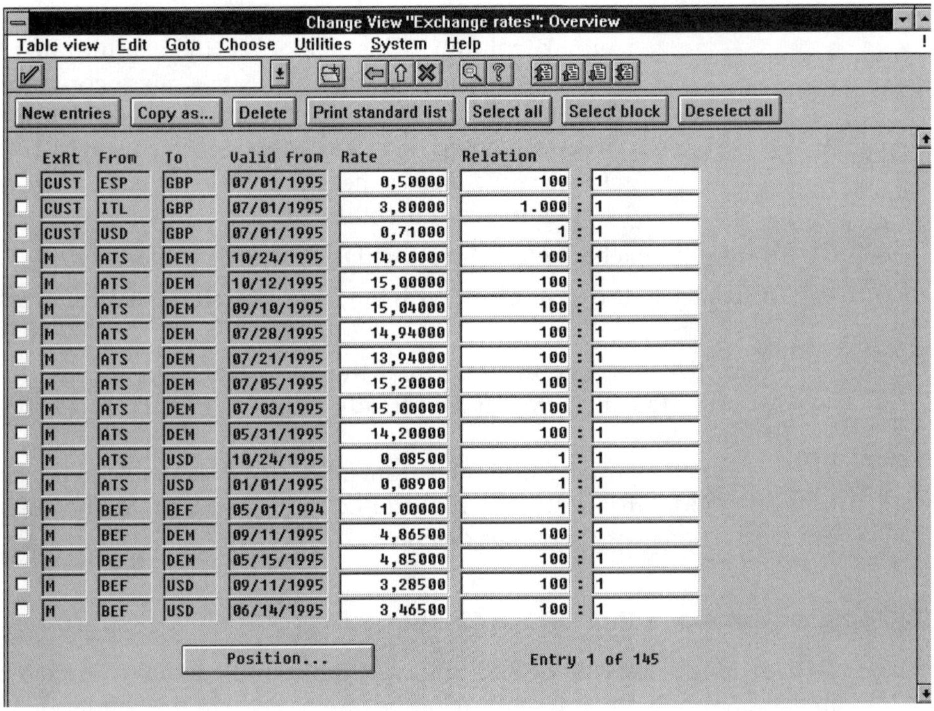

ExRt	From	To	Valid from	Rate	Relation	
CUST	ESP	GBP	07/01/1995	0,50000	100	1
CUST	ITL	GBP	07/01/1995	3,80000	1.000	1
CUST	USD	GBP	07/01/1995	0,71000	1	1
M	ATS	DEM	10/24/1995	14,80000	100	1
M	ATS	DEM	10/12/1995	15,00000	100	1
M	ATS	DEM	09/10/1995	15,04000	100	1
M	ATS	DEM	07/28/1995	14,94000	100	1
M	ATS	DEM	07/21/1995	13,94000	100	1
M	ATS	DEM	07/05/1995	15,20000	100	1
M	ATS	DEM	07/03/1995	15,00000	100	1
M	ATS	DEM	05/31/1995	14,20000	100	1
M	ATS	USD	10/24/1995	0,08500	1	1
M	ATS	USD	01/01/1995	0,08900	1	1
M	BEF	BEF	05/01/1994	1,00000	1	1
M	BEF	DEM	09/11/1995	4,86500	100	1
M	BEF	DEM	05/15/1995	4,85000	100	1
M	BEF	USD	09/11/1995	3,28500	100	1
M	BEF	USD	06/14/1995	3,46500	100	1

Exhibit 2.62 Exchange Rates Overview

enter a translation date in the transaction, then the program transfers the rate on the translation date.

Rate — Enter the rate, which is the number of units of currency in the To field to purchase one unit of the currency on the From field.

Relation — If either currency has small units (large numbers), such as Italian Lire, Spanish Pesetas, Greek Drachmas, Japanese

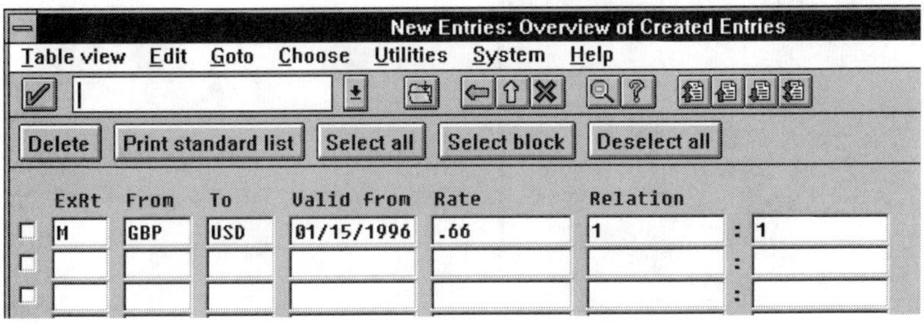

ExRt	From	To	Valid from	Rate	Relation	
M	GBP	USD	01/15/1996	.66	1	1

Exhibit 2.63 New Entries: Overview of Created Entries

Yen, or Korean Won, then you can enter a factor times in either column. This factor is then multiplied by the exchange rate. For example, if you were converting from ITL to USD and the exchange rate were 1600 ITL for 1 USD, then you could enter **ITL** as the From currency, **USD** as the To currency, **.625** as the exchange rate (Exch.rate), and **1000** in the first column of the Relation.

3. To store the exchange rate, press <F11> or the file folder icon.

4. To go back to the first screen with the table of exchange rates, press the left arrow.

5. Notice the Position pushbutton at the bottom of your screen. To find an exchange rate that you have already entered, first press Position. (See Exhibit 2.64.)

   To find all transaction rates from GBP to USD, enter **M** in the Exch.rate type field, **GBP** in the From currency field, and **USD** in the To currency field. Then press Continue or Enter.

Entering an Exchange Rate in the Header

To override an entry in the exchange rate table, or if you have no exchange rate in the table, you can enter an exchange rate directly in the header of a transaction. For example, you might have intercompany or commercial exchange rates in the table. If customs or VAT authorities specify certain exchange rates in certain transactions, these rates will surely differ from your intercompany rates. Enter the customs or VAT exchange rate in the header just to the right of the Currency/rate field in the transaction header as shown in Exhibit 2.65.

   Notice the Currency/rate field. In this example, the local currency is DEM and the transaction currency is USD and the exchange rate is .69 USD per unit of DEM (the functional currency of the company code where the transaction is posted). This exchange rate applies to all line items in the transaction. Later,

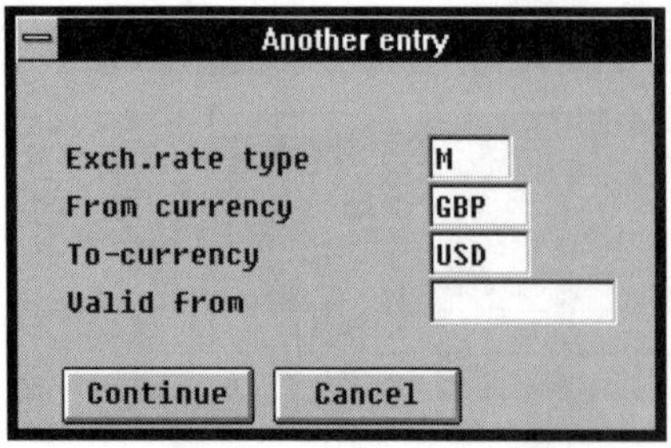

Exhibit 2.64 Finding All Exchange Rates for Two Currencies

```
┌─────────────────────────────────────────────────────────────────────────┐
│ ▬              Enter G/L Account Posting: Header Data          ▼ ▲         │
│ Document  Edit  Goto  Details  Options  Environment  System  Help      !  │
│ ┌──┐ ┌──────────────────┐ ┌─┐ ┌──┐ ┌─┬─┬─┐ ┌─┬─┐ ┌─┬─┬─┬─┐              │
│ │▨│ │                   │ │±│ │ ▨│ │←│↑│✕│ │Q│?│ │ │ │ │ │              │
│ └──┘ └──────────────────┘ └─┘ └──┘ └─┴─┴─┘ └─┴─┘ └─┴─┴─┴─┘              │
│ ┌─────────────────────┐ ┌──────────────────────┐                         │
│ │ Open held document  │ │  G/L item fast entry  │                         │
│ └─────────────────────┘ └──────────────────────┘                         │
│                                                                           │
│ Document date   [01/16/1996]  Doc.type  [GJ]  Company code   [GE20]        │
│ Posting date    [01/16/1996]  Period    [  ]  Currency/rate  [USD] [.69]   │
│ Document no.    [           ]                 Translation dte [        ]   │
│ Reference doc.  [           ]                                              │
│ Doc.header text [entry of ex rate in headr]                               │
│                                                                           │
│                                                                           │
│                                                                           │
│                                                                           │
│                                                                           │
│                                                                           │
│ ┌First line item─────────────────────────────────────────────┐           │
│ │ PostKey [50] Account [0100625      ] ▼  Sp.G/L [ ] Trans.type [ ] │       │
│ └──────────────────────────────────────────────────────────────┘         │
└───────────────────────────────────────────────────────────────────────────┘
```

Exhibit 2.65   Enter G/L Account Posting: Header Data

when displaying the overview of the transaction, you can switch between displaying the amounts in transaction currency and local currency. To switch the display from the transaction overview, press the Display currency pushbutton.

Entering a Long G/L Transaction Quickly

A long transaction is a transaction with many line items, such as a monthly payroll transaction or long expense accrual. You can enter up to 999 line items in any one transaction. To speed up data entry, you can enter a long transaction by entering line items line by line, instead of screen by screen.

To enter a long G/L transaction quickly:

1. Start to enter a G/L transaction as usual. This is documented in the previous section "Posting a G/L Transaction, Such as Petty Cash." From the General Ledger menu, select Document entry ➤ G/L account posting.

2. At the top of the screen, enter the transaction header. At the bottom of the screen, leave the PostKey and Account fields blank. If there are entries in either of these fields, delete them.

3. Still on the first screen, press the G/L item fast entry pushbutton. (See Exhibit 2.66.)

4. On this screen (Exhibit 2.66), enter a line item in each row. In each row, you have to enter at least the posting key in the PK column, the G/L account number in the Account column, and the tax code in the Ta column. In line items to a balance sheet account, enter ** in the Ta column. In line items to a P&L account, enter a valid tax code, depending on your configuration. You can also enter a business area (division) in the BusA column, a cost center, and an internal order. If the transaction is an intercompany transaction, you can enter the other company code in the CoCd column. If you enter an intercompany transaction, FI can only post the transaction if the debits equal the credits *in each company code.*

5. To review the transaction before you post, press the Overview pushbutton.

6. If any line items contain required entries that you did not enter line-by-line, double-click on the line item, enter the required field, and press Overview again.

7. To post the transaction, press <F11> or the file folder icon.

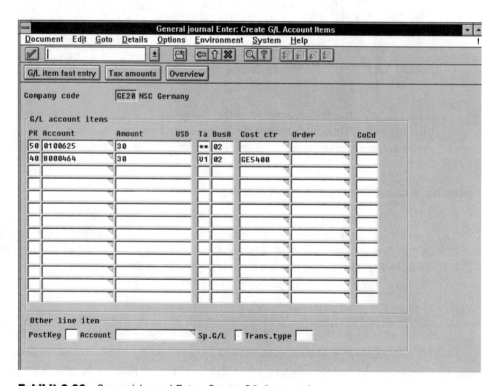

Exhibit 2.66   General Journal Enter: Create G/L Account Items

Reversing a G/L Transaction

To meet legal requirements in certain countries and for purposes of internal audits, you can never delete a transaction from the system. If you were ever allowed to delete a transaction, your books could become chaos. If you realize that you have made a mistake *before* you post the transaction, do not post the transaction. Simply exit the function by pressing the up arrow until you go back to the General Ledger menu. If you realize that you have made a mistake *after* you post the transaction, then you can reverse the transaction and enter it again. To reverse a G/L transaction:

1. From the General Ledger menu, select Document → Reverse. (See Exhibit 2.67.)

2. Enter the transaction (document) number. To display the transaction first before you reverse it (to check whether it is the transaction that you intend to reverse), press Display document.

3. To reverse the transaction, press <F11> or the file folder icon.

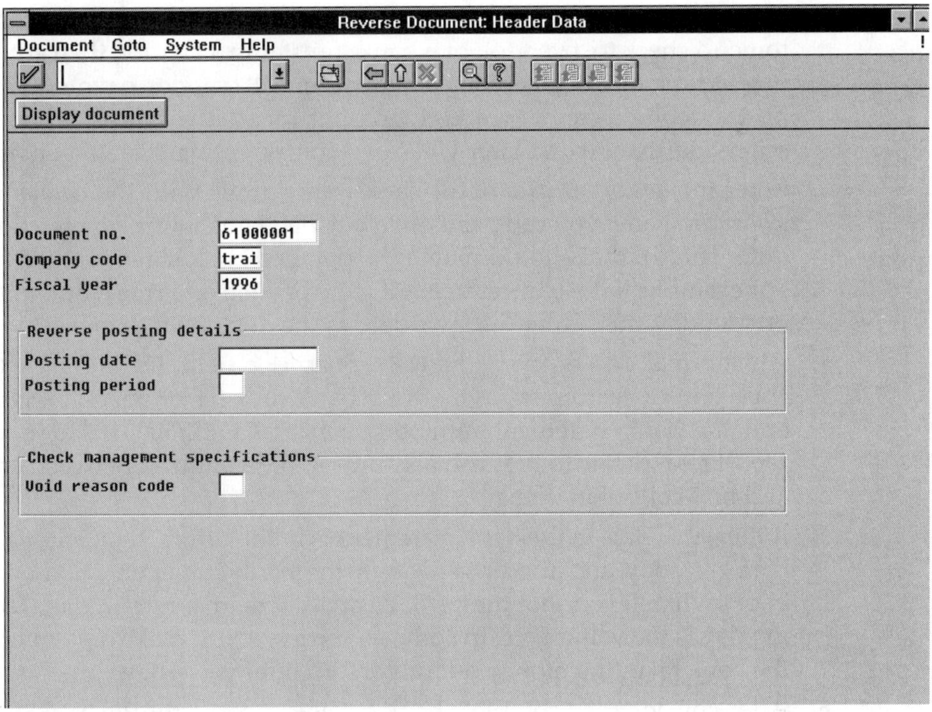

Exhibit 2.67   Reverse Document: Header Data

Posting Dividends Paid with Withholding

To record the payment of a dividend with tax withheld, enter a G/L transaction as usual. For example, assume that the dividend was 100 and that the dividend was subject to a 10% withholding tax. Credit the cash in transit account for 90. Credit the G/L account for withholding tax on dividends for 10. Debit the dividends paid account for 100.

Later, when you pay the withholding tax, credit cash in transit and debit the G/L account for withholding tax on dividends.

Entering a Bank Statement

After entering a complete bank statement, you can instantly reconcile the bank statement by comparing the bank balance in the system with the bank balance at the end of the bank statement. When entering and posting bank transactions, it is advisable to keep the following in mind:

1. If the transaction is in the bank statement, enter a document type of **BJ** (bank journal), depending on your configuration, and then post a debit or credit to a G/L account for *cash in the bank*.

2. If the transaction is not in the bank statement, such as a check from a customer, a check to a vendor, or a bank transfer to a vendor, then enter a document type of **CP** (customer payment) or **VP** (vendor payment) and then post a debit or credit to a G/L account for *cash in transit*. Although this seems like extra work, later you can reconcile the bank statement instantly.

3. Enter the *document date* of all bank transactions with the *date of the bank statement*. Later, you can print out a detailed bank journal by the document date. This journal should match the detailed bank statement for that day. For example, if the bank statement were printed on Friday, but you enter it on Monday, then enter Friday's date as the document date.

4. Always make an entry in the Reference doc field. If the transaction is a collection (a customer payment by bank transfer or check), enter **COLL** and the bank statement number, such as **COLL/50001**. Later, you can report total debits to the cash accounts and distinguish between collection and non-collection items.

5. If the value date in the bank statement is in the future, then enter a posting date of today and the *value date* in the bank statement. Sometimes the banks will tell you that they will clear an item on a certain day. This clearing day is the value date. In some countries, if you make a payment today, the bank takes the money out of your account yesterday.

6. After you enter the complete bank statement correctly, the bank balance in the system should be the same as the bank balance at the end of the bank statement.

7. You can use the treasury program to forecast your available bank balances. Based on the value dates of line items posted to G/L accounts, the forecast is for the next five days.

Note that there is some duplication in the following sections with the sections of the Accounts Receivable chapter. The organization determines whether the bank statement is posted in a Treasury Department or in Accounts Receivable.

Recording Control Totals. You can verify the correct entry of the complete bank statement. First, calculate the total debits and total credits that you expect to be posted for each bank account. Next, to record the control total for each bank account:

1. From the General Ledger menu, select Environment → Current options → Control totals. (See Exhibit 2.68.)

2. Enter the control totals as shown in Exhibit 2.68. At the bottom of the screen, in the AcTyp column, enter **S** for G/L account. In the From acct column, enter the G/L account for cash in the bank at that bank. In the Debit

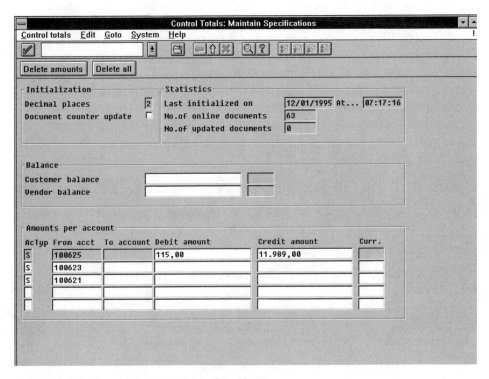

Exhibit 2.68 Control Totals: Maintain Specifications

amount column, enter the total debits (in your books) to be posted to your account from the bank statement. Note that the total debits in your books are the total credits in the bank's books for your account. In the Credit amount column, enter the total credits (in your books) to be posted to your account from the bank statement. Note, of course, that the total credits in your books are the total debits in the bank's books for your account. To define control totals for a series of customer accounts, enter **D** in the AcTyp column and then enter a series of customer accounts.

3. To store the control totals, press <F11> or the file folder icon.

4. Later, you can display the totals that were actually posted and the differences. To display the totals actually posted (after you store these control totals), select Goto ➤ Tot. actually posted.

Posting a Customer Payment Bank Transfer. A bank transfer is a domestic payment method found in many countries. Under this payment method, you give your bank account number to the customer, and then the customer directs his bank to make the payment to your account. You do not receive a check. Your bank statement shows when you receive the payment.

Using FI, you can use either of two functions to post a payment from a customer and close open invoices—payment fast entry and posting with clearing (longer). This section describes payment fast entry. Assume that the customer pays 1000 by bank transfer and that the bank charges 20 to receive the payment. You receive a net amount of 980, post it to your bank account, and clear an amount of 1000 in the customer account. These tasks will be done by the Accounts Receivable department, but they are part of entering and reconciling a bank statement. To post a payment from a customer by bank transfer, do as follows:

1. From the Accounts Receivable menu, select Document entry ➤ Payment fast entry. (See Exhibit 2.69.)

    The following is a summary of how to enter the header of a payment:

What You See on the Screen (Exhibit 2.69)	*What You Enter (Recommended)*
Company code	The company (legal entity) whose books you are keeping, depending on your configuration
Doc.type	**BJ** (for bank journal) or **CP** (customer payment by check), if this were a payment by check, depending on your configuration
Posting date	Today's date

```
┌─────────────────────────────────────────────────────────────────────┐
│ ▬                 Incoming Payments Fast Entry: Header Data      ▼ ▲  │
│ Specifications  Edit  Goto  Options  Environment  System  Help     ! │
│ ┌─┐┌──────────────┐ ┌±┐  ┌──┐ ┌─┐┌─┐┌─┐ ┌─┐┌─┐  ┌─┐┌─┐┌─┐┌─┐        │
│ │✔││              │ └─┘  │  │ │⇐││⇧││✗│ │Q││?│  │ ││ ││ ││ │        │
│ └─┘└──────────────┘      └──┘ └─┘└─┘└─┘ └─┘└─┘  └─┘└─┘└─┘└─┘        │
│ ┌─────────────┐ ┌────────┐                                           │
│ │Enter payments│ │ Delete │                                          │
│ └─────────────┘ └────────┘                                           │
│                                                                      │
│  ┌Specifications for the following incoming payments─────────────┐   │
│  │ Company code      │GE20│       Doc.type         │BJ│          │   │
│  │ Posting date      │02/19/1996│ Posting period    │9 │          │   │
│  │ Bank account      │100625    │▽                             │   │
│  │ Business area     │02│                                       │   │
│  │ Special G/L ind.  │  │                                       │   │
│  └──────────────────────────────────────────────────────────────┘   │
│                                                                      │
│  ┌Default data for the following incoming payments──────────────┐    │
│  │ Currency          │DEM │                                     │    │
│  │ Reference doc.    │bank stat. #│                             │    │
│  │ Document date     │02/19/1996│                               │    │
│  │ Value date        │02/19/96 │                                │    │
│  └──────────────────────────────────────────────────────────────┘   │
│                                                                      │
│  ┌Additional input fields───────────────────────────────────────┐   │
│  │ ☐ Possible selection by date                                  │   │
│  │ ☐ Reference number                                            │   │
│  │ ☑ Bank charges                                                │   │
│  └──────────────────────────────────────────────────────────────┘   │
│                                                                      │
└─────────────────────────────────────────────────────────────────────┘
```

Exhibit 2.69 Incoming Payments Fast Entry: Header Data

Posting period	Leave blank; the posting date always determines the posting period according to your configured fiscal year
Bank account	G/L account for cash in the bank or cash in transit, depending on your local chart of accounts
Business area	An internal division, such as **02,** depending on your configuration
Currency	Currency of the payment, which is usually the currency of the invoices that are being paid
Reference doc.	Bank statement number (for a bank transfer) or check number of a check
Document date	Date of the bank statement
Value date	Expected date of the payment receipt into your bank account; for a payment by bank transfer, this is usually the same date as the document date (bank statement date); for a payment by check, this is usually

	2–3 days after the receipt of the check; this field is used for the cash forecast
Possible selection by date	Leave blank for now, unless you wish to choose open invoices by date; then click on this field
Reference number	Leave blank for now, unless you wish to enter a bank statement number or a check number in each payment later
Bank charges	If there were bank fees for this transaction, click on this field and then enter the bank charges on the next screen

2. Enter fields as shown in Exhibit 2.69. Since this transaction is in the bank statement, you enter **BJ** (bank journal) in the Doc.type field. In the Bank account field, make sure that you enter a G/L account for cash in the bank at the bank that received the payment. Then press Enter payments and look for the screen in Exhibit 2.70—Incoming Payments Fast Entry.

3. Enter the customer number in the Customer field. If you are not sure what the customer number is, find the number with a matchcode by first press-

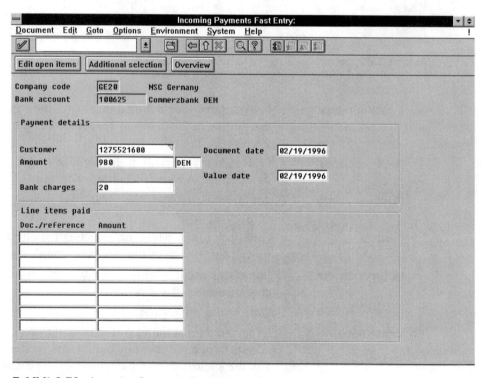

Exhibit 2.70 Incoming Payments Fast Entry

ing <F4> or the down arrow, then double-clicking on a type of matchcode, and then entering the data.

To match the payment to a specific invoice (optionally), enter the invoice number (SAP "document number" or "reference document number") in the Doc./reference field.

Then press <Enter> or Edit open items. The next screen contains all open items in the customer account. If you entered an invoice on the previous screen, then this screen also contains all open items for the customer with this open invoice. (See Exhibit 2.71.)

4. Notice that this screen, the open item processing screen (Exhibit 2.71), also known as the cash application screen, contains the open items selected on the previous screen. The Arrears column shows the number of days that each open item is in arrears. A negative number means that the item is not yet due. The value of the items is displayed in the currency of the payment from a previous screen. If the customer pays an item in full, simply double-click on the amount of the item.

Notice the Difference field in the lower-right corner of this screen. To post this payment, you have to make this amount zero (or almost zero if

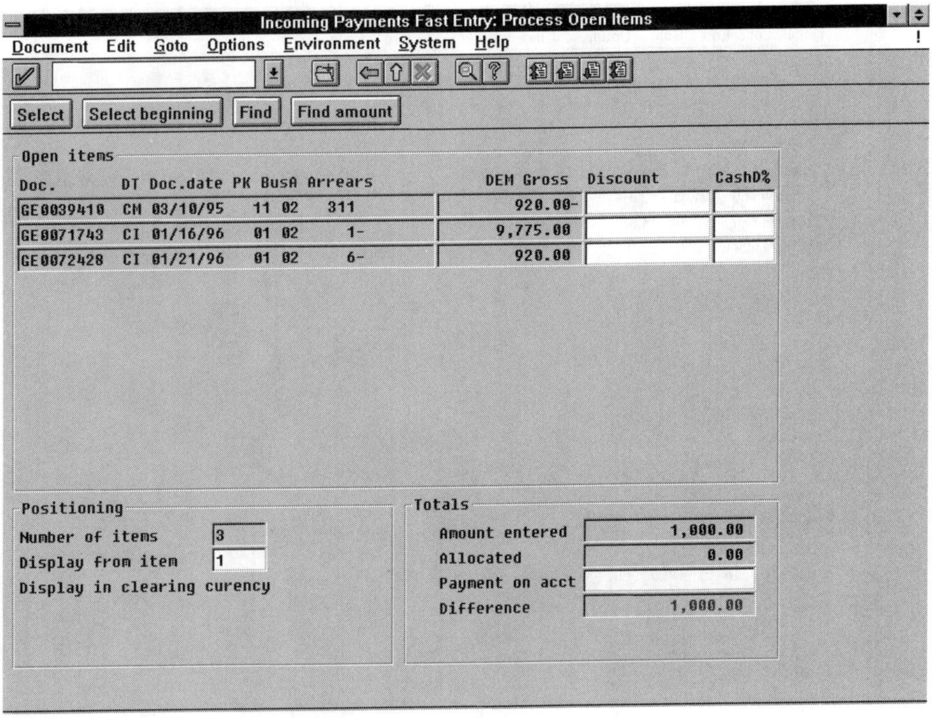

Exhibit 2.71 Incoming Payment Fast Entry: Process Open Items

you post small payment differences automatically, depending on your configuration). If the difference is zero (the debits equal the credits), then press <F11> or the file folder icon to post the payment and close one or more items. The Amount entered field shows the amount of the payment (entered on a previous screen).

Note that to start to post the payment and close (clear) open items, you first have to make one or more open items active by double-clicking on the amount of the specific open item (in the DEM Gross column in the example in Exhibit 2.71).

If the customer makes a *partial payment,* you can post the payment on account or as a residual item. A payment on account means that both the original invoice and the payment remain open items in the customer account. A residual item means that you close the original invoice and open a new item for the difference between the original invoice and the payment. Assume the customer made a partial payment and you wish to close the original invoice and open a new invoice for the difference (residual item). First, double-click on the amount of the open item and then select Goto ➤ Residual item screen. (See Exhibit 2.72.)

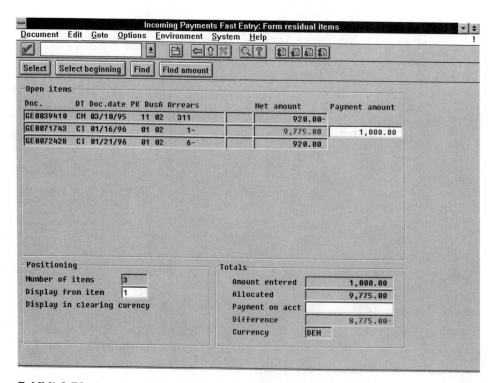

Exhibit 2.72   Incoming Payments Fast Entry: Form Residual Items

5. Enter the amount that the customer paid, including the bank fees, in the Payment amount column (Exhibit 2.72). Press <Enter>.

6. If the debits equal the credits (the difference is zero), press <F11> or the file folder icon to start to store the transaction. (See Exhibit 2.73.)

7. Notice that that the program automatically calculates and generates a line item for any valid cash discount (Exhibit 2.73). If the customer is making a partial payment, then the program calculates the valid cash discount in proportion to the amount of the payment as a percentage of the open item. In other words, if the customer is paying 50% of the open item, then the program calculates and generates an item for 50% of the cash discount that would be valid if the customer were paying the full amount. The validity of the cash discount depends on the baseline date of the invoice, the payment terms, any grace period, and the date of the payment. Cash discount applies mostly in countries where granting and taking cash discount is customary.

   When you enter a residual item, you always have to enter a description of the residual item—why the customer made the partial payment. To

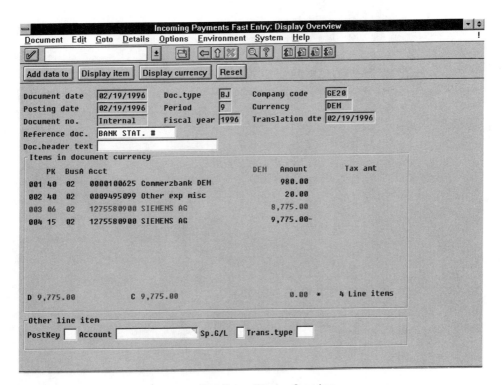

Exhibit 2.73 Incoming Payments Fast Entry: Display Overview

start to enter the text, first double-click on the residual item, usually shown in red or a lighter colored font, depending on your monitor, on the overview screen. (See Exhibit 2.74.)

8. Enter a note or other explanation in the Text field in the residual item (Exhibit 2.74).

9. Press <F11> or the file folder icon to post the transaction.

Posting a Cleared Check from the Customer.   First, assume that the customer paid 1000 by check. Next, assume that you already deposited the check in the bank and debited a G/L account for cash in transit at that bank. Last, assume that the bank has processed the check and credited your account in *the bank's records*. These tasks will be done by the Accounts Receivable department, but they are part of entering and reconciling a bank statement (Exhibit 2.75). To post a cleared check from a customer, assuming all these previous tasks have been done, do as follows:

1. From the General Ledger menu, select Document entry → Post with clearing. (See Exhibit 2.75.)

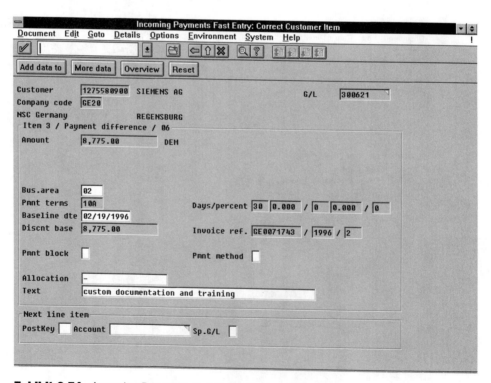

Exhibit 2.74   Incoming Payments Fast Entry: Current Customer Item

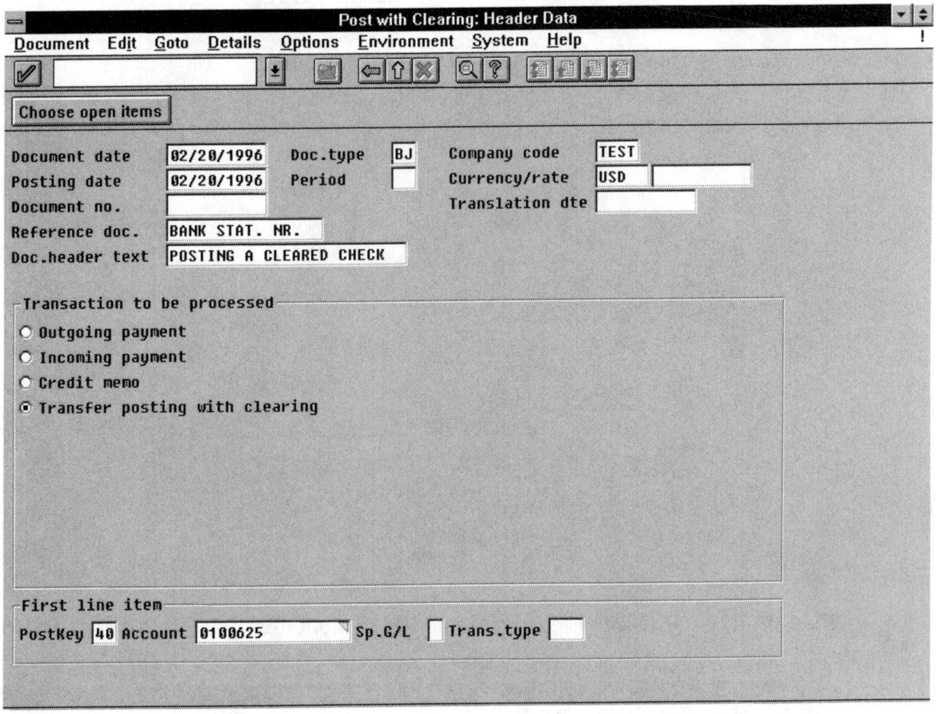

Exhibit 2.75   Posting a Cleared Check

2. Enter a document type of **BJ** (bank journal) and the bank statement number in the Reference doc. field. Also, click on the option Transfer posting with clearing at the end of the screen. Enter **40** to debit your G/L account for cash in the bank. Then enter the specific G/L account for cash in the bank at the bank that processed the check. Press <Enter>. The next screen is shown in Exhibit 2.76.

3. Enter the amount of the check and any other required field on this screen, depending on your configuration, and then press Edit open items (to start to process open items). The next screen looks like Exhibit 2.77.

4. In the Account field, enter the G/L account number for cash in transit at that bank. In the Account type field, enter **S** (hard-coded to mean G/L account). Press Edit open items again. Notice Exhibit 2.77.

5. Look at the screen in Exhibit 2.78. To make an item active, double-click on the amount of the open item for the check deposited. Depending on the configuration and data entry, checks deposited have the document type **CP** (customer payment), while the vendor payments have the document

```
┌─────────────────────────────────────────────────────────────────────────────┐
│ ▄                    Post with Clearing: Create G/L Account Item      ▼ ▲    │
│ Document  Edit  Goto  Details  Options  Environment  System  Help          ! │
│ ┌──┐ ┌──────────────────┐ ┌─┐  ┌─┐ ┌──────┐ ┌─┐ ┌──┐ ┌──────────┐          │
│ │▓▓│ │                  │ │±│  │▒│ │⇐⇑⇥✗│ │▒?│ │▒▒▒▒│                    │
│ └──┘ └──────────────────┘ └─┘  └─┘ └──────┘ └─┘ └──┘ └──────────┘          │
│ ┌────────────────┐ ┌────────────────┐ ┌───────────┐ ┌──────────┐           │
│ │Choose open items│ │Edit open items │ │More data  │ │Overview  │           │
│ └────────────────┘ └────────────────┘ └───────────┘ └──────────┘           │
│                                                                             │
│ G/L account       │100625  │  Commerzbank DEM                              │
│ Company code       │GE20│ NSC Germany                                      │
│                                                                             │
│ ┌Item 1 / Debit entry / 40────────────────────────────────────────────┐   │
│ │ Amount          │1000        │     USD                                │   │
│ │                               ▣ Calculate tax                         │   │
│ │                                                                        │   │
│ │ Business area   │02 │          Trading part.BA │      │               │   │
│ │                                                                        │   │
│ │                                                                        │   │
│ │ Value date      │02/20/1996│                                          │   │
│ │ Allocation      │                │                                    │   │
│ │ Text            │                                          │          │   │
│ └────────────────────────────────────────────────────────────────────┘   │
│ ┌Next line item──────────────────────────────────────────────────────┐   │
│ │ PostKey │  │ Account │                │ Sp.G/L │ │                   │   │
│ └────────────────────────────────────────────────────────────────────┘   │
└─────────────────────────────────────────────────────────────────────────────┘
```

Exhibit 2.76   Post with Clearing: Create G/L Account Item

```
┌─────────────────────────────────────────────────────────────────────────────┐
│ ▄                    Post with Clearing: Select open items            ▼ ▲    │
│ Document  Edit  Goto  Options  System  Help                                ! │
│ ┌──┐ ┌──────────────────┐ ┌─┐  ┌─┐ ┌──────┐ ┌─┐ ┌──┐ ┌──────────┐          │
│ │▓▓│ │                  │ │±│  │▒│ │⇐⇑✗│   │▒?│ │▒▒▒▒│                    │
│ └──┘ └──────────────────┘ └─┘  └─┘ └──────┘ └─┘ └──┘ └──────────┘          │
│ ┌────────────────┐ ┌────────────────┐                                      │
│ │Other selection │ │Edit open items │                                      │
│ └────────────────┘ └────────────────┘                                      │
│                                                                             │
│ ┌Open item selection──────────────────────────────────────────────────┐   │
│ │                                                                        │   │
│ │ Account         │0109625    │       □ Other accounts                 │   │
│ │ Account type    │S    │              □ Automatically search           │   │
│ │ Special G/L ind. │        │           ▣ Normal OI                     │   │
│ │                                                                        │   │
│ │ ┌Additional selections──────┐                                         │   │
│ │ │ ◉ None                     │                                         │   │
│ │ │ ○ Amount                   │                                         │   │
│ │ │ ○ Document no.             │                                         │   │
│ │ │ ○ Posting date             │                                         │   │
│ │ │ ○ Dunning area             │                                         │   │
│ │ │ ○ Reference doc.           │                                         │   │
│ │ │ ○ Collective invoice       │                                         │   │
│ │ │ ○ Doc.type                 │                                         │   │
│ │ │ ○ Business area            │                                         │   │
│ │ │ ○ Branch acct              │                                         │   │
│ │ │ ○ Currency                 │                                         │   │
│ │ └───────────────────────────┘                                         │   │
│ └────────────────────────────────────────────────────────────────────┘   │
└─────────────────────────────────────────────────────────────────────────────┘
```

Exhibit 2.77   Post with Clearing: Select Open Items

type **VP** (vendor payment). The exact document types depend on your configuration.

6. Assuming that the debits equal the credits (the Difference in the bottom-right corner of the screen is zero to the penny), press <F11> or the file folder icon to post this transaction. (See Exhibit 2.78.)

Posting a Cleared Vendor Payment.   First, assume that you have paid the vendor, either by check or by bank transfer. Further assume that you have posted the payment manually to the G/L and the vendor accounts or else had the automatic payment program post the vendor account and the G/L account for cash in transit, since the bank had not yet processed the payment. The payment program credits the G/L account that you specify, debits the vendor, and closes (clears) any paid invoices. Last, assume that you have received the bank statement and that the bank has processed the payment and debited your account in the bank's records.

The following procedure applies to processing payments that have been posted to a cash-in-transit account, assuming that these payments have now cleared the bank. You use the same screens to process a cleared payment to the

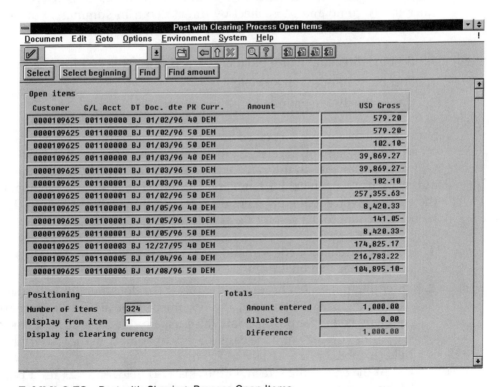

Exhibit 2.78   Post with Clearing: Process Open Items

vendor as the ones you used to process a cleared check from a customer. However, you enter a credit for the disbursement of cash from your bank account.

1. From the General Ledger menu, select Document entry ➤ Post with clearing.

2. Enter a document type of **BJ** (bank journal) and the bank statement number in the Reference doc. field. Also, click on the option Transfer posting with clearing. At the end of the screen, enter **50** to credit your G/L account for cash in the bank. Then enter the specific G/L account for cash in the bank at the bank that processed the payment to the vendor. Press <Enter>.

3. Follow the same steps as in the previous section to process a cleared check from the customer, except that you look for an item with the document type **VP** (vendor payment), depending on the configuration.

Posting a Vendor Payment by Direct Debit. In certain countries, direct debit is a routine domestic payment method. The vendor initiates the payment based on his invoice and your written permission to collect by direct debit. Many companies in Europe allow certain suppliers, such as telephone and other utility companies, to collect by direct debit. In summary, you process these payments (and the corresponding invoices) as follows:

1. Post the direct debit as a payment on account to the vendor's account.

2. Post the vendor invoice as usual.

3. Clear (match) the payment with the invoice.

Since the invoice might be posted after the payment, you post the direct debit on account. When you receive the bank statement, you enter a credit to the G/L account for cash in the bank and a debit to the vendor on account (without clearing any open items). Later, the Accounts Payable department matches the vendor invoice to the payment on account, clearing both. To post the payment on account to the vendor do as follows:

1. From the General Ledger menu, select Document entry ➤ G/L account posting. (See Exhibit 2.79.)

2. Enter the transaction header with at least the document date (usually the date of the bank statement), the document type **BJ** (bank journal), the company code, the posting date (also usually the date of the bank statement), the currency, and the bank statement number in the Reference doc. field (Exhibit 2.79).

    At the end of the screen, in the PostKey field, enter **25** for a payment (debit) to a vendor on account and then enter the vendor account. Press

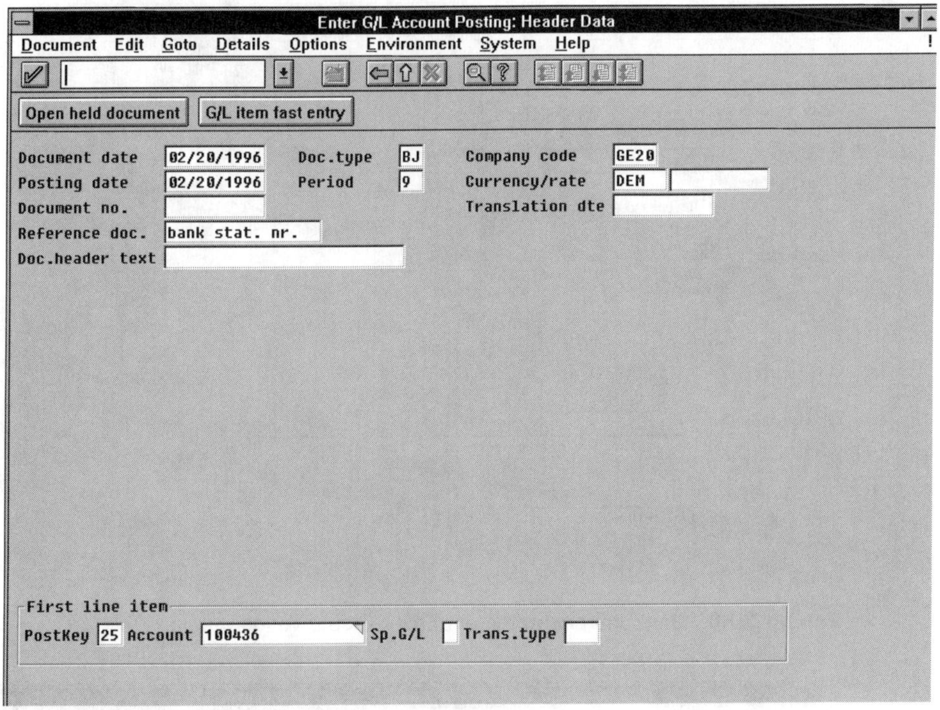

Exhibit 2.79 Enter G/L Account Posting: Header Data

<Enter>. The next screen lets you enter the amount and other fields required for this line item. (See Exhibit 2.80.)

3. Enter the amount of the payment. Click on the Calculate tax field and enter ** in the Tax code field. In general, always click on the Calculate tax field if it appears on the screen. The appearance of the Tax code field depends on your configuration. If the transaction is exempt from tax, enter a tax code with a zero percentage. For a list of the configured tax codes, put the cursor in the field and then click on the down arrow. The proper tax codes depend on regulations that the company code is under and on the configuration. Enter any other required fields, such as the business area (Exhibit 2.80).

4. At the end of the screen, in the PostKey field, enter **50** to credit the G/L account for cash in the bank. In the Account field, enter the G/L account number for cash in the bank. Press <Enter>. The next screen lets you enter the amount of this line item and any other required fields. (See Exhibit 2.81.)

5. Enter the amount and any other required fields, such as the business area and value date. Any required fields on this screen, depending on your configuration, are marked with a ? (Exhibit 2.81).

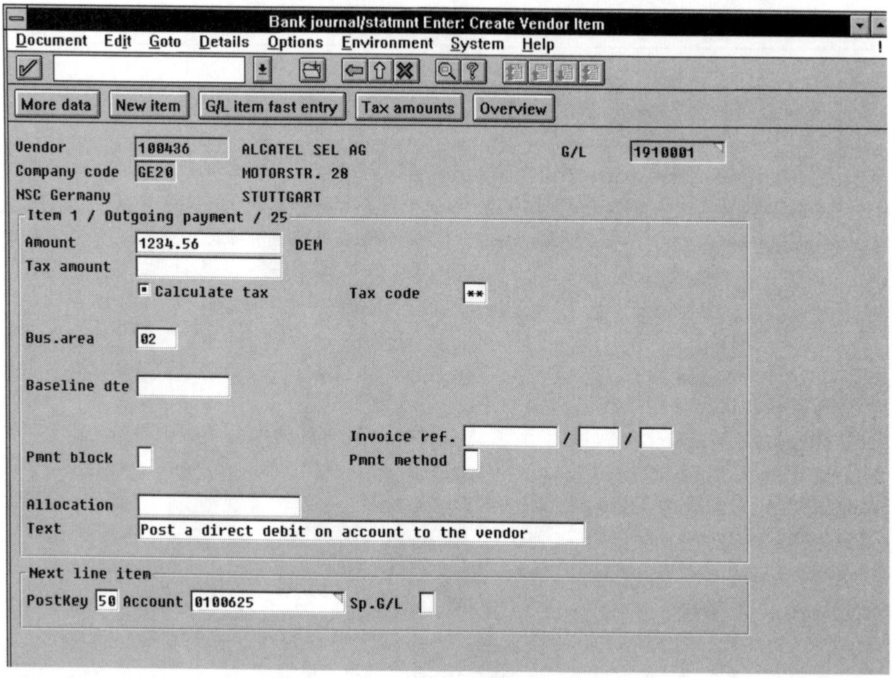

Exhibit 2.80 Bank Journal/Statement Enter: Create Vendor Item

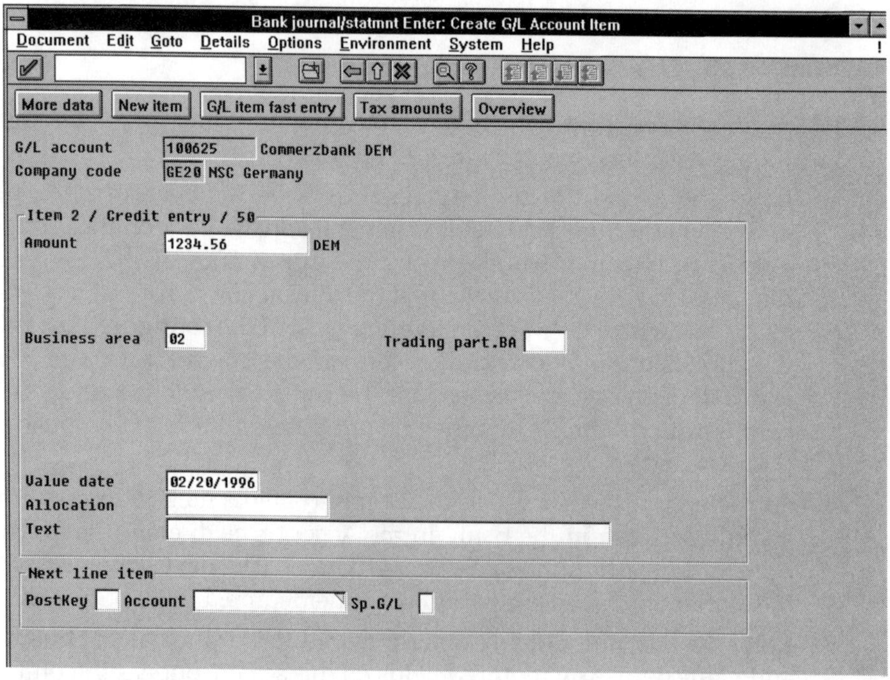

Exhibit 2.81 Bank Journal/Statement Enter: Create G/L Account Item

6. To post this transaction, press <F11> or the file folder icon.

Posting Miscellaneous Debits and Credits. Besides payments from customers and payments to vendors, bank statements also contain records of miscellaneous debits and credits, such as commissions for foreign exchange transactions, other bank fees, account maintenance fees, interest income, interest expense, and cash transactions with the bank. You post these transactions by reading the bank statement and then debiting or crediting the G/L account for cash in the bank and then crediting or debiting the offsetting account.

You post these transactions as G/L transactions. Use posting key **40** to debit a G/L account and **50** to credit a G/L account. For details, refer to the previous section, "Posting a G/L Transaction, Such as Petty Cash." From the General Ledger menu, select Document entry ► G/L account posting.

Posting a Receipt from a Vendor (Insurance). If you receive a payment from a vendor, such as an insurance payment for a loss or a repayment from a vendor for returned goods, post the receipt as a credit on account to the vendor. In this way, if you receive a debit memo from the vendor later, you can record the debit memo in one step and later close both the credit and debit items.

1. From the General Ledger menu, select Document entry ► G/L account posting (Exhibit 2.82).
2. Enter **BJ** in the Doc. type field, assuming that the payment is in the bank statement. If you receive the payment by check, enter **VP** instead. Enter the bank statement number in the Reference doc. field. Enter **35** in the PostKey field to record a credit in the vendor account for a payment. Enter the vendor account number in the Account field. Press <Enter> and enter the rest of the transaction as usual. If the receipt is by bank transfer, debit the G/L account for cash in the bank. If the receipt is by check, debit the G/L account for cash in transit. If the debits equal the credits, you can post the transaction as usual by pressing <F11> or the file folder icon.

Cancelling a Payment to a Vendor. If a mistake in the payment to the vendor is made, such as the vendor's name or bank account number, you can call the bank and cancel the payment. In your books, you can then cancel the payment and reinstate the vendor invoice in two steps. The first step it to reset the cleared (closed) items. The second step is to reverse the payment. To cancel a payment and reinstate the vendor invoice, do as follows:

1. From the General Ledger (or the Accounts Payable) menu, select Document ► Reset cleared items (Exhibit 2.83).

```
┌─────────────────────────────────────────────────────────────────────────────┐
│ ─                    Enter G/L Account Posting: Header Data            ▼ ▲    │
│ Document  Edit  Goto  Details  Options  Environment  System  Help          ! │
│ ┌─┐ ┌──────────────┐ ±  ▣  ⇐⇧✕  ⚲?  ▤▤▤▤                                    │
│ ┌─────────────────┐ ┌────────────────────┐                                   │
│ │ Open held document │ G/L item fast entry │                                 │
│                                                                               │
│ Document date   02/21/1996   Doc.type  BJ    Company code    ge20            │
│ Posting date    02/21/1996   Period          Currency/rate   DEM             │
│ Document no.                                  Translation dte                │
│ Reference doc.  bank stat. nr.                                               │
│ Doc.header text receipt from vendor                                          │
│                                                                               │
│                                                                               │
│                                                                               │
│  ┌First line item──────────────────────────────────────────────────┐        │
│  │ PostKey 35 Account 100539           Sp.G/L   Trans.type          │        │
│  └───────────────────────────────────────────────────────────────────┘      │
└─────────────────────────────────────────────────────────────────────────────┘
```

Exhibit 2.82   Enter G/L Account Posting: Header Data

```
┌─────────────────────────────────────────────────────────────────────────────┐
│ ─                           Reset Cleared Items                              │
│ Clear   Goto   System   Help                                                 │
│ ┌─┐ ┌──────────────┐ ±  ▣  ⇐⇧✕  ⚲?  ▤▤▤▤                                    │
│ ┌──────────────────┐ ┌──────────────────────┐                                │
│ │ Accompanying items │ Accompanying corrsp.  │                               │
│                                                                               │
│                                                                               │
│ Clearing doc.       67000001                                                 │
│ Company code        GE20                                                     │
│ Fiscal year                                                                  │
│                                                                               │
└─────────────────────────────────────────────────────────────────────────────┘
```

Exhibit 2.83   Reset Cleared Items

2. Enter the number of the clearing transaction. When you post payments to vendors, for example with the payment program, FI generates a clearing transaction. This transaction contains the credit to a G/L account for the disbursement of cash and a debit to the vendor account. To find the number of the clearing transaction, open another session, display the cleared items in the vendor account, and look for the payment of the invoice.

3. Press <F11> or the file folder icon to reset the clearing transaction. Look for the message at the end of the screen that says that the clearing transaction has been reversed.

4. Press the up-arrow to go back to the Accounts Payable menu.

5. From the General Ledger (or the Accounts Payable) menu, select Document → Reverse. (See Exhibit 2.84.)

6. Notice that you enter the same transaction number (the number of the clearing transaction). (See Exhibit 2.84.) Then press <F11> or the file folder icon to reverse the payment. In effect, this step then reinstates the vendor invoice.

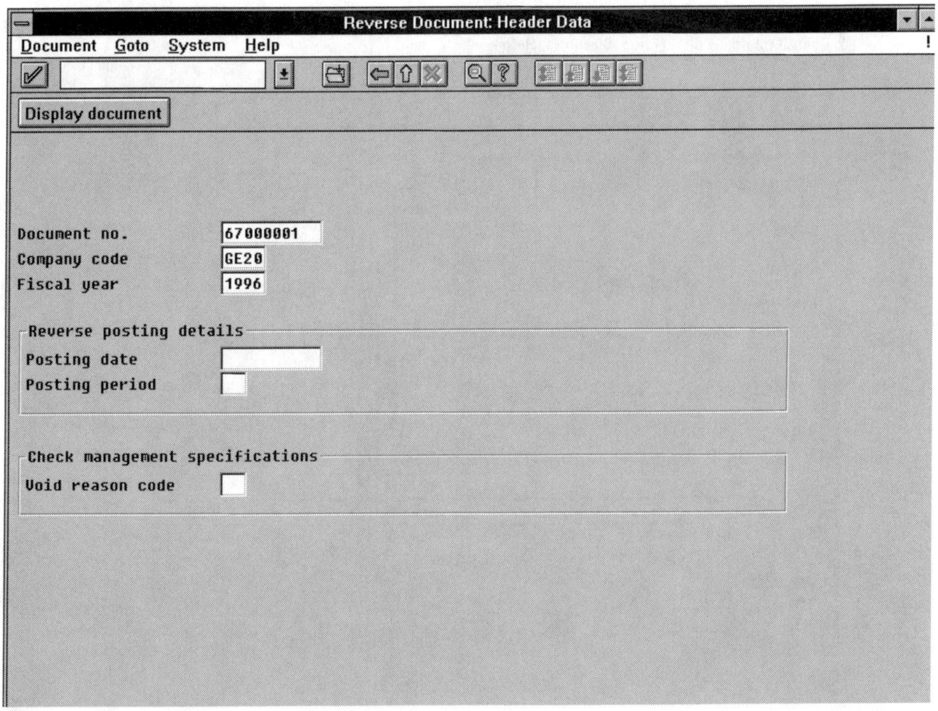

Exhibit 2.84 Reverse Document: Header Data

Note that you have to cancel a payment in two steps. First, you reset the clearing transaction that closed the open item. Second, you reverse the payment, reinstating the vendor invoice. The key to both of these functions is the number of the clearing transaction.

Displaying Control Totals and Posted Amounts. To verify that the bank statement was entered correctly, you can compare the control totals with the actually posted amounts. Assume that you have already entered control totals for each G/L account for cash in the bank, as described in the previous section. Also assume that you have entered the bank statement and posted these same G/L accounts. If you have calculated the control totals correctly and posted the bank statement correctly, then the difference between the control totals and the actually posted amounts is zero. To display the control totals and posted amounts:

1. From the General Ledger menu, select Environment ➤ Current options ➤ Control totals. (See Exhibit 2.85.)

2. Notice the title of this window—Control Totals: Display Posted Amounts (See Exhibit 2.85).

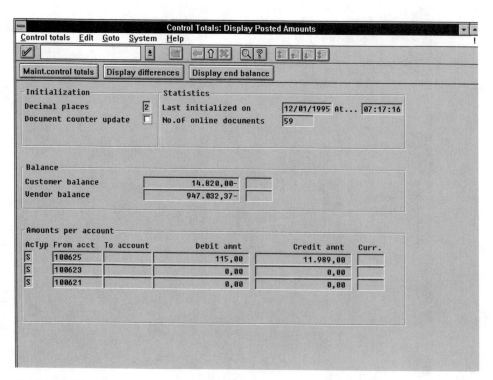

Exhibit 2.85 Control Totals: Display Posted Amounts

3. To see the differences between the control totals, select Goto → Display differences. The differences should be zero.

4. From the screen with the differences, go back to the control totals that you have already entered, select Goto → Displ. control totals. (See Exhibit 2.86.)

5. To go back, press the up arrow.

Reconciling the Bank Statement

After entering the complete bank statement correctly (Exhibit 2.86), the bank balance in the system should be the same as the bank balance at the end of the bank statement. There are various ways to reconcile the bank statement:

1. Compare the G/L account balance for cash in the bank in the system with the bank balance according to the bank.

2. Print out the bank journal in the system on the document date of the bank statement date [assuming all entries in the bank statement were entered

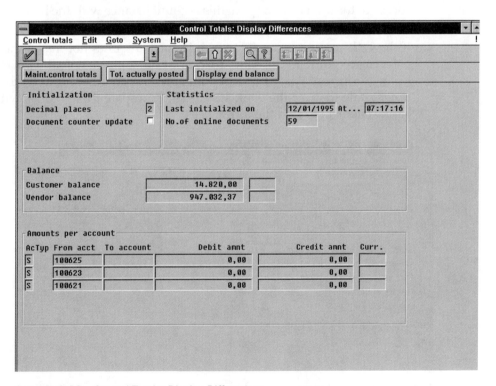

Exhibit 2.86 Control Totals: Display Differences

with a document date and a bank statement number (in the Reference doc. field) the same as the date of the bank statement].

3. Calculate and define control totals by G/L account before you enter the bank statement. Compare the control total to the amounts actually posted.

If there is a difference, then you have probably made an entry in the bank statement twice, omitted an entry, or mistyped a number. Rarely, the bank has made a mistake in the bank statement. To start to compare the G/L account balance for cash in the bank in the system with the bank balance according to the bank:

1. From the General Ledger menu, select Account ➤ Display balances. Compare the G/L account balance for cash in the bank in the system with the bank balance according to the bank. (See Exhibit 2.87.)

2. Enter the G/L account for cash in the bank, the fiscal year, * for all business areas, and the currency of the display (usually local currency) (Exhibit 2.87). Press <Enter>.

3. Look at the balance carryforward in the latest period (in the lower-right corner of the screen). Compare this account balance with the bank balance according to the bank. They should be the same.

4. If the G/L account balance for cash in the bank does not match the bank balance according to the bank, then print out a journal of all bank entries (with "document type" **BJ,** depending on your configuration) on the document date (date of the bank statement). Compare these entries with the bank statement to find the differences.

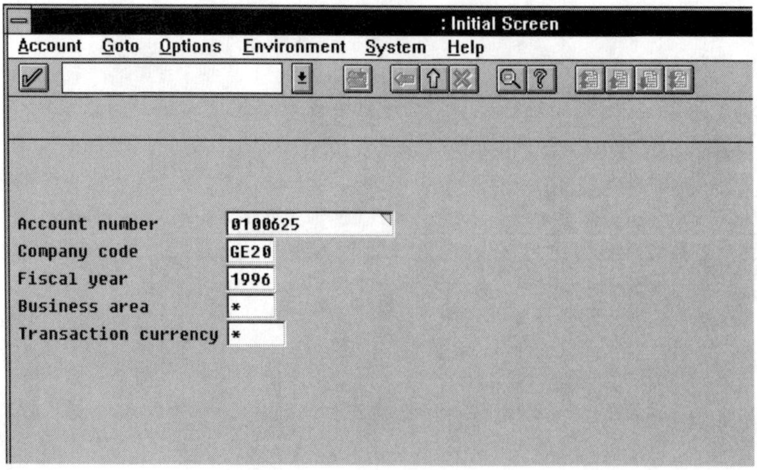

Account number	0100625
Company code	GE20
Fiscal year	1996
Business area	*
Transaction currency	*

Exhibit 2.87   Initial Screen: Account Balance

Printing the Bank Journal from the System

If the bank balance in the system does not match the bank balance according to the bank, then you can print a bank journal according to the system. Assume that you enter a posting date in each entry in the bank journal with the same date as the date of the bank statement. To reconcile the details of the bank statement, you print out a journal of the BJ journal (i.e., document type) on a specific posting date. To print out a bank journal on a specific posting date:

1. From the General Ledger menu, select Periodic processing → Month end reports → Compact journal. (See Exhibit 2.88.)

2. Enter at least the company code, document type, and the document date parameters (Exhibit 2.88). If you have multiple bank statements, make sure you enter the bank statement number in the Reference doc. field, then select the bank statement in the Reference number field when you start to print the journal, as shown in Exhibit 2.88. To go to the next screen of parameters, to enter an additional title of the report (for readability), press the + symbol in the lower-right corner of the screen.

3. To run the report, press the Execute pushbutton (Exhibit 2.89).

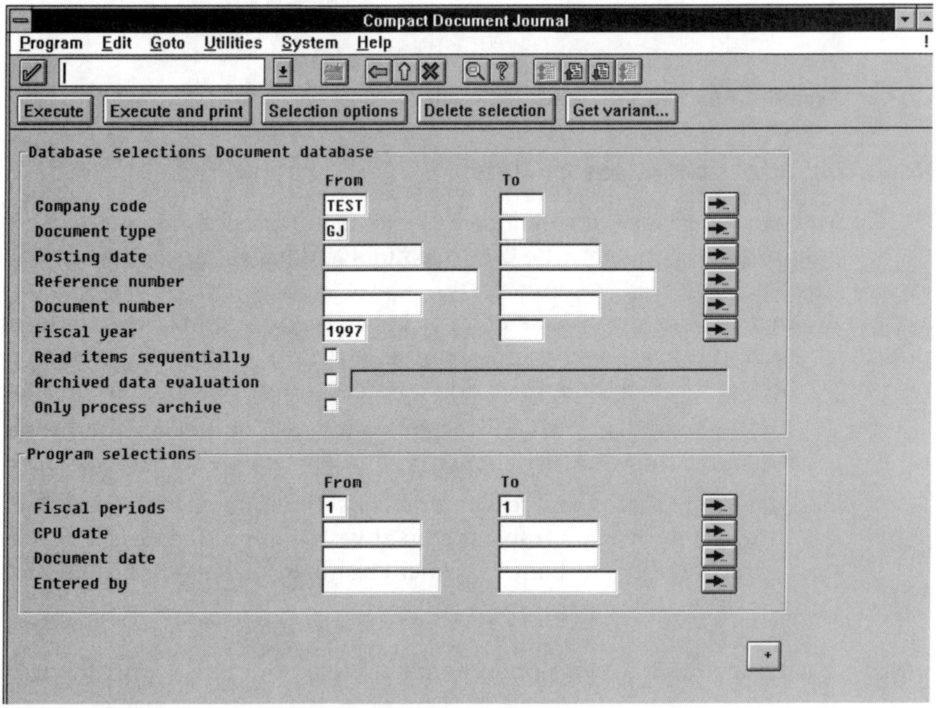

Exhibit 2.88   Compact Document Journal—Parameter Screen 1

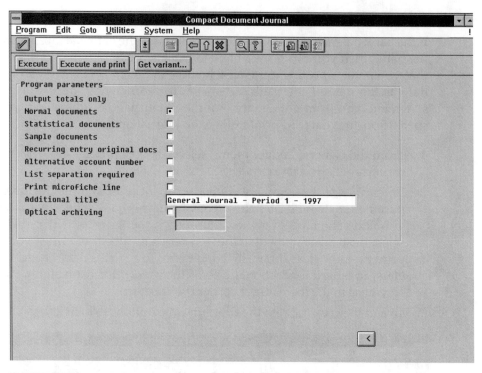

Exhibit 2.89 Compact Document Journal—Parameter Screen 2

Reporting Total Collections by Date

You can report total collections by date, using Excel as an auxiliary tool. This assumes that you enter the G/L accounts and bank transactions as follows:

1. In the G/L account master record of all cash accounts (cash in the bank and cash in transit), make sure that the Sort key (on the second screen of each account) is **009** (Reference document or External document number).

2. Make a work list of all G/L accounts for cash in the bank and cash in transit. Name the work list **CASH.**

3. Make sure that when you enter a collection or a customer payment either by check or by bank transfer, you always enter in the Reference doc. field COLL and then the bank statement number, such as **COLL/50015** as shown in Exhibit 2.90.

Later, when you display open items in the account, to report the total collections by date:

```
┌─                   Incoming Payments Fast Entry: Header Data        ▼ ▲
 Specifications  Edit  Goto  Options  Environment  System  Help          !
 ┌──┐ ┌─────────────┐ ┌─┐ ┌──┐ ┌──────┐ ┌────┐ ┌────────┐
 │✔ │ │             │ │±│ │  │ │←⇧✗│ │🔍?│ │        │
 └──┘ └─────────────┘ └─┘ └──┘ └──────┘ └────┘ └────────┘
 ┌──────────────┐ ┌──────┐
 │Enter payments│ │Delete│
 └──────────────┘ └──────┘

 ┌─Specifications for the following incoming payments────────────┐
 │ Company code      GE20          Doc.type         BJ           │
 │ Posting date      02/21/1996    Posting period   9            │
 │ Bank account      0100625 ▼                                   │
 │ Business area     02                                          │
 │ Special G/L ind.                                              │
 └──────────────────────────────────────────────────────────────┘

 ┌─Default data for the following incoming payments─────────────┐
 │ Currency          DEM                                         │
 │ Reference doc.    COLL/50015                                  │
 │ Document date     02/21/1996                                  │
 │ Value date                                                    │
 └──────────────────────────────────────────────────────────────┘

 ┌─Additional input fields──────────────────────────────────────┐
 │ ☐ Possible selection by date                                 │
 │ ☐ Reference number                                           │
 │ ☐ Bank charges                                               │
 └──────────────────────────────────────────────────────────────┘

                                    FIP (1)  scaix201  OVR  03:01PM
```

Exhibit 2.90 Incoming Payments Fast Entry: Header Data

1. Display open items for the work list **CASH.** From the General Ledger menu, select Account ➤ Display line items.

2. Enter the work list **CASH** and the company code and then press <Enter>.

3. With the basic list of line items displayed, select Edit ➤ Sort and then sort by Reference document (1) and Posting date (2).

4. Put the cursor on any entry in the Posting date column and press Total.

5. The totals by date include the non-collection items. Download the list to a spreadsheet and delete these non-collection items. Download this list to an Excel spreadsheet. From the menu, select Line items ➤ Transfer to Excel. To put the file in the Excel directory on your C: drive, name the file **c:\msoffice\excel\filename.xls** (or another filename).

6. Start up Excel. Open the file that you download. Select Fixed width, click just to the left of the second and following fields. Press Next. Select Text for the type of the fields.

7. Delete the non-collection items in the spreadsheet and calculate the totals by day again without the non-collection items.

Entering an Amount and Clearing Open Items

Assume you have one or more open items in an account, such as interest payable. Further assume that you wish to close the items and post some amount to another account, such as a loan payable account.

To post an amount to an account and clear open items in another account (Exhibit 2.91):

1. From the General Ledger menu, select Document entry ➤ Post with clearing. (See Exhibit 2.91.)

2. Start to enter a transaction as usual, starting with the transaction header. Enter the posting key and account number to which the entry will be posted. Press <Enter>. (See Exhibit 2.92.)

3. On the next screen, enter the line item and then press Edit open items. (See Exhibit 2.93.)

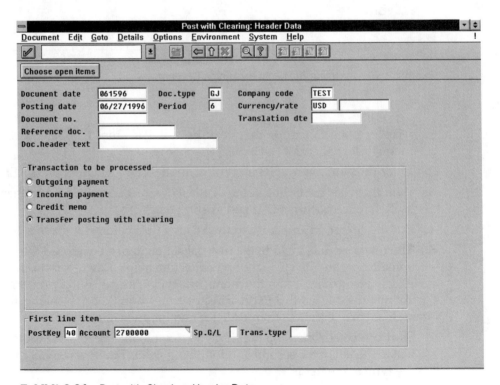

Exhibit 2.91   Post with Clearing: Header Data

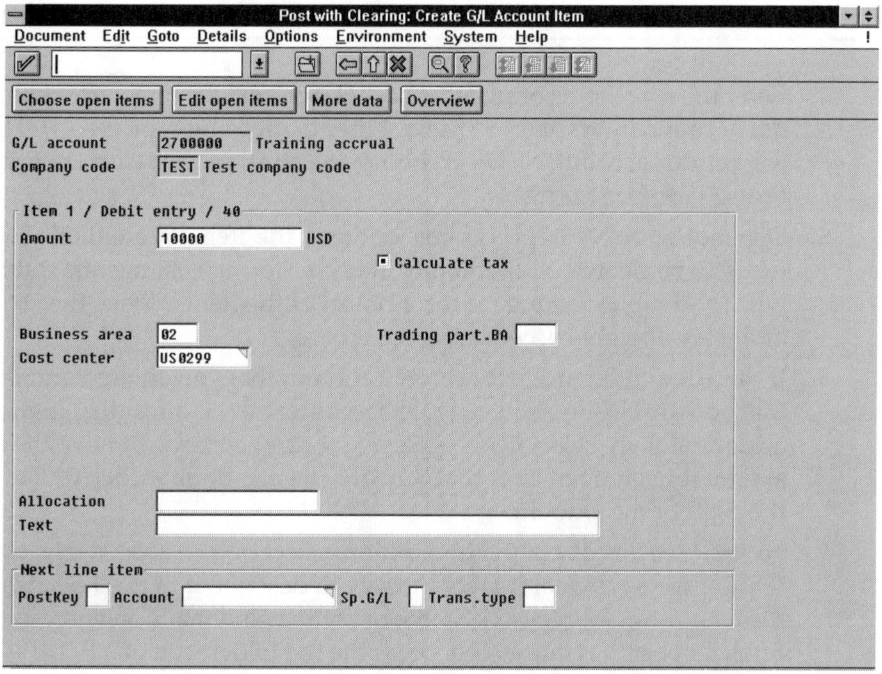

Exhibit 2.92 Post with Clearing: Create G/L Account Item

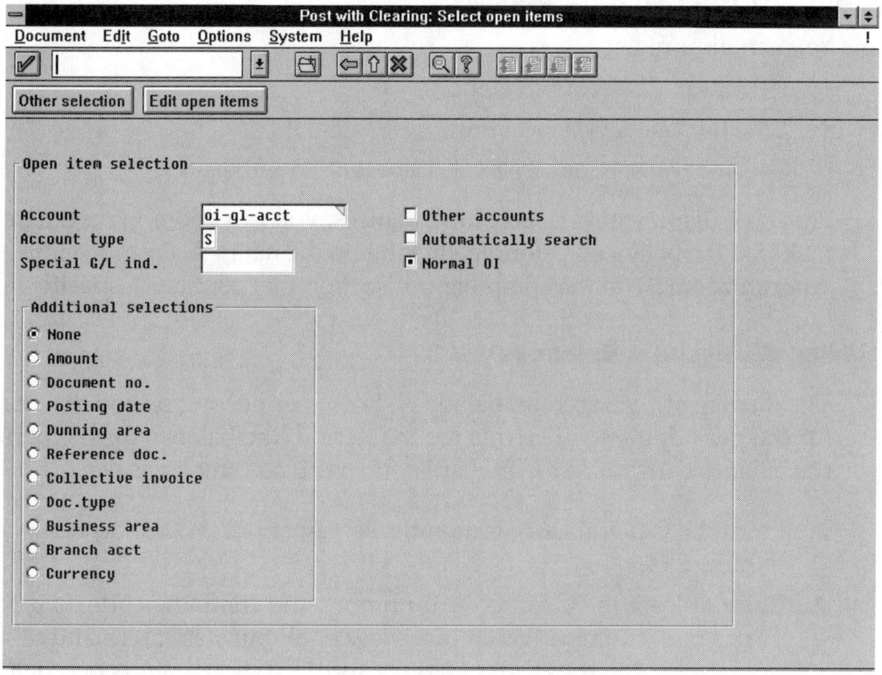

Exhibit 2.93 Post with Clearing: Select Open Items

4. Enter the specific account, either a G/L account, customer account, or vendor account, in the Account field. Enter the account type (S—G/L account; K—vendor account; or D—customer account) in the Account type field. Press Edit open items.

5. Depending on your processing options, the items are either all initially ready to be cleared or all initially inactive. You can change the status of the item by double-clicking on the amount of the item. Notice the Difference at the lower-right corner of the screen.

6. If there is a difference between the amount that you entered and the items that you are closing, you can post the difference as a residual item. To post a residual item, select Goto → Residual item screen. To have the amount assigned to an open item that you are closing, double-click on the field to the right of the amount.

7. To see the overview of the transaction, select Goto → Document overview. If you post a residual item, you have to describe it in the Text field. From the overview, double-click on the open item and make an entry in the Text field. To post the transaction, press the file folder icon or <F11>.

INQUIRING IN THE GENERAL LEDGER

You can inquire on:

- Periodic G/L account balances
- Line items in a G/L account
- Specific transactions by the "document" number

From the display of G/L account balances, you can zoom in on the items that make up the balance by double-clicking on the balance. From the line item list, you can zoom in on the complete transaction that contains a specific line item.

Displaying G/L Account Balances

The display of G/L account balances shows per posting period the total debits for the period, the total credits for the period, the balance for the period, and the balance carryforward. To display the G/L account balances:

1. From the General Ledger menu, select Account → Display balances. (See Exhibit 2.94.)

2. Enter at least the G/L account number, the company code, and the fiscal year. Press <Enter>. For an overview of all business areas and all transactions, enter * in the Business area and Transaction currency fields. Press <Enter>. (See Exhibit 2.95.)

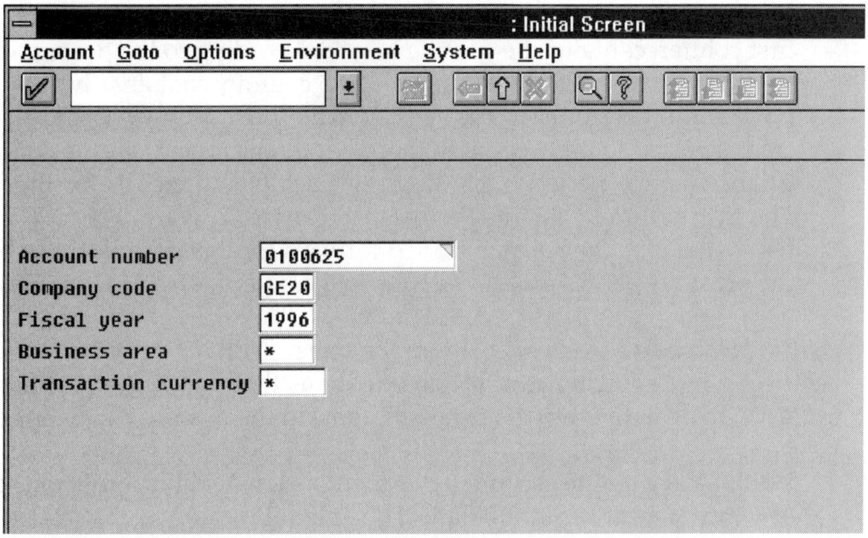

Exhibit 2.94 G/L Account Balances: Initial Screen

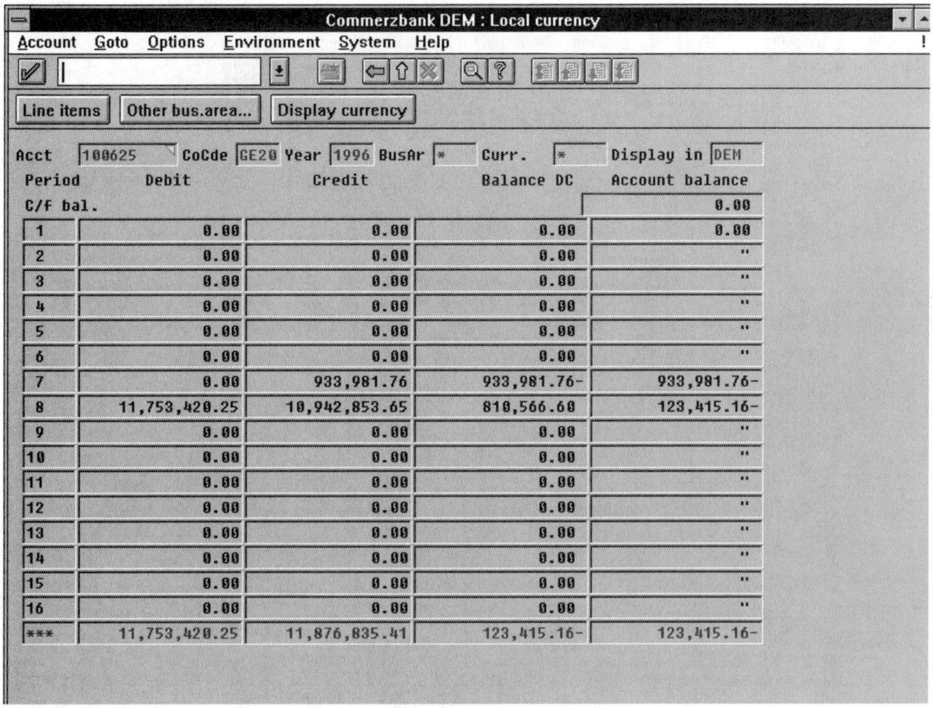

Period	Debit	Credit	Balance DC	Account balance
C/f bal.				0.00
1	0.00	0.00	0.00	0.00
2	0.00	0.00	0.00	"
3	0.00	0.00	0.00	"
4	0.00	0.00	0.00	"
5	0.00	0.00	0.00	"
6	0.00	0.00	0.00	"
7	0.00	933,981.76	933,981.76-	933,981.76-
8	11,753,420.25	10,942,853.65	810,566.60	123,415.16-
9	0.00	0.00	0.00	"
10	0.00	0.00	0.00	"
11	0.00	0.00	0.00	"
12	0.00	0.00	0.00	"
13	0.00	0.00	0.00	"
14	0.00	0.00	0.00	"
15	0.00	0.00	0.00	"
16	0.00	0.00	0.00	"
***	11,753,420.25	11,876,835.41	123,415.16-	123,415.16-

Exhibit 2.95 G/L Account Balances: Local Currency

3. Notice the five columns from left to right on this screen (Exhibit 2.95). The first column contains the posting period according to the posting date and the configured fiscal year. The second column contains the total debits posted to the account in that period. The third column contains the total credits posted to the account in that period. The fourth column contains the balance for the period (including only debits and credits for the period). The fifth column contains the balance carried forward from the previous fiscal year plus the balance carried forward for that period (the balance for the previous period plus any debits and credits posted in that period).

Drilling Down to Line Items.   From the screen with the periodic G/L account balances, you can drill down to the line items that make up any balance. For example, to drill down to the list of all items in the most recent balance:

1. Double-click on the account balance in the lower-right corner of the screen (the most recent account balance). (See Exhibit 2.96.)

2. Optionally use the Find, Sort, and Total pushbuttons to look for a specific line item, to sort the line items, or to total the line items.

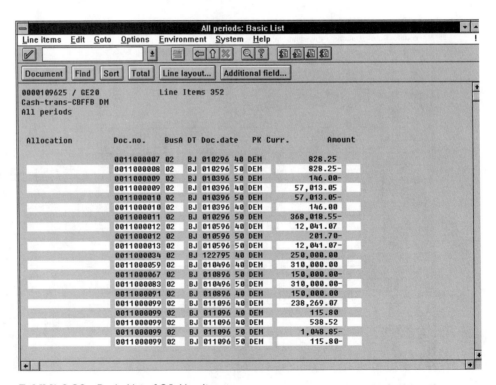

Exhibit 2.96   Basic List of G/L Line Items

Displaying a Transaction from a Line Item. From the screen with the list of line items, you can display the complete transaction that contains the line item. To display a transaction from a line item:

1. Put the cursor on the specific line item.
2. Press the Document pushbutton.
3. Notice the detailed screen with the line item. To see an overview of the complete transaction, press Document again.

Displaying Line Items in a G/L Account

If a G/L account is an open item account, then items in the account are open until you clear (close) them. If the account is not an open item account, then you can find all items as if they were open items.

To display line items in a G/L account (Exhibit 2.97):

1. From the General Ledger menu, select Account → Display line items. (See Exhibit 2.97.)

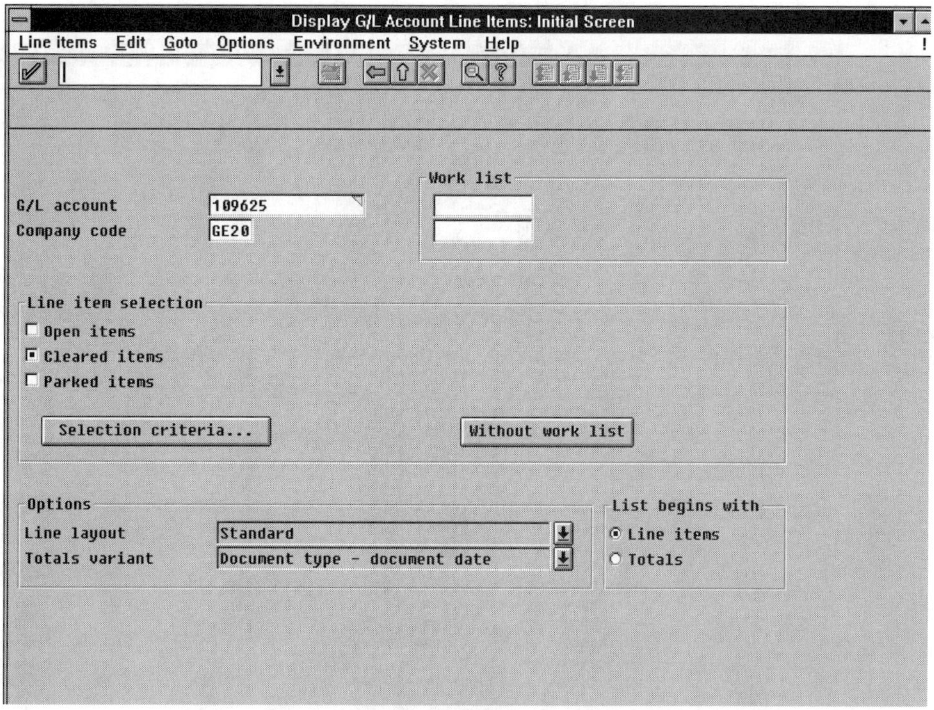

Exhibit 2.97 Display G/L Account Line Items: Initial Screen

2. Enter either a specific G/L account in the G/L account field or enter a work list of G/L accounts in the Work list field. Also enter the company code. Mark either Open items or Cleared items or both. Then press <Enter>. (See Exhibit 2.98.)

3. Optionally use the Find, Sort, and Total pushbuttons to look for a specific line item, to sort the line items, or to total the line items (Exhibit 2.98).

Displaying Open Items. To display open items in a G/L account, simply mark Open items only when you start to display items in a G/L account (Exhibit 2.99).

1. From the General Ledger menu, select Account → Display line items. (See Exhibit 2.99.)

2. Enter the G/L account and the company code. Click on Open items only. Press <Enter>.

   Notice that before pressing <Enter>, you can also select a line layout, a totals variant, and whether the list begins with the line items or the totals from this screen. The line layout and totals variants depend on your con-

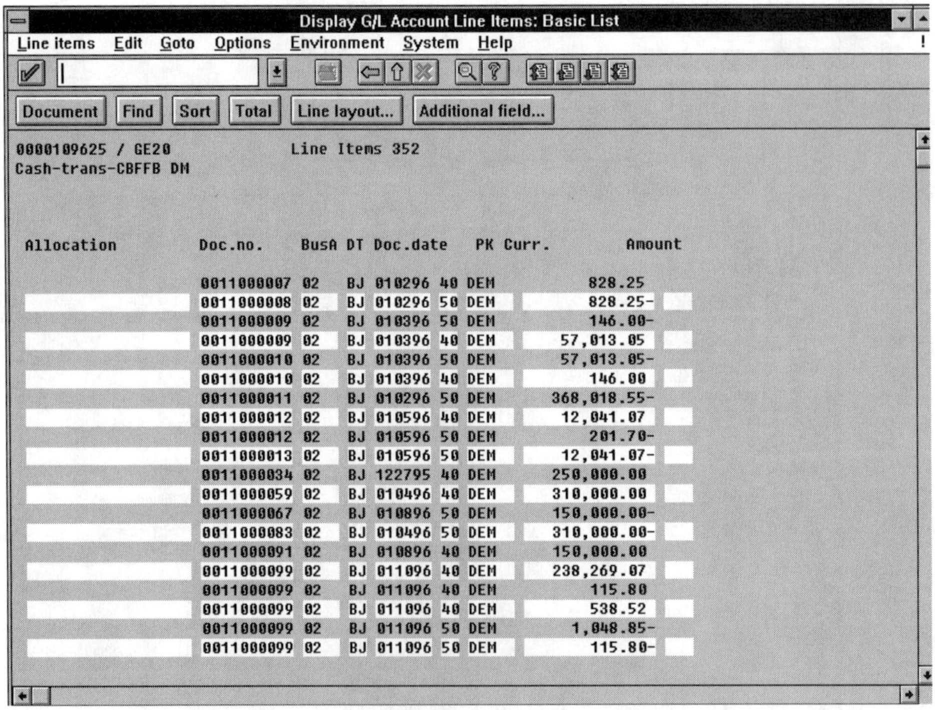

Exhibit 2.98 Display G/L Account Line Items: Basic List

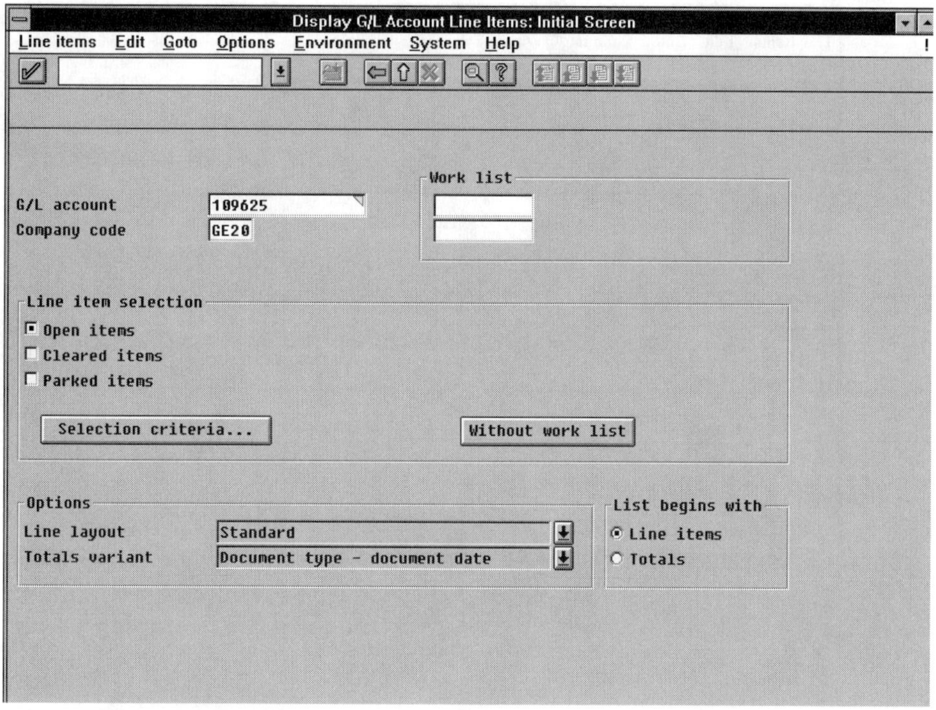

Exhibit 2.99   Display G/L Account Line Items: Initial Screen

figuration. To see the list of available line layouts or totals variants, put the cursor on the Line layout or Totals variant field and then press the down arrow.

Displaying Cleared (Closed) Items.   To display cleared items in a G/L account, simply mark Open items only when you start to display items in a G/L account.

1. From the General Ledger menu, select Account → Display line items. (See Exhibit 2.100.)
2. Enter the G/L account and the company code. Click on Cleared items only. Press <Enter>.

Displaying a Transaction

To display a specific G/L transaction:

1. From the General Ledger menu, select Document → Display. (See Exhibit 2.101.)

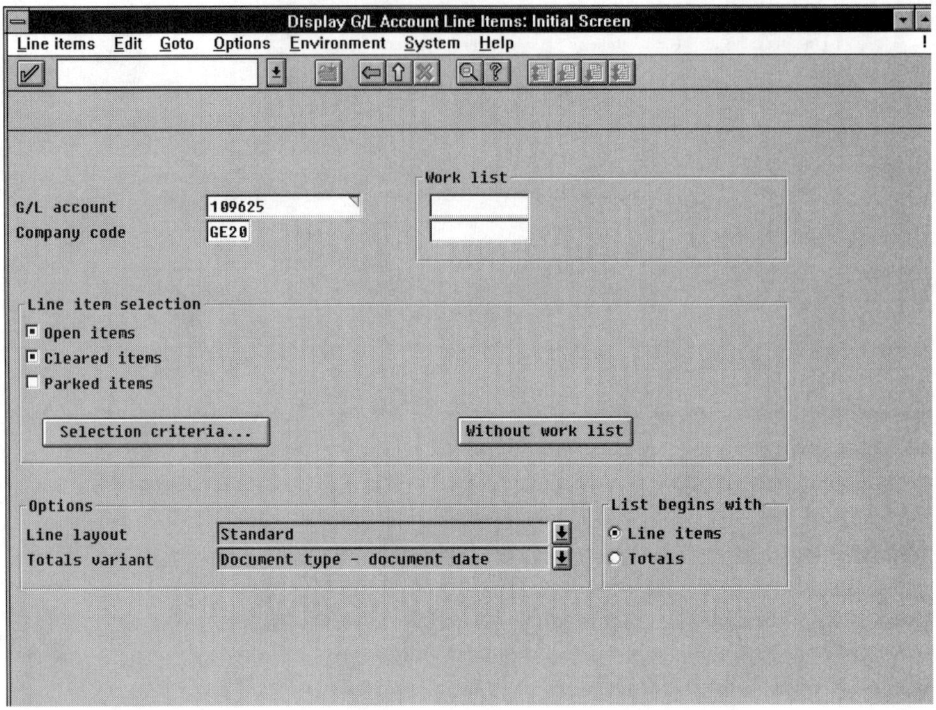

Exhibit 2.100 Initial Screen to Display Cleared Items

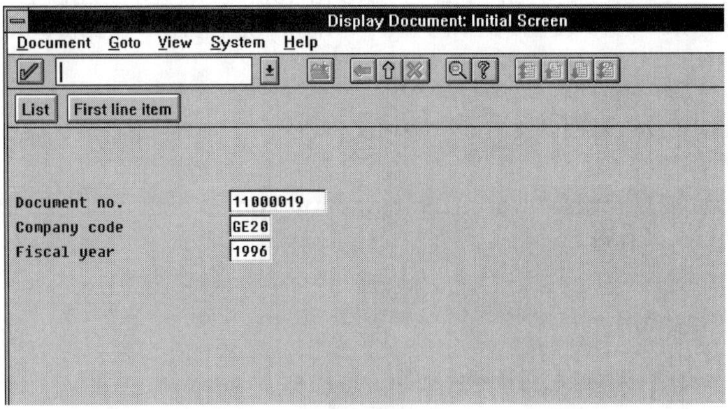

Exhibit 2.101 Display Document: Initial Screen

2. Enter the transaction (document) number, the fiscal year, and then press <Enter> (Exhibit 2.101). If you do not have the transaction number, press List. On the next screen (Exhibit 2.102), enter the parameters to list the transactions that you are looking for, and then press <F8> or Execute. (See Exhibit 2.102.)

3. To see the details of a line item, double-click on the line item or put the cursor on the line item and then press Choose.

   The amounts are displayed in transaction currency to begin with. To see the amounts in local currency or group currency, if different from transaction currency, press Display currency, then click on Loc.currency or Group currency, and press <Enter>. (See Exhibit 2.103.)

   To display the document header (Exhibit 2.104), with for example, the time the transaction was entered and the person who entered it, press Document header.

   Notice the fifth line on this window—Entered by. This shows the "transaction code" (function) used to enter the transaction and who entered it.

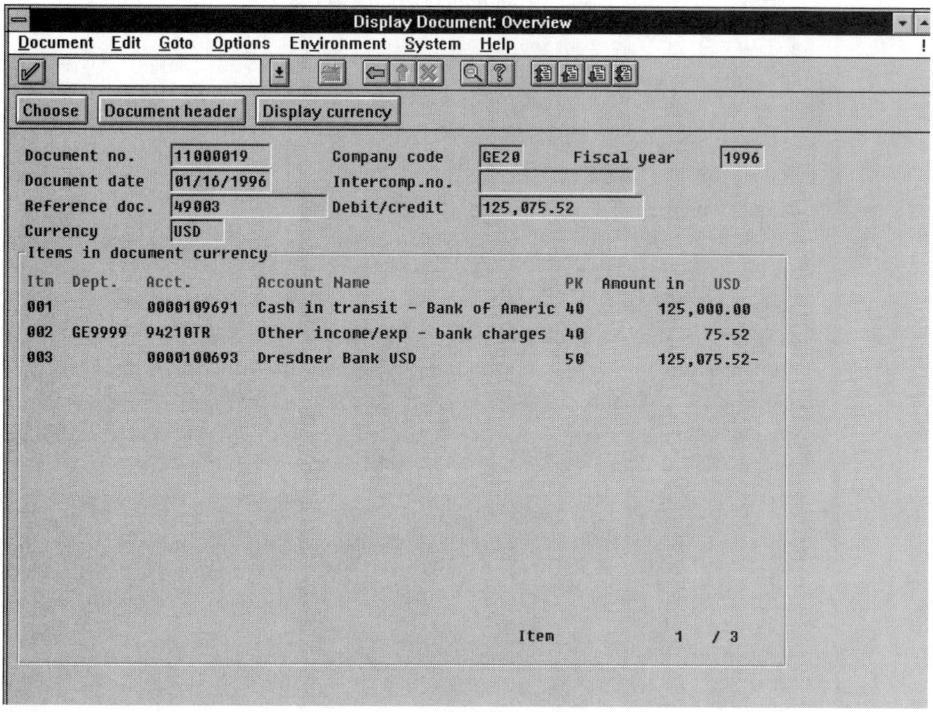

Exhibit 2.102   Display Document: Overview

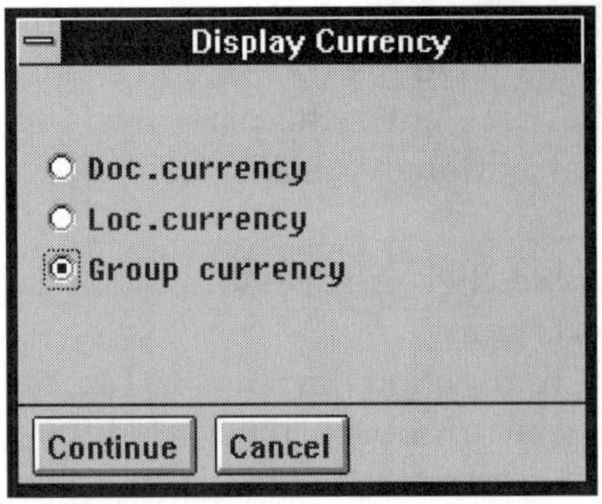

Exhibit 2.103   Display Currency

Displaying Transaction Amounts in Different Currencies.   Depending on the configuration, each and every transaction is recorded in up to three different currencies—transaction currency (specified in the header of the transaction), local currency (of the company code), and group currency such as USD or Euro. You can readily prepare financial statements in either local or group cur-

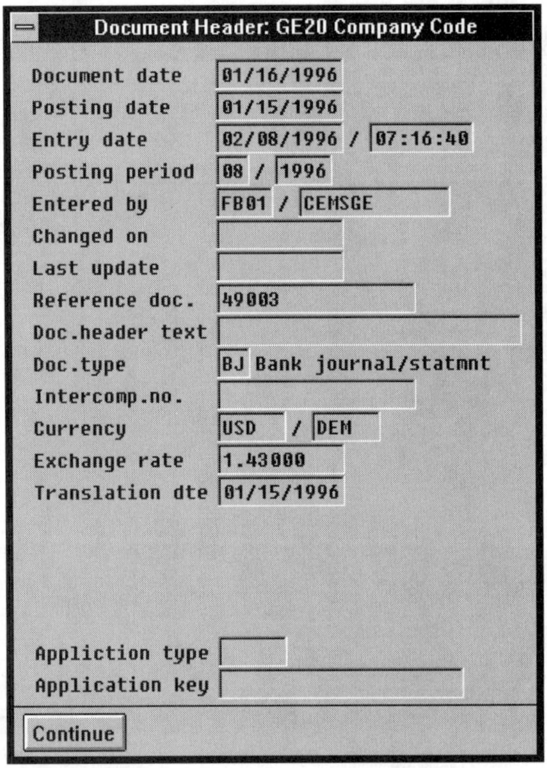

Exhibit 2.104   Document Header: Company Code

rency. To display a transaction in each of these currencies, first display the overview of the transaction. (See Exhibit 2.105.)

1. From the General Ledger menu, either display line items in an account or select Document → Display and then enter the transaction number, the company code, and the fiscal year. Press <Enter>.

2. To see the amounts in group currency, press Display currency. (See Exhibit 2.106.)

   To see the amounts in group currency, press Group currency and then press Continue.

INTERCOMPANY ACCOUNTING

Note that the following is only one possible method of intercompany accounting. In a consolidated financial statement, all intercompany account balances and transactions are to be eliminated. This applies most of all to intercompany receivables and payables. It also applies to any gains or losses from transfer-

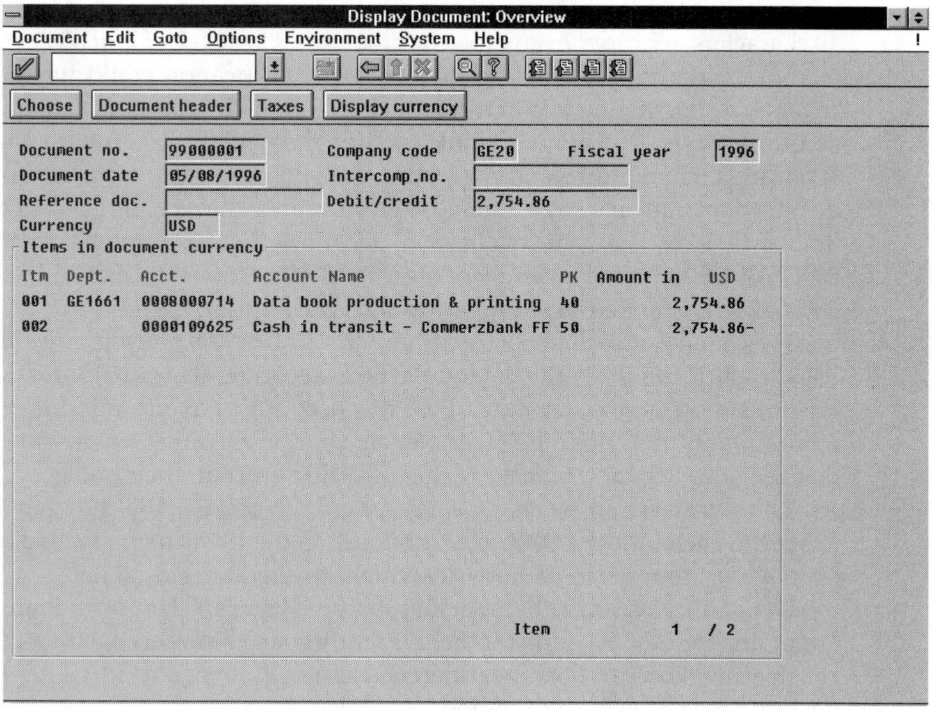

Exhibit 2.105 Display Document: Overview

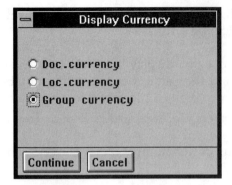

Exhibit 2.106 Display Currency

ring inventory from one location to another, gains or losses from transferring fixed assets between locations, and any investment by the head office in the equity of the subsidiary. It is advisable to have one and only one customer account and one and only one vendor account for each intercompany location, depending on your financial organization.

To prepare *aging reports* of intercompany receivables and payables, each location could have one (and only one) *customer account* and also one (and only one) *vendor account* (in each company's books). The account numbers could all have 10 characters, required in any interface, such as 00000006GE and 00000023GE.

For *transparency in the corporate ledger,* each location could have one *G/L account* (reconciliation account) for A/R and one G/L account (reconciliation account) for A/P. You could link each of these G/L accounts to the corresponding customer or vendor account. When you post to a customer or vendor account, the package immediately updates the account balance of the linked G/L account (reconciliation account). For example, the customer 00000006GE is linked to and updates the G/L account 06GE001. The vendor 00000023GE is linked to and updates the G/L account 23GE001.

To hold and then clear intercompany transactions before approval by both locations, each location could have a 05 G/L account, such as 05GE001. All 05 accounts are clearing accounts. Post this account to avoid any differences of opinion. You then post the customer or vendor account, when you are sure that the other location is making the offsetting entry in their books.

The *settlement* involves closing items that are usually, but not always, related to each other. If there is a difference in the items being settled, you can open a new item for the difference, which is called a residual item.

Depending on the settlement instructions, you can clear open items in customer and vendor accounts. If there is a difference between the items that you are clearing, you can post the difference as a new item, a residual item, with a posting date of the current period.

Keeping Intercompany Accounts

Intercompany accounts are separate by each company code, since you and any interface program always post each transaction to a specific company code.

To add another site, such as SG for Singapore, a sample way is to do as follows:

1. Enter *one and only one customer account* (with ten characters, including seven initial zeros), such as 00000006SG.

2. Enter *one and only one vendor account* (with ten characters, including six initial zeros), such as 00000023SG.

3. Enter *between five and seven G/L accounts,* depending on whether the other site is shipping or receiving and how much detail you require in the general ledger, as follows:
   - A reconciliation account for intercompany A/R, such as 06SG001
   - A reconciliation account for intercompany A/P, such as 23SG001
   - An open item account for clearing transactions, such as 05SG001 (a suspense account)
   - Margin-in, such as 46xx001 (to eliminate profits from intercompany transfers of inventory)
   - Margin-out, such as 56xx001 (to eliminate profits from intercompany transfers of inventory)
   - Intercompany revenue, such as 44xx001
   - Intercompany expense, such as 52xx001

4. If the other site is a brand-new site (not already in another company's books), then add the 05, 06, and 23 G/L accounts (open item accounts) to the list of open item accounts to be revalued (in the configuration).

To enter an intercompany customer account:

1. From the Accounts Receivable menu, select Master records → Create.

2. Enter the account number, the company code, and the account group **INTR,** depending on your configuration. Optionally, refer to the same account in another company code, if you have authorization to the other company code's customer accounts. Press <Enter>.

3. Enter the details of the other location, including at least the name, address, phone and fax numbers, reconciliation account, such as 06SG001, and payment terms.

To enter an intercompany vendor account:

1. From the Accounts Payable menu, select Master records → Create.

2. Enter the account number, the company code, and the account group **INTR,** depending on your configuration. Optionally, refer to the same account in another company code, if you have authorization to the other company code's vendor. Press <Enter>.

3. Enter the details of the other location, including at least the name, address, phone and fax numbers, reconciliation account, such as 23SG001, and payment terms.

To enter a G/L account:

1. From the General Ledger menu, select Master records → Create.

2. Enter the account number and your company code and then press <Enter>. To mark the account as an open item account (05xx001), go to the second screen and mark the Open item management field. To mark the account as a reconciliation account (06xx001 or 23xx001), go to the second screen and enter either **D** (for A/R) or **K** (for A/P) in the Recon.acct for acct type field.

Posting Intercompany Transactions

At the end of each posting period, you could transfer intercompany transactions by batch input to SAP A/R, A/P, and G/L. Enter all intercompany transactions in the same currency to avoid differences resulting from different exchange rates. In a large manufacturing company, the periodic product charge could have four transactions:

- Summary invoices (of products delivered and services performed)
- Returns
- Financial adjustments
- Samples

On the last day of each period, certain programs could automatically record batch input sessions and then post the transactions in these sessions to accounts, unless there is any "fallout" (errors) in the batch input session. A batch input session contains the transaction data.

Closing the Period

At period-end, each location has at least the following tasks:

1. Check that the batch input sessions for that location for that period have been processed. In other words, check that there has been no fallout from the batch input sessions.

2. Clear the 05xx001 G/L accounts and reduce the account balance to zero, either approving or disapproving the A/R or A/P.

3. Every other period, based on the settlement instructions, clear the intercompany customer (06) and intercompany vendor (23) accounts. You can clear the intercompany customer account and the intercompany vendor account for the same location separately or jointly. In other words, customer entries can be cleared with vendor entries, depending on your company policy and on the master data.

Checking the Batch Input Session. A batch input session contains data to be recorded in the system automatically, such as intercompany transaction data. These are to be posted with the intercompany transactions automatically on the last day of each period.

If there were any fallout or errors in the batch input session, such as missing accounts or product groups, then you would see the name of the batch input session in a list. If the batch input session were processed correctly, then the name would disappear from the list of batch input sessions. In other words, you are to look at the list of batch input sessions and verify that your batch input sessions are not in the list.

To list the batch input sessions:

1. From any menu, select System ➤ Services ➤ Batch input ➤ Edit.

2. Press Overview.

3. Look for the message No session found, which means that all of the batch input sessions have been processed. If you see a list of batch input sessions, then make sure your batch input sessions are not in the category Errors in sessions.

4. If there were errors in any of your batch input sessions, then put the cursor on the name of the session and then press Process. Then press Process with errors.

Clearing Open Items. At the end of each period, each location could reduce the account balance of all 05 accounts to zero. This is to accept or reject all intercompany transactions locally for further processing (settlement or payment). This involves clearing open items in a G/L account.

To clear open items in a G/L account:

1. From the General Ledger menu, select Account ➤ Clear.

2. Enter the account number, account type, and clearing in the common currency in your company. Press <Enter>.

3. To select an item to clear, simply double-click on the amount of the item. After you have selected all items to clear, if the difference between the debits and credits is zero, press <F11> or the file folder icon to record the clearing transactions.

Depending on the clearing instructions from your head office, match debit entries to credit entries, usually from the settlement items and other transactions already posted, such as invoices for products or services. You have to match open items in both the customer and vendor accounts, but do it separately or jointly according to your company policy. This involves clearing open items in customer and vendor accounts.

The package covers the following aspects of clearing open items:

- Automatic posting of exchange rate differences (in local currency)
- Small payment differences
- Posting payment differences by closing open items and opening a new item for the difference (a residual item)

Clearing involves matching and then closing open items in intercompany customer or vendor accounts. You can post any difference to a new item, called a residual item. The posting date of the residual item is the current period. If you are posting a difference, you should note the partial settlement and the original period in the Reference doc. field in the header of the clearing transaction.

Let all intercompany transactions posted by batch input (transferred from any other program) have the "document type" IC (intercompany).

This example assumes you clear intercompany customer entries separately from intercompany supplier entries.

To clear open items in a G/L account:

1. From the General Ledger menu, select Account → Clear.

2. Enter the account number, account type, and a common clearing currency for your companies. Press <Enter>.

3. To select an item to clear, simply double-click on the amount of the item. After you have selected all items to clear, if the difference between the debits and credits is zero, press <F11> or the file folder icon to record the clearing transactions.

To clear open items in a customer account:

1. From the Accounts Receivable menu, select Account → Clear.
2. Enter the intercompany customer account number, such as 00000006SG, and the account type
3. Process the items in this account, as you would if they were in an account for an external customer. Mark debit entries and credit entries to clear.
4. To post the difference, select Goto → Residual items. Then double-click on the right-most column of the item that is being partially cleared.
5. Press <F11> or the file folder to store the clearing transaction.

To clear open items in a vendor account:

1. From the Accounts Payable menu, select Account → Clear.
2. Enter the intercompany vendor account number, such as 00000023SG.
3. Process the items in this account, as you would if they were in an account for an external vendor. Mark debit entries and credit entries to clear.
4. To post the difference, select Goto → Residual items. Then double-click on the right-most column of the item that is being partially cleared.
5. Press <F11> or the file folder icon to store the clearing transaction.

Reporting Intercompany Account Balances

The aged A/R report is available from the package. You can run it from the A/R menu by selecting System → Services → Reporting, entering **RFDOPR10**, entering the parameters, and then pressing Execute.

The aged A/P (cash requirements) report is also available from the package. You can run it from the A/P menu by selecting System → Services → Reporting, entering **RFKOFW00**, then entering the parameters, and then pressing Execute.

You could also develop a program to show the total open items posted by intercompany account by posting period, excluding settlement and cash transactions (by the reference document). If you post a residual item with a payment difference, when you clear open items, then FI posts the residual item in the current period.

USING ADVANCED G/L FUNCTIONS

Processing Sample Transactions

You can use sample transactions as templates for long, detailed, regular transactions with slightly different amounts, such as periodic payroll transactions.

In a sample transaction, you define the company code, currency, debits, credits, accounts and amounts without posting the transaction to the accounts. Later, you can refer to the sample transaction and post an actual transaction, possibly changing the amounts of the items. In this way, a sample transaction can save you time on data entry. In other words, a sample transaction is a transaction that recurs, but the amounts or accounts vary slightly each time that you post the transaction.

Entering a Sample Transaction. To define a sample transaction:

1. From the General Ledger menu, select Document entry ➤ Reference documents ➤ Sample document. (See Exhibit 2.107.)

2. Enter and store the sample transaction, as if it were a real transaction. Note that when you store the sample transaction, it does not update G/L account balances. (See Exhibit 2.107.)

Posting with Reference to a Sample Transaction. To post a transaction based on a sample transaction, you post with reference to the sample transaction.

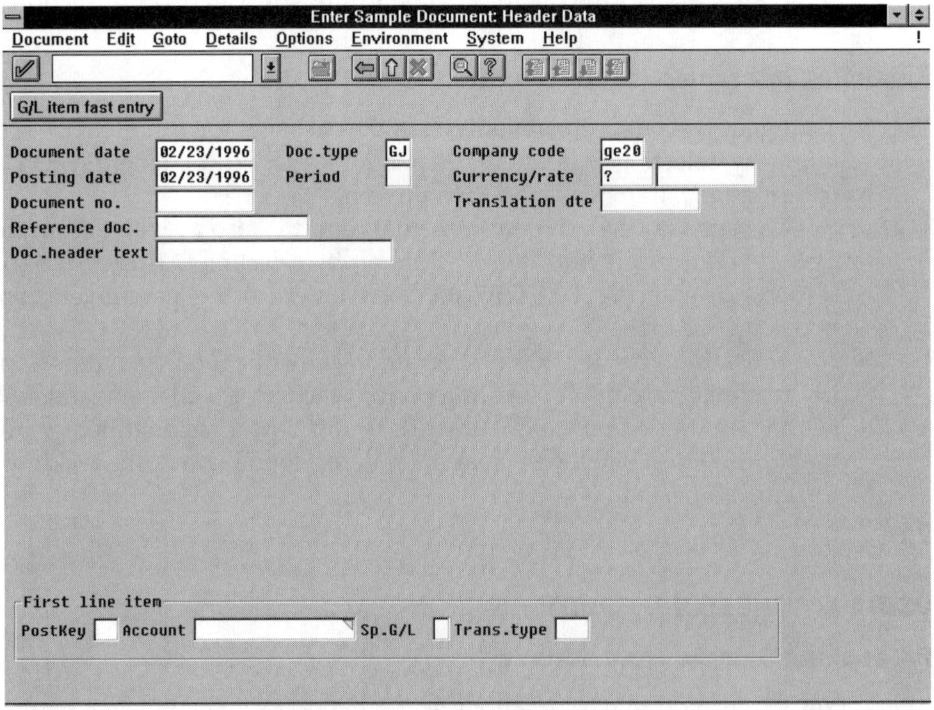

Exhibit 2.107 Enter Sample Document: Header Data

Note that you can also post with reference to an actual transaction that has already been posted.

1. From the General Ledger menu, select Document entry ➤ G/L account posting. (See Exhibit 2.108.)
2. Then select Document ➤ Posting with ref.
3. Enter at least the sample transaction number in the Document no. field and the company code. Notice from this screen that you have the following options:

Option	Meaning
Generate reverse posting	Proposes entries that reverse the transaction
Enter G/L account items	Restricts the sample transaction to items in G/L accounts and displays the G/L item fast entry screen (for editing longer transactions)

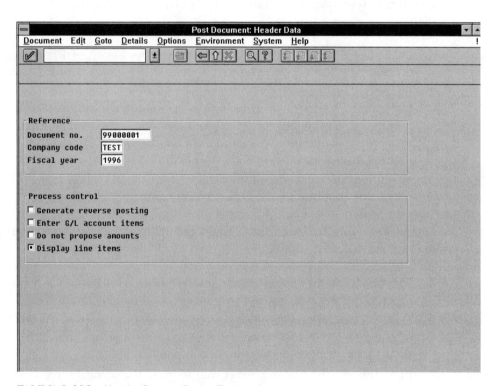

Exhibit 2.108 Header Data to Post a Transaction

| Do not propose amounts | Proposes only posting keys and accounts |
| Display line items | Display each detailed line item (otherwise, you see the header screen and then the overview screen) |

Note that you can also use an actual transaction (one posted to accounts) and not only a sample transaction as a reference for a transaction.

Processing Recurring Transactions

If you have transactions that are regularly repeated with the exact same accounts and amounts, such as rent payments, lease payments, or insurance payments, you can define a template with the recurring data. Later, in a second step, you can have FI read this template and generate a batch input session, which contains the line items and screens that are to be posted to the accounts. In a third step, you process the batch input session and post to the accounts.

Defining a Recurring Transaction.   To define a recurring transaction (the template):

1. From the General Ledger menu, select Document entry → Reference document → Recurring documents. (Exhibit 2.109 shows the next screen).
2. Enter the details of the recurring transaction, such as the first date and the last date that the transaction is to be posted, such as the 15th of every month. Depending on your configuration, you can also set various schedules for the recurring transactions, such as weekly posting. Enter the debits, credits, and accounts for the transaction.
3. Post the recurring transaction with <F11> or the file folder icon, but notice that it does not update the G/L account balances.

Listing Recurring Transactions.   To list recurring transactions (the templates) that you have already defined:

1. From the General Ledger menu, select Periodic processing → Month-end reports → Compact journal.
2. Enter parameters on the first screen, such as the company code. Optionally, enter no parameters on the first screen to find all recurring transactions that have been defined in all company codes.
3. Press the + in the lower-right corner to go to the second screen of parameters.

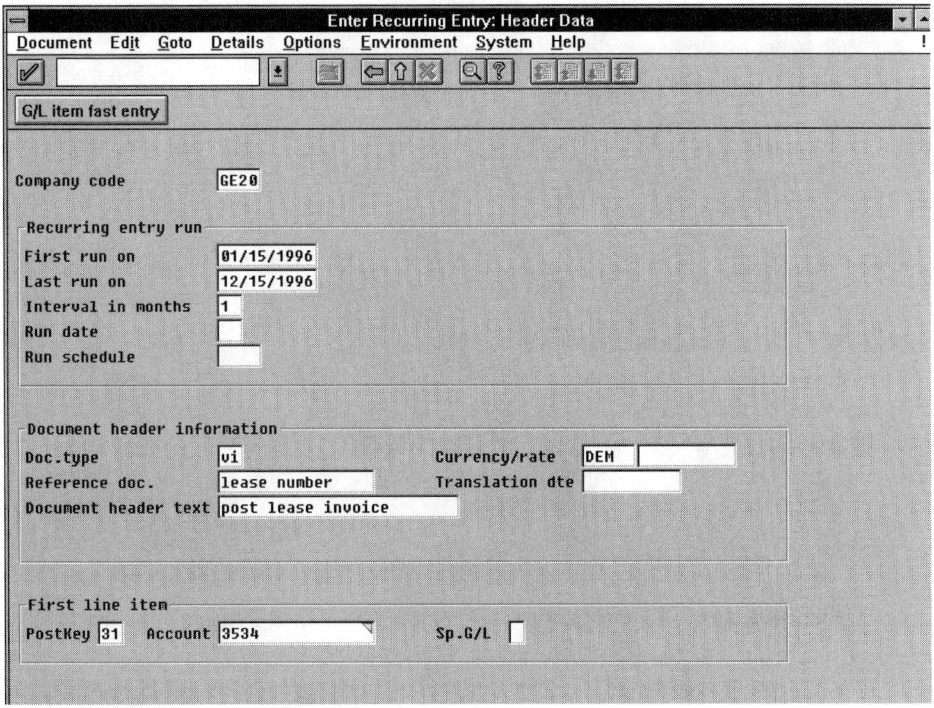

Exhibit 2.109 Enter Recurring Entry: Header Data

4. Mark Recurring entry original docs (the templates of the recurring transactions).

5. To run the report, press <F8> or Execute as usual. (See Exhibit 2.110.)

Generating the Recurring Transaction Data. To prepare to post the recurring transaction, for example on the 15th of every month:

1. From the General Ledger menu, select Periodic processing ➤ Recurring entries ➤ Proceed. The next screen is shown in Exhibit 2.111.

2. Enter at least the company code, one or more "document" types, the Calculation period (for which the transaction date is to be generated), and a name of the batch input session.

3. To generate the transaction data (the sequence of screens with the data pre-entered), press <F8> or Execute.

4. Look for the message in the lower-left corner of your screen (Exhibit 2.112). You specified the name of the session, before you ran the program to generate the session. If you do not see this (or a similar) message, then

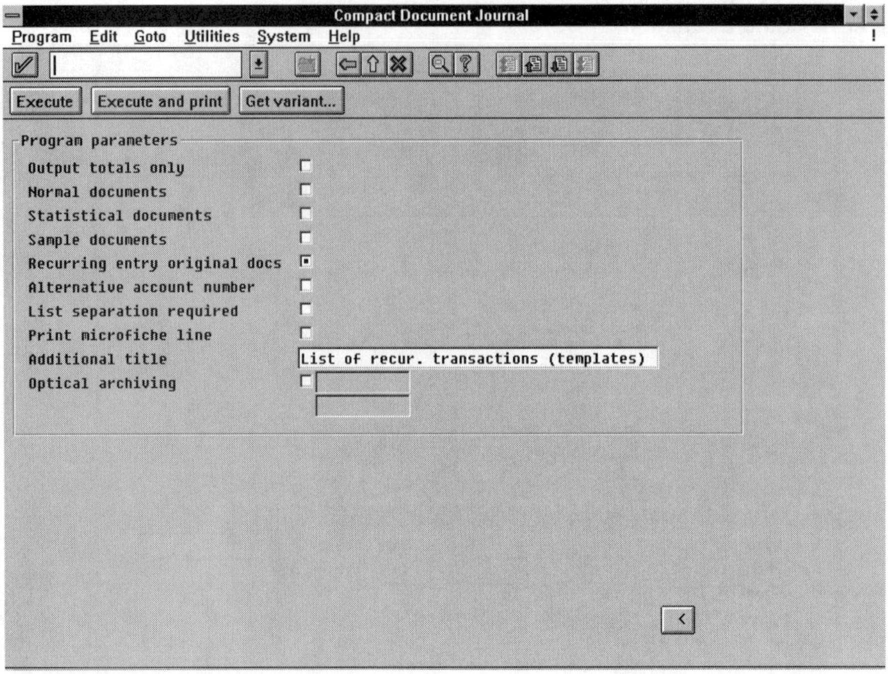

Exhibit 2.110   Compact Document Journal of Recurring Transactions—Screen 2

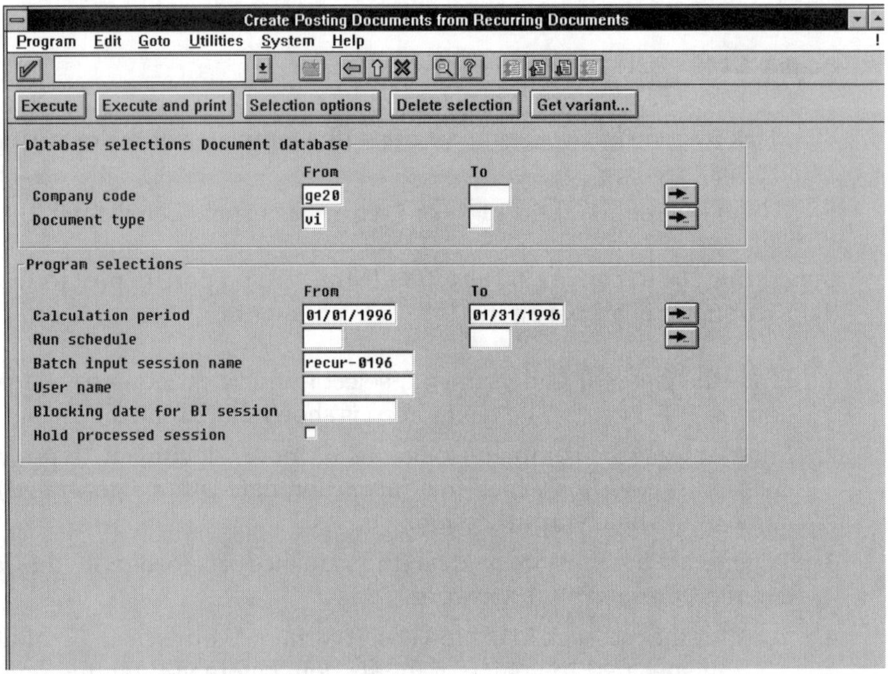

Exhibit 2.111   Create Posting Documents from Recurring Documents

Session RECUR-0196 was created

Exhibit 2.112 Session Message

there were either no recurring transactions to be generated in the Calculation period, or else there was an error generating the batch input session.

Posting the Recurring Transaction. Assuming that you have already generated the batch input session containing the recurring transactions, to post the transaction data (with one or more transactions) (Exhibit 2.113):

1. From any menu, select System ➤ Services ➤ Batch input ➤ Edit.
2. To see a list of the batch input sessions, press Overview (Exhibit 2.114).
3. To process the batch input session and post the transaction data, place the cursor on the line with the name of the batch input session and then press Process.

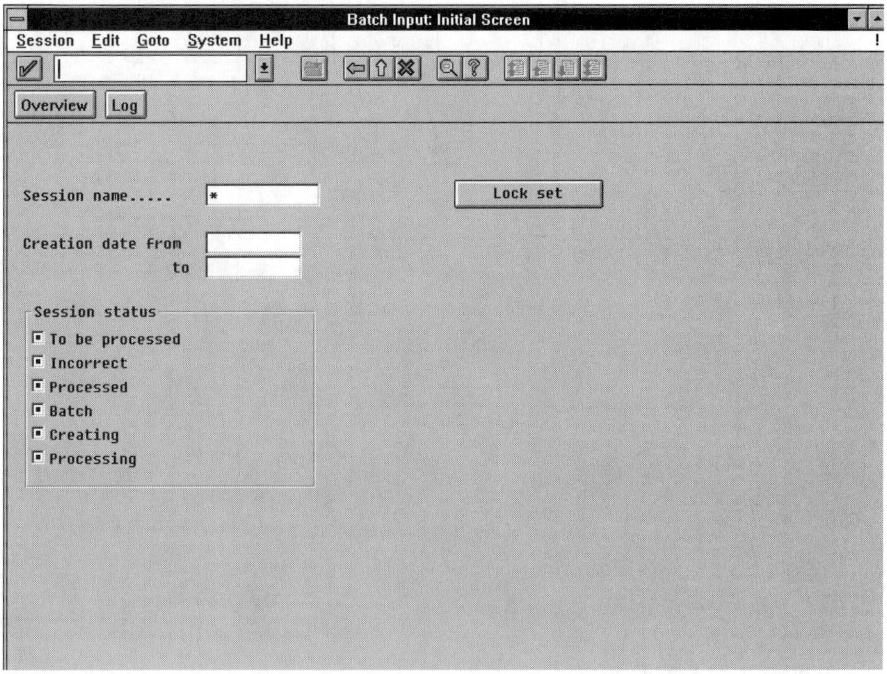

Exhibit 2.113 Batch Input: Initial Screen

4. To see only the screens with errors in them, click on Display errors only and press Process (Exhibit 2.115).

   If the batch input session were processed properly (without error and with all the transaction data posted to the accounts), you then see the message in Exhibit 2.116.

   Otherwise, if there were an error in the data (in the batch input session), you could either correct the error on-line, and then press <Enter> to continue, or select System → Services → Batch input → Cancel, or enter **/bend** in the command box to end the batch input session without processing the data.

5. To verify that the recurring transaction was posted properly, display the G/L account balances or the line items in the G/L accounts.

Deleting a Recurring Transaction. If the amount of the recurring transaction changes or you wish to delete the transaction (See Exhibit 2.117):

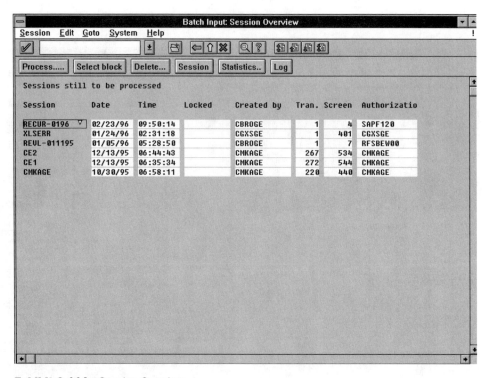

Exhibit 2.114 Session Overview

Exhibit 2.115 Process Session

1. From the General Ledger menu, select Document ➤ Reference documents ➤ Recurring document ➤ Delete.

2. Enter one or more company codes, one or more or a range of specific document numbers, **D** for recurring transactions, and then mark Test run.

3. To run the report, press <F8> or Execute (Exhibit 2.117).

Alternatively, you can delete the recurring transaction (the template), while you process the batch input session (See Exhibit 2.118). In this way, you post the transaction, but you prevent any more from being posted. To delete the recurring transaction (template):

1. Process the batch input session as usual. From the menu, select System ➤ Services ➤ Batch input ➤ Edit.

2. Press Overview.

3. Put the cursor on the batch input session and press Process.

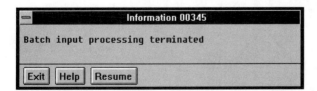

Exhibit 2.116 Information Message—Batch input

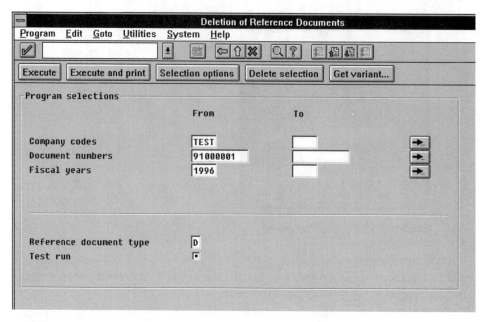

Exhibit 2.117   Deletion of Reference Documents

4. Select Process/foreground. (See Exhibit 2.118.) In this way, you see each screen. To go to the next screen, press <Enter>.

5. Mark Deletion ind. This prevents the transaction from being posted again in another batch input session. Press <Enter> to go to the next screen. Keep pressing <Enter> until you finish processing the batch input session (Exhibit 2.119).

Exhibit 2.118   Process Session

```
┌─────────────────────────────────────────────────────────────────┐
│ ═                  Realize Recurring Entry: Header Data      ▼ ▲ │
│  Document   Edit   Goto   Details   Options   Environment   System   Help              ! │
│  ┌──┐ ┌──────────────┐ ┌─┐ ┌──┐  ┌─┬─┬──┐ ┌─┬─┐  ┌──┬──┬──┬──┐      │
│  │✓ │ │              │ │±│ │🖩│  │⇐│⇧│✗│ │🔍│?│  │  │  │  │  │      │
│  └──┘ └──────────────┘ └─┘ └──┘  └─┴─┴──┘ └─┴─┘  └──┴──┴──┴──┘      │
│  ┌──────────────────┐ ┌──────────────────┐                        │
│  │ Open held document │ │ G/L item fast entry │                     │
│  └──────────────────┘ └──────────────────┘                        │
│                                                                   │
│  Document date    01/15/1996   Doc.type   GJ    Company code   TEST │
│  Posting date     01/15/1996   Period     6     Currency/rate  USD      │
│  Document no.                                    Translation dte        │
│  Reference doc.                                                    │
│  Doc.header text  recur. training accrual                          │
│                                                                   │
│                                                 Tax details    ☐  │
│                                                                   │
│  ┌─Recurring entry data ────────────────────────────────────────┐ │
│  │ Next run on     02/15/1996            Document no.   9100000000 │ │
│  │ Deletion ind.   ☒                     Fiscal year    1996     │ │
│  └──────────────────────────────────────────────────────────────┘ │
│                                                                   │
│                                                                   │
│  ┌─First line item ─────────────────────────────────────────────┐ │
│  │ PostKey 50 Account 0002700000      Sp.G/L ☐ Trans.type       │ │
│  └──────────────────────────────────────────────────────────────┘ │
└─────────────────────────────────────────────────────────────────┘
```

Exhibit 2.119 Realize Recurring Entry: Header Data

Matching (Clearing) Open Items

Open item accounts, also called clearing accounts or interim accounts, usually contain debit and credit items that exactly match. For example, assume you post a check received to a clearing account for cash in transit. Assume further that the bank clears the check and credits your account in their records for the full amount of the check. You then post the entry in the bank statement to the accounts for cash at the bank and cash in transit. You can then clear (close) items in the cash in transit account, but only if the debits exactly match the credits. Later versions may make it possible to post any differences on account. To clear (match) open items in G/L accounts:

1. From the General Ledger menu, select Account ➤ Clear. (See Exhibit 2.120.)
2. Enter at least the G/L account number, the clearing date, the company code, and the currency of the items to be cleared. Optionally, select a currency to display the open items in the Currency field. Otherwise, you will see the open items in either transaction currency or local currency, depending on the configuration and the line layout. Optionally, select open items by the additional criteria.

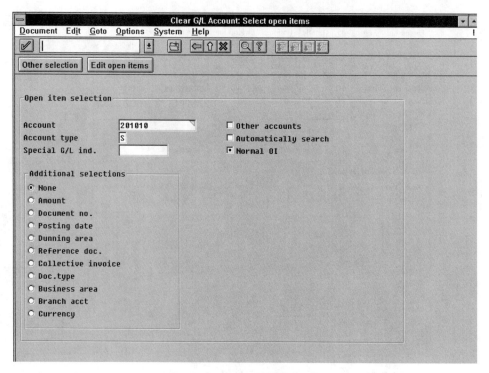

Exhibit 2.120   Clearing Open Items in Another Account

To start to process the open items, to select which ones to clear, press Edit open items.

3. From the list of open items, first select debit items that match credit items, such as checks in transit that match checks cleared by the bank. Whether open items are initially active or not depends on your processing options (for each user). Assuming that the open items are initially inactive, to select an item, double-click on the field with the amount of the item. After double-clicking on the amount of the item, notice that the color of the Amount field changes and that the subtotaled amount next to the Allocation and Difference fields changes. Note that to clear the open items, you have to select two or more items with a total Difference (between the debits and credits) or zero. Later versions may make it possible to post any differences on account.

4. To clear open items in another account, select Edit → Select more.

5. Enter at least the account number in the Account field and the type of the account (S—G/L account; K—vendor account; D—customer account) in the Account type field. Optionally, to clear any advances or other special G/L transactions, enter the code for the special G/L transaction in the Special

G/L ind. field. To clear regular transactions (without special G/L transactions), click on Normal OI. Select either Normal OI or Special G/L ind. transactions or both. Press <Enter> to see the list of open items in the accounts that you have selected.

6. Continue to select open items as you did with the first account.

7. After you select open items with a difference of zero (with total debits equal to total credits), press <F11> or the file folder icon to clear the open items.

    FI then stores a clearing transaction, which groups together the cleared items under a certain number. No account balance has changed.

    To reverse the clearing later, if required for a correction or an adjustment, from the General Ledger menu, select Document ➤ Reset cleared items and enter the clearing transaction number.

Making a Work List of G/L Accounts

If you display or clear line items in a set of related G/L accounts together, such as all cash accounts, you can combine these G/L accounts in a work list. You can define one or more work lists. You can also define work lists for customer accounts or vendor accounts. This work list of accounts is available for the functions to display line items and to clear open items.

To define a work list of G/L accounts:

1. From the General Ledger menu, select Environment ➤ Current options ➤ Work lists. (See Exhibit 2.121.)

2. Double-click on the line for General ledger accounts. (See Exhibit 2.122.)

3. To enter a new list, press Create. To edit a list that is already entered, double-click on the name of the list. (See Exhibit 2.123.)

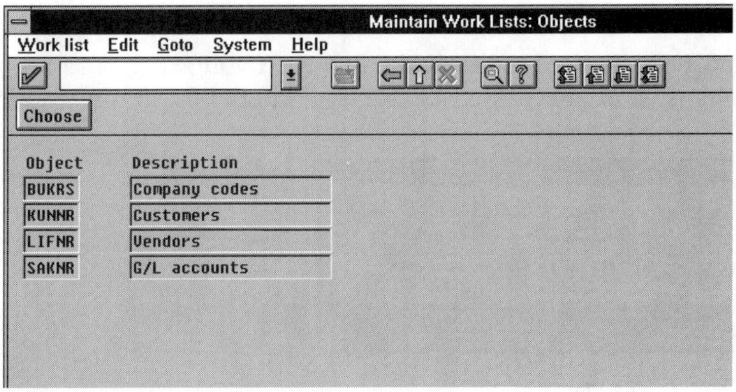

Exhibit 2.121 Maintain Work Lists: Objects

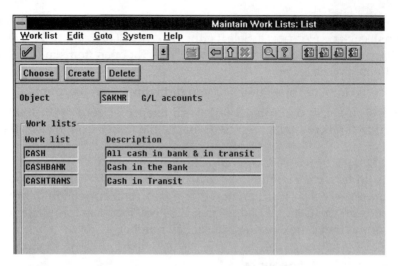

Exhibit 2.122   Maintain Work Lists: List

4. Enter a brief name of the new list and then press <Tab>. Enter a description and press <Enter>. (See Exhibit 2.124.)

5. Enter the specific individual accounts in the work list (with leading zeroes before the number and a total of ten digits per account number). To store the work list, press <F11> or the file folder icon. To go back to the General Ledger menu, press the up-arrow. To test the work list, select Account ➤ Display line items, leave the Account field blank, enter the brief name of the work list in the Work list field, and press <Enter>. Note that if you do not see an entry field for the work list, you first have to turn on the work list option. See the previous section "Setting Processing Options—Line Items" for how to turn on work lists.

Using Control Totals

Control totals can be used to verify data entry. If you expect a series of transactions to be entered and posted to certain accounts in certain amounts, you

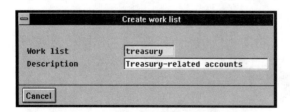

Exhibit 2.123   Create Work List

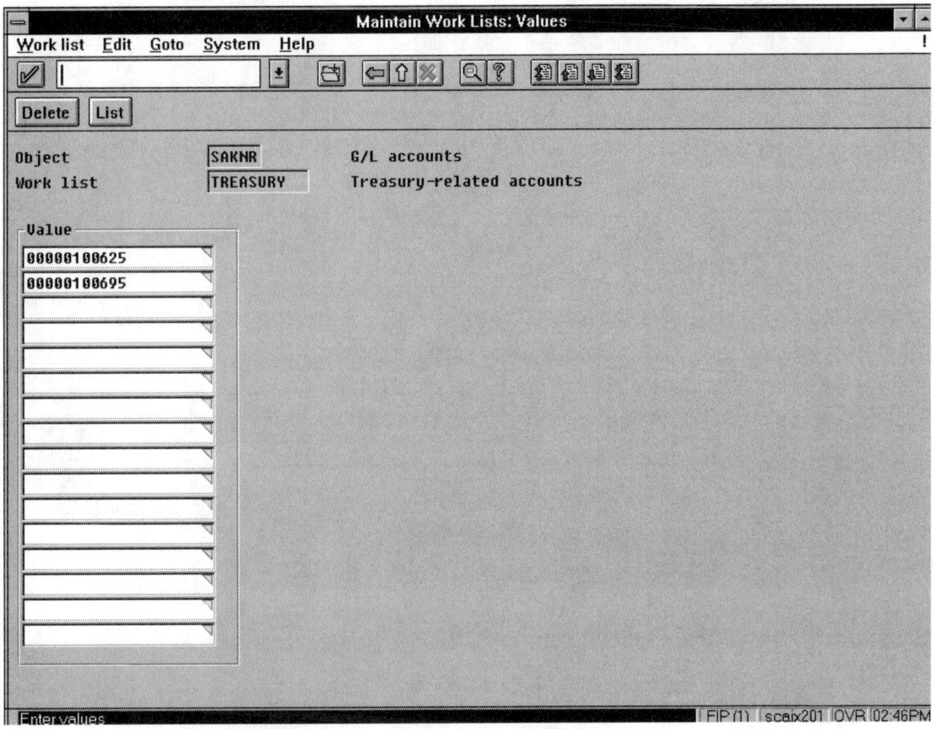

Exhibit 2.124 Maintain Work Lists: Values

can calculate and enter the control total before the entries are posted. FI then keeps track of the total amounts actually posted. After the data entry is complete, you can compare your control total with the amounts that were actually posted, displaying the differences. The control total should match the total actually posted. If not, then there has been a mistake in data entry or in calculating and entering the control total. Control totals most often apply to a series of entries in the bank statement, a batch of checks, or a series of invoices.

Maintaining Control Totals. Before entering the control totals (Exhibit 2.124), calculate what totals you expect to be posted from the series of (printed) documents in front of you, for example, entries in the bank statement. To enter control totals:

1. From the General Ledger menu, select Environment ➤ Current options ➤ Control totals.

2. Press Maint.control totals or select Goto ➤ Maint.control totals. (See Exhibits 2.125 and 2.126.)

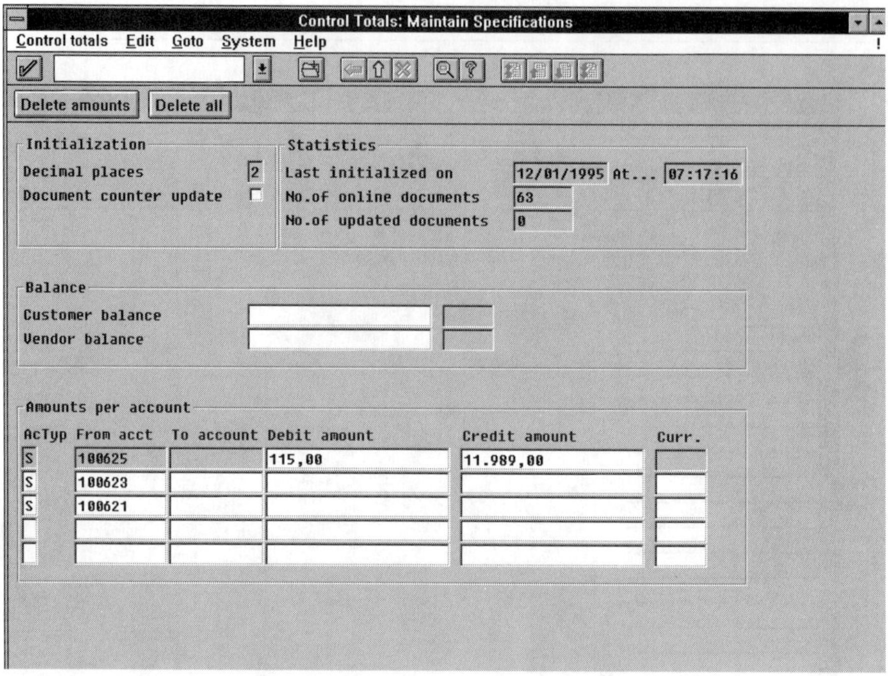
Control Totals: Maintain Specifications
Control totals Edit Goto System Help
Delete amounts
Delete all
Initialization
Decimal places 2
Document counter update
Statistics
Last initialized on 12/01/1995 At... 07:17:16
No.of online documents 63
No.of updated documents 0
Balance
Customer balance
Vendor balance
Amounts per account
AcTyp From acct To account Debit amount Credit amount Curr.
S 100625 115,00 11.989,00
S 100623
S 100621

Exhibit 2.125 Maintain Specifications

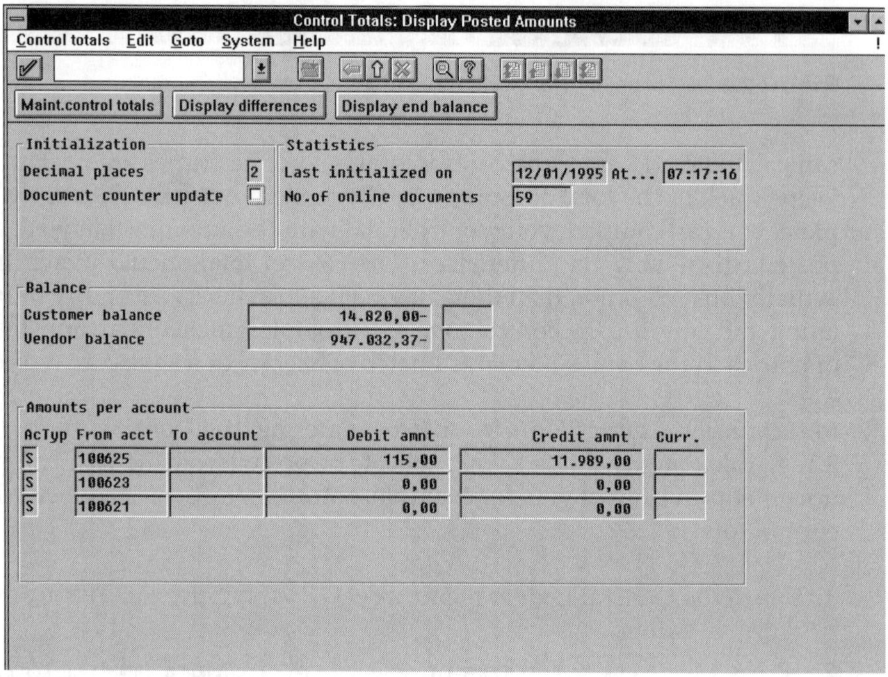
Control Totals: Display Posted Amounts
Control totals Edit Goto System Help
Maint.control totals
Display differences
Display end balance
Initialization
Decimal places 2
Document counter update
Statistics
Last initialized on 12/01/1995 At... 07:17:16
No.of online documents 59
Balance
Customer balance 14.820,00-
Vendor balance 947.032,37-
Amounts per account
AcTyp From acct To account Debit amnt Credit amnt Curr.
S 100625 115,00 11.989,00
S 100623 0,00 0,00
S 100621 0,00 0,00

Exhibit 2.126 Display Posted Amounts

3. Read the end of the screen and notice the control totals that were actually posted. To compare the control totals to the actually posted amounts, press Display differences or select Goto ➤ Display differences. (See Exhibit 2.127.)

4. The differences should be zero. If not, then someone has made a mistake entering and posting the data, or else you have made a mistake calculating and entering the control total.

5. If there were no differences between the control totals and the totals actually posted, you can delete either the amounts of the control totals only, if you control totals daily, or both the amounts and the accounts, if you did a one-time control of amounts.

   To start to delete the amounts, first press Maint.control totals or select Goto ➤ Maint. control totals. To delete the amounts only, press Delete amounts or select Edit ➤ Delete amounts.

   To delete the amounts and the accounts, press Delete all or select Edit ➤ Delete all.

Note that for each user, you can turn off the updating of control totals (the totals actually posted), for example, if you forgot to add an item to the control

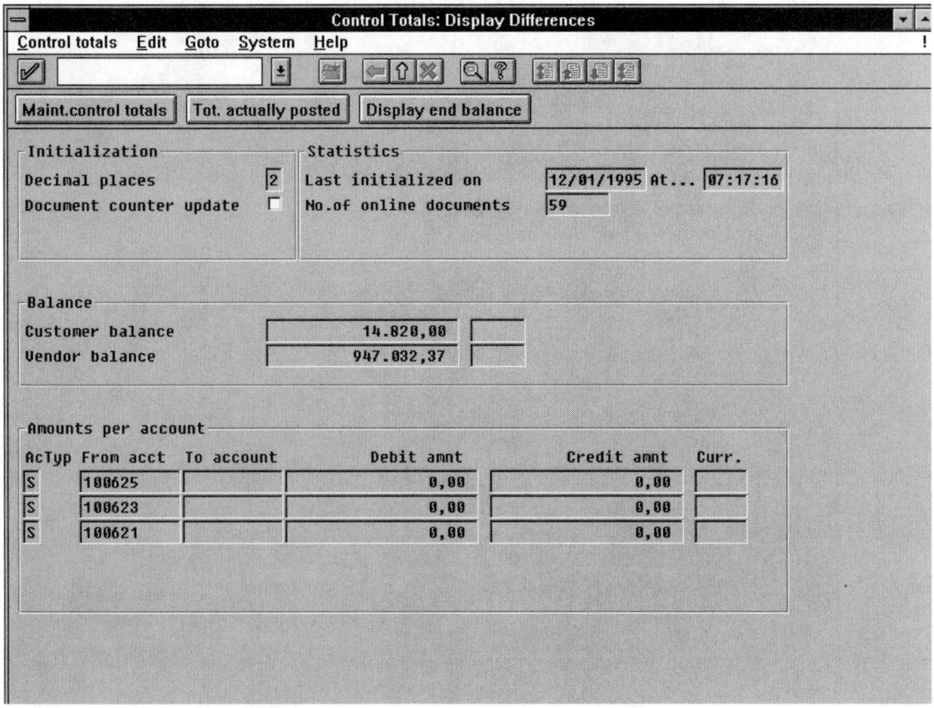

Exhibit 2.127 Display Differences

total, but wish to post the item anyway without affecting the calculation of the total actually posted. To turn off the update of the control total (the totals of the amounts actually posted):

1. From the General Ledger menu, select Environment → Editing options. (See Exhibit 2.128.)
2. Click on the Do not update control totals field.
3. To store the processing options, press <F11> or the file folder icon.

CLOSING

Each SAP module has its own period-end and year-end closing procedures. CO and AM have no specific period-end closing procedures, except for reporting (and depreciation) required by your company. In AM, there is a year-end

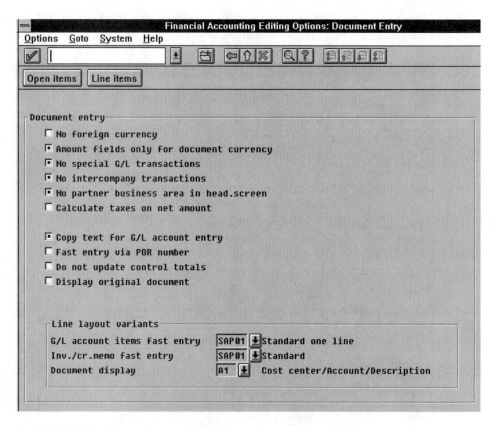

Exhibit 2.128   Financial Accounting Editing Options: Document Entry

closing procedure. In FI, there are no technical procedures to close the period and open another period. Unlike many mainframe software packages, FI lets you keep more than one period open at once. FI is an on-line system that continuously and completely integrates the general ledger with accounts receivable and accounts payable. At the beginning of a new period, you have to keep the current period open for new transactions, such as customer invoices, while you also have the previous period open for adjustments. In other words, the "housekeeping" or period-end programs found in many mainframe software packages are obsolete. The complicated, technical closing procedures to close the prior period, open the new period, and carry forward account balances, disappear. You can and should have two posting periods open at the same time—to make adjustments in the prior period before reporting the results at the same time that you post customer invoices or other data to the new period. SAP is an integrated system, so you cannot simply hold all invoices and wait for the prior period to be closed, before opening the new period.

Overview

During the first few days of a new period, all adjustments are usually to be posted to the prior period. Before closing the prior period, you can run a transaction journal of adjustments and accruals depending on the "document" type of adjustment entries, scan the journal, and make sure that all of these closing entries were posted to the prior period only.

If someone made a mistake and posted a closing entry to the new period, instead of to the prior period, then you can reverse the transaction and post it again to the prior period.

Closing the Period—Step-by-Step Procedure

The following is only a sample closing procedure. Your closing procedure depends on your company. Opening the new period and closing the previous period are two parts of the closing procedure. A possible procedure to close the period is as follows:

1. Coordinate closing with the purchasing department (MM), the cost accounting and internal reporting department (CO), and with fixed assets (AM).

2. In MM, you can post inventory movements only in the current period and the previous period. When you close the period in the purchasing department, using MM, you prevent posting of vendor invoices (invoice verification) and inventory movements in the closed period and permit posting of invoices in the new period. To close the period in MM:

    a. Select System ➤ Services ➤ Reporting from any menu.

    b. Then enter the **RFMMPERI** program.

    c. Lastly, press <F8> or the Execute pushbutton.

    d. Enter the company code twice, the next posting period, and press <F8> again. For details, read the on-line report documentation. You can also schedule this program to run in the background (as a batch job). If any material master records are locked, for example, by a goods receipt, then the program aborts without results. You also have to run the period closing program once before you go into production, using the initialization option.

3. It is usually advisable to enter the new intercompany exchange rates with a validity date of the beginning of the new period. Enter both exchange rates, in other words, the intercompany rate from transaction or group currency to local currency, such as from 1 USD to 1.5 DEM, and the reciprocal from local currency to the same transaction or group currency, such as from 1 DEM to .66667 USD.

4. When closing the period in the cost controlling department, using **CO,** enter the headcount in the form of "statistical ratios."

5. Post other accruals to be reversed automatically.

6. Post any management fees as G/L transactions.

7. Post reserves as G/L transactions.

8. If required, revalue open items and G/L accounts according to company policy or GAAP (FASB 52) regulations.

9. Optionally, revalue prepayments and accruals in local currency to group currency.

10. Post revaluation from previous step.

11. Run a transaction journal of the general journal and verify that no adjustments or closing entries were posted at the beginning of the new period.

12. Close the previous period. FI automatically carries forward the account balances to the next period (during the fiscal year). At the end of the year, you have to run two programs in FI. The first carries forward customer and vendor account balances. The second carries forward G/L account balances.

13. Prepare the sales tax report using third-party software, such as AVP or Vertex, or VAT report based on the report supplied by SAP. Make the VAT adjustment, posting VAT payable (or refundable) either manually or with the supplied VAT report. This adjustment makes the account balances in the input and output VAT accounts zero, so that the calculation for the next month starts at zero.

14. If required (at year-end), revalue open items and G/L accounts according to the local regulations and revaluation methods. If required, post no

translation gains (Germany and France). While payments were posted during the period, both of these countries require posting transaction gains and losses to separate G/L accounts.

15. With the local balance sheet format, print out the local balance sheet and P&L, if required.

16. Document briefly and clearly any changes to the procedure. Train everyone involved.

Opening the New Posting Period

To open the new posting period:

1. From the General Ledger menu, select Environment → Current options → Posting periods. (See Exhibit 2.129.)

2. For each company code, specify at least + in the second column to specify two possible ranges of open posting periods. Optionally, for each company code, you can specify by each type of account (A—assets; D—customers; K—vendors; S—G/L accounts) a range of accounts (or all accounts) and

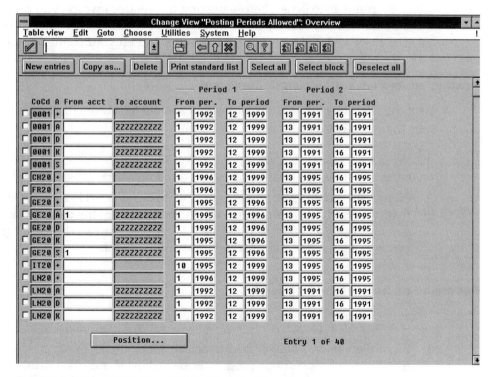

Exhibit 2.129 Change View "Posting Periods Allowed": Overview

two ranges of open posting periods. For example, you could keep one range of posting periods (From per. and To period) open for the period that you are closing and the new period and a second range open for adjustment periods in the previous fiscal year.

3. To open a posting period, simply include the posting period to one or the other possible range of posting periods. Then press <F11> or the file folder icon to store the posting periods.

Posting Adjustments

To post an adjustment (a closing entry), post a G/L transaction like any other. Debit one G/L account and credit another. To start to post an adjustment:

1. From the General Ledger menu, select Document entry → G/L posting.
2. Post the transaction as usual. See the section about entering and posting G/L transactions for details.

Posting an Expense Accrual without VAT

When accruing an expense, before posting the vendor invoice, you can record the expense without VAT by using a VAT code with a zero percentage, such as V0. The exact VAT codes and percentages depend on your configuration.

Posting an Accrual for Automatic Reversal

At the end of the period, you can post an accrual for automatic reversal in the next period. To post an accrual for automatic reversal:

1. From the General Ledger menu, select Periodic processing → Year-end reports → Balance sheet prep. → Enter accr/def doc. (See Exhibit 2.130.)
2. Note that you can enter an accrual either to be reversed in a prior period or to be reversed in a future period. Usually, you enter the date of the future reversal, but you enter it in the field labeled Pr.per.pst.dte (prior period posting date). Enter and post the transaction as usual.

Reversing an Accrual Automatically

To reverse an accrual that you have entered:

1. From the General Ledger menu, select Periodic processing → Year-end reports → Balance sheet prep. → Enter accr/def doc. (See Exhibit 2.131.)

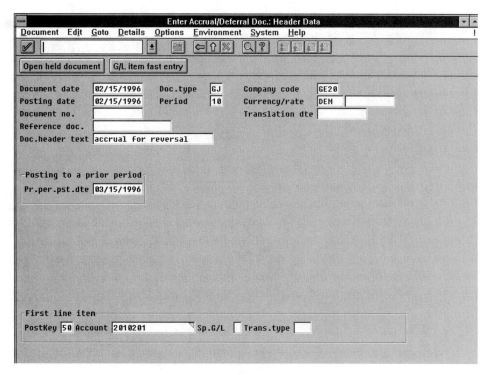

Exhibit 2.130   Enter Accrual/Deferral Header Data

2. To test the run, select Test run. Otherwise, to post the reversals, make sure Test run is not selected and then press Execute.

3. The next screen shows you which transactions would be reversed, if this were a test run, or which transactions were actually reversed, if this were not a test run.

Reporting Adjustments by Posting Date

Since both the previous posting period (for posting adjustments and accruals) and the new posting period (for posting customer invoices and payments) are open at the same time, it is possible that someone makes a mistake and posts an adjustment or accrual to the new posting period. Your staff should be properly trained that the posting date determines the posting period and that all adjustments and accruals should be posted to the prior period. Nevertheless, it is possible that they post to the mistaken period anyway. In this case, you can reverse the transaction and post it to the proper posting date and posting period.

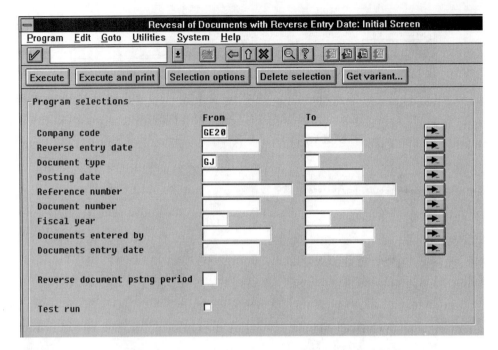

Exhibit 2.131   Reversal of Documents with Reverse Entry Date: Initial Screen

To make sure that all adjustments were posted to the proper date (in the previous period), you can report all adjustments (by one or more "document types") by the posting date as follows:

1. From the General Ledger menu, select Periodic processing ➤ Month end reports ➤ Compact journal. (See Exhibit 2.132.)

2. Enter at least the company code, one or more document types for adjustments depending on your configuration, and the posting dates that include the last few days of the prior period and the first few days of the new period. Alternatively, specify both posting periods in the Fiscal periods field. Press the + (plus symbol) at the lower-right corner of the screen to go to the next screen of parameters. (See Exhibit 2.133.)

3. Optionally, enter an additional heading in the report. To run the report, press Execute or press <F8>.

4. Scan the report. Make sure that the posting date of all adjustments and accruals was in the prior period. If any were posted to the new period by mistake, print the report, reverse the transaction by the number, and then post the transaction again with the proper posting date.

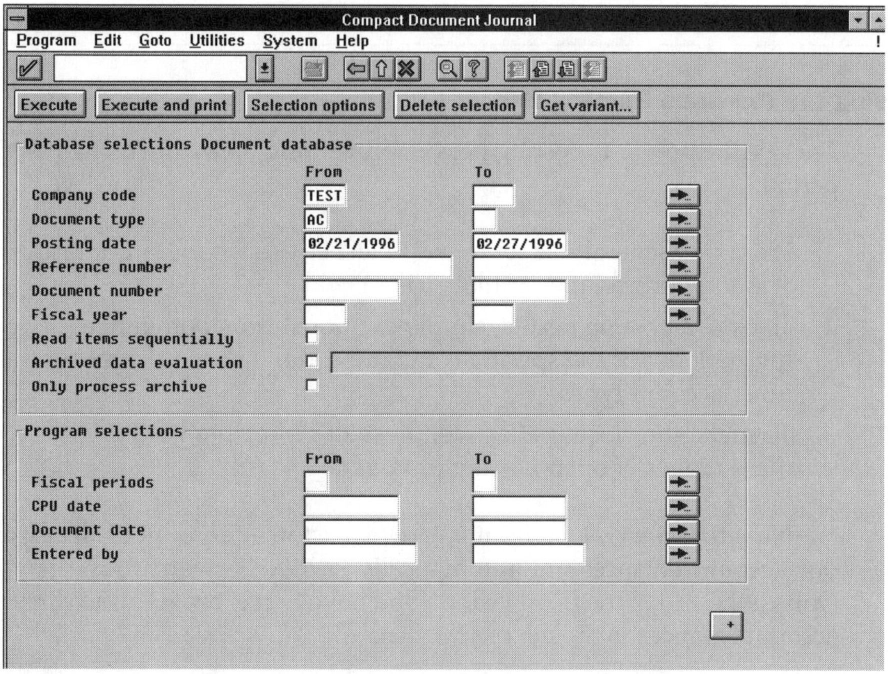

Exhibit 2.132 Compact Document Journal: Adjustments by Posting Date, Screen One

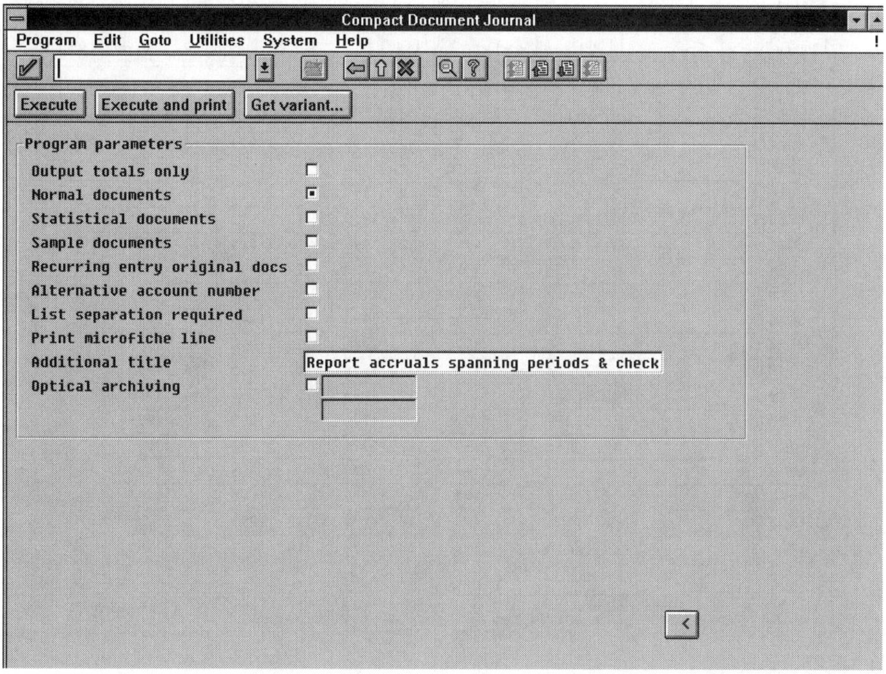

Exhibit 2.133 Compact Document Journal: Adjustments by Posting Date, Screen Two

Closing the Previous Posting Period

To close the previous posting period, preventing data from being posted to the period:

1. From the General Ledger menu, select Environment → Current options → Posting periods. (See Exhibit 2.134.)
2. To close a posting period, simply exclude it from both ranges of open posting periods for the specific company code, for the account type + and all other account types.
3. To make the closing effective, press <F11> or the file folder icon to store these ranges of open posting periods.

Note that the G/L account balances, customer account balances, and vendor account balances are automatically carried forward to the next period. Only at the end of the fiscal year do you have to run programs to carry forward account balances to the next fiscal year.

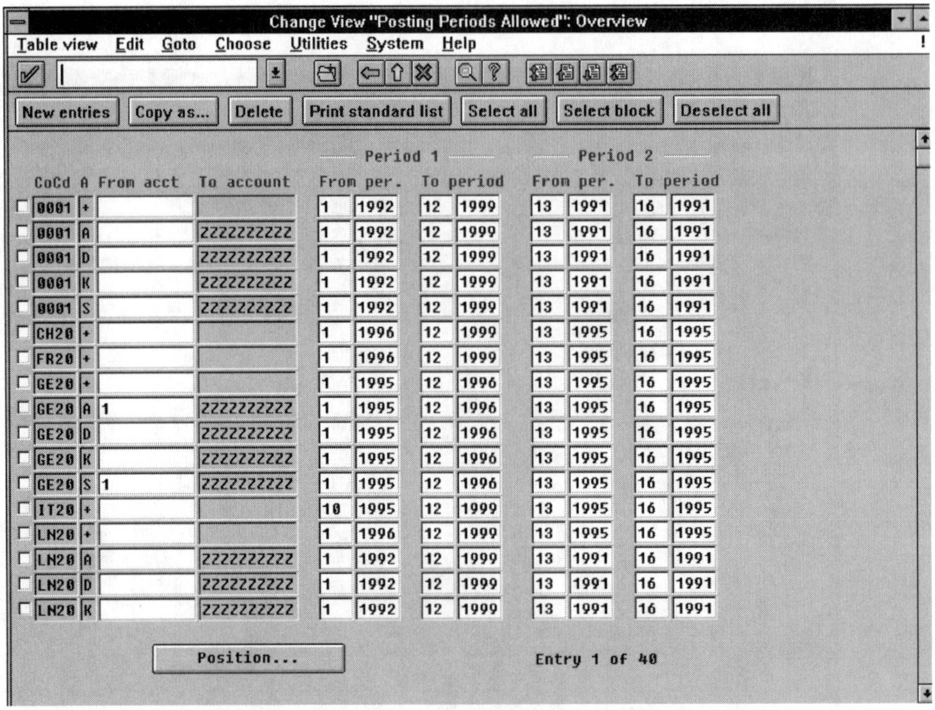

				Period 1				Period 2			
CoCd	A	From acct	To account	From per.		To period		From per.		To period	
0001	+			1	1992	12	1999	13	1991	16	1991
0001	A		ZZZZZZZZZZ	1	1992	12	1999	13	1991	16	1991
0001	D		ZZZZZZZZZZ	1	1992	12	1999	13	1991	16	1991
0001	K		ZZZZZZZZZZ	1	1992	12	1999	13	1991	16	1991
0001	S		ZZZZZZZZZZ	1	1992	12	1999	13	1991	16	1991
CH20	+			1	1996	12	1999	13	1995	16	1995
FR20	+			1	1996	12	1999	13	1995	16	1995
GE20	+			1	1995	12	1996	13	1995	16	1995
GE20	A	1	ZZZZZZZZZZ	1	1995	12	1996	13	1995	16	1995
GE20	D		ZZZZZZZZZZ	1	1995	12	1996	13	1995	16	1995
GE20	K		ZZZZZZZZZZ	1	1995	12	1996	13	1995	16	1995
GE20	S	1	ZZZZZZZZZZ	1	1995	12	1996	13	1995	16	1995
IT20	+			10	1995	12	1999	13	1995	16	1995
LN20	+			1	1996	12	1999	13	1995	16	1995
LN20	A		ZZZZZZZZZZ	1	1992	12	1999	13	1991	16	1991
LN20	D		ZZZZZZZZZZ	1	1992	12	1999	13	1991	16	1991
LN20	K		ZZZZZZZZZZ	1	1992	12	1999	13	1991	16	1991

Exhibit 2.134 Change View "Posting Periods Allowed": Overview

Note that, other than updating the open posting periods, there is no technical procedure to open the next posting period. In other words, the "housekeeping" program disappears.

Closing the Year and Carrying Forward Balances

Note that other SAP modules besides FI, such as AM (fixed assets) and MM (inventory management and purchasing), have specific procedures and programs required to close the fiscal year. This section describes carrying forward the account balances in FI to the next year. At the end of the fiscal year, you have to run two programs to carry forward the balances to the next fiscal year. One program carries forward the G/L account balances, while the other program carries forward the customer and vendor account balances. When running any carryforward program, make sure that nobody is posting entries to accounts. Also, run the carryforward program in the new year. After running the carryforward program, when you post a transaction to the previous year, the account balances in the current year are immediately updated.

To carry forward the G/L account balances to the next fiscal year:

1. From the General Ledger menu, select Periodic processing → Year-end reports → Bal. carried forward → General ledger. (See Exhibit 2.135.)

2. Enter at least the company code and the new fiscal year (in the Carry-forward to fiscal year field).

   Optionally, to test the program first, choose Test run. Otherwise, for a live run, make sure that this parameter is not selected.

   Optionally, to see the profit and loss account balances listed individually, click on Bal.carr.fwd acct individ.bals. Otherwise, the log includes only the balance sheet account balances and the total of the results carried forward to the next year.

   To carry forward the general ledger balances, press Execute or <F8>. The program extends the file of account balances. It then simply adds up the total debits and credits posted to all P&L accounts (by the P&L statement acct type in the G/L account) and posts this amount to the configured account for results to be carried forward. The program also simply copies balance sheet account balances from the end of one year to the beginning of the next year.

3. To carryforward the customer and vendor account balances, select Periodic processing → Year-end reports → Bal. carried forward → Customer/vendor. (See Exhibit 2.136.)

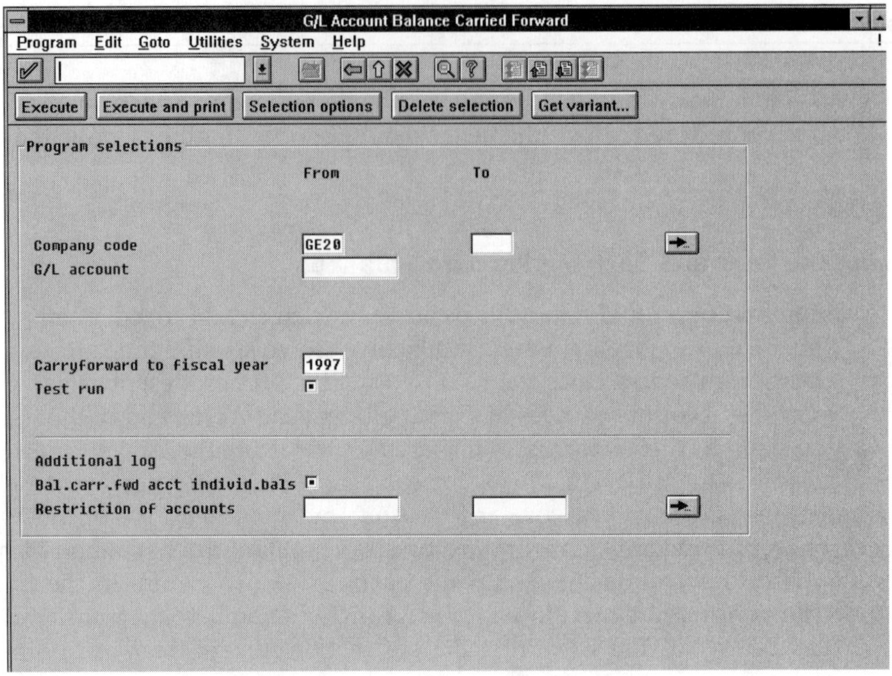

Exhibit 2.135   G/L Account Balance Carried Forward

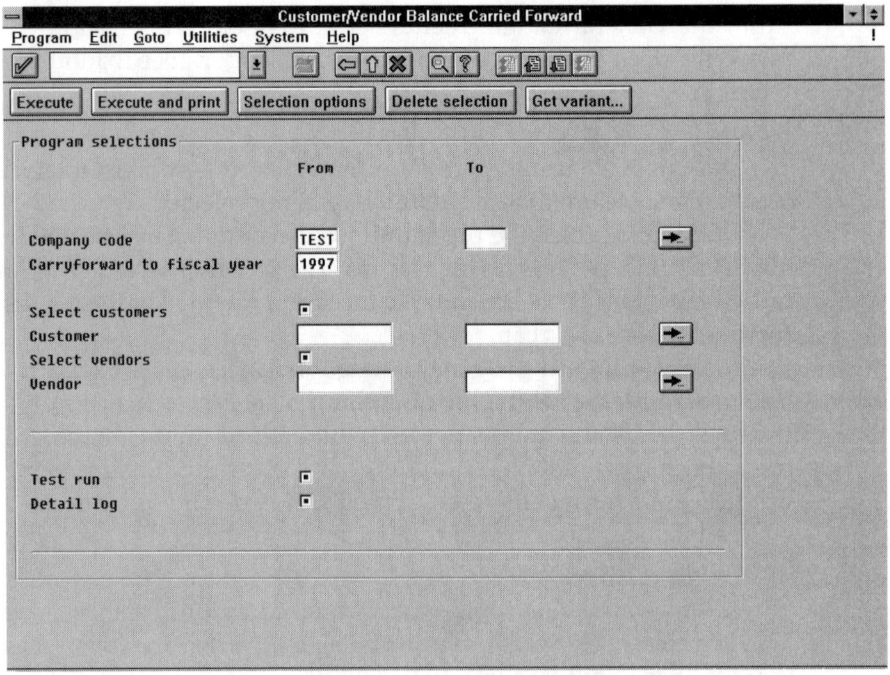

Exhibit 2.136   Customer/Vendor Balance Carried Forward

4. Enter the company code and the new fiscal year. Usually, carry forward all customer and all vendor account balances at the same time. To test, mark Test run. For a log, mark Detail log.

5. To run the program, press <F8> or Execute.

Archiving Data in R/3

A useful archive makes it possible for you to retrieve your data, even years later, even after you upgrade your equipment, operating system, database, and possibly R/3. Physically label all archive tapes. Archiving and restoring data with R/3 depends on your database software to record and retrieve the data. You also use the operating system to copy or move the archive file from the disk to tape and back. In practice, as with any archiving system, unless you clearly label the media and thoroughly test the archiving and retrieval to begin with, and also test it after you upgrade anything, you may end up with a tape that you cannot find, cannot read, or else cannot restore data from. If you have enough disk space and reliable disk drives, it is advisable to store five to ten years of data on-line and to archive your data as seldom as possible.

Archiving removes data from your on-line database and places it in an archive file that you can copy to a tape or other off-line media. R/3 is designed to archive master records (G/L accounts, customers, and vendors), account balances (transaction figures), and transaction data (documents). You can archive master records, only if:

- They do not have account balances
- They are marked for deletion
- There is no primary cost element for a G/L account master record
- There is no order entry, shipping, nor invoicing data for a customer record
- There is no purchasing data for a vendor master record
- The company code data of the master record has already been archived or selected to be archived (when you are archiving G/L account master records from the global chart of accounts or general data about customer and vendor master records)
- All transactions posted to a G/L account have already been archived (when you are archiving a G/L account master record in a company code)

You can never archive account balances in the current or the previous fiscal year. Account balances can be archived before the previous year, even if you have not yet archived the corresponding transaction data. Archive older account balances only if the posting periods that you are archiving are closed.

To start to archive transaction data:

1. From the General Ledger menu, select Periodic processing ➤ Archiving ➤ Documents ➤ Archive. (See Exhibit 2.137.)

2. To prevent anyone from posting any transactions during the archiving process, press Lock logon.

3. To start the archiving, press Start archiving. If you have already archived data, to see details of your previous archives, press Display admin.

4. After you press Start archiving, the next screen prompts you to specify which transactions to archive. (See Exhibit 2.138.)

5. Enter at least the company code and fiscal periods to archive. For a test run, select Test run.

6. To start the archiving program, press Execute or <F8>.

7. Using your database software and operating system, copy or move the archive file from disk to tape.

To archive master records for G/L accounts, customer master records, and vendor master records:

1. From the corresponding menu (General Ledger, Accounts Receivable, or Accounts Payable), select Periodic processing ➤ Archiving ➤ G/L accounts (or Customers or Vendors) ➤ Archive.

2. Follow the instructions on the screen.

To archive account balances:

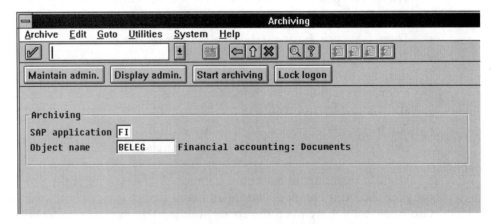

Exhibit 2.137   Archiving Data

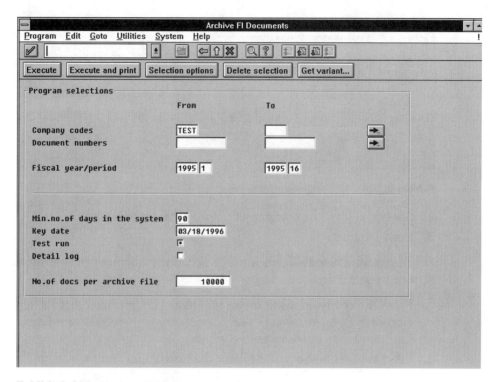

Exhibit 2.138 Archive FI Documents

1. From the General Ledger menu, select Periodic processing ➤ Archiving ➤ Transaction figures ➤ Archive.

2. Read the on-line help and follow the instructions on the screen.

Restoring Data from an Archive

As a practical matter, actually restoring data from an archive on tape depends on your operating system, your database, and which version of R/3 that you archived the data under. Assuming none of those changed from when you archived the data, and also assuming that you have labeled the archive tape and can find the tape later, it is a piece of cake to restore your archived data.

To start to retrieve archived transaction data:

1. Using your database and operating system, restore the archive file from tape to disk.

2. From the General Ledger menu, select Periodic processing ➤ Archiving ➤ Documents ➤ Reload. (See Exhibit 2.139.)

3. To retrieve the data, select Archive ➤ Start retrieval. (See Exhibit 2.140.)

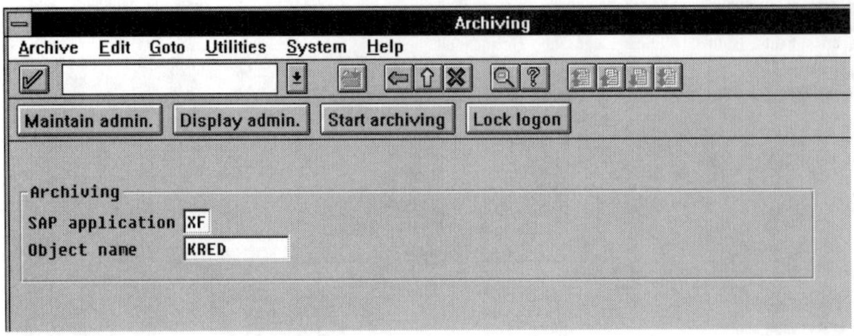

Exhibit 2.139   Archiving—Restoring Data

4. Specify at least the company code and the Archive key.
5. Press Execute.

To restore master records for G/L accounts, customer master records, and vendor master records:

1. From the corresponding menu (General Ledger, Accounts Receivable, or Accounts Payable), select Periodic processing ‣ Archiving ‣ G/L accounts (or Customers or Vendors) ‣ Reload.
2. Read the on-line help and follow the instructions on the screen.

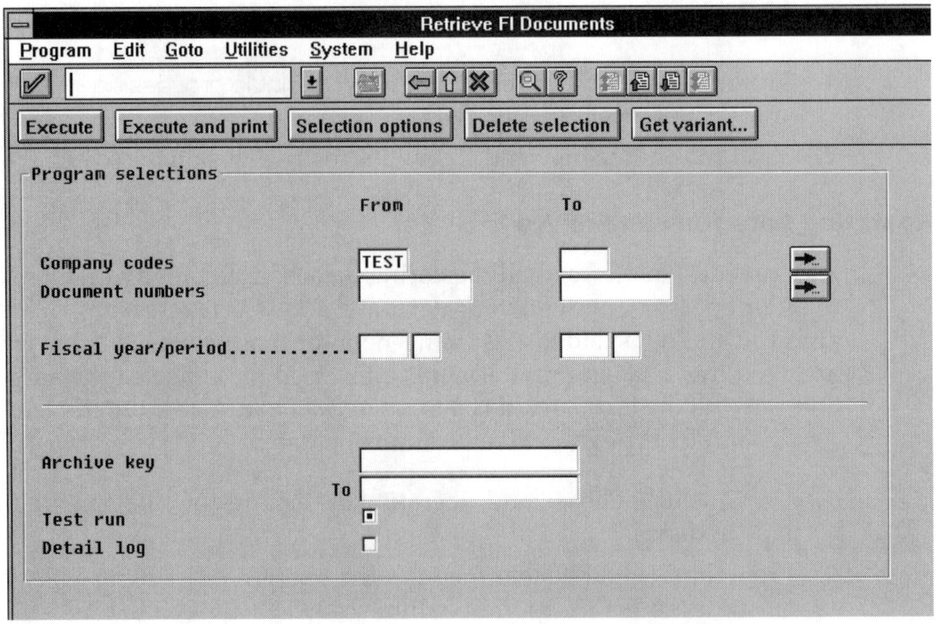

Exhibit 2.140   Retrieve FI Documents

REVALUING FOREIGN CURRENCY

Overview of Revaluation

For the purpose of revaluing amounts posted in foreign currency, there are two types of accounts:

1. *Open item accounts,* such as customer accounts, vendor accounts, intercompany customer accounts, intercompany vendor accounts, and cash in transit.
2. *Non-open item accounts* (balance forward accounts), such as bank accounts, prepayments, and expense accruals

For each type of account, a specific program is used to revalue either individual open items in the account or entire G/L account balances. Non-open item G/L accounts still contain line item details. The difference between an open item account and a G/L account with line item detail is that individual items are cleared and revalued in an open item account only. In other words, an open item account contains two types of line items—open items and cleared items.

You can use G/L to revalue both open items, such as customer invoices, vendor invoices, and intercompany invoices, and G/L accounts, such as bank accounts. Foreign currency is any other currency than the local reporting currency. What many companies call functional currency is what SAP calls group currency, depending on your configuration. You can revalue open items and G/L account balances both into local currency, if they were posted or defined in foreign currency, and group currency. These programs are designed to calculate and post certain exchange rate differences automatically, depending on your configuration.

Some countries (and US GAAP regulations) distinguish between *realized,* also known as transaction, gains and losses and unrealized, also known as translation, gains and losses. Other countries make no distinction between realized and unrealized gains and losses. Depending on the revaluation method, you can accommodate either type of regime.

When posting a payment (from a customer or to a vendor) and close an invoice, the Accounts Receivable or Accounts Payable program automatically calculates and posts a realized gain or loss. Depending on your configuration, the program posts a realized (transaction) gain or loss to a specific P&L account.

If you are holding invoices (or other open items such as cash in transit), you can revalue these invoices or open items in order to print a current, fairly stated balance sheet. A gain or loss that results from revaluing open items in foreign currency is known as an *unrealized gain or loss.* Usually, these gains or losses are posted to one or more balance sheet accounts. You run a specific program to revalue open items in foreign currency.

If you are holding bank accounts (or other G/L accounts) in foreign currency, you can revalue these G/L accounts in order to print a current, fairly stated balance sheet. A gain or loss that results from revaluing G/L accounts in foreign currency is known as a *realized gain or loss*. Usually, these gains or losses are posted to one or more P&L accounts. You run a second program to revalue G/L accounts in foreign currency.

In summary, FI is designed to calculate and post both unrealized gains or losses (on open items) and realized gains or losses (on G/L account balances). In addition, when you post a payment, the Accounts Receivable or the Accounts Payable program automatically calculates and posts an exchange rate difference.

Revaluing Foreign Currency—One Possible Method

At many international companies, there are two separate ledgers—a local ledger and a ledger in the currency of the head office. At the end of the period, each of the monetary account balances are revalued from local currency into the head office currency.

For example, under US GAAP, what many companies call *functional currency*, USD, is called *group currency* in SAP R/3 FI. *Local currency* in FI is the reporting currency of the company code, usually the legal entity. *Transaction currency*, also known as *document currency*, is the currency of a specific transaction, as specified in the header of each and every transaction, such as an invoice or a payment.

Depending on your configuration, you can set up only one combined ledger in local currency and group currency. However, you can use two programs to revalue currency amounts, both to group currency and to local currency. One program revalues open items, such as customer invoices. The other program revalues G/L account balances, such as bank accounts.

The following is a list of sample accounts that you could set up to be posted with exchange gains and losses:

Account	Purpose
93130TR	Gain or loss on revaluation of local currency account balances into group currency; offsets each revalued balance
93250TR	Unrealized gain or loss on revaluation of open items; can be posted in local and group currency; offsets a G/L account for revaluation of each open item account, such as intercompany receivables, intercompany payables, trade receivables, and trade payables

93260TR   Realized gain on closing (clearing) an open item; also contains realized gains on revaluation of G/L accounts not kept in local currency

93270TR   Realized loss on closing (clearing) an open item; also contains realized losses on revaluation of G/L accounts not kept in local currency

The possible revaluation procedure described here requires that all these G/L accounts be entered in local currency, even if they are not usually posted in local currency.

Revaluing with the New Procedure

Using SAP G/L, one possible revaluation procedure is as follows:

1. At the end of the month or period, enter the intercompany exchange rates. For the revaluation, enter the new intercompany exchange rates with an exchange rate type **REV** and the final day of the previous period as a validity date. The reason is to revalue the previous period's balances with the new exchange rate. For example, for a new DEM to USD rate for period 1 ending May 26, 1996 of .65789, you would enter as in Exhibit 2.141 (this says that 1 DEM = .65789 USD).

2. At the beginning of the next period, after closing the period but before preparing or transmitting your P&L and closing balance sheet, run the program to revalue open items into both local currency and into group currency. To revalue according to the lowest value method required in Germany and France, enter **TLV** (take lowest value) as the method for the company code currency depending on your configuration. Otherwise, enter **GAAP** (generally accepted accounting principles) as the revaluation method for the company code currency. Always enter a method of **GAAP** for the method of revaluation for group currency depending on your configuration and assuming your head office is in the United States. Make sure that these revaluation methods (TLV and GAAP or your specific revaluation methods) have been properly configured according to local requirements and your financial policy. Enter the last day of the previous period as the Balance sheet key date, depending on your fiscal year. For example, if this were P1, 1997, you enter the last day of P12, 1996 as the key date. Mark Postings requested. Enter the posting date of the fifteenth of the month of the new period. Enter the reversal date of the fifteenth of the next month. *Note that the following period must be open, so that you can then*

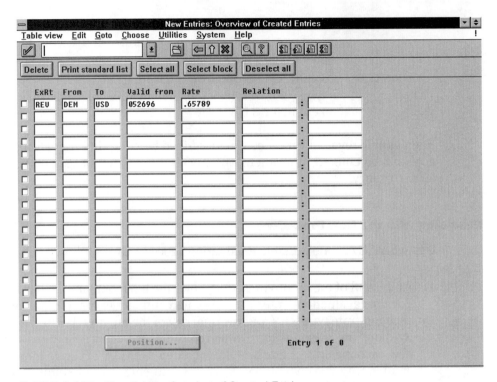

Exhibit 2.141   New Entries: Overview of Created Entries

reverse the revaluation posted in the current period. For details, read the following section "Revaluing Open Items."

The program then calculates and posts at least four separate transactions. The first two transactions record the revaluation of the open items into local currency and then reverse this revaluation. The second two transactions record the revaluation of the open items into group currency and then reverse this revaluation.

3. At the beginning of the next period, after closing the period, run the program to revalue G/L account balances. This program revalues both account balances kept in local currency, such as prepayments and accruals, and account balances kept in foreign currency, such as bank accounts in foreign currency. Enter **GAAP** as the revaluation method for both the company code currency and the group currency. Enter a key date of the last day of the previous period. For details, read the following section "Revaluing G/L Account Balances."

The program calculates and then posts in group currency, such as USD, to each account kept in local currency, such as prepayments and expense accruals in local currency, if the group currency value changed, offsetting these entries with entries to the configured account, such as 93130TR. The currency of the transaction header is local currency, although the amounts are zero in local currency. *This assumes that all local currency accounts (and only local currency accounts) have a blank in the* Exchange rate difference key *field in the G/L account master record.*

Separately, if the account is a foreign currency account, the program calculates and then posts each account in local currency and group currency, offsetting these entries with entries to the configured accounts, such as 93270TR with a loss or 93260TR with a gain. Some countries require separate accounts for currency gains and losses. *This procedure assumes that all local currency accounts (and only local currency accounts) have the proper* Exchange rate difference key *in the G/L account master record, depending on your configuration.*

4. When you close open items, for example, *when A/R posts a cash receipt and closes one or more customer invoices,* then the program automatically calculates and posts the realized exchange loss to 93270TR or the realized exchange gain to 93260TR—in both local currency and group currency. If both the invoice and the payment were in local currency, the program posts no exchange gain or loss in local currency, but does calculate and post an exchange gain or loss in group currency. This procedure requires a complete, error-free configuration.

Revaluing Open Items

To revalue open items, most of all customer invoices, vendor invoices, and intercompany receivables and payables:

1. From the General Ledger menu, select Periodic processing ➤ Month-end reports ➤ Balance sheet prep. ➤ For.curr.OI valuatn.

2. Enter at least the following parameters (Exhibit 2.142):

Parameter	*What to Enter*
Method for comp. code currency	Depending on your configuration, this code determines how the program revalues the open items. This parameter applies to open items posted in foreign currency that are to be revalued to local currency. In some countries, such as Germany and France, to take the lowest value, as required for the statutory balance sheet, enter **TLV**. This revaluation method results in posting nothing, if there is an unrealized gain. Otherwise, enter **GAAP** to have the program post an unrealized gain.

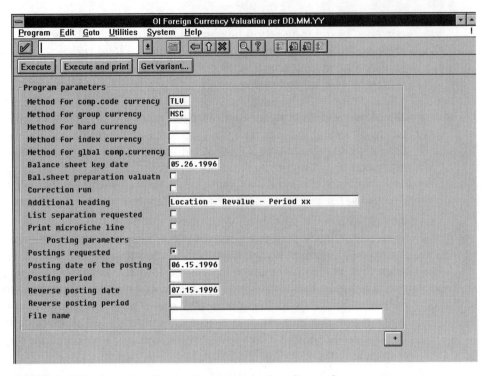

Exhibit 2.142   Open Item Foreign Currency Valuation, Screen One

Method for group currency	Depending on your configuration, this code determines how the program revalues the open items. This parameter applies to open items posted in foreign currency or in local currency and to be revalued into group currency. To comply with US GAAP and your company's financial policy, configure your revaluation methods properly.
Balance sheet key date	Cutoff date for open items. Any items cleared on or before this date will not be revalued. Usually, you enter today's date.
Additional heading	Optionally, enter a heading for the report.
Postings requested	To post the revaluation immediately, set this parameter on. To test the revaluation, leave this parameter off. The output of the program will show what would be posted, if you had posted something.

Posting date of the posting	Enter the posting date of the revaluation to be posted by this program. Usually, you enter today's date.
Reverse posting date	Enter the posting date of the transaction reversing the revaluation. This is required. Usually, you enter the fifteenth of the next posting period, if you prepare the balance sheet with the revaluation. Otherwise, enter a date that you know will be after the date of the next balance sheet including the revaluation.

3. Press +, in the lower-right corner of the screen, to go to the second screen of parameters. (See Exhibit 2.143.)

4. To revalue open items of a specific company code, enter the company code. Otherwise, the program will revalue open items in all company codes.

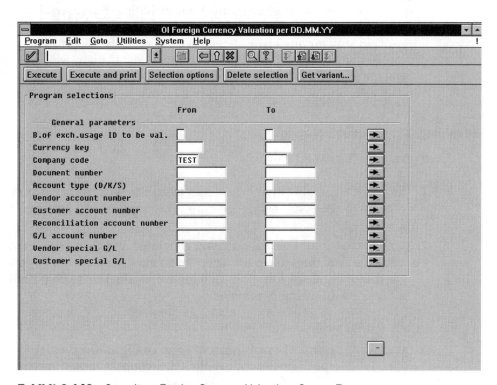

Exhibit 2.143 Open Item Foreign Currency Valuation, Screen Two

Optionally, restrict the revaluation to open items in specific currencies, in specific transactions (by the "document" numbers), in specific vendor accounts, in specific customer accounts, in specific reconciliation accounts (receivables, payables, or fixed assets control), in specific G/L accounts, or with specific special G/L codes (down payments, bills of exchange, and security deposits).

5. To start the revaluation, press <F8> or the Execute pushbutton.

    The program then calculates and posts at least four separate transactions. The first two record the revaluation of the open items into local currency and then reverse this revaluation. The second two record the revaluation of the open items into group currency and then reverse this revaluation. One method is to have all revaluation of open items be posted to 93250TR and to the corresponding offset account for the specific open item account.

6. After you run the open item revaluation program, note the message at the end of the screen—Document xxxxxxx was posted in company code yyyy. If a revaluation transaction were posted, this message indicates the number of the last posted transaction, including the reversal. Note also the results of the open item revaluation on the next screen. Scroll through the results to look for any errors. Scroll to the end of the report to look for the numbers of the posted revaluation transactions. If there were any errors, print the results and then correct the results. To print the report, press Print, select your printer, and then press Print again.

Revaluing G/L Account Balances

To revalue G/L account balances:

1. From the General Ledger menu, select Periodic processing → Month-end reports → Balance sheet prep. → For.curr.G/L acc.val. (See Exhibit 2.144.)

2. To see what would be posted if you generated and then posted the revaluation, do not mark the parameter Batch input requested. To generate a file (batch input session) that contains the revaluation to be posted, enter at least the following parameters:

Parameter	What to Enter
Company code	Depending on your configuration, enter the company code with G/L account balances to be revalued.
Key date	Enter a date to determine the posting period of the G/L account balances to be revalued. The key date

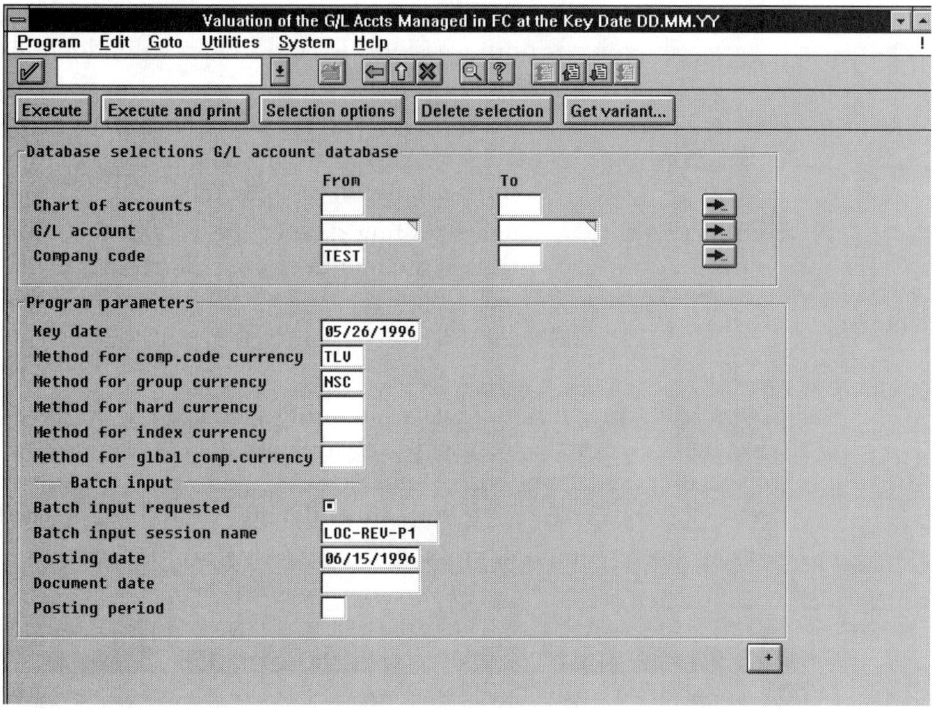

Exhibit 2.144 G/L Account Balance Revaluation

also determines the exchange rate that the program uses. If you enter a posting date in period 12, then the program will revalue G/L account balances in periods 13–16 also.

Method for comp. code currency

Depending on your configuration, enter the revaluation method, which determines how the G/L account balances are to be revalued into local currency. To take the lowest value, as required in Germany and France, enter **TLV.**

Method for group currency

Depending on your configuration, enter the revaluation method, which determines how the G/L account balances are to be revalued into group currency. To revalue according to US GAAP and your company's financial policy, configure the revaluation method properly.

Batch input requested

Set this parameter on to record a batch input session with the revaluation of the G/L account balances. To post the revaluation, you have to process the batch input session. To test the revaluation, leave this parameter blank.

Batch input
session name

Enter a name for the batch input session, such as **LOC-REVAL-PX**, where LOC is the location and PX is the period with the new rate.

Posting date

Enter a posting date of the revaluation, such as the fifteen of the month of the new period.

3. Press + to go to the second screen of parameters to this program (Exhibit 2.145).

4. Optionally, enter a note in each line of the revaluation in the Segment text field. Optionally, restrict the revaluation to G/L account balances in a specific Business area, Currency, or with one or more specific Exchange rate difference keys (revaluation key in the G/L account).

5. To start the revaluation, press <F8> or the Execute pushbutton.

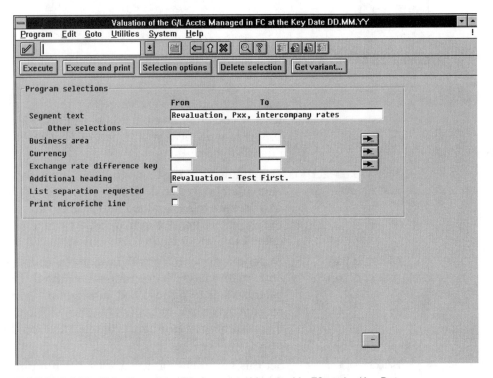

Exhibit 2.145   Valuation of the G/L Accounts Managed in FC at the Key Date

If a G/L account is not an open item account and is not kept in local currency, the program calculates and debits or credits the account in local currency, offsetting these entries with entries in the configured account, such as 93130TR.

Separately, if the account is kept in local currency, the program calculates and then debits or credits each account in group currency, offsetting these entries with entries to the configured accounts, such as either 93270TR with a loss or 93260TR with a gain.

6. To post process the batch input session and post the revaluation, from any menu, select System ➤ Services ➤ Batch input ➤ Edit. (See Exhibit 2.146.)

7. To see a list of all batch input sessions to be processed, press the Overview pushbutton (Exhibit 2.147).

8. To process a specific batch input session, first click on the name of the batch input session and then press the Process pushbutton (Exhibit 2.148).

9. The first time you process a batch input session, to see all the screens in the transaction as if you entered them by hand, click on Process/fore-

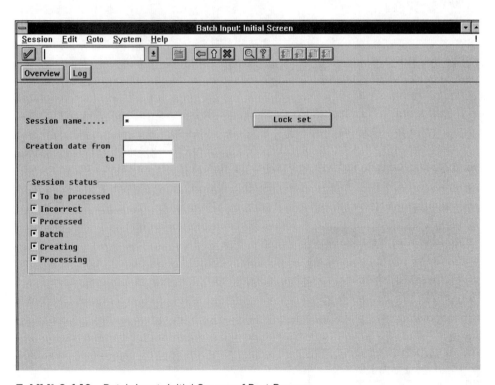

Exhibit 2.146 Batch Input: Initial Screen of Post Process

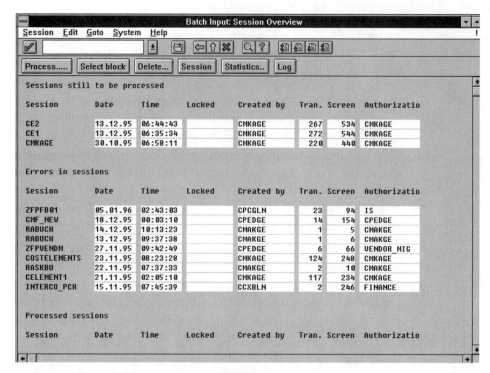

Exhibit 2.147 Batch Input: Session Overview List

ground·and then press Process. You can instead process the next batch input session more quickly if you click on Display errors only. You will then see only the screens in the batch input session containing an error.

10. Notice the data entry screen with the data already entered. Press <Enter> to go to the next screen. Process the batch input session completely.

Exhibit 2.148
Process a Specific Session

If there is an error in the batch input session, for example, in the configuration or a missing account, you should correct the mistake immediately and then continue to process the batch input session. Otherwise, only the revaluation before the error will be posted. In other words, the revaluation will be only partly posted. If you rerun the G/L balance revaluation program and process the batch input session again, then the revaluation before the error will be posted a second time.

To end a batch input session (to correct a mistake), select System ➤ Services ➤ Batch input ➤ Cancel. Whether you end the batch input session to correct a mistake or the batch input session ends itself by posting the transaction, you will see the message shown in Exhibit 2.149.

Unlocking the Open Item Revaluation

If you are running the program to revalue open items and are posting transactions, then you should never halt it. Otherwise, the transactions with the revaluation could be in error. However, if your system crashes or if you halt the open item revaluation unintentionally or during a test run, then the program is locked. This prevents you from running the program again.

To unlock the revaluation program:

1. From any menu, select System ➤ Services ➤ Table maintenance.
2. Enter **TBOKW** and then press Maintain.
3. Look for the line with SAPFI00. Put the cursor on this line and then press Delete line.
4. Press the left arrow to update the table and go back.

Forecasting Bank Balances in the Treasury

To control liquidity, you can forecast your bank balances using the treasury module. In this way, you have more accurate information about short-term liquidity (0–5 days). The program forecasts bank balances based on the value date entered in each line item posted to a G/L for cash in the bank (or cash in transit). You can also use the treasury submodule of F1 to forecast cash receipts from customers and cash disbursements to vendors. The cash receipts forecast

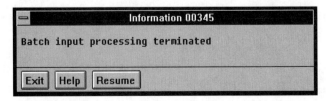

Exhibit 2.149 Information on Ending a Batch Input Session

is based on the customer payment history, which records the average days in arrears of each payment and whether or not the customer usually takes cash discount. The cash disbursements forecast is based on the due dates of vendor invoices. You can also make manual entries in the cash forecast, such as planned payroll and tax payments. You can forecast receipts and disbursements in this way up to 24 weeks or 6 months in the future.

This section describes a simplified use of the functions to forecast bank balances in the G/L only. Assume that you have three bank accounts. In each of these accounts, you record cash receipts, mostly from customers, and cash disbursements, mostly to employees, vendors, and tax authorities. Next, assume that the treasury program is properly configured. Last, assume that you wish to forecast the balances for today and the next five days.

To prepare this cash forecast:

1. From the R/3 Main Menu, select Accounting → Treasury → Cash man. + forecast. From the Cash Management and Forecast menu, select Cash management → Cash Management. position. (See Exhibit 2.150.)

2. Enter parameters in at least the Company code and Grouping fields. The Display as of parameter determines the start date of the forecast. You can

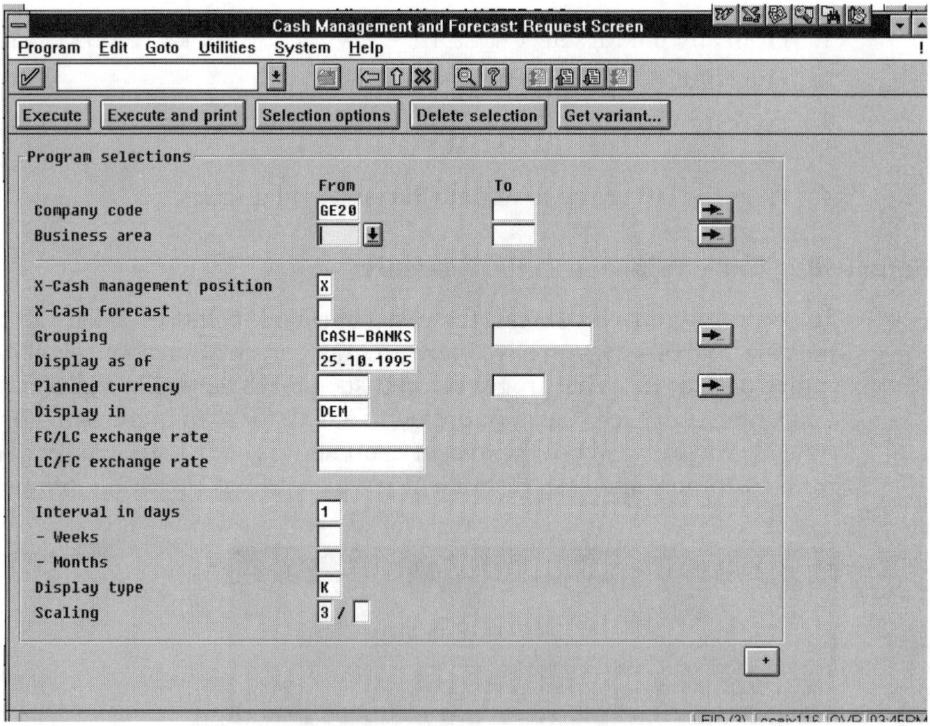

Exhibit 2.150 Cash Management and Forecast: Request Screen

determine the currency of the forecast using the Display in parameter. You can also use the Weeks and Months parameters to forecast up to 24 weeks or 6 months. Use the Display type parameter to control whether the program displays the forecast balances (**K**) or the changes (net flow) to the balances (**D**). (See Exhibit 2.152.)

A sample forecast looks like Exhibit 2.151.

3. Notice that each row in this sample forecast contains the forecast balances day-by-day of a specific G/L account. Each column contains the forecast G/L account balances for a specific day. This sample forecast is based on G/L accounts and the value dates in line items posted to these G/L accounts.

Forecasting Cash Receipts and Disbursements

You can also use FI to forecast cash receipts and disbursements, based on due dates of customer and vendor invoices and the number of days in transit for payments by check. This depends on your specific configuration.

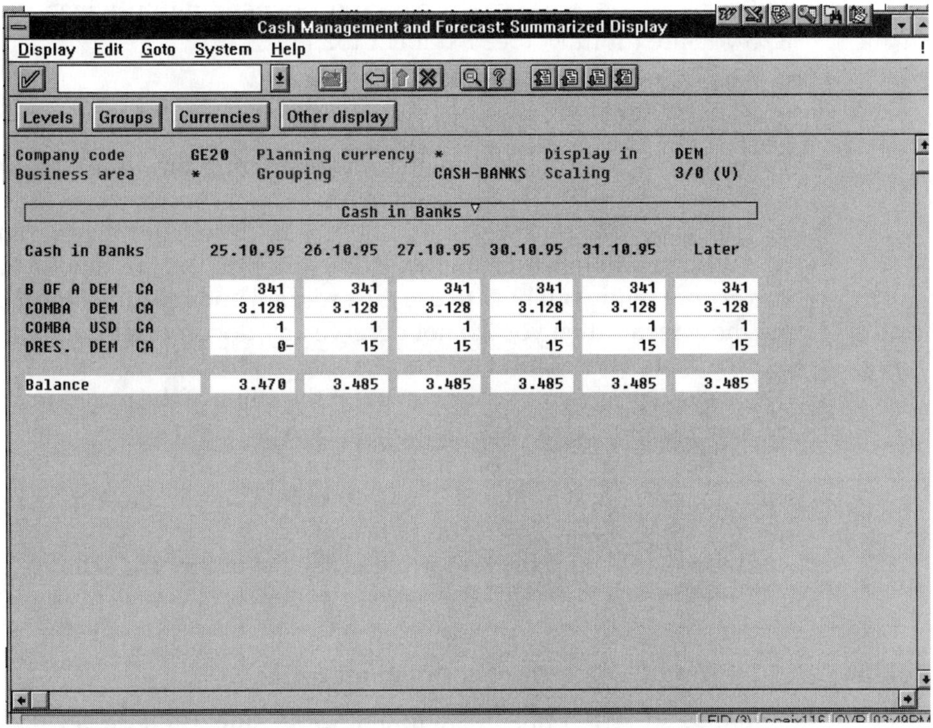

Exhibit 2.151 Cash Management and Forecast: Summarized Display

FINANCIAL REPORTING FROM THE GENERAL LEDGER

FI includes a series of ABAP/4 programs to prepare financial reports. Most of all, SAP designed these programs to meet the minimum legal requirements wherever they do business. For example, the primary financial reports are the trial balance, the balance sheet (always prepared with the profit and loss statement), and the report of transaction and tax subtotals by tax code (to prepare the VAT report). To calculate, post, and report sales tax, use a third-party package, such as AVP or Vertex. Although many other reports are also supplied with the package, you cannot assume that any specific financial report that you have in your current (or previous) system is available in FI. You can also develop custom reports, using the ABAP/4 programming language.

Listing Supplied FI Reports

To list available FI reports (reports prepared by ABAP/4 programs supplied with the package):

1. From any menu, select System ➤ Services ➤ Reporting.
2. From the ABAP/4: Execute program menu, select Utilities ➤ Find program or Environment ➤ Program directory, depending on which version of R/3 you are running. (See Exhibit 2.152.)
3. In the Program field, enter **RF***.
4. To list the report categories, press <F8> or Execute. (See Exhibit 2.153.)
5. To read the on-line documentation about a program, if the programmer wrote any documentation about the report, put the cursor on the name of the program and then press Documentation. Some of the programs have no documentation. Unfortunately, sometimes the programmer feels that if you cannot figure out how to use the program and read the report by reading the screens, then you do not deserve any documentation.

    To print the list, select System ➤ List ➤ Print.

    To run a program, put the cursor on the name of the program and press the Execute button at the left of the button bar or <F8>.

    To download the list of programs to a spreadsheet, depending on your software version, select List ➤ Download. SAP and Microsoft cooperate on integrating R/3 with Microsoft Office.

    To look for a specific text string in the list of reports, select System ➤ List ➤ Find.

Reading and Printing On-line Report Documentation

SAP supplies all report documentation on-line only. If you want the printed report documentation, then you must print it out. This reduces their costs of

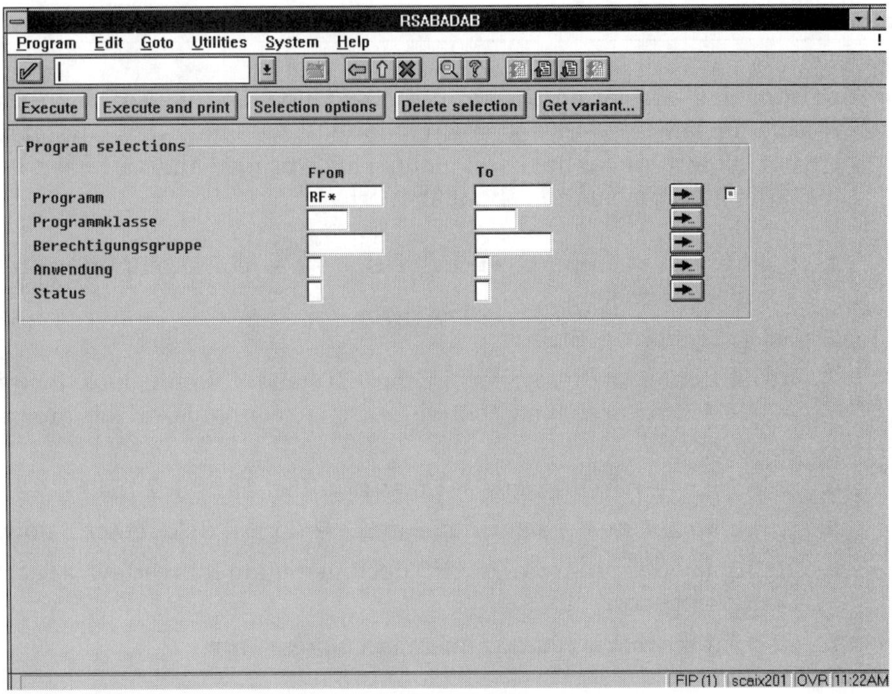

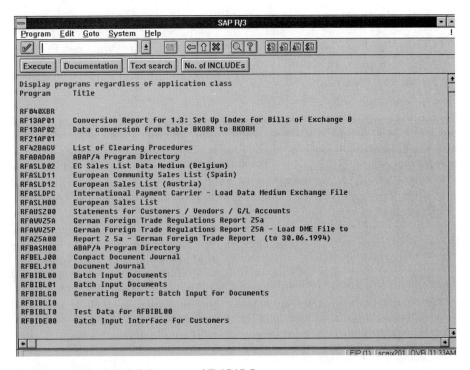

Exhibit 2.152 Obtaining a Directory of ABAP Programs

Exhibit 2.153 SAP R/3 Directory of FI ABAP Programs

printing and circulating printed documentation, and it also ensures that you receive the latest report documentation with the latest software release. You are not left waiting for the latest manual to be printed and sent to you. To print the on-line documentation about a report:

1. Start to run the report as usual. Display a screen prompting you to enter specific parameters.
2. Select System ➔ Status.
3. In the center of the screen in the left-hand column, look for the label ABAP/4 program. Find the (eight-character) name of the program and write it down.
4. Select System ➔ Services ➔ Reporting. (See Exhibit 2.154.)
5. If you do not see the same name in the Program field, enter it now.
6. To display this program (report) documentation for reading, select Goto ➔ Documentation.
7. To print the displayed documentation, press Print.

Printing Reports

To print reports from R/3 on your LAN or PC printer, make sure that you have the proper line printer daemon installed and properly configured. For example, to print reports to a PC printer attached to your Windows PC printer, you require a piece of software that runs under Windows called saplpd. Call or write SAP for details.

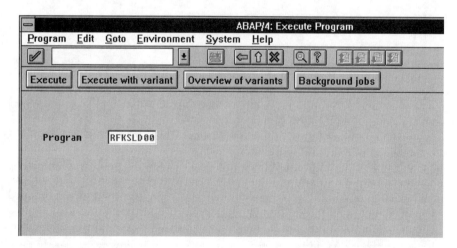

Exhibit 2.154   ABAP/4: Execute Program

When you have the report displayed on your screen, to print it, select Sys-tem ➤ List ➤ Print.

Downloading a Report to a Spreadsheet

You can download any report to a spreadsheet.

When you have the report displayed on your screen, to download it, select System ➤ List ➤ Download.

Finding a String in a Report

To find a string in a report:

1. Display the report and place your cursor at the beginning of the report
2. Select Edit ➤ Find
3. Enter the text string to search for
4. Press Continue

Checking the Printing in Process

The program places the report in a temporary file on the disk called a spool file. To check the printing in process:

1. From any menu, select System ➤ Services ➤ Output controller
2. Press <Enter> to see a list of print runs that you have done

Reporting Using a Reporting Tree

If you have the name of the ABAP program that produces a report, you can always start the report directly from any menu. To start any report:

1. From any menu, select System ➤ Services ➤ Reporting. (See Exhibit 2.155.)
2. Enter the name of the ABAP program, such as **RFBILA00,** the program to produce a balance sheet and P&L.
3. Press <F8> or the Execute (check mark) button to the left of the button bar.

The names of the primary financial reports available in G/L are as follows:

Report	*ABAP Program*
Global chart of accounts (general data)	RFSKPL00
Local chart of accounts (company code–specific)	RFSKVZ00

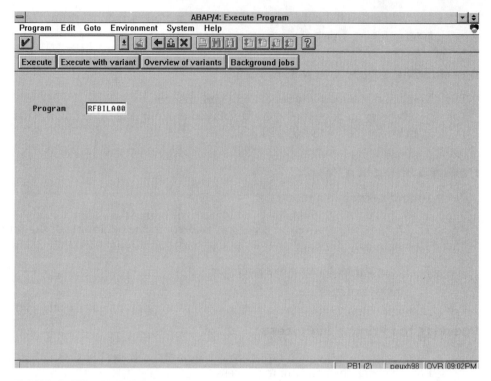

Exhibit 2.155   ABAP/4 Starting a Report

Transaction journal	RFBELJ00
Trial balance	RFSLD00
Balance sheet/P&L	RFBILA00
Balance audit trail	RFHABU00
Financial policy manual	RFSKTH00
Posting totals	RFBUSU00
Changes to G/L accounts	RFSABL00
Line item journal	RFEPOJ00

The above list is only a partial list of the supplied reports. SAP continuously maintains these reports and develops new reports.

You can also configure the menu of reports to include only the reports that you actually run, use, and read. How to configure this tree is out of the scope of this book. SAP supplies a reporting tree. These instructions are based on the supplied tree in version 3.0.

To start to run a G/L report using the supplied reporting tree:

1. From the General Ledger menu, select Periodic processing → Info system → Report selection. (See Exhibit 2.156.)

2. To turn on and off the display of the names of the nodes of the reporting tree and the names of the ABAP programs that produce your reports, select Settings → Tech. name on/off.

3. Notice the list of main nodes in the tree. If a node contains more nodes or reports, you see a small file folder to the left of the name of the node with a + symbol in the center. To expand the list of nodes or reports in any node in the tree, click once on the small file folder icon to the left of a line with the node. To contract the list, press the file folder containing the - symbol in the center. The ABAP programs that you can run have no file folder to the left of the line.

4. To choose an ABAP program from the reporting tree, put your cursor on the line and then press the Choose button at the left of the button bar or <F2>.

5. To run the report, enter the parameters and then press the Execute button at the left of the button bar or <F8>.

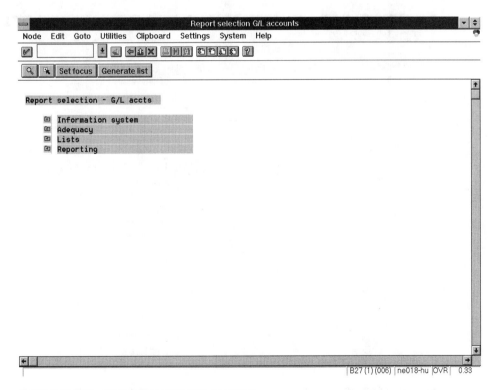

Exhibit 2.156   Report Selection G/L Accounts

Reporting the Global Chart of Accounts

Depending on your company and your terminology, the global chart of accounts is also known as the corporate chart of accounts. Most of all, it contains the name, number, and type of the account (balance sheet or P&L), but does not contain any posting details such as the currency, VAT category, open item status, or field status group.

To print the global chart of accounts:

1. From the General Ledger menu, select Periodic processing ➤ Info system ➤ Report selection.

2. Using your cursor and the reporting tree, select Lists ➤ Account.

3. Put your cursor in the Directory of chart of accts line and then press the Choose button or <F2>. (See Exhibit 2.157.)

4. Enter at least Chart of accounts parameter and then press the Execute button to the left of the button bar or <F8> (Exhibit 2.157).

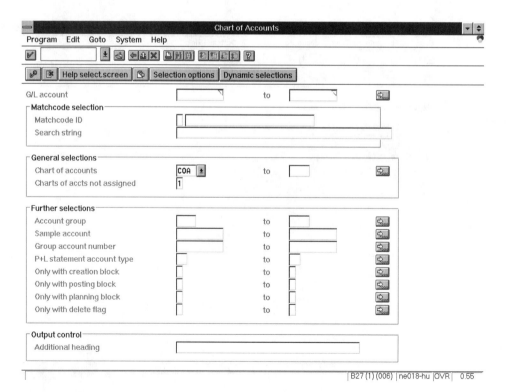

Exhibit 2.157 Chart of Accounts

Reporting the Local Chart of Accounts

The local chart of accounts is always contained in the global (corporate) chart of accounts. In SAP terminology, the local chart of accounts is the chart of accounts in the company code, while the global chart of accounts is the list of numbers and names of G/L accounts. You always post to a G/L account, customer account, or vendor account in a specific company code. Most of all, these accounts have details of the currency, the tax category if any, whether the account is an open item account, whether you always store line item details for this account, and which fields are required when you post a transaction to the account (field status group).

To print the local chart of accounts:

1. From the General Ledger menu, select Periodic processing ➤ Reporting ➤ Account list.

2. Enter at least the company code in the Company code field and the account sorting in the Account sorting field. To go to the next screen of parameters, press the + symbol (Exhibit 2.158).

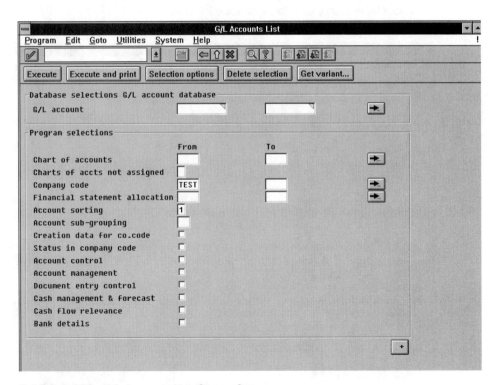

Exhibit 2.158   G/L Accounts List, Screen One

3. All of the parameters in this screen are optional (Exhibit 2.159). They are mostly self-explanatory. For example, you can use Opened in company code on and a range of dates to report new G/L accounts. Similarly, you can use the parameter Opened in company code by to find G/L accounts entered by a specific person (by their SAP login ID). To go to the next screen of parameters (Exhibit 2.160), press the + symbol.

4. To display the local chart of accounts, press Execute or <F8>.

Reporting a Transaction Journal

In some countries, the transaction journal is required by law to be in a specific format. The programs to prepare the journal in specifically required formats are country-specific programs either supplied with R/3 or available from the SAP branch in that country. The key to the transaction journal is the type of the transaction ("document type") that you enter in the header of each transaction.

To prepare the transaction journal:

1. From the General Ledger menu, select Periodic processing ➤ Month end reports ➤ Compact journal. (See Exhibit 2.161.)

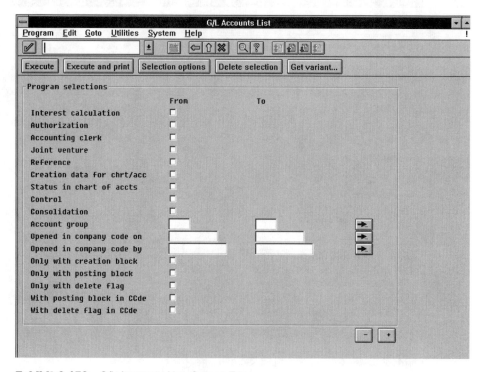

Exhibit 2.159 G/L Accounts List, Screen Two

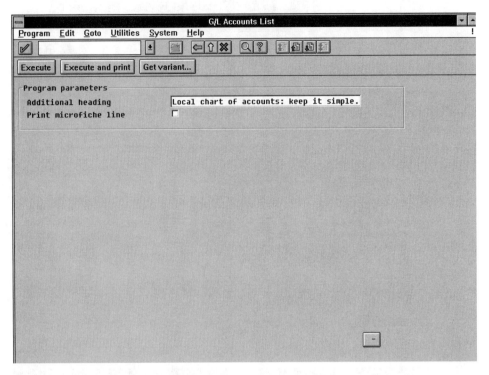

Exhibit 2.160   G/L Accounts List, Screen Three

2. Enter at least the company code, the fiscal year, and the fiscal periods (Exhibit 2.163). To specify a journal or a range of journals, enter the journal or range of journals in the parameter Document type. To go to the next page of parameters (Exhibit 2.162), press the + key.

3. Select Normal documents. In SAP terminology, this means all regular double-entry transactions and excludes sample transactions and recurring transactions. It is advisable to describe this report in the parameter Additional title. To run the report, press Execute or <F8>.

Reconciling Transactions and Account Balances

When you post a transaction, R/3 inserts the transaction in two logical files—one, a file of transactions and the other, a file of account balances. Occasionally, although rarely, a transaction is recorded in one file, but not in the other file. This can be due to an error in the program, or often it can be due to a delay in the network between updating the two files.

When you start using your system, you should make sure that the totals of the transactions in the transaction file are the same as the totals of the transactions in the account balance file. This is what it means to reconcile transactions

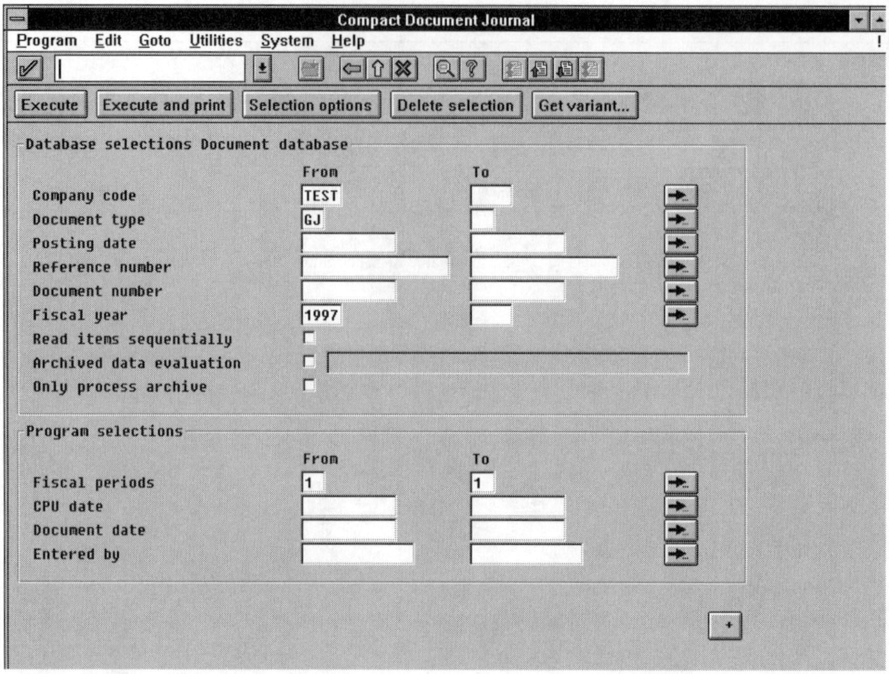

Exhibit 2.161 Compact Document Journal: Preparing the Transaction Journal

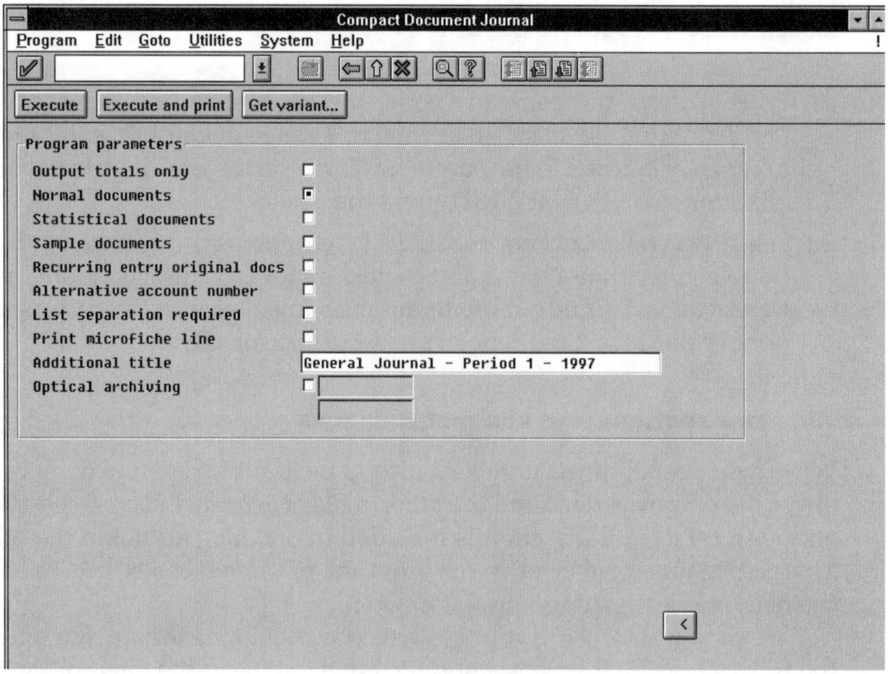

Exhibit 2.162 Compact Document Journal: Select Normal Documents

and account balances. This program is technically required to verify that the data was inserted correctly in both of these two logical files. Note that in SAP terminology transactions are called "documents" and account balances are called "transaction figures."

To reconcile the transactions and the account balances:

1. From the General Ledger menu, select Periodic processing ➤ Month-end reports ➤ Reconciliation. (See Exhibit 2.163.)

2. Select a currency in which to reconcile, usually company code currency. Then enter at least the company code, fiscal year, fiscal periods, and types of accounts to reconcile (Exhibit 2.163).

3. To carry out the reconciliation, press Execute or <F8>.

4. In the results of the report, look for the differences between the item file (transactions) and the master records (account balances) to be zero.

Reporting the Trial Balance

The trial balance contains the account balance carried forward from the previous period, the total debits for the period, the total credits for the period, and

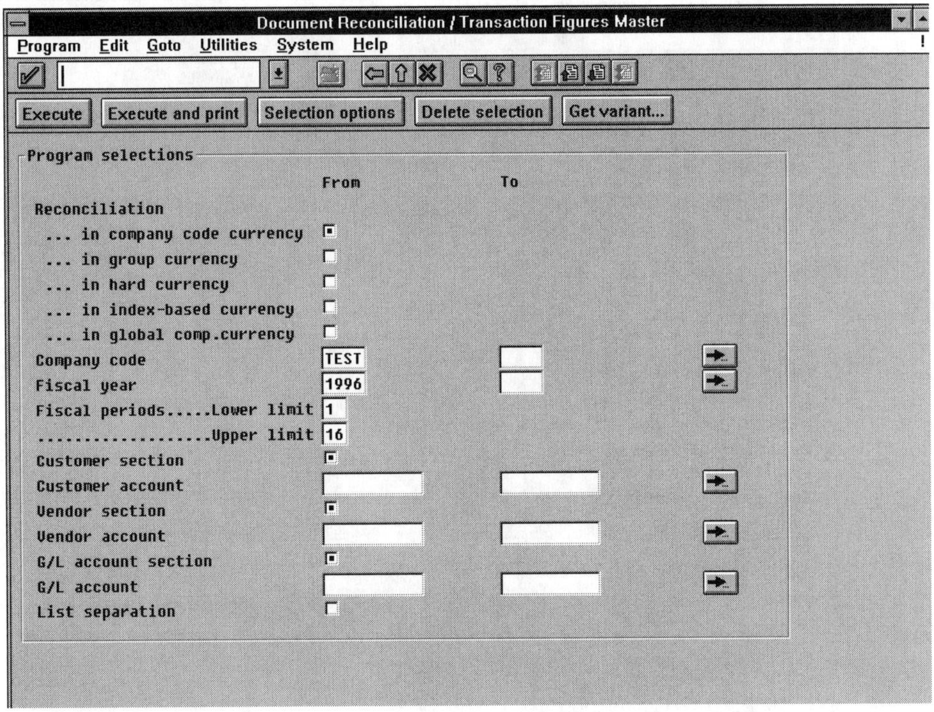

Exhibit 2.163 Document Reconciliation/Transaction Figures Master

the closing balance. You can use the trial balance to reconcile the opening balance sheet in the new system with the closing balance sheet of your previous system. Of course, you can also use the trial balance to begin to prepare a balance sheet. Often, the end-of-period closing procedure has the following steps:

1. Prepare the trial balance.
2. Enter closing adjustments, such as expense accruals and intercompany entries.
3. Prepare balance sheet and P&L.

To prepare the trial balance:

1. From the General Ledger menu, select Periodic processing → Reporting → Account balances. (See Exhibit 2.164.)
2. Enter at least the company code, the fiscal year, the summarization level (0, if you are not sure), and the fiscal periods to be included in the trial balance

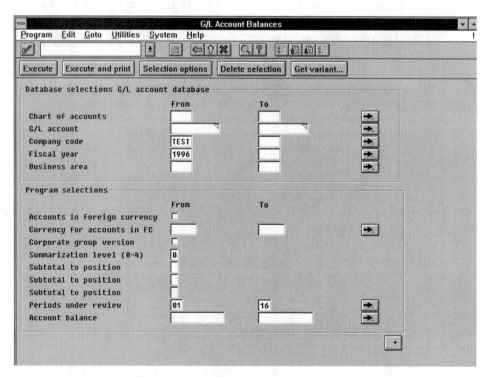

Exhibit 2.164 G/L Account Balances

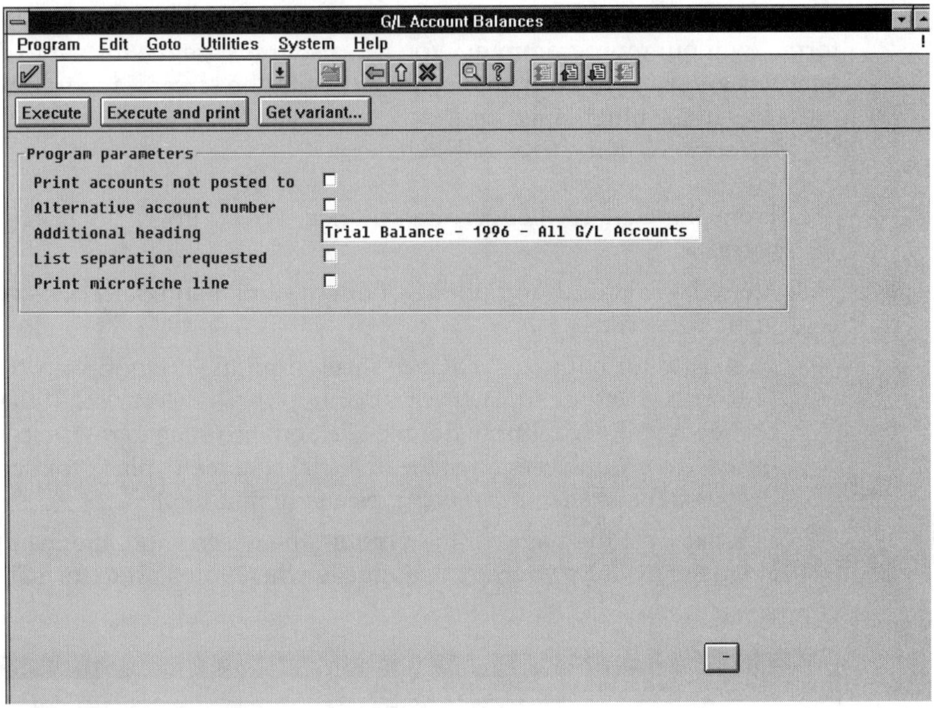

Exhibit 2.165 G/L Account Balances

(Exhibit 2.164). To go to the next screen of parameters, press +. (See Exhibit 2.165.)

3. All of the parameters in this screen are optional. To display the trial balance (list of G/L account balances), press Execute or <F8>.

Formatting a Financial Statement

To print a financial statement (a combined balance sheet and P&L statement), you first have to format the financial statement. In the format, you can define any headings, subheadings, account subtotals, and individual account balances that you wish. You can format one or more versions of a financial statement based on the same G/L account balances, for example to subtotal the account balances differently. When printing a financial statement later, the balance sheet always includes both a balance sheet and a P&L. When formatting the financial statement, assign all G/L accounts to the format. Any G/L accounts that you do not assign "fall out" at the end of the report, when you print it. Over time, you can revise the statement format or add a new statement format without reprogramming. You can also translate the format to different languages, even if you did not license R/3 with the screens, reports, and error messages in the other languages.

To start to format a financial statement:

1. From the General Ledger menu, select Environment → Configuration menu.

2. From the Financial Accounting Configuration menu, select Closing → Fin. stmt versions.

3. To start to format a new balance sheet, from the Change View "Financial Statement Versions": Overview menu, press New entries. If the format is already defined, simply double-click on it to start to revise it. Alternatively, to copy one version of the financial statement, place your cursor on the version and then press Copy. (See Exhibit 2.166.)

4. Enter at least the name of the version, the description, the maintenance language (usually your login language when you start to format the bal-

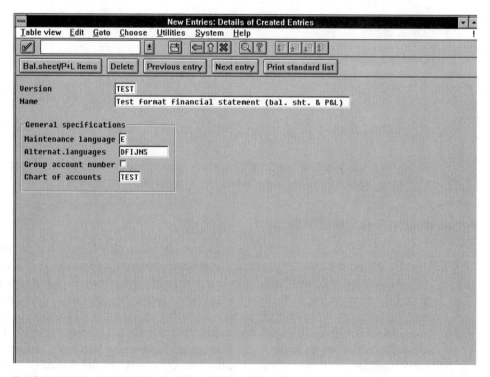

Exhibit 2.166   New Entries: Details of Created Entries

ance sheet), and the chart of accounts with the accounts to be assigned to the balance sheet. Optionally, enter alternate languages in the Alternat .languages field.

5. To start to define the headings and assign the G/L accounts, press Bal.sheet/P+L items or select Goto ➤ Bal.sheet/P+L items. (See Exhibit 2.167.)

6. An example of possible first-level headings is shown. First number and then name first-level headings in the Itm name and Short name columns. Note that the number in the format has nothing to do with the account numbers in the chart of accounts. If you are making a new format, define the numbers with at least as many digits as levels of headings that you would ever have in the balance sheet. For example, if you might have seven levels, define the numbers with at least seven digits. You can define up to nine levels of headings in total. Each heading contains either another level of headings or one or more G/L accounts. Only at the lowest level of a heading can you assign one or more specific G/L accounts. Along with the specific G/L accounts, you can assign starting text before

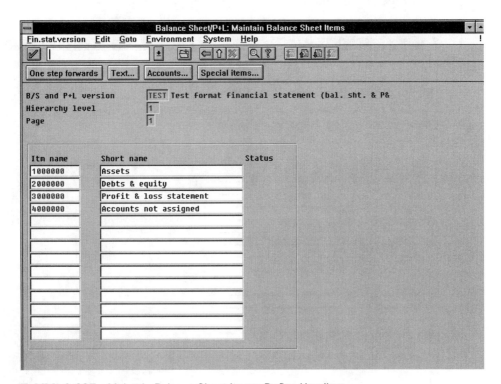

Exhibit 2.167 Maintain Balance Sheet Items: Define Headings

the group of G/L accounts or ending text after the group of G/L accounts. You can also optionally subtotal the G/L accounts assigned to a heading.

7. To go to the next level, simply double-click on a heading or place the cursor on the heading and press One step forwards or <F2>. For example, place the cursor on the heading with **Profit & loss statement** and press One step forwards. (See Exhibit 2.168.)

8. To assign specific G/L accounts to a heading, place the cursor on the heading and then press Accounts or <F6>. For example, put the cursor on the heading **Product revenues** and press Accounts. (See Exhibit 2.169.)

9. Specify one G/L account or a range of a G/L accounts. To have these account balances included, whether they are debit balances or credit balances, click on both ◻ (debit) and ⊏ (credit). To have the balances included only if a debit balance, then click on ◻ only. To have the balances included only if a credit balance, click on ⊏. This can be useful to put balance sheet accounts either in assets or in debts, depending on the type of the balance.

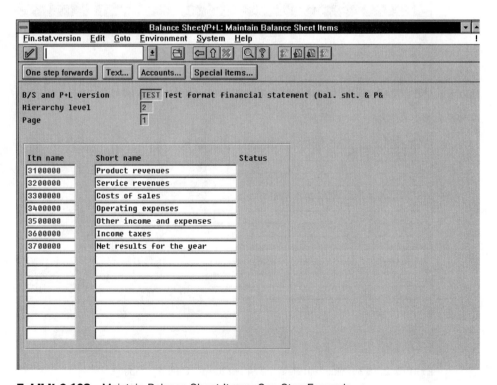

Exhibit 2.168   Maintain Balance Sheet Items: One Step Forwards

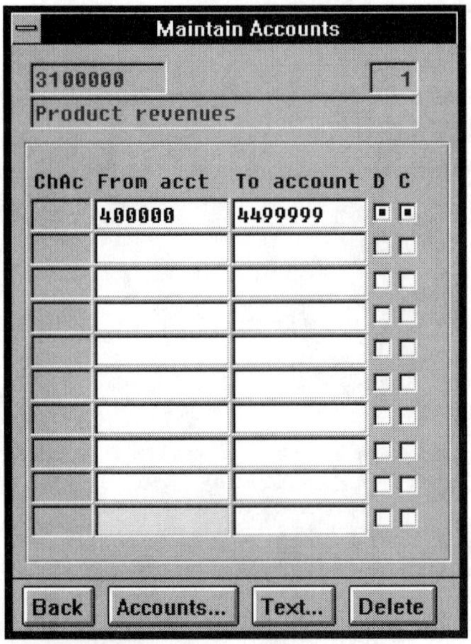

Exhibit 2.169   Maintain Accounts

10. To add text to this heading and group of G/L accounts, press Text (Exhibit 2.170).

11. Enter text either at the start of the group or at the end of the group or in both. Optionally, have the total of the G/L accounts that you assigned calculated and included in the balance sheet when you print it later. To go back, press Back or <F3>. (See Exhibit 2.171.)

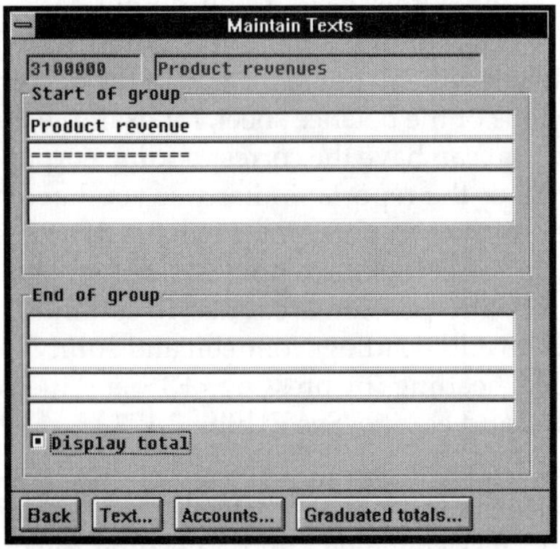

Exhibit 2.170   Maintain Texts

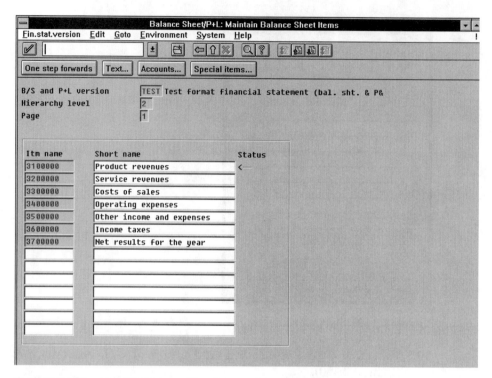

Exhibit 2.171 Maintain Balance Sheet Items: Completing the Assignment

12. Notice that headings with G/L accounts assigned have the left arrow symbol in the Status column to the right of the heading (←). To complete the G/L account assignments, assign all G/L accounts in the chart of accounts to a specific heading. Otherwise, if you do not assign a G/L account, or if you add a G/L account later and it is not included in any range of G/L accounts, then it will fall out at the end of the balance sheet. If you have different versions of the balance sheet, for example, local versions with local accounts, you can have the corresponding corporate G/L accounts fall out at the end of the report. Similarly, if you have a corporate version with only corporate accounts, you can have the corresponding local accounts fall out at the end of the report. Most often, this applies to fixed assets, depreciation, and pension accounts. To continue with the G/L account assignments, to add headings for debit and equity accounts, first go back to the first-level headings by pressing <F3>, and then double-click on the headings debts and equity. (See Exhibit 2.172.)

13. To finish the format, you have to assign certain headings, including assets, debts, year-to-date results from the balance sheet, year-to-date results from the profit and loss statement, and a heading to contain all

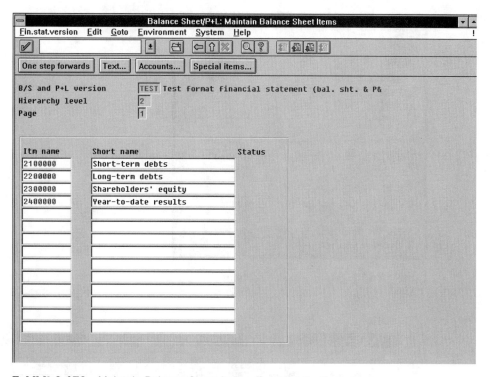

Exhibit 2.172 Maintain Balance Sheet Items: Finishing the Format

G/L accounts not assigned to the other headings, to specific line items in the financial statement. To assign these specific headings, press Special items or select Goto → Special items. (See Exhibit 2.173.)

14. These specific assignments depend on how you format this specific financial statement. The numbers refer to the numbers of the headings in the financial statement and not to the G/L account numbers. To finish the format, you have to fill in all entries. After making all six entries, press Continue.

15. To check that there are no overlapping intervals in the financial statement, which would make the statement nonsense, select Fin.stat.version → Check.

16. To store the financial statement, select Fin.stat.version → Save or press <F11> or press the file folder icon.

17. To display the format of the financial statement, including the headings and the assignment of the G/L accounts, select Environment → Display structure → List. (See Exhibit 2.174.)

18. To print the format of the financial statement, press Print.

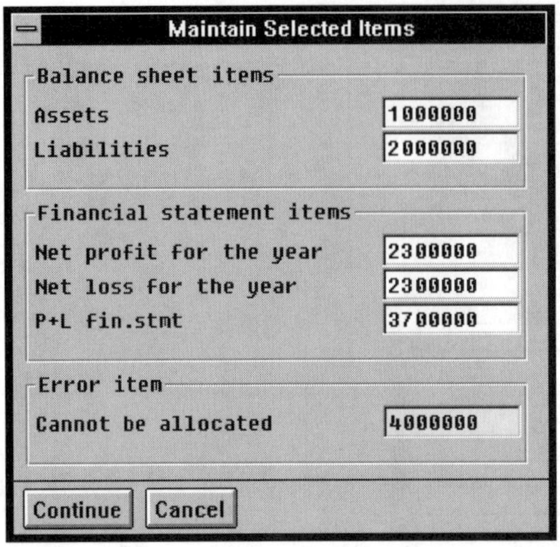

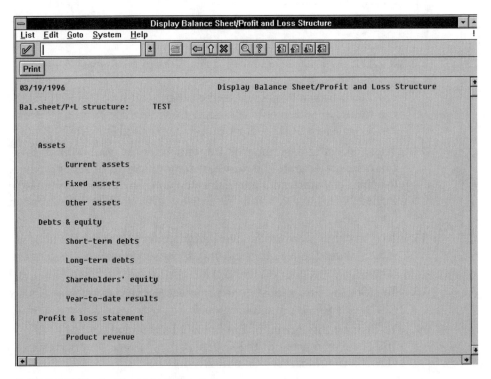

Exhibit 2.173   Maintain Selected Items

Exhibit 2.174   Profit and Loss Structure

Before you can print a financial statement, you have to define at least one financial statement format.

Translating a Financial Statement

Some countries, such as Belgium, Canada, and Switzerland, already have multiple official languages. Many international companies have to prepare financial statements in multiple languages. To receive the data entry screens, reports, error messages, and documentation in another language, you have to license R/3 in the other language from SAP. You then log in in the other language, and you see the screens, reports, and other text in the login language. You can translate the financial statement version (headings and subheadings) into another language before you log in in the other language.

To translate a financial statement:

1. From the General Ledger menu, select Environment → Configuration menu.
2. From the Financial Accounting Configuration menu, select Closing → Fin. stmt versions.
3. Place the cursor on the name of a financial statement version, and then select Goto → Foreign lang. texts. (See Exhibit 2.175.)
4. For a list of available languages, click on the down arrow. (See Exhibit 2.176.) For the latest details of available languages, required version, and required other software, such as code pages in operating systems, call your local SAP office. (See Exhibit 2.176.)
5. Select a language by double-clicking on the corresponding letter and then pressing Continue. (See Exhibit 2.177.)
6. To translate the headings, place the cursor on the line with the text and then press Foreign lang. texts. (See Exhibit 2.178.)
7. To translate the text at the end of the group, press End of group. To go back, press Back or <F3>.

Exhibit 2.175 Foreign Language Texts

Exhibit 2.176
Language Options

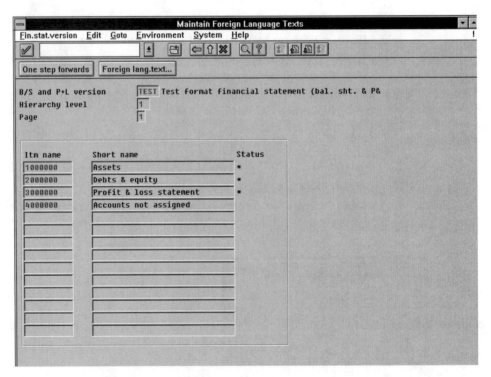

Exhibit 2.177   Maintain Foreign Language Texts

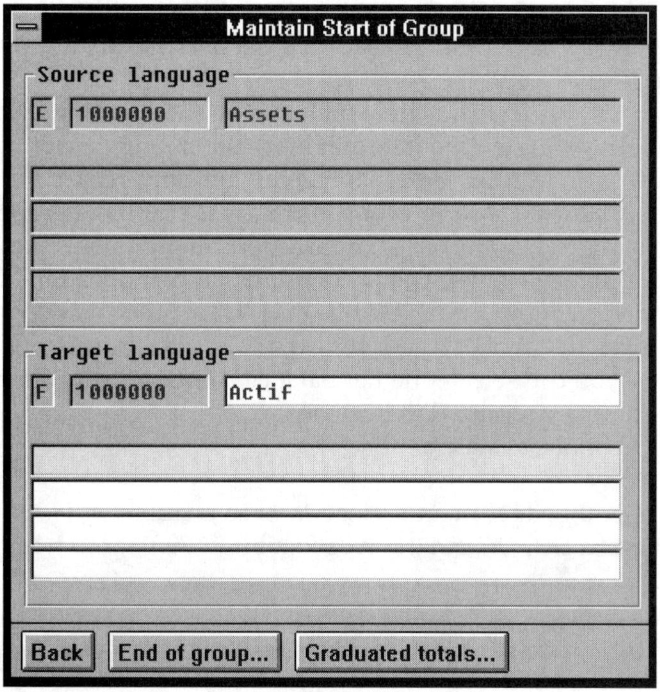

Exhibit 2.178 Maintain Start of Group

8. Continue this process for each and every heading and subheading in the format of the financial statement.

Reporting a Financial Statement

A financial statement always includes both a balance sheet and a profit and loss statement. In fact, the financial statement includes all G/L accounts in the chart of accounts for one or more company codes.

You can prepare a balance sheet at any moment. It is advisable to revalue open items and account balances in foreign currency before you prepare a balance, but it is not technically required. In fact, there is no technical preparation required. On the other hand, before preparing the financial statement, you may need to post various adjusting entries, based on legal and commercial requirements.

You usually prepare a financial statement for a specific company code, but you can also combine one or more company codes into one financial statement. If you combine company codes, however, the financial statement does not eliminate intercompany receivables, payables, revenue, expense, and other intercompany transactions, such as profit or loss on transferring inventory and the investment of the head office in the equity of the subsidiary. To eliminate these intercompany balances and transactions, set and use the Legal Consolidation submodule of FI.

You can prepare a financial statement sheet in another language, if you have entered the financial statement format in the other language or translated the balance sheet format to the other language. You can prepare the balance sheet in either local currency or in group currency, if you have properly configured the company code to record all transactions in group currency.

You can also prepare a statement of the sources and applications of funds. This statement includes only the net change in G/L accounts over certain posting periods. This statement does not include the balances carried forward from previous periods. You can select whether balance sheet accounts or profit and loss accounts or both are reported in this way.

To prepare the financial statement:

1. From the General Ledger menu, select Periodic processing → Month-end reports → Create bal. sheet/P+L. (See Exhibit 2.179.)

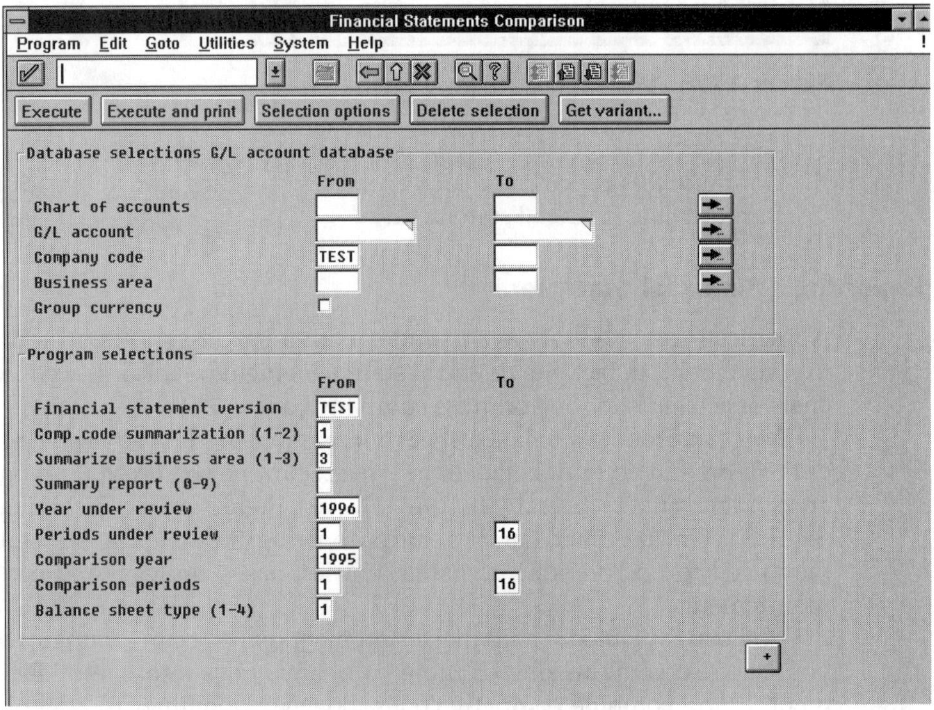

Exhibit 2.179   Financial Statements Comparison, Screen One

2. Enter at least the following parameters:

Parameter	*Meaning*
Company code	Usually a specific legal entity; you can also enter a series of company codes.
Financial statement version	Format of the financial statement, depending on your configuration
Comp.code summarization	Enter **1** for a separate financial statement for each company code or **2** for a combined financial statement.
Summarize business area	Usually, enter **3** for a financial statement combining business areas. Otherwise, enter **1** for separate financial statements by business area. To list the account balances by business area in the account, enter **2**.
Summary report	Leave this blank to see all G/L account balances. Otherwise, enter a level from the format of the financial statement to prepare a condensed financial statement that subtotals G/L account balances.
Year under review	Fiscal year, depending on your configuration
Periods under review	Posting periods, also depending on your configuration
Comparison year	To compare the financial statement to a prior year
Comparison periods	To compare the financial statements to one or more specific periods
Balance sheet type	To prepare an accumulated financial statement, including the balances carried forward, enter **1**. To prepare a statement of the sources and application of funds, which excludes the balances carried forward, enter **2**. To have balance sheet account balances reported with balances carried forward and profit and loss accounts reported without balances carried forward, enter **3**. To prepare an opening balance sheet, including only the balances carried forward and all G/L account balances, enter **4**.

3. To go to the next screen of parameters, press +. (See Exhibit 2.180.)
4. The primary parameters on this screen are:

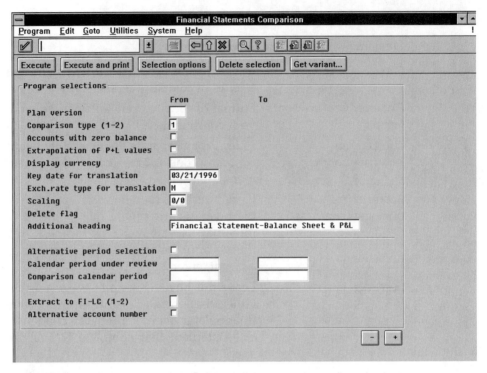

Exhibit 2.180   Financial Statements Comparison, Screen Two

Parameter	Meaning
Plan version	If you have formatted a plan version, you can specify it here for insertion into the report. You could have different plan versions for seasonal planning, compared with monthly planning. Otherwise, leave this field blank.
Accounts with zero balance	To include all G/L accounts mark this parameter.
Display currency	To display the balance sheet in a different currency than local currency or group currency, enter the ISO code for the currency of the display.
Key date for translation	If you display the financial statement in another currency than local currency or group currency, then this date determines the date on which the open items, usually customer invoices and vendor invoices, are revalued for the display.

Exch.rate type for translation	If you display the financial statement in another currency than local currency or group currency, then this is the type of exchange rate for the revaluation. If you are not sure, enter **M** in this field (for the average exchange rates).
Scaling	Use this parameter to format the numbers. For example, if you enter **3/0,** then the numbers would be displayed in thousands with no decimal places.
Delete flag	Includes all G/L accounts marked for deletion.
Additional heading	Enter your own description of the report.
Alternative period selection	If you report two or more company codes and the company codes have different fiscal years, then you can use this and the related parameters to adjust.
Extract to FI-LC	To extract the financial statement for the company code for the FI Legal Consolidation submodule, enter **1.** To extract the date for the business area, enter **2.**
Alternative account number	To prepare the financial statement based on the alternative account numbers, mark this parameter. This is useful in France, if you use the alternative account numbers for the French chart of accounts.

To go to the next page of parameters, press +.

5. To run the report and to prepare the financial statement, press Execute or <F8>.

Reporting an Audit Trail of an Account Balance

To audit an account, you are concerned with all the transactions that were posted to the account that make up the account balance. When you post a transaction, FI updates two files—one, with account balances and the other with transactions. For the audit trail (the detail of an account balance), you can display the G/L account balance and then double-click on the account balance with the details in which you are interested. For an audit trail, you can also prepare a detailed list of transactions by account from the transaction ("document") file.

To prepare the audit trail by account from the transaction file:

1. From the General Ledger menu, select Periodic processing ➤ Month-end reports ➤ Balance audit trail ➤ G/L bal.audit trail. (See Exhibit 2.181.)

2. Enter at least the company code, fiscal year, and fiscal periods (or posting dates). To see the balance audit trail for a specific G/L account, enter the G/L account in the G/L account field. To see the balance audit trail for all G/L accounts, leave the G/L account field blank. To go to the next page of parameters, press +. (See Exhibit 2.182.)

3. Optionally, enter a description of the report in the Additional heading field. To run the report, press Execute or <F8>.

Reporting an Audit Trail of an Open Item Account

All customer accounts and all vendor accounts are open item accounts. Depending on your chart of accounts, certain G/L accounts are usually also open item accounts, such as bank clearing or inventory clearing accounts.

To find an audit trail of any of these open item accounts, based on the transaction ("document") file:

Exhibit 2.181 General Ledger Database and Program Selections

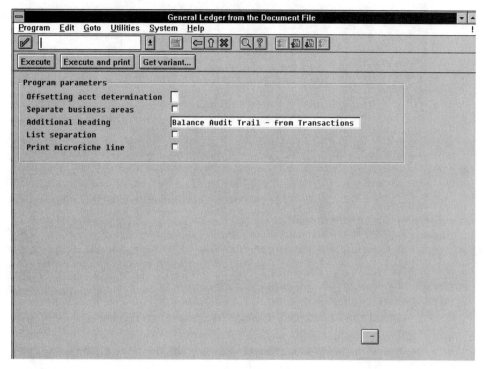

Exhibit 2.182 General Ledger Program Parameters

1. From the General Ledger menu, select Periodic processing → Month-end reports → Balance audit trail → Open items from doc. (See Exhibit 2.183.)

2. Enter at least the company code and fiscal year. Optionally, to trace the details of customer or vendor accounts, mark the corresponding parameters and specify one or more accounts. To see the details of all accounts, mark the corresponding parameter and specify the G/L accounts. To go to the next screen of parameters, press +. (See Exhibit 2.184.)

3. If you do not specify customer nor vendor accounts, then mark the parameter G/L account section and specify one or more G/L accounts.

4. To run the report, press Execute or <F8>.

Preparing the Tax Report (VAT)

Functions for calculating, posting, and reporting sales tax, as required in the United States, are supplied by third-party vendors, such as AVP and Vertex. You can use either of these companies' software with R/3 to prepare sales tax reports. Their service is competent and reliable.

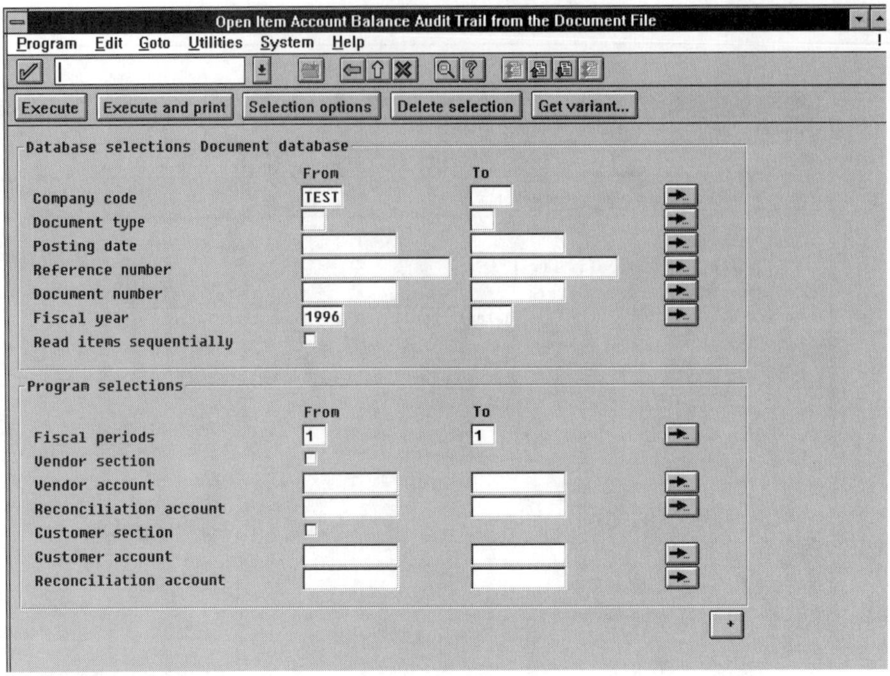

Exhibit 2.183　Account Balance Audit Trail, Screen One

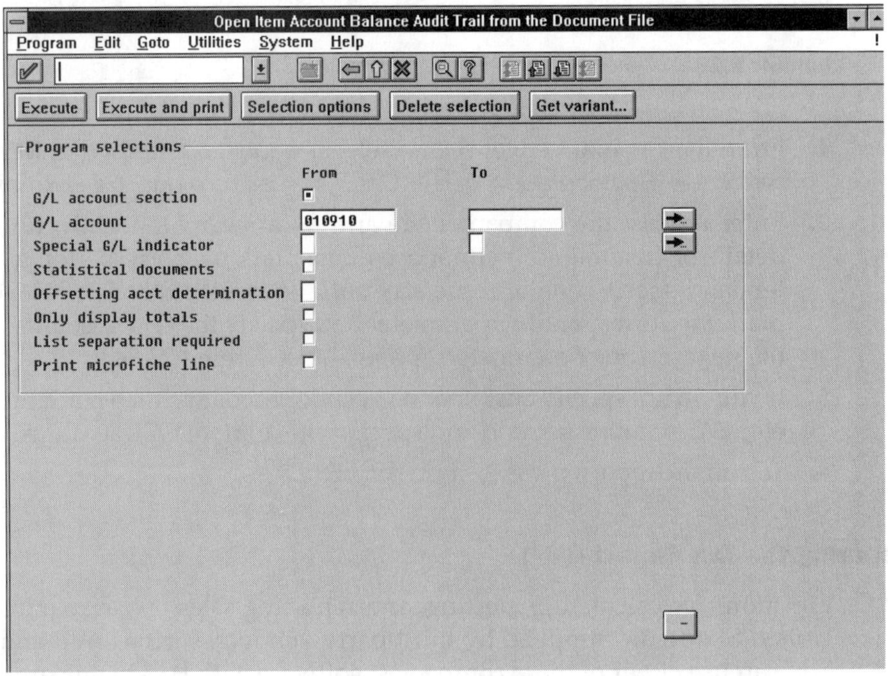

Exhibit 2.184　Account Balance Audit Trail, Screen Two

Output VAT is similar to sales tax, but in countries where VAT is applied, you can also usually deduct input VAT, which is paid on vendor invoices.

The VAT report that is supplied by the package is based on the VAT codes that you enter in transactions. The specific VAT codes depend on your configuration. The report subtotals both the base amounts (either revenue or expense) and the VAT amounts, based on the VAT codes. In other words, if you define enough detail in the VAT codes, then the report will contain enough detail to fill out the VAT form.

To prepare the VAT report:

1. From the General Ledger menu, select Periodic processing ➜ Month-end reports ➜ Tax on sales/purc. ➜ Advance tax report. (See Exhibit 2.185.)
2. Enter at least the company code, fiscal year, and fiscal period. Also mark either Select output tax or Select input tax or both. To go to the next screen of parameters, press +. (See Exhibit 2.186.)
3. To sort the report by the company code, enter **1** in the Sorting field. Mark Output tax line items or Input tax line items or both. To generate a batch input file containing the transaction that offsets both the input and output

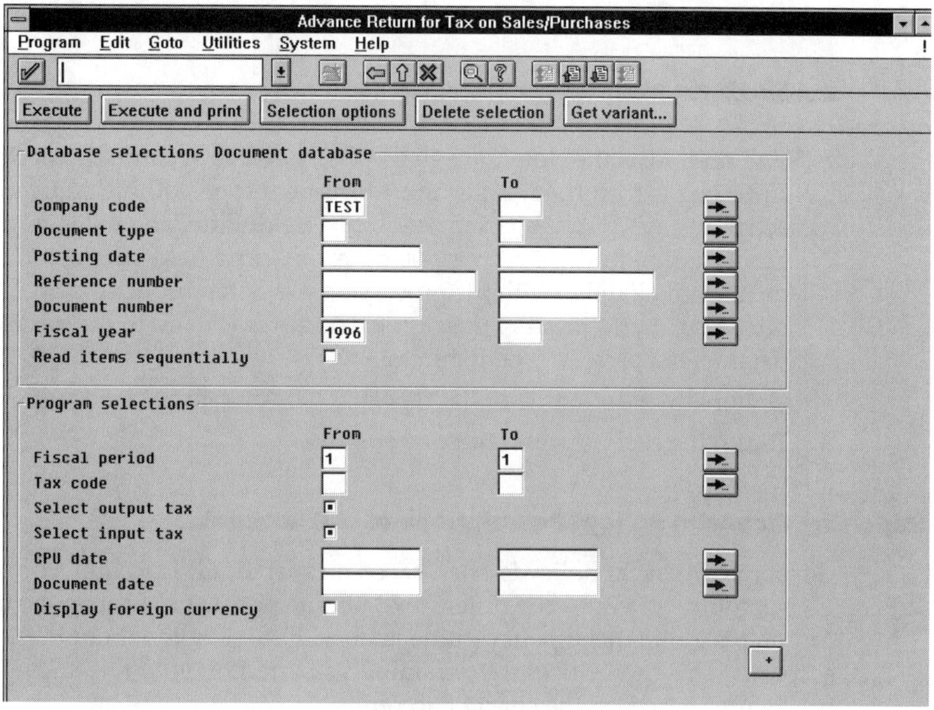

Exhibit 2.185   Return for Tax on Sales/Purchases, Screen One

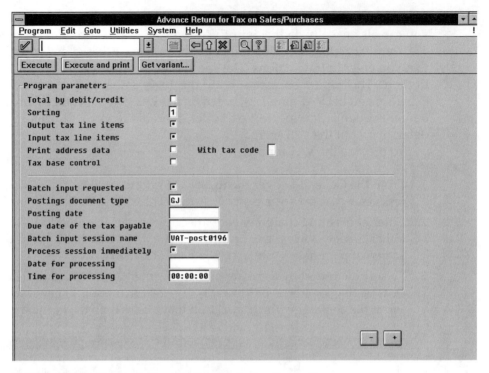

Exhibit 2.186   Return for Tax on Sales/Purchases, Screen Two

VAT and posts the difference to the VAT payable account, mark the Batch input requested field. Enter the "document type" of this adjusting transaction in the Postings document type field. Enter the name of the batch input session in the Batch input session name field. To post this adjustment immediately (without processing the batch input session in a separate step), mark Process session immediately. To go to the next screen of parameters, press +. (See Exhibit 2.187.)

4. Optionally, enter a title of the report in the Additional heading field.

5. To run the report, press Execute or <F8>.

Reporting Financial Policy (Descriptions of G/L Accounts)

Corporate financial policy is often based on specific G/L accounts or ranges of G/L accounts. If you write notes (text) about specific G/L accounts, then you can prepare a financial policy guide later with these notes about these specific accounts. This can be useful for training your staff on your specific policy and procedures based on the chart of accounts.

When entering notes about a G/L account, you can enter the notes either in the global chart of accounts (on the first screen, when you enter the account)

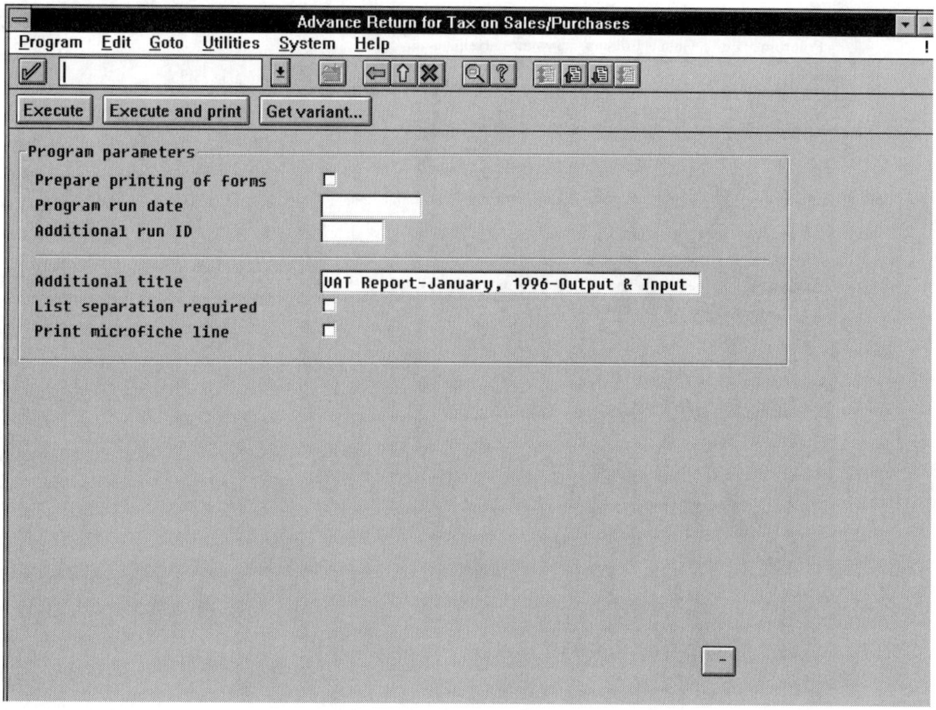

Exhibit 2.187   Return for Tax on Sales/Purchases, Screen Three

or in the local chart of accounts (on the second, third, or fourth screen) for a specific company code. You can then prepare the financial policy either for the global chart of accounts or for a specific company code.

Be careful when entering notes about G/L accounts that you enter them consistently, either in the global chart of accounts, in a specific company code, or in both. To prepare a financial policy guide:

1. From the General Ledger menu, select Periodic processing ➤ Reporting ➤ Acct assignment man. (See Exhibit 2.188.)

2. Enter either the chart of accounts or the company code. Also enter the code of the language and a text ID in the Acct assignment info text ID field, usually **0001,** if you entered only one type of text about each G/L account. Optionally, enter a title in the parameter Additional heading. Mark G/L account texts required. Press Execute.

Entering the Chart of Accounts by Batch Input

Use the RFBISA00 report.

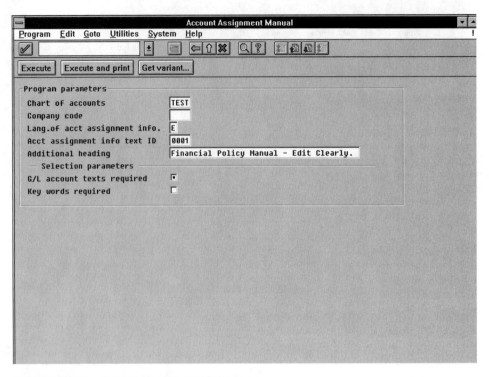

Exhibit 2.188   Account Assignment Manual

Using Line Item Layouts for Simple Reports

A line item layout is a formatted sequence of fields (columns of data) from left to right. You can choose the sequence and many aspects of the format, such as the length of the field and the spacing between columns. A line item layout is a type of display format. You can also format the display of open items to be cleared, items in the payment proposal, and the overview of a transaction. This section describes making and using line layouts in the G/L for displaying or printing account details.

You can use line item layouts to prepare simple reports. You could then select certain line items. Next, you could sort these line items. Lastly, you could switch the line item layout. All of these tasks you can do on-line. This is quicker and easier to maintain than developing ABAP reports. There are limitations on which fields you can include in line layouts, but you can often put the fields that you are looking for into a line layout that you can use.

Making a Line Item Layout.   To make a line item layout, it is often easier to copy an existing line layout, insert or delete fields that you require, label the headings, and then name the new line item layout. The example will show

how to make a line item layout with the number of the clearing transaction. This can show which invoices were paid with which payment, since both the invoice and the payment for that invoice have the same clearing transaction number if the payment also cleared (closed) the invoice. To make a line item layout:

1. From the General Ledger menu, select Environment ➤ Configuration menu and then select Business volume ➤ Payments ➤ Display format. (See Exhibit 2.189.)

2. Press Line item layout. (See Exhibit 2.190.)

3. Copy a line layout. First, put the cursor on a specific line item layout, such as **A0.** Then select Edit ➤ Copy. (See Exhibit 2.191.)

4. Enter a code name (abbreviation) of the new line layout, such as **CLR** for a line layout with the clearing transaction number. Press Continue. (See Exhibit 2.192.)

5. To insert a field in the line item layout, put the cursor on the name of a field and then select Edit ➤ Insert ➤ Insert before or Insert after. For

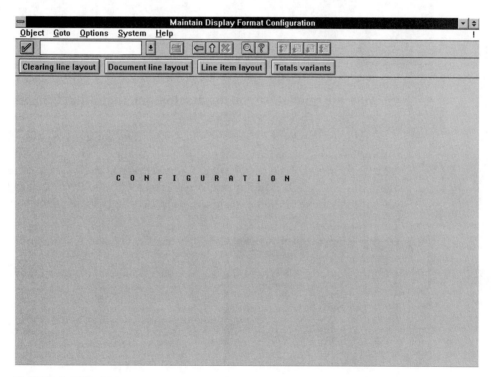

Exhibit 2.189 Maintain Display Format Configuration

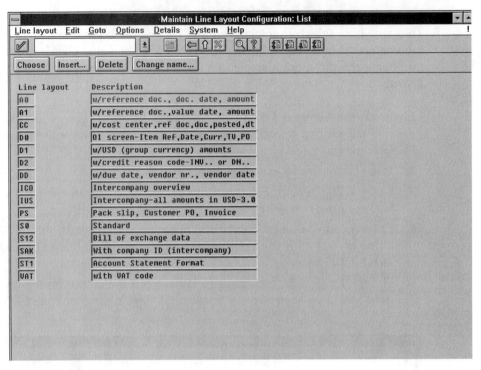

Exhibit 2.190   Maintain Line Layout Configuration: List

example, put your cursor on the first line and then select Edit ➤ Insert ➤ Insert before. (See Exhibit 2.193.)

6. You then see the list of fields available for the line item layout. To scroll through the list, use the <PageUp> and <PageDown> keys. To see the technical names of the fields, press Field names on/off. To see other fields available for the line item layout, press Special fields. To select a field, simply double-click on it. For example, to insert the field with the number of

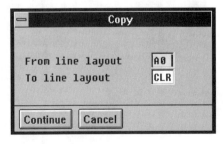

Exhibit 2.191   Copy

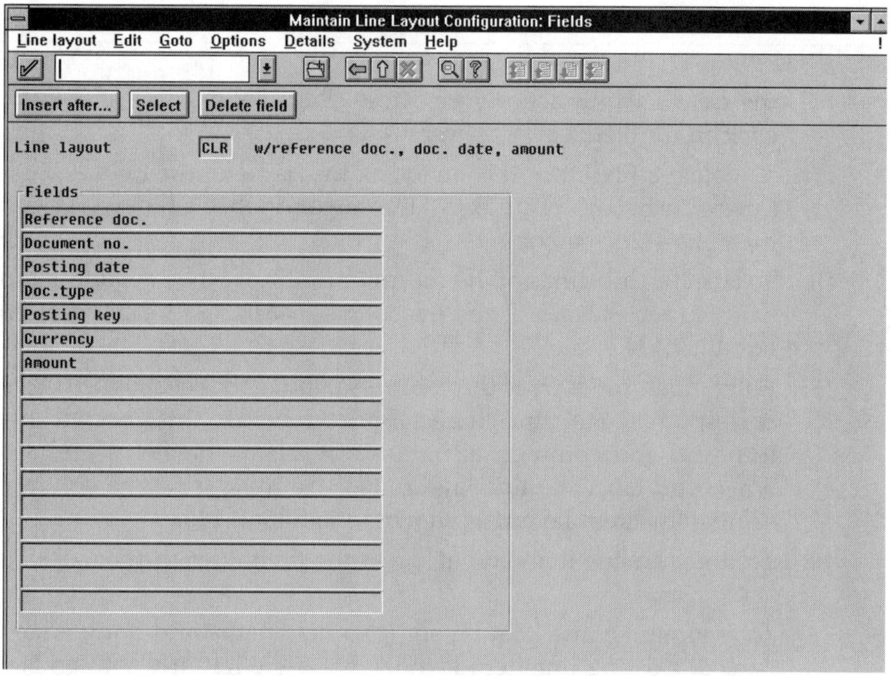

Exhibit 2.192 Maintain Line Layout Configuration: Fields

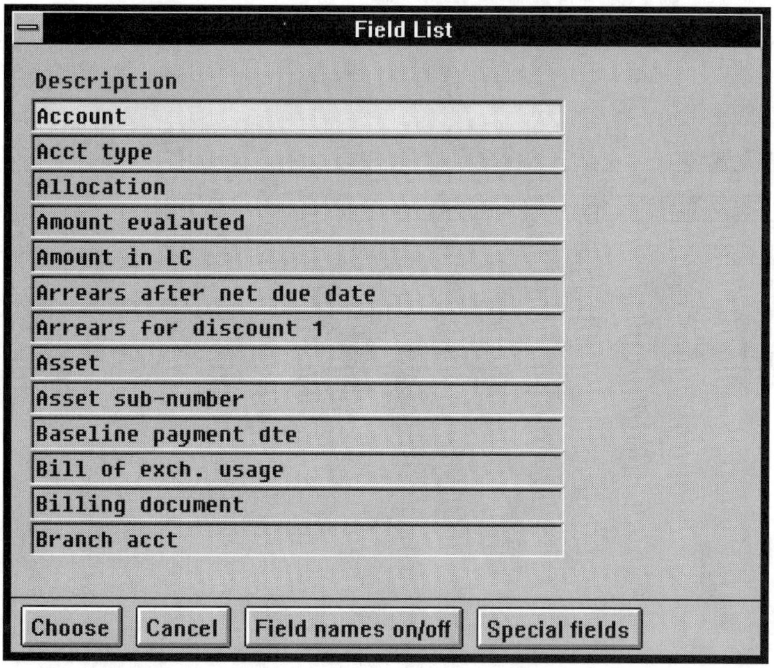

Exhibit 2.193 Field List

the clearing transaction, press the <PageDown> key and then double-click on the Clearing doc. field.

7. To delete a field, put the cursor on the name of the field and then press Delete field. For example, put the cursor on the Reference doc. field and then press Delete field.

8. To label the headings of the columns, first store the new line layout. Select Line layout ⇢ Save. Then select Edit ⇢ Texts ⇢ Column heading. (See Exhibit 2.194.)

9. Enter labels for each of the columns. Notice that each letter (A, B, C, etc.) corresponds to the first character of each field in this line item layout. The technical and commercial names of each of the fields are also shown when you label the line layout. For example, label the columns in this sample line item layout as shown in Exhibit 2.195.

10. To store the line item layout, press the file folder icon or select Line layout ⇢ Save.

11. To rename the line item layout (to a new name and not the name of the copied, existing line item layout), press the left arrow to go back to the

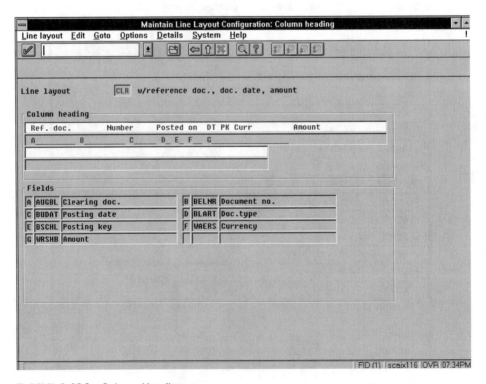

Exhibit 2.194 Column Headings

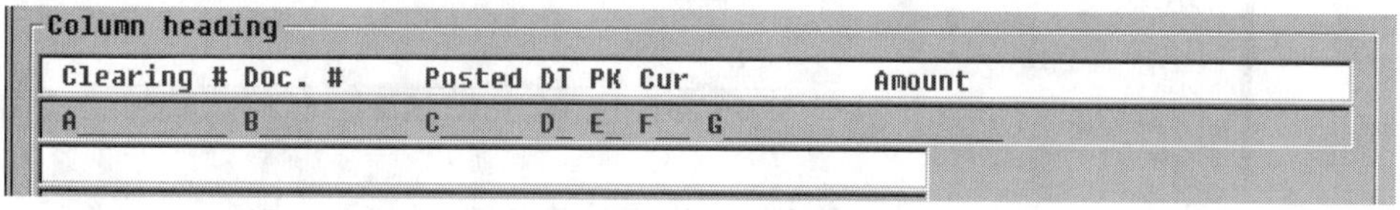

Exhibit 2.195   Column Heading

previous screen with the list of fields and then select Edit → Texts → Change name. (See Exhibit 2.196.)

12.   Enter the new name and then press Continue to store the new name of this line item layout.

13.   To make this line item layout available for specific account types (customer, vendor, or G/L account), select Edit → Usage. (See Exhibit 2.197.)

14.   Select one or more account types. This makes it possible for you to display line item detail (account detail) of the account type, using this line item layout. Press Continue.

15.   To store the line item layout with the account type, press the file folder icon once more or select Line layout → Save.

16.   To add spaces between columns, put the cursor on a specific field and then select Details → Display format. (See Exhibit 2.198.)

17.   To increase the number of spaces to the left of the field, increase the Distance parameter. To start the display of the field at a specific character, enter the number of characters before this in the Offset parameter. To display only part of a field, enter the Display length parameter. If you change the column spacing, you then should also change any column headings that you have already defined.

18.   To go back, keep pressing the up arrow until you reach the G/L menu or the menu from which you started.

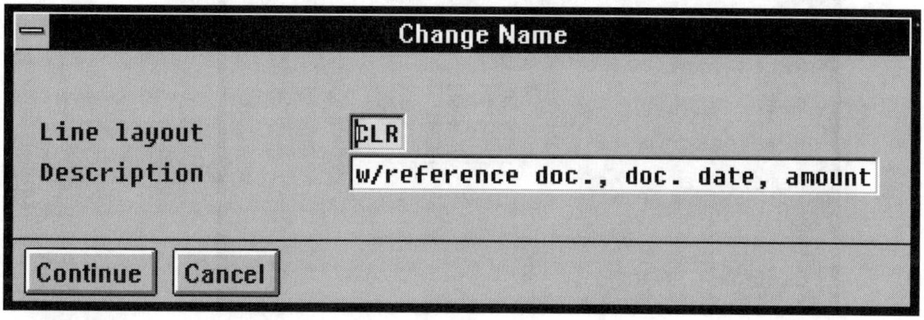

Exhibit 2.196   Change Name

```
┌──────────────────────────────────────────────────────────┐
│ ▄▄                    Line layout usage                    │
├──────────────────────────────────────────────────────────┤
│                                                            │
│  Line layout          ┌─────┐                              │
│                       │CLR  │                              │
│  Description          ┌─────────────────────────────────┐  │
│                       │w/reference doc., doc. date, amount│ │
│                                                            │
│  ┌Usage for the following account types──────────────────┐ │
│  │ ▣ Customer                                            │ │
│  │ ▣ Vendor                                              │ │
│  │ ▣ G/L account                                         │ │
│  └───────────────────────────────────────────────────────┘ │
│                                                            │
│  ┌To be reread───────────────────────────────────────────┐ │
│  │ □ Document header                                     │ │
│  │ □ Line item                                           │ │
│  │ □ Bill of exch.data                                   │ │
│  │ □ One-time data                                       │ │
│  └───────────────────────────────────────────────────────┘ │
│                                                            │
│  ┌──────────┐ ┌────────┐                                   │
│  │ Continue │ │ Cancel │                                   │
│  └──────────┘ └────────┘                                   │
└──────────────────────────────────────────────────────────┘
```

Exhibit 2.197   Line Layout Usage

```
┌──────────────────────────────────────────────┐
│ ▄▄               Display format                │
├──────────────────────────────────────────────┤
│  ┌────────────────────────────────────────┐   │
│  │Clearing doc.                           │   │
│  └────────────────────────────────────────┘   │
│                                                │
│  ┌Display format──────────────────────────┐   │
│  │ Offset              ┌───┐               │   │
│  │                     └───┘               │   │
│  │ Display length      ┌───┐               │   │
│  │                     │10 │               │   │
│  │ Distance            ┌───┐               │   │
│  │                     │1  │               │   │
│  └────────────────────────────────────────┘   │
│                                                │
│  ┌Field properties────────────────────────┐   │
│  │ Decimal places      ┌───┐               │   │
│  │                     │0  │               │   │
│  │ Data type           ┌─────┐             │   │
│  │                     │CHAR │             │   │
│  │ Reference table     ┌───────┐           │   │
│  │                     └───────┘           │   │
│  │ Reference field     ┌───────┐           │   │
│  │                     └───────┘           │   │
│  └────────────────────────────────────────┘   │
│                                                │
│  ┌──────────┐ ┌────────┐                       │
│  │ Continue │ │ Cancel │                       │
│  └──────────┘ └────────┘                       │
└──────────────────────────────────────────────┘
```

Exhibit 2.198   Display Format

In summary, making a line item layout is as simple as follows:

- Copy an existing line layout
- Insert and delete fields
- Define the column headings
- Rename the line item layout
- Store the line item layout

You can then use the line item to display or print line items in an account or a group (work list) of accounts.

AUDITING AND SECURITY

Keeping Your Password Private

Since each individual could be held responsible for entries by his or her own login ID, it is advisable to keep your password private. For internal security, do not write your password down near your PC.

Changing Your Password

It is also advisable to change your password occasionally.

If You Forget Your Password

Call the system administrator, and have him or her reset your password to an easy-to-remember password, such as password. Log in immediately under the reset password. The system prompts you to change your password the first time that you log in with a new password. Enter your new password, press <Tab>, enter it again, and then press <Enter>.

Authorizations and User Master Records

Each user is assigned one or more profiles. Each profile contains authorization objects with a specific authorization. The authorization objects and your profile determine what functions you can use. This will be the subject of another book.

Security Reporting

Use the STAT function to list all logins and functions used (SAP transaction codes) by person, date, and time. Put your cursor in the command box and enter **/nSTAT**.

CHAPTER 3

Accounts Receivable

SAP R/3 Accounts Receivable includes the following primary functions:

- Keeping customer master records
- Controlling customer credit
- Entering and posting customer invoices
- Applying cash and checks
- Inquiring about customer accounts
- Using other A/R functions
- Reporting from Accounts Receivable

STARTING TO USE ACCOUNTS RECEIVABLE

Setting User Defaults

For each SAP user ID you can set the start-up menu, print control parameters, date format, and decimal format. These settings are then valid each and every time you log in, until you change them. To set your user defaults:

1. Log in to R/3 with your user ID.
2. From any menu, select System ➤ User profile ➤ User defaults. (See Exhibit 3.1.)

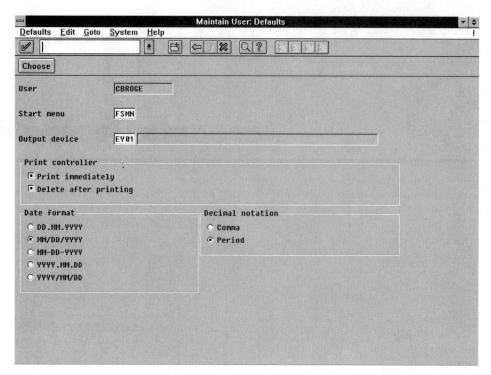

Exhibit 3.1   Maintain User: Defaults

3. To start up the Accounts Receivable menu each time you log in, enter
    FDMN in the Start menu field. In the Output device field, enter the four-
    character name of the printer in your R/3 system. To set up a printer, you
    first have to define it under your operating system—with maximum
    entries for the number of rows and columns per page. You then have to
    define the printer in R/3 with the applicable number of rows and columns
    per page. Click on a sample format in the Date format column. In the Dec-
    imal notation column, click on Comma or Period, to separate whole num-
    bers from fractions by either a comma or a period. To store these
    parameters, press <F11> or the file folder icon. Note that you can change
    these parameters later too.

Setting Processing Options

You can set various options to process transaction data. These options are
valid for each person until you change them. There are three sets of processing
options:

- Transaction entry and display
- Open item processing (for example, for cash application)
- Line item display

To set a processing option, you simply click on the option. To start to set processing options:

1. From the Accounts Receivable menu, select Environment → Current options → Editing options. (See Exhibit 3.2.)
2. The examples in this course assume that the processing options on this screen are set as shown. The primary transaction entry and display options are as follows:

Option	Meaning if Option is On
No foreign currency	If you enter and process transactions only in local currency, click on this option. In effect, this option suppresses entry of amounts in foreign currency.

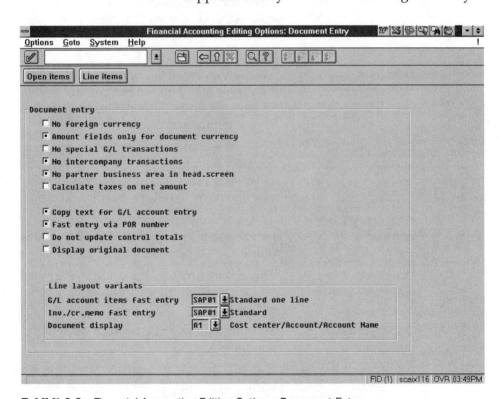

Exhibit 3.2 Financial Accounting Editing Options: Document Entry

Amount fields only for document currency	When you enter a transaction in foreign currency, you then enter the currency code in the transaction header and the amounts in the transaction currency only in each line item. If this option were off, then you could enter both the transaction currency amount and the local currency amount in each line item.
No special G/L transactions	This option suppresses entry of special G/L transactions, such as down payments, bills of exchange, security deposits, and others.
No intercompany transactions	This option suppresses entry of intercompany transactions in which two company codes buy or sell something jointly.
No partner business area in head.screen	This option suppresses the "partner business area" in the transaction header screen. If the transaction involves multiple business areas, then the receivables and payables between business areas are calculated and posted to and from the partner business area and the business areas in the transaction.
Calculate taxes on net amount	This option makes the program calculate transaction taxes based on the net amount in the revenue or expense entry. Otherwise, you enter the gross amount in the revenue or expense entry.
Copy text for G/L account entry	The option makes the program copy your entry in the text field from one G/L line item to the next when you enter a long G/L transaction, such as external payroll (not from HR).
Fast entry via POR number	This option is required only in Switzerland to enter vendor invoices based on the Swiss payment number.
Do not update control totals	This option turns off the update of control totals if you wish to control the totals of only certain users' entries.
Display original document	Turn this option on if you scan documents, such as vendor invoices.
G/L account items fast entry	Use the default (supplied) line layout to begin with. Depending on your requirements and your

configuration, you can change the line layout (the sequence of fields from left to right displayed on the screen).

Inv/cr.memo fast entry   Use the default (supplied) line layout to begin with. Depending on your requirements and your configuration, you can change the line layout (the sequence of fields from left to right displayed on the screen).

Document display   Use the default (supplied) line layout to begin with. Depending on your requirements and your configuration, you can change the line layout (the sequence of fields from left to right displayed on the screen). This determines how the overview of the transaction is displayed.

3. To set the open item processing options, press Open items. (See Exhibit 3.3.)

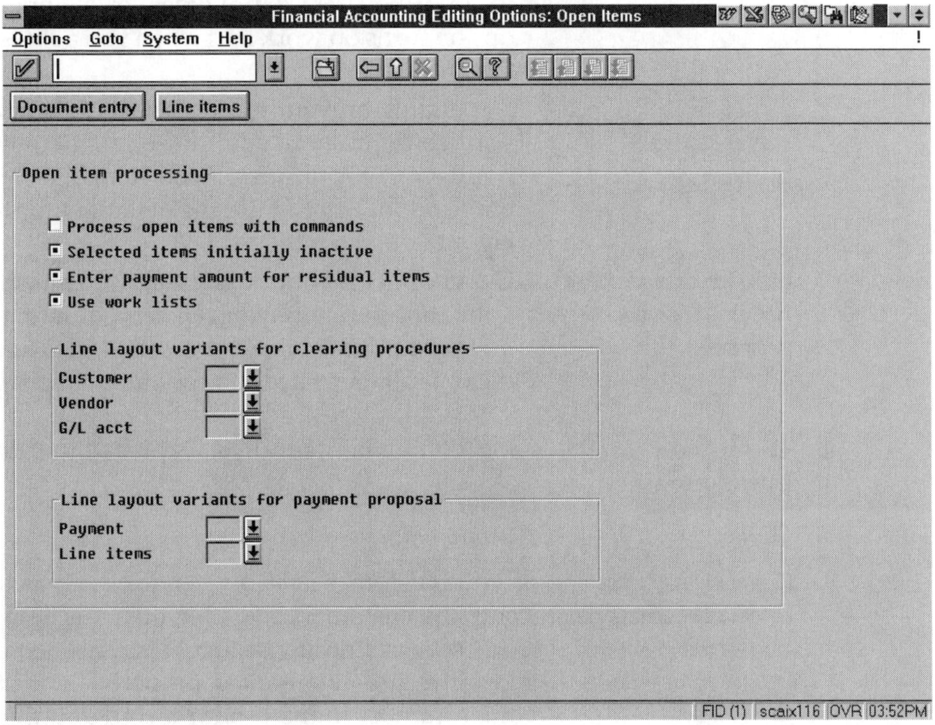

Exhibit 3.3   Financial Accounting Editing Options: Open Items

The following are the primary open item processing options:

Option	Meaning if Set On
Process open items with commands	If you set this option on, you can process open items with commands (in the left-most column). Otherwise, you use the mouse and double-click on an item to activate it.
Selected items initially inactive	If you set this option on, then all open items in the clearing screen (cash application screen) are not active (applied) until you activate them.
Enter payment amount for residual items	If you set this option on, you enter the amount of the payment in the residual item screen when you process a partial payment and close the original invoice. Otherwise, you enter the amount of the residual.
Use work lists	You can combine two or more customers into a work list—to display open items by a work list or to clear open items (apply cash) by a work list. This option turns on work lists when you process (clear) open items.
Line layout variants for clearing procedures	Depending on your business requirements and on your configuration, you can set a different default line layout for clearing open items, such as cash application. You can use the default (supplied) line layout to begin with.
Line layout variants for payment proposal	Depending on your business requirements and on your configuration, you can set a different default line layout for the payment proposal. You can use the default (supplied) line layout to begin with.

4. To set the processing option for line item display, press the Line items pushbutton.

Option	Meaning if Set On
Disp. customer and vendor items together	If your customer is also a vendor, such as an inter-company customer or vendor, then this item display both sets of line items together. This requires the master records be marked properly—with the customer number in the vendor record and the vendor number in the customer record.
Use work lists	You can combine two or more customers into a work list—to display open items by a work list or to clear

	open items (apply cash) by a work list. This option turns on work lists when you display open items.
Line layout variant —customers	Depending on your business requirements and on your configuration, you can set a different default line layout to display the customer (supplied) line layout to begin with.
Line layout variant —vendors	Depending on your business requirements and on your configuration, you can set a different default line layout to display vendor line items. You can use the default (supplied) line layout to begin with.
Line layout variant —G/L acct	Depending on your business requirements and on your configuration, you can set a different default line layout to display G/L line items. You can use the default (supplied) line layout to begin with.

5. To update your user master record with the processing options that you set, press <F11> or the file folder icon.

KEEPING CUSTOMER MASTER RECORDS

Customer records in FI have two parts—a general part that applies to all possible companies that this customer could buy from *and* a company code–specific part that applies only to a specific company code. Most of all, the general part of a customer master record contains the following data: the name, address, phone number, tax ID number, and bank account numbers of the customer. To collect by direct debit, you need the customer's written permission and the customer's bank account number. If the customer is also a vendor, such as an intercompany customer, also record the vendor number in the general part of the customer master record. Most of all, the company code–specific part of a customer master contains the following data: the G/L account for receivables from the customer (the reconciliation account), how to sort details automatically in this account when you display them later, and the payment terms to this customer.

Enter the general part of a customer master record on the first three screens. Then you enter the company code–specific part of a customer master record on the next four screens (screens four through seven). The customer master data is spread over these seven screens. It cannot be compressed onto one screen. If you have more than 1,000 customer master records in an existing A/R system, it could be quicker to enter them by batch input. These instructions are included so that you are familiar with the process of entering customer master records online. The screens are the same, when updating a customer master record.

Note that if you use SD (for order entry, shipping, and invoicing), you also enter customer master data. SD and FI use the same customer master records. In other words, you have a common, central customer database between order entry, shipping, invoicing, and accounts receivable. Depending on your organization and your configuration, you enter customer master data in SD into one or more sales areas. A sales area is a combination of sales organization (usually geographic, but possibly related to product liability), a distribution channel (for example, wholesale, retail, or direct), and a division (usually a product grouping). In addition, you enter customer master data in FI. If you centralize your credit and collection, you can enter one customer in FI with multiple sales areas in SD. A sales organization in SD is always linked to one and only one company code in FI, so when you enter an order in SD by a sales area, it is always clear to which company code you will post the revenue and receivable.

Entering a Customer Master Record

If you are thinking of implementing SAP, your IT department will probably offer to transfer customer records by batch input. This section describes the fields in a customer record, as if they were entered by hand. Depending on your business requirements and your configuration, specific fields in customer master records are either required, optional, or suppressed. If you require a specific field that is not available in all of the possible fields in a customer master record, try to use another field to contain your specific field. In this way, you use the software as supplied by SAP. As a last resort, it is possible to modify the format and the entry of a customer record, but this can complicate an upgrade to the next version of the software.

To enter a customer master record:

1. From the Accounts Receivable menu, select Master records ➔ Create. (See Exhibit 3.4.)
2. Enter at least the name, search term (matchcode), city, postal code, country, and language of the customer. Press <Enter>. (See Exhibit 3.5.)
3. Enter at least the VAT registration number of the customer. Press <Enter>. (See Exhibit 3.6.)
4. If you collect by direct debit from this customer, enter the customer's bank account numbers. Otherwise, press <Enter> to go to the next screen. (See Exhibit 3.7.)
5. Always enter a reconciliation account and a sort key for the customer. If the customer invoice always includes VAT, then enter the appropriate G/L

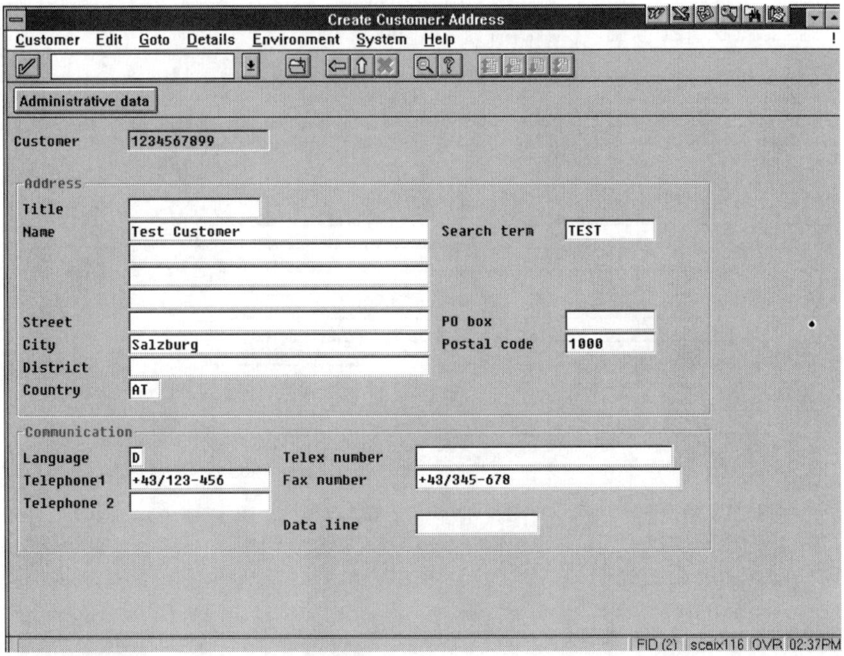

Exhibit 3.4　Create Customer: Address

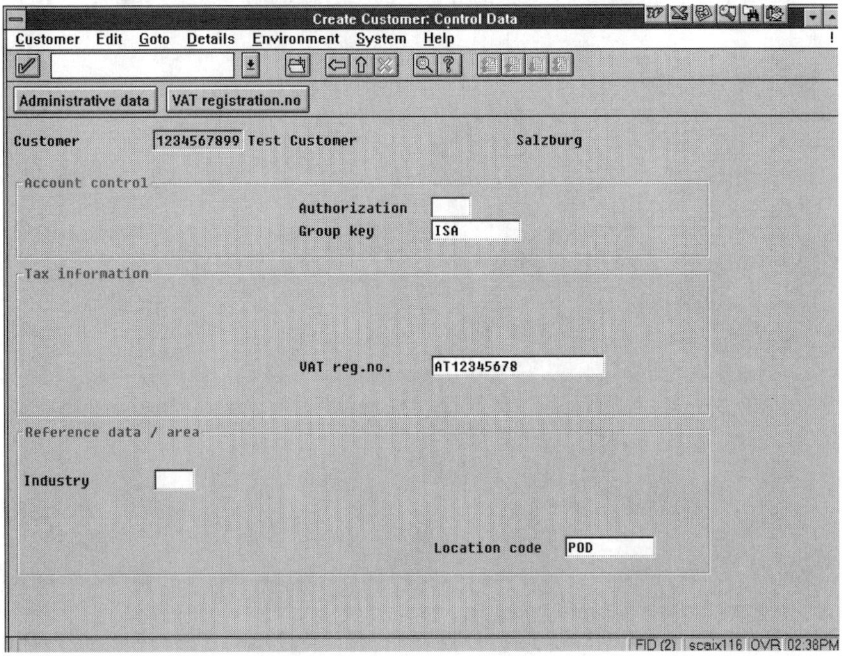

Exhibit 3.5　Create Customer: Control Data

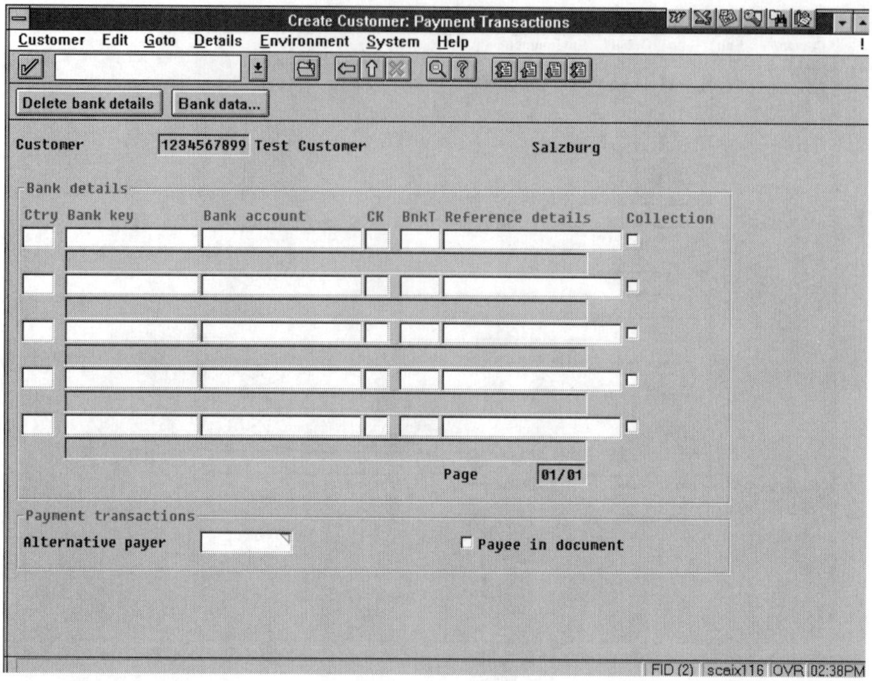

Exhibit 3.6   Create Customer: Payment Transactions

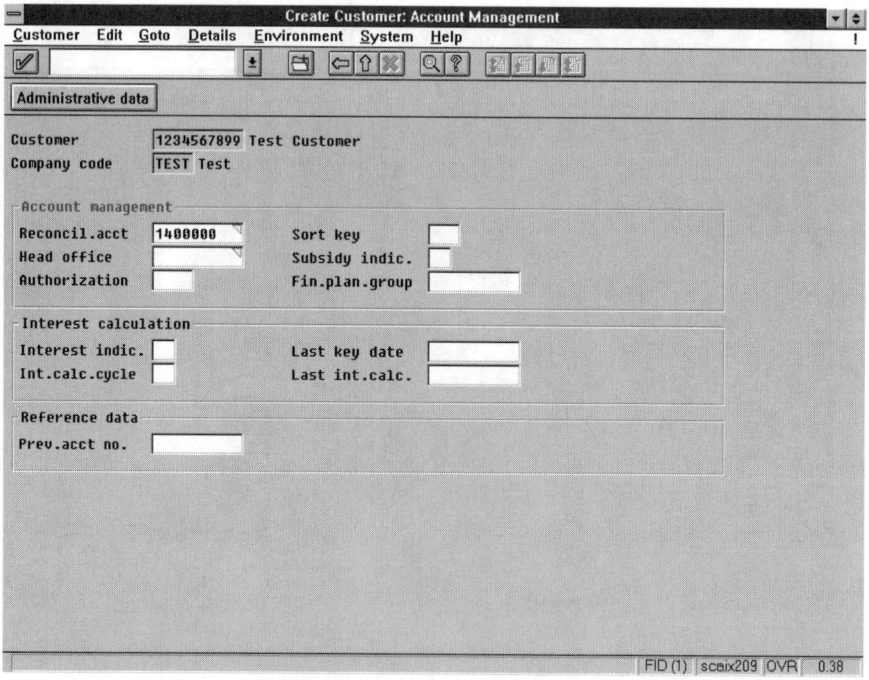

Exhibit 3.7   Create Customer: Account Management

account for receivables in the Reconcil.acct field, such as **1400000** for the domestic receivables, depending on your specific chart of accounts. Depending on your business requirements and configuration, make an entry in the Sort key field to determine how line items in the account will be automatically sorted after you post transactions later. Press <Enter>. (See Exhibit 3.8.)

6. Always enter the payment terms that the customer receives. Always mark record payment history. Press <Enter>. (See Exhibit 3.9.)

7. To dun the customer, enter **DAIL** in the Dunn.procedure field, depending on your configuration. In the Acctg clerk field, enter the two-letter initials of the credit analyst or accounting clerk. In the Acct statement field, enter **2** to send the customer monthly statements or **1** to send the customer weekly statements.

8. To store the customer record, press <F11> or the file folder icon.

Entering Notes in a Customer Master Record. You can enter notes (text) about a customer to describe how the customer is organized, who the officers

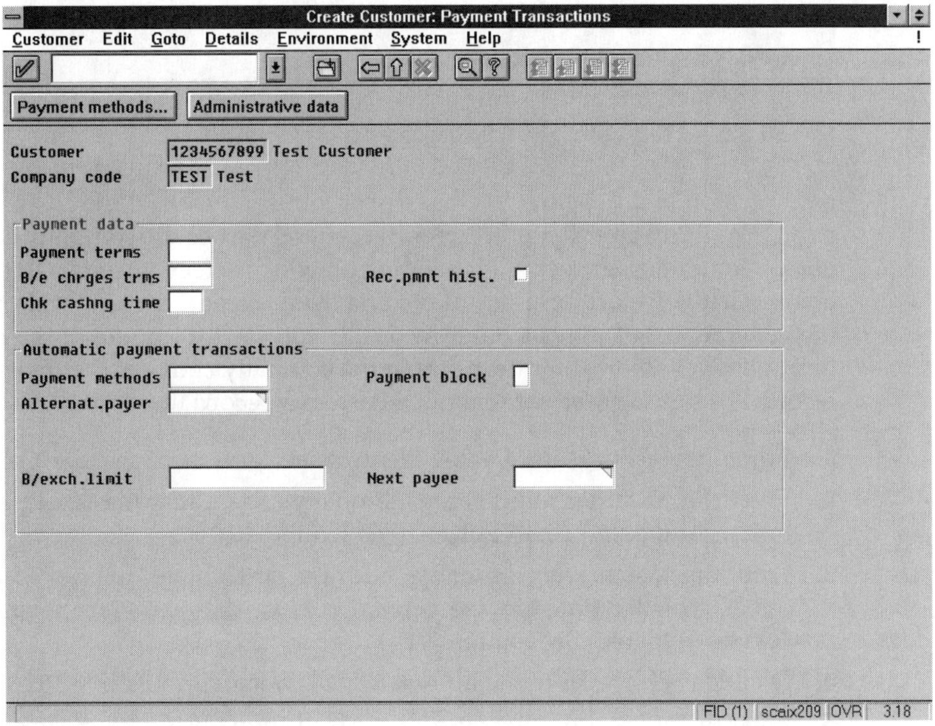

Exhibit 3.8   Create Customer: Payment Transactions

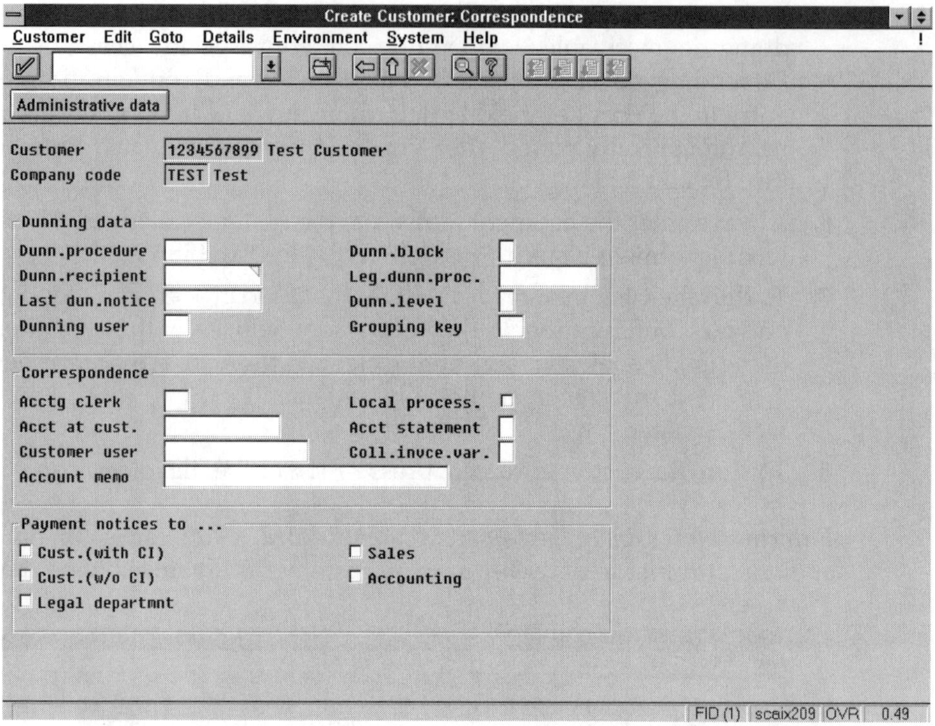

Exhibit 3.9 Create Customer: Correspondence

of the customer are, who is in charge of accounts payable at the customer, and so on. Notes can be entered in either the general part or the company code part of a customer master record, depending on which screen you start to enter the text from. If you start from one of the first three screens, then enter the notes in the general part of the customer record. If you start from one of screens four through seven, then enter the notes in the company code part of the customer record. To start to enter notes about a customer record that is already entered:

1. From the Accounts Receivable menu, select Master records → Change.

2. Enter the customer number and company code. Press the Select all push-button, and then press <Enter>. (See Exhibit 3.10.)

3. From the screen with the name, address, and phone number of the customer, to enter notes in the general part of the customer record, select Details → Texts. (See Exhibit 3.11.)

4. Double-click on the line with Accounting note. (See Exhibit 3.12.)

5. Enter the notes about the customer. This is done using the SAPScript line-oriented text editor. Keep the following in mind when using SAPScript:

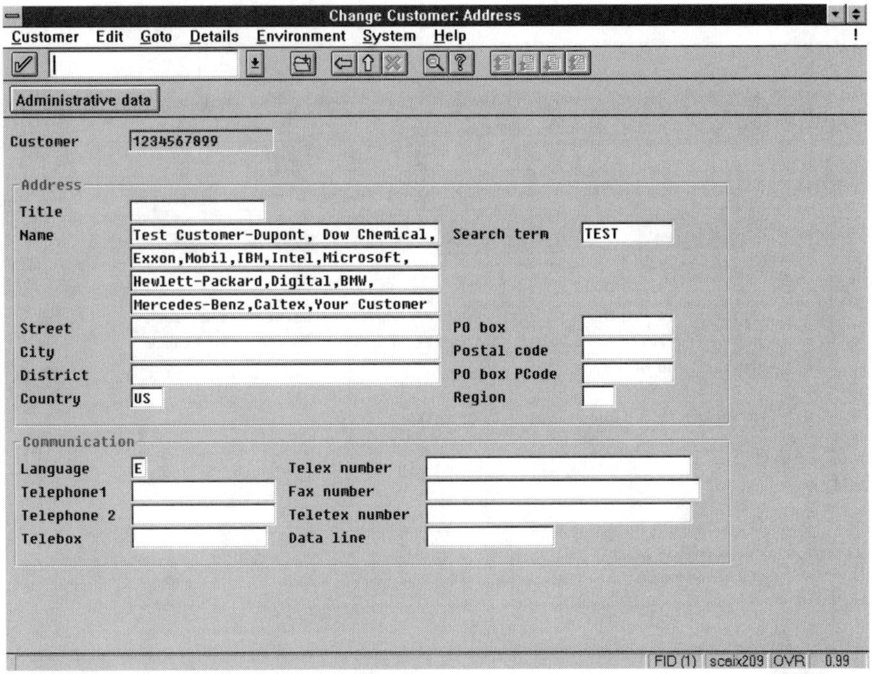

Exhibit 3.10 Change Customer: Address

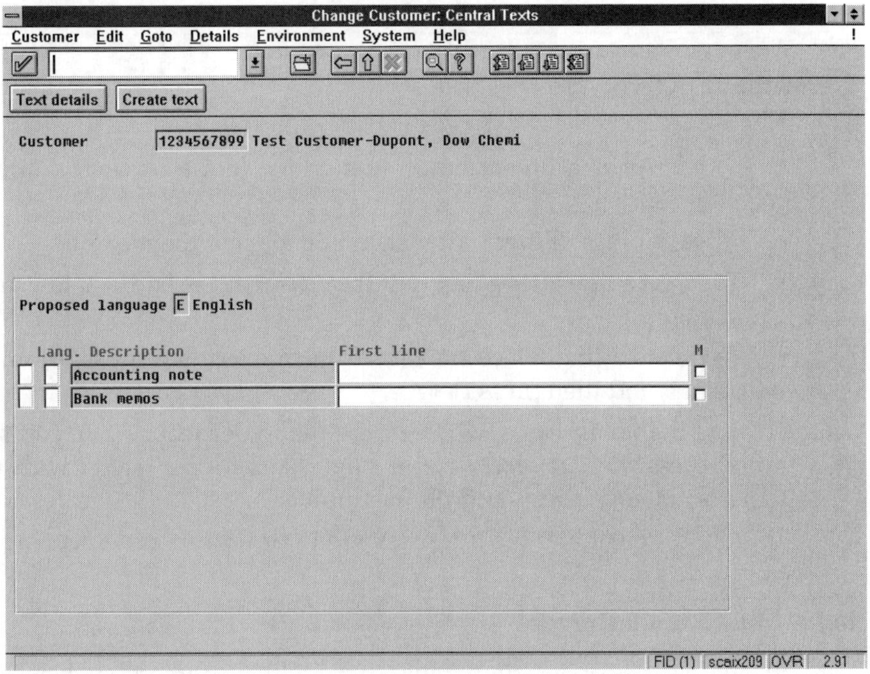

Exhibit 3.11 Change Customer: Central Texts

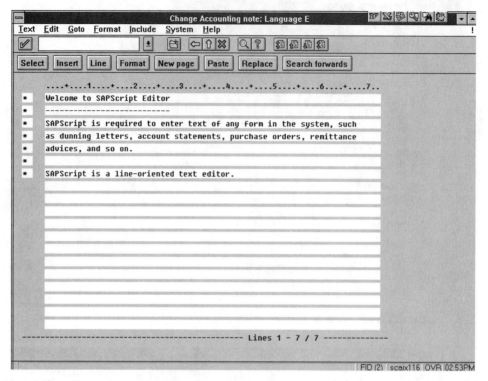

Exhibit 3.12   Change Accounting Note

- SAPScript is a line-oriented text editor (not a screen-oriented word processor).
- Always press <Enter> after each line to go to the next line.
- To insert a line after a line, put the cursor at the end of a line and press <Enter>.
- To delete a line, place the cursor in the very left-most column, press Select, and then press Delete.

6. To store the notes, press <F11> or the file folder icon. After you store the notes, press the left arrow twice to go back to the screen with the customer's name, address, and phone number.

7. To store the customer record, press <F11> or the file folder icon again.

Entering a One-time Customer

If you have a series of one-time transactions with customers, such as claims on insurance companies or retail transactions, you can enter a one-time customer master record. This avoids entering a series of customer master records that you post to only once. In this way, you enter one one-time master record and then you post the invoice to the one-time customer master record. When entering the invoice, you have the option to enter the specific name and address of the customer in the second screen of the invoice. To enter a one-time customer record:

1. From the Accounts Receivable menu, select Master records → Create. (See Exhibit 3.13.)

2. In the Customer field, enter a valid name or number of the customer, such as **onetime-gb,** a valid company code, and a valid customer account group. The validity of all of these entries depends on your configuration. Press <Enter>. (See Exhibit 3.14.)

3. Enter all required fields, depending on your configuration. On another screen, Create Customer: Account Management, also make sure that you enter a reconciliation account and a G/L account to be posted with any receivables from this one-time customer.

4. To store the master record after entering all required fields, press <F11> or the file folder icon.

Finding a Customer Number by Name, City, or Index

If you do not have the customer account number, you can find it by the name, city, or other index field predefined by SAP. On any screen where you are prompted to enter a customer account number, whether updating a cus-

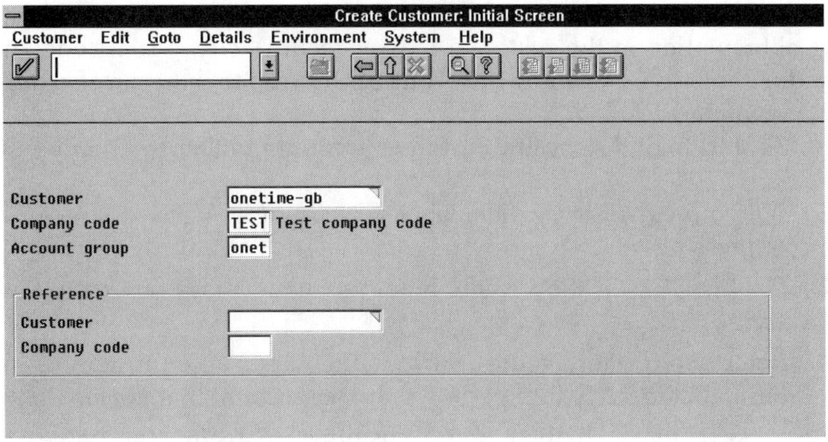

Exhibit 3.13 Create Customer: Initial Screen

```
 ─                          Create Customer: Address                      ▼ ＋
   Customer   Edit   Goto   Details   Environment   System   Help                  !
  ☑ │            │  ±   ▦  ⇐⇧☒   ◎?   ▤▤▤▤
  ┌─────────────────────┐
  │ Administrative data │
  └─────────────────────┘
   Customer      │ONETIME-GB        │

  ┌─Address──────────────────────────────────────────────────────────────┐
  │                                                                        │
  │  Name       │Onetime Customer - Britain     │   Search term  │onetime-gb│
  │             │                               │                          │
  │                                                                        │
  │                                                                        │
  │                                                                        │
  │  Country    │GB│                                                       │
  └────────────────────────────────────────────────────────────────────────┘
  ┌─Communication─────────────────────────────────────────────────────────┐
  │  Language    │E│                                                       │
  │                                                                        │
  │                                                                        │
  └────────────────────────────────────────────────────────────────────────┘
```

Exhibit 3.14   Create Customer: Address

tomer master record, entering a customer invoice, or entering a customer payment, you can look up the customer number using a matchcode. A matchcode is simply an index to a file, like a card in a card catalog in a library. All the customers are indexed by their name, search term (short name or abbreviation in the customer master record), city, postal code (zip code), and other fields. Depending on your configuration, you can also define your own matchcodes.

To start to find a specific customer account number by an index:

1. Put your cursor in the field labeled Account and click on the down arrow or press <F4>.
2. Double-click on the specific index, such as ☐ Customers [by company code].
3. Enter one or more values, such as the name, account number, or search term, that identify the specific customer account that you are looking for.
4. Press <Enter>. If there is no customer matching the values that you entered, you see a message. If there is only one customer that matches your criteria, then the program puts this account number in the Account field.

If there is a set of customers that match your criteria, then you see this set on your screen.

Note that you can also define fields other than the ones predefined by SAP as index fields, but that is beyond the scope of this book, since it requires analysis and competent configuration, which are already assumed in this book.

Displaying a Customer Master Record

To display a customer record:

1. From the Accounts Receivable menu, select Master records ➤ Display.
2. Enter the customer number and company code. To see all seven screens about the customer, press the Select all pushbutton, and then press <Enter>. To see a specific screen, click on the name of that specific screen, and then press <Enter>.
3. Press <Enter> to go to the next screen, if you have selected it from the very first screen.

Updating a Customer Record

If you have a separate customer file in an external order entry system, it is advisable to coordinate updates to the customer files. If you use SD for order entry, shipping, and invoicing, it is advisable to restrict who can update customer master data. To edit (update) a customer record in FI:

1. From the Accounts Receivable menu, select Master records ➤ Change.
2. Enter the customer number and company code. To edit all seven screens about the customer, press the Select all pushbutton, and then press <Enter>. To edit data on a specific screen, click on the name of that specific screen, and then press <Enter>.
3. Press <Enter> to go to the next screen, if you have selected it from the very first screen.

Printing a Customer List

To print or display the customer list, using the program supplied by SAP:

1. From the Accounts Receivable menu, select Periodic processing ➤ Reporting ➤ Account list. (See Exhibit 3.15.)
2. Enter at least the company code, and then press <F8> or the Execute pushbutton to run the program. Press the + in the lower-right corner to go to the next screen of parameters. (See Exhibit 3.16.)

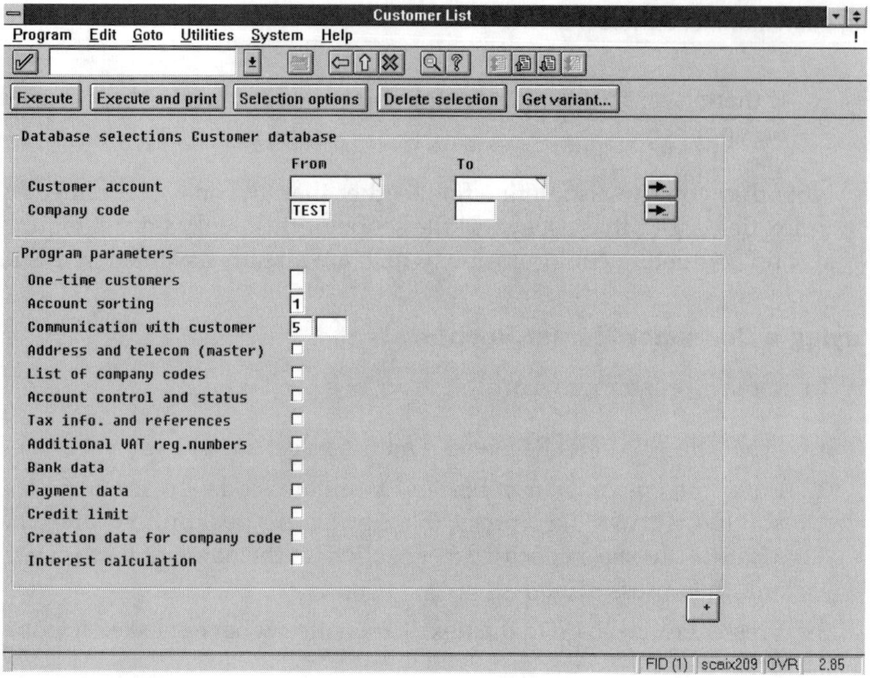

Exhibit 3.15   Customer List, Screen One

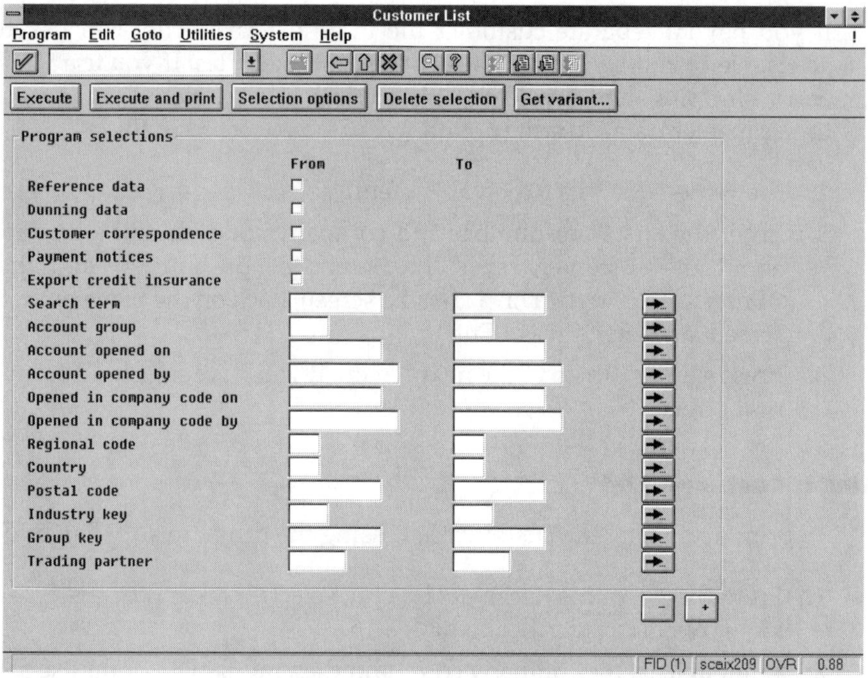

Exhibit 3.16   Customer List, Screen Two

3. Optionally, enter one or a range of parameters to select a portion of your customer list. Press + to go to the next screen of parameters or - to go to the previous screen of parameters. For now, press +. (See Exhibit 3.17.)

4. Optionally, enter parameters to restrict your search. To run the program and print the list, press Execute and print.

Checking the Printing in Process

The program places the report in a temporary file on the disk called a spool file. The concept is the same as a mainframe spool file. To check the printing in process:

1. From any menu, select System → Services → Output controller. Press <Enter> to see a list of print runs that you have done.

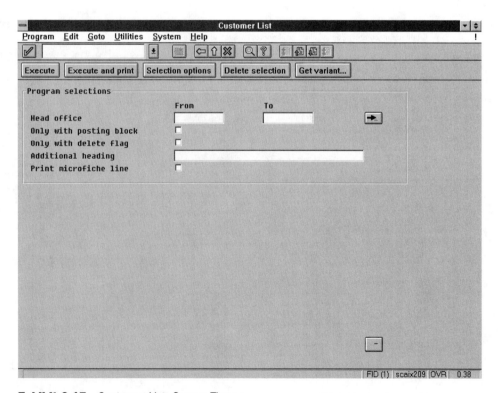

Exhibit 3.17 Customer List, Screen Three

CONTROLLING CUSTOMER CREDIT

You enter a credit limit either in an individual customer account or in a credit account, which is a set of related customer accounts. A credit account is also called a reference customer.

Entering an Individual Credit Limit

To enter an individual credit limit:

1. From the Accounts Receivable menu, select Master records → Credit management → Maintain. (See Exhibit 3.18.)
2. Enter the customer account number in the Customer field and the credit control area in the Credit control area field. Click on Select all. Press <Enter>. (See Exhibit 3.19.)
3. Keep pressing <Enter> to see the credit data screens that you selected (all five in this example). The next two screens are shown in Exhibits 3.20 and 3.21.

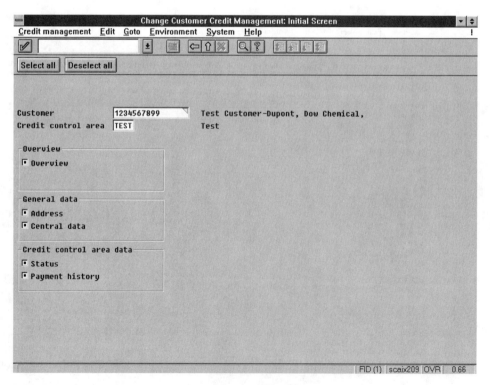

Exhibit 3.18   Change Customer Credit Management: Initial Screen

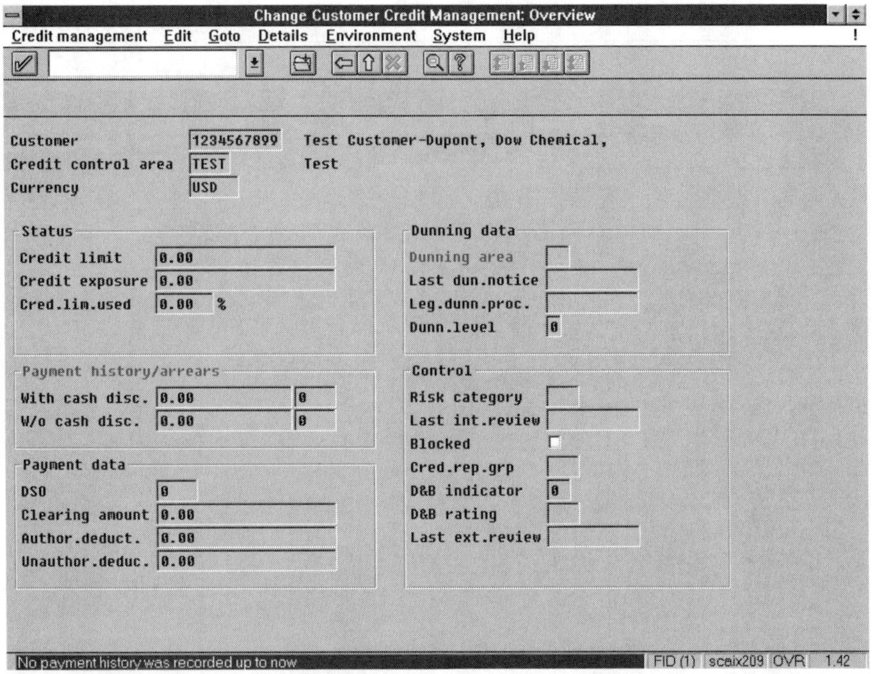

Change Customer Credit Management: Overview

Credit management   Edit   Goto   Details   Environment   System   Help   !

Customer   1234567899   Test Customer-Dupont, Dow Chemical,
Credit control area   TEST   Test
Currency   USD

Status

Credit limit   0.00
Credit exposure   0.00
Cred.lim.used   0.00   %

Dunning data

Dunning area
Last dun.notice
Leg.dunn.proc.
Dunn.level   0

Payment history/arrears

With cash disc.   0.00   0
W/o cash disc.   0.00   0

Control

Risk category
Last int.review
Blocked
Cred.rep.grp
D&B indicator   0
D&B rating
Last ext.review

Payment data

DSO   0
Clearing amount   0.00
Author.deduct.   0.00
Unauthor.deduc.   0.00

No payment history was recorded up to now   FID (1)   scaix209   OVR   1.42

Exhibit 3.19   Change Customer Credit Management: Overview

Change Customer Credit Management: Address

Credit management   Edit   Goto   Details   Environment   System   Help   !

Customer   1234567899

Address

Title
Name   Test Customer-Dupont, Dow Chemical,   Search term   TEST
     Exxon,Mobil,IBM,Intel,Microsoft,
     Hewlett-Packard,Digital,BMW,
     Mercedes-Benz,Caltex,Your Customer
Street   PO box
City   Postal code
District   PO box PCode
Country   US   Region

Communication

Language   E   Telex number
Telephone1   Fax number
Telephone 2   Teletex number
Telebox   Data line

FID (1)   scaix209   OVR   0.66

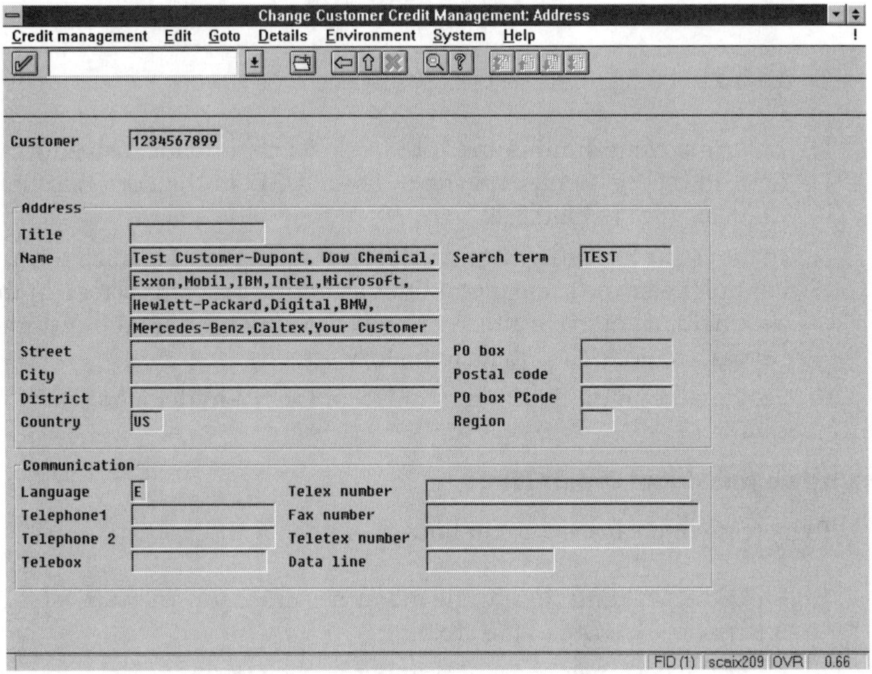

Exhibit 3.20   Change Customer Credit Management: Address

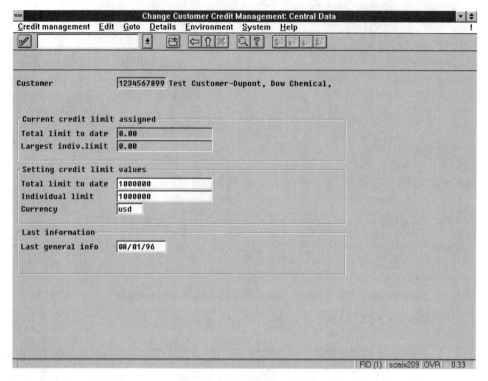

Exhibit 3.21   Change Customer Credit Management: Central Data

4. Enter the credit limit in the Total limit to date field. Also enter the same limit in the Individual limit field. Enter **USD** in the Currency field. Press <Enter>. (See Exhibit 3.22.)

5. In the Credit limit data section, depending on your organization and credit control, enter the same credit limit as on the previous screen in the Credit limit field. If you have already received payments from the customer, press <Enter> to go to the Payment history screen.

6. To store the credit limit, press <F11> or the file folder icon.

Changing an Individual Credit Limit

To increase or decrease a credit limit:

1. From the Accounts Receivable menu, select Master records → Credit management → Maintain. (See Exhibit 3.23.)

2. Enter the customer account number in the Customer field and the credit control area in the Credit control area field depending on your organization. Click on Central data and Status. Press <Enter>.

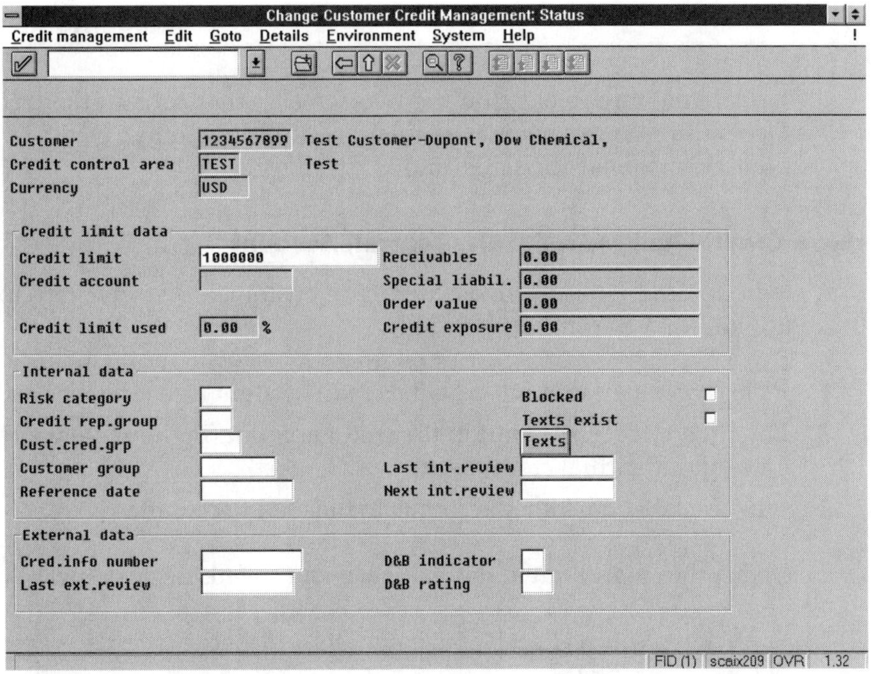

Exhibit 3.22 Change Customer Credit Status

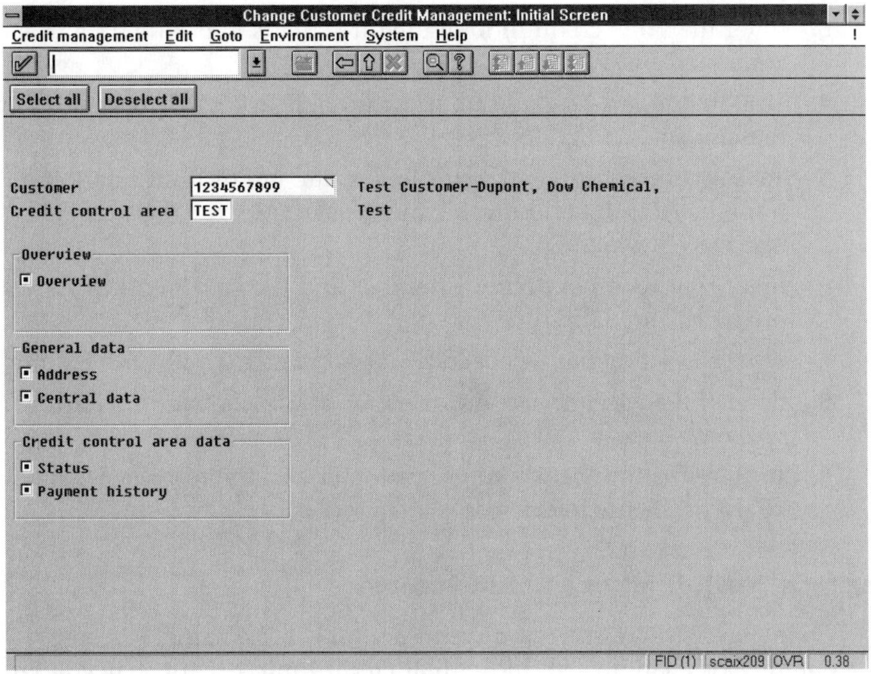

Exhibit 3.23 Change Customer Credit Limit

3. Update the three fields (on the two screens) that contain the credit limit. Depending on how your company controls customer credit, it may be advisable to enter the same amount in all three fields.

Entering a Credit Limit for a Credit (Central) Account

A credit account is also called a reference customer. Step by step, to enter a credit limit for a credit account, you:

1. Pick a customer account to be the credit account (the reference customer).
2. Enter the total credit limit in the credit account (in the same way that you enter an individual credit limit).
3. Link the other customer accounts to the credit account.

First, enter the credit limit in the credit account (reference customer) as follows:

1. From the Accounts Receivable menu, select Master records ➤ Credit management ➤ Maintain.
2. Enter the customer account number and the credit control area, and then press <Enter>. Click on Central data and Status. (See Exhibit 3.24.)
3. Enter the same credit limit in the three fields in both the Central data and Status screens.
4. To store the central credit limit in the credit account, press <F11> or the file folder icon.
5. To link an individual account to a group credit limit in another account, from the Accounts Receivable menu select Master records ➤ Credit management ➤ Maintain.
6. Enter the customer account number and the credit control area and then press <Enter>. Click on Status.
7. From the action bar, select Edit ➤ Change reference. (See Exhibit 3.25.)
8. Enter the customer account number of the central (reference) customer. Press <Enter>.
9. To store the link between this customer and the reference customer, press <F11> or the file folder icon.

Changing a Credit Limit of a Credit Account

Changing a credit limit of a credit account is the same, screen-by-screen, as entering or changing an individual credit limit, except that you change the credit limit of the credit account (reference customer) only.

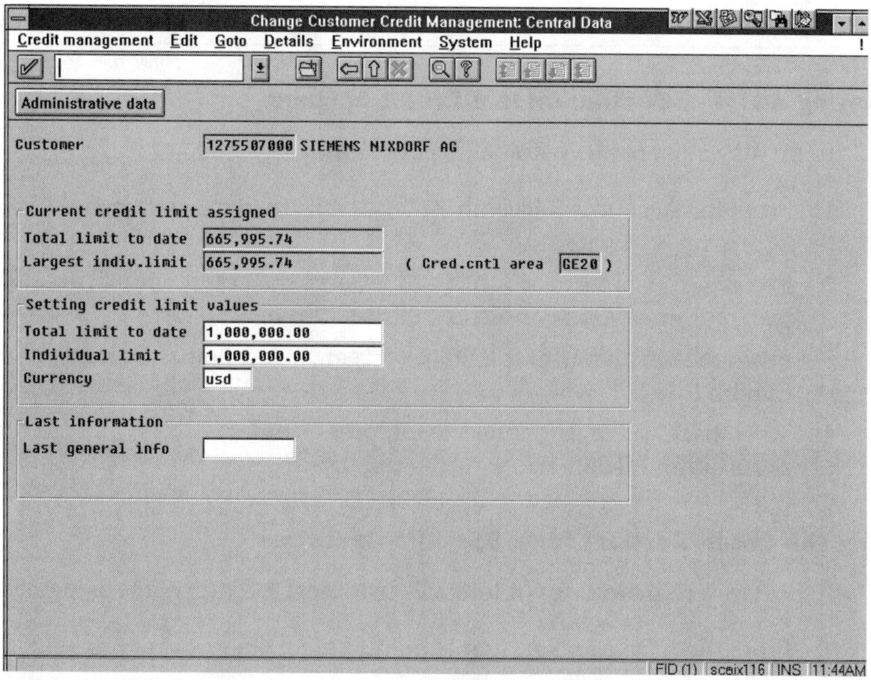

Exhibit 3.24 Change Customer Credit Management: Central Data

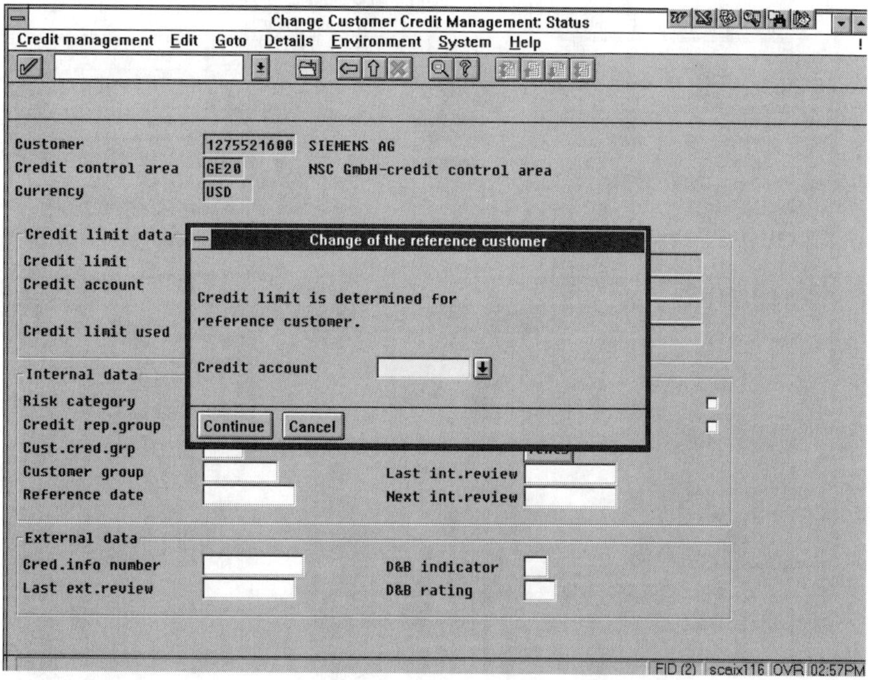

Exhibit 3.25 Change of the Reference Customer

Displaying a List of Customers in a Credit Account

To display a list of all customer accounts in a credit account:

1. From the Accounts Receivable menu, select Master records → Credit management → Maintain.

2. Enter the customer account number and the credit control area, and then press <Enter>. Click on Status. Press <Enter>.

3. From the action bar of the Status screen, select Edit → Reference list. (See Exhibit 3.26.)

4. To go back to the previous screen, press <Enter>. To go back to the menu, press either the left arrow or the up arrow.

Finding the Credit Account for a Specific Customer

To find the credit account (reference customer) for a specific customer account:

1. From the Accounts Receivable menu, select Master records → Credit management → Maintain.

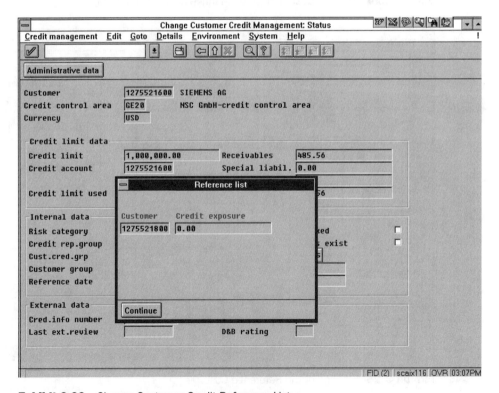

Exhibit 3.26   Change Customer Credit Reference List

2. Enter the customer account number and the credit control area, and then press <Enter>. Click on Status. Press <Enter>.

3. Look in the Credit account field for the credit account (reference account) number.

Reporting Credit Limits by Customer

To display a brief list of customers (individual customer accounts and credit accounts) and their credit limits:

1. From the Accounts Receivable menu, select Periodic processing ➤ Credit management ➤ Reporting ➤ Brief overview. (See Exhibit 3.27.)

2. Enter a customer or a range of customers in the Customers for credit limit field. Alternatively, to see all customers and their credit limits in a specific company code, enter the company code in the Company code field. To run the program, press <F8> or the Execute pushbutton. (See Exhibit 3.28.)

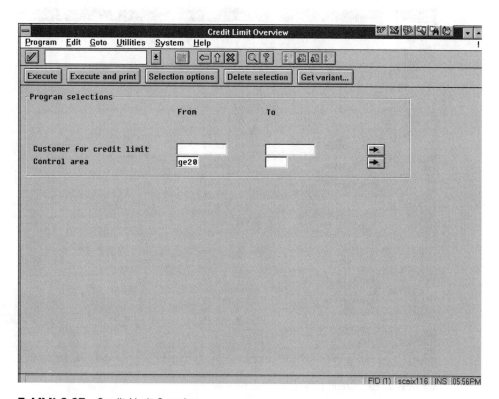

Exhibit 3.27   Credit Limit Overview

Reporting Credit Limits and Balances by Customer

To display a list of customers, their credit limits, and the total balance for each customer (individual customer accounts and credit accounts):

1. From the Accounts Receivable menu, select Periodic processing → Credit management → Reporting → Overview. (See Exhibit 3.29.)
2. To see the credit limits and account balances for all customers in the control area, enter the control area in the Control area field. To run the program, press <F8> or the Execute pushbutton. (See Exhibit 3.30.)

ENTERING AND POSTING CUSTOMER INVOICES

If you are thinking of implementing SAP, it may be desirable for you to do it step by step, starting with your general ledger, accounts receivable, and accounts payable only. In this first step, you enter and post customer invoices

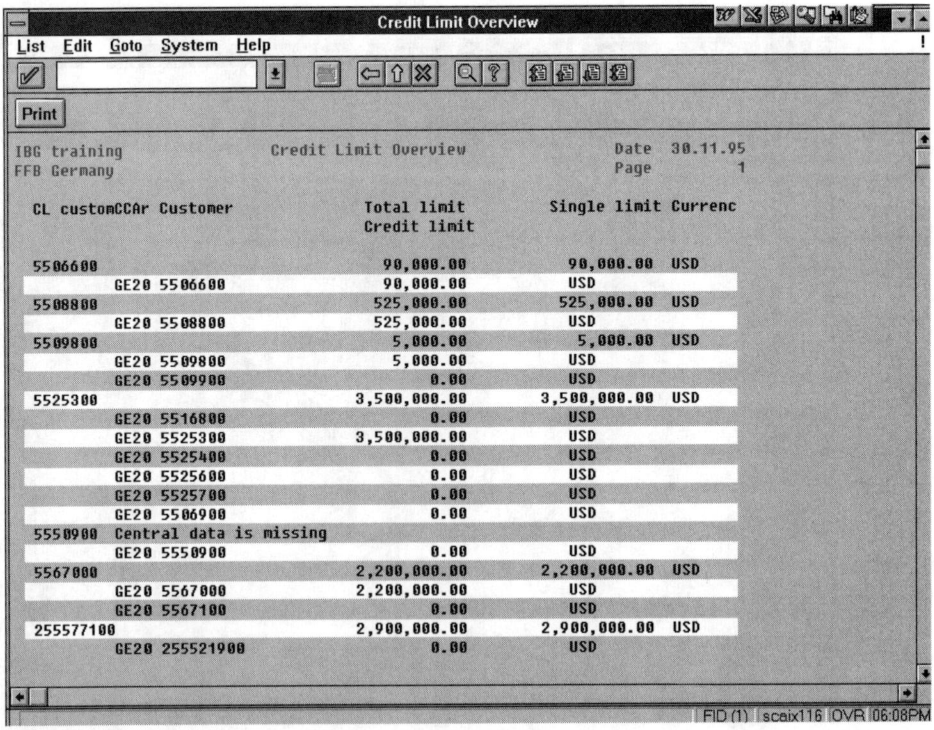

Exhibit 3.28 Credit Limit Overview: Result

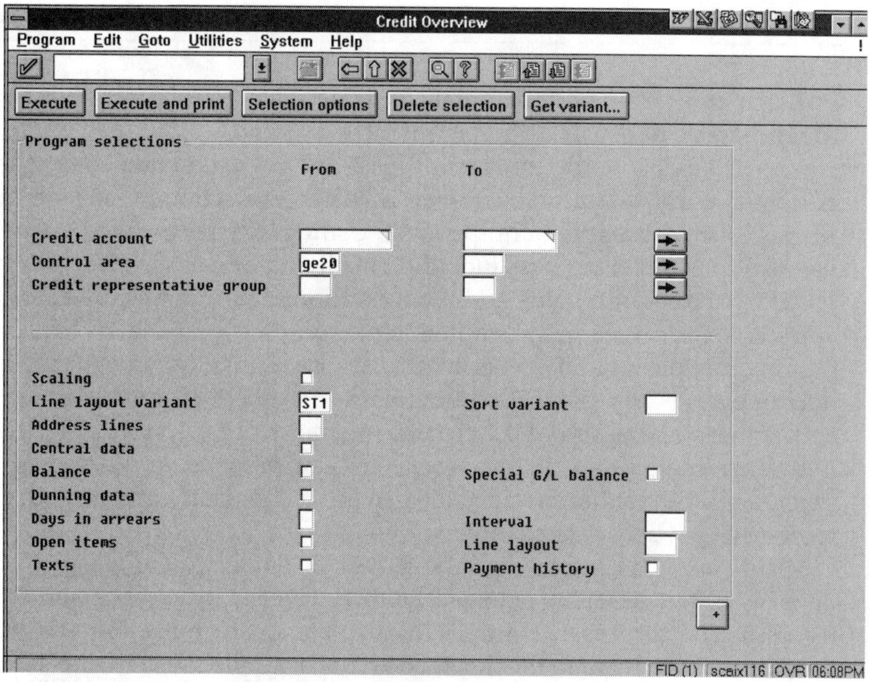

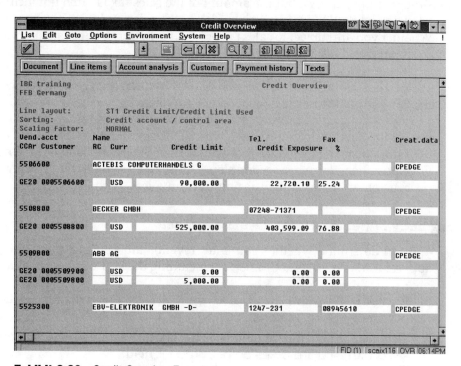

Exhibit 3.29   Credit Overview in Control Area

Exhibit 3.30   Credit Overview Executed

by batch input from your external invoicing system. This section is applicable to companies that enter customer invoices by hand.

A customer invoice contains at least one revenue entry and at least one customer entry. Usually, customer invoices also contain one or more tax entries, such as sales tax or output VAT. Using FI, there can be a total of 999 line items in a customer invoice, including tax items. Depending on your country-specific legal requirements and configuration, FI automatically calculates the applicable tax and generates a line item. You then post the invoice. To post a customer invoice (or any other regular transaction), you have to comply with only one absolute technical requirement—that the total amount of the debits equals the total amount of the credits. In other words, you cannot post an out-of-balance transaction. In this way, you can prepare an up-to-date balance sheet almost immediately, since the general ledger is integrated with accounts receivable and accounts payable.

Sales tax is a country-specific aspect of entering and posting customer invoices. Often, sales tax is levied on three levels: city, county, and state. SAP recommends third-party routines to calculate, post, and report sales tax. With this in mind, and due to the fact that VAT is a simpler system, the examples in this book assume that you are calculating and posting output VAT. Sales tax is similar to output VAT, but the amount of the sales tax is often not included in the price, while VAT is usually included in the price, unless otherwise marked. Whether you are subject to sales tax or VAT, make sure your system is properly configured and tested.

You might already have an external system to print invoices. In this case, you can post these invoices by batch input. First, convert the invoice records to the batch input format and then load the invoices by batch input.

If you are using SD (sales and distribution) for order entry, shipping, and invoicing, enter and post invoices with SD. Depending on the billing type in SD, either post an SD invoice that you print in SD immediately to accounts in FI, or post the invoice in a second step. This section assumes that you enter and post customer invoices, such as non-trade invoices, with FI.

Setting Entry of Net (or Gross) Revenue Amounts

You can determine whether you enter revenue amount gross, including any applicable VAT or sales tax, or net, not including the VAT or sales tax as follows:

1. From the Accounts Receivable menu, select Environment ➤ Current options ➤ Editing options.

2. To enter the net amount (and base the tax calculation on the net amount), select the Calculate taxes on net amount field.

Posting a Customer Invoice in Local Currency

You enter and post an invoice as follows:

1. Start the function by selecting Document entry ➟ Invoice from the Accounts Receivable menu.
2. Enter the invoice header.
3. Enter two or more line items (up to 999).
4. Post the invoice.

This section describes each of these steps.

1. From the Accounts Receivable menu, select Document entry ➟ Invoice. See Exhibit 3.31 for the first screen.
2. The top half of the screen contains the transaction header. The following five fields are always required in a transaction header:

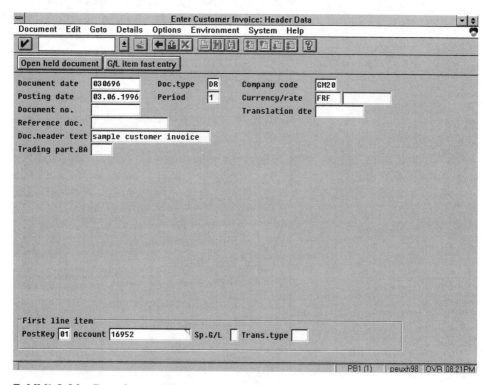

Exhibit 3.31 Enter Customer Invoice: Header Data

Field	*Note*
Document date	This is usually today's date, but could be different.
Doc.type	This is an SAP term for a journal. The most frequently used journals in Accounts Receivable are CI (customer invoices), CM (credit memos), and CP (customer payments).
	With your cursor in this field, press the down arrow for a list of available journals (i.e., document types) in your configuration.
Company code	Enter the company whose books you are keeping.
Posting date	This is also usually today's date, but could be different. The posting date determines the period in which FI updates the account balances, after you post the invoice.
Currency/rate	Enter a code for the currency of the transaction. Use the ISO code for the currency, which always has three characters. The first two characters represent the country. The third character represents the currency. The following are commonly used currency codes:

ATS	Austrian shillings
AUD	Australian dollars
BEF	Belgian francs
CAD	Canadian dollars
CHF	Swiss francs
CNY	Chinese yuan
DEM	German marks
DKK	Danish krona
ESP	Spanish pesetas
FIM	Finnish marks
FRF	French francs
GBP	British pounds
HKD	Hong Kong dollars
ILS	Israeli shekels
INR	Indian rupees
ITL	Italian lire
JPY	Japanese yen
KPW	Korean won

MXN	Mexican new pesos
MYR	Malaysian ringgit
NLG	Dutch guilders
NOK	Norwegian krona
SEK	Swedish krona
SGD	Singapore dollars
THB	Thai baht
TWD	Taiwan dollars
USD	US dollars

For a complete list of the currency codes, put your cursor in this field and then click on the down arrow just to the right of this field. Foreign currency is any currency that is different from the local reporting currency of the company code where you are posting the transaction. If you enter a code for a foreign currency, then you can also enter an exchange rate in the field immediately to the right of the field with the currency code.

Ignore the Period field. FI automatically determines the posting period based on the posting date and your fiscal year as configured. Assuming that your configuration has a "document type" CI (customer invoice) and that these transactions are set up to be numbered internally (automatically by FI when you post), then leave the Document no. field blank. Immediately after posting the invoice, FI assigns the invoice a number, based on the available number range. You can enter a reference number, such as a printed invoice number from an external system in the Reference doc. field. Your system can also be set up so you can enter the printed invoice number into the Document no. field (external invoice numbering). The "document" must always be a unique number for each invoice, whether you use internal numbering or external numbering. Optionally, you can describe the transaction briefly, using the Doc. header text field.

3. At the end of this screen, enter the posting key in the PostKey field. To debit a customer account, enter a posting key of **01.** Also enter a customer account number in the Account field.

4. Press <Enter>. The program then validates all the data on the first screen and determines the posting period. Among other validations, FI verifies that you have entered the dates correctly. It also verifies that the posting period is open, that the company code and currency code exist, and that the posting key and G/L account exist. Assuming that all of these and other conditions are true, then you see the screen shown in Exhibit 3.32.

5. On the second screen to enter a customer invoice, enter the amount in the Amount field. Note that, at the end of the previous screen, you have already specified whether this amount is a debit or a credit and in which account you are entering this amount. Also enter the Business area (division). Optionally, enter a description of this line item in the Text field. At the end of this screen, enter the posting key and account of the second line item. For example, to enter a credit to a revenue account, enter **50** in the PostKey field and enter a G/L account number for revenue, such as **701100,** in the Account field.

6. Press <Enter>. The program validates the data entered on this screen and then displays the next screen shown in Exhibit 3.33.

7. To see an overview of the customer invoice, press the pushbutton (on the fourth row of the window) marked Overview. The overview looks like the screen shown in Exhibit 3.34.

8. Note that the total debits appear near the lower left corner of the screen just to the right of the letter D, while the total credits appear just to the right of the letter C. If the debits equal the credits, then the balance of the

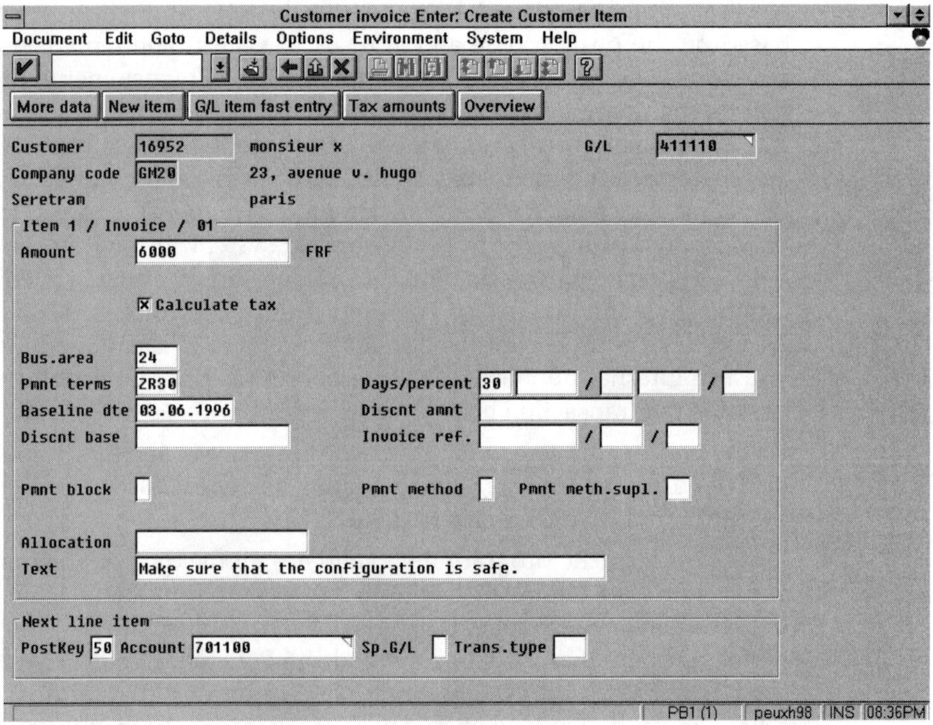

Exhibit 3.32   Customer Invoice Enter: Create Customer Item

```
Enter G/L account document: Create G/L Account Item                    _ 🗗 ✕
Document  Edit  Goto  Extras  Settings  Environment  System  Help
✔ [        ▼] 🖪 ← ⬆ ✕ 🖪🖩🖾 🖪🗂🗂🗂 ?
👤 🖪 🖪 🗋 | More data | Act assgnmt model... | G/L item fast entry | Tax amounts
```

G/L account   701100   VENTES DE PRODUITS FINIS – A
Company code   TEST TEST

┌ Item 1 / Credit entry / 50 ─────────────────────────────
  Amount   6000   FRF
  Tax code   A0   ☑ Calculate tax

  Business area   test   Trading part.BA [   ]
  Cost center   [▽]

  Purchasing doc. [▽]
  Value date   [   ]
  Allocation   [   ]
  Text   sample GL entry for sales of finished product [±]

┌ Next line item ──────────────────────────────────────
  PstKy [   ] Account [▽] Sp.G/L [ ] Trans.type [ ] New co.code [   ]

```
                                    P11 (2) (003) | axp4100 | INS |11:01PM
```

Exhibit 3.33 Customer Invoice: Create G/L Line Item

invoice is zero and □ appears on the same line. Also note that you can enter another line item by entering a posting key and an account number at the bottom of this screen. To delete a line, double-click on the line and then enter zero in the amount on the line item screen. If a mistaken amount is entered, double-click on the item in this overview, and then re-

```
─                        Display Document: Overview                    ▼ ◆
Document   Edit   Goto   Options   Environment   System   Help
✔ [        ±] 🖪 ← ⬆ ✕ 🖪🖩🖾 🖪🗂🗂🗂 ?
| Choose | Document header | Taxes | Display currency |
```

Document no.   1800000010   Company code GM20   Fiscal year 1997
Document date 03.06.1996   Intercomp.no.
Reference doc. [   ]   Debit/credit   6,000.00
Currency   FRF
┌ Items in document currency ─────────────────────────

Itm	PK	BusA	Acct no.	Description	TC	Tax	Amount in	FRF
001	01	24	0000016952	monsieur x			6,000.00	
002	50	24	0000701100	Sales-training & do	A4		4,975.13-	
003	50		0000445710	TVA COLLECTEE	A4		1,024.87-	

Exhibit 3.34 Display Customer Invoice

enter the amount on the next screen. If you have entered a mistaken posting date in the transaction header, it cannot be changed on this screen. You must exit this function without posting the invoice and then enter the transaction again with the correct posting date. This is due to the fact that the program has already validated the posting date and determined the posting period from the invoice header that you entered on the first screen.

9. To post the customer invoice, either press <F11> or press the file folder icon. Note that you can often do the same thing in two ways.

   The program then validates the invoice. Most of all, the program verifies that the total debits equal the total credits. It also checks whether the tax code is valid and then calculates the tax and posts the tax item. Calculating, posting, and reporting transaction taxes (VAT or sales tax) depend on country-specific legal requirements and also on the configuration. Calculating, posting, and reporting sales tax is usually done with third-party software routines. Last, if you have internal transaction numbering, the program assigns a number to the invoice and updates the customer and G/L account balances in the posting period.

Displaying the Last Posted Invoice

To verify that the invoice is properly posted, display the last posted transaction. From the Enter Customer Invoice: Header Data menu, select Document → Display.

The overview of the customer invoice looks like the screen shown in Exhibit 3.35.

Entering an Invoice in Foreign Currency

Foreign currency is any currency that is different from local currency, which is the reporting currency of the company code to which you are posting the transaction. To enter an invoice in foreign currency, enter the currency of the invoice in the header. You can then enter the exchange rate of this invoice in one of three ways:

1. Enter exchange rates in a table of exchange rates by validity dates. FI then automatically transfers the most recent exchange rate valid on or before the posting date of the invoice. You can also override the transfer on the posting date by entering a translation date in the header of the invoice.

2. Enter an exchange rate directly in the invoice by entering the number of units of local currency per unit of foreign currency.

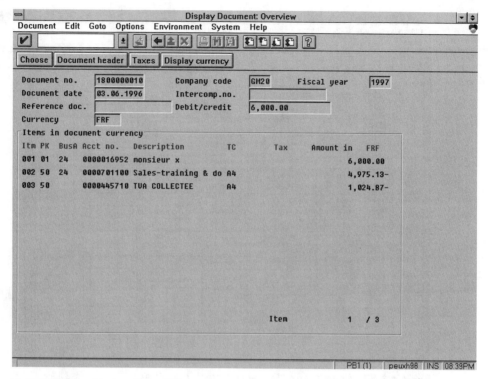

Exhibit 3.35 Display Customer Invoice

3. Enter the local currency amount and the foreign currency amount in each line item.

Note that a transaction can be entered in any currency, but you can only enter a transaction in one currency. For example, if you have a credit card invoice with line items in various currencies, you have to enter each line in the credit card invoice as a separate transaction.

Entering an Exchange Rate in the Rate Table. To enter an exchange rate in the rate table:

1. From the Accounts Receivable menu, select Environment → Current options → Exchange rates. (See Exhibit 3.36.)
2. To start to add a new entry to the table, press New entries. (See Exhibit 3.37.)
3. To add a new entry, first enter the exchange rate type. An exchange rate type of **M** is always used for revaluing all transactions posted. Depending on your configuration, you can define other exchange rate types for other

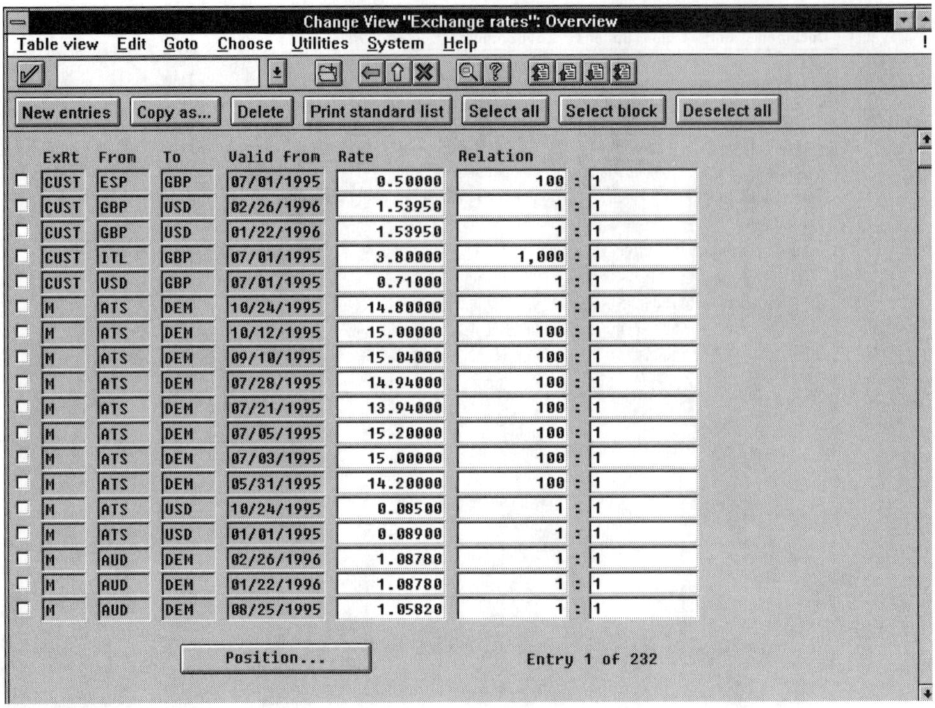

	ExRt	From	To	Valid from	Rate	Relation		
☐	CUST	ESP	GBP	07/01/1995	0.50000	100	:	1
☐	CUST	GBP	USD	02/26/1996	1.53950	1	:	1
☐	CUST	GBP	USD	01/22/1996	1.53950	1	:	1
☐	CUST	ITL	GBP	07/01/1995	3.80000	1,000	:	1
☐	CUST	USD	GBP	07/01/1995	0.71000	1	:	1
☐	M	ATS	DEM	10/24/1995	14.80000	1	:	1
☐	M	ATS	DEM	10/12/1995	15.00000	100	:	1
☐	M	ATS	DEM	09/10/1995	15.04000	100	:	1
☐	M	ATS	DEM	07/28/1995	14.94000	100	:	1
☐	M	ATS	DEM	07/21/1995	13.94000	100	:	1
☐	M	ATS	DEM	07/05/1995	15.20000	100	:	1
☐	M	ATS	DEM	07/03/1995	15.00000	100	:	1
☐	M	ATS	DEM	05/31/1995	14.20000	100	:	1
☐	M	ATS	USD	10/24/1995	0.08500	1	:	1
☐	M	ATS	USD	01/01/1995	0.08900	1	:	1
☐	M	AUD	DEM	02/26/1996	1.08780	1	:	1
☐	M	AUD	DEM	01/22/1996	1.08780	1	:	1
☐	M	AUD	DEM	08/25/1995	1.05820	1	:	1

Position...   Entry 1 of 232

Exhibit 3.36   Change View "Exchange Rates": Overview

purposes. Then enter the From and To currencies. The From currency is usually the foreign currency of the transaction, while the To currency is usually local currency. Enter the validity date. When you enter a transaction in foreign currency (a currency different from local currency), the program takes the most recent exchange rate on or before the posting date of

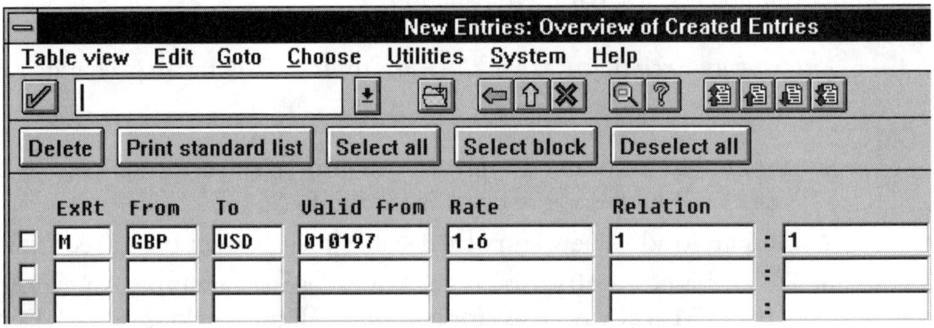

	ExRt	From	To	Valid from	Rate	Relation		
☐	M	GBP	USD	010197	1.6	1	:	1
☐							:	
☐							:	

Exhibit 3.37   New Entries: Overview of Created Entries

the transaction, if you do not specify a translation date for the transaction. Last, enter the exchange rate in units of the To currency to be exchanged for one unit of the From currency. Optionally, use the Relation field as a factor of the exchange rate to enter exchange rates related to currencies with unusually large numbers (small units), such as Italian lire (ITL), Spanish Pesetas (ESP), or Korean Won (KPW).

4. To store the new exchange rate, press <F11> or the file folder icon.

Setting Entry of Transaction Currency Only. If, when entering transactions in foreign currency, you always enter the amounts in foreign currency only, then you can simplify the data entry by suppressing the fields for the amounts in local currency from the screen.

To enter transaction amounts in transaction currency only,

1. Select Environment → Current options → Editing options. (See Exhibit 3.38.)
2. Click on the option Amount fields only for document currency.
3. Press <F11> or the file folder icon.

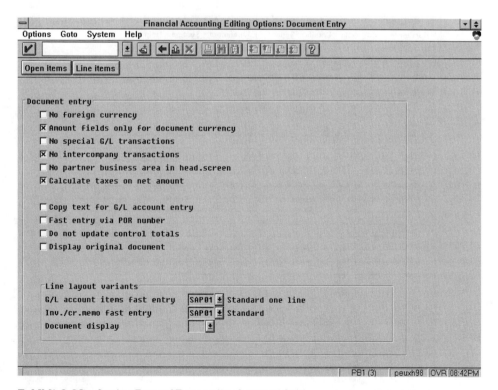

Exhibit 3.38 Setting Entry of Transaction Currency Only

Entering an Exchange Rate in the Invoice

Entering G/L Items in an Invoice Quickly.   Assume you have an invoice with a series of G/L entries, such as revenue entries. You can enter the series of G/L entries on one screen, instead of entering each line on a separate screen. This can speed up data entry.

To enter G/L items in a customer invoice quickly:

1. Start to enter a customer invoice as usual. From the Accounts Receivable menu, select Document entry ➤ Invoice.

2. At the top of the screen, enter the invoice header. At the bottom of the screen, enter the posting key and account for the first line item. Press <Enter> to go to the second screen.

3. On the second screen to enter an invoice, enter the amount of the customer entry. Click on the Calculate tax field, if it appears on your screen. Enter any other required fields in the customer entry.

4. Press the G/L item fast entry pushbutton. (See Exhibit 3.39.)

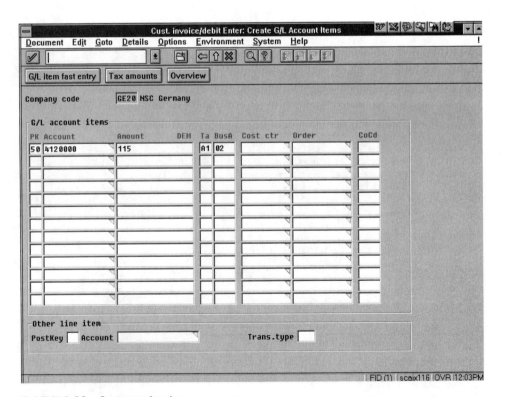

Exhibit 3.39   Customer Invoice

5. Note that you can enter a line item on each line. In each line, enter at least the posting key in the PK column, the G/L account number in the Account column, and the tax code in the Ta column. You can also enter a business area (division) in the BusA column, a cost center, and an internal order. If the invoice is an intercompany invoice, you can enter the other company code in the CoCd column. If you enter an intercompany transaction, FI can only post the transaction if the debits equal the credits in each transaction in each company code.

Entering a One-time Customer Invoice

The purpose of entering and posting a one-time customer invoice is to avoid filling up your customer file with customers' names and addresses that you post to only once. This assumes that you have already entered a master one-time customer master record. If not, then enter a one-time customer master record first. To enter a one-time customer invoice:

1. Enter and post the invoice as usual. From the Accounts Receivable menu, select Document entry → Invoice.

2. When prompted for a customer account number, enter the account number of the one-time customer master record, such as **ONETIME-GB**. On ... optionally enter the name and address of the one-time customer if you wish to keep this data.

3. If the total debits equal the total credits, post the invoice as usual. Press <F11> or the folder icon.

Reversing an Invoice

If you make a mistake posting an invoice, you can never delete it. You also cannot change the amounts nor the accounts. The simplest way to correct a mistake is to reverse the invoice. Reversing an invoice is also known as canceling an invoice. When you reverse an invoice (or any other transaction), FI changes a credit to a debit and a debit to a credit. You can then enter and post the invoice again.

If a customer invoice has already been posted with the SD (sales and distribution) module and you wish to cancel the invoice, always use SD to cancel the invoice. Otherwise, the invoice numbering will contain errors and your customer invoice totals will be inconsistent between FI and SD.

Assume you have entered a customer invoice with FI. You can reverse it as follows:

1. From the Accounts Receivable menu, select Document → Reverse. (See Exhibit 3.40.)

```
Huntley Bookstore
Of the Claremont Colleges
175 E. Eighth St.
Claremont CA. 91711
Phone# 909-621-8168

340  3877058118752  3877058   118.75
     USING SAPR3 F1

            SUB TOTAL  118.75
                DISC     0.00
           SALES TAX     9.80
               TOTAL   128.55
CASH                   130.00
                         0.00
          CHANGE DUE     1.45

SALE  1201 001 13:06:58 05/27/98 4274
Your Clerk Was: CELIA
CHECKS ARE SUBJECT TO A 14 DAY
WAITING PERIOD FOR CASH REFUND!

Thanks for shopping at Huntley.
```

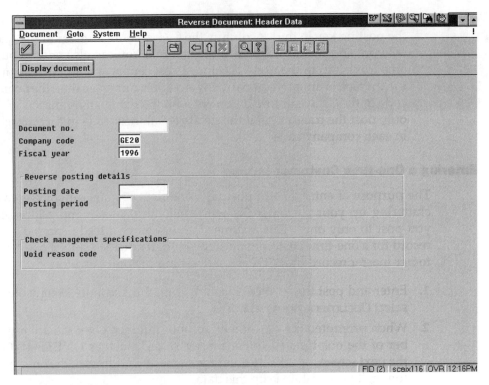

Exhibit 3.40 Reverse Document: Header Data

2. Enter the SAP "document" number in the Document no. field. Optionally, enter a posting date of the reversing transaction in the Posting date field. If you leave this field blank, then FI reverses the transaction on the same posting date as the original transaction. FI automatically determines the posting period from the posting date. Note that you can only reverse the transaction with internally assigned "document" numbers (numbers assigned by FI).

3. Press <F11> or the file folder icon to post the reversing transaction.

Note that, after you post, the system displays a message on the very last line of your screen. The message contains the "document" number and company code where FI posted the reversing transaction. To display the reversing transaction, from Reverse Document: Header Data menu, select Document ➤ Display.

INQUIRING IN ACCOUNTS RECEIVABLE

You can easily display the following information about a customer account:

- Open items
- Cleared (closed) items
- Account balances (by period and year-to-date)
- Total account balance with bills of exchange

When displaying line items (open or cleared), you can look for a specific item, sort, or subtotal the line items. When displaying customer account balances, you can drill down to the line items that make up an account balance. When a line item is displayed on your screen, you can go to the complete transaction containing that line item.

Displaying Monthly (Periodic) Account Balances

Customer account balances include period by period for the entire fiscal year the total debits for the period, the total credits for the period, and the balance for the period. The account balance screen also includes the fiscal year-to-date balance.

To display customer account balances:

1. From the Accounts Receivable menu, select Account → Display balances. (See Exhibit 3.41.)
2. Enter the customer account number, the company code, and the fiscal year. Press <Enter>. (See Exhibit 3.42.)
3. Notice the five columns of information on this screen. The first column is the posting period, according to the configuration of the company code. The second column contains the total debits posted to that customer in that posting period (in that fiscal year in that company code). The third column contains the total credits posted to that customer in that posting period (in that fiscal year in that company code). The fourth column contains the balance in that posting period. The fifth column contain the balance carried forward, including the balance of all previous periods. Notice that the most recent balance carried forward is also displayed in red in the lower-right corner of your screen.
4. To see the details of any of these balances, simply double-click on any balance. You then see the line items that make up the balance.

Displaying Line Items in a Customer Account

All customer accounts are open item accounts. You can display either open item or cleared (closed) items or both. The cleared items are displayed in a sep-

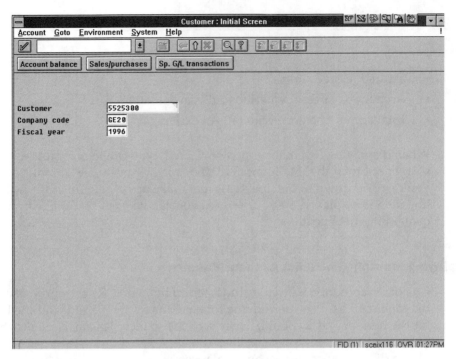

Exhibit 3.41   Customer: Initial Screen

Customer : Account Balance

Account   Edit   Goto   Details   Environment   System   Help

Line items | Account balance | Sales/purchases | Sp. G/L transactions

Customer 5525300 EBU-ELEKTRONIK GMB CoCde GE20 Year 1996 Currency DEM

Period	Debit	Credit	Balance DC	Account balance
C/f bal.				0.00
1	0.00	0.00	0.00	"
2	0.00	0.00	0.00	"
3	170,829.59	20,982.80	149,846.79	149,846.79
4	0.00	0.00	0.00	"
5	5,388,895.48	1,222,058.50	4,166,836.98	4,316,683.77
6	244,823.56	0.00	244,823.56	4,561,507.33
7	98,101.42	0.00	98,101.42	4,659,608.75
8	0.00	0.00	0.00	"
9	0.00	0.00	0.00	"
10	0.00	0.00	0.00	"
11	0.00	0.00	0.00	"
12	0.00	0.00	0.00	"
13	0.00	0.00	0.00	"
14	0.00	0.00	0.00	"
15	0.00	0.00	0.00	"
16	0.00	0.00	0.00	"
***	5,902,650.05	1,243,041.30	4,659,608.75	4,659,608.75

FID (1) scaix116 INS 12:12PM

Exhibit 3.42   Customer: Account Balance

arate list after the list of open items. You can also display line items for a set of accounts together by using a work list of customer accounts, depending on your configuration.

Displaying Open Items.   To display open items in a customer account:

1. From the Accounts Receivable menu, select Account → Display line items. (See Exhibit 3.43.)
2. Enter customer account number in the Customer field. Alternatively, enter a name of a work list of customers (named set of customers, depending on your configuration) in the Work list field. Enter the company code in the Company code field, or enter a work list of company codes (named set of company codes) in the Work list field. To see the open items only, click on the box to the left of Open items. To see the cleared items, click on the box to the left of Cleared items. To see both open and cleared items, click on both. Last, press <Enter>. (See Exhibit 3.44.)

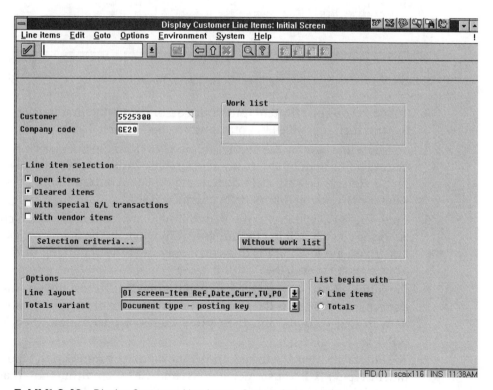

Exhibit 3.43   Display Customer Line Items, Screen One

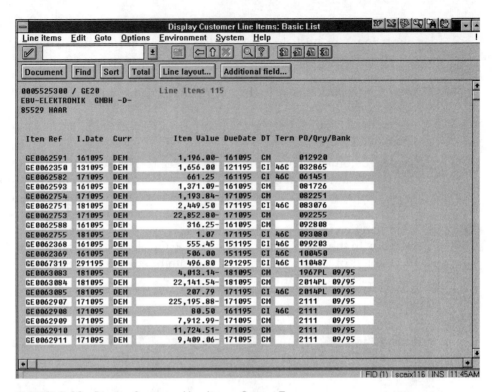

Exhibit 3.44   Display Customer Line Items, Screen Two

3. To look for a specific item, put your cursor before the first line item in the list and then press the Find pushbutton. (See Exhibit 3.45.)

4. To find a line item by the invoice number, click on the Document no. field. To find a line item by the customer purchase order or query number, click on the Reference doc. field depending on your configuration. Then press <Enter> or click on Proceed. (See Exhibit 3.46.)

5. Enter the specific entry in the item that you are looking for. Then click on String, if you are looking for this entry anywhere in the field, or click on Initial, if you are looking for this entry only in at the beginning of the field. Then press Proceed. (See Exhibit 3.47.)

6. Press the left-arrow to go back to the original list. To sort the line items by a specific field, such as the purchase order number, place your cursor on an item in that column, and then press the Sort pushbutton. (See Exhibit 3.48.)

7. To subtotal the items in the account, for example by transaction type ("document type") (**CI** = customer invoice and **CM** = credit memo), place the cursor in that field, and then press Total. (See Exhibit 3.49.)

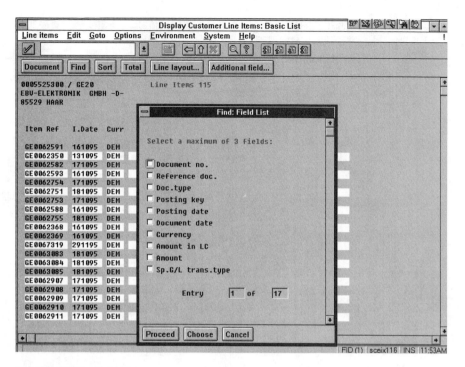

Exhibit 3.45 Field List

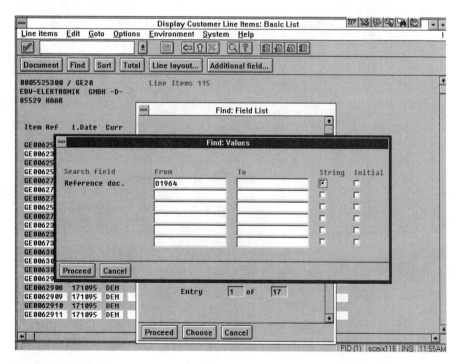

Exhibit 3.46 Values

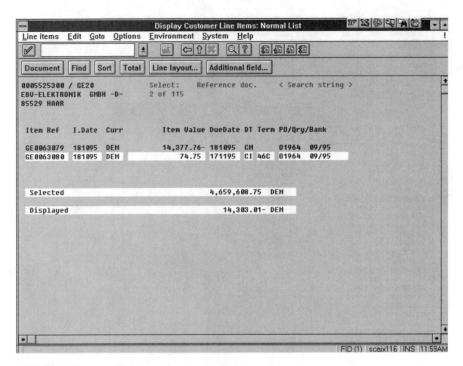

Exhibit 3.47 Display Customer Line Items: Normal List

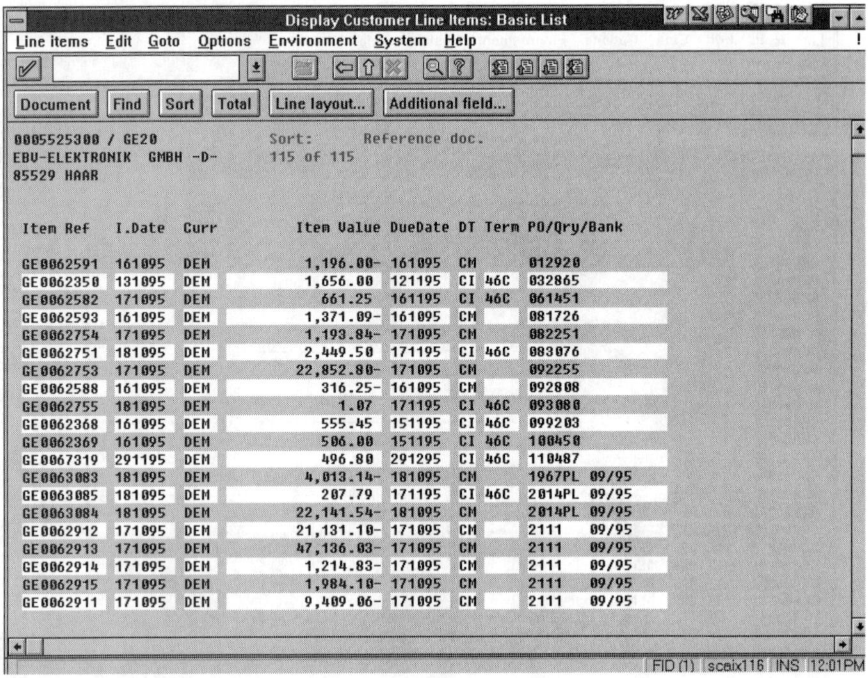

Exhibit 3.48 Display Customer Line Items: Basic List

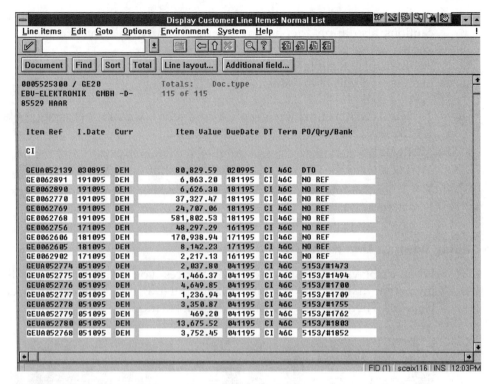

Exhibit 3.49 Display Customer Line Items: Normal List

8. Note that you can find items, sort, and subtotal one step at a time, so the resulting list includes all steps.

Displaying Cleared (Closed) Items. To display cleared (closed) items in a customer account:

1. From the Accounts Receivable menu, select Account ➤ Display line items.
2. Follow the same steps as when you displayed the open items, except that you select Cleared items only.

Note that you can also display open and cleared items together.

Displaying the Total Balance with Bills of Exchange

A bill of exchange is a payment method commonly found in France, Italy, Spain, and South Korea. It is similar to a postdated check. The credit risk of a bill of exchange can be high, since if you cash it before it is due and then the customer goes bankrupt, the bank recovers the payment from you. Other precautions also apply, depending on the country. Bills of exchange are also known as drafts.

To display the total customer balance, including invoices, payments, credit memos, and bills of exchange:

1. From the Accounts Receivable menu, select Account → Display balances. (See Exhibit 3.50.)

2. Enter the customer account number, the company code, and the fiscal year. Then press the Sp. G/L transactions pushbutton. (See Exhibit 3.51.)

3. To see the details of any balance on this screen, simply double-click on the balance.

Drilling Down to Line Items from a Balance

When displaying customer account balances, you can drill down to the line items that make up an account balance. First, display the customer account balances. Then double-click on an account balance.

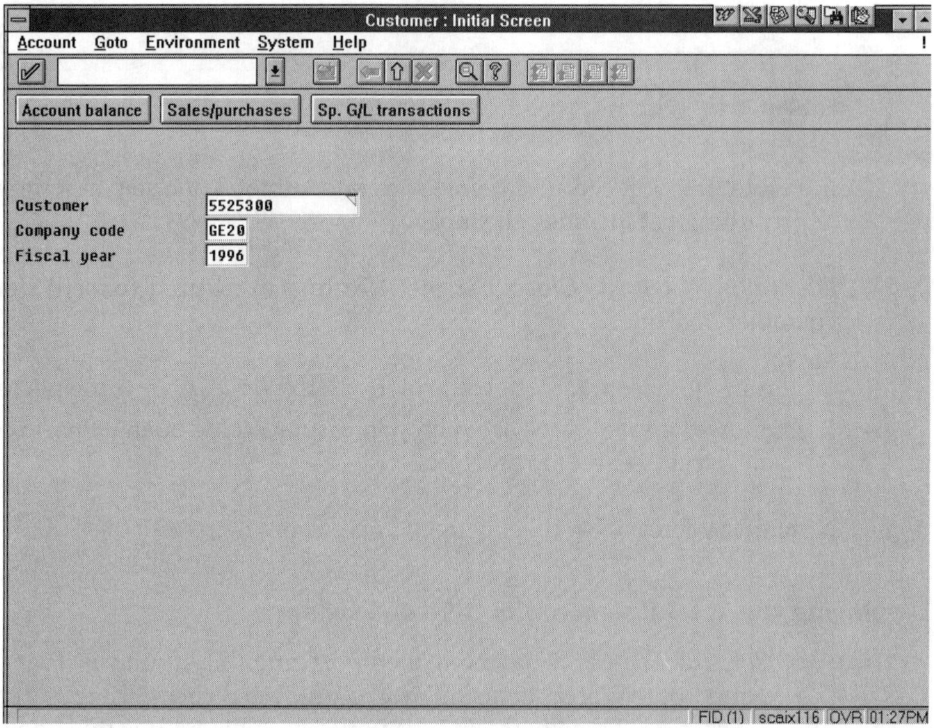

Exhibit 3.50   Customer: Initial Screen

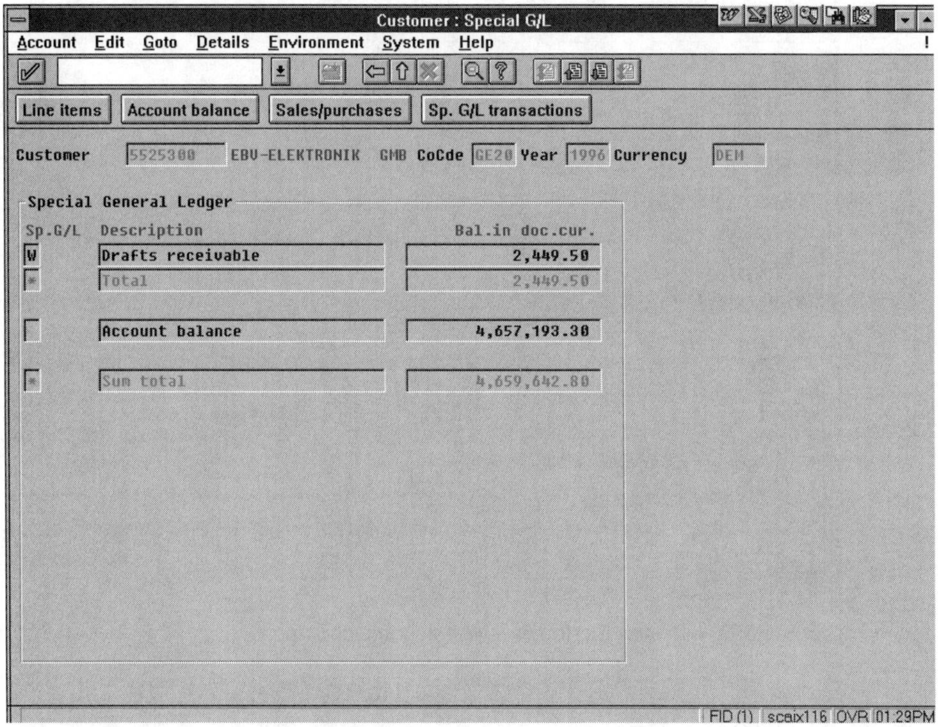

Exhibit 3.51 Customer: Special G/L

Displaying a Transaction from a Line Item

To see the complete transaction of a specific line item, first display the line items, then double-click on the specific item as follows:

1. From the Accounts Receivable menu, select Account → Display line items. (See Exhibit 3.52.)

2. Enter the customer account number in the Customer field, or enter a work list of customers (named set of customers, depending on your configuration) in the Work list field. Enter the company code in the Company code field, or enter a work list of company codes (named set of company codes) in the Work list field. To see the open items only, click on the box to the left of Open items. To see the cleared items, click on the box to the left of Cleared items. To see both open and cleared items, click on both. Press <Enter>. (See Exhibit 3.53.)

3. To display the details of a specific line item, double-click on the item. You also can do the same thing by placing the cursor on the line item and then pressing Document. (See Exhibit 3.54.)

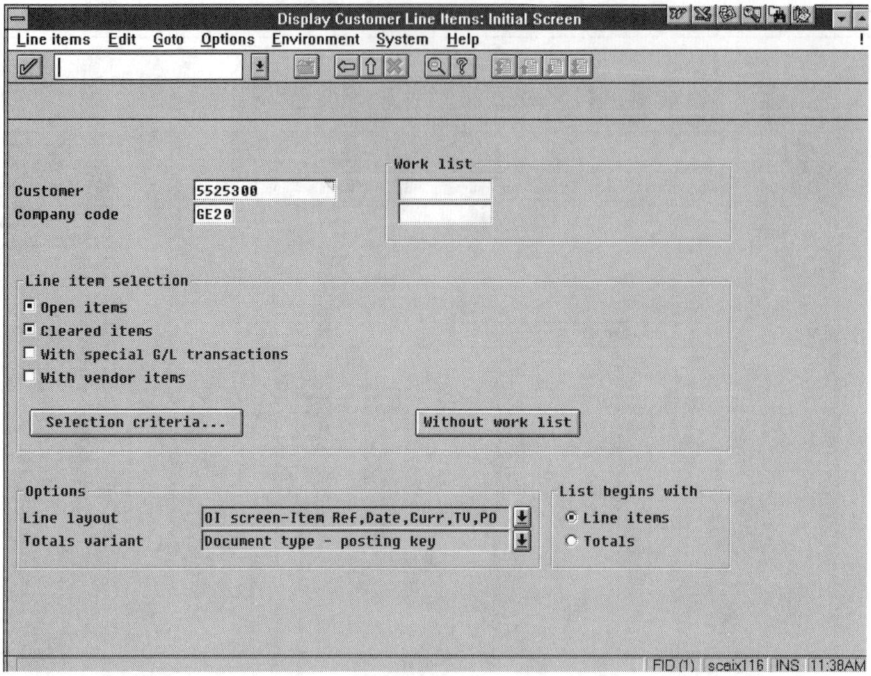

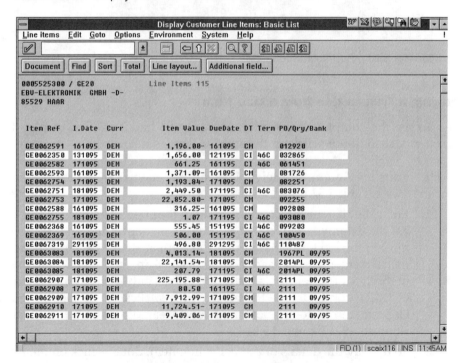

Exhibit 3.52 Display Customer Line Items: Initial Screen

Exhibit 3.53 Display Customer Line Items: Basic List

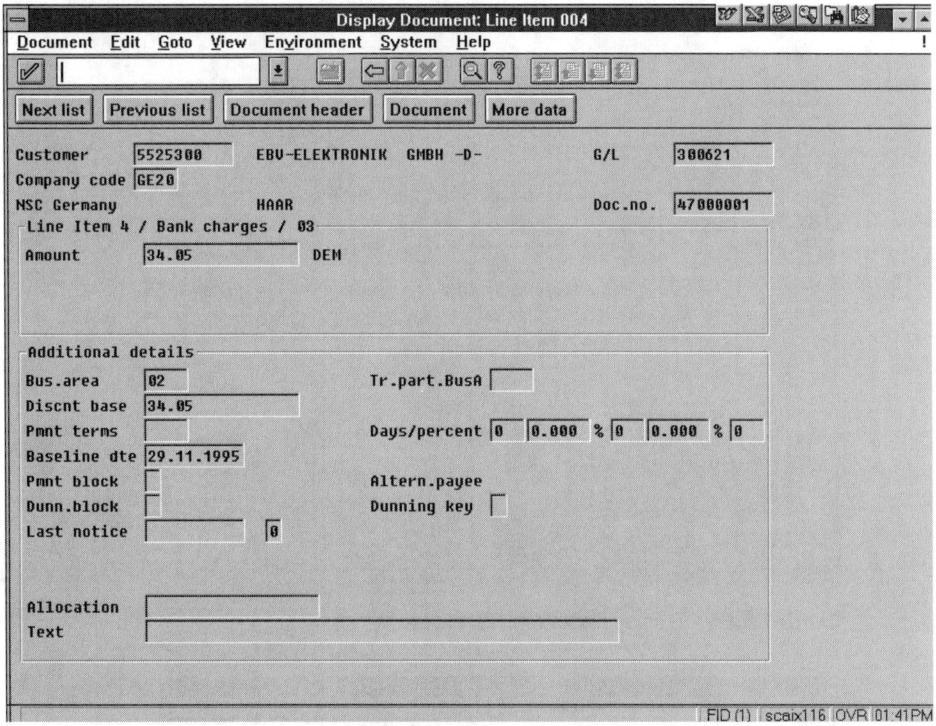

Exhibit 3.54   Display Document: Specific Line Item

4. This screen shows you the details of the specific line item. To see the complete transaction, press Document again. (See Exhibit 3.55.)

Displaying Customer Payment History

The payment history is by posting period. FI totals up the amount of the line items that were paid when the customer paid and took the valid cash discount (from the payment terms, date of the payment, and grace days from the configuration). The program also totals up the amount of the line items that were paid when the customer paid and did not take the cash discount, although it would have been valid. To display this payment history:

1. From the Accounts Receivable menu, select Account → Analysis. (See Exhibit 3.56.)

2. Enter the customer number, company code, and fiscal year. Select Goto → Payment history. (See Exhibit 3.57.)

3. Notice that this screen contains by type of payment (with discount, if valid or without discount, although valid) the total of the payments and the

```
 ─                        Display Document: Overview        ip |XS|⊕|⊡|⊡|⊡  ▼|▲
 Document   Edit   Goto   Options   Environment   System   Help                    !
 ☑ |                    ± |   ▦ | ⇦|⇧|⊠ | ⚲|? | ▦|▦|▦|▦ |

 Choose    Document header    Next document

 Document no.     47000001       Company code    GE20     Fiscal year      1996
 Document date    29.11.1995     Intercomp.no.
 Reference doc.                  Debit/credit     2,483.55
 Currency         DEM
 ─Items in document currency
 Itm  Cost ctr Acct      Description                    PK Amount in   DEM
 001           0005525300 EBV-ELEKTRONIK GMBH -D- / HAAR  09        2,449.50
 002  GE9999   0009431099 Other income/expense - fixed ass 50         29.05-
 003  GE9999   0009431099 Other income/expense - fixed ass 50          5.00-
 004           0005525300 EBV-ELEKTRONIK GMBH -D- / HAAR  03         34.05
 005           0005525300 EBV-ELEKTRONIK GMBH -D- / HAAR  15      2,449.50-
 006  GE02TR   0009325000 Transaction gain/loss on payment 50          0.00




                                             Item          1   / 6


                                                     FID (1)  scaix116  OVR 01:44PM
```

Exhibit 3.55   Display Document: Overview

```
 ─                    Account Analysis Customer : Initial Screen  ip|XS|⊕|⊡|⊡|⊡ ▼|♦
 Account   Goto   Environment   System   Help                                    !
 ☑ |                    ± |   ▦ | ⇦|⇧|⊠ | ⚲|? | ▦|▦|▦|▦ |

 Account balance    Sales/purchases    Sp. G/L transactions



 Customer          5525300
 Company code      GE20
 Fiscal year       1996












                                                     FID (1)  scaix116  OVR 06:11PM
```

Exhibit 3.56   Account Analysis Customer: Initial Screen

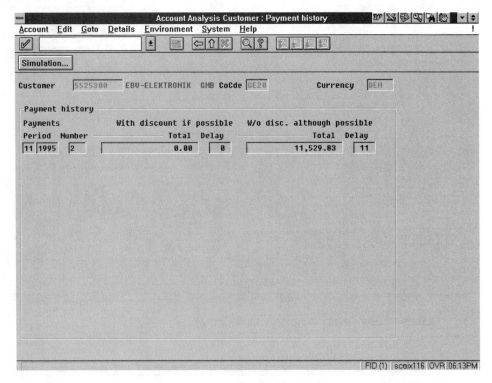

Exhibit 3.57   Account Customer Analysis: Payment History

average days in arrears. The calculation of the average days in arrears is internal to FI and is weighted by the amount of the item.

Displaying a Transaction

You can display any transaction by the "document" (transaction) number. To display a specific transaction:

1. From the Accounts Receivable menu, select Document ➤ Display. (See Exhibit 3.58.)

2. If you do not have the transaction number, press the List pushbutton. (See Exhibit 3.59.)

3. To select specific invoices, enter the search criteria for the invoices. Otherwise, enter the company code in the Company code field and **ci** in the Document type field. To run the report to list the transactions, press the Execute pushbutton. (See Exhibit 3.60.)

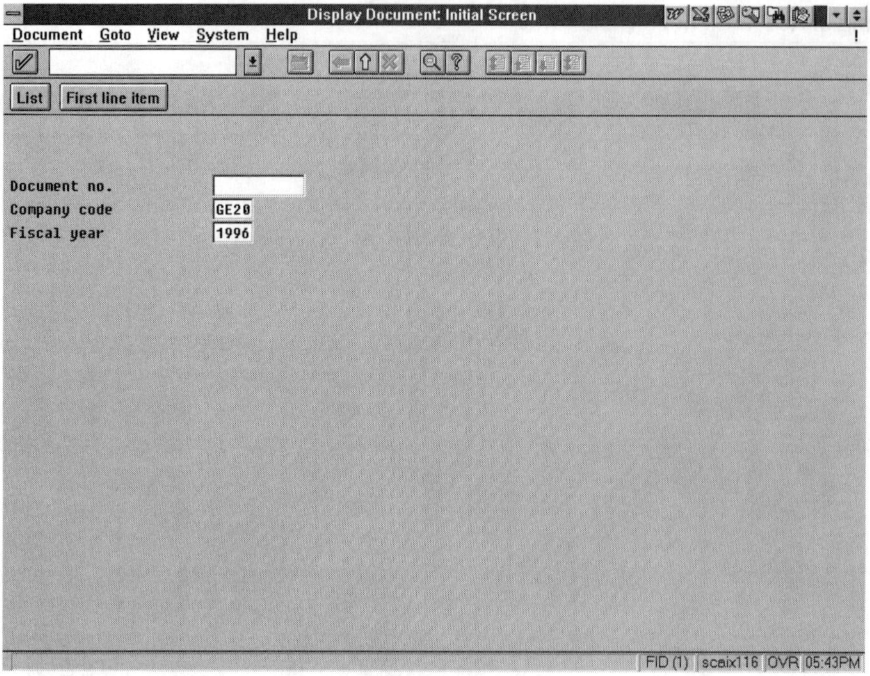

Exhibit 3.58 Display Document: Initial Screen

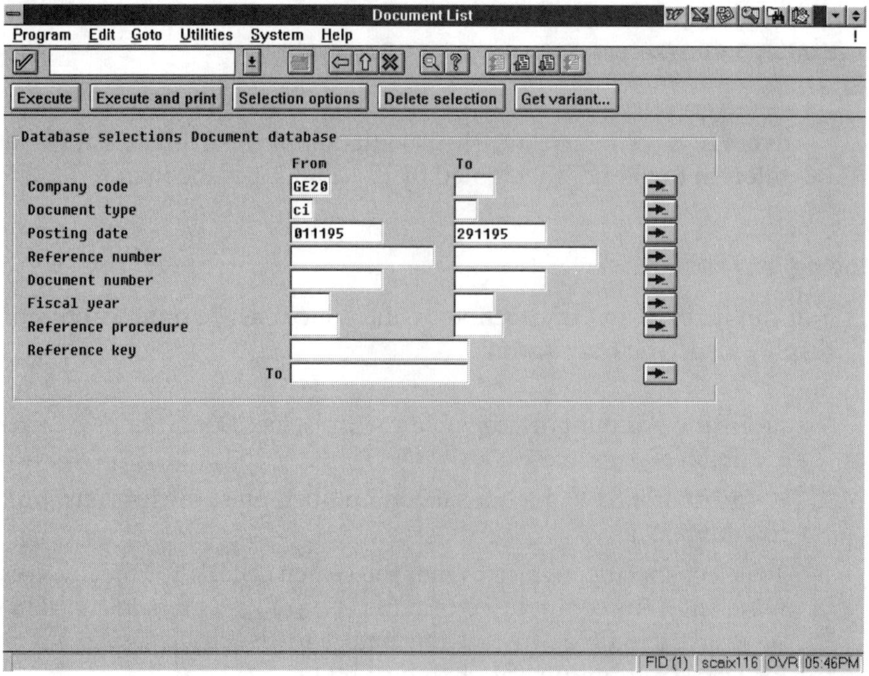

Exhibit 3.59 Document List

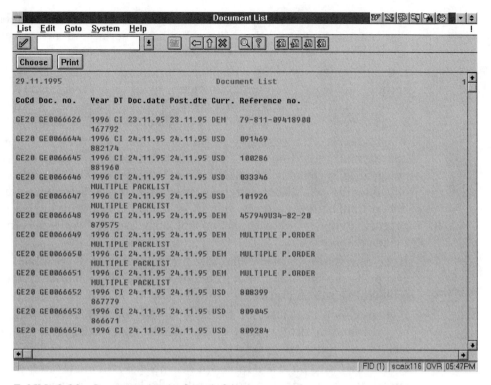

Exhibit 3.60 Document List by Search Criteria

4. To display a specific transaction, place your cursor on the invoice and then press Choose. To print a specific transaction, place your cursor on the invoice and then press Print.

Finding a Customer Number from an Invoice

Assume that you have an invoice number and are looking for the customer number. You can display the transaction and then find the customer number.

To find the customer number from an invoice:

1. From the Accounts Receivable menu, select Document → Display.
2. Enter the company code and fiscal year as usual.
3. Press <Enter>.

APPLYING CASH

You can apply cash in any form, usually either bank transfers or checks, to open items in a customer account. When you apply cash, please keep the following in mind:

- If a certain customer is paying for a set of customer accounts together, then you can make a work list for this set of customer accounts. You can then apply the payment to the *work list* of customer accounts.

- If the customer is making a *partial payment*, you can post the payment on account and leave the original invoice or invoices open (a *partial payment*), or you can close the original invoice and record a new item for the difference between the original item and the payment (a *residual item*).

- When you record a customer payment and the customer takes any valid *cash discount* according to the payment terms of the invoice, the program automatically calculates and posts the cash discount. You can also manually enter the cash discount in each line item that the customer is paying. If the customer makes a partial payment of an invoice with valid cash discount, then the program apportions the cash discount by the percentage of the partial payment.

- If there are *small payment differences*, the program automatically calculates and posts the small payment differences to a G/L for small payment differences, depending on your configuration.

- If you accept the *bank fees* for the customer payment, then you can have the program automatically post the bank fees to the expense account for bank fees.

- When you post a payment in *foreign currency* (any other currency than local currency), the program automatically calculates and posts the exchange rate differences.

- If it is not clear which invoice or invoices the customer is paying, you can post a *payment on account.*

If you cannot identify which customer made the payment, then post to an account for an unidentified customer.

There are two ways of posting a payment and clearing invoices. One way is longer and has more screens but is more flexible. This book will cover only the fast method of entering payments and clearing invoices.

Posting a G/L Account for Cash or in Transit

When posting a bank transfer from the bank statement, post to the G/L account for cash in the bank. When posting a check, post to the G/L account for cash in transit. Your treasury department will inform you of which G/L account to post.

Applying Cash (Accounts Receivable)

The overview of a possible procedure to enter the A/R-related entries in the bank statement, to apply cash, and to reconcile the bank statement is as follows:

1. The treasury department prints the bank statement or receives the printed bank statement daily in the morning.

2. The treasury department makes a copy of the bank transfers from customers in the bank statement.

3. For each batch of payments by bank account by currency, the treasury department fills in a header sheet and brings it to A/R. The header sheet contains:
   a. Bank account (G/L account number—**0100xxx** for bank transfers and **0109xxx** for payments by check or other payments not in the bank statement, depending on your chart of accounts)
   b. Document type—either **BJ** for entries to be posted to 0100xxx or **CP** for entries to be posted 0109xxx depending on your configuration
   c. Reference document—the bank statement number, preceded by **C** for collections, to record collections by day and week
   d. Document date—date of the bank statement
   e. Value date—date of available liquidity at the bank
   f. Currency—of the payments
   g. Total payment amount—of payments in this batch

4. The treasury department enters control totals by G/L account of the subtotals by bank account in the bank statement.

5. With reference to the header sheet, A/R enters the header of each payment in this batch of payments. A/R processes open items, including cash discount based on the net total of invoices paid minus credit memos deducted.

6. A/R applies cash the same day as received from the treasury department.

7. To reconcile the bank statement, the treasury department compares the bank balance in each bank account (according to the end of the bank statement) with the G/L *account balance* for each bank account in the system. If they are not equal, then the treasury department prints a bank journal (Doc. type **BJ**) on the date of the bank statement to find the differences in the *posted transactions*. The treasury department also checks the control totals by G/L account.

Using a Work List. If your processing options are set properly, you can apply cash to a series of related customer accounts (a work list). For details about processing options, read the previous section on setting processing options "Setting Processing Options." For example, if a customer pays centrally, you can apply cash to all related accounts through the work list. You first have to define a work list, which is described in the section about other A/R functions, "Making a Work List of Customer Accounts."

Note that there are some differences about how to use the work list, depending on which function you are using, as follows:

- When applying cash with the payment fast entry function, enter the work list name (or the individual customer account number) in the same field—the Customer field. (See Exhibit 3.61.)

- When displaying line items in a customer account (or a work list of accounts), enter the work list name in the separate Work list field. (See Exhibit 3.62.)

Applying a Bank Transfer. Assume that you have one or more invoices to apply cash to. Also assume that the invoices are in local currency and that the payment is a full payment of all invoices. Further assume that there are no bank fees. To enter the payment and apply the cash to the open invoices:

1. From the Accounts Receivable menu, select Document entry → Payment fast entry. (See Exhibit 3.63.)
2. Fill out this screen and then press Enter payments. (See Exhibit 3.64.)
3. Fill out this screen and then press Edit open items. Note that you can enter either a customer number *or* a work list name in the Customer field. Note that if you do not have the customer number, you can specify the invoice

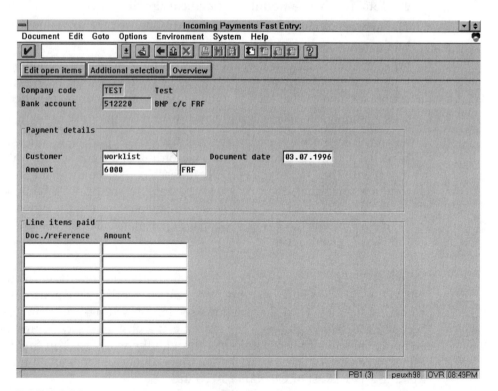

Exhibit 3.61 Incoming Payments Fast Entry for a Worklist

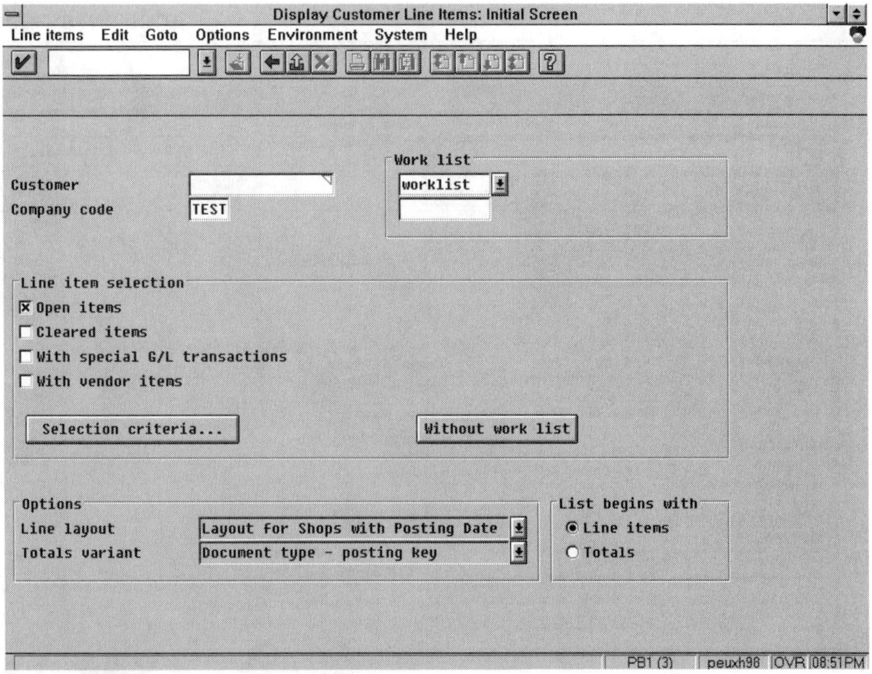

Exhibit 3.62   Displaying Customer Line Items for a Worklist

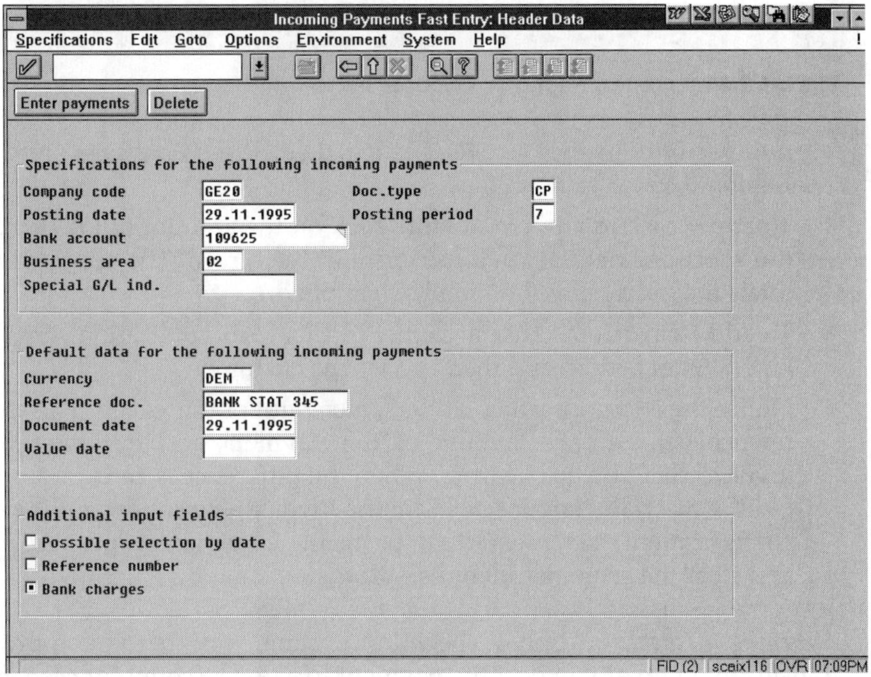

Exhibit 3.63   Incoming Payments: Enter Payments

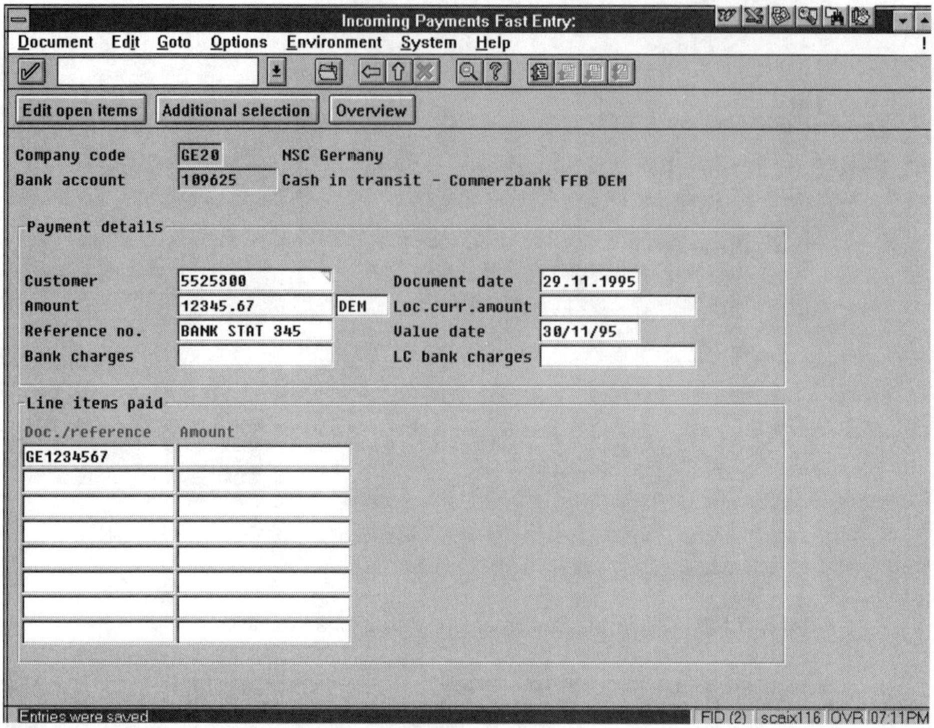

Exhibit 3.64   Incoming Payments: Edit Open Items

number only in the Doc./Reference field. Press Edit open items. (See Exhibit 3.65.)

4. To apply cash to an item, double-click on the amount of the item. Notice the Allocated field at the lower-right of the screen. The allocated amount totals the open items that you have applied.

5. To add items from other accounts to this cash application screen, select Edit ➤ Select more and then specify the customer.

6. Notice the Difference field at the lower-right of the screen. This is the difference between the amount of the payment and the amount of the invoices that you are clearing. When the difference is zero, or almost zero (within a certain amount or 1% of the invoice amount depending on your configuration), then press <F11> or the file folder icon to post the payment and clear the customer invoices.

Applying a Check.   Apply a check in the same way that you apply a bank transfer, except that you post the payment to a G/L account for cash in transit (**0109xxx**), depending on your chart of accounts.

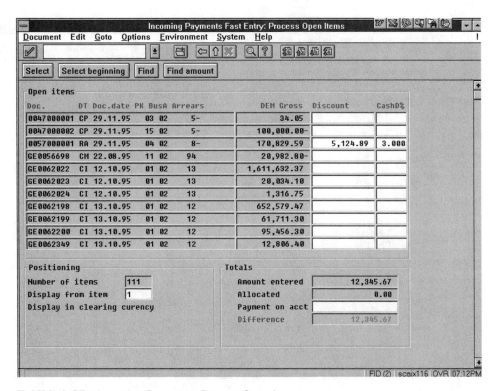

Exhibit 3.65 Incoming Payments: Process Open Items

Selecting Additional Items or Accounts.   While you are applying cash to a customer or to a work list, you can select either an additional item by the invoice number or a specific additional customer account. The program then adds one or more items to your list of open items on the cash applications screen.

To select additional items or an additional account:

1. From the Incoming Payments Fast Entry: Process Open Items screen, select Edit → Select more. (See Exhibit 3.66.)
2. To find an invoice, click on Document no. and then press Edit open items. Alternatively, to find all open items in a specific account, enter the customer account number in the Account field and then press Edit open items.
3. Continue to process open items and apply cash as usual.

Entering and Posting a Debit Note.   If the customer makes a partial payment, you can close the original invoice and make a new item for the difference

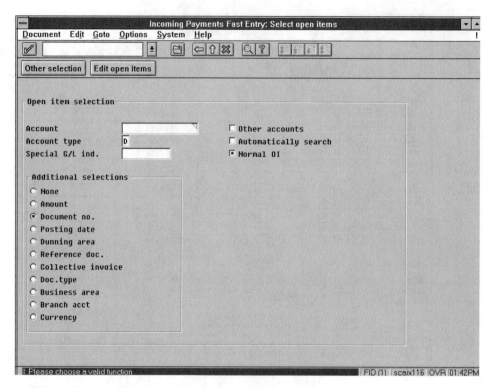

Exhibit 3.66 Incoming Payments Fast Entry: Select Open Items

between the payment and the original invoice. Similarly, if you issue the customer a debit note, you can close the original invoice and open a debit note. To do this, you apply cash, you mark the open items being paid. You then enter one or more debit notes for the difference between the invoice and the payment.

1. From the Accounts Receivable menu, select Document entry → Payment fast entry. (See Exhibit 3.67.)

2. Fill in the screen as shown. Press Enter payments. (See Exhibit 3.68.)

3. Fill in the screen as shown. To match to a specific invoice without the customer number, enter the invoice number in the column Doc./reference. Otherwise, if you have the customer account number, enter it in the Customer field. Alternatively, if you are applying cash to a customer paying centrally (a work list of customers), enter the name of the work list in the Customer field. To process the open items, press Edit open items. (See Exhibit 3.69.)

4. Notice that the invoice that you specified is highlighted in red (on the screen). If no invoices are highlighted, you first have to activate each item

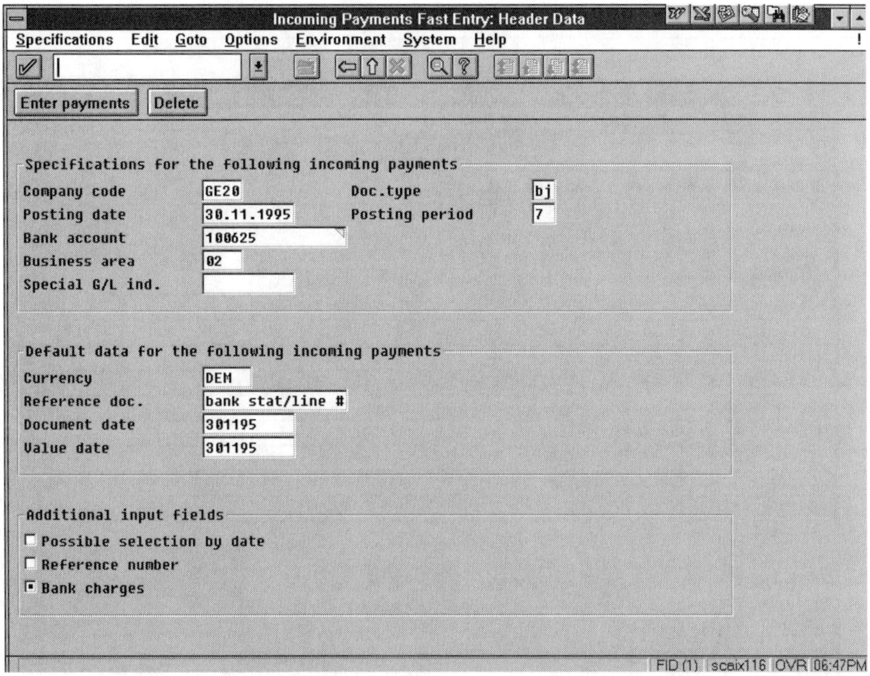

Exhibit 3.67 Incoming Payments Fast Entry: Header Data

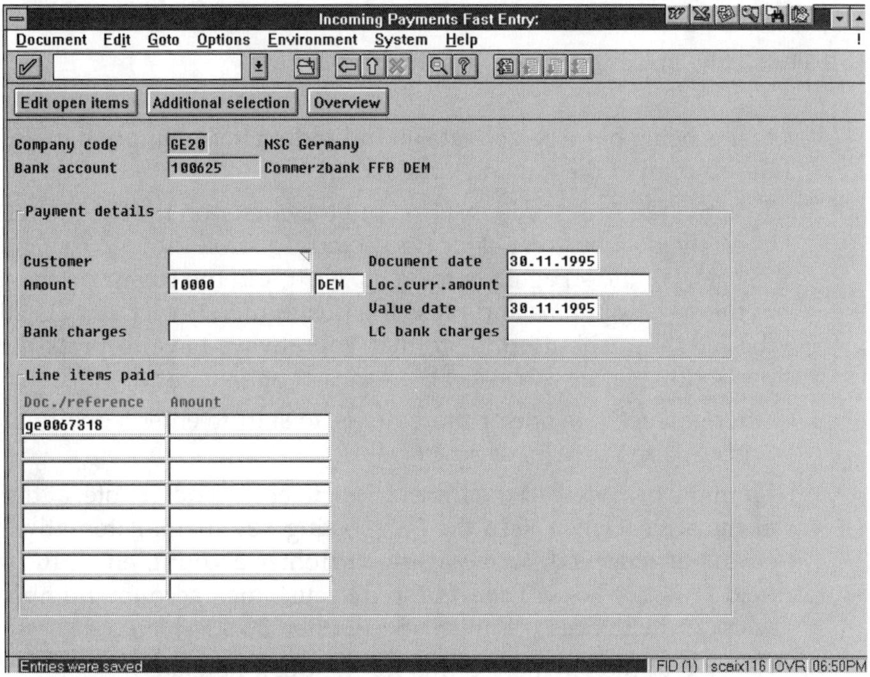

Exhibit 3.68 Incoming Payments Fast Entry

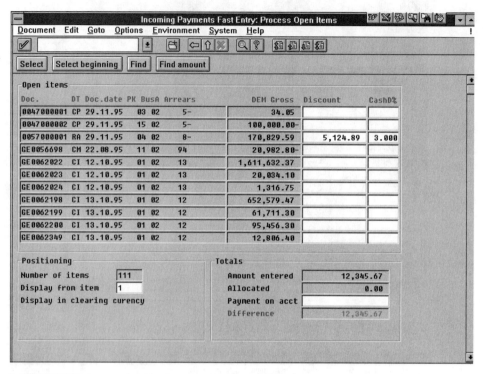

Exhibit 3.69 Incoming Payments: Process Open Items

that is being paid. To activate an individual item, simply double-click on the amount of the item on your screen.

5. To activate a series of items, first put the cursor on the first item and then press the pushbutton Select beginning. To scroll through the list, use the <PageUp> and <PageDown> keys. Next, put the cursor on the last item in the series of items and press the pushbutton Select end. Lastly, press the Active pushbutton. Note that you always have to press the Active pushbutton, after you select the series of open items.

6. After you activate one or more items, to start to enter a debit note, select Goto → Document overview.

7. From the overview of the transaction, to enter a debit note, at the bottom of the screen enter **06** in the PK (posting key) field. Alternatively, if the customer overpaid, to credit the customer account, enter **16** in the PK field. Press <Tab>. Then enter the customer account number in the Account field. Press <Enter>. (See Exhibit 3.70.)

8. Check that the payment terms for the debit note are net 30. If not, enter **10A** in the Pmnt terms field. You can never post a debit without enter-

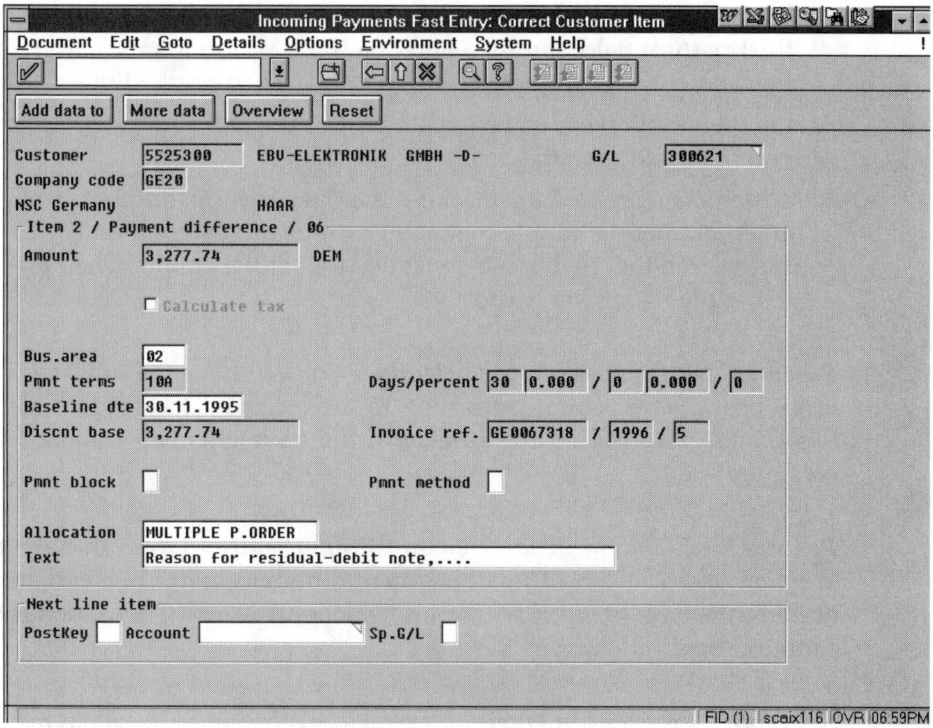

Exhibit 3.70 Incoming Payments: Correct Customer Item

ing some explanation of the reason for the debit note in the Text field on the detailed line item entry screen.

9. To see the overview of the transaction, press Overview. This shows the total debits and total credits in the transaction. You can never post a transaction without the debits being equal to the credits.

10. To post the transaction, press <F11> or the file folder icon.

Entering Multiple Debit Notes with One Payment. You can enter one or more debit notes if the customer makes a partial payment and you wish to close an invoice and open one or more specific debit notes. In SAP, a debit note is called a residual item.

To enter multiple debit notes:

1. Enter the payment as usual. Mark open items as usual.

2. From the cash application screen, select Goto → Document overview.

3. From the transaction overview screen, select Document → Simulate.

4. To start to enter a debit note (residual item) manually, place the cursor in the PostKey field and then enter **06** (for a residual item). In the Account field, enter the customer account number. Then press <Enter>.

5. On the next screen, enter the amount of the debit note. In the Text field, enter **DN** and then the debit note number.

6. To see the overview again, press the Overview pushbutton. You can then enter another debit note manually by repeating steps 4 and 5. To post the transaction the total debits must equal the total credits. Then press <F11> or the file folder icon to post.

Posting Cash Discount Automatically.   You can have the program automatically post cash discount, according to the payment terms, date of the payment, and grace period for a delay in the payment. This depends on your configuration.

Posting Small Payment Differences Automatically.   You can have the program automatically post small payment differences—up to a certain amount or percentage of the invoice amount, whichever is less. This depends on your configuration.

Applying a Payment in Foreign Currency.   When entering a payment in foreign currency, simply enter a different ISO currency code on the first screen. The program automatically calculates and then posts, based on your configuration, the gain or loss from the change in the exchange rate between the date of the invoice and the date of the payment. The posting date determines which exchange rate is transferred from the table of exchange rates, unless you enter an overriding exchange rate in the header of the transaction.

Posting Bank Fees.   If you cover the bank fees and accept the net amount of the payment (minus the bank fees) to clear the gross amount of the invoice, then simply enter the net amount of the payment (what you receive) and the bank fees. The bank should include both of these amounts in each entry in your bank statement. When you post the transaction, the program automatically posts the bank fees to the expense account and clears the total amount (net payment plus bank fees) with one or more open items that you specify.

1. From the Accounts Receivable menu, select Document entry ➤ Payment fast entry. (See Exhibit 3.71.)

2. Fill in the screen as shown. Make sure you click on the Bank charges field at the end of the screen. Press Enter payments. (See Exhibit 3.72.)

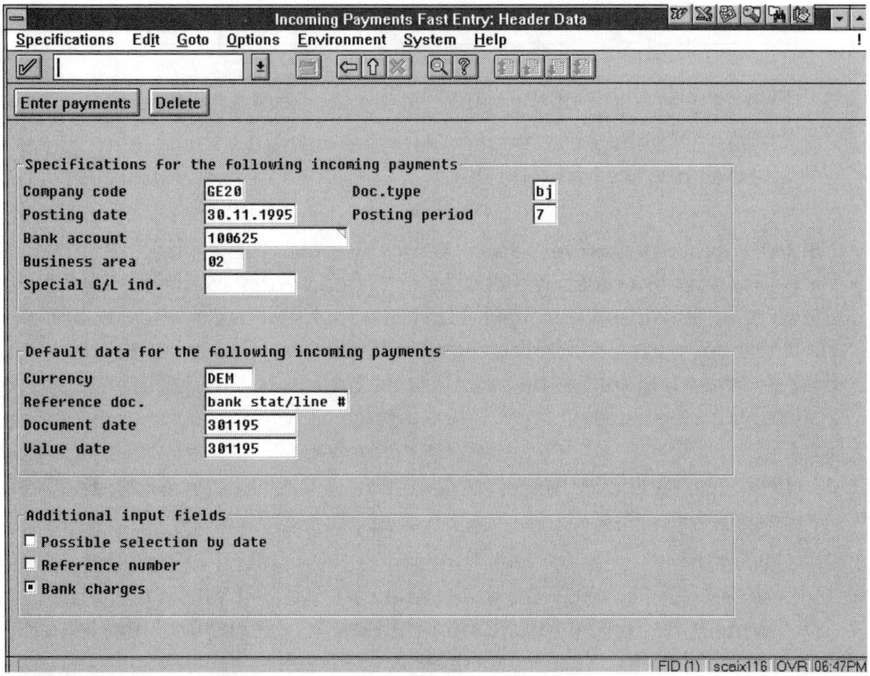

Exhibit 3.71 Incoming Payments: Header Data

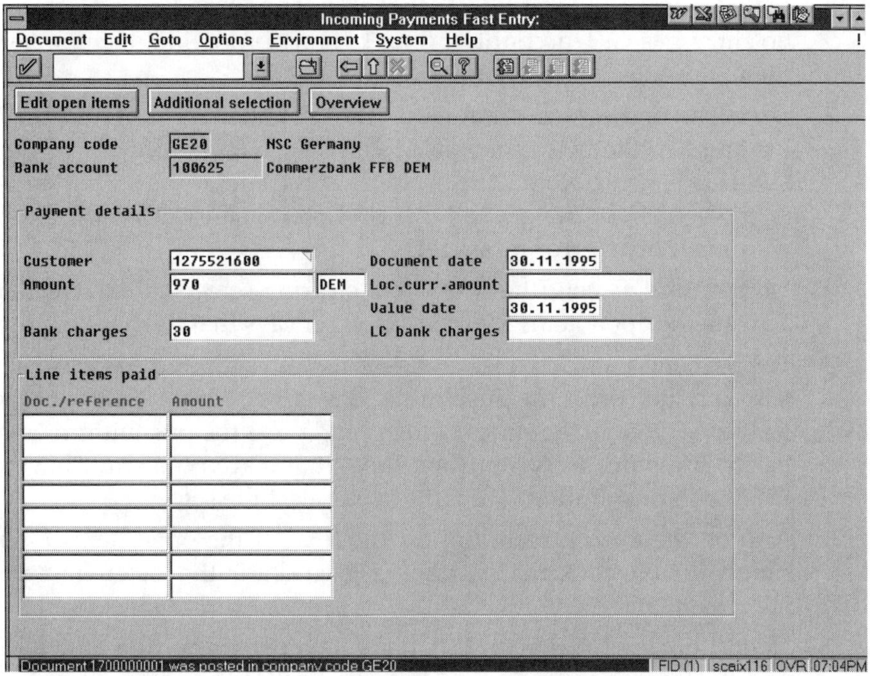

Exhibit 3.72 Incoming Payments: Bank Charges

3. Enter the amount of the bank fees in the Bank charges field.

4. Process the payment as usual. In this example, this payment would clear an open invoice of 1000 DEM.

Entering and Processing a Remittance Advice.   To enter a remittance advice, you close open invoices and enter a new debit entry in the customer account for the total of the closed invoices. The customer balance does not change, but you close the open invoices in the remittance advice. This assumes that you believe the customer will make the payment according to the remittance advice.

Enter and process a remittance advice as follows:

1. From the Accounts Receivable menu, select Document entry → Payment fast entry.

2. On the first screen of this function, make sure that you enter the transaction header properly for a remittance advice. If you have already used the payment fast entry function in this session, then press the left-arrow to go back to the first screen. On the first screen, in the Document date field, enter the date of the remittance advice. Enter the document type **RA** (for remittance advice) in the Doc.type field depending on your configuration. In the Account field, enter a G/L account number, although you will make no entry to a G/L account. In the Reference doc. field, enter **Await Payment.** Press Enter Payment.

3. On the second screen, enter either the customer account number or work list name in the Customer field. Enter a payment amount of zero. Press Edit open items. Notice the message at the end of the screen–W: Amount is zero—line will be ignored. Press <Enter>, since this message is only a warning (not an error message).

4. On the third screen (the open item clearing screen), first select and then activate the open items that the customer says that they are paying.

5. To select and then activate a series of items, first put the cursor on the first item and then press the pushbutton Select beginning. Next, put the cursor on the last item in the series of items and press the pushbutton Select end. Lastly, press the Active pushbutton. Note that you always have to press the Active pushbutton, even after you select the set.

6. Also on the third screen, to post the total of the open items on account, simply double-click on Payment on account in the lower-right portion of the screen.

7. Notice that the Difference is **0** in the lower-right portion of the screen. To post the transaction, press <F11> or the file folder icon.

The procedure may differ from country to country, depending on the reliability of the remittance advice.

Posting a Payment on Account. If the customer made a payment, but you are not sure which open items were being paid, then you can post the payment on account.

To post a payment on account:

1. From the Accounts Receivable menu, select Document entry → Payment fast entry.
2. On the first screen of this function, make sure that you enter the transaction header properly for a payment. If you have already used the payment fast entry function in this session, then press the left-arrow to go back to the first screen. On the first screen, in the Document date field, enter the bank date of the payment. Enter either the document type **BJ** (for bank journal) or **CP** (for customer payment by check) in the Doc.type field depending on your configuration. In the Account field, enter a G/L account number for the cash or cash in transit account at the bank that receives the payment. In the Reference doc. field, enter the bank statement number, preceded by **C** or the check number. Press Enter Payment.
3. On the second screen, enter either the customer account number or work list name in the Customer field. Enter the payment amount. Press Edit open items.
4. On the third screen (the open item clearing screen), enter the amount of the payment in the Payment on account field in the lower-right portion of the screen.

Entering Unapplied Cash (Unidentified Customer). If you cannot be sure which customer made the payment, nor which invoice was being paid, enter the payment on account to a customer for unapplied cash (an unidentified customer).

Matching Debits and Credits (Clearing). Matching open items is also known as clearing open items. In effect, you remove one or more line items from the list of open items and add the same line item to the list of cleared items. Usually, you do this when you enter and then match a payment to one or more invoices. If you already have both debit entries and credit entries as open items in a customer account, such as invoices and credit memos, you can clear them in one step. The only requirement is that the total of the debits exactly equal the total of the credits.

USING OTHER A/R FUNCTIONS

Entering a Credit Memo

If the customer either returns the goods or does not accept your invoice with a reason, you can enter and post a credit memo. This reduces the customer's debit to your company.

To enter a credit memo:

1. From the Accounts Receivable menu, select Document entry → Credit memo.
2. Enter the debits and credits as usual. A posting key of all 11 is a credit to a customer account.

Note that if you use SD to post the customer invoice, you should use SD to post the credit memo.

Making a Work List of Customer Accounts

You can use a work list to display customer line items (open or cleared) of a set of related customers. You can also use a work list to clear open items of a set of related customers.

To make a work list:

1. From the Accounts Receivable menu, select Environment → Configuration menu.
2. From the Financial Accounting Configuration menu, select Environment → Employees → Work lists. (See Exhibit 3.73.)
3. Double-click on KUNNR Customers to start to define a work list of customers. (See Exhibit 3.74.)
4. To start to define a new work list, press Create.
5. Enter the brief name and description of the work list. Press <Enter>.
6. Enter the complete ten-digit account numbers of the customers in the work list.
7. To store the work list, press <F11> or the file folder icon.

Refunding a Credit Balance (Negative Cash)

If you have issued one or more credit memos to the customer and then have paid a refund to the customer, you can record a refund to the customer (a cash disbursement) and close the credit memo.

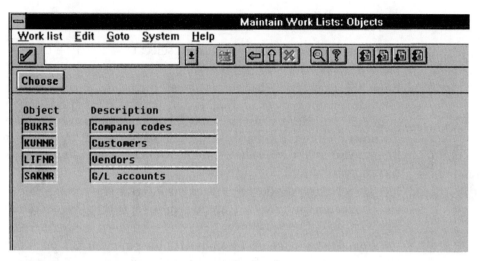

Exhibit 3.73   Maintain Work Lists: Objects

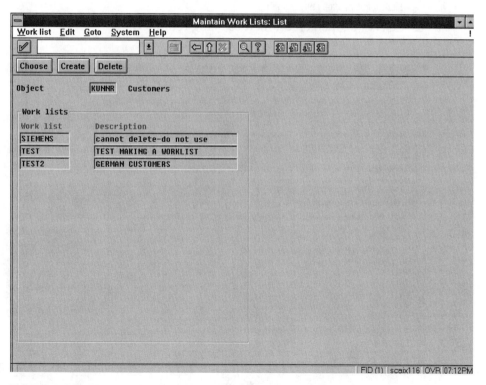

Exhibit 3.74   Maintain Work Lists: List

To record a refund to the customer and close a credit memo:

1. From the Accounts Receivable menu, select Document ➤ Others ➤ Posting with clearing. (See Exhibit 3.75.)

2. Enter the transaction header as usual, including at least the document date, document type (**BJ** for bank transfer or **CP** for check depending on your configuration), company code, posting date, currency, and reference document (either the bank statement reference or the check number) fields. Also, make sure that you click on Outgoing payment to start to record the refund to the customer.

3. At the end of the screen, enter **50** in the PostKey field (for a credit entry to a G/L account) and the G/L account number (for the bank account) in the Account field. Press <Enter>.

4. On the next screen, enter the amount of the payment as a positive number. Click on Calculate tax. Press Edit open items.

5. Specify the customer account with the credit memo being paid. Then press Edit open items again.

6. Select the open credit memos being refunded.

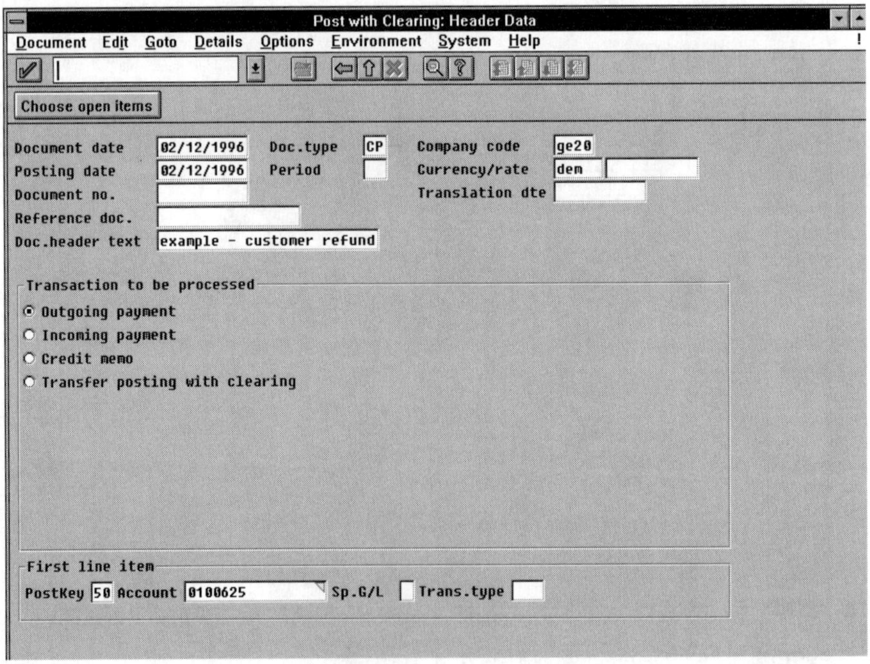

Exhibit 3.75   Post with Clearing: Header Data

7. To see an overview of the transaction, press Overview.

8. To post the transaction, press <F11> or the file folder icon.

Reversing a Payment

Sometimes you need to reverse a payment that has already closed (cleared) an invoice (for example, if the check bounces). If you have posted a payment that has closed one or more invoices, you have to reverse it in two steps:

1. Reverse the clearing (of the open invoices).

2. Reverse the payment, reinstating the open invoices.

Note that to reverse the payment and reinstate the invoice, you have to first reverse the clearing and then reverse the payment.

Reversing the Clearing.   To reverse the clearing,

1. From the Accounts Receivable menu, select Document ➤ Reset cleared items. (See Exhibit 3.76.)

2. Enter the transaction number of the clearing transaction (not the invoice). To reverse the clearing, press <F11> or the file folder icon.

3. Look for the message at the end of the screen—Clearing reversed.

At this moment, both the payment and the invoice are open. The next step is to reverse the payment, so that only the invoice is still open.

Reversing the Payment and Reinstating the Invoice.   To reverse the payment, after you have already reversed any clearing:

1. From the Accounts Receivable menu, select Document ➤ Reverse. (See Exhibit 3.77.)

2. Enter the same number as the clearing transaction number in the Document no. field.

3. To reverse the payment, press <F11> or the file folder icon.

4. Look for the message Document xxxxxx was posted in company code xxxx, where the transaction number and company code are the same as the payment being reversed.

Changing the Due Date of an Open Item

You can change the due date of an open item but only by changing the item's baseline date for payment. The baseline date for payment is the date on which

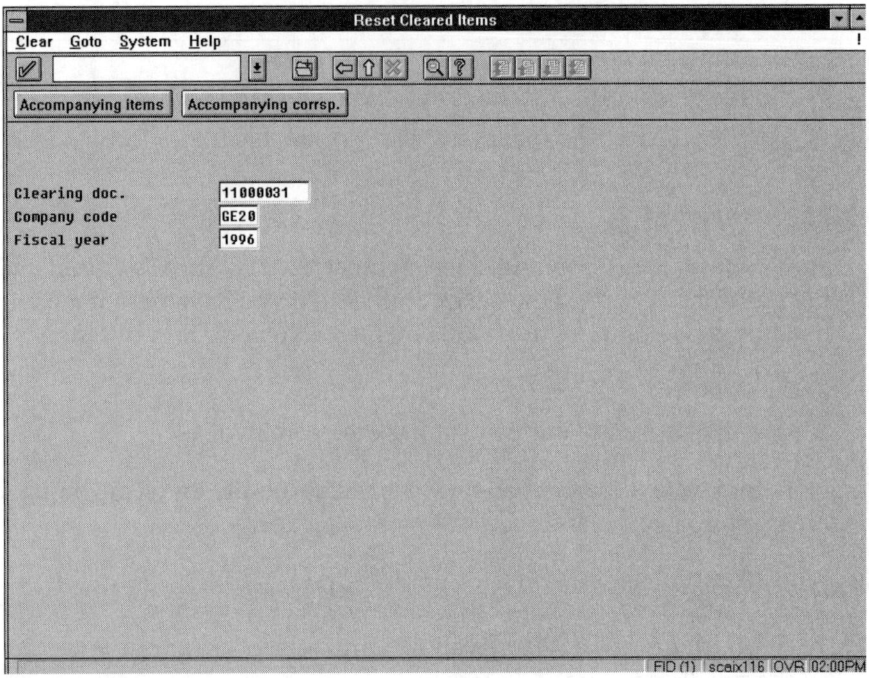

Exhibit 3.76 Reset Cleared Items

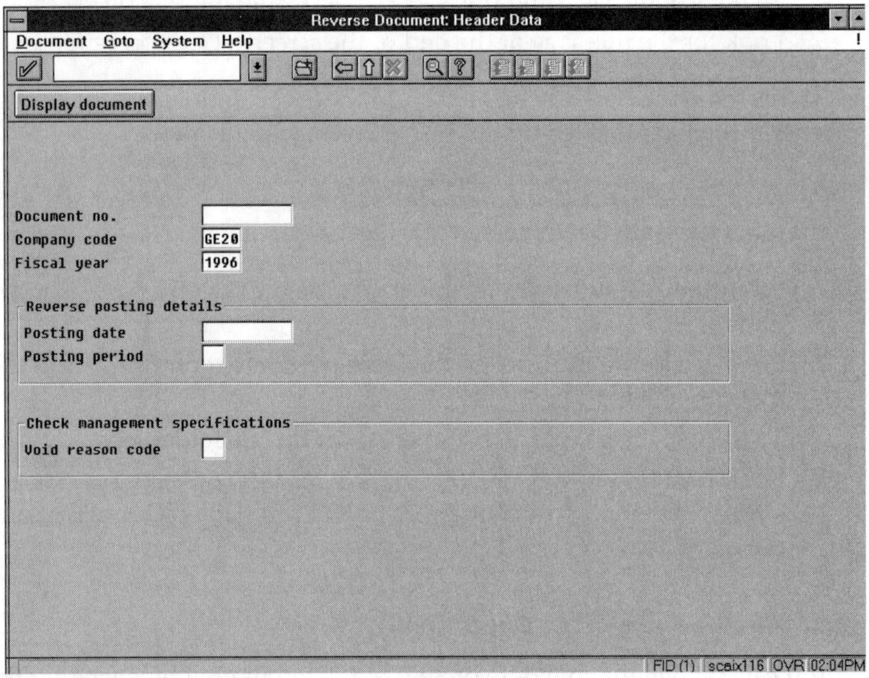

Exhibit 3.77 Reverse Document: Header Data

the calculation of the due date starts. The exact due date of an open item is always derived from the baseline date and the payment terms. In other words, an open item does not contain a due date; it only contains a baseline date for payment and a certain payment terms code. Depending on your business requirements and configuration, the baseline date is derived from either the document date or the posting date in the invoice header.

After posting a transaction, you can never change the amounts, posting keys, or accounts of a transaction. If you make a mistake posting a transaction without clearing open items, you have to reverse the transaction and then re-enter it. If you make a mistake, or the check bounces, and you have already cleared open items, you have to first reset the cleared items and then reverse the transaction.

Changing a Series of Open Items

You can change some fields in a series of line items at once. You can change the following fields:

- Payment terms
- Payment block
- Payment method
- House bank
- Date of last dunning notice
- Dunning level
- Dunning block

To change a series of line items at once:

1. From the Accounts Receivable menu, select Account ➤ Change line items.
2. Enter the customer account number and company code and then press <Enter>.
3. From the list of open items, select Edit ➤ Mass changes.
4. Place cursor on the open item and then press Activate/deactivate.
5. Press New values to set the new fields in the open items.

Recording a Repayment to the Customer

If the customer has one or more credit memos that exceed the value of open invoices, then the customer has a credit balance. In this case, you owe the customer for the credit balance. Assuming that you have written a check or a bank transfer to repay the customer, you record the repayment by crediting a G/L account for cash or cash in transit, debiting the customer, and closing the credit memos. Specifically, record a repayment to the customer as follows:

1. From the Accounts Receivable menu, select Document ➤ Others ➤ Posting ➤ with clearing. (See Exhibit 3.78.)

2. Enter the transaction header as usual. Click on Outgoing payment. At the end of the screen, enter a posting key of **50** in the PostKey field to start to record a credit. In the Account field, enter the G/L account number for cash in transit at the bank that you used to pay the customer, depending on your chart of accounts. Enter the amount of the payment. Press <Enter>.

3. Choose customer open items (one or more credit memos) to clear with the payment.

Dunning

You can send dunning letters to remind one or more customers to pay their outstanding and overdue invoices to you. The program features multilevel

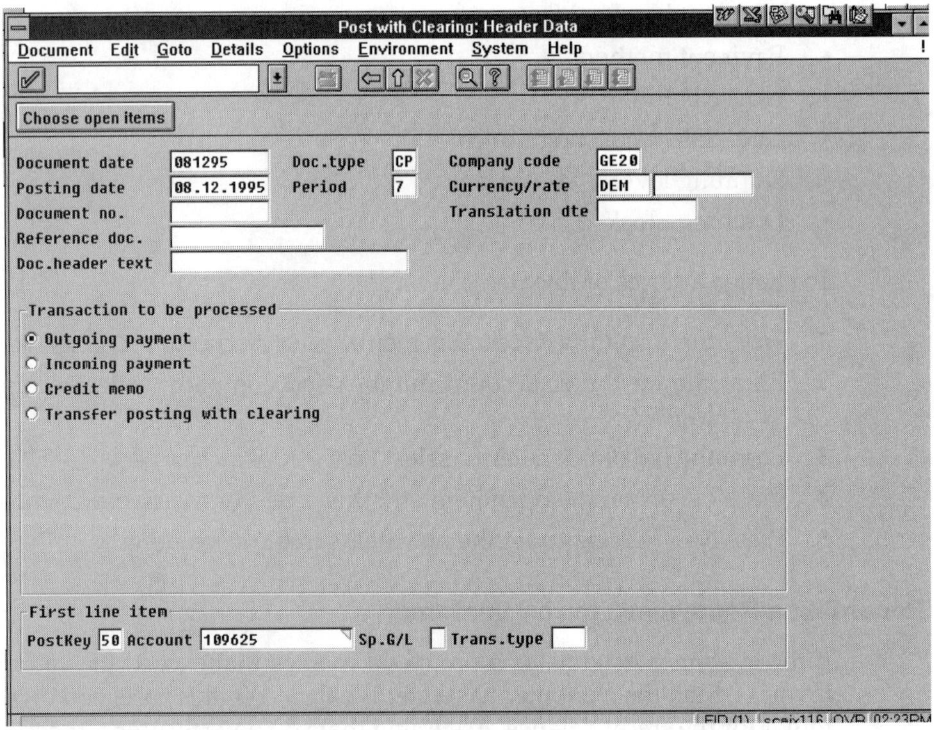

Exhibit 3.78   Post with Clearing: Recording a Credit

dunning. In this way, you can enter various, more sharply worded, collection letters. Later, depending on your configuration and on the dunning level of the customer account, you can have a different dunning letter printed. Assume that you have customer invoices that are overdue. Further, assume that the dunning program is properly configured. Last, assume that your printer is properly installed and configured for R/3. In summary, you dun customers as follows:

1. First, write and format the text of the letter with the SAPScript line-oriented text editor. SAPScript is also required to write any other text to be printed as a form, such as account statements, check forms, payment remittance advices, purchase orders, and customer invoices. This is not described here due to the complexity and changeability of SAPScript.

2. Run the dunning program and generate a dunning proposal based on due dates of outstanding invoices.

3. Optionally, block items from being dunned.

4. Print the dunning letters.

Blocking a Customer from Being Dunned. If you have an agreement with a customer that overrides the due dates of individual invoices, such as an agreement with a large, regular customer, you can block the customer from being dunned. This prevents this customer from being included in the dunning proposal, no matter what the amounts and due dates of outstanding invoices to this customer.

To block a customer from being dunned,

1. From the Accounts Receivable menu, select Master records → Change. (See Exhibit 3.79.)

2. Click on the Correspondence box only. Press <Enter>. (See Exhibit 3.80.)

3. Enter a code for the dunning block in the Dunn.block field, depending on your configuration. For a list of codes, put the cursor in this field and then press the down arrow.

4. To update the customer master record, press <F11> or the file folder icon.

Running the Dunning Program. Based on the due dates of outstanding invoices, the dunning level of each customer from the previous run, and the configuration, the dunning program generates a dunning proposal. This proposal contains a list of open invoices that the programmer would suggest you dun if he were sitting there with you. To start the dunning program:

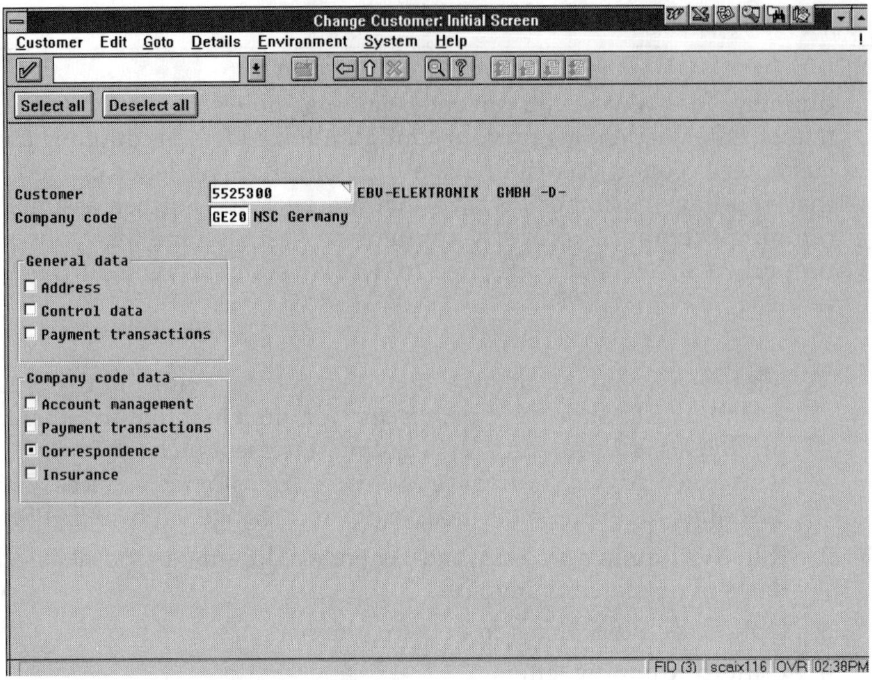

Exhibit 3.79   Change Customer: Initial Screen

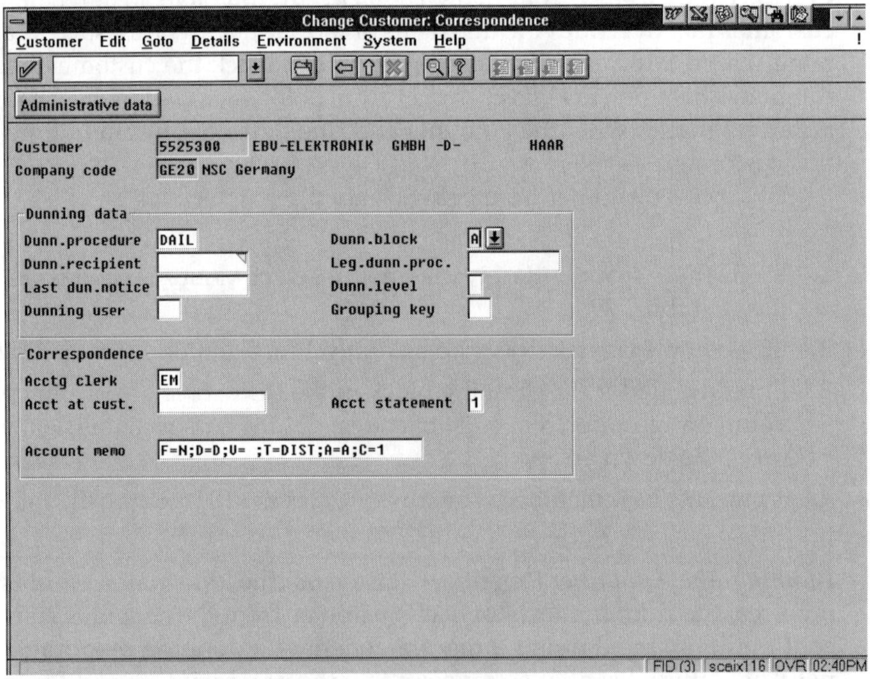

Exhibit 3.80   Change Customer: Correspondence

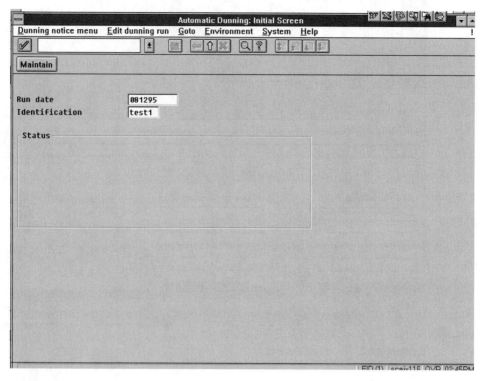

Exhibit 3.81   Automatic Dunning: Initial Screen

1. From the Accounts Receivable menu, select Periodic processing → Dunning. (See Exhibit 3.81.)

2. Usually, you enter today's date in the Run date field and some short name of this dunning run in the Identification field. Press the Maintain pushbutton. (See Exhibit 3.82.)

3. To store the parameters, press <F11> or the file folder icon.

4. From the initial screen, to start the dunning run, press Schedule. (See Exhibit 3.83.)

5. To see the latest status of the dunning run, keep pressing <Enter> until you see the message "dunning run is ready."

6. To edit the dunning run (changing the dunning level of an invoice of blocking an invoice), press Change dunn.notices and then press <Enter>. (See Exhibit 3.84.)

7. To store the dunning run, press <F11> or the file folder icon.

8. To print the dunning letters, press Schedule. (See Exhibit 3.85.)

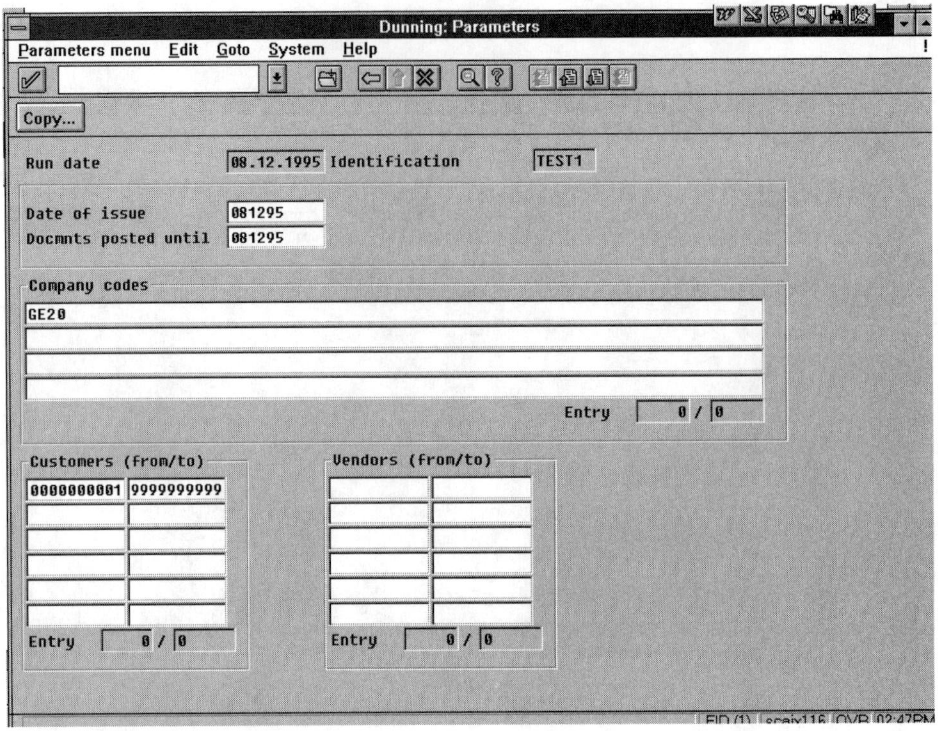

Exhibit 3.82 Dunning: Parameters

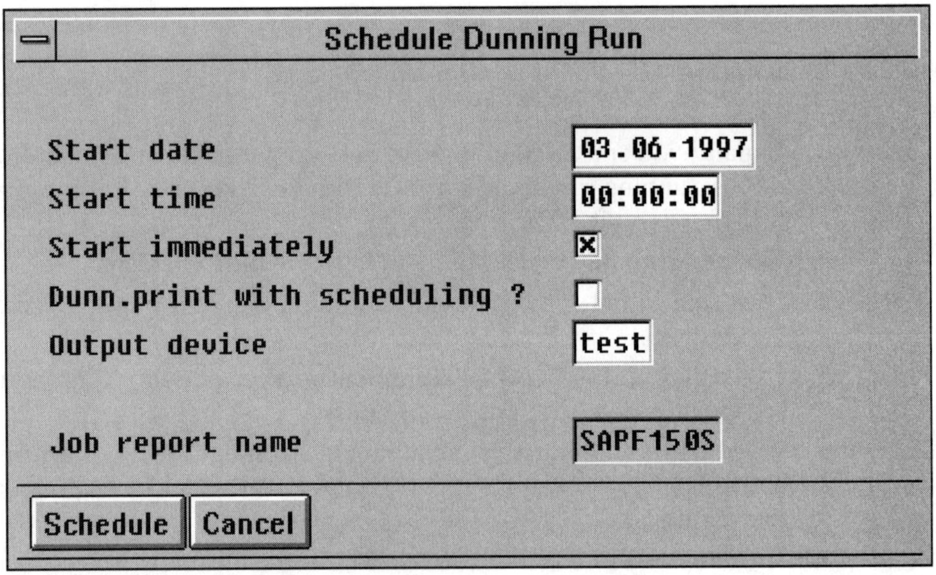

Exhibit 3.83 Timetable for the Dunning Run

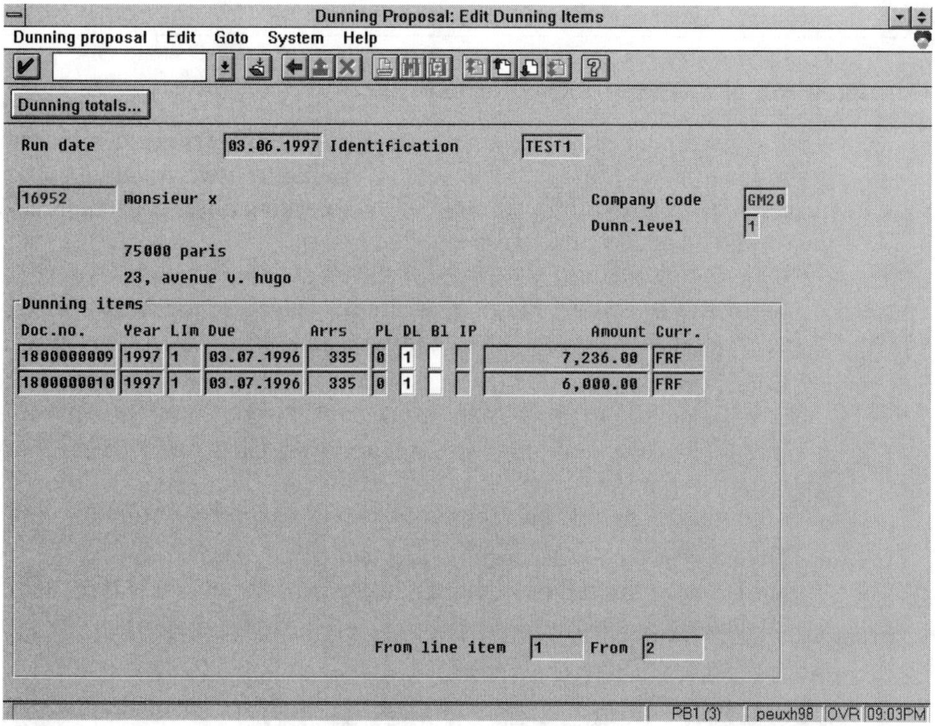

Exhibit 3.84 Dunning Proposal: Edit Dunning Items

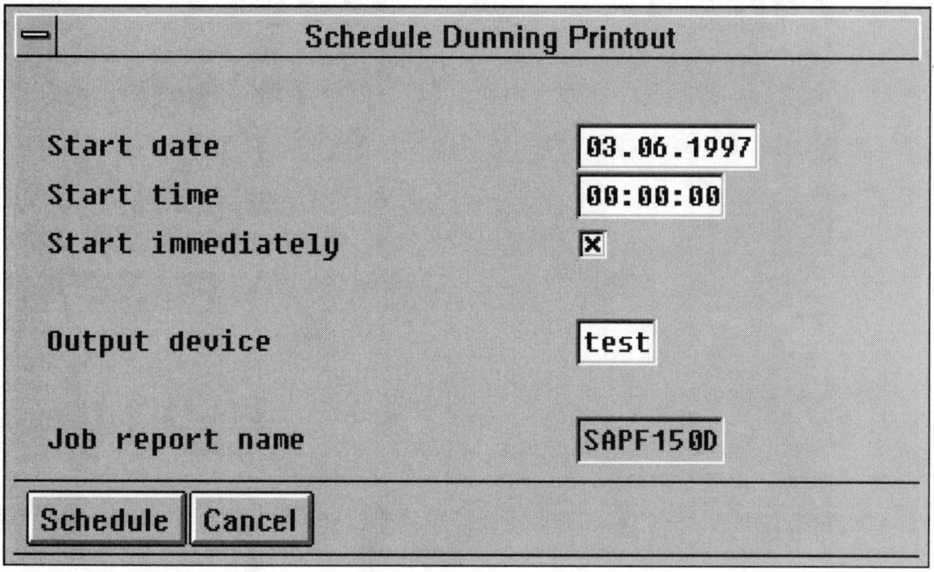

Exhibit 3.85 Timetable for Printing Dunning Letters

Posting a Bill of Exchange Receipt in France

A bill of exchange is a common payment method in France, Italy, and Spain. It is similar to a postdated check. It is advisable to have reliable, current credit information about your customer before accepting a bill of exchange. To record the receipt of a bill of exchange:

1. From the Accounts Receivable menu, select Document entry ➤ Bill of exchange ➤ Payment. (See Exhibit 3.86.)

2. Enter a posting key **09** (for a special G/L debit to a customer account, a specific customer, and **W** in the Sp. G/L field). Enter the bill of exchange into the specific customer account and then close the invoices that the customer is paying with the bill of exchange. The program then decreases accounts receivable and increases bills of exchange receivable.

3. To keep the bank fees and interest charges to a minimum, it may be advisable to hold the bill of exchange in the drawer until it is due, usually 60 or 90 days after it is issued.

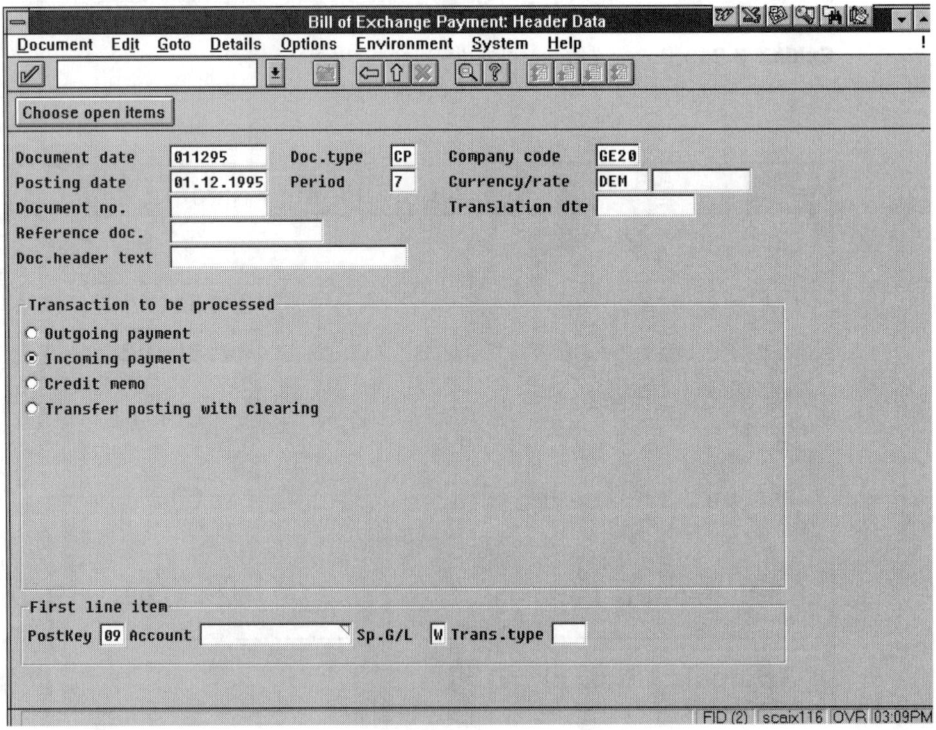

Exhibit 3.86 Bill of Exchange Payment: Header Data

Displaying a Customer Balance with Bills of Exchange

In each customer account, bills of exchange are recorded separately from invoices and payments (so-called normal items). In SAP terminology, bills of exchange like down payments and security deposits are "special G/L transactions."

To display bills of exchange in a customer balance:

1. From the Accounts Receivable menu, select Account → Display balances.
2. Enter the customer number, company code, and fiscal year, as usual. Press <Enter>.
3. To see the total of the bills of exchange in this customer account, from the account balance display, press Sp. G/L transactions.

In general, special G/L transactions update another G/L account balance than the one you assign to the customer as the reconciliation account in the customer master record.

Displaying Open Items with Bills of Exchange

In each customer account, bills of exchange are recorded separately from invoices and payments (so-called normal items). In SAP terminology, bills of exchange are "special G/L transactions."

To display open items in a customer account, including bills of exchange:

1. From the Accounts Receivable menu, select Account → Display items.
2. Mark the With special G/L transactions field. Press <Enter> and display the open items as usual.

Reporting Bills of Exchange in France by the Due Date

Use the RFWEKO01 ABAP program. From any menu, select System → Services → Reporting.

REPORTING FROM ACCOUNTS RECEIVABLE

SAP supplies certain reports. You can print out or display these reports on your screen. However, all the reports on the screen were intended for 132-column printers, so you have to use the horizontal scroll bar to scroll left and right to see parts of the report. To see the entire report all at once, print out the report and read the printed report. If your printer is not yet installed properly, you can download any report to a spreadsheet, such as Microsoft Excel, and print from the spreadsheet. ABAP programs, developed with the SAP-proprietary programming language, produce reports. SAP never supplies reports that begin with the letter Z.

If your company is already using SAP, you may have developed and maintained other reports. You should make sure that all of your company's ABAP programs begin with the letter Z (and only with the letter Z). Since SAP never supplies reports that begin with the letter Z, you can be sure that your reports will never be overwritten, even after an upgrade or release change.

Listing Available Custom A/R Reports

To list any custom reports that your company has developed:

1. From any menu, select System ➤ Services ➤ Reporting.
2. From the ABAP/4: Execute Program screen, select Environment ➤ Program directory. (See Exhibit 3.87.)

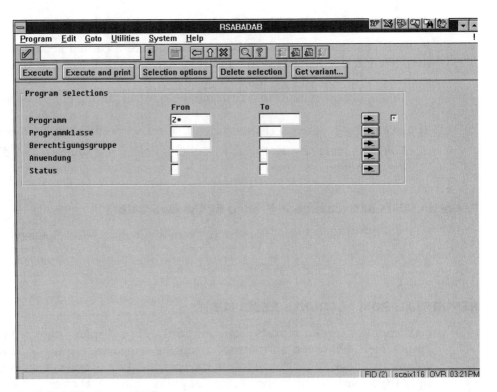

Exhibit 3.87 Program Directory

3. In the Program field, enter **Z***. Press <F8> or the Execute pushbutton. Press <Enter> on the next screen.

4. On the next screen, double-click on the line Display programs regardless.

5. The next screen contains a list of all your company's custom programs. If the programmers have documented the program, you can read the report documentation on-line. Place the cursor on the line with the report and then press the Documentation pushbutton.

6. To run a report, place the cursor on the line with the name of the report and then press <F8> or the Execute pushbutton.

Reading and Printing On-line Report Documentation

SAP supplies all report documentation on-line only. If you want SAP's printed report documentation, then you must print it out. This reduces their costs of printing and circulating printed documentation, and it also ensures that you receive the latest report documentation with the latest software release. You are not left waiting for the latest manual to be printed and sent to you. To find the name of and then print the on-line documentation about a report:

1. Start to run a report as usual from a menu. Display a screen prompting you to enter specific parameters (the first screen of parameters).

2. Select System → Status.

3. Halfway down the screen, in the left-hand column, look for the name ABAP/4 program. Find the (eight-character) name of the program and write it down. For example, the name of the program to print a financial statement (list of G/L account balances) is RFBILA00.

4. Select System → Services → Reporting. (See Exhibit 3.88.)

5. If you do not see the same name in the Program field, enter it now.

6. To display this program (report) documentation for reading on-line, select Goto → Documentation.

7. To print the displayed documentation, press Print.

Printing Reports

To print reports from R/3 on your LAN or PC printer, make sure that you have the proper line printer daemon installed and properly configured. For example, to print reports to a PC printer attached to your Windows PC printer, you require a piece of software that runs under Windows called saplpd. (Call or write SAP for details.)

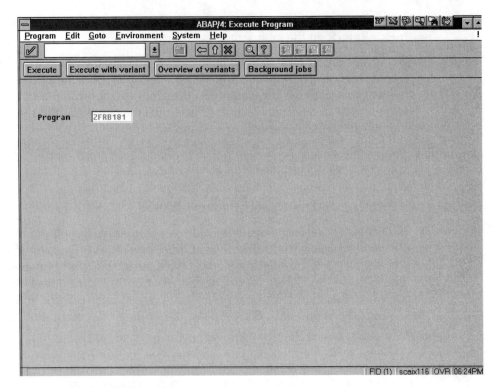

Exhibit 3.88   Execute Program

When you have the report displayed on your screen, to print it, select
System → List → Print.

Downloading a Report to a Spreadsheet

You can download any report to a spreadsheet.

When you have the report displayed on your screen, to download it, select
System → List → Download.

Finding a String in the Report

To find a string in the report:

1. Display the report and place your cursor at the beginning of the report.
2. Select Edit → Find.
3. Enter the text string to search for.
4. Press Continue.

Checking the Printing in Process

The program places the report in a temporary file on the disk called a spool file. To check the printing in process:

1. From any menu, select System ➤ Services ➤ Output controller.
2. Press <Enter> to see a list of print runs that you have done.

Printing the Customer List

To print the customer list with the SAP-supplied report:

1. From the Accounts Receivable menu, select Periodic processing ➤ Reporting ➤ Account list. (See Exhibit 3.89.)
2. Enter at least the company code, and then press <F8> or the Execute pushbutton to run the program.

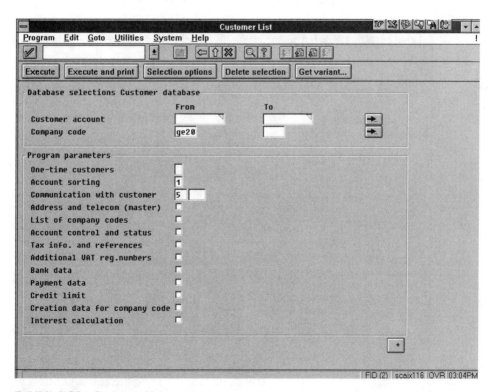

Exhibit 3.89 Customer List

Customer Balances

To print the customer balances, using the program supplied by SAP:

1. From the Accounts Receivable menu, select Periodic processing ➤ Reporting ➤ Account balances. (See Exhibit 3.90.)
2. Enter at least the company code, and then press <F8> or the Execute pushbutton to run the program.

Customer Open Items and Balances by Currency

To report the customer balances by currency:

1. From the Accounts Receivable menu, select Periodic processing ➤ Reporting ➤ Open items. (See Exhibit 3.91.)
2. Enter at least the company code. De-select Line items required, and select Total by currency.
3. To run the report, press <F8> or the Execute pushbutton.

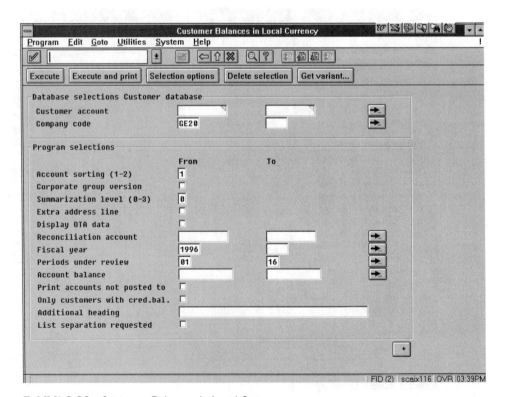

Exhibit 3.90 Customer Balances in Local Currency

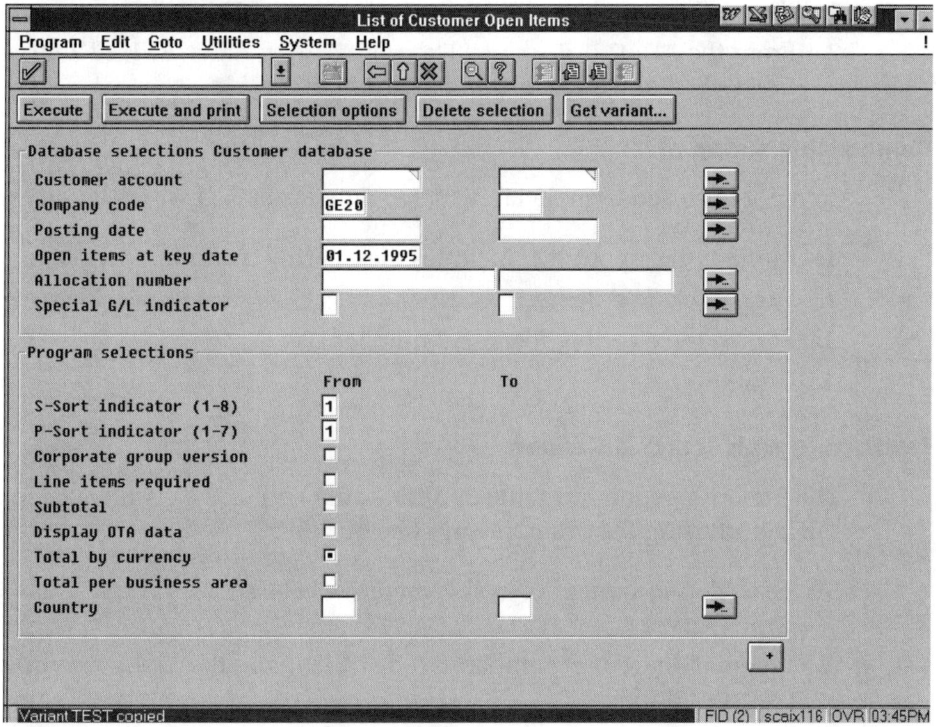

Exhibit 3.91   List of Customer Open Items

Aged Receivables Summary

To print this report with the program supplied by SAP, use the report **RFDOPR10,** with the **1 1 1** parameters in the OI sorted list, Summarization, and OI list summarization parameters.

The aged A/R is then sorted by the ranges of 1–15, 16–30, 31–60, and over 60 days overdue.

Aged Receivables Detail

To print this report with the program supplied by SAP, use the report **RFDOPR00,** with the **1 0 1** parameters in the OI sorted list, Summarization, and OI list summarization parameters. On the second screen of parameters you can specify a range of due dates.

Bills of Exchange Report

To report the bills of exchange sorted by the due date:

1. From any menu, select System ➤ Services ➤ Reporting.
2. From the ABAP/4: Execute Program screen, enter **RFWEKO01** and then press <F8> or the Execute pushbutton.

Closed Item Detail

To report a closed item detail (which payments closed which invoices):

1. Make a line layout that includes the clearing document number.
2. Display cleared items.
3. Sort by the clearing document number.
4. Print this list.

Customers with Credit Balances

This report is required by the auditor at the end of the fiscal year. To prepare this report using the program supplied by SAP:

1. From the Accounts Receivable menu, select Periodic processing ➤ Reporting ➤ Account balances.
2. Enter at least the company code. Click on the Only customer with cred.bal. option.
3. To run the report, press <F8> or the Execute pushbutton.

Controlling Transaction Data Interfaces

Use the **RFBUSU00** report to verify totals posted. You can use this to verify transaction data posted from external systems by batch input.

Recording Control Totals

A control total is a total that you have calculated in advance by hand and that you expect to be posted to one or more accounts, such as customer accounts or G/L accounts for cash in the bank. To record one or more control totals:

1. From the Accounts Receivable menu, select Environment ➤ Current options ➤ Control totals.
2. Press the Maint. control totals pushbutton.

Running Custom Reports

If your company has developed custom reports, you can run them as follows:

1. From any menu, select System ➤ Services ➤ Reporting. (See Exhibit 3.92.)

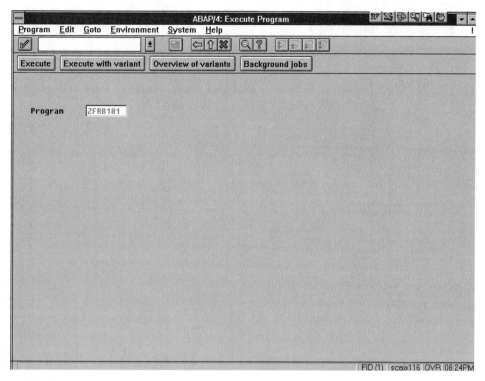

Exhibit 3.92   Execute Program

2. In the Program field, enter the name of the ABAP program, such as **ZFR-Bxxxx.** To run the report, press <F8> or the Execute pushbutton.

Running Reports Quickly with Variants

A variant is a set of report parameters that you can store and retrieve as a set. This can be useful if you regularly run the same report, with the same or similar parameters. You can store the parameters in a variant and then retrieve the variant the next time that you run the report.

Storing a Report Variant.   To store a report variant:

1. After you enter the report parameters, but before you run the report, select Goto ➤ Variant ➤ Save.
2. Enter a brief name, press <Tab>, and then enter a description of the report variant.
3. To store the variant, press <F11> or the file folder icon.

Running a Report with a Variant.   To retrieve a variant:

1. From the report parameter screen, before you run the report, press Get variant.

2. Enter the name of the variant and press <Enter>. Alternatively, for a list of variants already defined, press the down arrow.

CHAPTER 4

Accounts Payable

This chapter describes using the SAP R/3 Accounts Payable program to keep track of vendor master records, to process and pay vendor invoices, and to prepare required reports, such as a vendor invoice journal, vendor line item listings (open items and paid items), and vendor account balances. You can post vendor invoices in either local currency or foreign currency. You can also use Accounts Payable to keep track of employee travel advances and expenses. To do this, enter a vendor master record for each employee. Then record a travel advance to an employee, as if it were a down payment to a vendor. Later, you record the employee travel expenses as if they were vendor invoices. You can also post invoices to employees, as if they were travel advances, so that a receivables account contains the transaction. Accounts Payable includes an automatic payment program to pay vendors (or employees) according to the due dates of their invoices. To pay the vendor by bank transfer, enter both the vendor's bank account and the payment method for bank transfer in the vendor master record.

Accounts Payable is integrated with the General Ledger module in FI and with the Invoice Verification module in the MM module. If you want to match vendor invoices to purchase orders, then use MM to enter a purchase order, to enter a packing list (of goods received), and then to enter, verify, and post the vendor invoice. This chapter describes entering and posting vendor invoices with FI only.

To go to Accounts Payable, from the SAP R/3 main menu (with the title SAP R/3), select Accounting ➤ Financial accounting ➤ Accounts payable. (See Exhibit 4.1.)

323

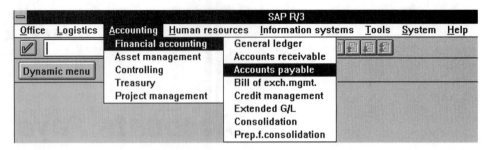

Exhibit 4.1 Getting to Accounts Payable

STARTING TO USE ACCOUNTS PAYABLE

Setting User Defaults

For each SAP user ID, you can set the start-up menu, print control parameters, date format, and decimal format. These new settings are valid after you log off and log in again. They are then valid each and every time you log in after you change them. You can change your user defaults at any time, but you have to log off and then on again to make the new settings valid. To set your user defaults:

1. Log in to R/3 with your user ID.
2. From any menu, select System ➤ User profile ➤ User defaults. (See Exhibit 4.2.)
3. To start at the Accounts Payable menu each time you log in, enter **FKMN** in the Start menu field. In the Output device field, enter the four-character name of the printer in your R/3 system. To set up a printer, you first have to define it under your operating system—with maximum entries for the number of rows and columns per page. You then have to define the printer in R/3 with the applicable number of rows and columns per page. Click on a sample format in the Date format column. In the Decimal notation column, select on Comma or Period to separate whole numbers from fractions by either a comma or period. To store these parameters, press <F11> or the file folder icon. Note that you can change these parameters later too.

Setting Processing Options

You can set various options to process transaction data. These options are valid for each person until you change them. There are three sets of processing options:

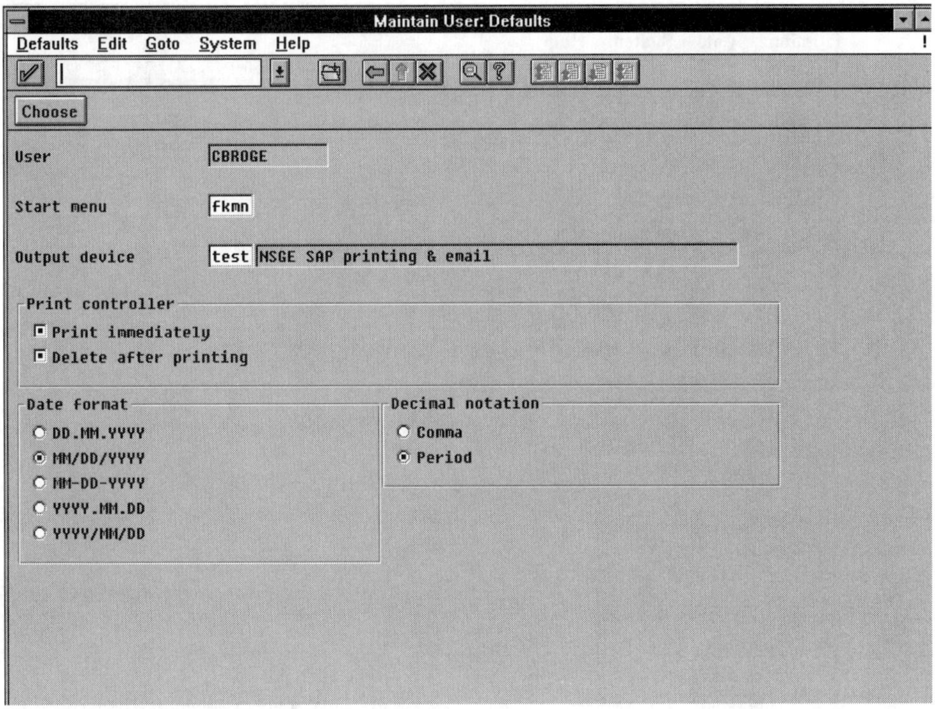

Exhibit 4.2 Maintain User: Defaults

- Transaction entry and display
- Open item processing (for example, for cash application)
- Line item display

To turn on a processing option, you simply click on the box next to the option, so that a mark appears in the box. To turn off an option, click on the box, so that the mark disappears. To start to set processing options:

1. From the Accounts Receivable menu, select Environment ➤ Current options ➤ Editing options. (See Exhibit 4.3.)

   All of the examples in this course assume that the processing options on this screen are set as shown. The primary transaction entry and display options are as follows:

Option	Meaning if option is on
No foreign currency	If you enter and process transactions only in local currency, click on this option. In effect, this option suppresses entry of amounts in foreign currency.

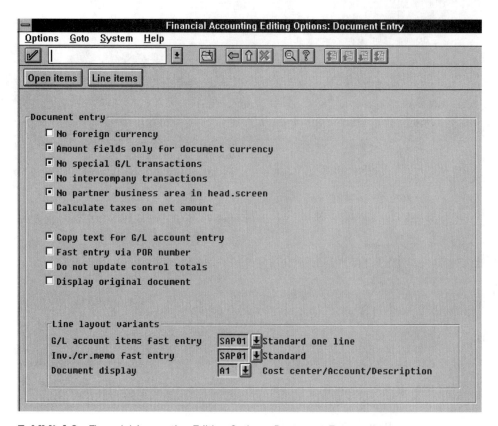

Exhibit 4.3 Financial Accounting Editing Options: Document Entry

Amount fields only for document currency	When you enter a transaction in foreign currency, then you enter the currency code in the transaction header and the amounts in the transaction currency only in each line item. If the option were off, then you could enter both the transaction currency amount and the local currency amount in each line item.
No special G/L transactions	This option suppresses entry of special G/L transactions, such as down payments, bills of exchange, security deposits, and others.
No intercompany transactions	This option suppresses entry of intercompany transactions in which two company codes buy or sell something jointly.

No partner business area in head. screen	This option suppresses the partner business area in the transaction header screen. If the transaction involves multiple business areas, then the receivables and payables between business areas are calculated and posted to and from the partner business area and the business areas in the transaction.
Calculate taxes on net amount	This option makes the program calculate transaction taxes based on the net amount in the revenue or expense entry. Otherwise, you enter the gross amount in the revenue or expense entry.
Copy text for G/L account entry	The option makes the program copy your entry on the text field from one G/L line item to the next, when you enter a long G/L transaction such as external payroll (not from HR).
Fast entry via POR number	This option is required only in Switzerland to enter vendor invoices based on the Swiss payment number.
Do not update control totals	This option turns off the update of control totals, if you wish to control the totals of only certain user's entries.
Display original document	Turn this option on, if you scan documents such as vendor invoices.
G/L account items fast entry	Use the default (supplied) line layout to begin with. Depending on your requirements and your configuration, you can change the line layout (the sequence of fields from left to right displayed on the screen).
Inv/cr.memo fast entry	Use the default (supplied) line layout to begin with. Depending on your requirements and your configuration, you can change the line layout (the sequence of fields from left to right displayed on the screen).
Document display	Use the default (supplied) line layout to begin with. Depending on your requirements and your configuration, you can change the line layout (the sequence of fields from left to right displayed on the screen). This determines how the overview of the transaction is displayed.

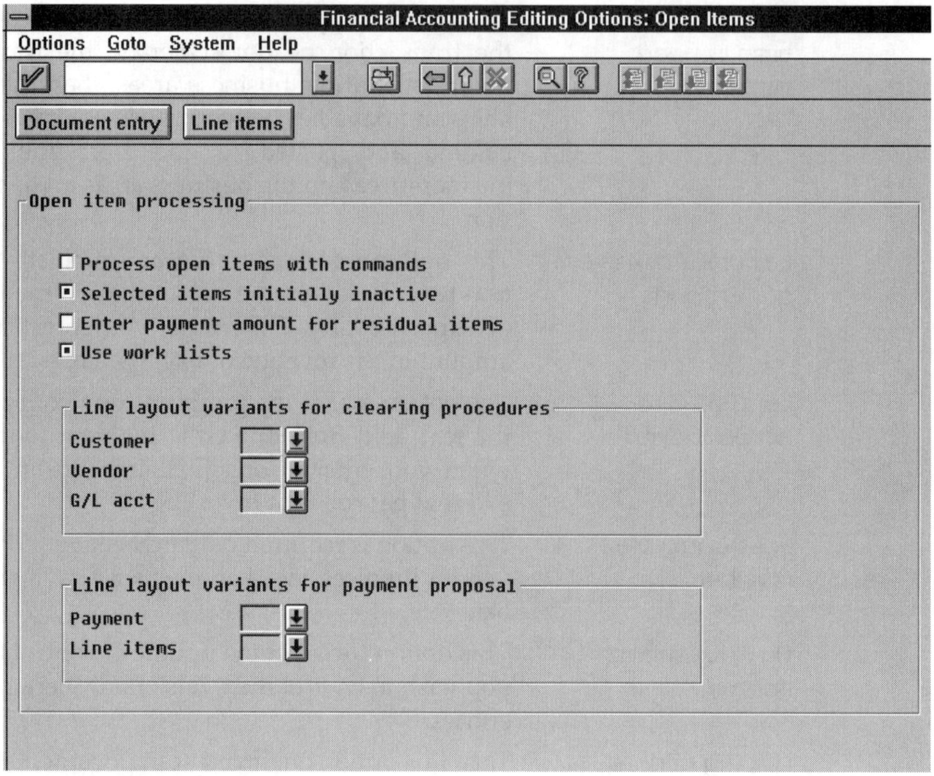

Exhibit 4.4 Financial Accounting Editing Options: Open Items

2. To set the open item processing options, press Open items. (See Exhibit 4.4.) The following are the primary open item processing options:

Option	Meaning if Set On
Process open items with commands	If you set this option on, you can process open items with commands (in the left-most column). Otherwise, you use the mouse and double-click on an item to activate it.
Selected items initially inactive	If you set this option on, then all open items in the clearing screen (cash application screen) are not active (applied), until you activate them.
Enter payment amount for residual items	If you set this option on, you enter the amount of the payment in the residual item screen when you process a partial payment and close the original invoice. Otherwise, you enter the amount of the residual item.

Use work lists	You can combine two or more customers into a work list—to display open items by a work list or to clear open items (apply cash) by a work list. This option turns on work lists when you process (clear) open items.
Line layout variants for clearing procedures	Depending on your business requirements and on your configuration, you can set a different default line layout for clearing open items, such as cash application. To begin with, use the default (supplied) line layout.
Line layout variants for payment proposal	Depending on your business requirements and on your configuration, you can set a different default line layout for the payment proposal. To begin with, use the default (supplied) line layout.

3. To set the processing option for line item display, press the Line items pushbutton. (See Exhibit 4.5.)

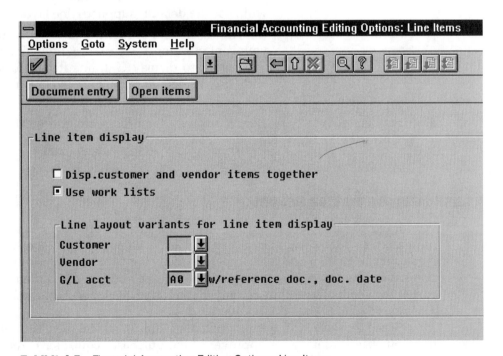

Exhibit 4.5   Financial Accounting Editing Options: Line Items

Option	Meaning if Set On
Disp.customer and vendor items together	If your customer is also a vendor, such as an inter-company customer or vendor, then this item display both sets of line items together. This requires the master records be marked properly—with the customer number in the vendor record and the vendor number in the customer record.
Use work lists	You can combine two or more customers into a work list—to display open items by a work list or to clear open items (apply cash) by a work list. This option turns on work lists when you display open items.
Line layout variants—Customer	Depending on your business requirements and on your configuration, you can set a different default line layout to display customer line items. To begin with, use the default (supplied) line layout.
Line layout variants—vendors	Depending on your business requirements and on your configuration, you can set a different default line layout to display vendor line items. To begin with, use the default (supplied) line layout.
Line layout variants—G/L acct	Depending on your business requirements and on your configuration, you can set a different default line layout to display G/L line items. To begin with, use the default (supplied) line layout.

4. To update your user master record with the processing options that you set, press <F11> or the file folder icon.

KEEPING VENDOR MASTER RECORDS

Vendor records in FI have two parts—a general part that applies to all possible companies that this vendor could supply *and* a company code–specific part that applies only to a specific company code being supplied. Vendor records also have a third part, purchasing data about the vendor. You can enter this part of the vendor master record only if you have licensed and set up the purchasing program in the MM module.

You can then use MM to enter purchase requisitions and then to enter and print purchase orders (after approval of the purchase requisition). You then record the deliveries according to the vendors' pack lists and your inspections, comparing the goods that you received with what you ordered. To complete the process, you enter the vendor invoice in MM, comparing the invoiced quantities with the received quantities and the invoice prices with the prices in the purchase orders.

Most of all, the general part of a vendor master record contains the following data: the *name, address, phone number, tax ID number,* and *bank account numbers* of the vendor. To pay the vendor by bank transfer, you need the vendor's bank account number. This is a valid payment method in many countries and is often simpler than printing checks. If the vendor is also a customer, such as an intercompany vendor, you also record the customer number in the general part of the vendor master record.

The company code-specific part of a vendor master contains the following data: the reconciliation account for the vendor (G/L account for payables), how to sort details in this account when you display them later, the *payment terms* from this vendor, and one or more *payment methods* you use to pay the vendor, such as bank transfer or check. To pay the vendor by bank transfer, you have to enter both the vendor's bank account and the payment method for bank transfer in the vendor master record.

Most companies use bank transfers to pay vendors in Germany, the United Kingdom, France, and Italy. This book does not include details of printing checks. Due to the complexity, error-prone nature, and variable configuration required to print checks to pay vendors, this chapter will assume that you pay vendors by bank transfer. In regions or countries where a check is the main payment method, such as North America and Southeast Asia, first make sure that the payment program is properly configured and tested.

Entering a Vendor Master Record

You enter the general part of a vendor master record in FI on the first three screens. Then you enter the company code–specific part of a vendor master record on the next three screens (screens four through six). The vendor master data is spread over these six screens. You cannot compress it onto one screen.

When you enter a vendor master record, you have to enter a *reconciliation account* (accounts payable to the vendor) for the vendor on the fourth screen. This integrates accounts payable with the general ledger. When you post a vendor invoice or a vendor payment, then FI automatically and transparently updates both the vendor account and the G/L account for accounts payable to that vendor. You should also enter at least the payment terms from the vendor and the payment method that you use to pay the vendor.

You can also enter a single vendor master record for one-time vendors, such as restaurants, hotels, and other one-time services. The purpose of a one-time vendor master record is to avoid cluttering up your data files with vendor master records that you only use once. When you post a vendor invoice to a one-time vendor master record, you enter the name, address, and possibly the bank account of the vendor (for payment by bank transfer) in the invoice.

If you have an international company, you might have three or four types of vendors and seven vendor account groups—*external* vendors (**VEND**), *intercompany* vendors (**INTR**), *employees* by country with travel expenses (**EMGE, EMLN, EMFR, EMIT**), and *one-time vendors* (**OTXX** where **XX** represents the country where the vendor is located, such as **OTGE, OTFR, OTUK,** and so on). Assuming your system is properly configured for local and global requirements, enter a vendor master record:

1. From the Accounts Payable menu, select Master records → Create. (See Exhibit 4.6.)

    When entering a vendor master record, do not enter a vendor account number in the Vendor field. It may be advisable to number ven-

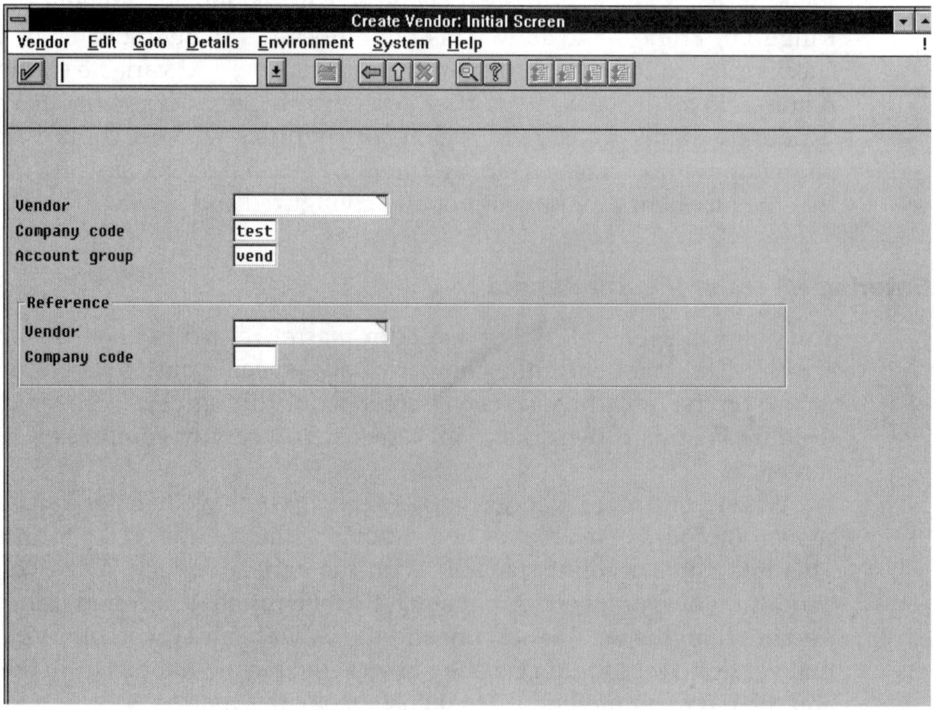

Exhibit 4.6   Create Vendor: Initial Screen

dors internally with no logic in the vendor number. In other words, you could have FI number the vendors according to a defined, worldwide vendor number range (1–999,999). FI automatically assigns a vendor number after you store the vendor. On the other hand, depending on your configuration, it is also possible to number the vendors externally. The following fields are always required to enter a vendor header:

Field	Note
Company code	Enter the company code that this vendor supplies, such as **GE20**.
Account group	Enter an account group for this vendor. The account group determines how vendors in this account group are numbered (internally by FI or externally by you according to vendor numbers in some external system).

Press <Enter>. The next screen prompts you to enter the name, address, and phone numbers of the vendor, with all possible fields shown in Exhibit 4.7.

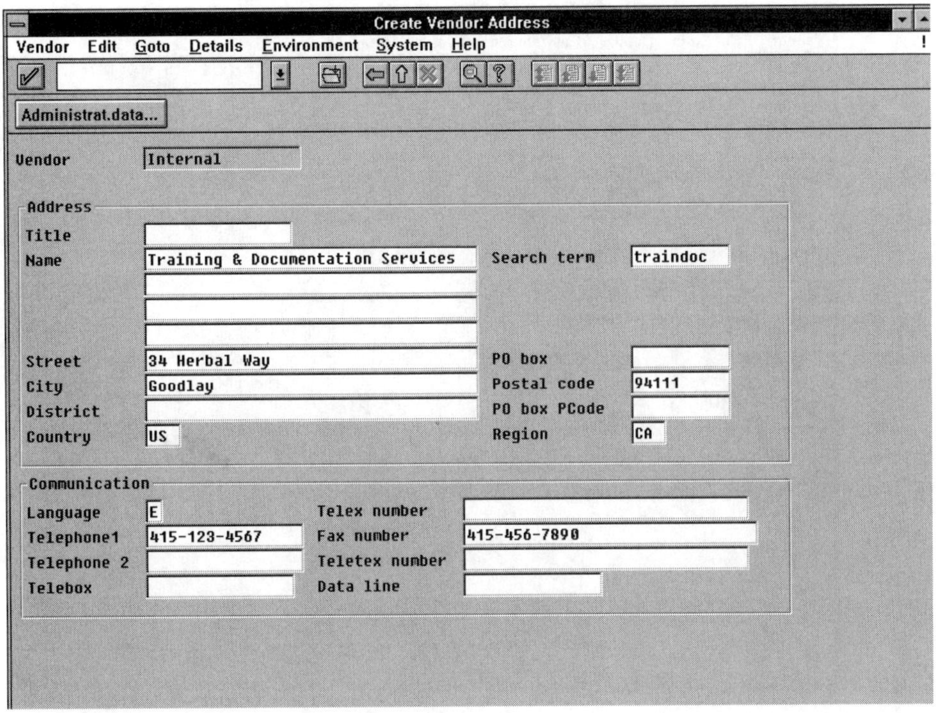

Exhibit 4.7 Create Vendor: Address

2. Enter your vendor data. Note that the exact fields that you see when you enter a vendor master record depend on your specific configuration. Also note that any field on any screen that contains a question mark is a required field, depending on your configuration. The Search term field lets you enter a short name for the vendor and then find the vendor account number later by the short name, if you do not remember the vendor account number. Other fields, such as the Postal code, may be required, but do not have a question mark in them. Press <Enter>. The next screen is shown in Exhibit 4.8, with all possible fields shown for illustration.

3. If the vendor is also a customer, such as an intercompany vendor, enter the customer number in the Customer field. The Tax code 1 field is used in France, Italy, Belgium, and Spain. Use the VAT reg.no. field to record the vendor's number in the Common Market (European Union). Press <Enter>. The next screen prompts you to enter the vendor's bank data, in order to pay the vendor by bank transfer. (See Exhibit 4.9.)

4. If you do not pay vendors by bank transfer, press <Enter> to go to the next screen. If you do pay vendors by bank transfer, enter the country of

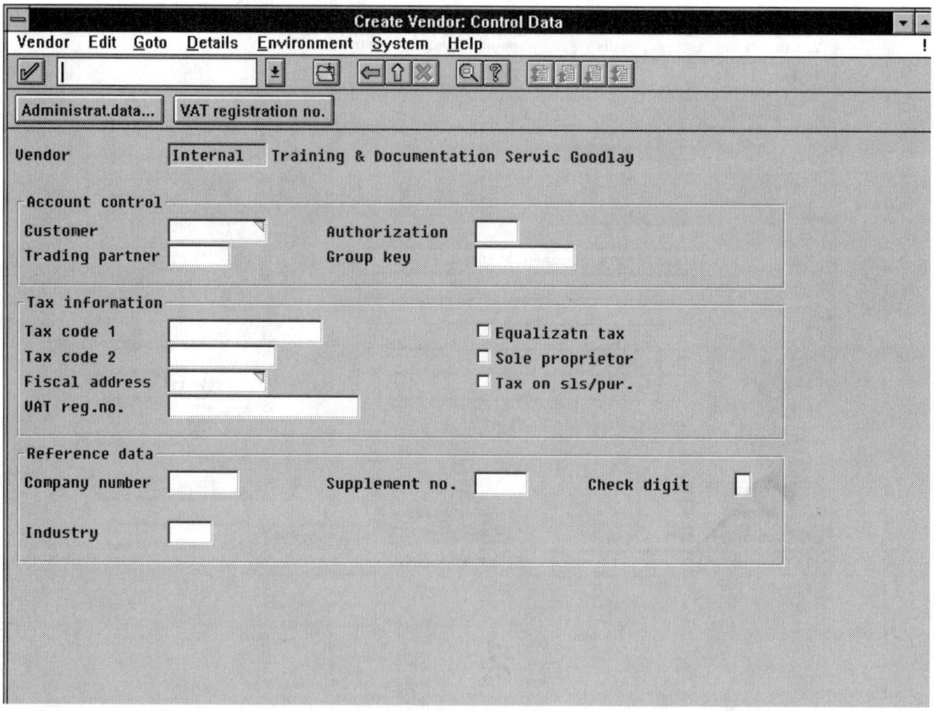

Exhibit 4.8   Create Vendor: Control Data

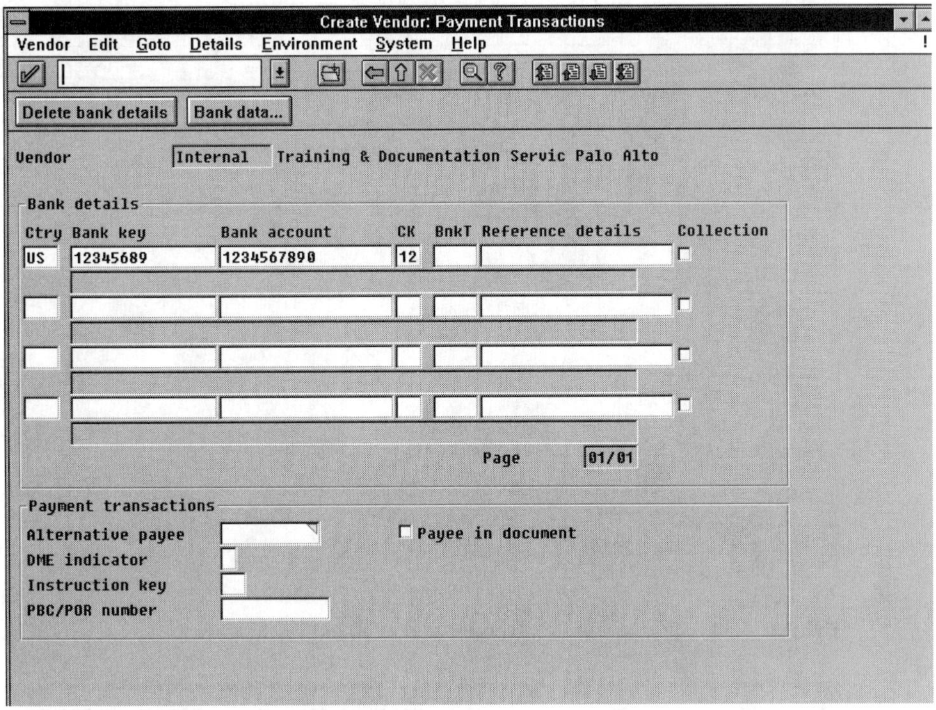

Exhibit 4.9 Create Vendor: Payment Transactions

the vendor's bank in the Ctry field, a bank key (sort code) of the vendor's bank in the Bank key field, and a bank account number in the Bank account field. The CK field is used in France to verify a correct bank account number. You can enter more than one bank account, if the vendor has more than one. To pay foreign vendors by international bank transfer, you have to include the SWIFT (Society for Worldwide Interbank Financial Telecommunications) address of the bank in the bank master record. The SWIFT number uniquely identifies the bank for international payments. If you do not have the vendor's bank details, call the vendor and have them give you their bank account number and the SWIFT address of their bank. In the United Kingdom, if the vendor has a bank account at a building society, enter the building society's sort code and bank account number at a clearing bank in the Reference details field. Press <Enter>. (See Exhibit 4.10.)

5. In the Reconcil.account field, enter the G/L account for accounts payable to this vendor. If you do not have the G/L account number, you can look it up using a matchcode. Put the cursor in the Reconcil.acct field and press the down arrow. (See Exhibit 4.11.)

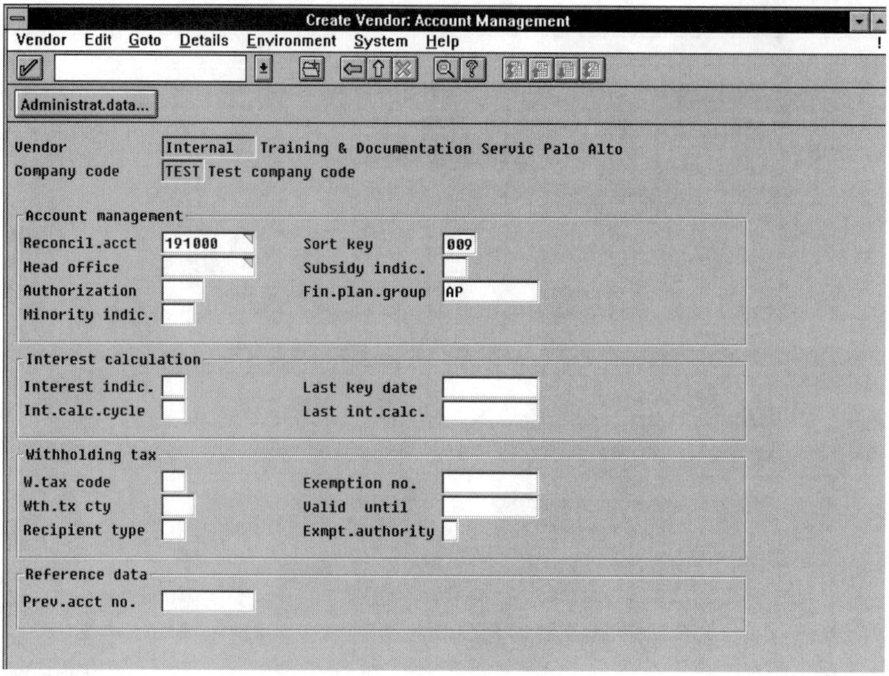

Exhibit 4.10 Create Vendor: Account Management

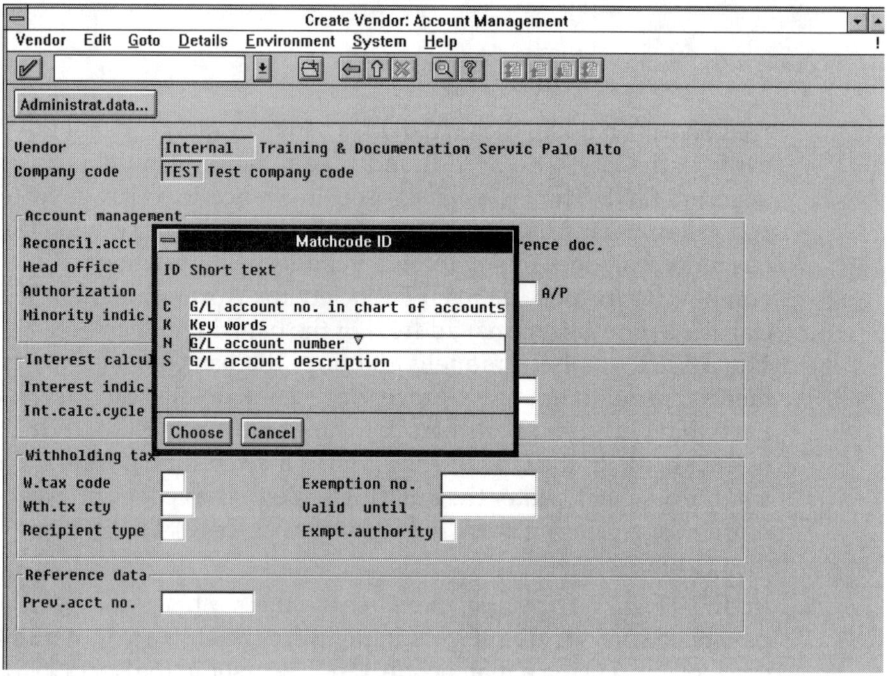

Exhibit 4.11 Create Vendor: Account Management

6. To find the G/L account number in the company code, double-click on the third line (N G/L account number). (See Exhibit 4.12.)

7. In the pop-up window, enter the first two digits of the G/L account number, if you have them, and then an asterisk, such as **19***, in the *first G/L account* field. In the *Company code* field, enter the company code. Then press <Enter> or the *Continue* button to see the list of G/L accounts with these criteria in this company code.

8. If there is only one G/L account that matches your specification, then the program puts this G/L account number in the *Reconcil.account* field. If there is a series of G/L accounts matching the specifications, you will see a list of these accounts. In the window listing the G/L accounts, select a G/L account by double-clicking on it.

9. In the *Sort key* field, enter **009** to sort the vendor account details later by the vendor's invoice number. The sort key is only useful later, after you have posted a series of vendor invoices to a vendor account. The sort key that you enter now determines later how FI sorts line items in the basic list of line items posted to this vendor account. In the *Prev.acct no.* field,

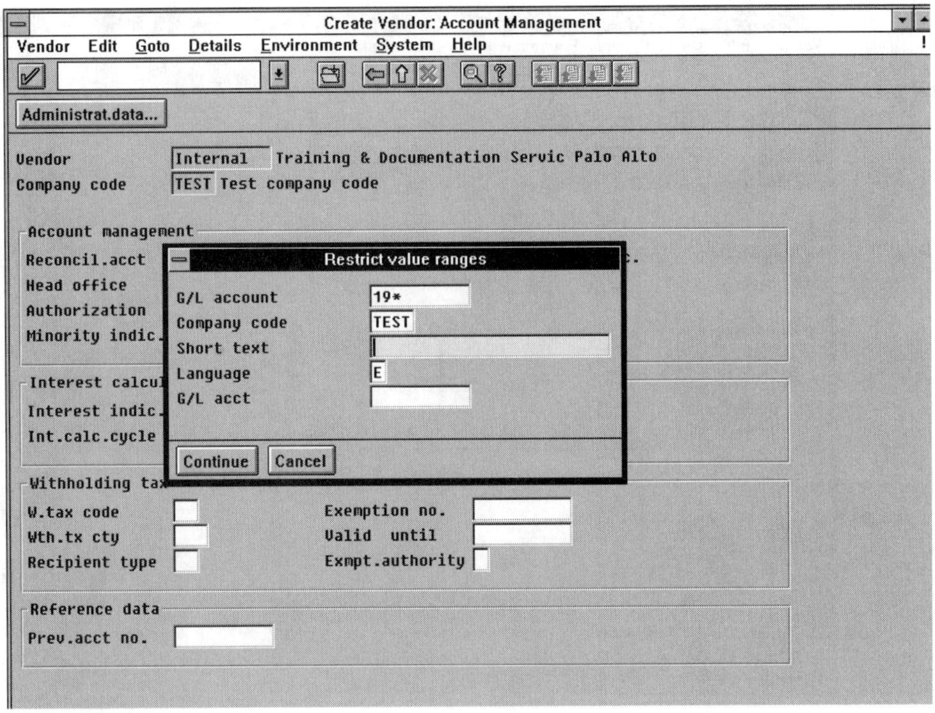

Exhibit 4.12   Restrict Value Ranges

enter the previous account number of the vendor, if you are entering this vendor data from a previous system. Press <Enter>. (See Exhibit 4.13.)

10. Enter the payment terms in the Payment terms field, such as **D10** for 2/10 net 30. Always click on the Chk. double inv. field. FI then issues a message if you enter two vendor invoices with the same document date, currency, reference document number (vendor number and invoice number), and amount. Always enter at least one payment method in the Payment methods field. For a list of valid payment methods in the country of the company code, press the Payment methods pushbutton, after you enter something in the Payment method field. Press <Enter>. (See Exhibit 4.14.)

11. In the Acctg clerk field, enter the name of the accounting clerk in your company who is responsible for this vendor. In the User at vendor field, enter the person at the vendor who is responsible for their accounts receivable. Alternatively, if you receive vendor invoices by EDI, enter the name of the EDI invoice administrator at the vendor. In the Account memo field, enter a brief note about the vendor. To enter more detailed text about the

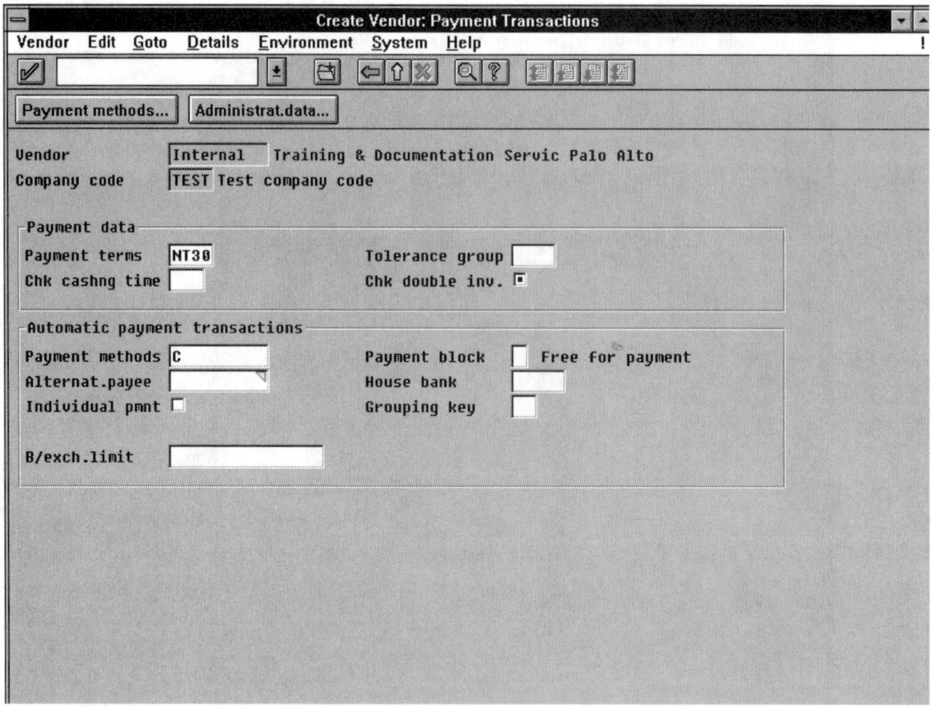

Exhibit 4.13   Create Vendor: Payment Transactions

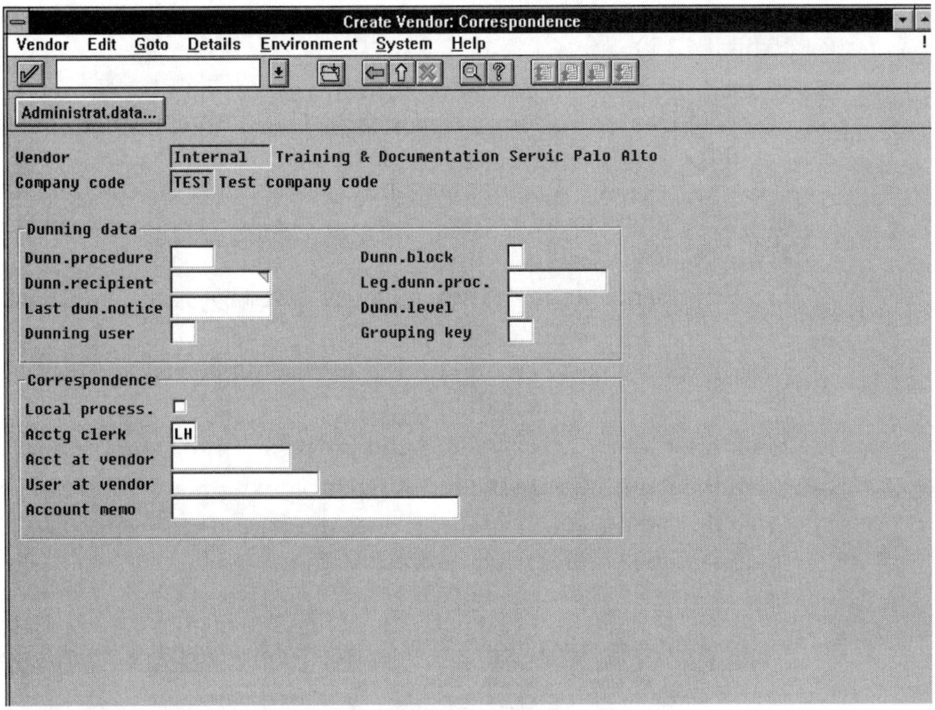

Exhibit 4.14 Create Vendor: Correspondence

vendor, read the next section, "Entering notes about a vendor." Press <F11> or the file folder icon to store this vendor master record on the disk.

Note that the exact fields that you see when you enter a vendor master record depend on your specific configuration.

FI then assigns the vendor a number and records the vendor master record on the disk.

Entering Notes about a Vendor. To describe a vendor, you can enter text about a vendor. For example, you could describe how the vendor is organized, or include specific purchasing behavior or payment instructions required by the vendor. You can enter text about a vendor either in the general part of the vendor master record, in the company code–specific part of the vendor master record or in both. Often, you enter text about a vendor after entering the vendor master record. However, you can also enter text about a vendor at the same time that you enter the vendor master record.

Assume that you have already entered a vendor master record. To enter text about a vendor:

1. From the Accounts Payable menu, select Master records → Change. (See Exhibit 4.15.)

2. In the Vendor field, enter the vendor account number. In the Company code field, enter the company code that this vendor supplies. To enter text about the vendor in the general part of the vendor master record, click on the Address field. To enter text about a vendor in the company code part of the vendor master record, click on the Account management field. Press <Enter>. (See Exhibit 4.16.)

3. From the menu bar on this screen, select Details → Texts. (See Exhibit 4.17.)

4. Notice that this window lists possible types of text that you can enter. To start to enter text in an accounting note, double-click on the description Accounting note. (See Exhibit 4.18.)

5. Enter the text about the vendor and press <F11> to store the text.

6. From the window with the list of types of text, press Continue.

7. From the data screen where you started, press <F11> or the file folder icon to update the vendor master record with the text.

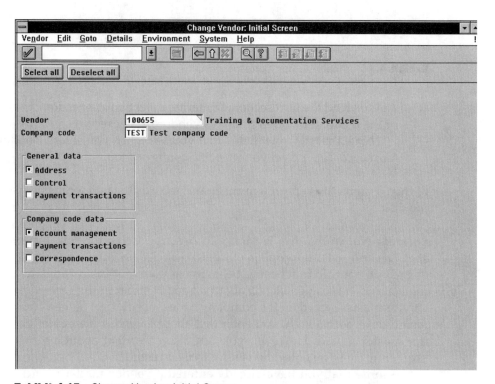

Exhibit 4.15   Change Vendor: Initial Screen

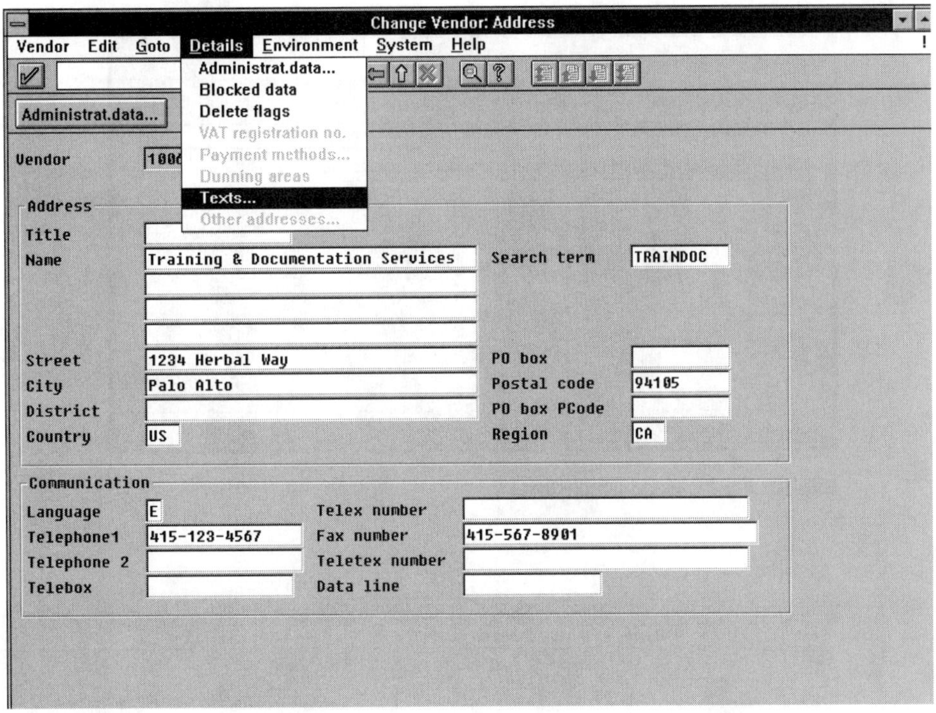

Exhibit 4.16   Change Vendor: Address

Note that you have entered text in the general part of a vendor master record. To enter text in the company code part of a vendor master record, first go to a screen containing company code data about the vendor. From the action bar, select Details ➙ Texts and enter the text in the same way.

Entering an Intercompany Vendor

In order to make intercompany accounting more clear, to reconcile intercompany accounts in various companies in the group, and to prepare intercompany aging reports, enter all companies in the group as vendors. At the same time, also enter all companies as customers. Intercompany vendors are numbered separately from external vendors. The purpose of entering intercompany vendors and customers separately is to reconcile and consolidate intercompany payables and receivables later. The screens to enter an intercompany vendor are usually almost the same as the screens to enter an external vendor, depending on your configuration.

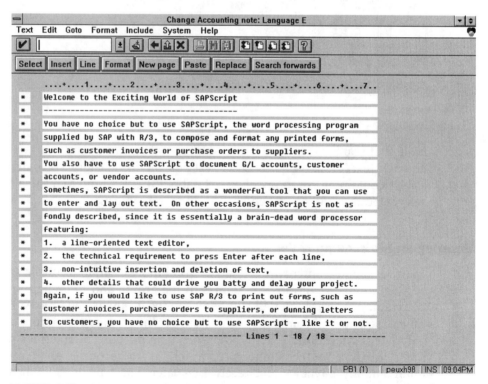

Exhibit 4.17 Head Office Texts

```
┌─────────────────────────────────────────────────────────────────────┐
│                          Head Office Texts                            │
│                                                                        │
│ Proposed language E English                                           │
│                                                                        │
│   Lng Description                    1st line                      M  │
│ ┌┐ E │Accounting note      │        │Note organization structure first.│ ☐│
│ ┌┐   │Purchasing memo      │        │                                 │ ☐│
│ ┌┐   │Payment instructions │        │                                 │ ☐│
│                                                                        │
│                                                                        │
│ │Continue│ │Cancel│ │Detail text│ │Delete text│ │Create text│         │
└─────────────────────────────────────────────────────────────────────┘
```

```
┌─────────────────────────────────────────────────────────────────────┐
│                 Change Accounting note: Language E               ▼ ▲│
│ Text  Edit  Goto  Format  Include  System  Help                      ●│
│ ✔ [          ] ± ⬚ ←⬚✕ ⬚⬚⬚ ⬚⬚⬚⬚ ?                                  │
│ │Select│ │Insert│ │Line│ │Format│ │New page│ │Paste│ │Replace│ │Search forwards││
│                                                                        │
│      ....+....1....+....2....+....3....+....4....+....5....+....6....+....7..│
│   *  Welcome to the Exciting World of SAPScript                       │
│   *  ------------------------------------------                       │
│   *  You have no choice but to use SAPScript, the word processing program│
│   *  supplied by SAP with R/3, to compose and format any printed forms,│
│   *  such as customer invoices or purchase orders to suppliers.       │
│   *  You also have to use SAPScript to document G/L accounts, customer │
│   *  accounts, or vendor accounts.                                    │
│   *  Sometimes, SAPScript is described as a wonderful tool that you can use│
│   *  to enter and lay out text.  On other occasions, SAPScript is not as│
│   *  fondly described, since it is essentially a brain-dead word processor│
│   *  featuring:                                                        │
│   *  1.  a line-oriented text editor,                                 │
│   *  2.  the technical requirement to press Enter after each line,    │
│   *  3.  non-intuitive insertion and deletion of text,                │
│   *  4.  other details that could drive you batty and delay your project.│
│   *  Again, if you would like to use SAP R/3 to print out forms, such as│
│   *  customer invoices, purchase orders to suppliers, or dunning letters│
│   *  to customers, you have no choice but to use SAPScript - like it or not.│
│  ------------------------------------------- Lines 1 - 18 / 18 -------------│
│                                                                        │
│                                       │PB1 (1)│ │peuxh98│ │INS│ │09:04PM││
└─────────────────────────────────────────────────────────────────────┘
```

Exhibit 4.18 Change Accounting Note: Language E

To enter an intercompany vendor:

1. From the Accounts Payable menu, select Master records → Create. (See Exhibit 4.19.)
2. In the Vendor field, enter a four-character account number of an intercompany vendor, such as **23LN, 23GE,** and so on. For purposes of transparency and later consolidation, these numbers could be the same as the current G/L account numbers. In the Company code field, enter the company code that this vendor is supplying. In the Account group field, enter **intr** (for intercompany vendor). Press <Enter>.
3. Depending on your configuration, the following screens look like the screens to enter an external vendor. Enter at least the name, address, phone number, and fax number on the first screen. On the second screen, enter at least the customer account number. On the fourth screen, enter at least the reconciliation account number (for intercompany payables). On the fifth screen, enter the payment terms (net 60) for the other company in the group. The exact screens and fields depend on your configuration.

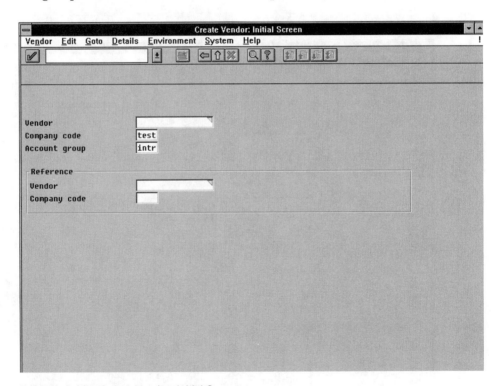

Exhibit 4.19   Create Vendor: Initial Screen

Entering a One-time Vendor

A one-time vendor is someone who supplies you once and only once, such as a restaurant, hotel, taxi, or entertainment. FI makes it possible for you to enter a vendor master record for one-time vendors. In this way, you do not clutter up your vendor file with vendor accounts that you post to only once. The screens and fields required to enter a one-time vendor depend on your configuration. Number one-time vendors with a name, such as **ONETIME-XX,** where **XX** is the country where the vendor is located. If you have one-time vendors in different countries, you should enter a one-time vendor master record for each country, since the address formats are different. The only purpose of entering a one-time vendor master record is to avoid cluttering up your vendor file with vendors that you post to only once.

To enter a one-time vendor master record:

1. From the Accounts Payable menu, select Master records → Create. (See Exhibit 4.20.)

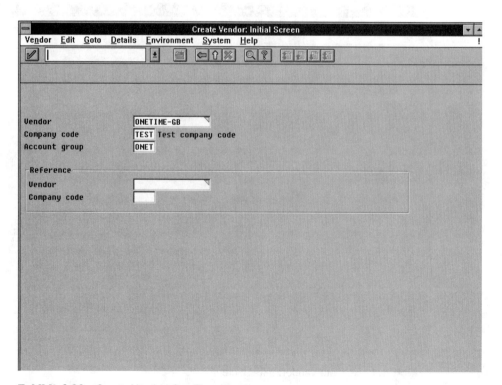

Exhibit 4.20   Create Vendor: One-Time Vendor

2. In the Vendor field, enter a name or number for the one-time vendor, such as **ONETIME-GB** for a one-time vendor master record for Great Britain. In the Company code field, enter the company code that this vendor is supplying. In the Account group field, enter **OTXX** where **XX** represents the country where the vendor is located (for one-time vendors). Press <Enter>. (See Exhibit 4.21.)

3. Enter the name, search term, and country of the vendor. Note that the exact fields that you see when you enter a vendor master record depend on your specific configuration and account group. Later, the search term makes it possible for you to find the vendor account number if you do not remember it. Press <Enter>. (See Exhibit 4.22.)

4. In the Reconcil.acct field, enter the G/L account number for accounts payable to vendors. In the Sort key field, enter **022** to sort details in the one-time account later by the name and city of the one-time vendor. Press <Enter>. Optionally, in the Prev.acct no. field, enter the vendor account number from your previous accounts payable system. (See Exhibit 4.23.)

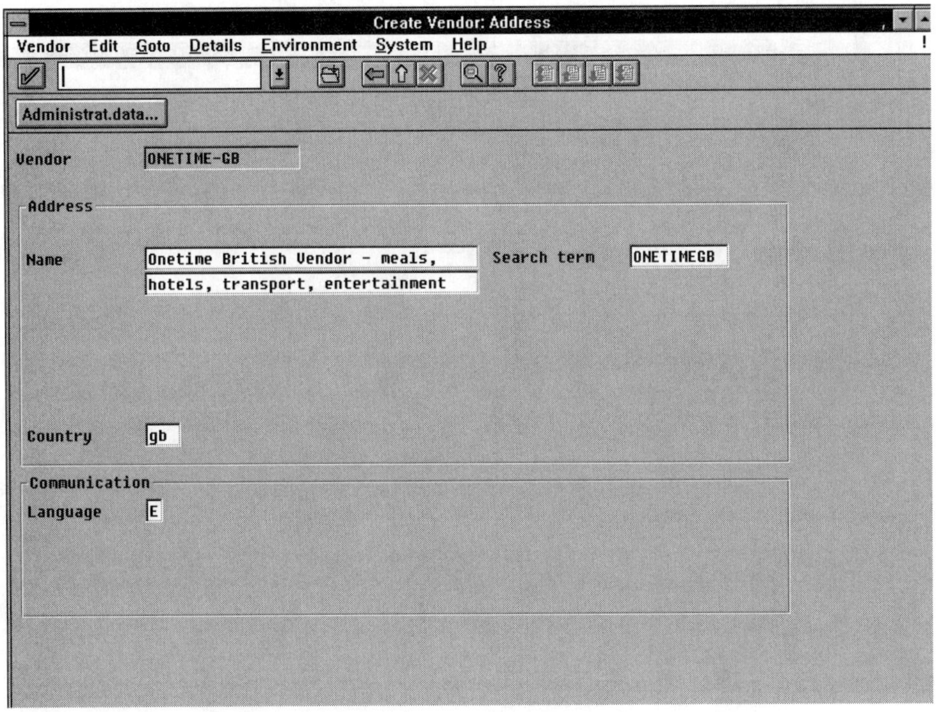

Exhibit 4.21 Create Vendor: Address

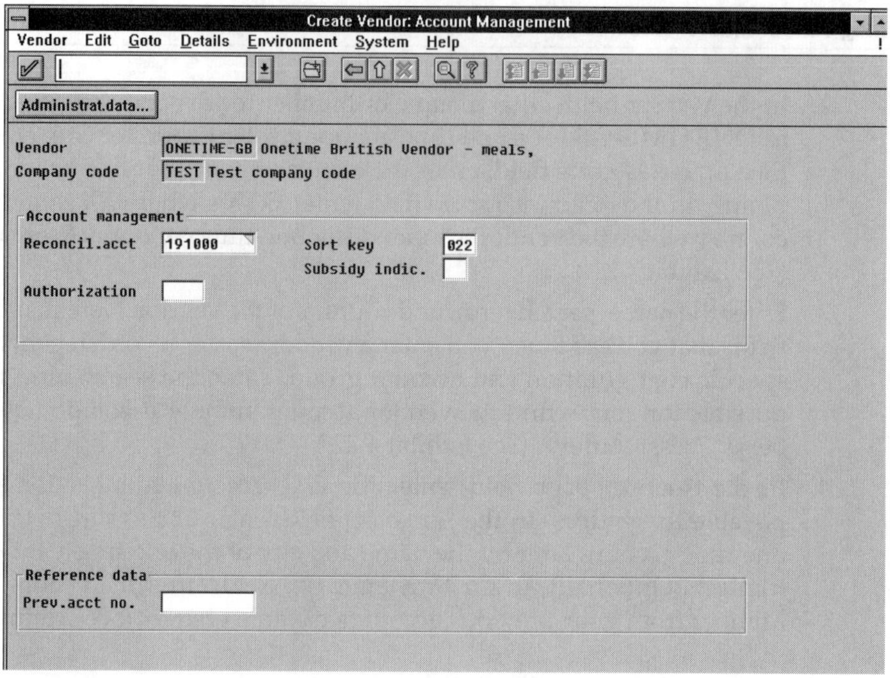

Exhibit 4.22 Create Vendor: Account Management

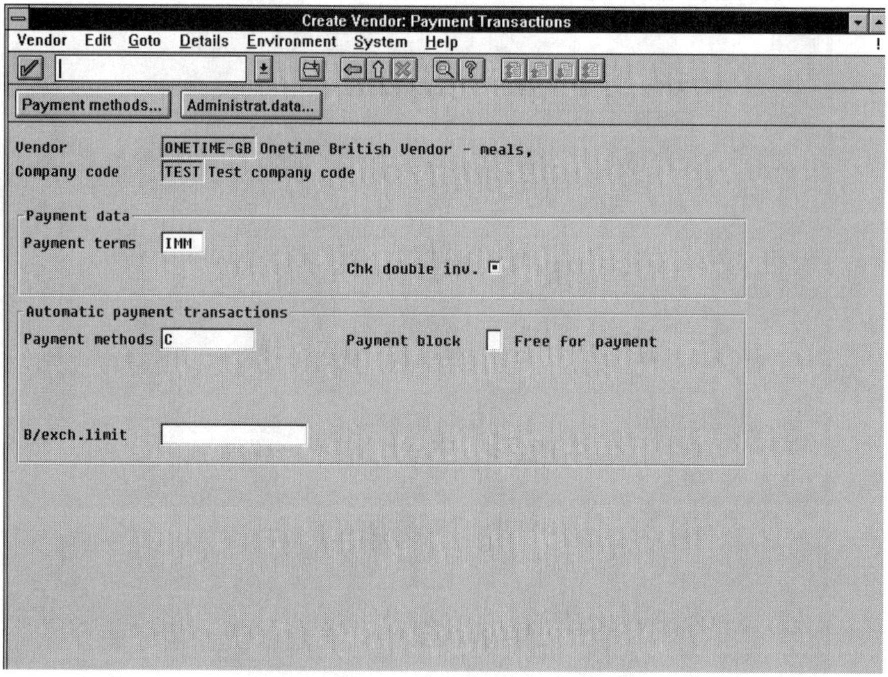

Exhibit 4.23 Create Vendor: Payment Transactions

5. Enter the payment terms, such as **IMM** (for due immediately), depending on your configuration. Click on the Chk double inv. field to have the system flag vendor invoices with the same document date, currency, reference document number, and amount. To pay one-time vendor invoices by check or bank transfer, enter the country-specific payment method for check (**C** in the United States) or bank transfer (**T** in the United Kingdom, **U** in Germany, or **V** in France). Press <Enter>. (See Exhibit 4.24.)

6. In the Acctg clerk field, enter the initials of the person responsible for these one-time vendor transactions, depending on your configuration. To store the vendor master record, press <F11>. Note the message on the last line on your screen. (See Exhibit 4.25.)

Entering a Vendor Who Factors Invoices

Some companies sell their receivables to banks or finance companies. This practice is known as factoring. If your vendor does this, they ask you to send the payment for their invoice to another company. To pay the factoring company, you should do as follows:

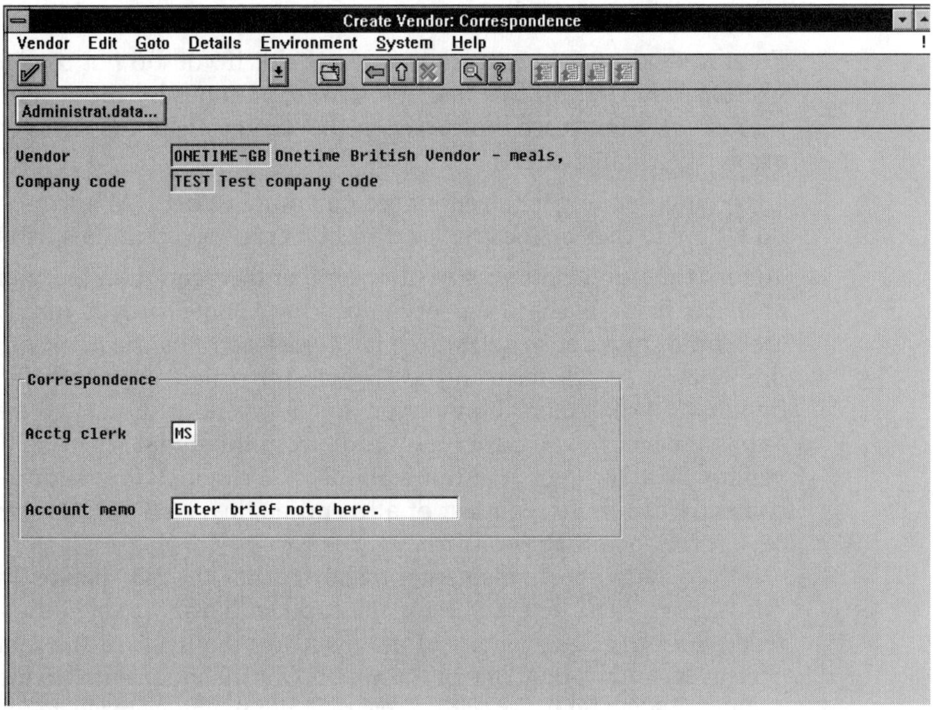

Exhibit 4.24 Create Vendor: Correspondence

Account ONETIME-GB has been created for company code TEST

Exhibit 4.25   Screen Message

1. Enter a vendor master record for the factoring company, including the bank account of the factoring company. Note the account number.

2. Enter a vendor master record as usual. In the screen to enter the bank account number, enter the bank account number (for a bank transfer) of the vendor, if required. Also enter the account number of the vendor's factoring company in the Alternative payee field.

3. When you pay the vendor's invoice, the payment program will substitute the bank details or address (to print a check) of the alternative payee account, the factoring company.

Displaying a Vendor Master Record

To display a vendor master record:

1. From the Accounts Payable menu, select Master records ➤ Display. (See Exhibit 4.26.)

2. Enter a vendor number in the Vendor field. If you do not remember the vendor number, you can find the vendor number by the name, using a matchcode. First place the cursor in the Vendor field and press the down arrow. (See Exhibit 4.27.)

3. To continue looking for a vendor account number, in the Matchcode ID window, double-click on the line Vendors by company code. (See Exhibit 4.28.)

4. To find the vendor number by the name of the vendor, in the Name field, enter the first few characters of the vendor's name, such as **train***. To find the vendor number by the search term, instead of by the name of the vendor, enter a search term in the Search term field. A search term is an optional 10-character abbreviation for the vendor. Enter (or verify the automatic entry of) the company code from the initial screen to display a vendor. With the proper authorizations, you can look for vendors in other company codes. To see a list of all vendors, leave all fields, except Company code, blank. Press Continue. (See Exhibit 4.29.)

    Note that you can also enter a shortcut for the matchcode directly in the Account field. To enter the matchcode with a shortcut, in the Account field, enter the equals sign (=), followed by the letter of the matchcode, such as **K,** followed by one or more dots (for the index entry in the matchcode), followed by the specific entry to look for. For example, to find a vendor account number, assuming that the name starts with "train," enter **=K....train** in the Account field.

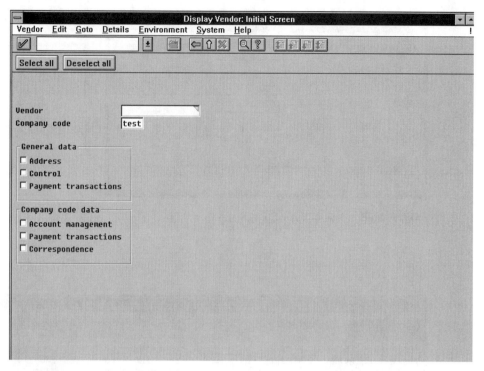

Exhibit 4.26   Display Vendor: Initial Screen

5. To select a vendor to display, double-click on the line with that vendor.
    You will then see the initial screen to display a vendor. FI enters the vendor number in the Vendor field. (See Exhibit 4.30.)

6. Note that each vendor master record contains six possible screens of data. Each line on this screen, from Address to Correspondence, represents a

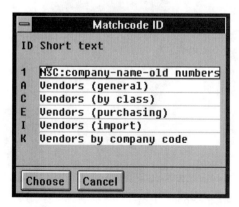

Exhibit 4.27   Matchcode ID

```
┌────────────────────────────────────────────────────┐
│ ▭              Restrict value ranges                │
├────────────────────────────────────────────────────┤
│ Search term          [              ]               │
│ Postal code          [              ]               │
│ City                 [              ]               │
│ Name                 [train*                      ] │
│ Vendor               [              ]               │
│ Company code         [test  ]                       │
│                                                     │
│ [ Continue ]  [ Cancel ]                            │
└────────────────────────────────────────────────────┘
```

Exhibit 4.28   Restrict Value Ranges

```
┌─────────────────────────────────────────────────────────────────────────────┐
│ ▭        Matchcode K: Display Data for Search Term 'K.TRAIN*.....TEST'        │
├─────────────────────────────────────────────────────────────────────────────┤
│ SearchTerm  Post.code   City           Name                  Vendor    CoCd   │
│                                                                               │
│ TRAIN-FR    75018       PARIS          TRAINING - FORMATION   100656    TEST   │
│ TRAIN-SPAN  09000       BARCELONA      TRAINING - FORMACION   100657    TEST   │
│ TRAINDOC    94105       PALO ALTO      TRAINING & DOCUMENTA   100655    TEST   │
│                                                                               │
│                                                                               │
│                                                                               │
│ [ Choose ]  [ Cancel ]  [ New selection ]                                     │
└─────────────────────────────────────────────────────────────────────────────┘
```

Exhibit 4.29   Matchcode K: Display Data for Search Term

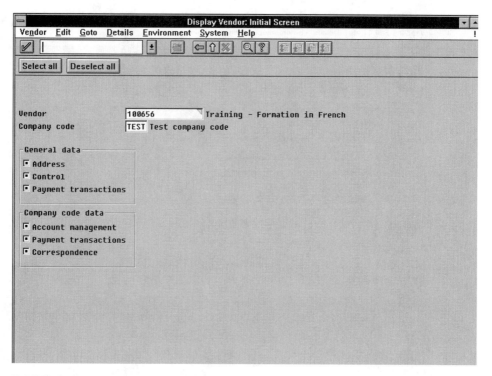

Exhibit 4.30 Display Vendor: Initial Screen

specific screen. To see a specific screen, click on the box to the left of the name of the screen. For example, to see the name, address, and phone number of the vendor, click to the left of Address. To see all screens one after the other, press the Select all pushbutton. Then press <Enter>. (See Exhibit 4.31.)

7. You will then see the first screen that you selected. To go to the next screen, press <Enter> or select Goto ➤ Next screen.

8. To go back to the previous screen, select Goto ➤ Previous screen. To go back to the Accounts Payable menu, keep pressing the back arrow (green in color).

Updating a Vendor Master Record

Since FI is multiuser software (not PC software), only one person can update a vendor master record at a time. If this were not so, then two people could update a record at the same time, and the second person to store the record would overwrite the first person's update. Transparently to the user, FI performs record-locking on all master records and transaction records.

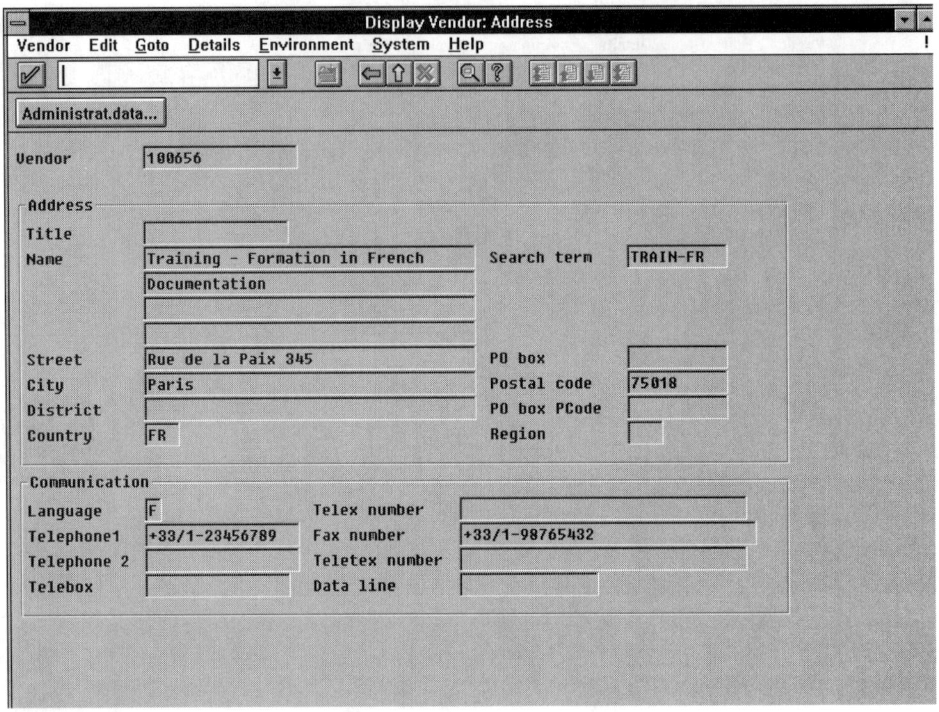

Exhibit 4.31 Display Vendor: Address

To update a vendor master record:

1. From the Accounts Payable menu, select Master records ➤ Change.
2. Enter the vendor number in the Vendor field and select the screen that contains the vendor data you wish to update. If you are not sure which contains the data to update, press the Select all pushbutton and then press <Enter>.
3. To go to the next screen, press <Enter> or select Goto ➤ Next screen from the Change Vendor menu.
4. Press <F11> or the file folder icon to store the vendor with the updates.

Displaying Changes to a Vendor Master Record

To display changes to a single master record:

1. From the Accounts Payable menu, select Master records ➤ Display changes. (See Exhibit 4.32.)

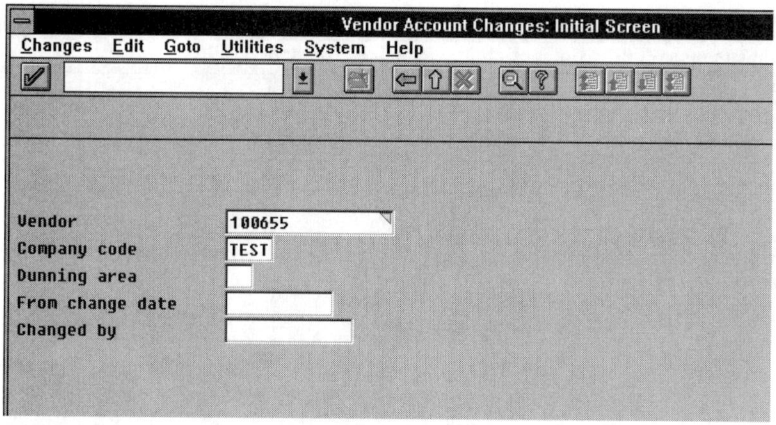

Exhibit 4.32 Vendor Account Changes: Initial Screen

2. Enter at least the vendor account number in the Vendor field and the company code in the Company code field, as if you were displaying a vendor master record. Optionally, make entries in the Dunning area, From change date, and Changed by (SAP login ID) fields. Press <Enter>. (See Exhibit 4.33.)

3. This screen contains a list of the fields that were changed in this specific vendor master record. To display details of a specific field change (the date of the change and both the old and new entries), double-click on the field or place the cursor on the line and then press Choose. (See Exhibit 4.34.)

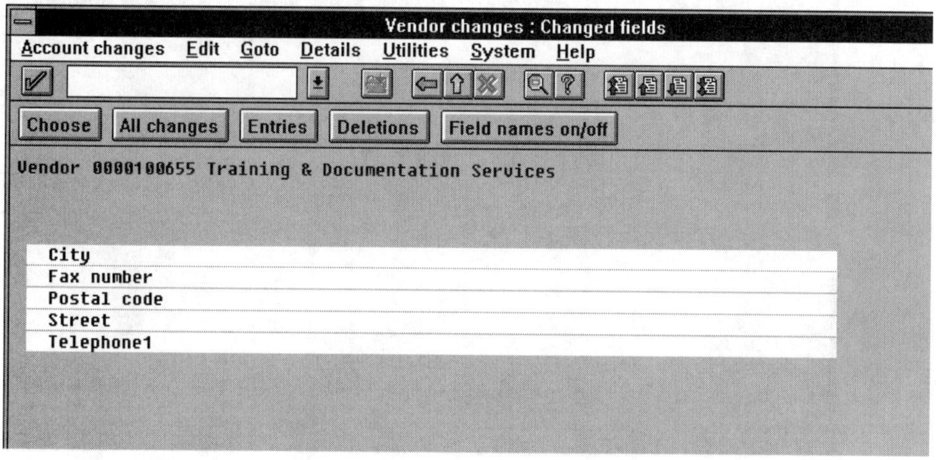

Exhibit 4.33 Vendor Changes: Changed Fields

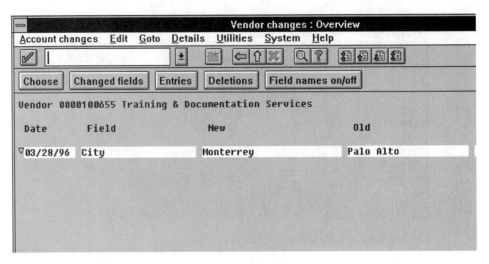

Exhibit 4.34   Vendor Changes: Overview

4. In this example, the vendor moved from Palo Alto to Monterey. To see further details about the change, such as who made the change and the exact date and time, double-click on the line with the name of the field or place the cursor on the line and press Choose. (See Exhibit 4.35.)

     Note that you can also display changes to vendor master records, while you display the vendor master record, by selecting Environment → Account changes.

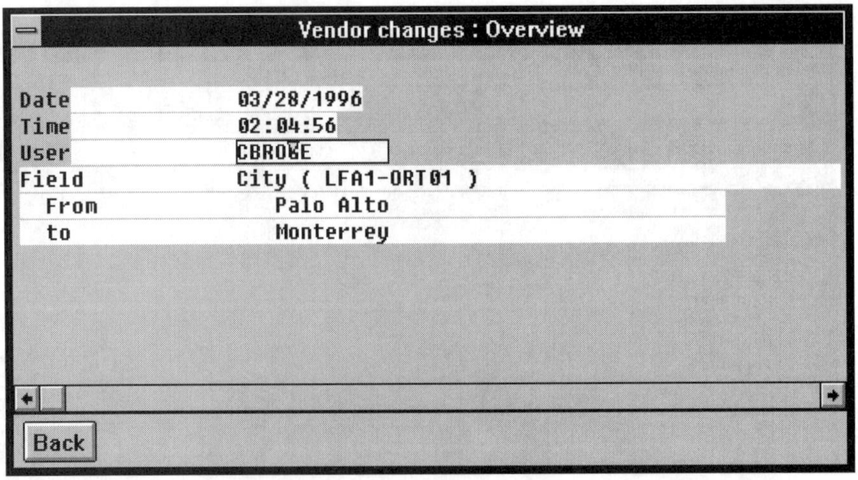

Exhibit 4.35   Vendor Changes: Overview

Blocking a Vendor Master Record

If you do not accept invoices from nor make payments to a specific vendor, you can prevent (block) a vendor account from being posted. In general, there are four possible ways to prevent the posting of invoices or payments to a specific vendor:

1. Block the vendor account, which prevents the posting of any new transactions (invoices, credit memos, and payments) to the vendor.

2. Block the vendor account from payment, which prevents all invoices from being paid, but does not prevent new invoices and credit memos from being posted.

3. Block one or more specific invoices from being paid, either when you enter the invoice or before you run the payment program.

4. When you run the payment program, after generating the payment proposal, block one or more specific vendor invoices from being paid in the payment proposal **for this payment run.** It does not prevent the invoice from being included in the next payment proposal, nor does it prevent the posting of any new invoices to the vendor.

Blocking a vendor account can be useful, if you have a dispute with the vendor that you expect will never be resolved. In this way, you close the account, preventing any new entries, but keeping the account and transaction detail online. To block a vendor account from being posted:

1. From the Accounts Payable menu, select Master records ➤ Block/unblock.

2. On the next screen, enter the vendor account number and company code of this vendor to be blocked. Press <Enter>. (See Exhibit 4.36.)

3. To prevent posting invoices to all company codes, click on the All company codes field. To prevent posting invoices to a specific company code, select Selected company code.

4. To store the block on this account, press <F11> or the file folder icon.

5. Press either the left arrow or the up arrow to go back to the Accounts Payable menu. Note that from this and many other screens, pressing either of these keys does the same thing. The difference depends on how the programmer was feeling on the day that he or she developed the function.

6. To verify the vendor account is blocked, try to post an invoice or pay an invoice to this account. You then see a message on the screen (or in the log of the payment proposal) that this account is blocked for posting.

7. To unblock a vendor account, permitting posting of invoices and payments to this account again, start the same function. From the Accounts Payable

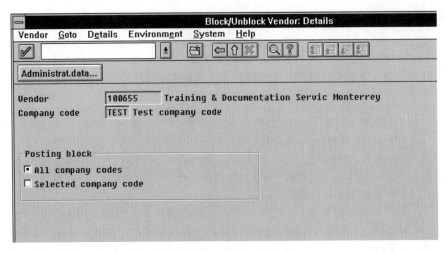

Exhibit 4.36   Block/Unblock Vendor: Details

menu, select Master records ➤ Block/unblock. Click on one or both fields to remove any blocks. Then press <F11> to store the unblocked vendor account.

Blocking Payments to a Vendor

By putting a payment block on the vendor account, you permit posting invoices from this vendor, but prevent payment of all invoices, including ones that you have already posted. This can be useful if you have a dispute with the vendor that you expect will be resolved. In this way, you can continue to post invoices and credit memos but make no payments to this vendor.

Note that blocking a vendor account does not prevent paying any vendor invoices that you have already posted to this account. To put a payment block on the vendor account, blocking all payments to the vendor of invoices that you have already posted:

1. From the Accounts Payable menu, select Master records ➤ Change. (See Exhibit 4.37.)

2. Specify the vendor account and company code. In the Company code data section, click on the Payment transactions line. Press <Enter>. (See Exhibit 4.38.)

3. In the Payment block field, enter a valid code to block payments, depending on your configuration. For a list of valid codes, put the cursor in the field and then press the down arrow. Do not worry, if the text next to the field still indicates the vendor will be paid, even after you enter a code to

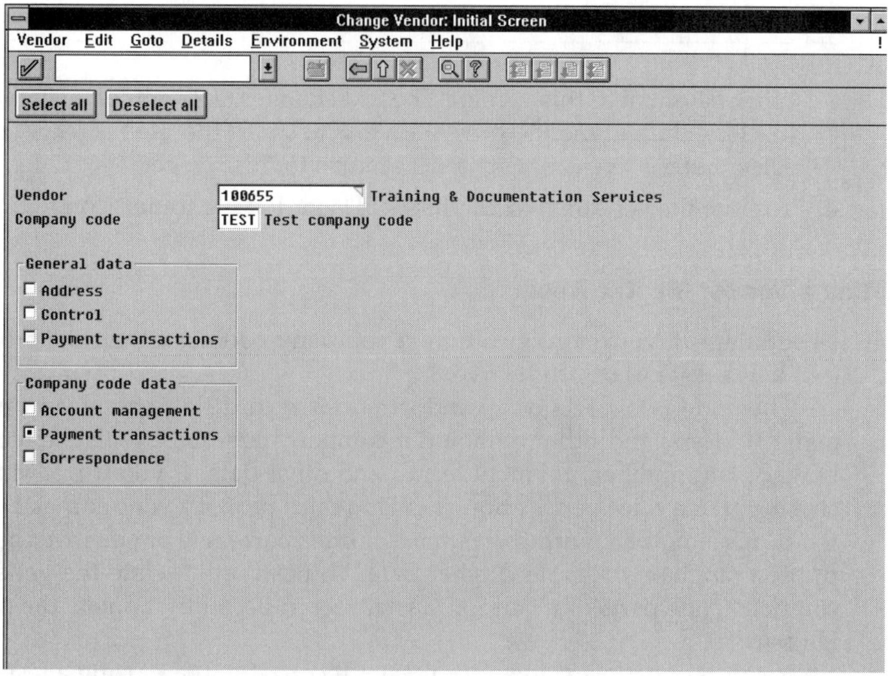

Exhibit 4.37 Change Vendor: Initial Screen

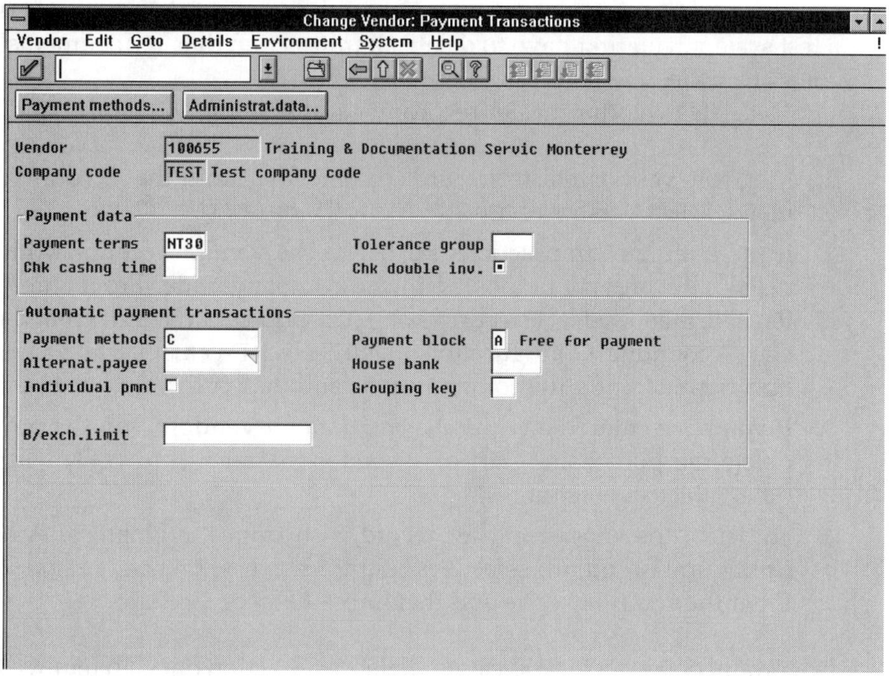

Exhibit 4.38 Change Vendor: Payment Transactions

block payment to this vendor. The text changes after you enter a valid code to block the payments, press <Enter> to go to the next screen, and then select Goto → Previous screen to return to this screen.

4. To store the vendor record, press <F11> or the file folder icon.

Deleting a Vendor Master Record

Depending on your configuration, a company code is either not productive (not a test system) or productive.

There are two parts of a vendor master record—a general part with the name, address, and other data and a company code part with the reconciliation account number, payment terms, and other data. If you use MM for purchasing and invoice verification, there is a third part of a vendor master record, the purchasing part with the purchase order currency, payment terms in the printed purchase order, and other data. You can only delete the general and company code parts of a vendor master record if you first delete the purchasing part.

You can only delete a vendor master record if you are using a test system. In this way, the account is removed from the system with little trace. Also, you can only delete a vendor master record if there are no transactions posted to the account in the current or any previous month. To delete a master record in a test system, you first have to delete all transaction data ("documents") in the company code.

To delete a vendor master record in a test system:

1. Mark the vendor master record for deletion. From the Accounts Payable menu, select Master records → Mark for deletion.

2. If there are any transactions posted to the vendor account, you have to delete all transactions posted in the company code. From the Accounts Payable menu, select Environment → Configuration menu. From the Financial Accounting Configuration menu, select Productive start → Delete documents. Enter the company code and then press <F8> or Execute.

3. If you have entered any purchasing data for vendors, run the program to delete the purchasing part of a vendor master record (LFM1 in 2.2 and other tables in version 3.0).

4. To delete the vendor master record, also from the Financial Accounting Configuration menu, select Productive start → Delete master records. Enter the company code and then press <F8> or Execute.

In a production system, you cannot delete transaction data. To remove the vendor master record in a production system, you must first archive the record.

However, you can only archive a vendor master record if the account has a zero balance and if both the account and any previous transactions posted to it have exceeded a minimum residence in the system. You can configure a minimum residence. By default, FI keeps all master records for two years (730 days). After two years, you can archive a vendor master record as follows:

1. Make sure that there are no open items in the vendor account and that the vendor account balance is zero. Also make sure that two years have passed since you entered the vendor.
2. From the Accounts Payable menu, select Master records → Mark for deletion.
3. From the General Ledger menu, select Periodic processing → Archiving → Accounts payable. (See Exhibit 4.39.)
4. Press Start archiving. (See Exhibit 4.40.)
5. Click on the Archive vendors parameter and select the vendor (or vendors) to be archived with the Vendors parameter. Click on the General master records and Financial accounting parameters. Specify a company code. To archive the purchasing data, click on the Purchasing parameter and specify a purchasing organization. To see a test run, click on Test run.
6. Press <F8> or the Execute pushbutton to run the program.

Displaying/Printing a Vendor List

To display or print a list of vendors:

1. From the Accounts Payable menu, select Periodic processing → Reporting → Account list. (See Exhibit 4.41.)

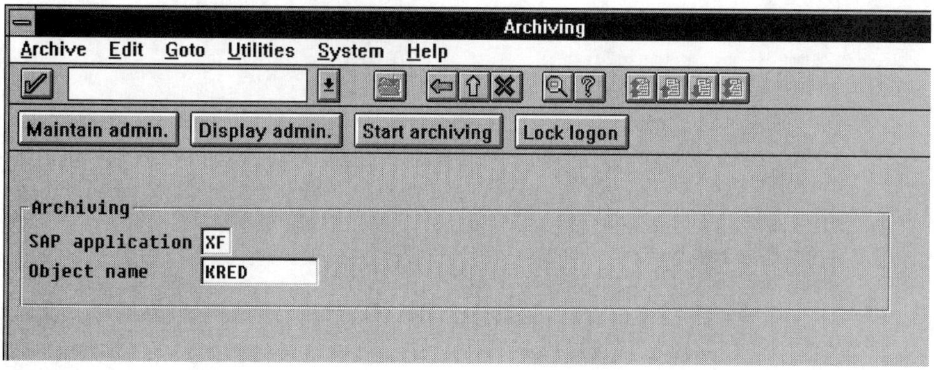

Exhibit 4.39   Archiving

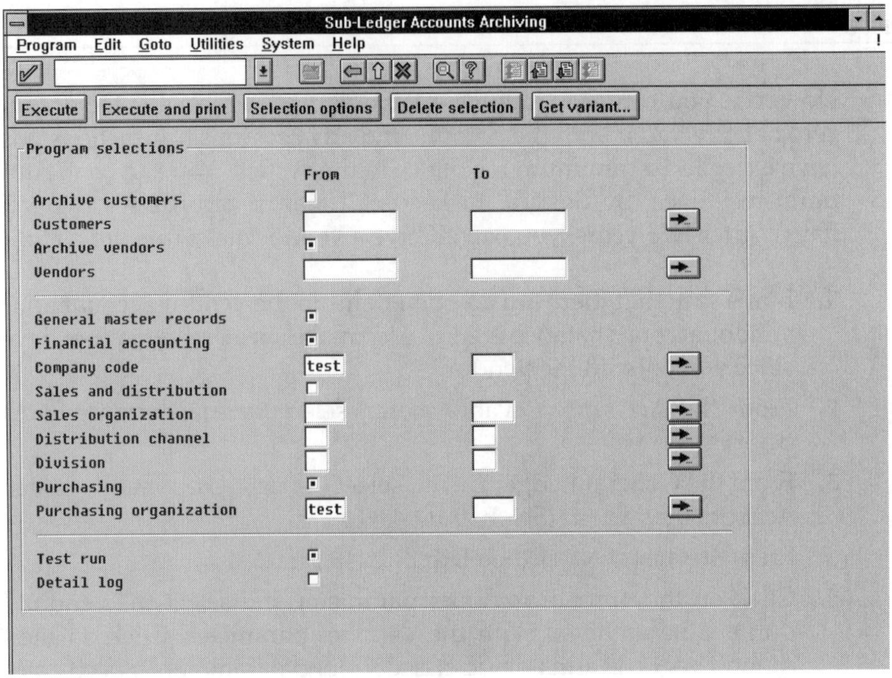

Exhibit 4.40   Sub-Ledger Accounts Archiving

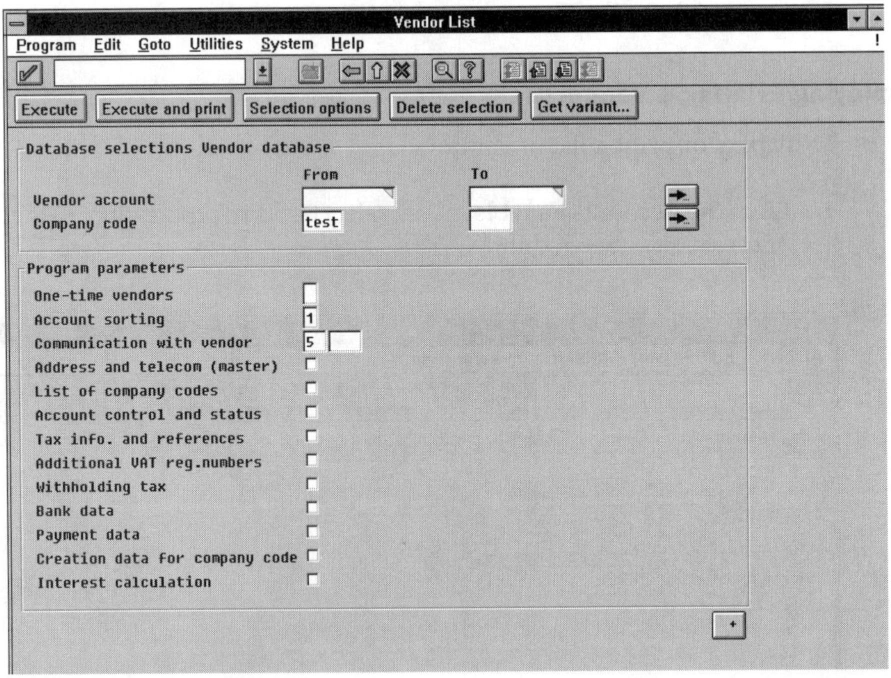

Exhibit 4.41   Vendor List, Screen One

2. Enter at least the company code and parameters in the Account sorting and Communication with vendor fields. For a description of each parameter, place the cursor in the field and then press <F1>.

3. Optionally, to go to the next screen of parameters, press the + symbol in the lower-right corner of the screen. (See Exhibit 4.42.)

4. Optionally select the vendors by any of these parameters. For example, to select vendors by the country, enter one or a range of countries in the Country field. You can also specify a list of individual countries by pressing the right arrow, entering the list, and then pressing the left arrow. Optionally, to go to the next screen of parameters, press the + symbol in the lower-right corner of the screen. To go to the previous screen of parameters, press the – symbol. (See Exhibit 4.43.)

5. To display the report with the vendor listing, press <F8> or the Execute pushbutton. To print the report, press the Execute and print pushbutton. (See Exhibit 4.44.)

6. In the Output device field, enter the 4-character name of the printer. To make sure that the your report is printed now, click on the Print immed.

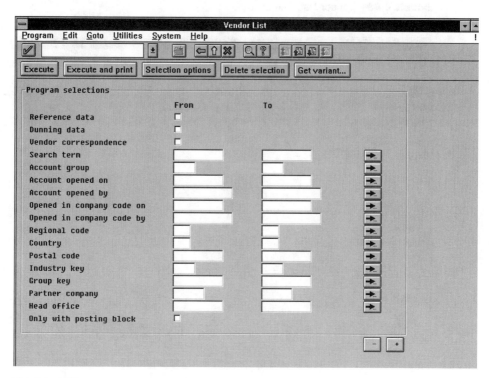

Exhibit 4.42 Vendor List, Screen Two

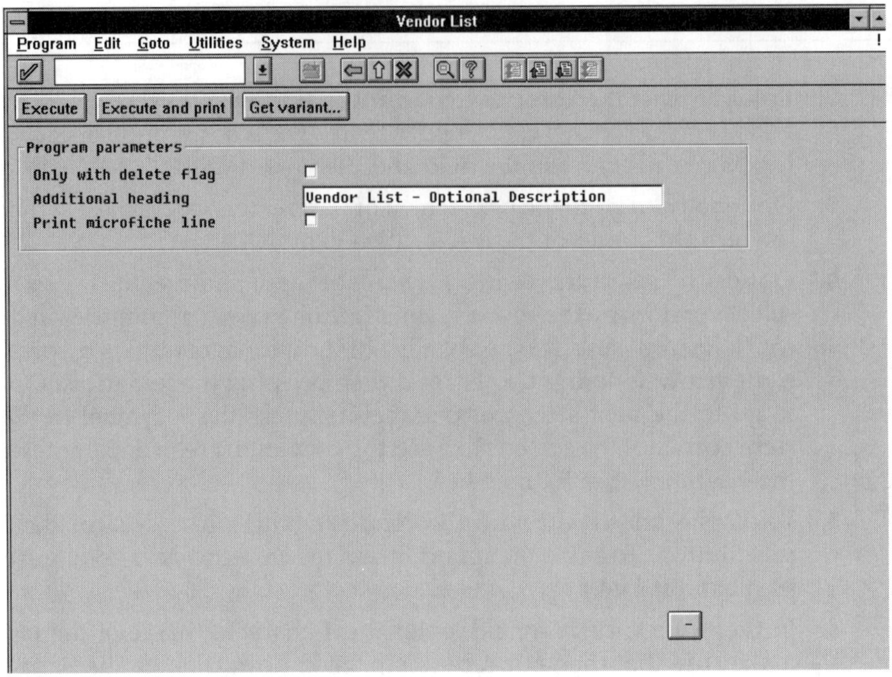

Exhibit 4.43 Vendor List, Screen Three

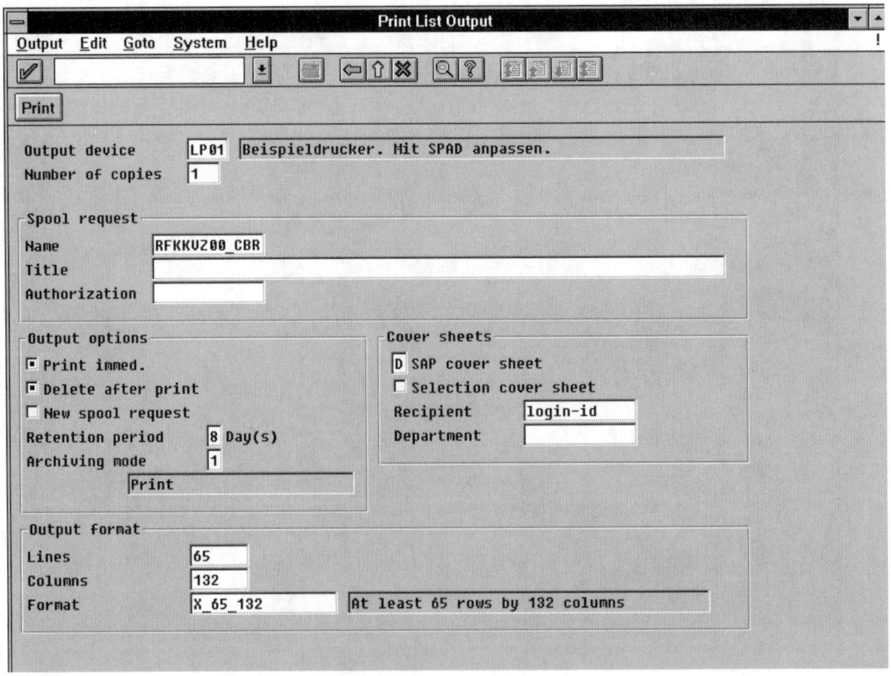

Exhibit 4.44 Print List Output

field. To prevent overfilling the spool file, click on Delete after print field. Last, press the Print pushbutton again.

Checking the Printing

First, make sure that your printer is properly installed. You then must configure the printer in the operating system of the machine running FI. Next, you have to configure the printer in R/3 using Basis functions. Make sure that the configured page size in the operating system (rows and columns) exceeds or equals the configured page size in R/3 Basis. You may have to install the printer in your local LAN.

Assume that your printer is properly installed and configured. After you start to print a report, the system places the report in a spool file. FI then prints the report from this spool file. To monitor the spooling and printing:

1. From any menu, select System → Services → Output controller. (See Exhibit 4.45.)

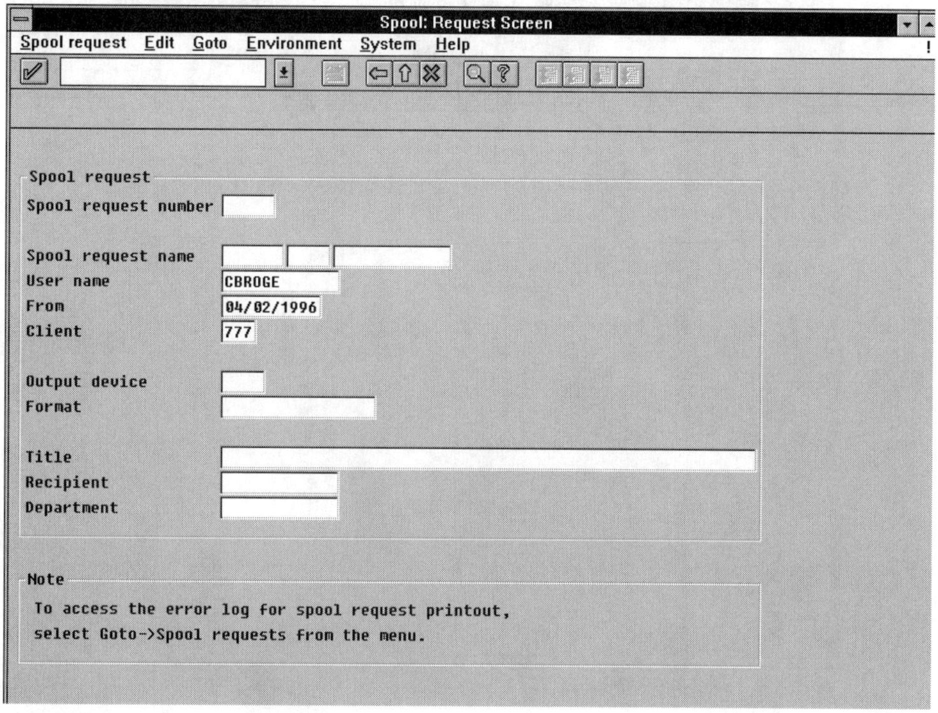

Exhibit 4.45 Spool Screen

2. From the Spool: Request Screen, press <Enter> to see the entry in the spool file.

3. If the report is already printed, then you see a message at the end of the screen that says there are no spool requests for your selection. Otherwise, you see the entries in the spool file. (See Exhibit 4.46.)

4. Notice the columns with the reference number of the spool file entry (Spool No.), the data and time of the spool file entry (Generation Date and Time), the Output Status (In proc means in process), the Size (in pages), the printer that you specified, and the name of the program that prepares this report (Title).

Reporting New Vendors

To display or print a list of new vendors:

1. Run the program to list vendors. From the Accounts Payable menu, select Periodic processing ➤ Reporting ➤ Account list.

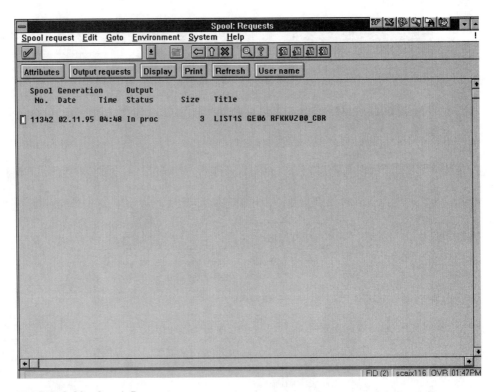

Exhibit 4.46 Spool: Requests

2. Go to the second screen of parameters by pressing the + symbol in the lower-right corner of the screen.

3. In the Account opened on parameter, enter the cutoff date for new vendors in the From column. Enter today's date in the To column of the same parameter. For example, if you wish to see all vendors entered on or after June 6, 1996, enter **060696** in the From column and today's date in the To column.

4. Press <F8> or the Execute pushbutton.

Printing Changes to Vendor Master Records

You print a list of changes to vendor master records, such as which fields were changed, by whom, and on what dates. Depending on the number of vendors and vendor transactions, you might run this report before you run the payment program. To print changes to vendor master records, run the RFKABL00 program as follows:

1. To run an ABAP program, from any menu, select System → Services → Reporting. On the next screen, ABAP/4: Execute Program, enter **RFK-ABL00** in the Program field and then press <F8> or the Execute pushbutton. (See Exhibit 4.47.)

2. Enter a vendor account number or a range of vendor account numbers in the Vendor parameter. Enter a change date or a range of change dates in the Change date parameter. You can sort the list of changes in various ways. For details, place the cursor on the Sorting parameter and press <F1>. Specify either General data or Company code data by clicking on the one or both parameters. If you specify company code data, enter a company code, such as **GE20**.

3. To run the report, press <F8> or the Execute pushbutton. If there were no changes to vendor master records between these dates, then the ABAP/4: Execute Program screen is shown again with a message at the end of the screen that no changed records were found.

ENTERING AND POSTING VENDOR INVOICES

You can use either MM or FI to post vendor invoices. To verify vendor invoices, you have to use MM to compare the invoice with the purchase order (prices and amounts) or the packing list (quantities and delivery dates) or both.

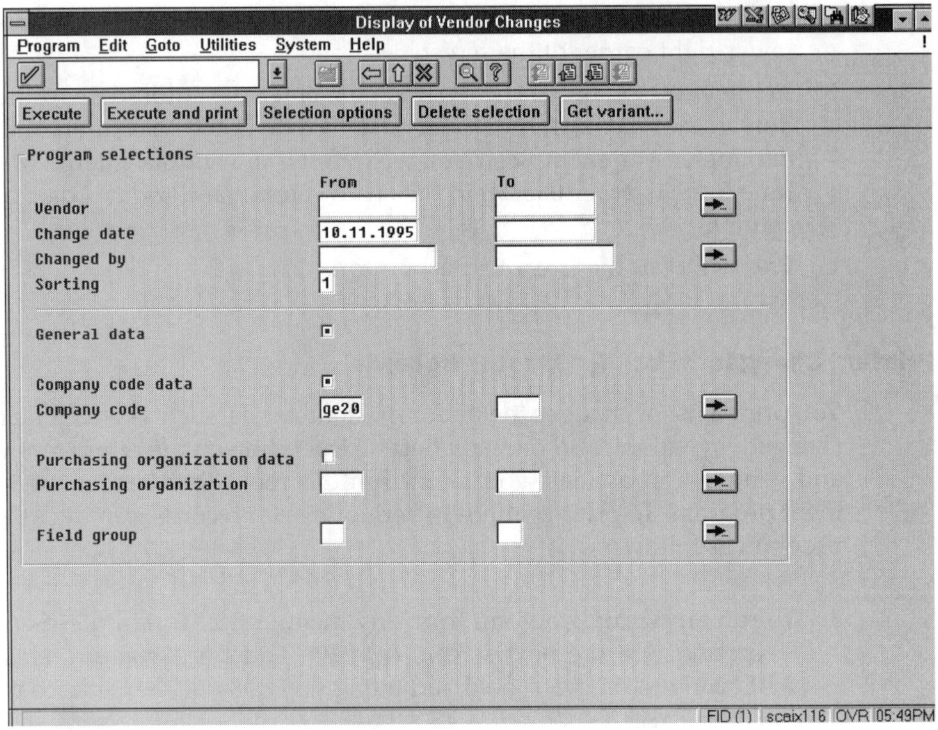

Exhibit 4.47   Display of Vendor Changes

This section handles entering and posting vendor invoices that do not have a matching purchase order. Some companies enter and post the following invoices without a purchase order:

- Cafeteria
- Car repairs
- Freight forwarders (shipping companies)
- Telephone
- Utilities
- Electricity
- Contract labor
- Travel agency summary invoices
- Leasing invoices
- Intercompany invoices
- Recurring invoices

- Reversing transactions
- Communications services

Assuming you do not wish to match these invoices to a purchase order, use FI to enter and post these invoices.

Setting Entry of Net (or Gross) Expense Amounts

Some invoices contain many expense items and only one total VAT amount. To enter these invoices with the net amount of the expense, instead of the gross amount including the VAT, you have to set entry of net amounts.

To set entry of expense amounts:

1. From the Accounts Payable menu, select Environment → Current options → Editing options.
2. Click on the parameter Calculate taxes on net amount (Exhibit 4.48).
3. To store the parameters, press <F11> or the file folder icon.

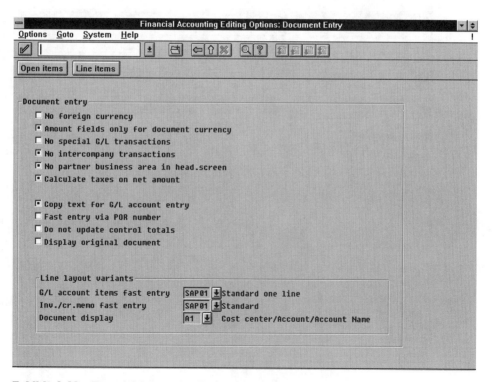

Exhibit 4.48 Financial Accounting Editing Options: Document Entry

Note that you can change this setting between net entry and gross entry. The new setting takes effect immediately after you store the parameter.

Posting a Vendor Invoice without a PO

In summary, to post a vendor invoice do the following:

1. Start the function
2. Enter the invoice header
3. Enter two or more line items (up to 999)
4. Post the invoice

Step by step, enter and post a vendor invoice with FI:

1. From the Accounts Payable menu, select Document entry ➤ Invoice. (See Exhibit 4.49.)

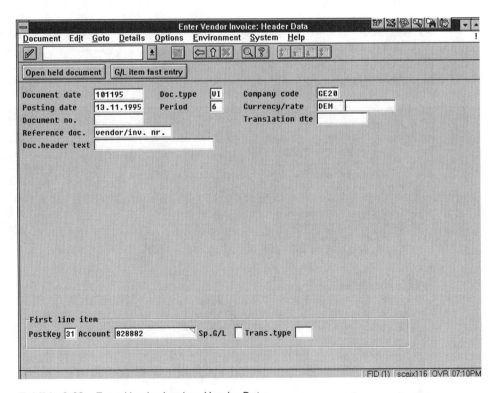

Exhibit 4.49   Enter Vendor Invoice: Header Data

2. The top half of the screen contains the transaction header. The following five fields are always required in a transaction header:

Field

Note

Document date

Usually, enter the vendor's date of the invoice in this field.

Doc.type

This is an SAP term for a journal. The most frequently used journals in Accounts Payable are **VI** (vendor invoices), **VM** (vendor memos), and **VP** (vendor payments). With your cursor in this field, press the down arrow for a list of available journals (i.e., document types), depending on your configuration.

Company code

Enter the company whose books you are keeping.

Posting date

This is also usually today's date, but could be different. The posting date determines the period in which FI updates the account balances, after you post the invoice.

Currency/rate

Enter a code for the currency of the transaction. Use the ISO code for the currency, which always has three characters. The first two characters represent the country. The third character represents the currency. The following are commonly used currency codes:

ATS	Austrian schillings
AUD	Australian dollars
BEF	Belgian francs
CAD	Canadian dollars
CHF	Swiss francs
CNY	Chinese yuan
DEM	German marks
ESP	Spanish pesetas
FRF	French francs
GBP	British pounds
HKD	Hong Kong dollars
ILS	Israeli shekels
INR	Indian rupees
ITL	Italian lire
JPY	Japanese yen

KPW   Korean won

MXN   Mexican new pesos

NLG   Dutch guilders

SGD   Singapore dollars

TWD   Taiwan dollars

USD   US dollars

For a complete list of the currency codes, put your cursor in this field and then press the down-arrow just to the right of this field. Foreign currency is any currency that is different from the local reporting currency of the company code. If you enter a code for a foreign currency, then you can also enter an exchange rate in the field immediately to the right of the field with the currency code.

Ignore the Period field. FI automatically determines the posting period based on the posting date and your fiscal year as configured. Assuming that your configuration has a "document type" **VI** (vendor invoice) and that these transactions are set up to be numbered internally (automatically by FI when you post), then leave the Document no. field blank. Immediately after you post the invoice, FI assigns the invoice a number, based on the available number range. Always *enter your customer number at the vendor (if printed on the invoice), a slash (/), and the vendor's invoice number* in the Reference doc. field, such as **12345/6789.** This will identify to the vendor in the payment file which of their customers (i.e., your company) is paying and which invoice is being paid. Your system can also be set up, so you can enter the printed invoice number into the Document no. field. The "document" must always be a unique number for each invoice, whether you use internal numbering or external numbering. Optionally, you can describe the transaction briefly, using the Doc.header text field.

3. At the end of this screen, enter the posting key in the PostKey field. To credit a vendor account, enter a posting key of **31.** Also enter a vendor account number in the Account field.

4. Press <Enter>. The program then validates the data on the first screen and determines the posting period. Among other validations, FI verifies that you have entered the dates correctly. It also verifies that the posting period is open, that the company code and currency code exist, and that the posting key and vendor account exist. Assuming that all of these and other conditions are true, then you see the screen shown in Exhibit 4.50.

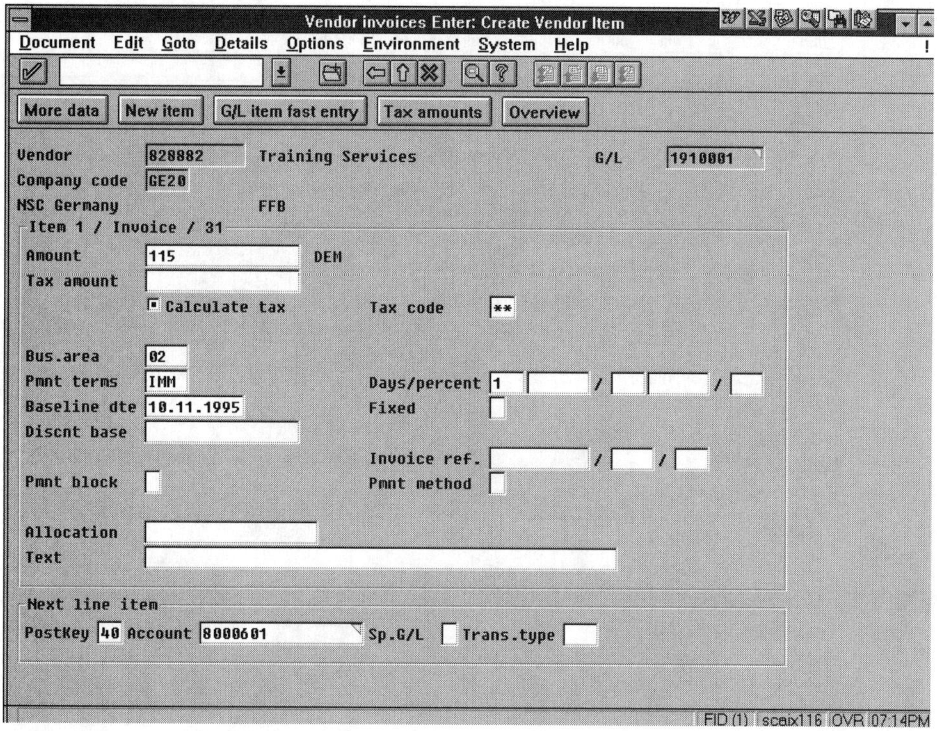

Exhibit 4.50   Vendor Invoices Enter: Create Vendor Item

5. On the second screen to enter a vendor invoice, enter the amount in the Amount field. Always click on the Calculate tax field, if it appears on your screen. Enter any other required fields in the vendor entry. Note that at the end of the previous screen, you have already specified whether this amount is a debit or a credit and in which account you are entering this amount. Also enter the Bus.area (business area). Later, you can prepare an internal balance sheet and P&L by business area. Optionally, enter a description of this line item in the Text field. At the end of this screen, enter the posting key and account of the second line item. For example, to enter a debit to an expense account, enter **40** in the PostKey field and enter a G/L account number for an expense, such as **8000601** in the Account field.

6. Press <Enter>. The program validates the data entered on this screen and then displays the next screen to enter a G/L account entry. (See Exhibit 4.51.)

7. Enter the amount of the expense in the Amount field. Always enter a tax code in the Tax code field, even if the rate is zero. If displayed, always

```
┌──────────────────────────────────────────────────────────────────────────────┐
│ ═        Vendor invoices Enter: Create G/L Account Item          ▼│ ♦│
│ Document  Edit  Goto  Details  Options  Environment  System  Help        !│
│ ☑ [          ]  ± │ 🖫 │ ⇦⇧✖ │ 🔍❓ │ 🔳🔳🔳🔳 │
│ ┌─────────┐┌──────────┐┌──────────────────┐┌─────────────┐┌──────────┐  │
│ │More data││ New item ││ G/L item fast entry ││ Tax amounts ││ Overview │  │
│ └─────────┘└──────────┘└──────────────────┘└─────────────┘└──────────┘  │
│                                                                      │
│ G/L account     [8000601]  Professional fees                         │
│ Company code    [GE20] NSC Germany GmbH                              │
│                                                                      │
│ ┌Item 2 / Debit entry / 40────────────────────────────────────────┐ │
│ │ Amount       [115        ]  DEM                                   │ │
│ │ Tax code     [v1]                                                 │ │
│ │                                                                   │ │
│ │                                                                   │ │
│ │ Business area  [02  ]         Trading part.BA [   ]               │ │
│ │ Cost center    [100003  ]▾    Order           [        ]▾         │ │
│ │                                                                   │ │
│ │                                                  ☐ More           │ │
│ │                                                                   │ │
│ │ Allocation     [            ]                                     │ │
│ │ Text           [                              ]                   │ │
│ └───────────────────────────────────────────────────────────────────┘ │
│ ┌Next line item──────────────────────────────────────────────────┐   │
│ │ PostKey [ ]  Account [            ]▾                             │   │
│ └─────────────────────────────────────────────────────────────────┘   │
└──────────────────────────────────────────────────────────────────────────────┘
```

Exhibit 4.51   Vendor Invoices Enter: Create G/L Account Item

click on the Calculate tax field. Enter any other required fields (fields that contain a question mark), such as the Business area (division) and Cost center (department) (Exhibit 4.51).

8. If you do not have the cost center, you can hold an invoice without posting it. First, enter a dummy cost center, such as **GE9999,** depending on your organization in CO and then select Document ➔ Hold. Enter a number to hold the invoice in the Temporary document number field. Find out the cost center. To complete the entry of the invoice, from the Enter Vendor Invoice: Header Data screen, select Document ➔ Open held document. Enter the temporary number under which you want the invoice held. Press <Enter>. Complete the entry of the invoice as usual.

9. To see an overview of the vendor invoice, press the pushbutton (on the fourth row of the window) marked Overview. The overview is shown in Exhibit 4.52.

10. Note that the total debits appear near the lower-left corner of the screen just to the right of the letter D, while the total credits appear just to the right of the letter C. If the debits equal the credits, then the balance of the

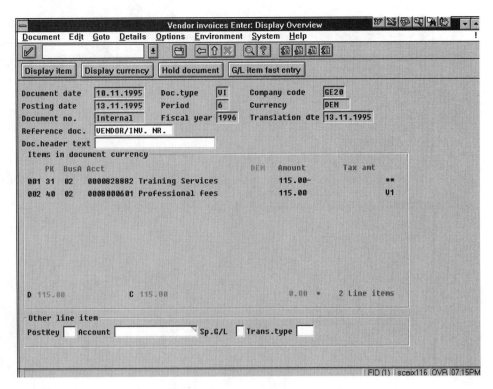

Exhibit 4.52 Vendor Invoices Enter: Display Overview

invoice is zero and □ appears on the same line. Also note that you can enter another line item by entering a posting key and an account number at the bottom of this screen. To delete a line, double-click on the line and then enter zero as the amount on the line item screen. If you enter a mistaken amount, double-click on the item in this overview, and then re-enter the amount on the next screen. If you have entered a mistaken posting date in the transaction header, you cannot change it on this screen. You must exit this function without posting the invoice and then enter the transaction again with the correct posting date. This is due to the fact that the program has already validated the posting date and determined the posting period from the invoice header that you enter on the first screen.

11. To see the tax entries that FI generates automatically, select Document → Simulate. (See Exhibit 4.53.)

12. To post the vendor invoice, press either <F11> or the file folder icon. Note that you can often do the same thing in two ways.

   The program then validates the invoice. Most of all, the program verifies that the total debits equal the total credits. It also checks whether the

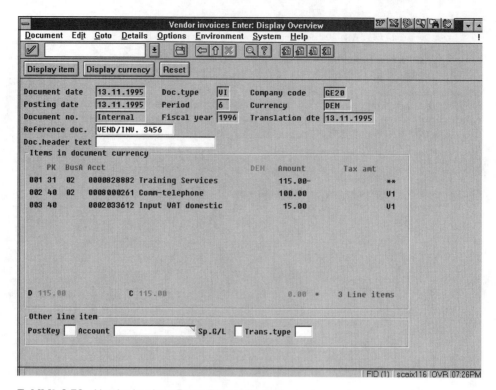

Exhibit 4.53   Vendor Invoices Enter: Display Overview

tax code is valid and then calculates the tax and posts the tax item. Calculating, posting, and reporting transaction taxes (VAT or sales tax) depend on country-specific legal requirements and also on the configuration. Calculating, posting, and reporting sales tax are usually done with third-party software routines, such as Vertex or AVP. Last, if you have internal transaction numbering, the program assigns a number to the invoice and updates the vendor and G/L account balances in the posting period.

Displaying the Last Posted Invoice

To verify that the invoice is properly posted, you can display the last posted transaction. From the Enter Vendor Invoice: Header Data screen, select Document → Display.

The overview of the vendor invoice looks like the overview in the previous screen. (See Exhibit 4.54.)

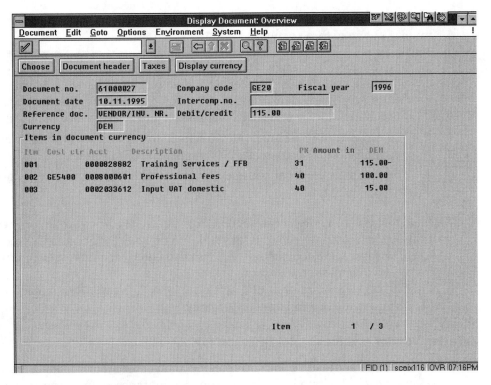

Exhibit 4.54 Display Document: Overview

Entering an Invoice with Two Tax Codes

To enter an invoice with two or more tax codes:

1. Set the processing options to enter either net amounts or gross amounts in the expense line items, as previously described.
2. Enter the transaction as usual. In the vendor line item screen, enter ** in the Tax code field.
3. In each expense line item screen, enter the specific applicable tax code, depending on the configuration, such as **V1** for input VAT regular and **VO** for input VAT exempt.

Entering an Invoice in Foreign Currency

Foreign currency is any currency that is different from the local currency. Local currency is the reporting currency of the company code to which you are posting the transaction. To enter an invoice in foreign currency, you enter the currency of the invoice in the header. You can then enter the exchange rate of this invoice in one of three ways:

1. You can enter exchange rates in a table of exchange rates by validity dates. FI then automatically transfers the most recent exchange rate valid on or before the posting date of the invoice. You can also override the transfer on the posting date by entering a translation date in the header of the invoice.

2. You can enter an exchange rate directly in the invoice by entering the number of units of local currency per unit of foreign currency.

3. You can enter the local currency amount and the foreign currency amount in each line item.

Note that you can enter a transaction in any currency, but you can only enter a transaction in one currency. For example, if you have a credit card invoice with line items in various currencies, you have to enter each line in the credit card invoice as a separate transaction.

For the details, refer to the section in the Accounts Receivable chapter, "Entering an Invoice in Foreign Currency."

Entering Vendor Invoices Quickly

If you have a series of vendor invoices, you can enter them quickly. This avoids entering each line item in the invoice on a separate screen. You can also use this function to quickly enter a long vendor invoice (with a series of G/L entries). The purpose is to speed up data entry.

To enter vendor invoices quickly:

1. Start to enter a vendor invoice as usual. From the Accounts Payable menu, select Document entry → Iv/Cr.mem.fast entry. (See Exhibit 4.55.)

2. At the top of this screen, fill in at least the Company code, Doc.type, and Posting date fields. Then fill in the Currency and Document date fields. Press the Enter inv./cr.memo pushbutton to go to the second screen. (See Exhibit 4.56.)

 On the second screen, always enter your company's customer number at the vendor (if printed on the invoice) and the vendor's invoice number in the Reference doc. field, such as **vend/inv.nr.** This will identify to the vendor in the payment file which of their customers (your company) paid and which invoice your company is paying. In the Vendor posting section of the screen, enter at least the vendor account number in the Account field, the division in the Business area field, and the total amount (transaction tax- and configuration-dependent) due to the vendor in the Amount field. Click on the Calculate tax box.

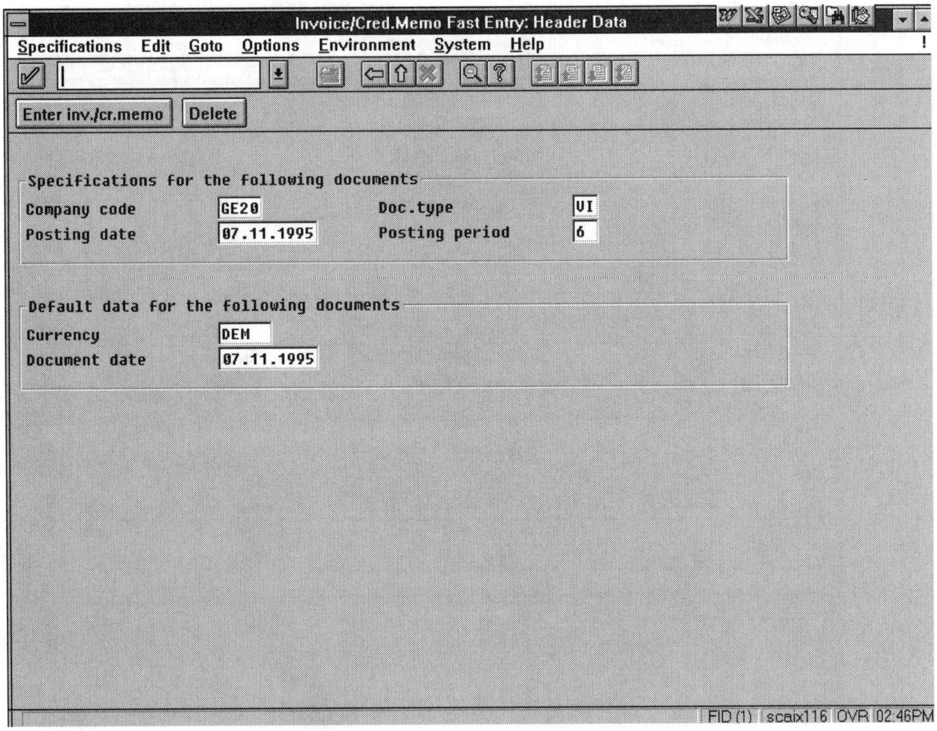

Exhibit 4.55   Invoice/Credit Memo

Note that you enter a line item on each line in the Offsetting items section of the screen. In each line, you have to enter at least the G/L account number in the Account column, and the tax code in the Ta column. You can also enter a business area (division) in the BusA column, a cost center, and an internal order.

To go to the overview, press the Overview pushbutton. If the debits equal the credits, you can post the transaction immediately. To post the transaction, press <F11> or the file folder icon.

Posting a One-time Vendor Invoice

To enter and post a one-time invoice from a vendor, you first have to enter a one-time vendor master record. The sole purpose of entering a one-time vendor master record is to avoid cluttering up your vendor master file with vendor accounts that you post to only once. When you enter a one-time vendor invoice, you enter the vendor's address, phone number, and bank account (if paying the invoice by bank transfer). You can use the quick entry function to

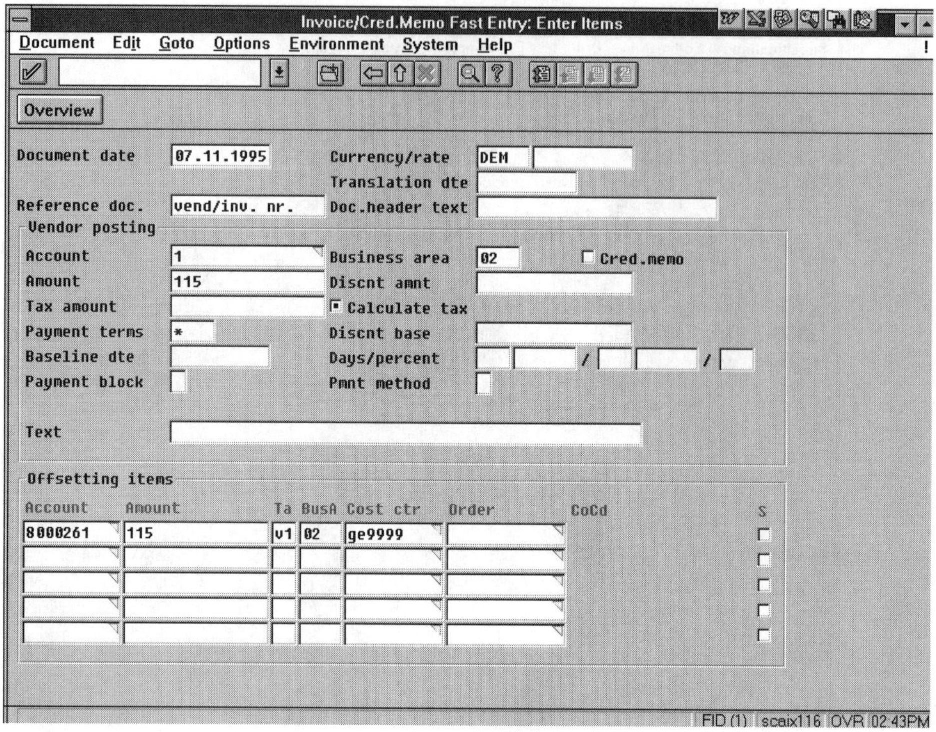

Exhibit 4.56   Invoice/Credit Memo: Enter Items

post a vendor invoice to a one-time vendor. To start to enter and post a one-time vendor invoice:

1. Select Document entry ➤ Invoice/Cred.Memo Fast Entry. (See Exhibit 4.57.)

2. At the top of the screen, fill in at least the Company code, Doc. type, and Posting date fields. Then fill in the Currency and Document date fields. Press the Enter inv./cr.memo pushbutton to go to the second screen.

3. On the second screen, enter the vendor's account and invoice number in the Reference doc. field. In the Vendor posting section of the screen, enter at least the vendor account number in the Account field, the division in the Business area field, and the total amount (transaction tax- and configuration-dependent) due to the vendor in the Amount field. Click on the Calculate tax box.

   Note that you enter a line item on each line in the Offsetting items section of the screen. In each line, enter at least the G/L account number in the Account column, and the tax code in the Ta column. You can also enter a business area (division) in the BusA column, a cost center, and an internal order. To continue, press <Enter>. (See Exhibit 4.58.)

```
┌─────────────────────────────────────────────────────────────────────┐
│ —                    OI - List of Due Dates (Vendors)          ▼ ▲   │
│ Program  Edit  Goto  Utilities  System  Help                      !  │
│ ✔ │                    │  ±  │ 🖩 │⇦⇧✖│ 🔍?│ 🗐🗐🗐🗐                    │
│ ┌Execute┐ ┌Execute and print┐ ┌Selection options┐ ┌Delete selection┐ ┌Get variant...┐ │
│                                                                        │
│ ┌─Database selections Vendor database─────────────────────────────┐   │
│ │  Vendor account         ┌──────────┐▽  ┌──────────┐▽      ➡     │   │
│ │  Company code           │TEST      │   │          │       ➡     │   │
│ │  Posting date           ┌──────────┐   ┌──────────┐       ➡     │   │
│ │  Open items at key date │05/30/1996│                             │   │
│ │  Allocation number      ┌──────────┐   ┌──────────┐      ⬇➡     │   │
│ │  Special G/L indicator  ┌─┐           ┌─┐          ⬇➡            │   │
│ └─────────────────────────────────────────────────────────────────┘   │
│ ┌─Program parameters──────────────────────────────────────────────┐   │
│ │  Output totals only     ☑                                        │   │
│ │  Due date I until       ┌──────┐ 8                               │   │
│ │  Due date II until      ┌──────┐ 30                              │   │
│ └─────────────────────────────────────────────────────────────────┘   │
│                                                                        │
└─────────────────────────────────────────────────────────────────────┘
```

Exhibit 4.57 Invoice/Credit Memo Header Data

4. The next screen prompts you to enter the name, address, phone number, and possibly bank account number of the vendor. Enter at least the Name and City fields. Press <Enter>.

5. To see the overview, press <Enter>. To post the transaction, press <F11> or the file folder icon.

Posting a Shipping Invoice with Customs and VAT

In general, invoices from shipping companies for shipments from abroad include both customs charges (tariffs) and VAT. They may also include an administrative fee from the shipping company for having made a payment to customs on your behalf. They do not always have the value of the goods being shipped. To post these invoices, post directly to the VAT account and to the customs accounts, entering the amount of the charge and the base amount of the goods. Calculate the base amount of the goods by dividing the charge by the percentage of the tax code. For example, if the charge were 12 and the percentage were .15, then the base amount that you calculate is **75**.

Otherwise, you post these invoices as you would any other vendor invoices. For example, the vendor item is illustrated in Exhibit 4.59.

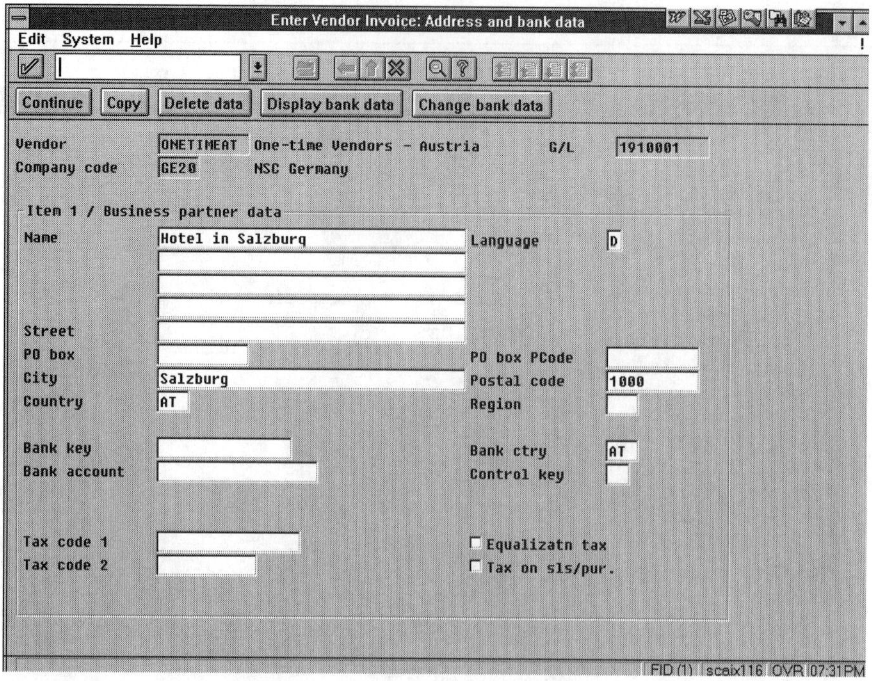

Exhibit 4.58 Enter Vendor Address and Bank Data

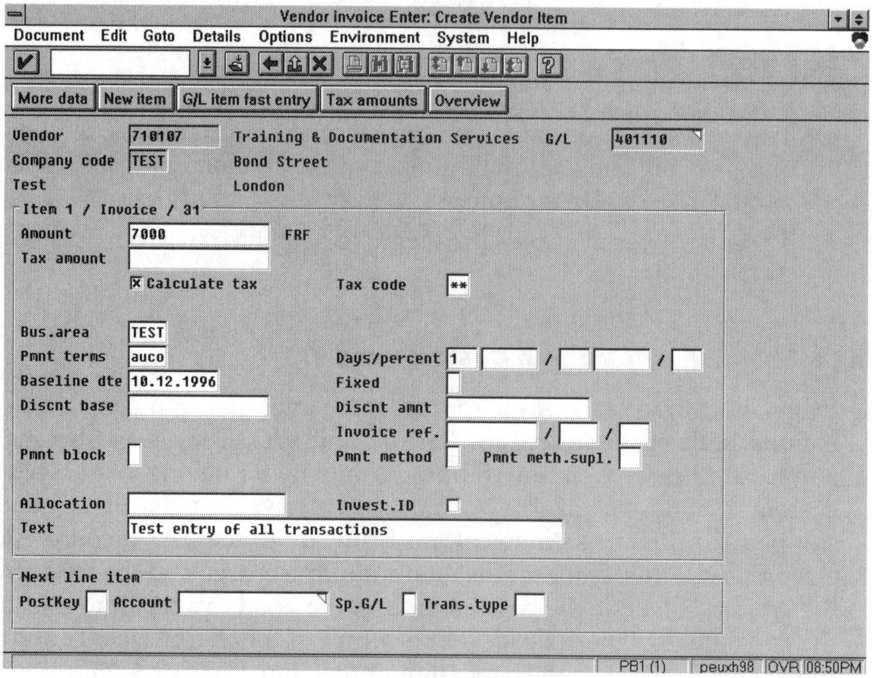

Exhibit 4.59 Vendor Invoice Enter: Create Vendor Item

Entering an Invoice with Withholding Tax

In many countries, when you pay invoices from certain vendors, the tax regulations require you to make a partial payment of the invoice and then send the payment difference to the authorities. This difference is called withholding tax. It most often applies to invoices from small vendors, such as self-employed vendors, professional service firms, or construction companies.

Depending on your configuration of the withholding tax codes and the vendor master records, you can have the withholding tax automatically calculated and posted, but only when you make the payment. In this way, you enter the gross amount due the vendor, including the withholding tax, when you enter the invoice. You then can enter separate amounts for the withholding tax base and the amount exempt from withholding tax. In all other ways, enter a vendor invoice with withholding tax in the same way as any other vendor invoice. Before posting the invoice with withholding tax, make sure that the vendor master record contains the proper withholding tax code (in the account management screen). To enter an invoice with withholding tax:

1. From the Accounts Payable menu, select Document entry ➤ Invoice.

2. Enter the invoice header as usual, including at least the document date (usually the vendor's date), the "document type," the company code, the posting date (usually today's date), the currency of the invoice, and the reference document (usually the vendor's invoice number). At the end of the screen, enter the posting key **31,** the vendor account number, and then press <Enter>. (See Exhibit 4.60.)

3. For example, assume that 19% VAT and 19% withholding tax are applicable to the invoice. Further assume that withholding tax code **40** represents 19% withholding tax. In other words, the net payable to the vendor is **10,000** in this example. In the vendor item, in the Amount field, enter the total amount with VAT, withholding tax, and the expense. In the W.tax base field, enter the expense amount with the withholding tax contribution. In the W.tax exempt field, enter any input VAT amount. Press <Enter> to go to the next screen.

4. In the expense item, in the Amount field, enter the total expense amount with the withholding tax contribution. If you enter invoices net, do not include the VAT amount. If you enter invoices gross, include the VAT amount.

Entering an Invoice for Payment Abroad (Germany)

In the Federal Republic of Germany, the state requires that international payments be coded with the purpose of the payment, such as imports of raw

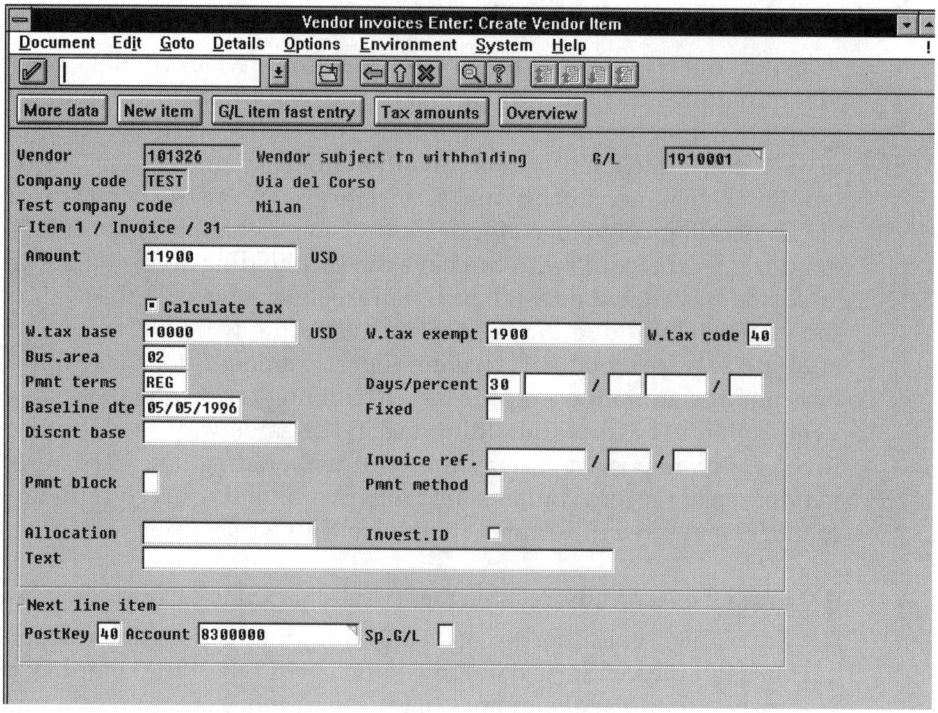

Exhibit 4.60   Vendor Invoices Enter: Create Vendor Item

materials, and the supplying country. This data is used to prepare statistical information. To pay the vendor by diskette, you have to enter the code for the purpose of the payment when you enter the invoice.

First, *make sure that the vendor master record contains the vendor's complete bank details, including the Society for Worldwide Interbank Financial Telecommunications (SWIFT) code of the vendor's bank, and also the payment method for international bank transfer (**L** in the Federal Republic of Germany).* If this data is not complete in the vendor's master record, then you cannot generate a file to pay the vendor by sending a diskette to your bank.

When you enter an invoice with FI Accounts Payable:

1. From the full screen to enter the vendor item (the payables item), first enter the amount of the invoice and any other required data. Then press More data. (See Exhibit 4.61.)

2. On the next screen, enter the central bank code for the payment in the Cen.bank ind field (the code for the purpose) and the country code in the Suppl. cntry field. For a list of valid codes, put the cursor in the field and press <F4>.

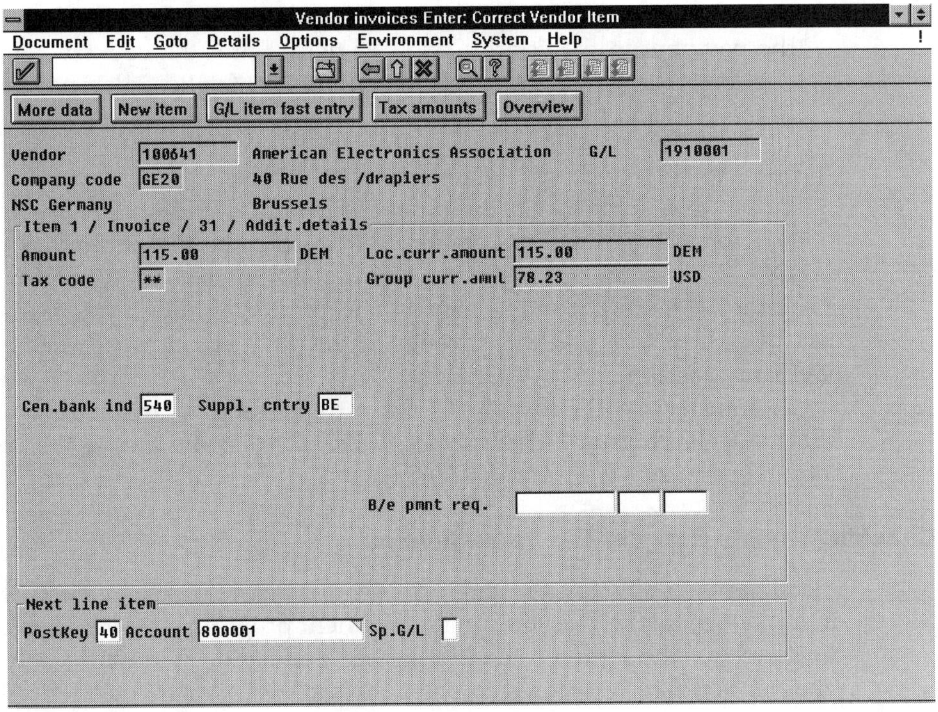

Exhibit 4.61 Vendor Invoices Enter: Correct Vendor Item

When you post an invoice with MM Purchasing or Invoice Verification:

1. While you are entering the vendor item on the very first vendor item screen, first enter the amount of the invoice and any other required data. Then press Details. (See Exhibit 4.62.)

Exhibit 4.62 Additional Data: Vendor

2. On the next screen (the pop-up window), enter the central bank code for the payment in the Central bank ID field. Enter the country code of the vendor in the Supplying cntry field. For a list of valid codes, put the cursor in the field and then press <F4>.

Continue to enter and post the invoice as otherwise.

To pay the invoice, run the payment program and specify the payment method for international payments: **L.** To record the file of the disk, run the RFFOD__L program. Specify **DME** ("data medium exchange," which is SAP-speak for file transfer), and specify a valid printer, although you are writing a disk file. Make sure that the currency of the payment is already set up in the payment program.

To transfer the file to your C: drive depending on the country, run the RFFODOWN program. Always specify **DTAZV0** as the Target file (for international payments from Germany).

Checking Double Entry of the Same Invoice

It is always possible to enter the same vendor invoice twice by mistake. If you do not notice this before you run the payment program, you then pay the vendor twice for the same product or service delivered. FI automatically checks whether you have appeared to enter the same vendor invoice twice by mistake. If you enter a vendor invoice with the same document date, currency, and reference document number, FI flags this and prompts you whether to continue entering the invoice. Note that FI does not prevent you from posting the invoice twice. It merely flags an apparent duplicate and issues a message at the end of the second screen that you may have entered a duplicate invoice.

Copying a Screenful of Data in a Long Invoice

If you are entering a long invoice, with a series of similar line items, such as expense items for the same amount of account fees for cellular phones to a series of cost centers, you can copy a screenful of data to a series of screens. In this way, you hold the data from the first screen in the series, then have this data copied to each next screen, and then change the cost center only. The purpose is to enter a long invoice quickly, saving time on the data entry. This technique applies to any data entry screen, and not only to data entry screens for vendor invoices.

To copy a screenful of data:

1. On any data entry screen, enter the data that you would like copied to each next screen, such as the amount, tax code, business area, a posting key of **40,** and G/L account number for the expense.

2. From any data entry screen, select System → User profile → Hold data.

3. Notice the message at the end of the screen that the data was held.

4. Press <Enter> to go to the next screen. During your login session (until you log off or reset the held data), each time that you go to the same screen on which you have previously held the data, the program copies the data that you held into the new data entry screen.

5. Notice that the data has been copied to the next screen. Change the cost center, in this example.

6. On the last screen in the series, remove the posting key and G/L account number to avoid having to enter another screen after you press <Enter>.

7. Post the transaction as usual.

8. To reset the held data, so that it does not appear on the same data entry screen again, select System → User profile → Release data.

Reversing a Vendor Invoice

If you mistake posting an invoice, you can never delete it. You also should not change the amounts nor the accounts. The simplest way to correct the mistake is to reverse the invoice. Reversing an invoice is also known (in English) as canceling an invoice. When you reverse an invoice (or any other transaction), FI switches a credit to a debit and a debit to a credit. You can then enter and post the invoice again. If you have already posted a vendor invoice with the MM (materials management) module and you wish to cancel the invoice, always use MM to cancel the invoice.

Assume you have entered a vendor invoice with FI. You can reverse it as follows:

1. From the Accounts Payable menu, select Document → Reverse. (See Exhibit 4.63.)

2. Enter the SAP "document" number in the Document no. field. Optionally, enter the posting date of the reversing transaction in the Posting date field. If you leave this field blank, then FI reverses the transaction on the same posting date as the original transaction. FI automatically determines the posting period from the posting date. Note that you can only reverse transactions with internally assigned "document" numbers (numbers assigned by FI). If you wish, press Display document to look at the transaction, before you reverse it.

3. Press <F11> or the file folder icon to post the reversing transaction.

Note that after you post, the system displays a message on the very last line of your screen. The message contains the "document" number and company code to which FI posted the reversing transaction. To display the reversing transaction, from the Reverse Document: Header Data menu, select Document → Display.

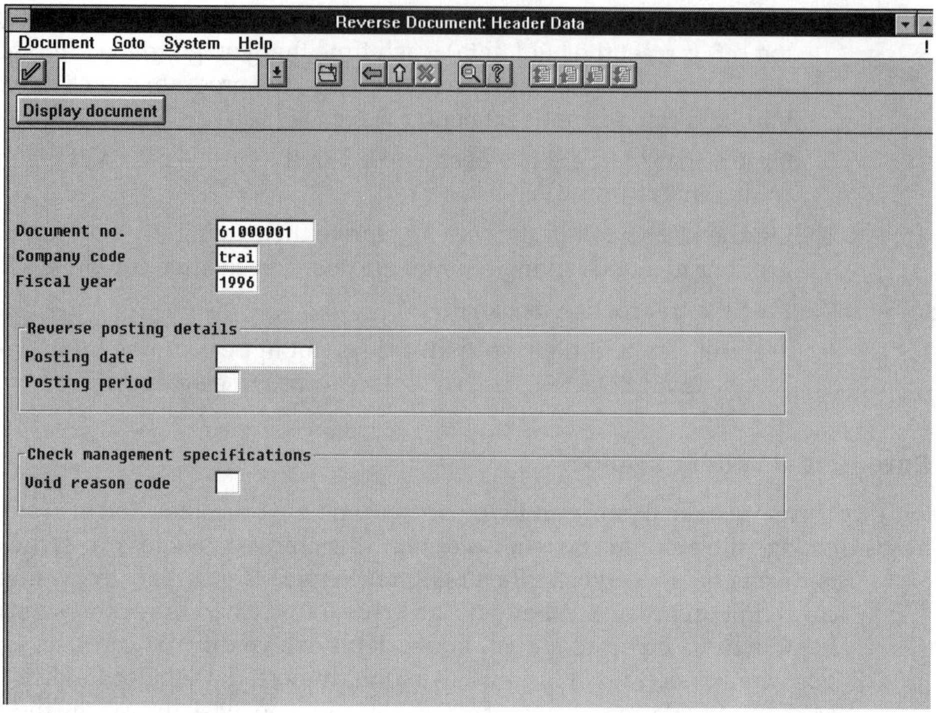

Exhibit 4.63   Reverse Document: Header Data

Holding an Incomplete Invoice (without Posting)

If you are missing data needed to enter a transaction, such as a cost center or other detail of the transaction, you can hold the invoice. FI then does not post the invoice to the accounts. Note that the configuration requires a cost center, so first enter a dummy cost center. Then store the incomplete invoice. To hold an incomplete invoice:

1. Enter an invoice as usual and display the header.
2. Select Document → Hold from the overview of the invoice. (See Exhibit 4.64.)
3. Enter a number in the Temporary document number field.
4. Press the Hold document pushbutton.

Posting a Held Vendor Invoice

If you have already held an incomplete invoice, you can complete it and then post it. To open a held invoice:

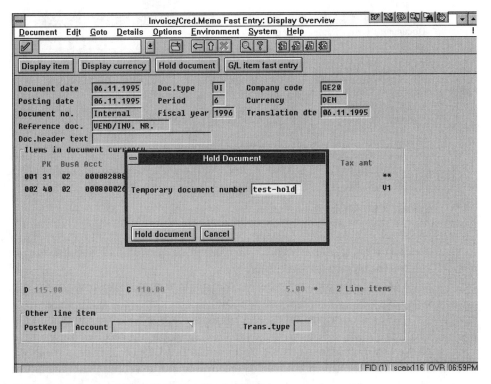

Exhibit 4.64   Invoice/Credit Memo: Display Overview

1. From the Accounts Payable menu, select Document entry ➤ Invoice.

2. From the Enter Vendor Invoice: Header Data menu, select Document ➤ Open held document. (See Exhibit 4.65.)

3. Enter the number that you already gave to the transaction when you held it and your SAP login ID. To complete the transaction, press Edit. Optionally, if you do not remember the number, press the List pushbutton and then double-click on the specific held transaction from the list.

4. Complete the transaction. Press <F11> or the file folder icon to post the transaction.

Parking a Vendor Invoice

A parked invoice is one that you have entered and stored, but not yet posted to G/L and vendor accounts. In other words, when you park an invoice, it does not update account balances. There are two reasons to park an invoice— if the invoice is awaiting approval by a certain department or if you wish to

```
─                              Post Parked Document: Header Data
  Document  Goto  System  Help
  ┌─┐ ┌─────────────────┬─┐  ┌──┐ ┌─┬─┬─┐ ┌─┬─┐ ┌─┬─┬─┬─┐
  │✓│ │                 │±│  │  │ │←│↑│✕│ │🔍│?│ │ │ │ │ │
  └─┘ └─────────────────┴─┘  └──┘ └─┴─┴─┘ └─┴─┘ └─┴─┴─┴─┘
  ┌────┐ ┌────┐ ┌──────┐ ┌───────────┐
  │Edit│ │List│ │Delete│ │ New entry │
  └────┘ └────┘ └──────┘ └───────────┘



  Temporary  document  number  ┌──────────┐
                               └──────────┘
  User                         ┌──────────┐
                               │login-id  │
                               └──────────┘
```

Exhibit 4.65   Post Parked Document

deduct any applicable input VAT from your output VAT liability without posting the invoice to the accounts.

Parking an invoice is also known as preliminary posting. In SAP terminology, these terms are interchangeable.

Note that held invoices, as previously described, are specific to a user and
can only be reported by the user who held the invoice, while you can report
parked invoices for all users. You should hold invoices if you are looking for a
piece of information to quickly complete the invoice. Otherwise, you might
forget that you had held the invoice. On the other hand, you should park
invoices if they are awaiting approval that might take days.

To park an invoice:

1. From the Accounts Payable menu, select Document entry ⇝ Preliminary
   posting. (See Exhibit 4.66.)

2. Enter the vendor invoice as usual. If the invoice is in foreign currency, to
   have the amounts converted when you post the transaction later, click on
   Doc.currency. Otherwise, to have the amounts converted now, when you
   enter the invoice, do not click on this parameter.

3. To store the invoice, without posting it to the accounts, press <F11> or the
   file folder icon.

Note that preliminary posting in FI is similar to parking an invoice in MM. The
concept is the same. Enter and store the transaction without posting it to vendor and G/L accounts. The advantage of this is that you enter these invoices at
the end of the month and run a program to deduct the input VAT even before
you have approved the invoice and posted it to G/L accounts.

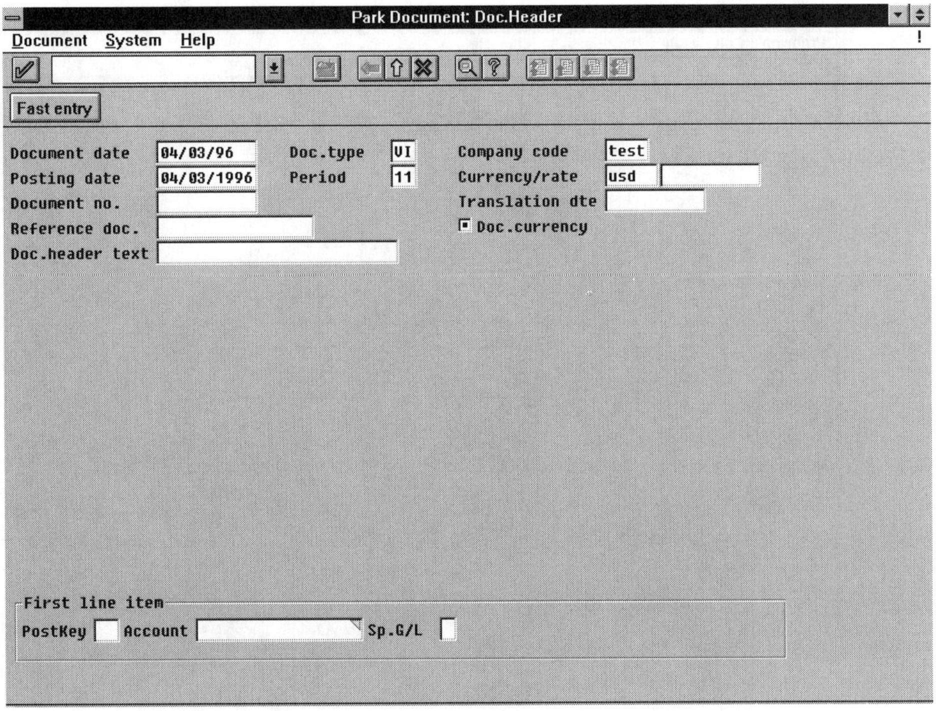

Exhibit 4.66 Park Document

Reporting Parked Invoices

To list all parked invoices, including invoices parked in both FI and MM:

1. From the Accounts Payable menu, select Document ➤ Parked documents ➤ Post.
2. Press List. (See Exhibit 4.67.)
3. Enter the company code and, optionally, other parameters, such as the "document type" and user login ID, to select the parked transactions.
4. Press <F8> or the Execute pushbutton.

Posting a Parked Invoice

To update the vendor and G/L account balances with a parked invoice, you have to post the parked invoice.

1. From the Accounts Payable menu, select Document ➤ Parked documents ➤ Post. (See Exhibit 4.68.)

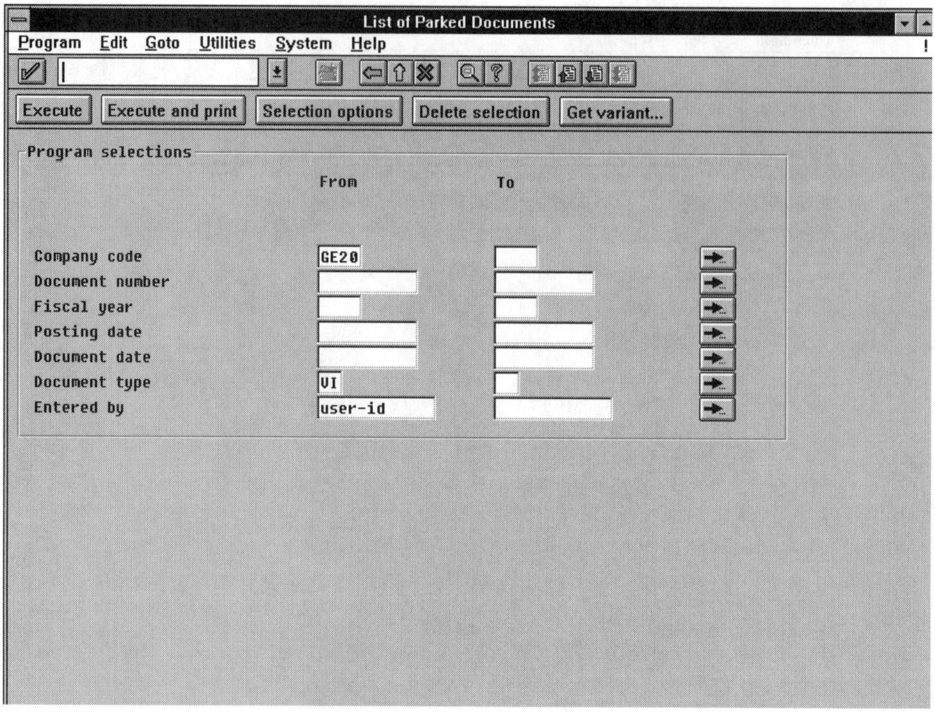

Exhibit 4.67 List of Parked Documents

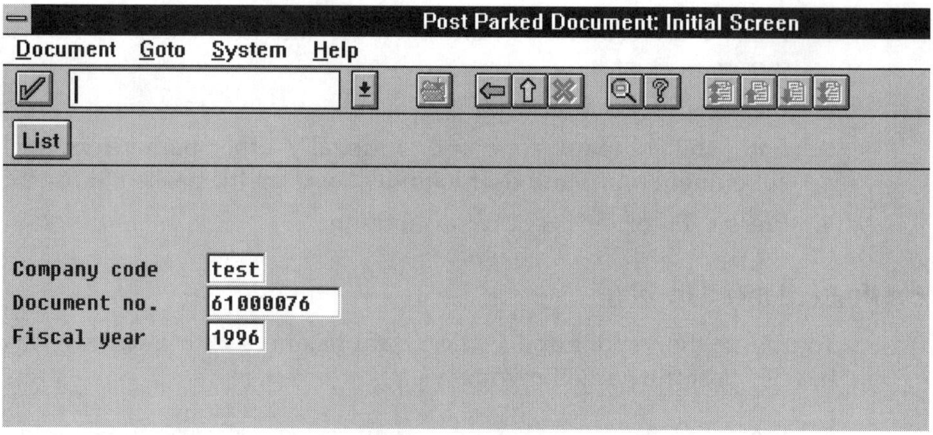

Exhibit 4.68 Post Parked Document: Initial Screen

2. Enter the company code, the transaction (document) number, and the fiscal year. Press <Enter>. (See Exhibit 4.69.)

3. From the overview of the transaction, press <F11> or the file folder icon to post the transaction.

Blocking an Invoice from Payment

You can block a specific invoice from being paid. After posting a transaction, you can never change the posting keys, accounts, or amounts of any line item. However, you can change certain other fields in line items, depending on your configuration, such as the payment block. In this way, you prevent the invoice from being processed by the payment program, until you remove the payment block.

To block a specific invoice from being paid:

1. From the Accounts Payable menu, select Document ➤ Change. (See Exhibit 4.70.)

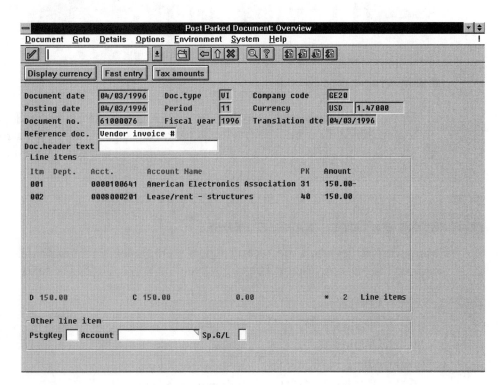

Exhibit 4.69 Post Parked Document: Overview

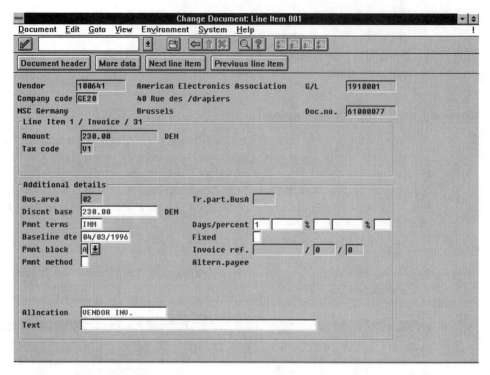

Exhibit 4.70　Change Document

2. In the Pmnt block field, enter a valid code to block the payment, depending on the configuration. For a list of valid codes, press the down arrow.

3. To store the updated invoice with the payment block, press <F11> or the file folder icon.

PROCESSING EMPLOYEE TRAVEL EXPENSES

Many companies use FI to record and pay employee travel expenses. Enter each employee as a vendor. The employee numbers could be the following:

Number Range	Type
00000G0001–00000G9999	German employees
00000L0001–00000L9999	British employees
00000FR001–00000FR999	French employees
00000IT001–00000IT999	Italian employees
000000S001–000000S999	Swedish employees

Note that the complete employee number for travel expenses has ten characters.

Note that to process employee travel expenses, the company keeps only the name of the employee and their bank account number. In this system, the company does not keep any personal data about the employee, except in the United Kingdom, where this is required on the address of remittance advices.

Entering an Employee Master Record

You can enter the employee master records by hand or by batch input, as you would enter a vendor master record. Depending on the country, enter only the name and bank account number of the employee. The system should not contain private information about the employee, such as the address or telephone number. Otherwise, keeping employee master records is the same as keeping vendor master records.

Entering a Request for a Travel Advance

Record travel advances as if they were down payments to vendors. If the employee is asking for a travel advance, you can record the request. The next time you run the payment program, you can pay the requested travel advance. To enter a request for a travel advance:

1. From the Accounts Payable menu, select Document entry ➤ Down payment ➤ Request. (See Exhibit 4.71.)

2. In the Account field, enter the employee number, based on the badge number, preceded by five zeroes. Since the account number has both a character and digits, you have to enter the five zeroes before the employee number. Enter a target special G/L indicator (Trg.sp. G/L ind.) **A** (for advance). Press <Enter>. The next screen prompts you to enter the amount of the request. Depending on your configuration, the system posts a one-sided entry to one G/L account only.

3. When you run the payment program, the program may suggest paying this request for advance, depending on the due date and the date of the next payment run. When you post the payment, depending on your configuration, the program credits cash in transit and debits the employee account.

Posting an Employee Travel Advance

If you have already paid the employee a travel advance by check, bank transfer, or in cash (not using the payment program), you can post the advance. The system posts a debit to the employee account. To post an advance to an employee for travel expenses:

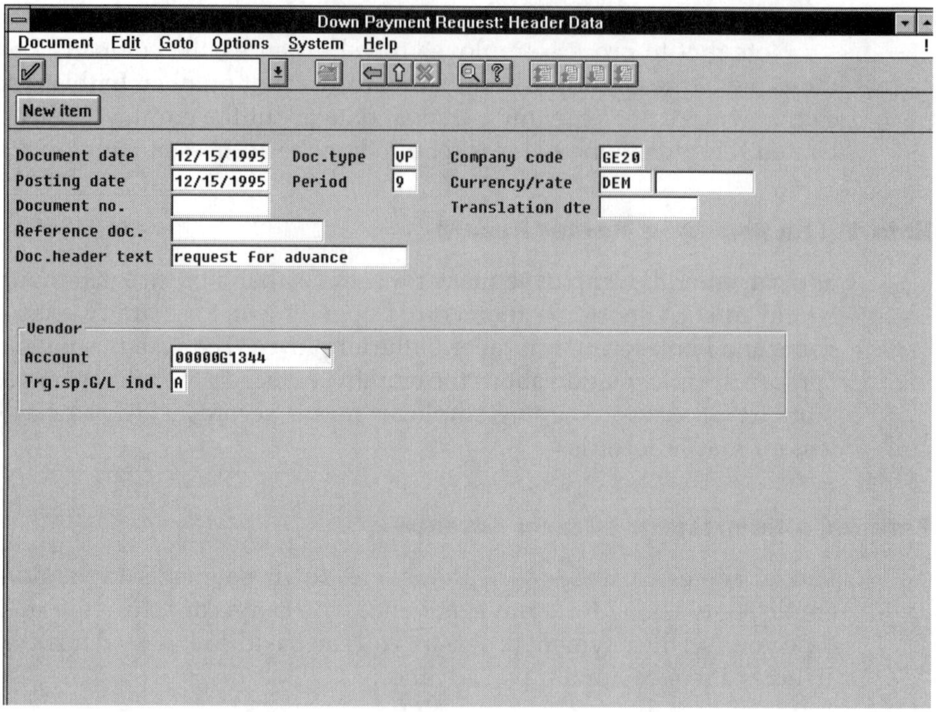

Exhibit 4.71   Down Payment Request: Header Data

1. From the Accounts Payable menu, select Document entry ➤ Down payment ➤ Post. (See Exhibit 4.72.)
2. Enter the transaction header as usual, except that you enter the "document type," depending on the configuration, as **EA** (employee advance).

    In the Vendor section, enter the employee number in the Vendor field. To enter a *permanent advance,* also known as a "float," which will not be processed in the payment run (subtracted from expense sheets), enter **P** (permanent advance) in the Special G/L ind field, depending on your configuration.

    To enter a *regular advance,* which will be subtracted from expense sheet totals in the payment run, enter **A** in the Special G/L ind field, depending on your configuration.

    In the Bank section, enter the G/L account (for petty cash, cash in the bank, or cash in transit, depending on the payment method) in the Account field. Enter the division in the Business area field. Enter the total amount of the disbursement, including any possible bank fees, in the Amount field. If there were any bank fees, then enter the bank fees for the down payment in the Bank charges field. In other words, the program posts the bank fees separately from the advance, assuming that the com-

Exhibit 4.72 figure:

```
─                     Post Vendor Down Payment: Header Data              ▼ ◆
 Document  Edit  Goto  Details  Options  Environment  System  Help                    !
 ✓ [            ]  ± [▣] [⇐][⇧][✕] [🔍][?] [▣][▣][▣][▣]

 [ New item ] [ Requests ] [ Overview ]

 Document date   12/15/1995   Doc.type  EA    Company code   GE20
 Posting date    12/15/1995   Period    9     Currency/rate  DEM  [      ]
 Document no.    [         ]                   Translation dte [      ]
 Reference doc.  [             ]
 Doc.header text entering a travel advance

 ┌Vendor────────────────────────────────────────────────────────────┐
 │ Account        00000G1344     ▼           Special G/L ind A        │
 └───────────────────────────────────────────────────────────────────┘

 ┌Bank──────────────────────────────────────────────────────────────┐
 │ Account        0100625        ▼           Business area   02       │
 │ Amount         610                                                 │
 │ Bank charges   5                                                   │
 │ Value date     12/15/1996                                          │
 └───────────────────────────────────────────────────────────────────┘
```

Exhibit 4.72 Post Vendor Down Payment: Header Data

pany pays any bank fees. To go to the next screen, press <Enter> as usual. (See Exhibit 4.73.)

3. Enter the amount. Click on the Calculate tax field. Enter the division in the Bus.area field.

   To see the overview of the transaction, press on the Overview pushbutton. (See Exhibit 4.74.)

4. Look at the next line after the list of items in the transaction. Make sure that the total debits (D) equal the total credits (C). To post the transaction, press <F11> or the file folder icon.

5. The advance is automatically blocked for payment (not included in open item processing during the payment run). To have the down payment deducted from any expense sheets later (included in the payment run when calculating the amount of the payment), change the transaction and remove the payment block. To change the down payment, immediately after you post it:

   a. Select Document ➤ Change.

   b. From the overview of the transaction, double-click on the employee item. (See Exhibit 4.75.)

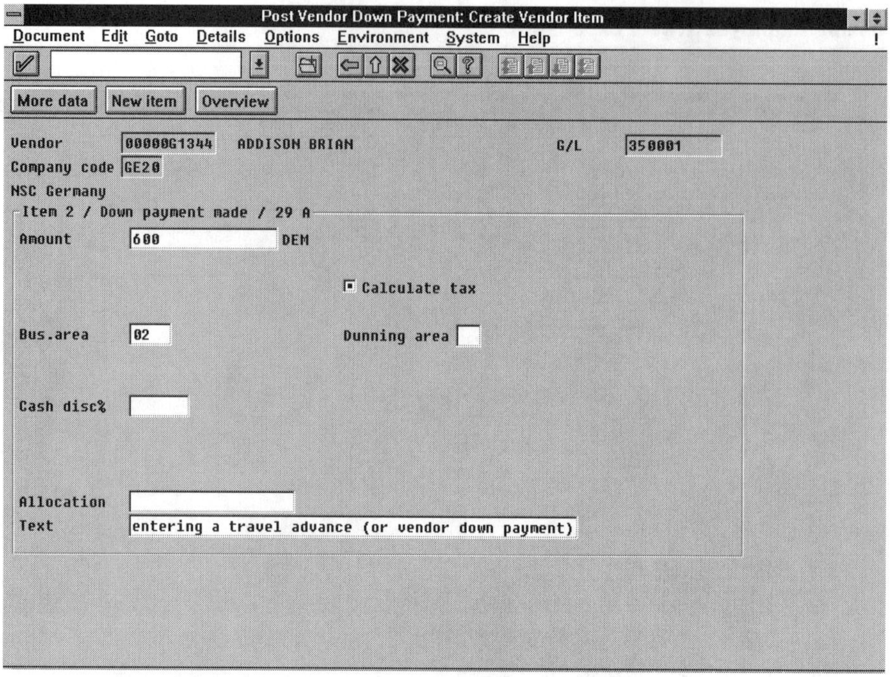
Post Vendor Down Payment: Create Vendor Item
Document Edit Goto Details Options Environment System Help
More data
New item
Overview
Vendor 00000G1344 ADDISON BRIAN
G/L 350001
Company code GE20
NSC Germany
Item 2 / Down payment made / 29 A
Amount 600 DEM
Calculate tax
Bus.area 02
Dunning area
Cash disc%
Allocation
Text entering a travel advance (or vendor down payment)

Exhibit 4.73 Post Vendor Down Payment: Create Vendor Item

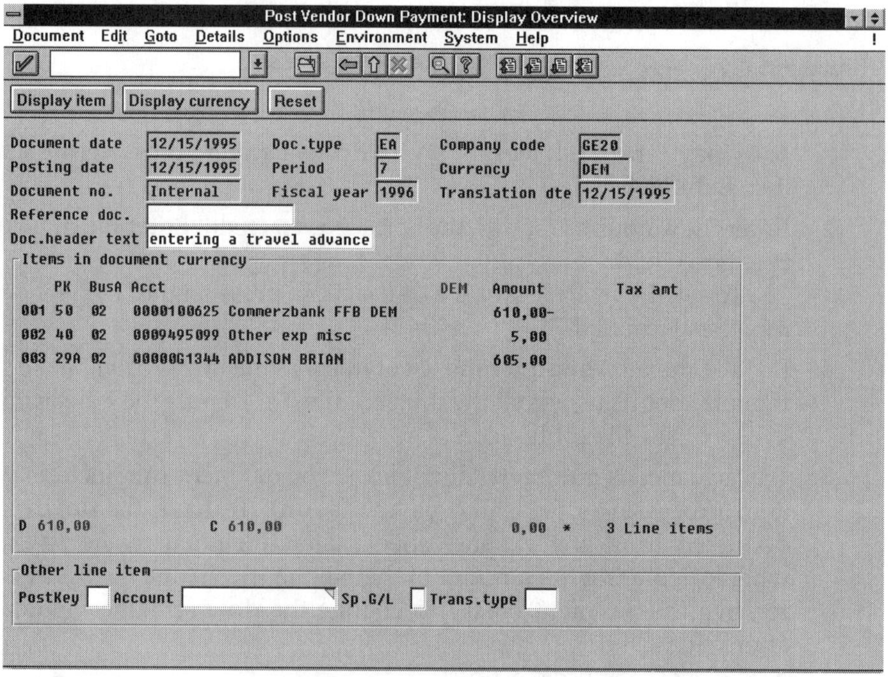
Post Vendor Down Payment: Display Overview
Document Edit Goto Details Options Environment System Help
Display item
Display currency
Reset
Document date 12/15/1995
Doc.type EA
Company code GE20
Posting date 12/15/1995
Period 7
Currency DEM
Document no. Internal
Fiscal year 1996
Translation dte 12/15/1995
Reference doc.
Doc.header text entering a travel advance
Items in document currency
PK BusA Acct DEM Amount Tax amt
001 50 02 0000100625 Commerzbank FFB DEM 610,00-
002 40 02 0009495099 Other exp misc 5,00
003 29A 02 00000G1344 ADDISON BRIAN 605,00
D 610,00 C 610,00 0,00 * 3 Line items
Other line item
PostKey Account Sp.G/L Trans.type

Exhibit 4.74 Display Vendor Down Payment: Display Overview

```
┌──────────────────────────────────────────────────────────────────────────┐
│ ▬                    Change Document: Line Item 003                  ▼│▲│
│ Document  Edit  Goto  View  Environment  System  Help                    !│
│ ┌─┐ ┌────────────────────┐ ┌─┐ ┌─┬─┬─┐ ┌─┬─┐ ┌─┬─┬─┬─┐                  │
│ │✓│ │                    │▼│ │🖫│ │←│↑│✕│ │🔍│?│ │▣│▣│▣│▣│                  │
│ └─┘ └────────────────────┘ └─┘ └─┴─┴─┘ └─┴─┘ └─┴─┴─┴─┘                  │
│ ┌───────────────┐ ┌───────────┐ ┌───────────────┐ ┌───────────────────┐ │
│ │Document header│ │ More data │ │ Next line item│ │ Previous line item│ │
│ └───────────────┘ └───────────┘ └───────────────┘ └───────────────────┘ │
│                                                                          │
│ Vendor...... 0000061344   ADDISON BRIAN              G/L    350001       │
│ Comp.code   GE20                                                         │
│ NSC Germany                                          Doc.no. 21000003    │
│ ┌─Line Item 3 / Down payment made / 29 A──────────────────────────────┐ │
│ │ Amount        605,00                                                 │ │
│ │                                                                      │ │
│ │                                                                      │ │
│ └──────────────────────────────────────────────────────────────────────┘ │
│ ┌─Additional details──────────────────────────────────────────────────┐ │
│ │ Due on       12/15/1995        Bus.area    02                        │ │
│ │ Pmnt method  ┌─┐               Pmnt block  ┌─┐                        │ │
│ │ Cash disc%   0,000                                                   │ │
│ │                                                                      │ │
│ │                         0                                            │ │
│ │                                                                      │ │
│ │ Allocation   ┌─────────────┐   Disp.envirn. ┌────┐ / 0 / 000         │ │
│ │ Text         entering a travel advance (or vendor down payment)      │ │
│ └──────────────────────────────────────────────────────────────────────┘ │
└──────────────────────────────────────────────────────────────────────────┘
```

Exhibit 4.75 Change Document

    c. Remove the payment block from the Pmnt block field. If the advance is a permanent advance, leave the payment block on, which excludes the permanent advance from the net due calculation in the payment program.

    d. Store the transaction by pressing <F11> or the file folder icon.

Posting Expense Sheets

Post employee travel expenses as if they were vendor invoices. You credit the employee (vendor) and debit the expense. Follow the instructions about entering and posting vendor invoices. To start to enter an employee expense sheet:

1. From the Accounts Payable menu, select Document entry → Invoice. (See Exhibit 4.76.)

2. To record the travel expenses in a separate journal, enter **EE** (employee expenses) in the Doc.type field, depending on your configuration. Enter or make sure that the posting key is **31** (to credit a vendor account). Enter the vendor account number for the employee.

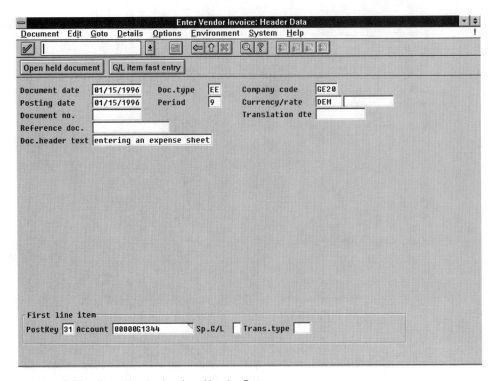

Exhibit 4.76   Enter Vendor Invoice: Header Data

3.   Enter and post the expense sheet as if it were a vendor invoice. Credit the vendor (employee) account and debit the expense account.

Posting an Invoice to an Employee

In a sample balance sheet, employee receivables could be reported in G/L account 0350099, separately from travel paybacks (expense sheets payable) in 1910103. At the same time, all employees could be set up as vendor accounts, such as 00000G1234 (German employee). If the company splits an expense with the employee, such as moving costs, or even uses its purchasing power on behalf of the employee, you can record the invoice to the employee as a debit to the employee, using a special G/L code **Y** and credit to both the expense and the input VAT accounts. In this way, employee receivables and travel expense payables are reported in separate G/L accounts, but all transaction detail is stored in the employee's (vendor) account.

Posting a Permanent Advance

Post a travel advance as already described. Do not unblock the payment. It will not be processed in the payment run.

Paying Employee Travel Expenses

To pay employee travel expenses, run the payment program and specify the employee account numbers, instead of the vendor account numbers. To include any travel advances in the payment run (to deduct the advance from the expense sheet and pay the employee the net balance), first unblock the travel advance, if you have not already done this. Employees and vendors can both be included in the same payment run.

Reviewing the Employee Account Detail

Since all employee transactions (expense sheets, invoices to employees, travel advances, and permanent advances) are recorded in the employee (vendor) account, you can display all these details in one account. The invoices and advances are displayed separately from the expense sheets (open items), the paid expense sheets, and any travel advances already applied to expense sheets (cleared items). To review the employee account detail:

1. From the Accounts Payable menu, select Account ➤ Display items. (See Exhibit 4.77.)

2. Enter the employee account number in the Vendor field and the company code in the Company code field. To see open (unpaid) items only, click on the Open items box and then press <Enter>. To see both open and cleared (paid and reimbursed) items, also click on Cleared items and press <Enter>. To see the parked items (expense sheets entered but not yet posted), click on Parked items. To see advances and invoices in the detail, depending on your configuration, select With special G/L transactions. Press <Enter>. (See Exhibit 4.78.)

3. To see the details of a specific line item, place the cursor on that line and then press the Document pushbutton. From the screen with the details of the line item, to see the overview of the complete transaction, press the Document pushbutton again. To go back to the basic list of line items, press the left arrow.

   To sort the list of line items, place the cursor on the column that you wish to sort by and then press the Sort pushbutton.

   To print the list, select Line items ➤ Print.

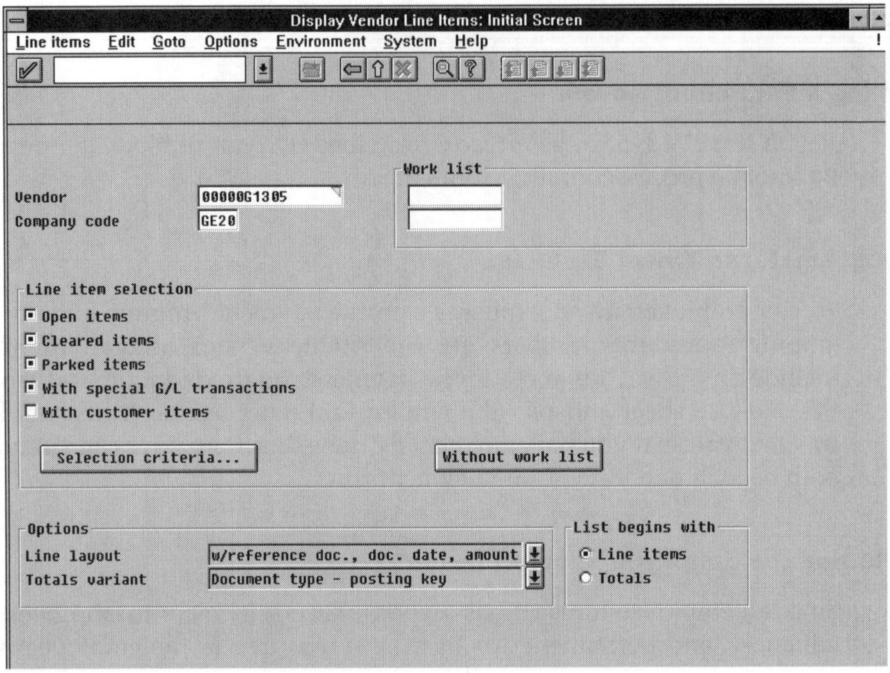

Exhibit 4.77   Display Vendor Line Items: Initial Screen

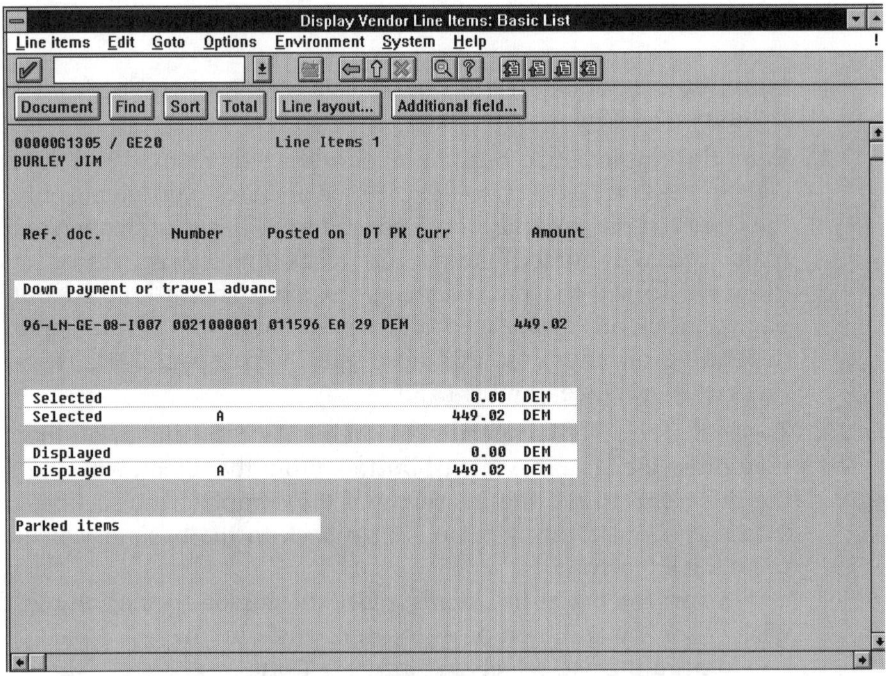

Exhibit 4.78   Display Vendor Line Items: Basic List

400

To transfer the list to a spreadsheet, select Line items ➤ Download. This transfer was developed first to Excel, but also functions with 1-2-3 in later versions.

To look for a specific line item, if you have a lot of open items, press the Find pushbutton. (See Exhibit 4.79.)

To continue to look for a specific item, click on a field to search by. Then press the Proceed pushbutton or <Enter>. (See Exhibit 4.80.)

To continue to look for a specific item, enter the item that you are looking for and press the Proceed pushbutton or <Enter>.

To go back to the basic list of line items, press the left arrow. (See Exhibit 4.81.)

From the basic list, you can also subtotal amounts of line items. To subtotal line items by a specific field, such as the posting date, place your cursor on any entry in the Posted on column and then press the Total pushbutton. This depends on the configuration of your line layouts.

The line layout is the sequence of specific fields from left to right on each line. Your configuration can include alternate line layouts. To switch

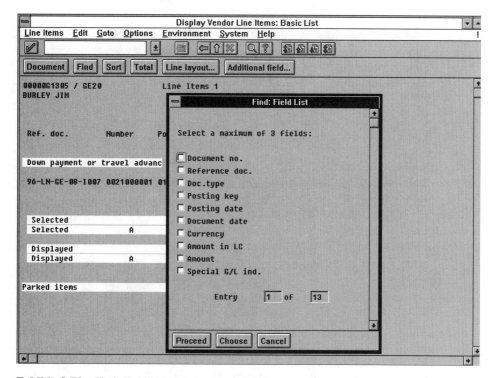

Exhibit 4.79   Find: Field List

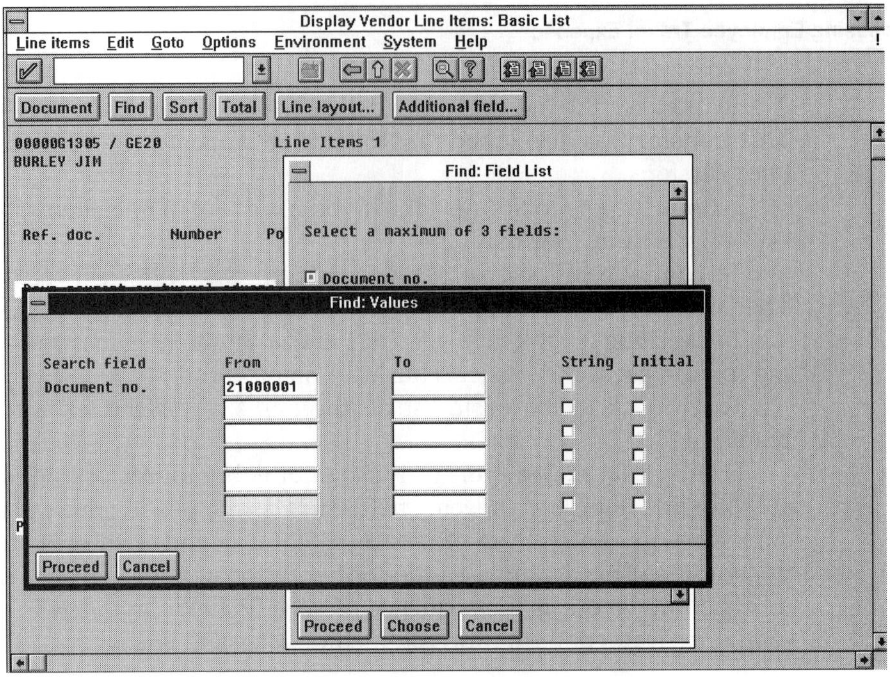

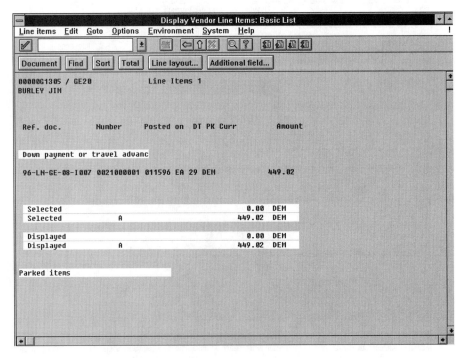

Exhibit 4.80   Find: Values

Exhibit 4.81   Display Vendor Line Items: Basic List

to a different line layout, if included in your configuration, press the Line layout pushbutton and then double-click on a line layout description.

4. To go back to the Accounts Payable menu from the basic list of line items, press the up arrow.

INQUIRING IN ACCOUNTS PAYABLE

Various functions are available to query accounts payable transactions and vendor account balances. The most frequently used functions are:

- Displaying monthly account balances
- Displaying a transaction
- Displaying line items in an account

Displaying Periodic Vendor Account Balances

To see monthly (periodic) account balances:

1. From the Accounts Payable menu, select Account → Display balances. (See Exhibit 4.82.)

2. Enter the vendor name (or account number) in the Vendor field. Also enter the company code and the fiscal year. Then press <Enter>. (See Exhibit 4.83.)
    Note that the first column contains the posting periods, according to your fiscal year as configured. The second column contains the total debits posted to this account in each posting period, according to the *posting date* of the transaction. The third column contains the total credits posted to this account in each posting period, also according to the posting date of the transaction. The fourth column contains the balance (debit or credit) for that posting period. The fifth column contains the balance carried forward for each period, including that period and all previous periods. Notice that the current balance (the most recent balance carried forward) is also always displayed in the very lower-right portion of the screen.

Drilling Down to Line Items from a Balance

Assume you still have the vendor account balances on your screen. You can instantly drill down to the basic list of line items that make up any account balance.

1. From the Vendor: Account Balance screen, simply double-click on any balance, such as the current balance in the lower-right corner. (See Exhibit 4.84.)

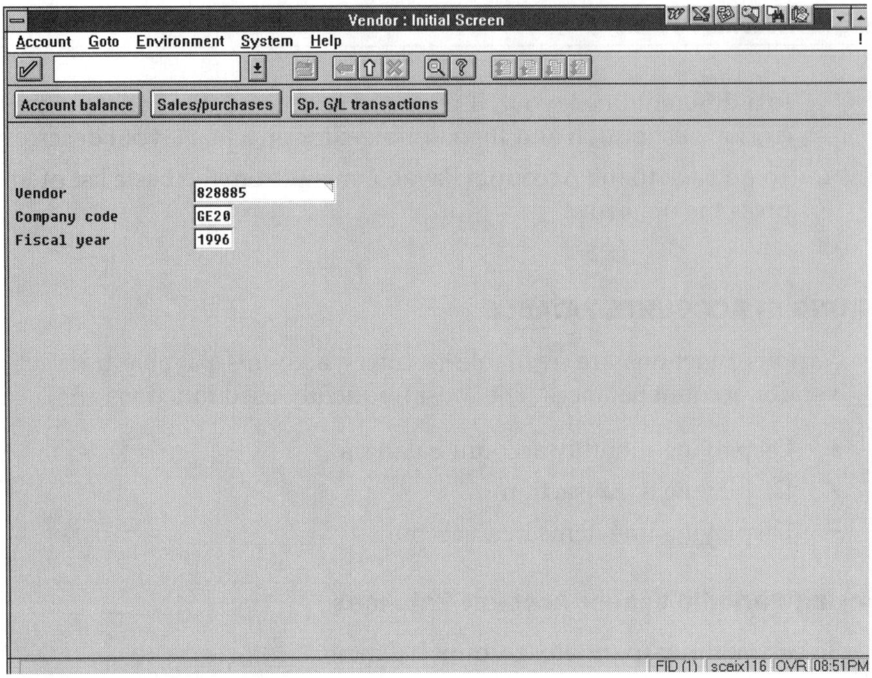

Exhibit 4.82   Vendor: Initial Screen

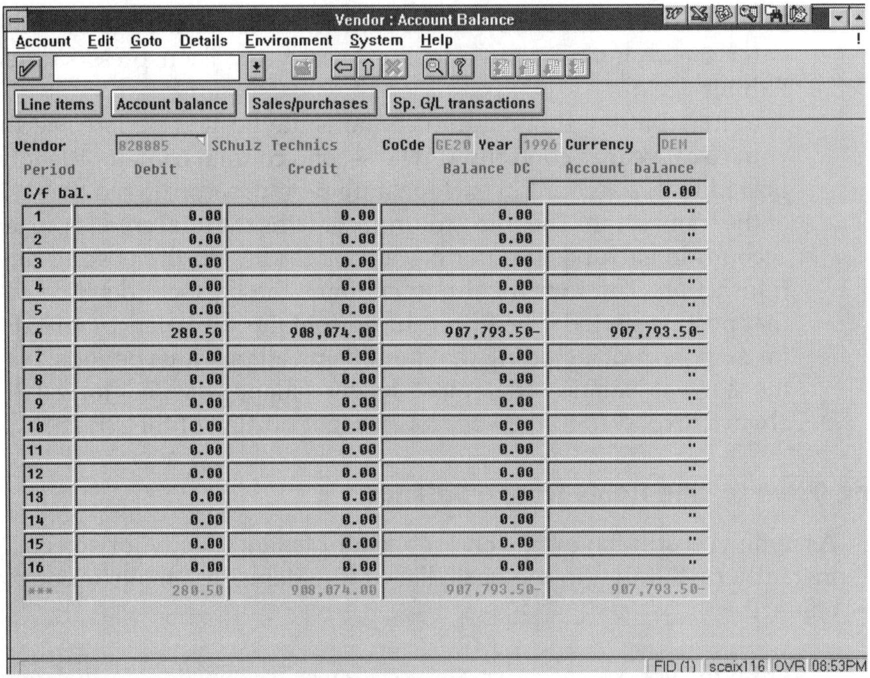

Exhibit 4.83   Vendor: Account Balance

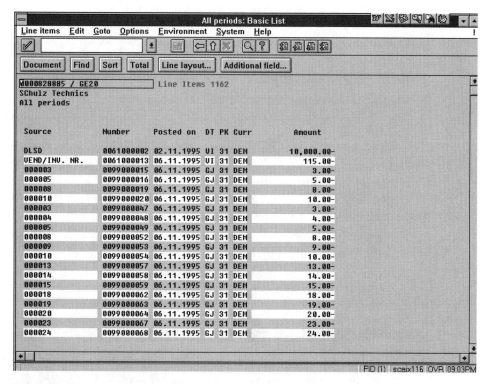

Exhibit 4.84 All Periods: Basic List

2. From the basic list, you have the same functions available to sort, find, subtotal, and change the line layout of line items that were described in the previous section, "Reviewing Employee Account Detail."

Displaying a Transaction from a Line Item

Assume you have the Basic List of line items on your screen. To look at the complete transaction for a specific line item:

1. Place the cursor on a specific line item and then press the Document pushbutton.
2. From the detail screen of the line item, press the Document pushbutton again.

The next screen shows the complete transaction, including all the debits and credits.

Displaying a Transaction

To display a transaction:

1. From the Accounts Payable menu, select Document ➤ Display.
2. On the next screen, enter the transaction number and press <Enter>. If you do not remember the transaction number, press the List pushbutton. (See Exhibit 4.85.)

   The screen shown in Exhibit 4.85 prompts you to specify the transaction you are looking for. Always enter the company code in the Company code field. To find vendor invoices, enter **VI** in the Document type field depending on your configuration. Press <F8> or the Execute pushbutton for a list of vendor invoices. (See Exhibit 4.86.)
3. From the list of vendor invoices, double-click on a line to see that specific invoice. (See Exhibit 4.87.)
4. To go back to the list, press the left arrow. From the list, to go back to the Accounts Payable menu, press the up arrow twice.

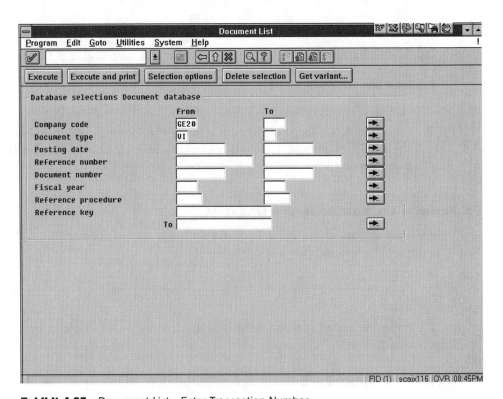

Exhibit 4.85   Document List—Enter Transaction Number

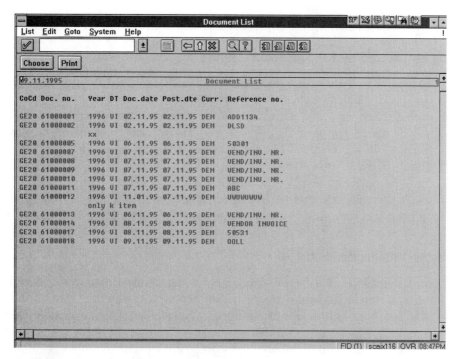

Exhibit 4.86   Document List—View a Specific Invoice

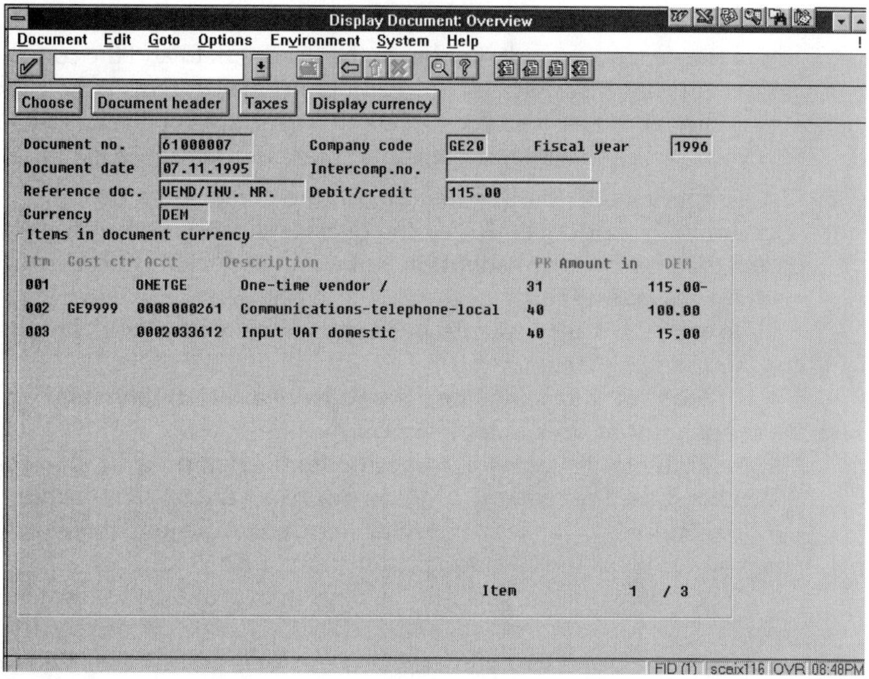

Exhibit 4.87   Display Document

Finding an Invoice by the Reference Number

To find an invoice by the reference number (usually the vendor's invoice number), use the transaction ("document") journal report. Enter the vendor's invoice number in the parameter Reference doc. Run the report as usual. For details about running this report, see the section "Reporting a Transaction Journal" in the General Ledger chapter. The output of the report shows the details of the transaction.

Alternatively, display the line items in a vendor account. Make sure that the Reference doc. field is in a specific column in the line layout. Sort by this column and then find the invoice, or use the Find function to find the invoice.

Displaying Vendor Open Items

In a vendor account, you can display open (unpaid) items, cleared (paid) items, or both. To display items in a set of accounts together, first define a work list. See the section about defining a work list, "Making a Work List of Accounts," in the General Ledger chapter. Then enter the work list instead of the vendor account number.

1. From the Accounts Payable menu, select Account → Display items. (See Exhibit 4.88.)

2. Enter the vendor account number in the Vendor field and the company code in the Company code field. To see open (unpaid) items only, click on the Open items box and then press <Enter>. To see both open and cleared (paid) items, also click on Cleared items and press <Enter>. (See Exhibit 4.89.)

3. To see the details of a line item, place the cursor on a line and press the Document pushbutton. To see the overview of the complete transaction, press the Document pushbutton again. To go back to the basic list of line items, press the left arrow.

    To sort the basic list, place the cursor on a field and press the Sort pushbutton.

    To look for a specific item, if you have a lot of open items, press the Find pushbutton. (See Exhibit 4.90.)

    To continue to look for a specific item, click on a field to search by. Then press the Proceed pushbutton or press <Enter>. (See Exhibit 4.91.)

    To continue to look for a specific item, enter the item that you are looking for and press the Proceed pushbutton or press <Enter>.

    To go back to the basic list of line items, press the left arrow. (See Exhibit 4.92.)

    From the basic list, you can also subtotal amounts of line items. To subtotal line items by a specific field, such as the posting date, place your cursor on the Posted on field and then press the Total pushbutton.

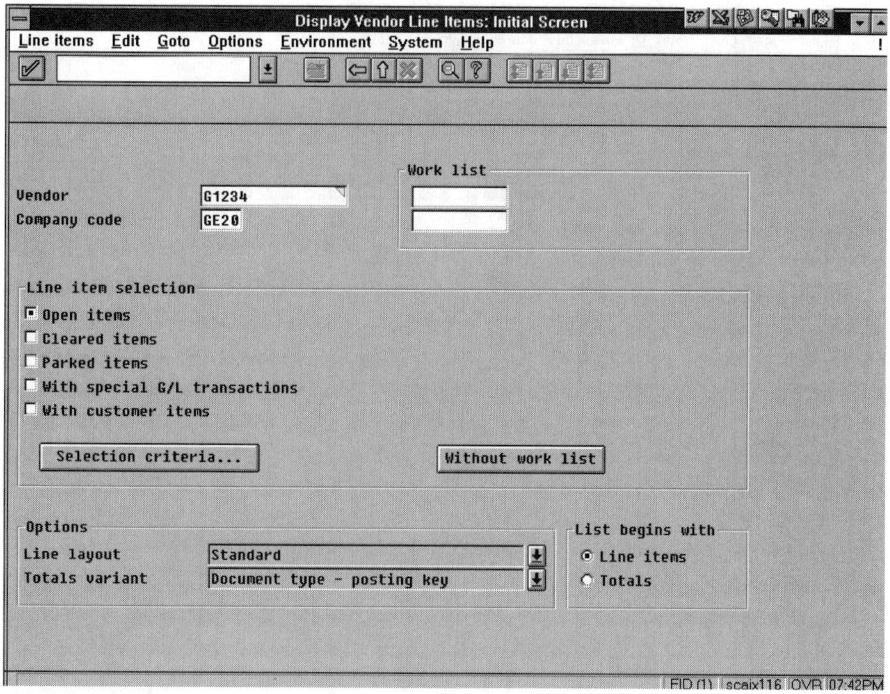

Exhibit 4.88 Display Vendor Line Items: Initial Screen

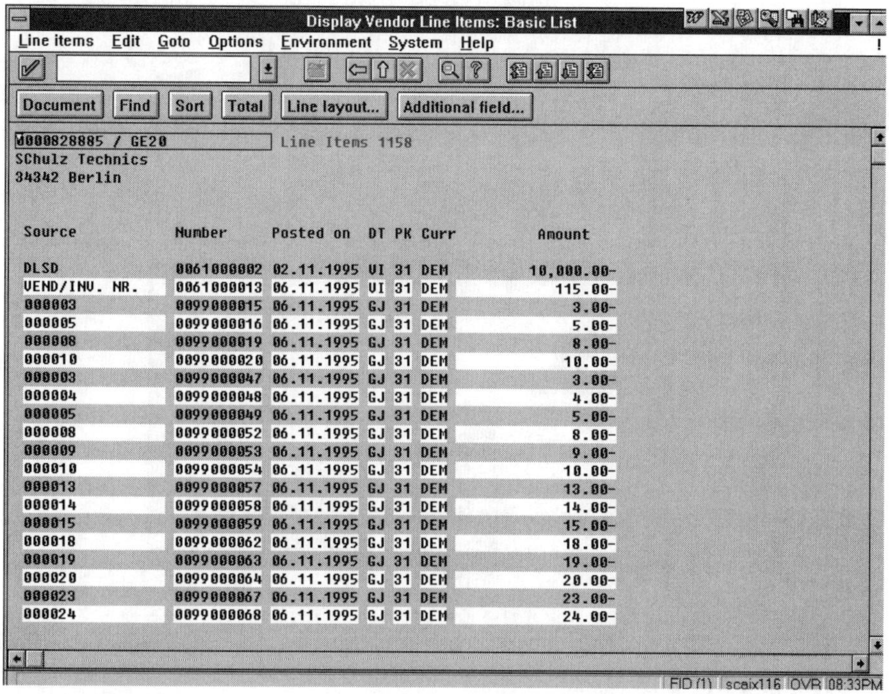

Exhibit 4.89 Display Vendor Line Items: Basic List

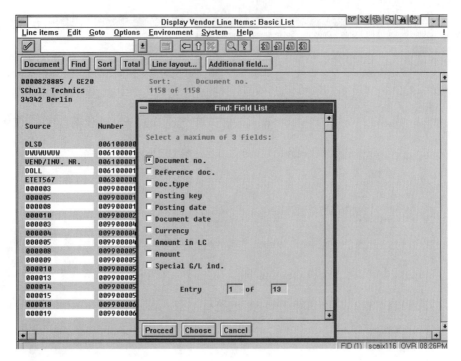

Exhibit 4.90 Find: Field List

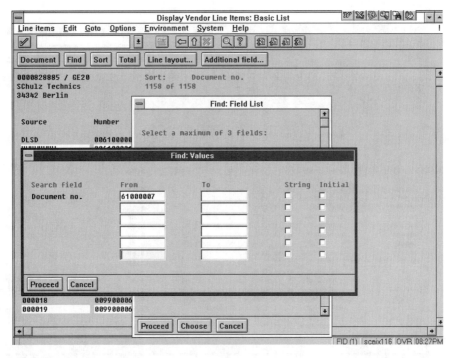

Exhibit 4.91 Find: Values

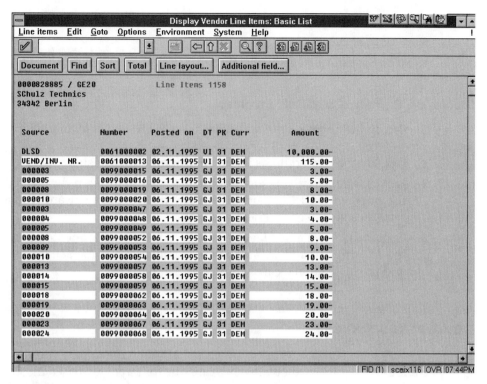

Exhibit 4.92 Display Vendor Line Items

The line layout is the sequence of specific fields from left to right on each line. Your configuration can include alternate line layouts. To switch to a different line layout, if included in your configuration, press the Line layout pushbutton and then double-click on a line layout description.

To go back to the Accounts Payable menu, from the basic list of line items, press the up arrow.

Printing Vendor Line Items

To print out the line items in a vendor account from the display of the line items, simply select Line Items ➤ Print.

Downloading Vendor Line Items to Excel

For further processing, to download the line items in a vendor account from the display of the line items:

1. Simply select Line Items ➤ Download.

2. Enter a valid directory filename on your C: (or other PC) drive.

3. Press Send.

4. Wait for the message confirming that the file has been sent.

Displaying Payments and Paid Invoices

To display the payment to the vendor and which invoices were paid:

1. Display the cleared items in the vendor account as usual.

2. Notice that before you sort, subtotal, or search through the cleared items, the payment and the paid invoices with this payment are displayed in sequence next to each other.

3. Optionally, have a line layout configured for vendor line items to include the clearing "document" number. This number is the same for invoices and payments that cleared those specific invoices.

PAYING VENDOR INVOICES

If you have a series of vendor invoices that you have to pay, you can use the payment program to calculate which are due for payment, based mostly on the payment terms, and to generate a payment proposal automatically. Whether the invoice is included in a payment proposal or postponed until the next payment run depends on the baseline date for payment, usually the vendor's invoice date, the payment terms, today's date, the date of the next payment run, and the configuration. With the payment proposal, you can optionally block specific open items from being paid. When you are satisfied with the payment proposal, you can post the payments. To prepare the payment media (for example, to prepare the disk file of bank transfers or to print checks), you then have to run another program.

In summary, to pay vendors with the payment program, do as follows:

1. Enter the payment program *parameters*

2. Run a payment *proposal*

3. Optionally, process the payment proposal, blocking one or more vendor invoices from being paid

4. *Post the payments.* The payment program then credits the configured G/L accounts, debits the vendors, and clears (closes) the open invoices

5. Run a separate program to *record a file* of payment instructions on the disk (or to print checks)

6. *Transfer the file* to your PC

7. Put the payment file on a disk and *send it to the bank by courier* or transfer it to the bank by modem

Note that SAP does not supply the software for the last step. Use the PC operating system to put the file on the diskette or some external vendor to transmit the file to the bank or clearinghouse, such as BACS in the United Kingdom.

Employee travel expenses are paid in the same way as vendor invoices. Simply specify a different range of vendor account numbers.

Running the Payment Program

Assume that the payment program is properly configured for your company. Furthermore, assume that you have overdue invoices, according to the payment terms of the vendor invoice and today's date. To start to run the payment program:

1. From the Accounts Payable menu, select Periodic processing → Payments. (See Exhibit 4.93.)

2. On the first screen, enter the date of the payment run, usually today's date, in the Run date field. In the Identification field, enter any 1–5 character ID for this payment run, such as **test1**. Note that you will need these two values later to prepare the payment media (bank transfer file or checks). Press <Enter>. (See Exhibit 4.94.)

3. On the next screen, notice the area labeled Status. In this area, FI keeps you informed about this payment run. Press <F5> or the Maintain parameters pushbutton to enter the parameters of this payment run. (See Exhibit 4.95.)

4. On the parameters screen, you have to enter at least the following fields:

Field	Meaning
Posting date	When you post the payments, they will have this posting date.
Docs entered up to	Cut-off date of the invoices to be analyzed in this payment run, according to the entry date
Company codes	The company code that is paying
Pmnt meths	The payment method according to your configuration, such as **U** for domestic bank transfers in the Federal Republic of Germany or **L** for international bank transfers in the Federal Republic of

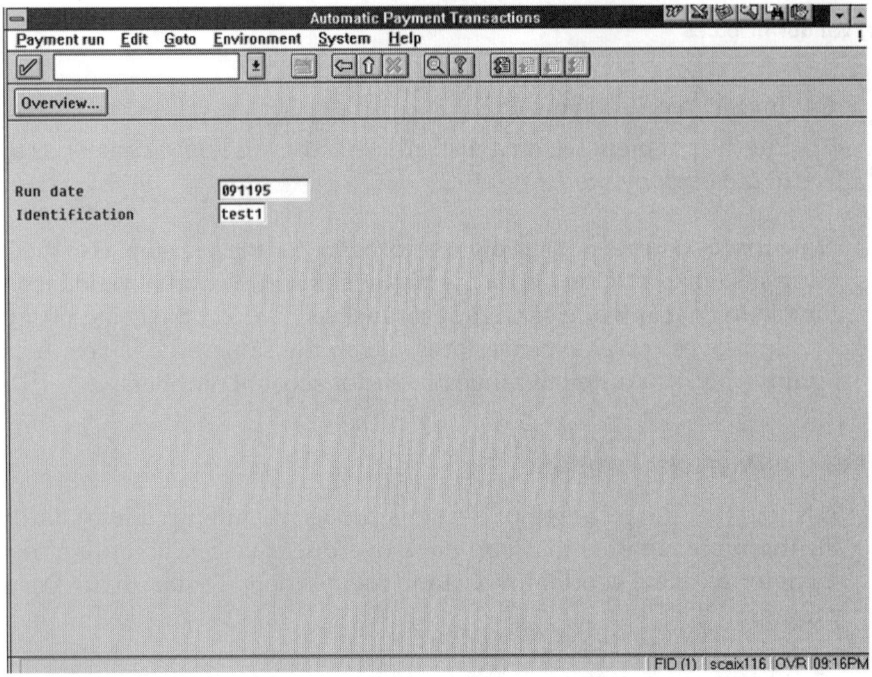

Exhibit 4.93 Automatic Payment Transactions, Screen One

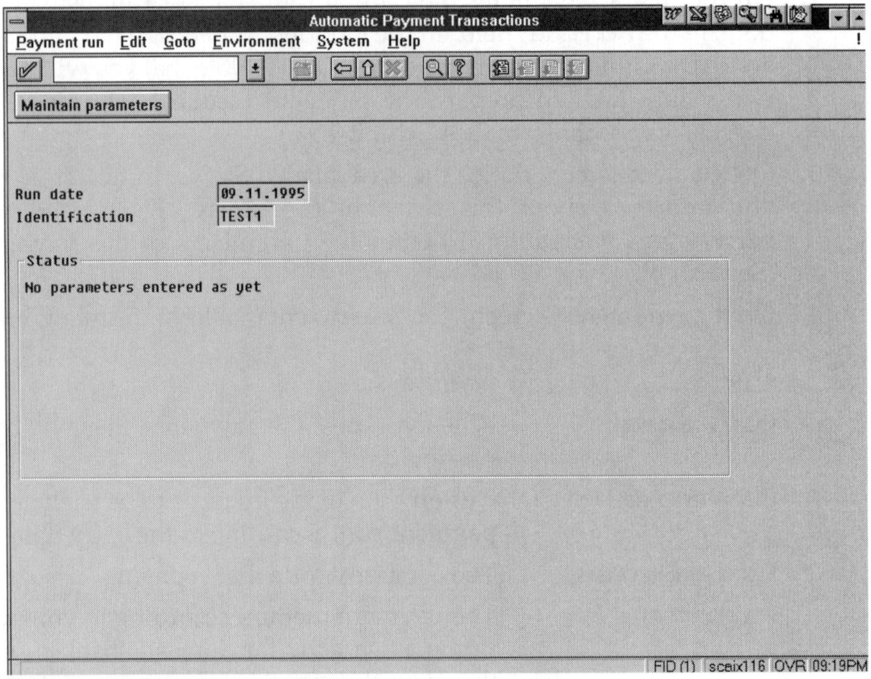

Exhibit 4.94 Automatic Payment Transactions, Screen Two

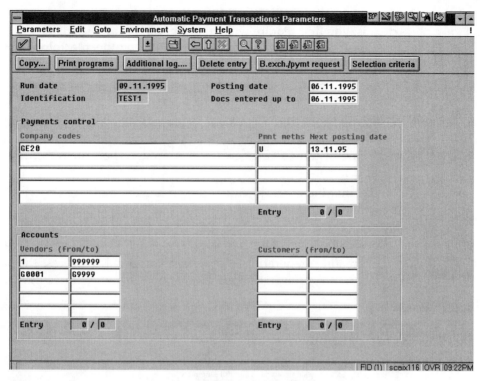

Exhibit 4.95   Automatic Payment Transactions: Parameters

	Germany, depending on the country and your configuration. In other words, payment methods are country specific and company code specific.
Next posting date	Date of the next payment run. The program uses this date to determine whether to postpone the proposed payment.
Vendors	Enter a vendor or a range of vendors to be paid. Optionally, enter an employee or range of employees to be paid. You can process both vendor payments and employee payments in the same run.

Note that you can also specify a customer or a range of customers in order to collect from customers by direct debit. This is allowed in some countries, mostly in Europe, and requires written permission from the customer. You can then generate a file in the specific required format. You then send this file to your bank and your bank collects the payment. To repeat, to collect by direct debit, in whatever country you might wish to do this, you first require written permission from the customer.

To store the parameters, press <F11> or the file folder icon. (See Exhibit 4.96.)

5. From the control (status) screen of the payment program, press the Schedule proposal pushbutton. (See Exhibit 4.97.)

6. To start running the proposal now, click on the Start immediately button. Otherwise, you can schedule the proposal run according to the date and time of the CPU where FI is running. Then press Schedule. (See Exhibit 4.98.)

7. Notice that the control (status) screen has the message Proposal is running after the message Parameters have been entered. To see the latest message, press <Enter>. Keep pressing <Enter> until the proposal run is finished, and you see the message Payment proposal has been created.

8. After creating (generating) the payment proposal, to process the payment proposal, press the Edit proposal pushbutton. (See Exhibit 4.99.)

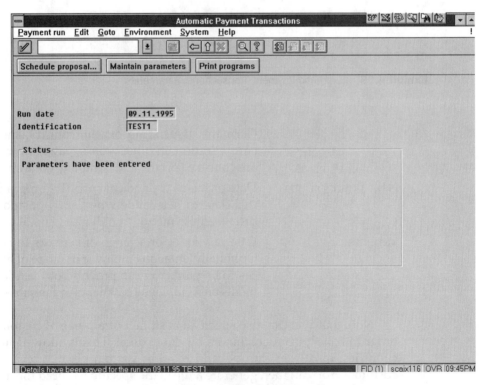

Exhibit 4.96 Automatic Payment Transactions: Parameters Entered

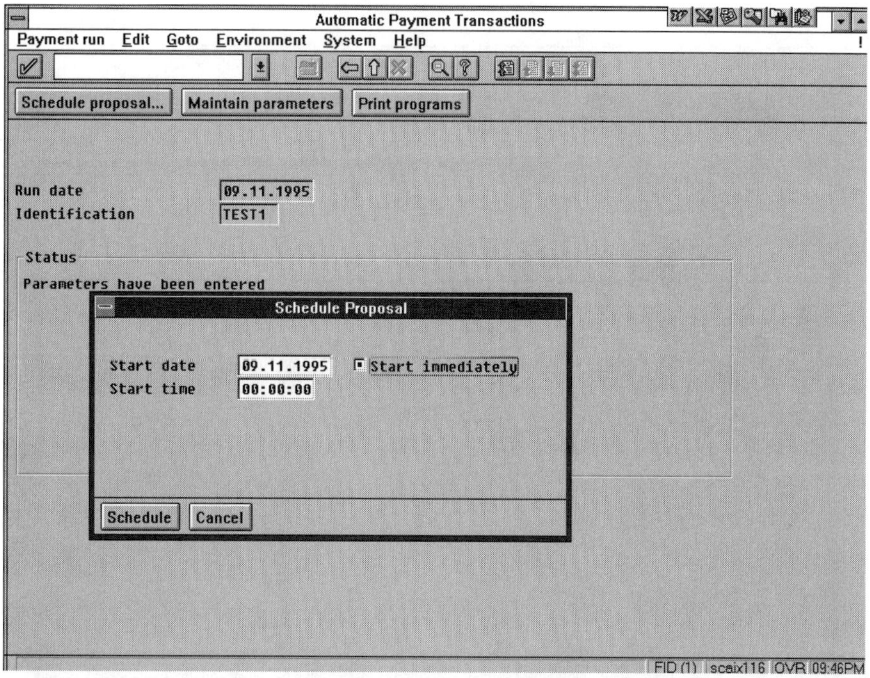

Exhibit 4.97 Schedule Proposal

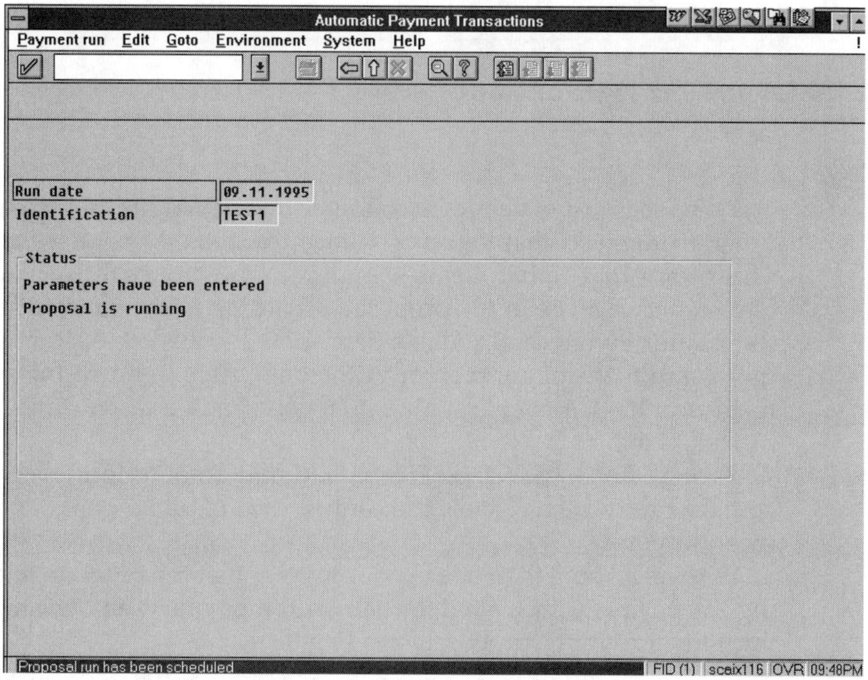

Exhibit 4.98 Automatic Payment Transactions

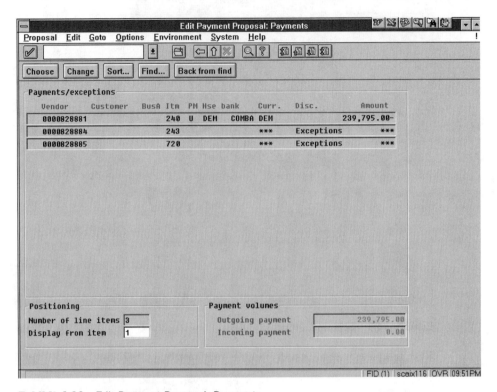

Exhibit 4.99   Edit Payment Proposal: Payments

9. You then see a list of vendor accounts and the amounts that the payment
    program suggests that you pay. Notice the entry *** Exceptions ***.
    This means that certain items were not in the proposal that you might
    have expected to be in the proposal, according to the payment terms of
    the vendor invoice and today's date. Usually, this message indicates a
    mistake in the configuration or in the data, such as a missing payment
    method or bank account number (to pay by bank transfer) in the vendor
    master record.

    Notice the Outgoing payment field and amount in the lower-right
    corner of the screen. This is the control total of all amounts in the pay-
    ment proposal.

    If there is more than one vendor invoice that the program is suggest-
    ing for payment, then double-click on the payment amount to see the
    open invoices in the proposal. (See Exhibit 4.100.)

10. To start to block a specific invoice from being paid, double-click on that
    invoice. (See Exhibit 4.101.)

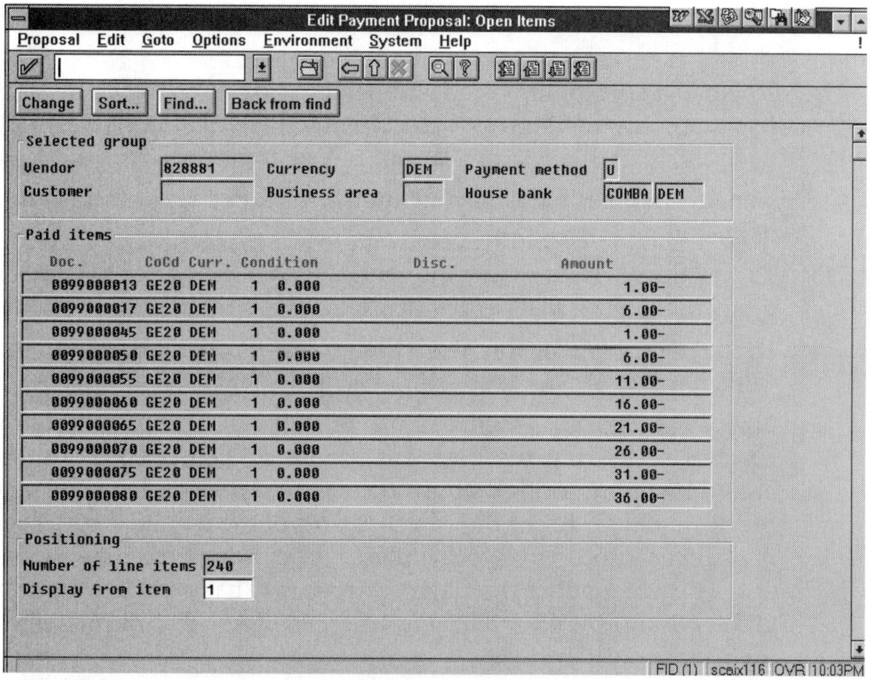

Exhibit 4.100 Edit Payment Proposal: Open Items

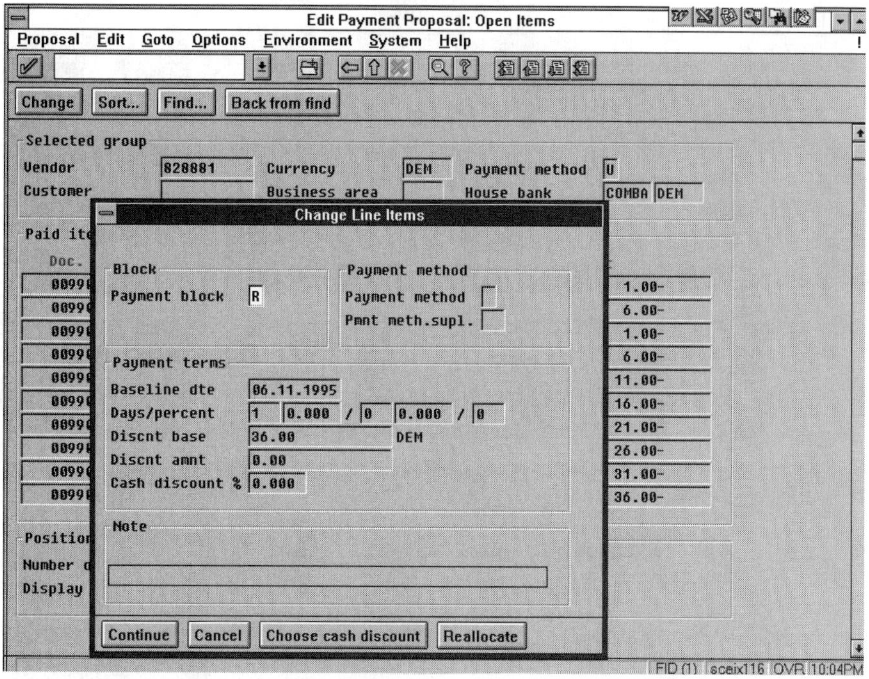

Exhibit 4.101 Change Line Items

419

11. To block a specific invoice from being paid, enter the code for the payment block in the Payment block field. Then press Continue.

12. To process the payment proposal, optionally block other items from being paid. Press the left arrow until you reach the control (status) screen of the payment program.

13. To post the payments from the control (status) screen of the payment program, press Schedule payments. (See Exhibit 4.102.)

14. To start the payment run now, click on Start immediately and then press <Enter> or Schedule. (See Exhibit 4.103.)

15. Notice the message Payment run is running. This means that the program is processing the payment proposal, then posting the payments according to the configuration, and clearing the vendor invoices (closing the open items). To see the current status of the payment run, keep pressing <Enter> until you see the message Payment run has been carried out. This means that the payment program has credited the configured G/L account, debited the vendor or vendors, and cleared the vendor invoices.

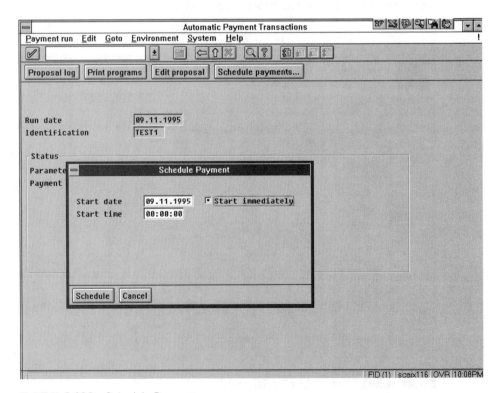

Exhibit 4.102   Schedule Payment

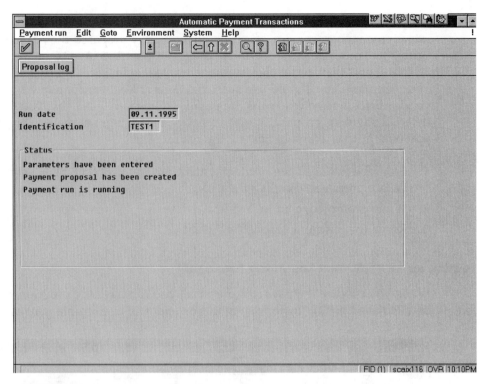

Exhibit 4.103 Automatic Payment Transactions

Why Overdue Invoices Are Not in the Proposal

If some overdue items are not in the proposal, make sure that you have entered all required data in the vendor master record, such as the *vendor's bank account number* and one or more *payment methods* to pay the vendor. Also, make sure that the *invoice is overdue* according to the baseline date for payment, the payment terms, and the grace days (in the configuration). If this due date is on or after the *date of the next payment run* (in the payment program parameters), then the payment program postpones the proposed payment until that payment run. Also, make sure the payment methods, banks, and accounts are configured properly. Last, make sure that the available amount of cash, depending on the configuration, does not restrict the payment. Possibly, the available amount of cash should restrict the payment, if your company is not sufficiently liquid but is paying certain open items anyway.

Deleting the Payment Proposal and Rerunning

If you made a mistake in the payment program configuration or the program parameters, you can delete the proposal, correct your mistake, and then rerun the payment proposal. In a similar way, if you wish to add an invoice or an advance to a payment run, after you have already prepared the payment proposal, you can delete the payment proposal, post the invoice or request for advance, and then rerun the payment proposal. To keep internal control in your company, you should use authorizations at least to separate who posts a vendor invoice from who runs the payment program. Note that you can only delete a payment proposal if you have not posted the payments. To delete a payment proposal (before posting the payments):

1. From the initial screen of the payment program, select Edit ➤ Proposal ➤ Delete proposal. (See Exhibit 4.104.)

2. When prompted, click on Yes and delete the payment proposal.

3. Rerun the payment proposal as usual.

Turning on an Additional Log in the Proposal

When you prepare the payment proposal, you can have the program record a detailed (additional) log for one or more vendors. For example, you could use

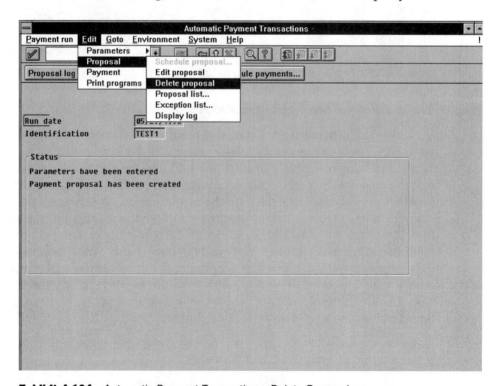

Exhibit 4.104   Automatic Payment Transactions: Delete Proposal

this log to trace why an item was or was not included in the payment proposal. Recording the log slows down the processing. To turn on the additional log of the payment proposal:

1. Start to run the payment program as usual. From the Accounts Payable menu, select Periodic processing → Payments. Enter the run date and ID. Press <Enter>. Then press Maintain parameters. (See Exhibit 4.105.)

2. From the screen to maintain the payment program parameters, press Additional log or select Edit → Additional log. (See Exhibit 4.106.)

3. To verify how the payment program calculates the due date, click on Due date check. To verify how the payment method was selected, if the item was not in the payment proposal (due to an invalid payment method or due to a mistake in the configuration), click on Payment method selection if not successful. To see the line items (credits, debits, accounts, and amounts) in the additional log, click on Line items of the payment documents. Also, specify one or more vendors in the columns for the vendors. Note that you have to enter the range of vendors twice—once in the

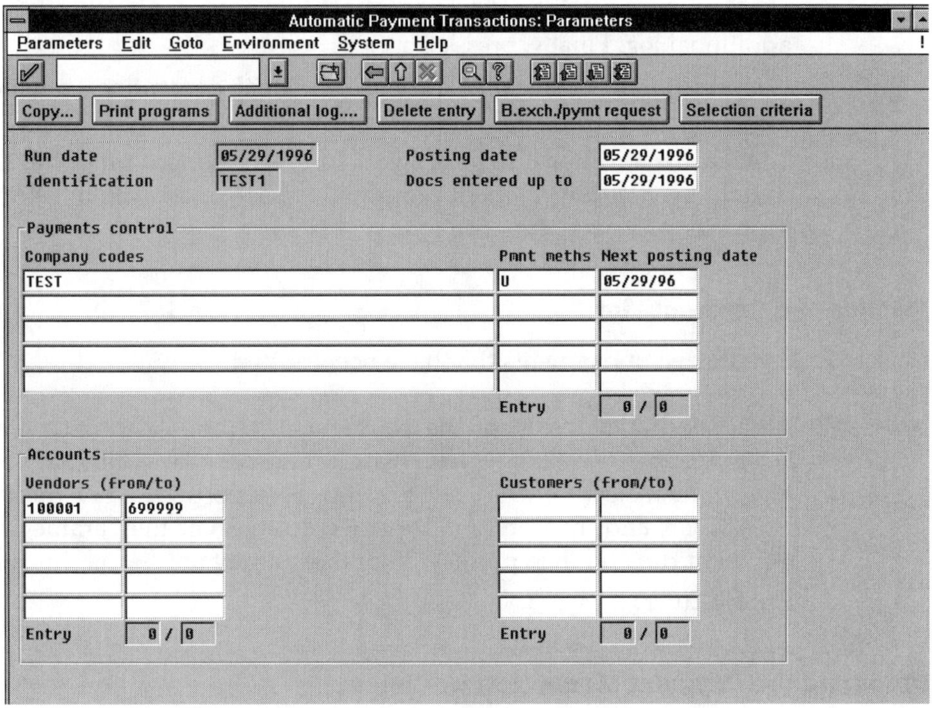

Exhibit 4.105   Automatic Payment Transactions: Parameters

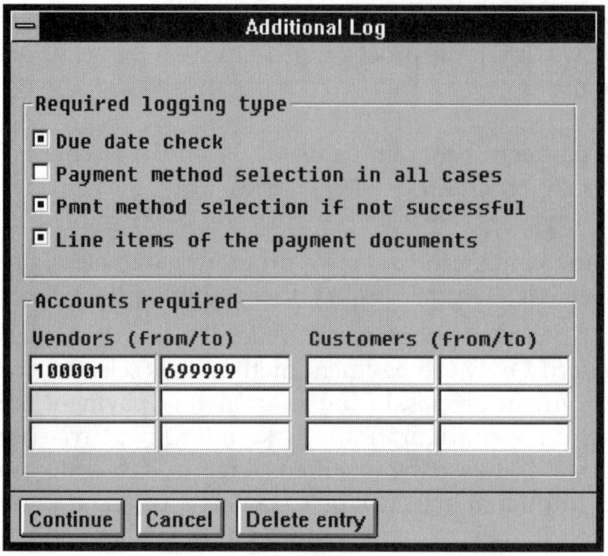

Exhibit 4.106   Additional Log

parameters (on the previous screen) and once in the specifications of the
additional log. Finally, press Continue.

4. Continue to run the payment program as usual, generating a payment proposal.

5. To read the additional log after you run the payment proposal, from the
   initial screen of the payment program, press Proposal log or select Edit →
   Proposal → Display log. (See Exhibit 4.107.)

Printing the Payment List

To print the list of payments that have been posted:

1. From the initial screen of the payment program, Automatic Payment
   Transactions, select Edit → Payment → Payment list. Alternatively, from
   any menu, select System → Services → Reporting, enter the program
   RFZALI00, and then press <F8> or Execute. Enter the parameters of the
   payment run and then press <F8> or Execute again.

2. Press <Enter>.

Preparing the Payment Media (File or Checks)

The exact payment media, such as printed checks or data files to send to the
bank, depend on the country where you are making the payment. In some

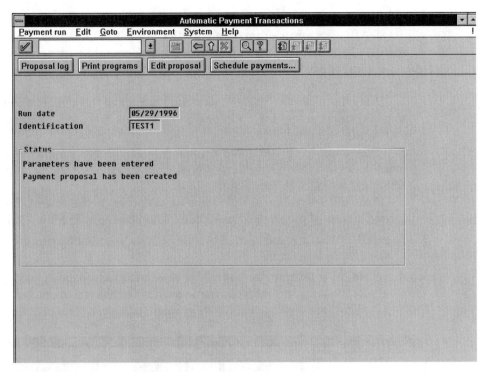

Exhibit 4.107 Automatic Payment Transactions

countries where the banks receive payment instructions by file transfer, different banks require different formats, even in the same country. Most countries have one standard format for domestic payments. Some countries also have a standard format for international payments.

1. From any menu, select System → Services → Reporting. To prepare the file of bank transfers or to print checks, you have to run a country-specific and payment method–specific ABAP program as follows:

Country	Payment Method	ABAP Program
Germany	Domestic bank transfer (Multicash)	RFFOD__U
	International bank transfer	RFFOD__L
UK	Domestic bank transfer (BACS)	RFFOGB_T
France	Domestic bank transfer	RFFOF__V
Italy	Bank transfer (to be delivered with version 3.0)	RFFOIT_B
US	Printed Check (pre-numbered)	RFFOUS_C

For a complete list of all ABAP programs to prepare payment media, list all ABAP programs that start with the letters RFFO*, as described in the section "Listing Supplied FI Reports" in the General Ledger chapter.

For example, to record the file of domestic payments in Germany, enter the parameters in RFFOD_U as shown in Exhibit 4.108.

Press the + symbol in the lower-right corner of the screen. The second screen of parameters for a file of domestic bank transfers in Germany is shown in Exhibit 4.109.

Alternatively, if you have recorded international payments in Germany, to record the file of international bank transfer, set the parameters to RFFOD_L as follows. (See Exhibit 4.110.)

Press the + symbol in the lower-right corner of the screen. Enter the second screen of parameters to RFFOD_L as shown in Exhibit 4.111.

2. To run the program and record the file on the diskette or print the checks, press <F8> or Execute.

3. If the file for international payments was recorded properly, you see the results of the program with the name of the file that was recorded and the

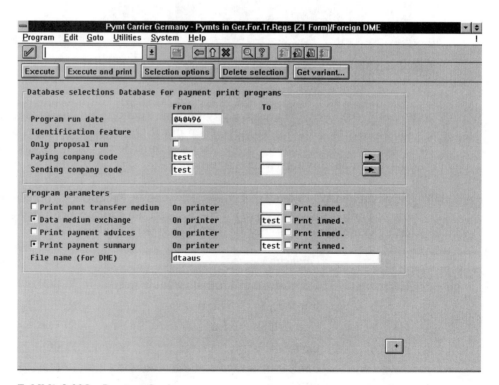

Exhibit 4.108 Payment Carrier

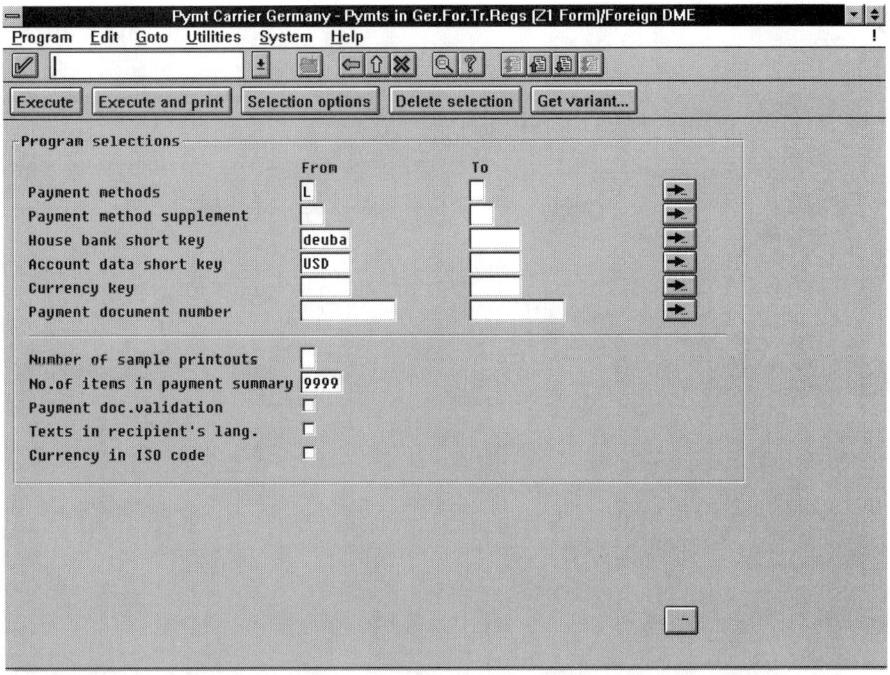
Pymt Carrier Germany - Pymts in Ger.For.Tr.Regs (Z1 Form)/Foreign DME
Program Edit Goto Utilities System Help
Execute
Execute and print
Selection options
Delete selection
Get variant...
Program selections
From
To
Payment methods
L
Payment method supplement
House bank short key
deuba
Account data short key
USD
Currency key
Payment document number
Number of sample printouts
No.of items in payment summary
9999
Payment doc.validation
Texts in recipient's lang.
Currency in ISO code

Exhibit 4.109 Payment Carrier—Transfers, Debits, Collections

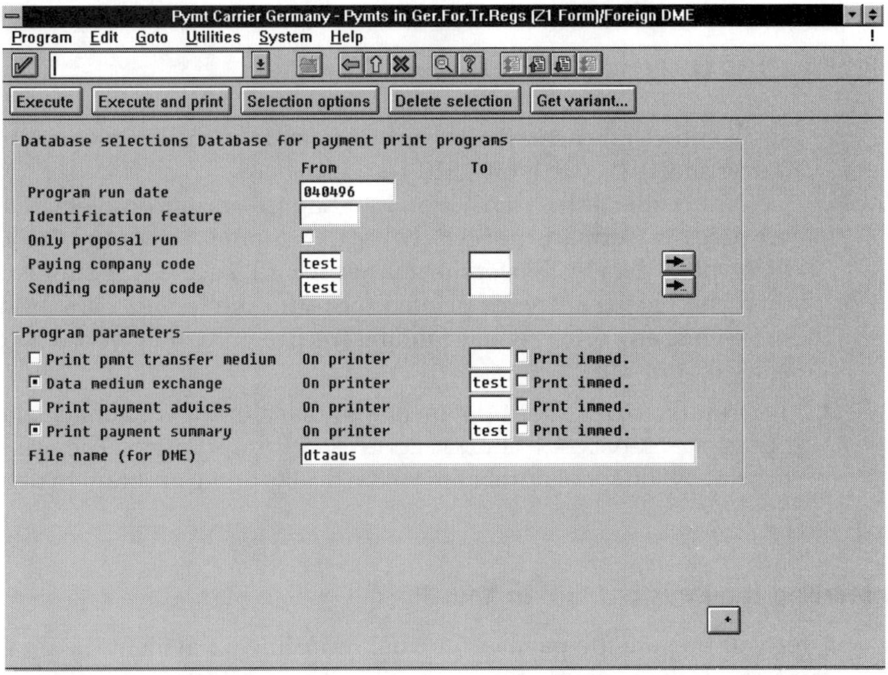
Pymt Carrier Germany - Pymts in Ger.For.Tr.Regs (Z1 Form)/Foreign DME
Program Edit Goto Utilities System Help
Execute
Execute and print
Selection options
Delete selection
Get variant...
Database selections Database for payment print programs
From
To
Program run date
040496
Identification feature
Only proposal run
Paying company code
test
Sending company code
test
Program parameters
Print pmnt transfer medium
On printer
Prnt immed.
Data medium exchange
On printer
test
Prnt immed.
Print payment advices
On printer
Prnt immed.
Print payment summary
On printer
test
Prnt immed.
File name (for DME)
dtaaus

Exhibit 4.110 Payment Carrier—Record File of International Bank Transfer

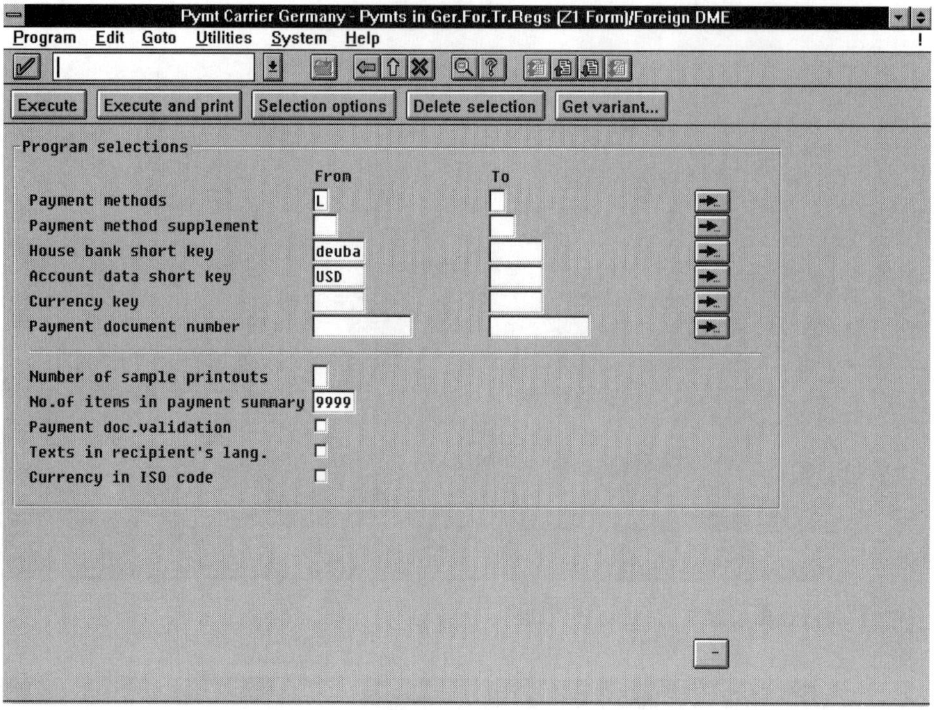

Exhibit 4.111 Payment Carrier Parameters, Screen Two

spool entries for the payment summary and the disk accompanying sheet (cover sheet). (See Exhibit 4.112.)

Notice that, if the translation into English was incomplete, the screens are partly in German, the SAP central development language. If there were incomplete data in the vendor master record, such as missing bank data, then you see the entry for printed forms for the foreign bank transfers. If there were any errors while running the program, then you would see an entry for error log.

4. To print the cover sheet, payment summary, or other spool entries, select System → Services → Output controller. Press <Enter>. Then select what to print by the spool number from the results of the program to prepare the media.

Transferring the Payment File to Your PC

After you prepare the payment media, recording a payment file on the disk, you transfer the payment file to your PC. You can transfer this file, using the ABAP program RFFODOWN, but you have to specify a target filename that

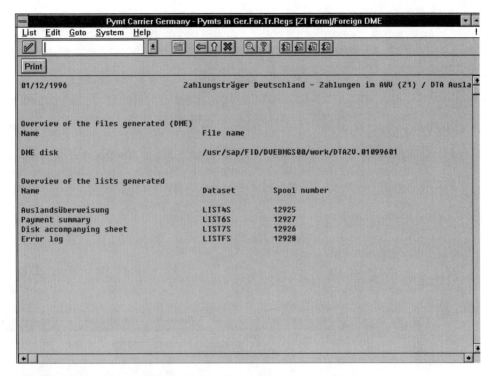

Exhibit 4.112   Payment Carrier Results Screen

depends on the country and the payment method. Alternatively, you can use ftp (the file transfer program supplied with your TCP/IP software), log in to the machine where the file is stored, and transfer it to your PC.

To transfer the file to your PC with ftp, you need to know the following about the payment file:

- The exact machine name (node for ftp login)
- The exact directory
- The exact filename that you specified when you ran the program to record the file with the payments

If the RFFODOWN program does not function properly (due to incompatible network drivers, for example), log in to the machine where FI is installed and use the ftp program to transfer the file directly.

If you do not have the exact directory where the file is stored, log in to the machine where FI is installed and use an operating system command, such as the UNIX Find command (or Windows NT equivalent), to look for the file by the filename. (Consult the UNIX or Windows NT documentation for details.)

When you transfer the file from the UNIX or NT box, delete the file. Keep any necessary previous versions of the payment file on your PC.

To transfer the file to your PC using RFFODOWN:

1. From any menu, select System ➤ Services ➤ Reporting.

2. Enter **RFFODOWN** and then press Execute or <F8>. Select Get variant, enter a properly configured variant, and then press Open. (See Exhibit 4.113.)

3. Make sure that the name of the source file in the Source file parameter is the same as the name of the file that you recorded with the previous program (RFFOD__U for domestic payments in the Federal Republic of Germany and RFFOD__L for foreign payments in the Federal Republic of Germany).

   If you are transferring the file with domestic payments, **DTAUS0** is required in the Target file field.

   If you are transferring the file with foreign payments, **DTAZV0** is required in the Target file field. German banks require these file names to

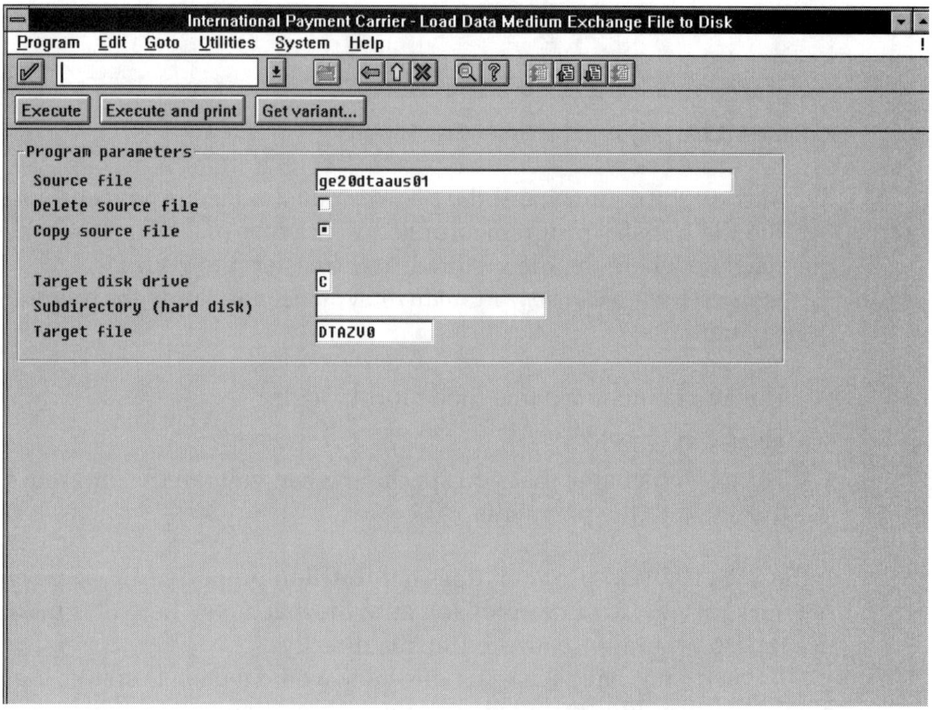

Exhibit 4.113   International Payment Carrier—Load Data File to Disk

process files and carry out the payments, so one or the other exact file name is required. To download the file to your PC, press Execute or <F8>.

4. After you have the payment file on your local disk drive, you have to transfer it to the bank, using software not supplied by SAP. Depending on the country, the bank, and the payment method, either put the file on a diskette and send the diskette to the bank by courier or use a modem and communications software to dial up the bank or clearinghouse and to transfer them the file.

Sending the File

Before you send the file to the bank for processing:

1. If you are sending a file with international payments in Germany (**DTAZV0**) and if you are paying with a multicurrency account (***** in the currency field), edit the file with a text editor and substitute **USD** for ***** as the currency of the account. Replace exactly the characters "*****" (asterisk and two blanks) with **USD,** so the sequence of characters in the file does not change.

2. Using MS-DOS or Windows, move the file to a diskette, deleting it from the disk drive of your PC. Put each file on a separate diskette until the bank approves submitting two files on one diskette.

3. Scan the diskette for viruses.

4. Print the cover sheet.

5. Send the diskette to the bank.

Adding a Currency to the Payment Run

If you receive an invoice from a vendor in another currency than the currencies which the payment program was configured to pay, you have to add the currency to the payment program configuration. Step by step, in summary, to add a currency to the payment program configuration:

1. Add the currency to the list of banks selected (ranking order).

2. Add the currency (and maximum total payment in that currency in any one run) to the list of available amounts.

3. Specify, for this currency, the bank account (by account ID) from the list of bank accounts and the G/L account to be credited, when posting payments using the payment program.

Step by step, in detail, to add the currency to the list of banks selected, available amounts, and G/L accounts posted:

1. From the Accounts Payable menu, select Environment → Configuration menu.
2. From the Financial Accounting Configuration menu, select Business volume → Payments → Payment program → Configuration.
3. From the Payment Program Configuration: Initial Screen, select Banks → Bank selection.
4. Put the cursor on the company code making the payments and then press Ranking order.
5. To add the currency to the list, press Create. (See Exhibit 4.114.)
6. Depending on your existing configuration, enter the payment method and the currency to be added. Always use the ISO codes for the currency. If you only use one bank to make payments in this currency, enter 1 in the Rank.order field. Depending completely on your configuration, enter the bank key in the House bank field. To continue, press Proceed.
7. From the Maintain Payment Program Configuration: Bank Selection menu, press Available amounts.
8. Depending completely on your configuration and list of bank accounts (Exhibit 4.115), enter the code for the house bank and account to pay in this currency. The Days until value date field applies to payments by bill of exchange, which are found in France, Italy, and Spain. If you do not make payments by bill of exchange or you are not sure, enter **999** in this field. The Available for outgoing payment field restricts the total payment in this

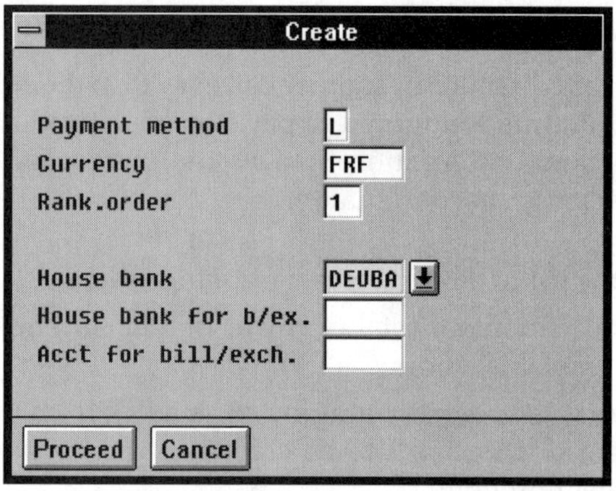

Create	
Payment method	L
Currency	FRF
Rank.order	1
House bank	DEUBA
House bank for b/ex.	
Acct for bill/exch.	

Proceed   Cancel

Exhibit 4.114 Add Currency

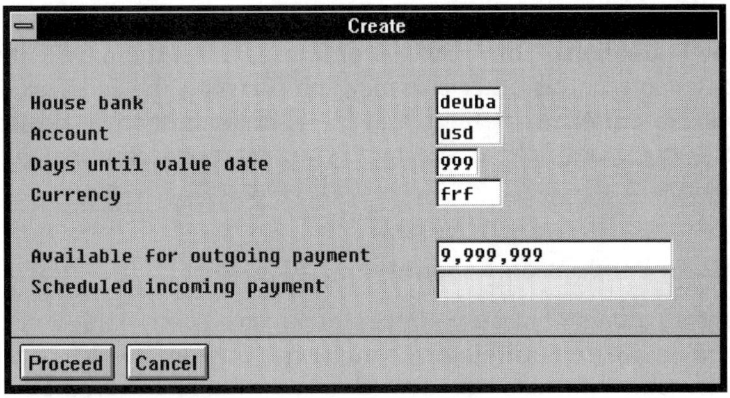

Exhibit 4.115 Available Amounts

currency during any one payment run. If your funds are severely limited, you can enter an amount in this field. The payment program will then disburse no more than this amount, no matter what the amounts and due dates of the outstanding invoices are. If you are not in a cash squeeze, then enter a high amount in this field. To continue, press Proceed.

9. From the Maintain Payment Program Configuration: Available Amounts menu, to specify which G/L account is posted when you post the payments, press Accounts. (See Exhibit 4.116.)

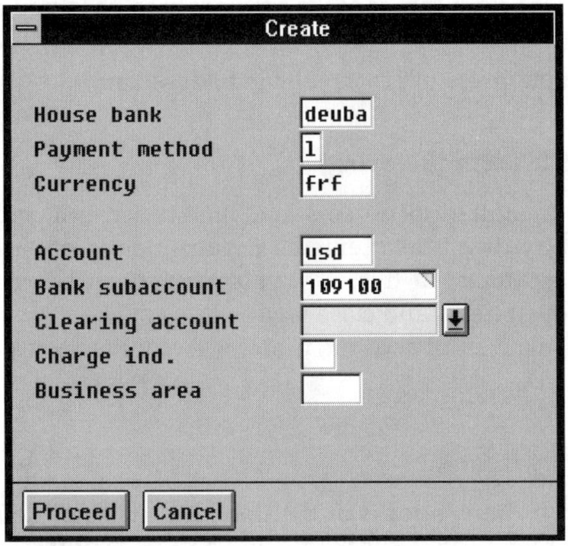

Exhibit 4.116 Create

10. Also depending completely on your configuration, enter at least the code for the house bank from your list of house banks, the payment method for payments in this other currency, the currency, the code for the bank account in the Account field, and the G/L account to be posted in the Bank subaccount field according to your chart of accounts. To continue, press Proceed.

Posting Payments to Vendors on Account

If you make a payment before you post the invoice being paid, you can post the payment on account. In this way, you do not close an invoice because you do not yet have an invoice to close. You debit the vendor and credit the vendor account. For example, if you pay the vendor by direct debit, you can post the payment on account. Later, after you post the invoice, you can clear (close) items in the vendor account, matching debit items to credit items. If you make a payment to a vendor based on a pro forma invoice, or if you have not yet processed and entered the vendor invoice, post the payment on account.

1. From the Accounts Payable menu, select Document entry → Outgoing payment → Post. (See Exhibit 4.117.)
2. Enter the transaction header as usual.
3. Press the Edit open items pushbutton. (See Exhibit 4.118.)
4. Double-click on the Payment on acct field in the lower-right corner. If the Difference in the lower-right corner of the screen is zero, then you can post the transaction.
5. To post the transaction, press <F11> or the file folder icon

Matching Vendor Debits and Credits (Clearing)

If you have equal and offsetting open items in a vendor account, such as an invoice and a payment by direct debit entered independently of each other, you can clear these open items. In this way, you remove equally offsetting items from the vendor open items and close them.

To clear open items in a vendor account, from the Accounts Payable menu, select Account → Clear.

Posting One-time Payments by Check

Posting the Payment.   If the vendor is at the door and will not deliver the goods without a check, then write a check by hand and present it to the vendor. To record this one-time payment:

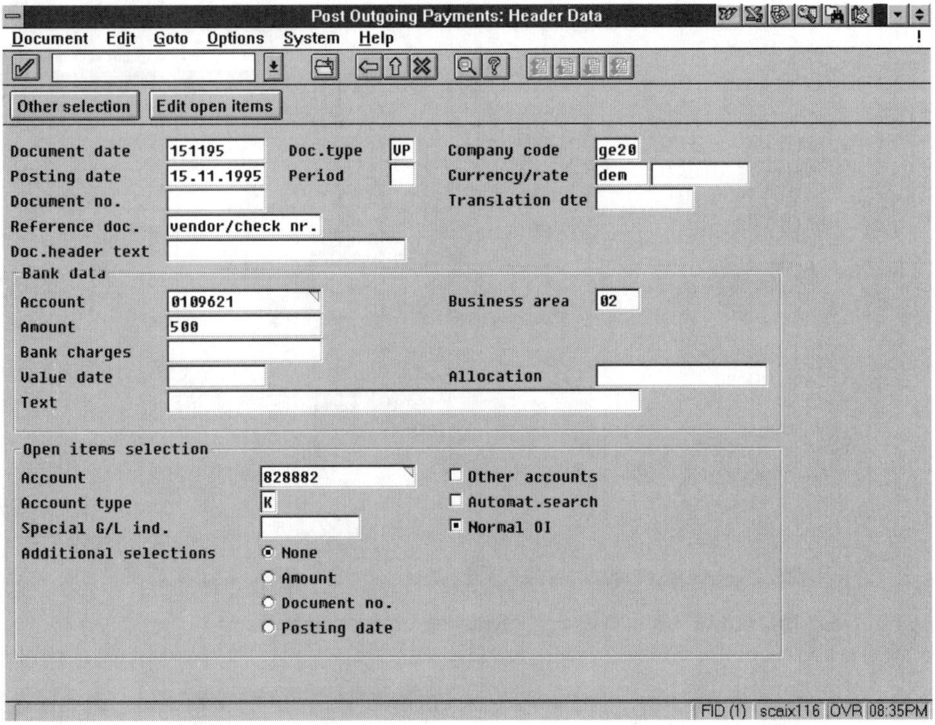

Exhibit 4.117   Post Outgoing Payments: Header Data

1. From the Accounts Payable menu, select Document entry ⇥ Outgoing payment ⇥ Post. (See Exhibit 4.119.)

2. Enter the header of the payment transaction as usual. Next, in the Account field of the Bank data section, enter the G/L account for cash in transit for the bank account that you are using to issue the check. Then enter the amount of the check and a value date, such as two or three days after you wrote the check. Last, enter the vendor account number in the Account field of the Open items selection and press the Edit open items pushbutton. (See Exhibit 4.120.)

3. To clear (close) an invoice (marking it as paid), double-click on the amount field in that invoice. If you are paying the vendor on account, enter the amount of the check, followed by a minus symbol, in the Payment on acct field in the lower-right portion of the screen or double-click on the Payment on acct field. Make sure that the value of the Difference (between debits and credits) is zero.

4. To post the payment, assuming the debits equal the credits (the Difference is zero), press <F11> or the file folder icon.

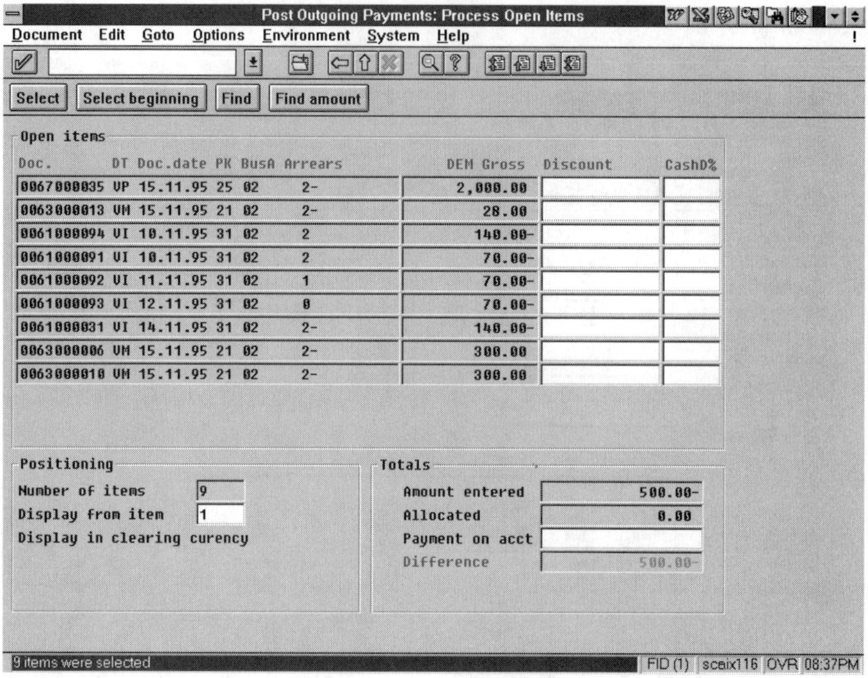

Exhibit 4.118 Post Outgoing Payments: Process Open Items

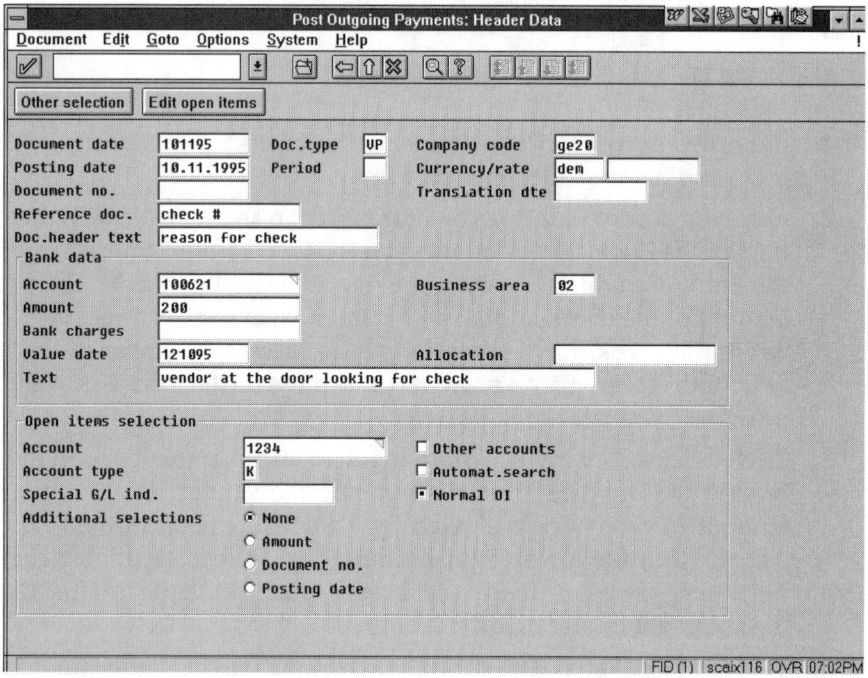

Exhibit 4.119 Post Outgoing Payments: Header Data

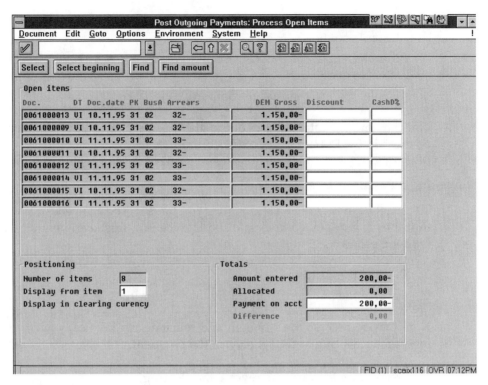

Exhibit 4.120   Post Outgoing Payments: Process Open Items

Posting a Partial Payment.   You can only post a partial payment to a vendor manually (not with the payment program).

Posting and Printing the Payment.   You can also post and print a check in one step. If you have a low volume of checks, it is sometimes simpler to write the check by hand than to set up the system to print these infrequent checks. Printing prenumbered checks was added to the original development, so it is not described in this book.

Restricting the Total Disbursement

If your company has very limited liquid resources or is in a work-out situation, you can restrict the total disbursement by the payment program. To restrict the total amount disbursed from a bank account (in other words, no matter what vendor invoices are due when), you can reconfigure the payment program.

To restrict the total disbursement, do as follows:

1. Start the payment program as usual. From the Accounts Payable menu, select Periodic processing → Payments.

2. From the Automatic Payment Transactions screen, select Environment ➤ Maintain config.

3. From the Payment Program Configuration: Initial screen, select Banks ➤ Available amounts.

4. Double-click on the paying company code.

You can limit the total amount of the disbursement, always by bank and bank account, in the Outgoing payment column.

Reversing a Payment to a Vendor

To cancel a payment to a vendor after you have closed the vendor invoice (for example, if you posted and paid the invoice in a mistaken vendor account), follow these two steps:

1. Reverse the clearing.
2. Reverse the payment, reinstating the vendor invoice.

Note that, to reverse the payment and reinstate the invoice, you have to first reverse the clearing and then reverse the payment.

Reversing the Clearing.   To reverse the clearing,

1. From the Accounts Payable menu, select Document ➤ Reset cleared items. (See Exhibit 4.121.)

2. Enter at least the transaction number ("document number") of the payment and the company code.

3. To reverse the clearing, press <F11> or the file folder icon and notice the message at the end of the screen that the clearing has been reversed.

Reversing the Payment and Reinstating the Invoice.   To reverse a payment, after you have already reversed any clearing:

1. From the Accounts Payable menu, select Document ➤ Reverse. (See Exhibit 4.122.)

2. Enter at least the same transaction number ("document number") and company code as the payment and the company code with the clearing that you reversed in the previous step.

3. To reverse the payment and reinstate the invoice, press <F11> or the file folder icon and notice the message at the end of the screen that the transaction has been reversed.

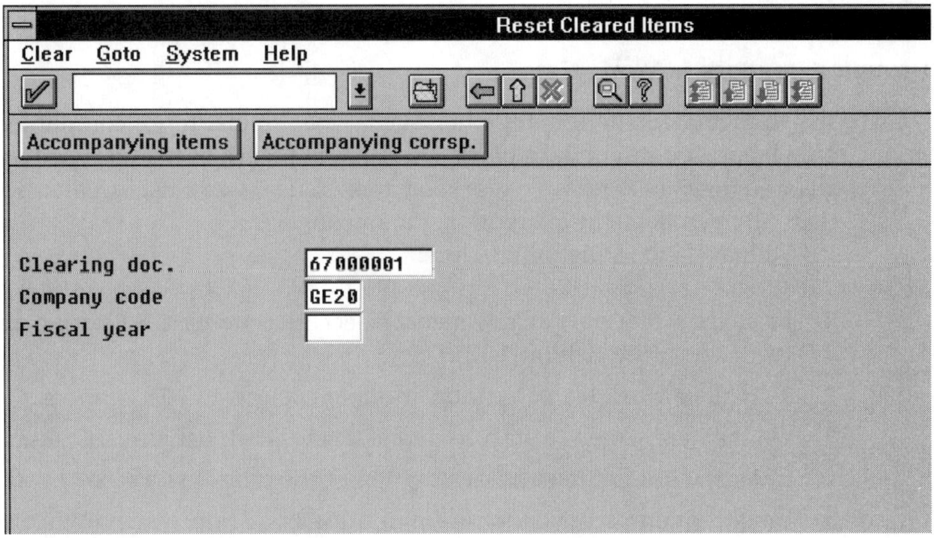

Exhibit 4.121 Reset Cleared Items

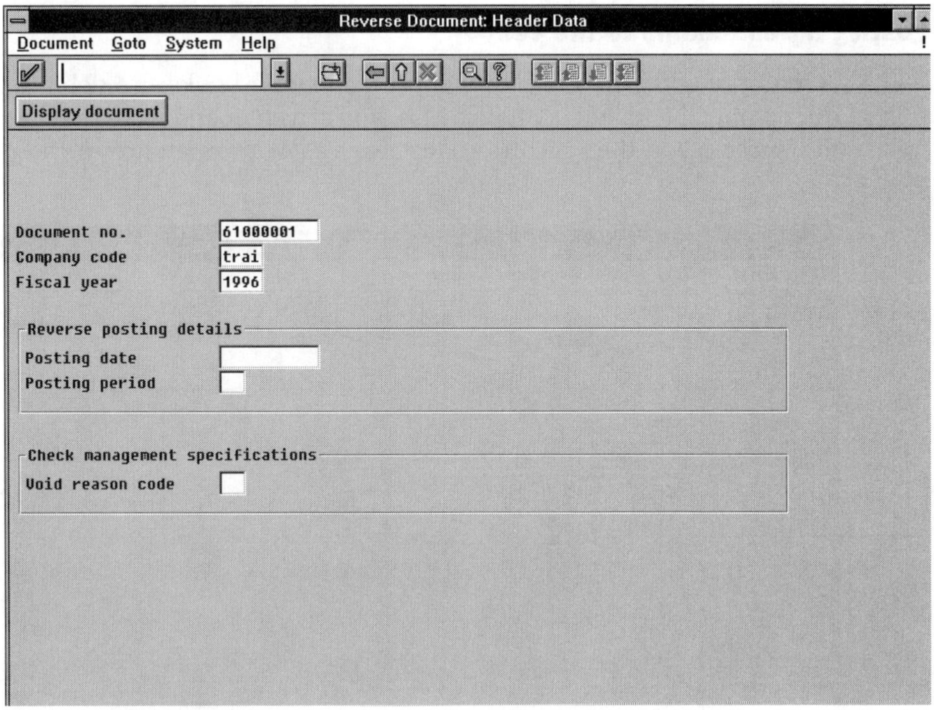

Exhibit 4.122 Reverse Document: Header Data

USING OTHER ACCOUNTS PAYABLE FUNCTIONS

Grouping Vendors in Work Lists

To group related vendors together, such as health insurance companies or contract labor, you can make a work list. Later, the work list can be used to display all open items in the whole work list at once. The work list can also be used to clear all open items in the work list at once.

To make a work list of vendors:

1. From the Accounts Payable menu, select Environment → Current options → Work lists. (See Exhibit 4.123.)
2. To make a work list of vendors, double-click on LIFNR Vendors.
3. On the next screen to start to define a new work list, press Create.
4. Enter the brief name and description of the work list. Press <Enter>.
5. Enter the complete vendor account numbers, or press the down arrow and use the matchcode to select the vendor account numbers.
6. To store the work list, press <F11> or the file folder icon.

Posting a Debit Memo to the Vendor

A return of goods to the vendor is posted in your books as a debit to the vendor account. Note that if you use MM, you can enter and print purchase orders to vendors. You then record goods received with reference to the purchase

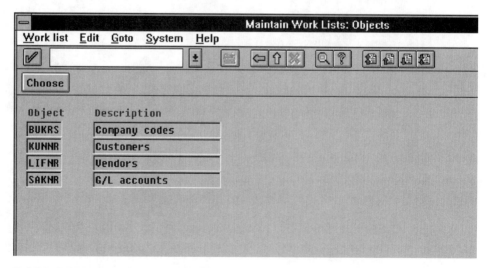

Exhibit 4.123   Maintain Work Lists: Objects

order. Lastly, you record the vendor invoice (in MM), controlling the invoice by comparing the quantities invoiced with the quantities received and the prices invoiced with the prices in the purchase orders. Note that if you have already posted a vendor invoice in MM (for goods received) and if you wish to return the goods, such as returnable packaging, you first have to record a credit memo in MM. This example assumes that you are not yet using MM.

To post a debit memo, which is called a credit memo by SAP in FI, for example, if you return damaged goods:

1. From the Accounts Payable menu, select Document entry ➤ Credit memo.
2. Notice the Document type **VM** and the posting key **21.** Other than these two automatic entries, enter and post a debit memo in a similar way (with similar screens) to posting a vendor invoice.
3. Press <F11> or the file folder icon to post the debit memo.

Posting a Down Payment to the Vendor

If you pay the vendor a down payment in anticipation of receiving goods or services, record the payment as a debit to the vendor account. FI then updates a separate G/L account (reconciliation account) for down payments to vendors depending on your configuration. In effect, your down payment to the vendor is a claim on the vendor. The vendor owes you the goods or services. To post a down payment to a vendor:

1. From the Accounts Payable menu, select Document entry ➤ Down payment ➤ Post. (See Exhibit 4.124.)
2. Enter the transaction header, the vendor account number, the G/L account number for the payment, the amount of the payment, and the value date. Press the New item pushbutton to enter the amount to debit to the vendor account and to credit to the G/L account. (See Exhibit 4.125.)
3. Enter the amount of the payment and the division (business area).
4. To post the payment, press <F11> or the file folder icon.

Changing a Transaction

After you post a transaction, whether an invoice, a payment, or an adjustment, you can never change the posting keys, amounts, or accounts posted in that transaction. However, you can change certain other details, such as the value date, allocation (sorting key), payment terms, payment block, and text in the line items of a transaction. To change a transaction:

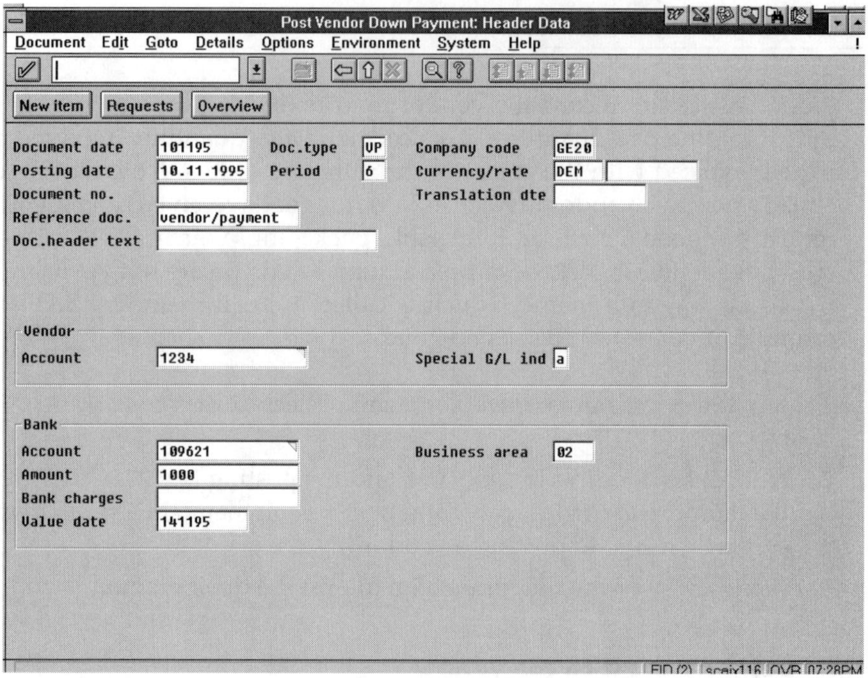

Exhibit 4.124 Post Vendor Down Payment: Header Data

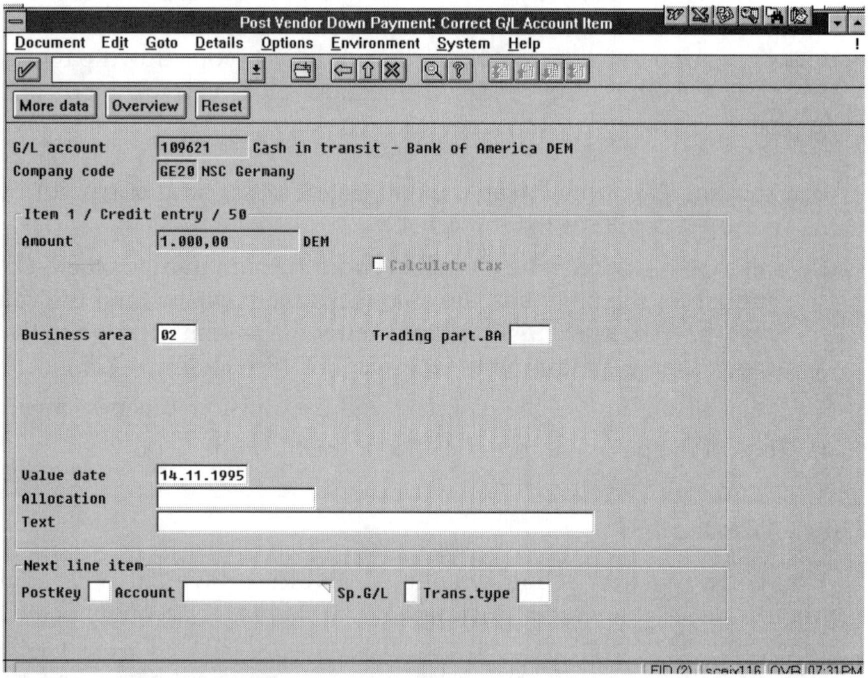

Exhibit 4.125 Post Vendor Down Payment: Correct G/L Account Item

1. From the Accounts Payable menu, select Document → Change.

2. Enter the transaction number, the company code, and the fiscal year. Press <Enter>.

3. From the overview, double-click on a line item to display the details of that line item.

4. You can add or edit certain fields in each line item. Note that you cannot change the cost center, since the CO module has already recorded this line item and updated subtotals by cost center.

Changing the Cost Center after Posting

After you post an invoice, you cannot change the cost center. You could enter a G/L transaction to debit and credit the same account, but with different cost centers. However, using the CO (cost accounting) module, you can transfer costs from one cost center to another cost center for the amount of an invoice. This assumes that CO has been properly installed and configured. It also assumes that the G/L account has been flagged as a cost element. To transfer costs from one cost center to another:

1. From the R/3 main menu, select Accounting → Controlling → Cost center acctg.

2. From the Cost Center Accounting menu, select Actual postings → Transfer costs → Enter.

3. Press the List screen pushbutton.

4. Enter the cost center that you are relieving of costs (Send. Cctr), the cost center that is being burdened with the costs (Rec. Cctr), the G/L account (Cost elem.), and the amount of the transfer.

5. Press <F11> or the file folder icon to store the transfer of costs.

See the CO documentation for more details. Using CO, including cost center accounting, profit center accounting, and product costing, is beyond the scope of this book. CO, Cost Center Accounting is intended for internal reporting only, based on your internal organization (hierarchy), budgeted and actual costs and cost allocations and transfers.

Processing Recurring Vendor Transactions

A recurring transaction is one that is repeated with the exact same amounts at regular intervals, such as monthly car lease, insurance, or rent payments. To post recurring transactions, first define the interval at which the transaction recurs (the schedule). Then specify which accounts to debit and credit (the entries). Depending on the interval, you periodically run a program that generates a batch input file containing the recurring transaction. Finally, process the batch input file to post the vendor and G/L accounts.

Scheduling and Entering a Transaction.   To schedule the recurring transaction:

1. From the Accounts Payable menu, select Document entry ➤ Reference document ➤ Recurring document. (See Exhibit 4.126.)
2. Enter the interval and the accounts to be debited and credited, starting with **31** as the posting key and the vendor account number.
3. Store the specifications. Note that you have not posted any accounts.

Posting a Transaction.   To post the transaction:

1. From the Accounts Payable menu, select Periodic processing ➤ Recurring entries ➤ Proceed.

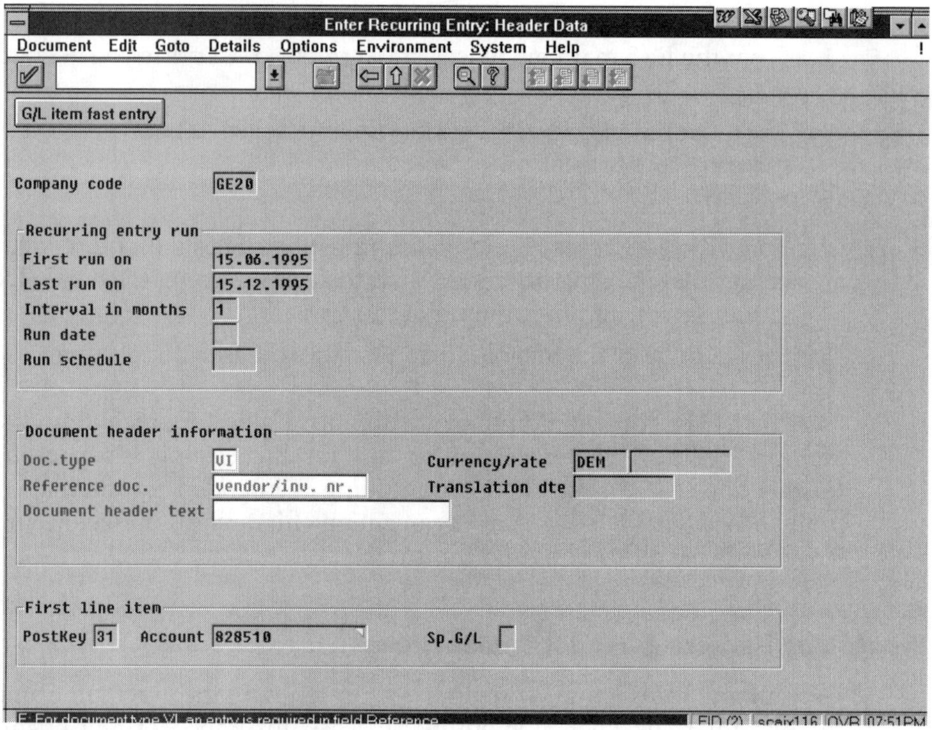

Exhibit 4.126   Enter Recurring Entry: Header Data

2. Generate the batch input file.

3. To post the transactions contained in the batch input file, select System ➤ Services ➤ Batch input ➤ Edit from any menu.

Changing a Recurring Transaction. You can change certain details of a recurring transaction, such as the last run, the interval in months, the run date, and the schedule (if other than monthly). Before you can delete a recurring transaction, you have to change the recurring transaction and mark it for deletion.

To change a recurring transaction:

1. From the Accounts Payable menu, select Document ➤ Reference document ➤ Recurring document ➤ Change.

2. Enter the recurring transaction number, the company code, and the fiscal year. Press <Enter>.

3. From the overview of the transaction, select Goto ➤ Recurr. entry data. (See Exhibit 4.127.)

4. To change the recurring entry data, enter the new value and then press Save. To prepare to delete the recurring transaction, enter an x in the Deletion indicator field and then press Save.

5. At the bottom of the screen look for the message Changes have been saved.

Exhibit 4.127 Change Recurring Document: Recurring Entry Data

Deleting a Recurring Transaction. If the amounts of the recurring transaction change (for example, if the rent goes up), then you can delete the recurring transaction. Optionally, you can enter another recurring transaction. To delete a recurring transaction:

1. First change the recurring transaction and mark it for deletion, as described in the previous section.

2. From the Accounts Payable menu, select Document ➤ Reference document ➤ Recurring document ➤ Delete. (See Exhibit 4.128.)

3. Enter at least the company code, recurring transaction (document) number, the fiscal year, and **D** (for recurring transactions). Optionally, click on Test run to see what would be deleted, if you were not running a test.

4. To run the program, press Execute or <F8>.

Posting Sample Vendor Transactions

A sample transaction is a transaction template. If certain transactions recur regularly but the amounts differ slightly, enter a sample transaction.

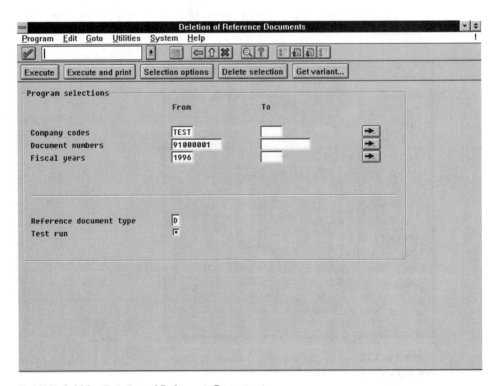

Exhibit 4.128 Deletion of Reference Documents

Entering a Sample Transaction. From the Accounts Payable menu, select Document entry ‣ Reference documents ‣ Sample document. (See Exhibit 4.129.)

Enter a sample transaction as you would enter any other transaction. Note that the G/L account balances are not updated and the compact journal does not contain the sample transaction with the list of posted transactions.

Posting a Sample Transaction. To post a sample transaction:
From the Accounts Payable menu, select Document entry ‣ Invoice.
Then select Document ‣ Posting with ref. (See Exhibit 4.130.)

Enter a sample transaction as you would enter any other transaction. Note that the G/L account balances are not updated and the compact journal does not contain the sample transaction with the list of posted transactions.

Reversing Transactions, Such as Accruals, en Masse

You can reverse a series of transactions en masse (as a set), if you can identify the set of transactions, for example, by the transaction ("document") numbers. This can be useful if there is an error in a series of transactions entered by batch input. To reverse a set of transactions:

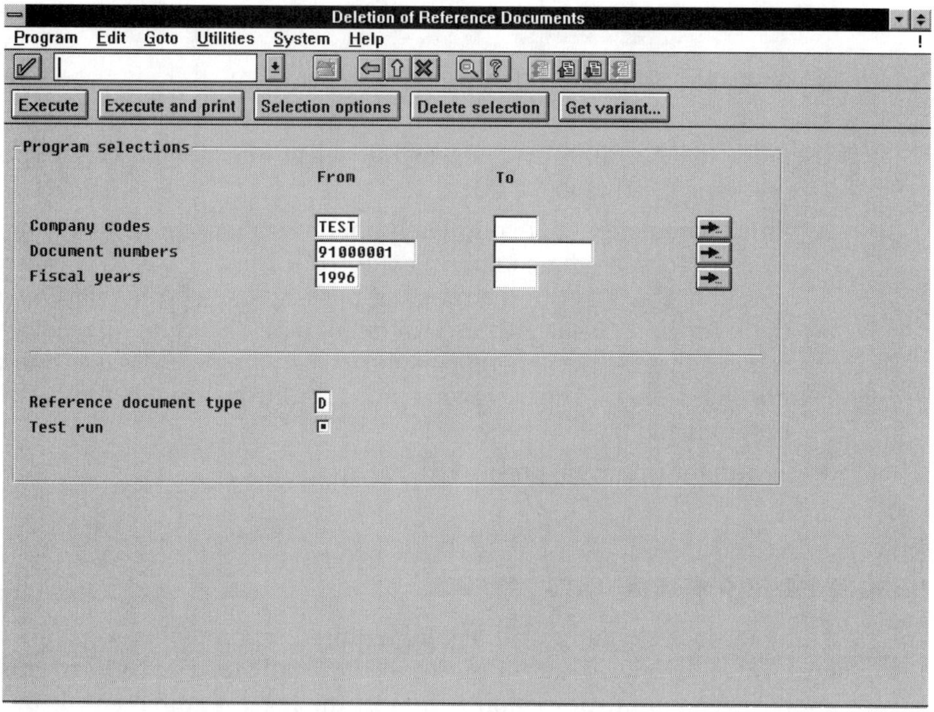

Exhibit 4.129 Deletion of Reference Documents

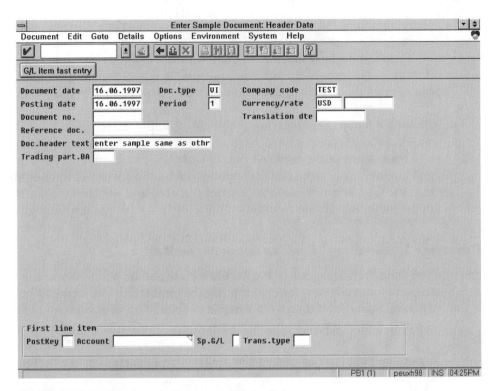

Exhibit 4.130 Entry Sample Document: Header Data

1. From the Accounts Payable menu, select Periodic processing → Mass reversal. (See Exhibit 4.131.)

2. Enter parameters that completely identify transactions that you wish to reverse, such as the company code, "document type" (AC = accrual, if posted in this way), and a range of posting dates. Note that you can post the reversing transactions on a different date, according to what is entered in the Reverse document posting date parameter. Make sure that the posting period of the reversing transactions is open, before you run the program and try to reverse.

3. To run the program, press <F8> or Execute.

REPORTING FROM ACCOUNTS PAYABLE

SAP endeavors to supply all legally required reports wherever they do business. Often, if they do not supply a specific legally required report, you can use another general-purpose report to meet the legal requirement. If the regula-

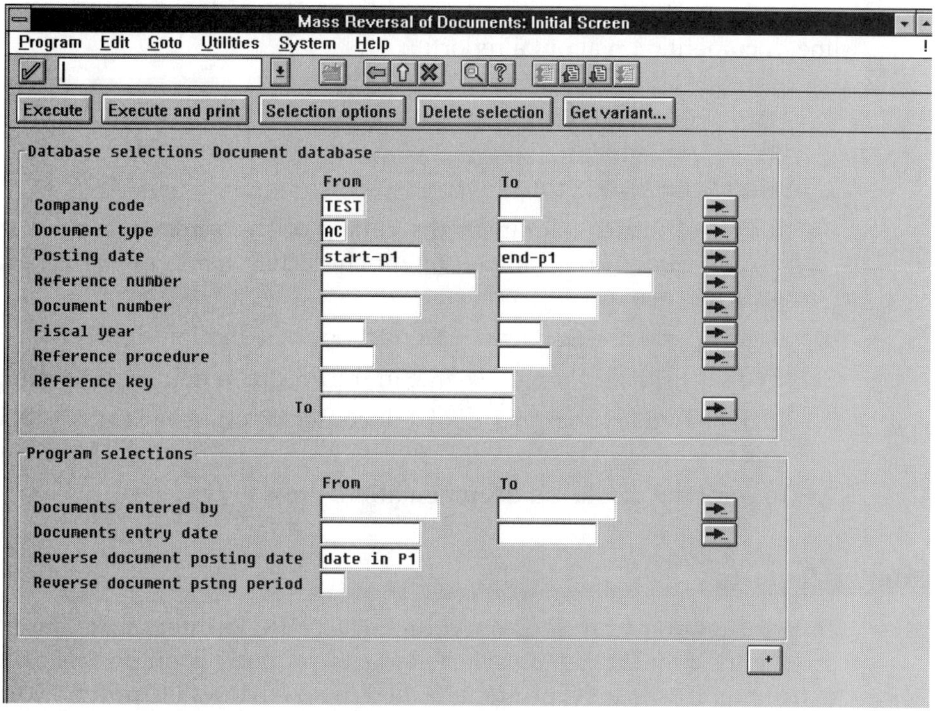

Exhibit 4.131 Mass Reversal of Documents

tions or legal requirements change, expect SAP to enhance the supplied report or to supply the newly required report when they upgrade FI.

Some companies develop custom reports, such as a report of parked invoices, including certain details about each invoice and a specific budget-actual report, including expenses and fixed asset purchases by project (internal order).

Reading On-line Report Documentation

While entering report parameters, before running the report, to read the on-line documentation about a report, select Help ➤ Extended help.

Printing On-line Report Documentation

SAP supplies all report documentation on-line only. If you want the printed report documentation, you must print it out. This reduces their costs of printing and circulating printed documentation, and it also ensures that users receive the latest report documentation with the latest software release, and are not left waiting for the latest manual to be printed and sent. To print the on-line documentation about a report:

1. Start to run the report as usual. Display a screen prompting you to enter specific parameters.
2. Select System → Status.
3. In the left-hand column in the center of the screen, look for the label ABAP/4 program. Find the (eight-character) name of the program and write it down.
4. Select System → Services → Reporting. (See Exhibit 4.132.)
5. If you do not see the same name in the Program field, enter it now.
6. To display this program (report) documentation, select Goto → Documentation.
7. To print the displayed documentation, press Print.

Printing Reports

To print reports from R/3 on your LAN or PC printer, make sure that the proper line printer daemon is installed and properly configured. For example, to print reports to a PC printer attached to a Windows PC printer, you require a piece of software that runs under Windows called saplpd. Call or write SAP for details.

When you have any report displayed on your screen, to print it, select System → List → Print.

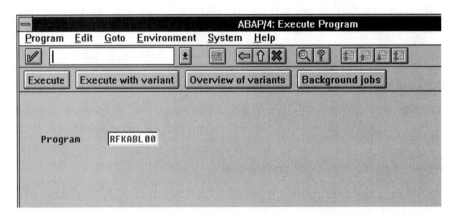

Exhibit 4.132   Execute Program

Downloading a Report to a Spreadsheet

You can download any report to a spreadsheet, such as Microsoft Excel.

When you have the report displayed on your screen, to print it, select System → List → Download.

Finding a String in the Report

To find a string in any report:

1. Display the report and place your cursor at the beginning of the report
2. Select Edit → Find
3. Enter the text string to be found
4. Press Continue

Checking the Printing in Process

When you print a report, The program places the report in a temporary file on the disk called a spool file. To check the printing in process:

1. From any menu, select System → Services → Output controller.
2. Press <Enter> to see a list of print runs that you have done.

Reporting the Vendor List

A list of reliable, satisfactory vendors is invaluable. To report the vendor list:

1. From the Accounts Payable menu, select Periodic processing → Reporting → Account List. (See Exhibit 4.133.)
2. If you leave the Vendor account parameters blank, the program selects all vendors. Enter at least the company code in the Company code field, the account sorting in the Account sorting field, and the number of lines per vendor in the first Communication with vendor field. Optionally, in the second Communication with vendor field, enter the country code for domestic vendors to format the domestic addresses according to the domestic format in that country.
3. To go to the second screen of parameters, press the + button in the lower-right corner of the screen. (See Exhibit 4.134.)
4. Optionally, to include reference, dunning, or vendor correspondence data, mark one or more of these parameters. Also optionally, enter parameters on the second screen to select specific vendors in the list.

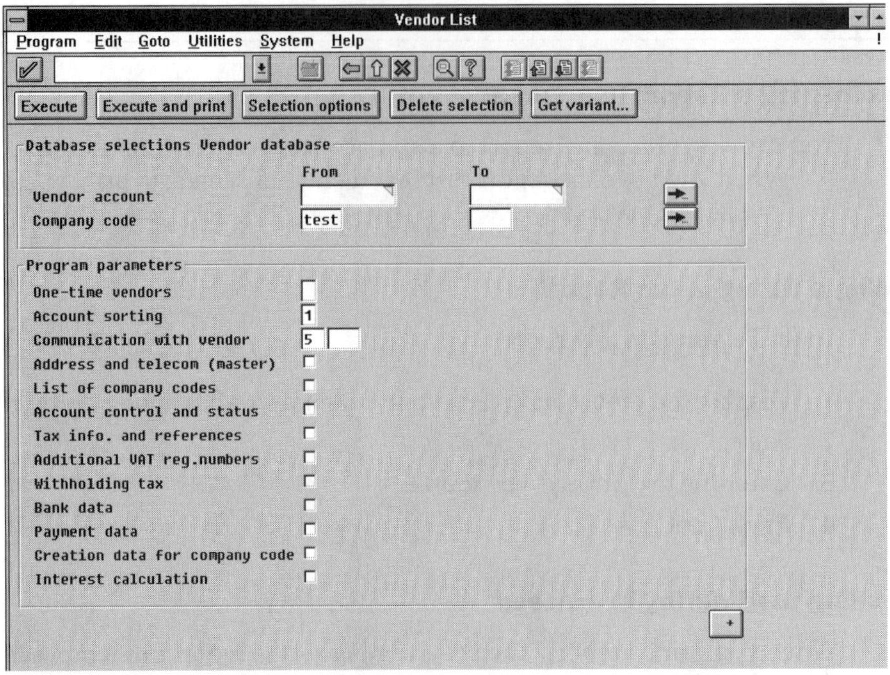

Exhibit 4.133   Vendor List: Account List

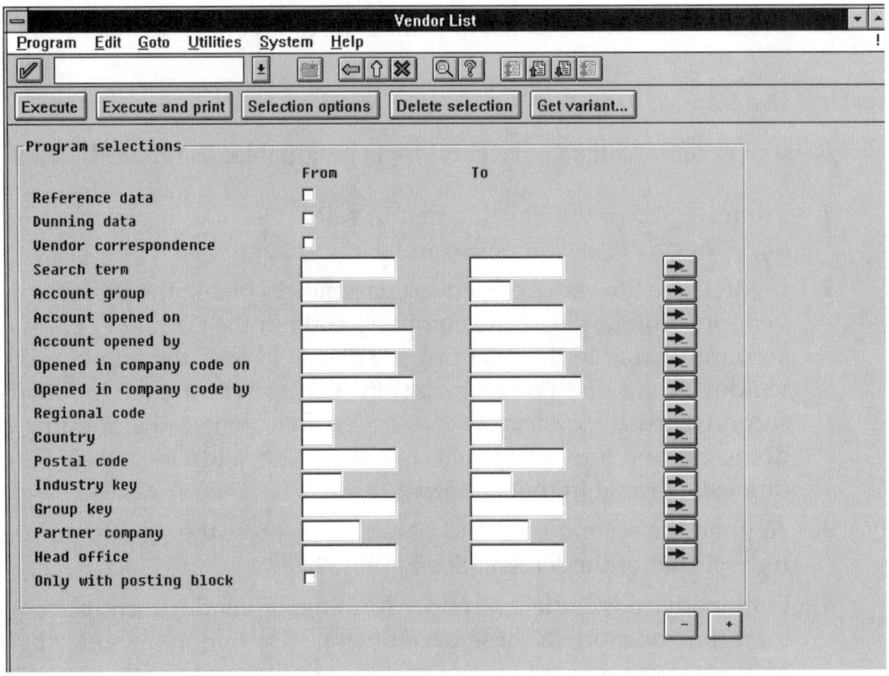

Exhibit 4.134   Vendor List: Data Screen

For example, to select vendors in a certain country, enter the ISO code of that country in the Country parameter.

5. To run the report, press Execute or <F8>.

Reporting New Vendors

To report new vendors, first run the program to list the vendors. Then specify all accounts opened between a range of dates or all accounts opened in a company between a range of dates. Optionally, you can also specify one or more SAP login IDs to select the new vendors opened by one or more specific individuals.

To report new vendors:

1. Start to report the vendor list as usual. From the Accounts Payable menu, select Periodic processing ➤ Reporting ➤ Account list. The screens are the same as those shown in the previous section, "Reporting the Vendor List."

2. On the first screen, enter at least the parameters for the company code, account sorting, and communication with the vendors.

3. Press + in the lower-right portion of the first screen to go to the second screen of parameters.

4. On the second screen, to see the new vendors by the date, the name, and the address (and any other general data) they were first entered, enter a range of dates in the Account opened on parameter. To see the new vendors in the company code, enter a range of dates in the Opened in company code on parameter.

5. To run the report, press Execute or <F8>.

Reporting Changes in Vendor Master Records

To list changes to vendor master records:

1. From any menu, select System ➤ Services ➤ Reporting. (See Exhibit 4.135.)

2. In the Program field, enter **RFKABL00** and then press Execute. (See Exhibit 4.136.)

3. Enter at least the range of dates in the Change date field, the sorting order in the Sorting field (time, account, person, or field group of change), and one or more sets of data that may have changed—general data (name, address, tax ID, bank account number, and so on), company code data (reconciliation account, payment terms, payment methods, and so on), or pur-

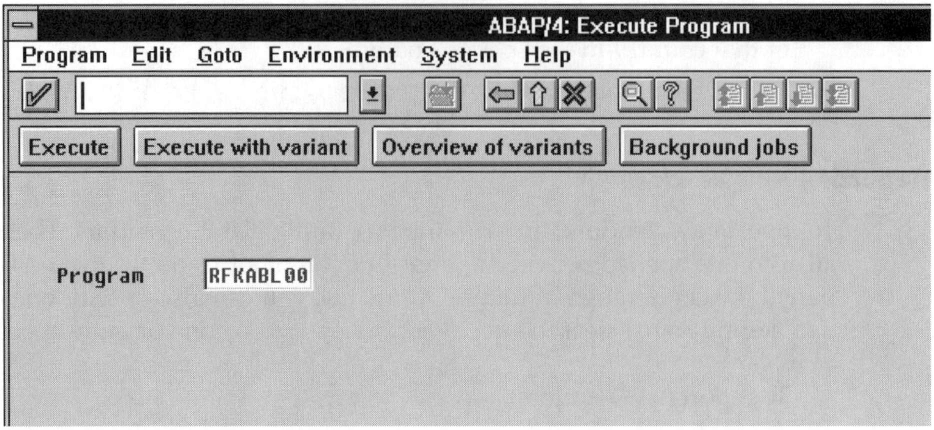

Exhibit 4.135   List Changes to Vendor Master Record

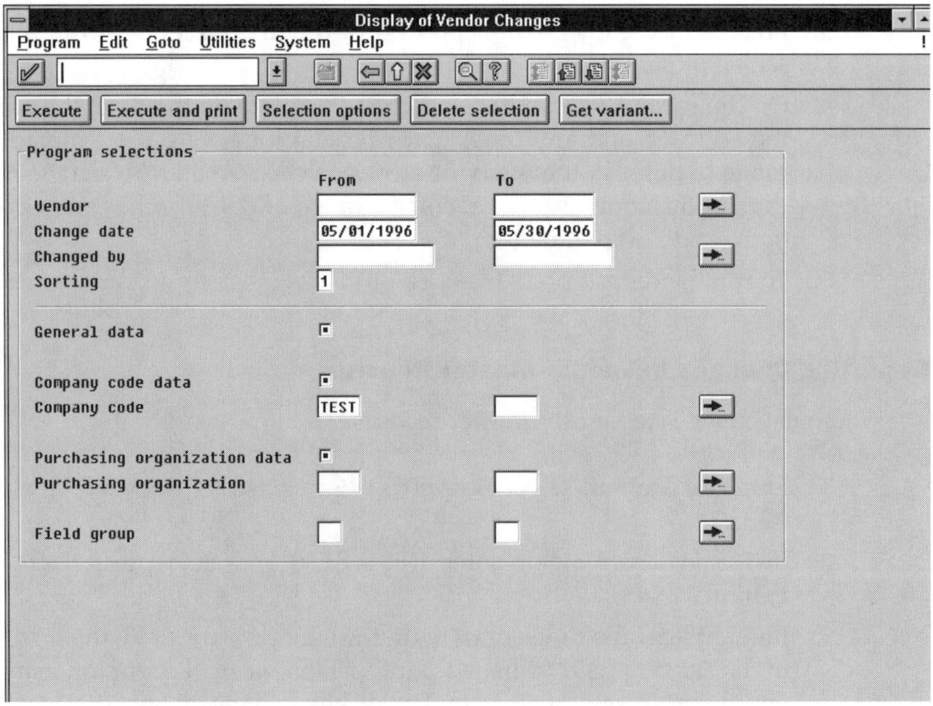

Exhibit 4.136   Display of Vendor Changes

chasing organization (currency of the purchase orders to this vendor, payment terms to the vendor, shipping instructions, and so on).

4. To run the report, press Execute or <F8>.

Reporting Vendor Account Balances

Vendor account balances include all outstanding invoices to the vendor and any other open items, such as credit memos or payments on account that did not close (clear) invoices.

To report vendor balances:

1. From the Accounts Payable menu, select Periodic processing → Reporting → Account balances. (See Exhibit 4.137.)

2. Enter at least the parameters for the company code, account sorting, summarization level, fiscal year, and posting periods. Optionally, enter an additional heading to appear in the report output.

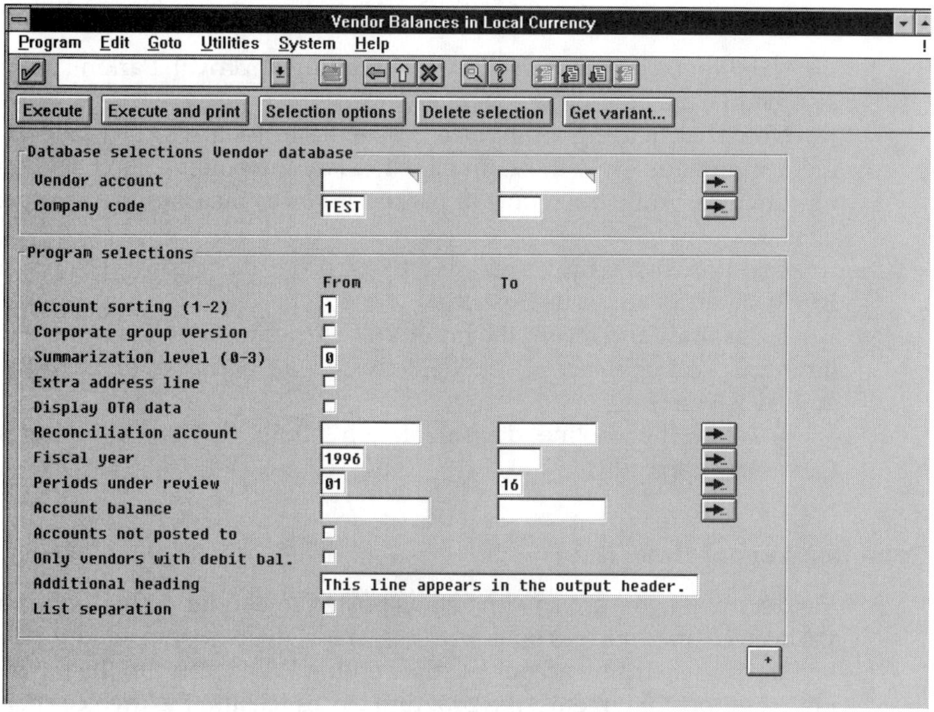

Exhibit 4.137 Vendor Balances in Local Currency

Note that you can obtain the vendor account balances from the previous year by entering the previous fiscal year and the complete range of posting periods.

3. To run the report, press Execute or <F8>.

Reporting Vendors with Debit Balances

This report is often required by auditors. If the vendor has a debit balance, then your company owes the vendor. To prepare a report of vendors with debit balances:

1. Run the report of vendor account balances as described in the previous section, "Reporting Vendor Account Balances."
2. Enter the parameters as usual. Click on the parameter Only vendor with debit bal.
3. To run the report, press Execute or <F8>.

Reporting Parked Invoices

A parked invoice is a vendor invoice awaiting approval. Parking an invoice is also known as preliminary posting.

Note that holding an invoice is specific to each user. The report of held invoices includes only those invoices held by the person who held that particular invoice, while the report of parked invoices includes invoices parked by all users.

To report parked invoices, select System ➤ Services ➤ Reporting, enter **RFPVEB**, and then press Execute.

To generate and record the input VAT entries for invoices entered with preliminary posting, select System ➤ Services ➤ Reporting, enter **RFPUMSOO** and click Execute.

To read the on-line documentation about the report, select Help ➤ Extended help.

Reporting Vendor Open Items

Vendor open items are any line items posted to vendor accounts that have not yet been cleared, such as open invoices, credit memos from vendors, advances, and any payments on account to the vendor. When you run the payment program and post payments, the program closes (clears) the invoices being paid. Cleared items do not appear in the report of vendor open items. To report vendor open items:

1. From the Accounts Payable menu, select Periodic processing → Reporting → Open items list. (See Exhibit 4.138.)

2. Enter at least the company code, a date in the Open items at key date field, the S-Sort indicator (how to sort the list of vendors in the output) and the P-Sort indicator (how to sort the list of open items in the account, if the line items are displayed). To display the line items, click on Line items required. To display the subtotals by the open items sort parameter, click on Subtotal. To go to the second screen of parameters, press + in the lower-right portion of the screen. (See Exhibit 4.139.)

3. Usually, you should make sure that Normal documents is selected. "Normal documents" is an SAP term that means regular transactions, not one-sided entries, sample transactions, recurring transactions, or parked invoices. To go to the third screen of parameters, press +. To go back to the first screen of parameters, press –. The third screen of parameters is shown in Exhibit 4.140.

4. Optionally, select one of these parameters. To run the report, press Execute or <F8>.

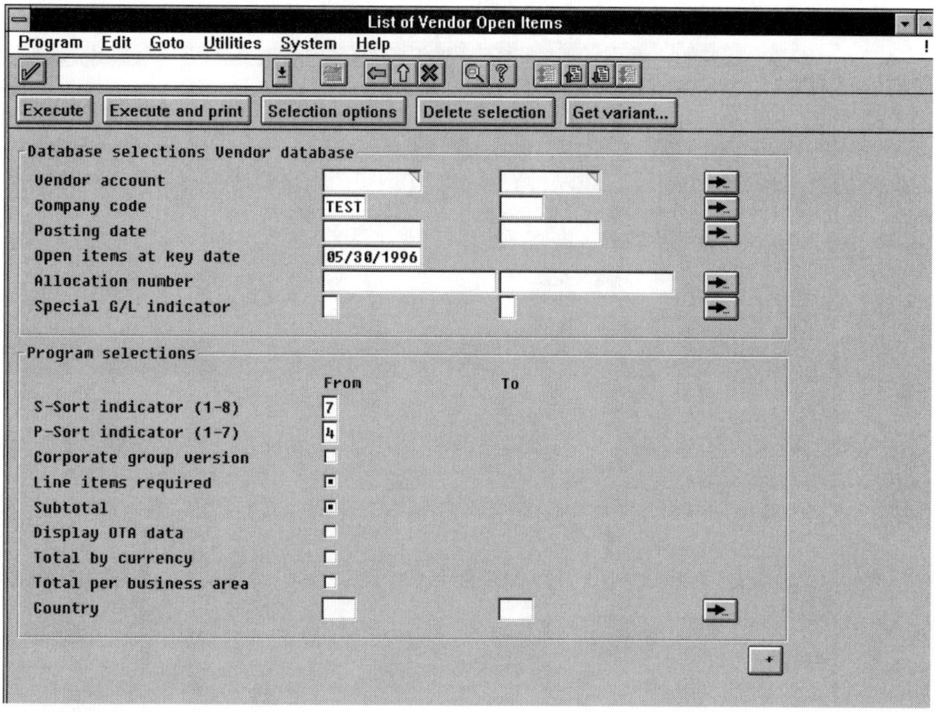

Exhibit 4.138 List of Vendor Open Items, Screen One

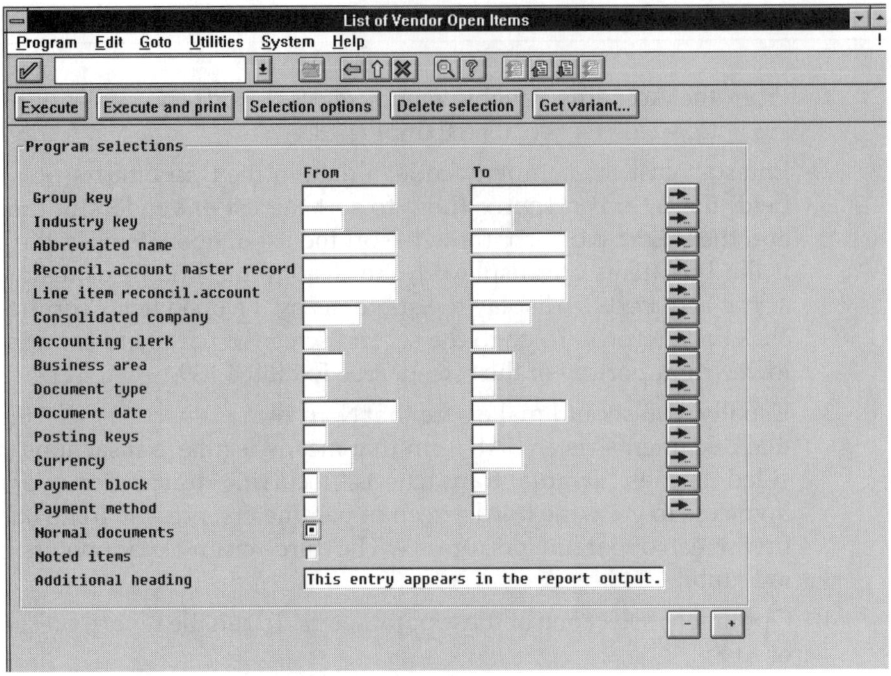

Exhibit 4.139 List of Vendor Open Items, Screen Two

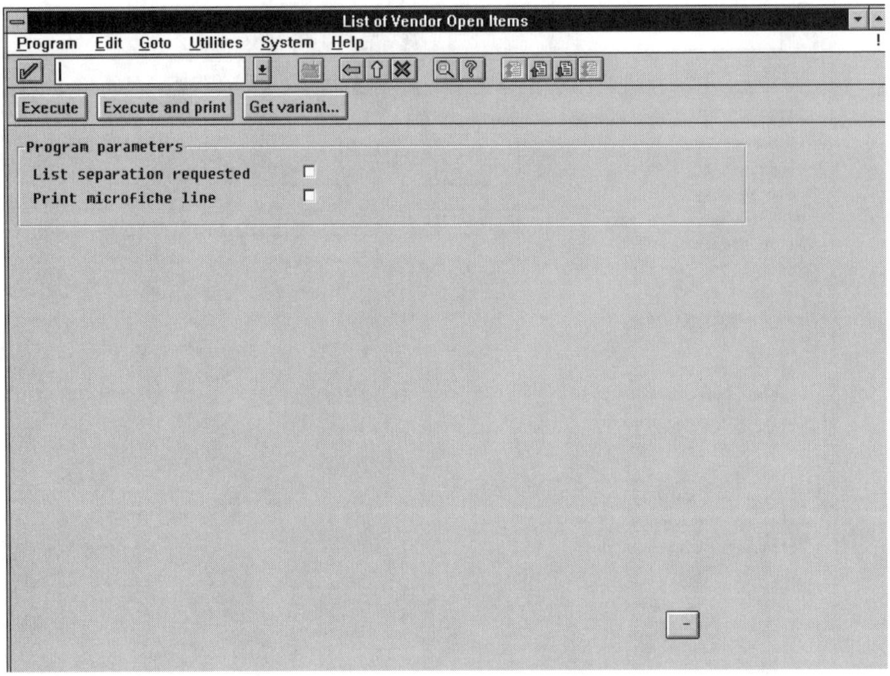

Exhibit 4.140 List of Vendor Open Items, Screen Three

Reporting Blocked Invoices

To block an invoice from being paid, enter a one-character code for the reason for blocking the invoice. You can block invoices either when running the payment proposal, when entering the invoice, or when updating the invoice. If you block an invoice in the payment proposal, then the block is only valid for that payment run. In other words, the next time that you run the payment program, the invoice will not be blocked. If you block an invoice, when you enter or update the invoice, by entering a code in the Pmnt block field, the invoice is blocked each and every time that the payment program is run, until you unblock the invoice.

To select vendor invoices that have been blocked for payment:

1. Run the program to report vendor open items as described in the previous section, "Reporting Vendor Open Items."
2. Enter the parameters as usual.
3. On the second screen of parameters, in the Payment block parameter, enter one or more codes for the reason that the invoice was blocked.
4. To run the report, press Execute or <F8>.

Reporting Total Payables by Currency

If you purchase goods or services in different currencies, you have to manage your payables and liquidity in different currencies. To report the total payables by currency:

1. Run the program to report vendor open items as described in the previous section, "Reporting Vendor Open Items."
2. Enter the parameters as usual.
3. On the first screen of parameters, click on the Total by currency parameter.
4. To run the report, press Execute or <F8>.
    Note that if you purchase from the same vendor in different currency, the output subtotals the payables to that vendor by currency. At the end of the report, the output totals the payables by currency for all vendors.

Reporting Vendor Open Items by Due Date

1. Run the program to report vendor open items as described in the previous section, "Reporting Vendor Open Items."
2. Enter the parameters as usual.

3. In the first screen of parameters, enter **4** in the P-Sort indicator parameter.

4. To run the report, press Execute or \<F8>.

Reporting Vendor Transaction Journals

In some countries (such as France, Italy, and others), you are required to submit a complete transaction journal to the authorities. The details depend on your configuration. To prepare this report, use the G/L report described in the section in the General Ledger chapter, "Reporting a Transaction Journal." Note that other reports may also be required to meet country-specific requirements.

Forecasting Cash Requirements

To forecast cash requirements based on due dates of vendor invoices:

1. From any menu, select System ⟶ Services ⟶ Reporting.

2. In the Program field, enter **RFKOFW00** and then press Execute or \<F8>. (See Exhibit 4.141.)

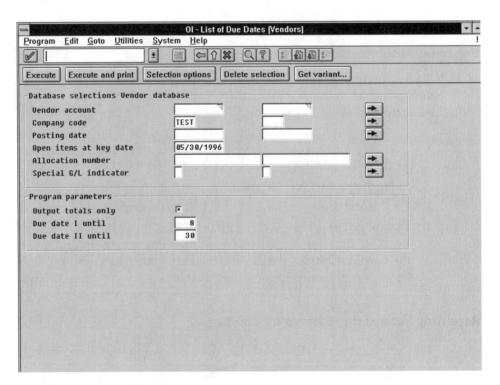

Exhibit 4.141   List of Due Dates

3. Enter at least the company code and the date on which the items are opened in the Open items at key date field, usually today's date. In the Due date I until parameter, enter the number of days (usually in the future, after a key date of today) for which you wish to calculate liabilities after the key date. The program then forecasts cash requirements from the key date until this date. In the Due date II until parameter, enter the number of days in the future for which you wish to calculate liabilities. The program then forecasts cash requirements from the due date I until this day. Optionally, to output the totals by company code only, click on Output totals only.

CHAPTER 5

Basics of System Administration

SAP system administration most often involves:

- Understanding the technical design (processes) of the R/3 package
- Adding users with authorizations
- Resetting forgotten passwords
- Maintaining authorization profiles
- Transporting custom programs, any source code changes, and configuration changes between machines and between clients

Transporting program and configuration changes is beyond the scope of this text. To set up the transport system, use transaction code **SE06.** To prepare to carry out the transport, use **SE01.** For information about the transport system, use **SE05.** Various other useful functions are also briefly described here.

DISPLAYING PROCESSES

A process, technically speaking, is a program running in memory. In this sense, R/3 has the following main types of processes, which correspond to processes in your operating system, such as UNIX or NT:

Type of Process	*Function*	*Abbreviations*
Dialog	Data entry and validation	DIA
Update	Read and write data table	VB
Enqueue	Record-locking	ENQ
Batch job	Background processing	BTC
Spool	Print spooling	SPO

Depending on the number of users and patterns of usage, you can and should have multiple processes of each type running at the same time.

To display the running processes:

1. From the R/3 main menu, select Tools ➤ Administration.

2. From the System Administration menu, select Monitoring ➤ System monitoring ➤ Process overview. (See Exhibit 5.1.)

```
┌─────────────────────────────── Overview of Processes ──────────────────────── ▾│▴
 Process   Program   User session   Edit   Goto   System   Help                    !
┌──┐ ┌──────────────┐ ┌▾┐  ┌──┐ ⇦⇧✕  ⌕?  📧📧📧📧
│✓ │ │              │ └─┘  └──┘
└──┘ └──────────────┘
┌────┐ ┌─────────┐ ┌────────────────┐ ┌───────────┐                              ▴
│CPU │ │ Refresh │ │ Delete session │ │ Debugging │                              ▓
└────┘ └─────────┘ └────────────────┘ └───────────┘
                                                                                  ▓
 No.Ty. PID      Status   Cause Start Err Sem CPU      Time   Program  Cl. User        Action

 0  DIA 19312    Run            Yes                            RSMON000 610 CBUOGE
 1  DIA 20338    Wait           Yes
 2  DIA 20596    Wait           Yes
 3  DIA 20854    Wait           Yes
 4  DIA 21112    Wait           Yes
 5  DIA 21370    Wait           Yes
 6  DIA 21628    Wait           Yes
 7  VB  21886    Wait           Yes
 8  VB  22144    Wait           Yes
 9  ENQ 22402    Wait           Yes
 10 BTC 22660    Wait           Yes
 11 BTC 22918    Wait           Yes
 12 BTC 23176    Wait           Yes
 13 SPO 23434    Wait           Yes


                                                                                  ▾
┌─┐┌─┐                                                                         ┌─┐
│◄││ │                                                                         │►│
└─┘└─┘                                                                         └─┘
```

Exhibit 5.1   Overview of Processes

ADDING A USER

R/3 is a multiuser application. Users must be added to the application. You do not have to add them to the operating system, unless they require specific access to the operating system. To add a user:

1. From the System Administration menu, select User maintenance → Users. (See Exhibit 5.2.)

2. Enter the person's login ID in the User field and press Create/change. (See Exhibit 5.3.)

3. Enter an initial password in the Initial password field, press <Tab>, and then enter the very same initial password again (Exhibit 5.3). Make sure that you spell the passwrod exactly the same in both fields. Then assign one or more profiles to each user. The profiles determine which functions and data that user is allowed to use. Defining authorization profiles is beyond the scope of this text. For a list of available profiles, press Profiles. (See Exhibit 5.4.)

4. Click on Active only and then press List. (See Exhibit 5.5.)

5. To select a profile and add it to the user master record, simply double-click on the profile. (See Exhibit 5.6.)

6. Optionally enter validity dates for this user. For example, if you are having external people train your users, you could limit their access to one or more days by entering the Valid from and Valid to fields. To store the user master record with the profile, press <F11> or the file folder icon.

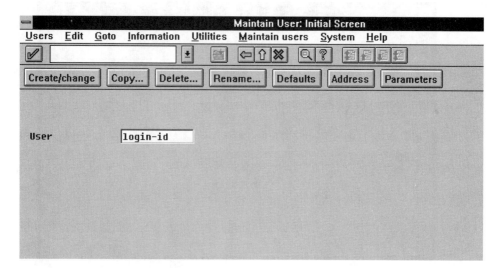

Exhibit 5.2   Maintain User: Initial Screen

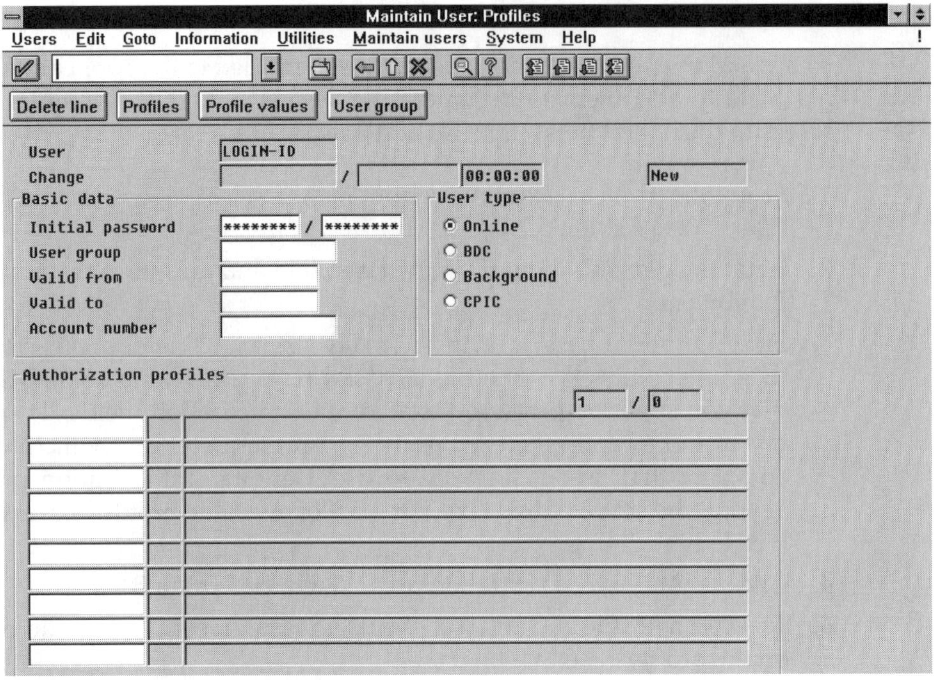

Exhibit 5.3 Maintain User: Profiles

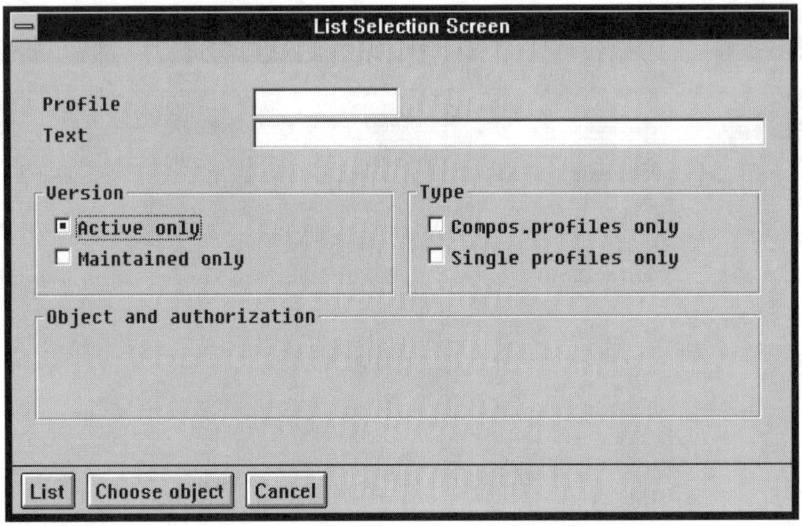

Exhibit 5.4 List Selection Screen

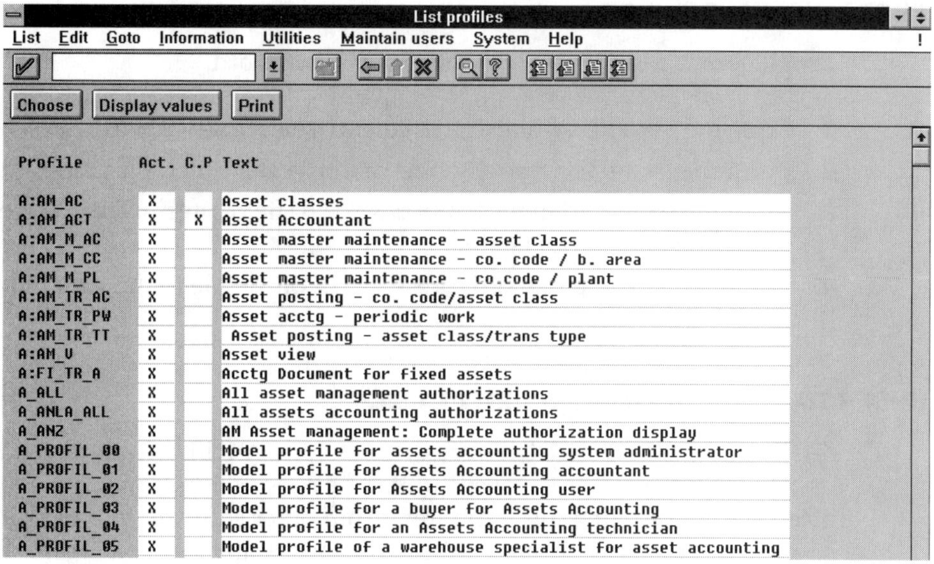

Exhibit 5.5   List Profiles

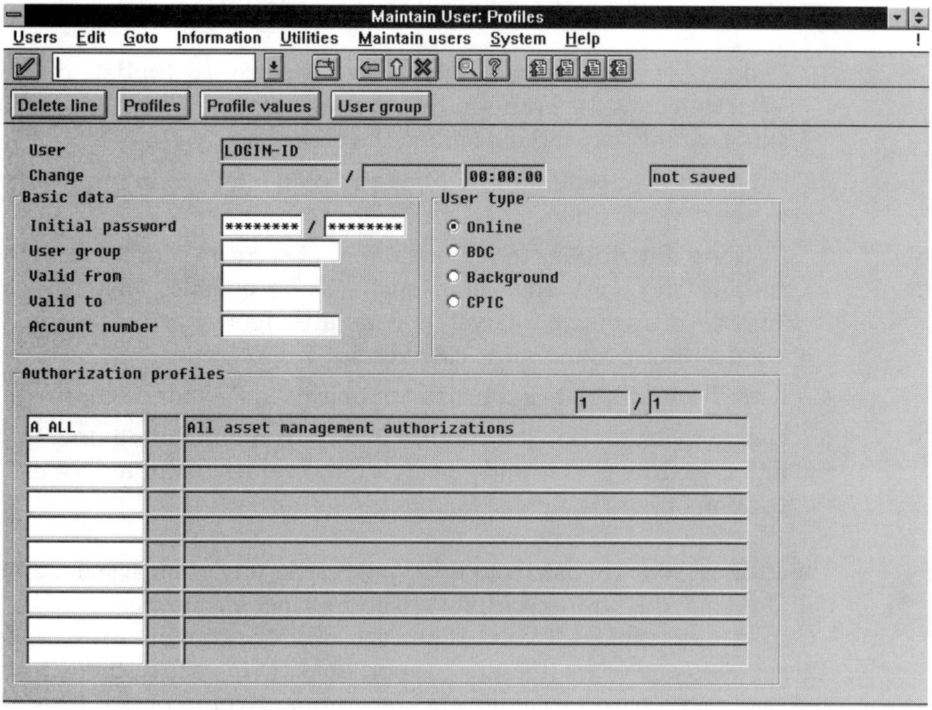

Exhibit 5.6   Adding a Profile to User Master Record

RESETTING A PASSWORD

People forget passwords. To reset a user's password:

1. From the System Administration menu, select User maintenance → Users.
2. From the Maintain User: Profiles menu, select Goto → Change password.
3. Enter the password in the Initial password field, press <Tab>, and enter the same exact password again.
4. To store the new password, press <F11> or the file folder icon.

UNDERSTANDING SYSTEM SECURITY IN SAP

SAP is designed to restrict all access, unless you specifically permit someone (a user ID) to have access to specific data or a specific function (an authorization object). This concept may be different from other software that permits everyone to have access to all data, unless you specifically prohibit access. This concept also makes it possible to design very complicated security schemes that can become difficult to maintain. To prepare to set up security profiles for your accounting system by user under R/3, it is advisable to:

1. Make a list of your users, what data they process (update or view), and what functions they use—in the form of a matrix of individuals along one axis and function and data along the other axis.
2. On paper first, combine functions and data into a set of profiles applicable to your organization.
3. Develop descriptions (documentation) of security profiles from the sets of specific functions and data, such as "receivables invoicing analyst," "payables invoicing analyst," "general ledger analyst," "cash disbursement authorization," and "cash receipt authorization."
4. Find the appropriate authorization objects in R/3 for each profile.
5. Define the authorization profiles in R/3, combining authorization objects into a security profile and specifying the values permitted for each authorization object.

The greatest security risk to an R/3 system, like any other system, is not external. It is from disgruntled employees and former employees.

In summary, in SAP, you assign each user one or more profiles. Each profile contains one or more authorization objects. To each authorization object, you assign one or more values, such as company codes or display and update authorizations.

UNDERSTANDING AUDIT AND INTERNAL CONTROL

To keep internal control of your accounting function, you only need to follow one rule: separate duties. Specifically, the same individual who records the payment of an invoice, whether a customer invoice or a vendor invoice, should not also be allowed to post the invoice. If you issue purchase orders, receive goods, and post invoices in comparison to the purchase orders and goods received, then you should also separate the duties for purchasing, receiving and recording the vendor invoice. In smaller organizations, your people are on vacation and subsitute for each other. As a practical matter, you cannot always separate duties. To keep internal control in a large organization, there should be no exception to the separation of duties. Any other arrangement creates a temptation and risks misuse of the system.

FINDING A MISSING AUTHORIZATION QUICKLY

If you receive a message that you are not authorized to use a certain function or update or display certain data, then put the cursor in the command box in the upper-left portion of your screen and enter **/NSU53**.

Finding Out Required Authorization Objects

If you are setting up user authorizations, you first need to outline the separation of duties in your organization in the form of a matrix. Let the horizontal axis be a list of specific duties (one or more user functions), such as post a vendor invoice, post a payment to a vendor, and so on. Let the vertical axis be a list of users. To find out the required authorization objects for a function (either a user function or an ABAP program), do the following:

1. From any menu, select System → Utilities → ABAP/4 trace.
2. Enter the four-character user function ("transaction code"), such as **F-43** to enter a vendor invoice, or the eight-character ABAP program in the Transaction/report field. To find out the transaction code for a specific user function, start the function from a menu, then select System → Status, and look in the Transaction field.
3. Press the Execute pushbutton.
4. Use the function. Carry out all steps (for example, to post a vendor invoice).
5. From any menu, select System → Utilities → ABAP/4 trace again.
6. Enter (or check entry of) the same user function or ABAP program.
7. Press the Analyze pushbutton.
8. Press the Authorization objs pushbutton.

Displaying or Printing Hypertext

SAP supplies very little printed documentation. R/3 includes various hypertext documents (on-line books). If you want a printed version of the hypertext, you can print it out. If you do not have the title of the document, you can look for it. To look for and then display a hypertext document:

1. From the R/3 main menu, select Tools → Hypertext → Structures. (See Exhibit 5.7.)
2. In the Structure field, enter the title of the hypertext document, if you have it. If you do not have the title of the document, press <F4> for a list of available documents. For now, press <F4>. (See Exhibit 5.8.)
3. To see the complete list of available hypertext documents by language, press Continue.
4. With the list displayed, double-click on a document to see the outline of the document. (See Exhibit 5.9.)
5. To print out the whole book, select Structure → Print → Book.
6. To read a chapter, place the cursor on the line with the name of the chapter and press Read module.

Releasing Locked Records

If R/3, the operating system, or the database crashes while you are entering or changing data, R/3 sometimes does not release the locked records when you start up the system again. The locked records must be released directly. To release locked records:

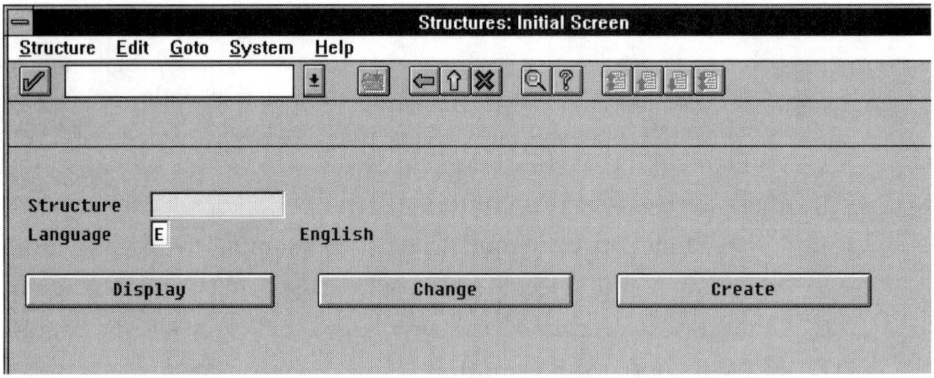

Exhibit 5.7   Structures: Initial Screen

Exhibit 5.8 Find Structure

1. From the System Administration menu, select Monitoring ➤ Lock entries. (See Exhibit 5.10.)

2. To see a list of all locked records, press List. (See Exhibit 5.11.)

3. If there are locked records, to see who was logged in while the record was locked and when it was locked, put the cursor on the locked record and press Details. To release a locked record, put the cursor on a locked record and then press Delete. From the menu on this screen, to release all locked records, select Lock entry ➤ Delete all.

Note that you should only release locked records if there has been a system crash and if you know what you are doing. Otherwise, if you release locked records that your users still have active, then there is a possibility that two users will update the same record at the same time, and the second one to store the update will overwrite the first update.

Broadcasting a System Message

You can broadcast an immediate system message (for example, to ask users to log off before bringing the system down for maintenance). When any logged

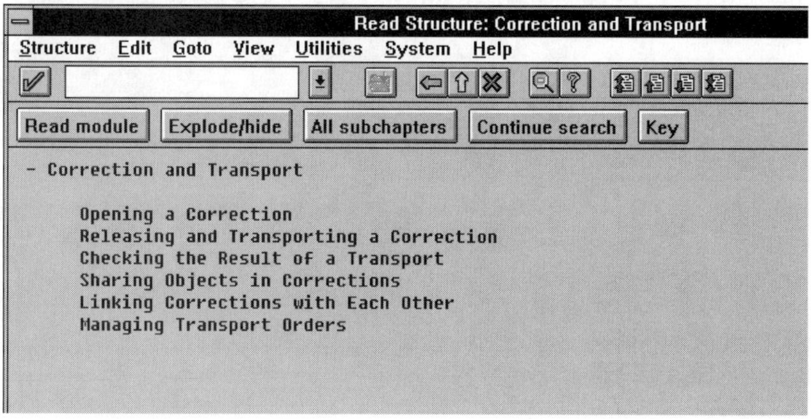

Exhibit 5.9 Read Structure

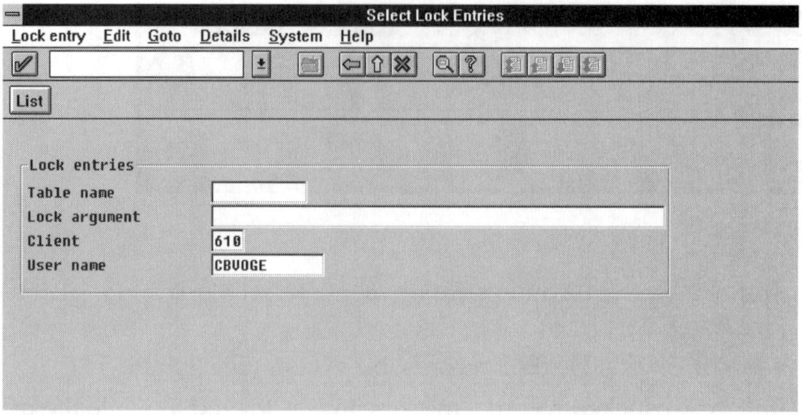

Exhibit 5.10   Select Lock Entries

user does anything, such as pressing a mouse button or a key on the keyboard, or logs in, then the user sees the system message. To send a system message:

1. From the System Administration menu, select Administration → System messages. (See Exhibit 5.12.)
2. To start to enter a message, press Create. (See Exhibit 5.13.)
3. Enter a one-line message and press <Enter>. When a user does anything, such as pressing a key or a mouse button or logging on, then the user sees the message entered in the Text field.

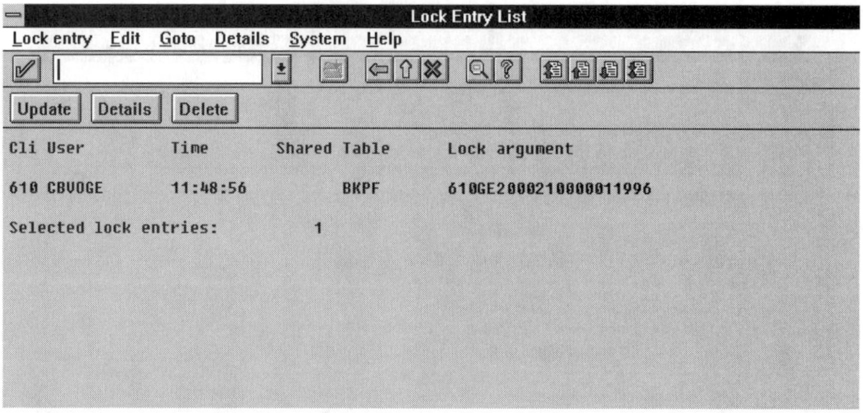

Exhibit 5.11   Lock Entry List

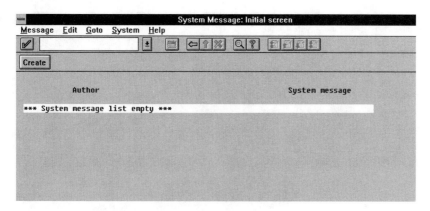

Exhibit 5.12 System Message: Initial Screen

Displaying Records Not Yet Recorded

Entering data and storing data are, technically speaking, asynchronous processes. In other words, when you press <F11> or the file folder icon, and see a message that the master record or transaction record ("document") has been stored, it has not yet been stored. R/3 transfers the record to the update process, which then writes the record to the disk. If there is a delay in this transfer (for example, in a congested network), then there is a delay in this update. Sometimes, one process or another simply times out and the record is in limbo, not yet recorded. This does not happen often, but it can happen, particularly in a transcontinental network where non-dedicated data lines are shared (leased). Sometimes, although rarely, the update process simply fails and data is entered, but not yet stored on the disk. You can then manually prompt the update process to record the data again.

To display and manually update records that have not yet been recorded:

1. From the System Administration menu, select Monitoring ➤ Update. (See Exhibit 5.14.)

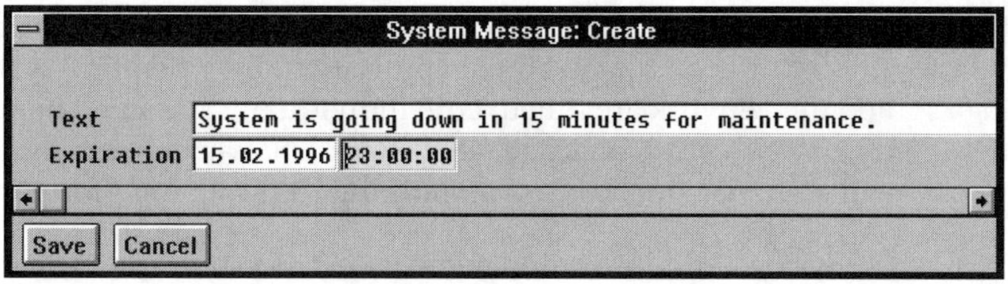

Exhibit 5.13 System Message: Create

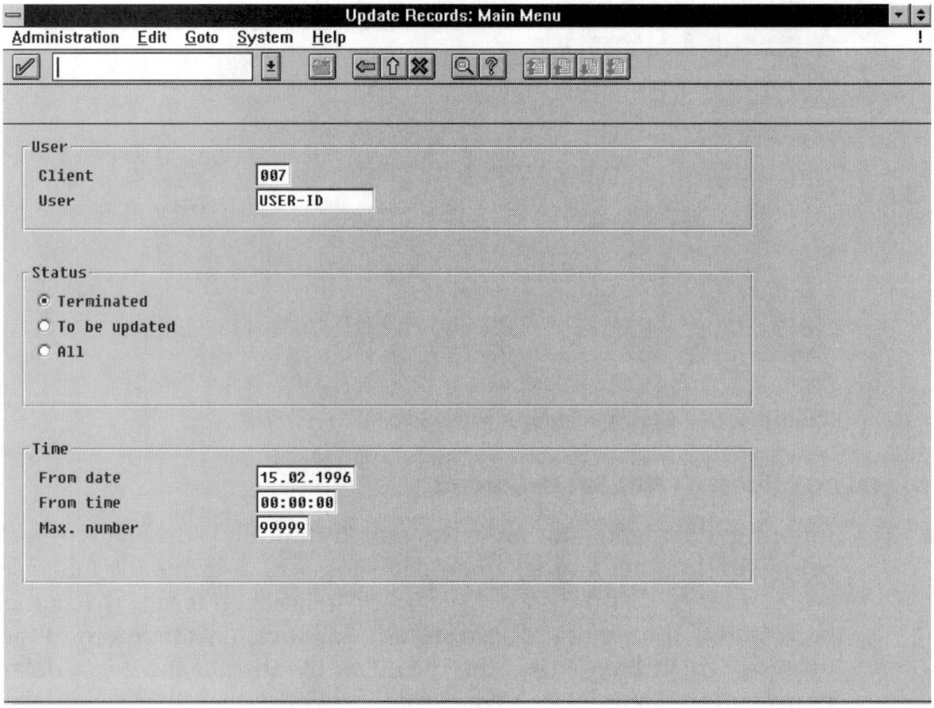

Exhibit 5.14   Update Records

2. Enter the client and user that may have records that have not yet been updated ("update records"). Press <Enter>.

    To update all records, select Administration ➤ Update ➤ All records. To delete all update records (for example, if the system crashed and your users have already entered the data again), select Administration ➤ Delete ➤ All records.

Monitoring Performance

You can monitor the system performance, including response time and "hit ratios" of records found in memory without reading the disk. Much of system performance depends on how well the application, the operating system, the database, and the network are tuned, both individually and in relation to each other. Tuning is beyond the scope of this text; however, you can start to improve your response time by first monitoring the system performance.

1. From the System Administration menu, select Monitoring ➤ Performance.

2. From the Performance Monitoring menu, select Setup/buffers ➤ Buffers. (See Exhibit 5.15.)

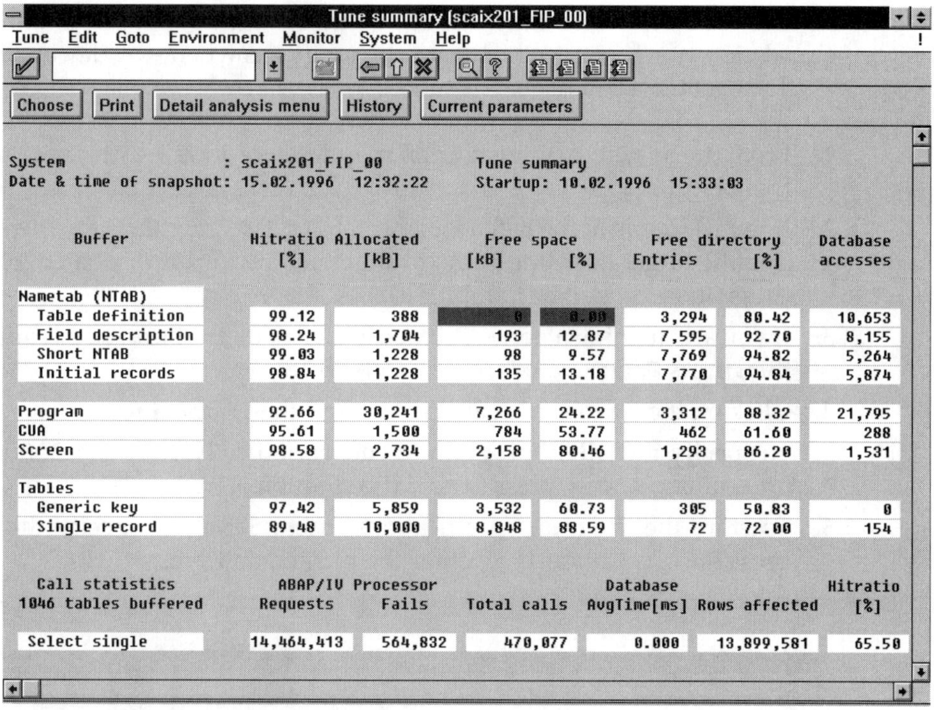

Tune summary (scaix201_FIP_00)

Tune Edit Goto Environment Monitor System Help

Choose | Print | Detail analysis menu | History | Current parameters

System : scaix201_FIP_00 Tune summary
Date & time of snapshot: 15.02.1996 12:32:22 Startup: 10.02.1996 15:33:03

Buffer	Hitratio [%]	Allocated [kB]	Free space [kB]	Free space [%]	Free directory Entries	Free directory [%]	Database accesses
Nametab (NTAB)							
Table definition	99.12	388	0	0.00	3,294	80.42	10,653
Field description	98.24	1,704	193	12.87	7,595	92.70	8,155
Short NTAB	99.03	1,228	98	9.57	7,769	94.82	5,264
Initial records	98.84	1,228	135	13.18	7,770	94.84	5,874
Program	92.66	30,241	7,266	24.22	3,312	88.32	21,795
CUA	95.61	1,500	784	53.77	462	61.60	288
Screen	98.58	2,734	2,158	80.46	1,293	86.20	1,531
Tables							
Generic key	97.42	5,859	3,532	60.73	305	50.83	0
Single record	89.48	10,000	8,848	88.59	72	72.00	154

Call statistics 1046 tables buffered	ABAP/IV Processor Requests	ABAP/IV Processor Fails	Database Total calls	Database AvgTime[ms]	Database Rows affected	Hitratio [%]
Select single	14,464,413	564,832	470,077	0.000	13,899,581	65.50

Exhibit 5.15 Tune Summary

3. Look for the hit ratio to be over 90% for all types of buffered records. Do not attempt to analyze this performance data or to tune your system without the proper training.
4. To see an analysis of the response time, go back to the Performance Monitoring menu and then select Workload → Analysis.
5. To analyze the database performance, go back to the Performance Monitoring menu and then select Database → Activity.

Scheduling a Batch (Off-line) Job

A batch job is a program that you schedule to run at a later time. The concept is the same as a batch job in mainframe systems. You can use batch jobs to balance the system load of producing periodic reports or processing large volumes of data periodically. For example, you could schedule a printout of the customer invoice journal to run once a week overnight. You can schedule an ABAP program and a variant. However, as obvious as it seems, if you have a centralized, international installation that spans three continents, your company never sleeps! To balance the load with batch jobs, you should first take a global view of who runs which periodic programs when—by day and by hour.

To schedule a batch job:

1. From the System Administration menu, select Jobs ➤ Job definition. (See Exhibit 5.16.)
2. Enter the name of the batch job, the batch class (enter **C** if you are not sure), and the target host (the name of the machine to run this batch job). Then press Start time. (See Exhibit 5.17.)
3. If you are defining a periodic batch job, click on the Periodic job button and then press Period values. (See Exhibit 5.18.)
4. Click on the period, such as Weekly, and then press Save.
5. To specify the ABAP program to run periodically, from the Define Background Job screen, press Steps. (See Exhibit 5.19.)
6. To store the program specifications, press Save. To specify the printer, press Print specifications, enter the printer, and press <F11>.

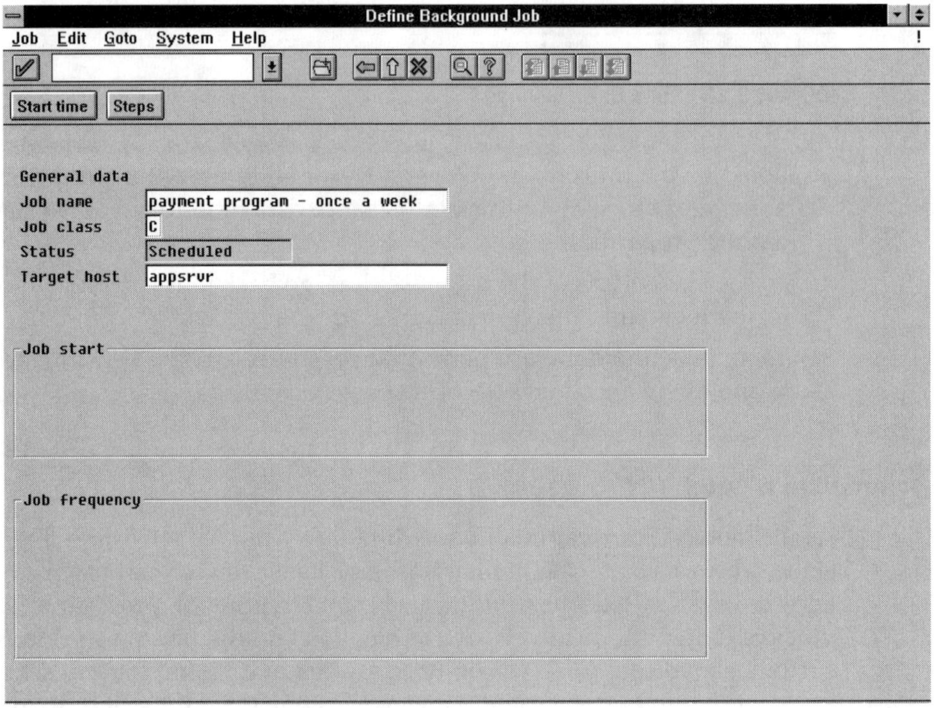

Exhibit 5.16 Define Background Job

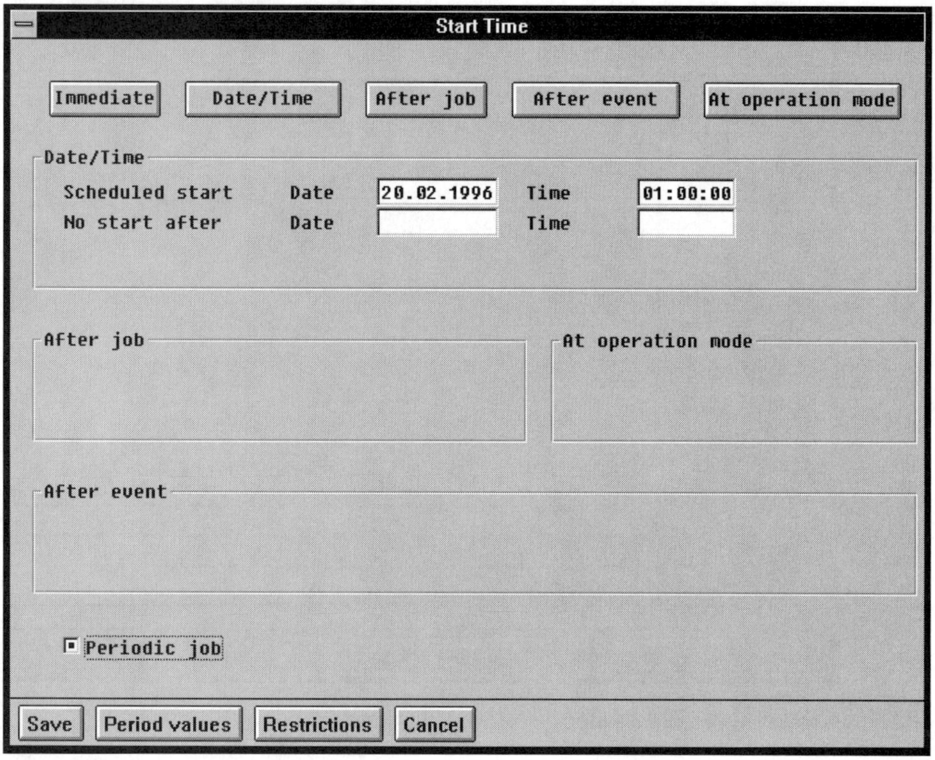

Exhibit 5.17 Start Time

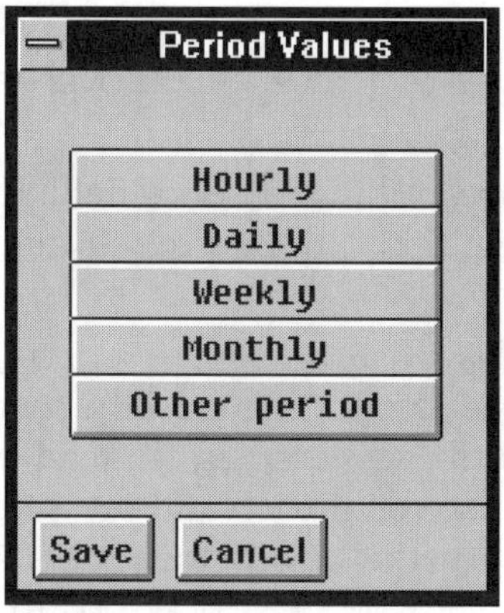

Exhibit 5.18 Period Values

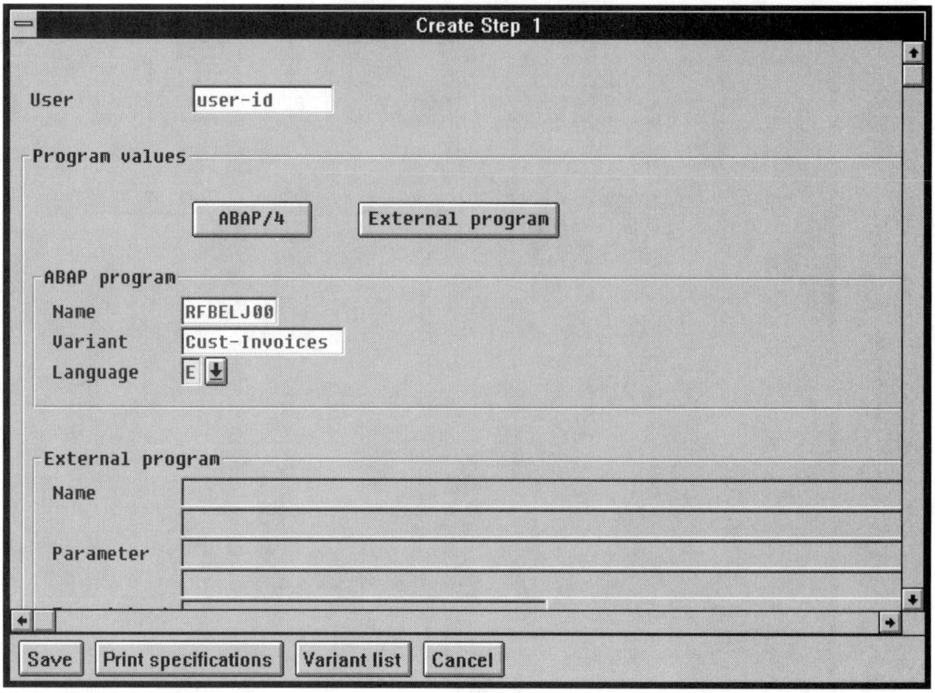

Exhibit 5.19   Create Step 1

Displaying Batch Jobs

All batch jobs are either scheduled, released, ready (in a queue), active (running), finished, or canceled (sometimes due to program error or errant variant). To display batch jobs:

1. From the System Administration menu, select Jobs → Job overview. (See Exhibit 5.20.)

2. Enter the name of the job or * for all jobs in the Job name field. Enter the user name or * for all users in the User name field. Press Execute. (See Exhibit 5.21.)

3. To read the log of a job that has finished (with an X in the Finished column), place the cursor on the job and then press Job log. To read the schedule of a batch job, put the cursor on the job and press Display. To read the steps (ABAP programs) in the job, put the cursor on the job and press Steps. To release a job in the queue, put the cursor on the job and then press Release. To cancel a job (to stop the execution), select Job → Cancel job. To delete a job, select Job → Delete.

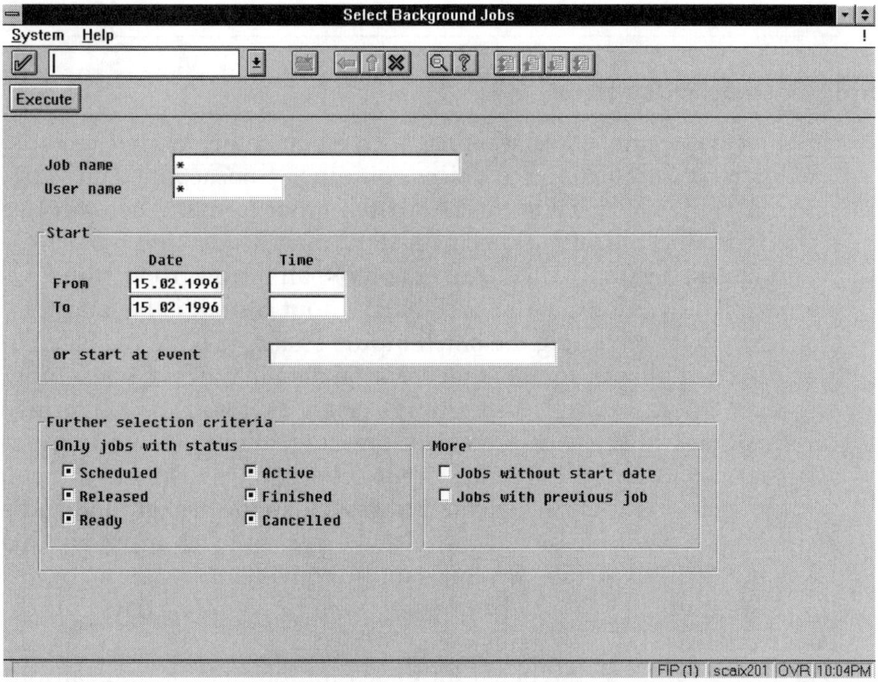

Exhibit 5.20 Select Background Jobs

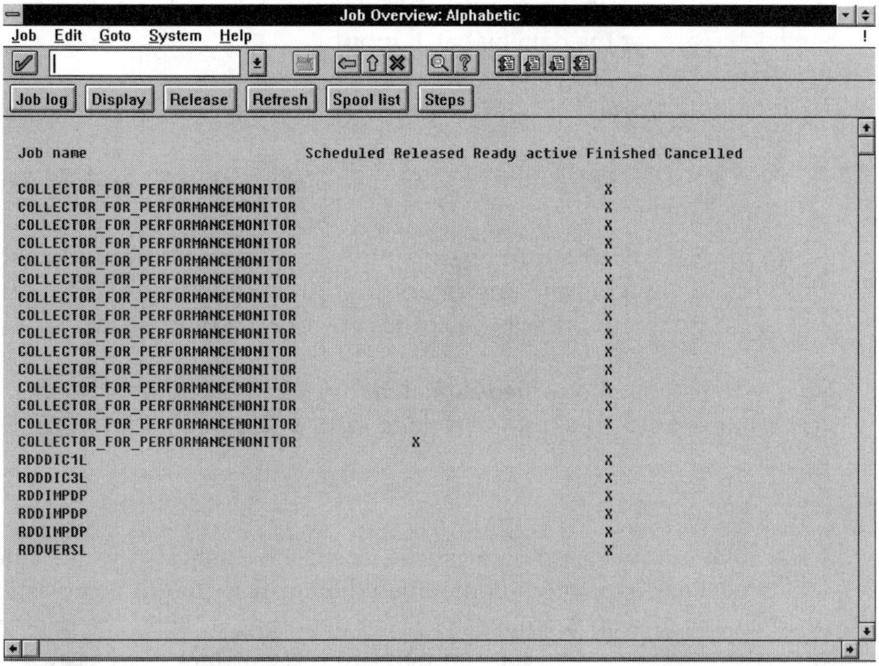

Exhibit 5.21 Job Overview: Alphabetic

Entering Data by Batch Input

To enter data from other systems, such as customer master records, vendor master records, customer invoices, or other transaction data, first convert (reformat) the records into the SAP batch input format. Then record this converted data in a file with a specific SAP format (header and footer) known as a batch input session. This conversion is an error-prone, time-consuming process. (Converting data to SAP batch input format is beyond the scope of this text.) After recording the batch input session, process the batch input session. SAP supplies programs that read the data in the SAP batch input session and then enters it into R/3 screen-by-screen, as if you were entering the data on-line. You can see each screen by pressing <Enter> to go to the next one. Alternatively, process the batch input session only displaying the errors, or you can process the entire batch input session in the background and place the errors in a separate session. Most often, errors in batch input are due to mistakes in the original data, mistakes in the conversion program, or mistakes in the configuration. In effect, batch input simulates on-line data entry. Note that batch input is different from a batch (background) job. You can schedule a batch job to process the batch input session off-line, or you can process the batch input session on-line. Assume that you have already converted your data into SAP batch input format, recorded this converted data in a batch input session, and that you wish to enter the data by batch input without a batch job. To enter the data by batch input:

1. From any menu, select System ➤ Services ➤ Batch input ➤ Edit. (See Exhibit 5.22.)
2. Press <Enter> to list all batch input sessions with any possible status. (See Exhibit 5.23.)
3. To process a batch input session, put your cursor on the session and press Process. If there were any errors after processing the batch input session, the program put the session in the category Errors in session.

Note that you can also schedule batch input in a batch job. Use the ABAP/4 program RSBDCSUB to process one or more batch input sessions.

Displaying the System Log

If you have a technical problem, such as a system crash, always read the log for details of what happened. Sometimes the crash is due to inconsistencies or other incompatibilities among R/3, the operating system, the database, and the network. The system log can point to these or other error-causing occurrences.

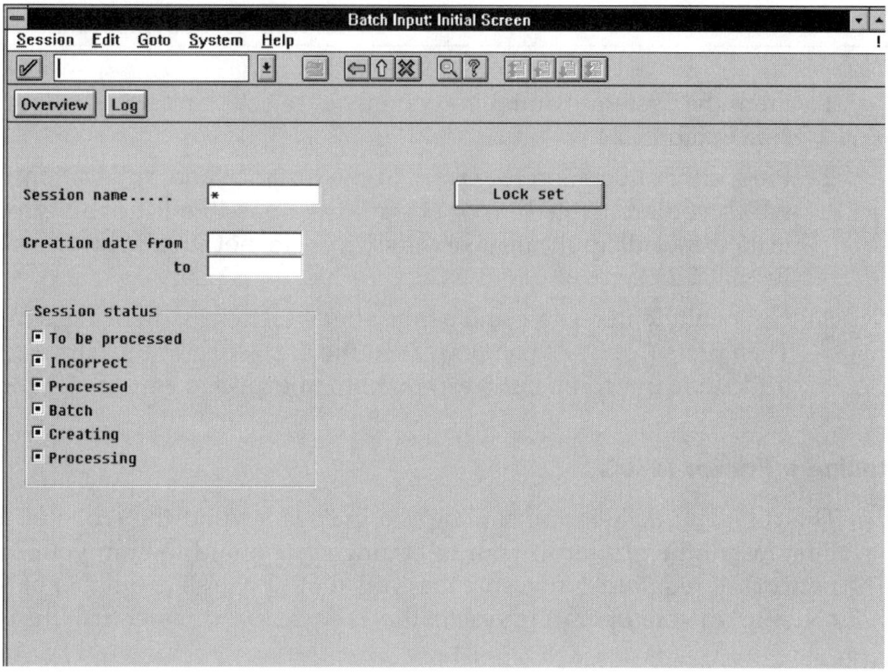

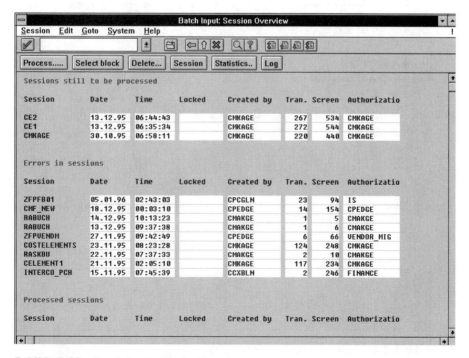

Exhibit 5.22 Batch Input: Initial Screen

Exhibit 5.23 Batch Input: Session Overview

1. From the System Administration menu, select Monitoring ➤ System log. (See Exhibit 5.24.)

2. Press either Local log (of errors in the instance and application server to which you are logged in) or Central for a possible list of all errors on all instances of all application servers. If you are not sure, press Local log. (See Exhibit 5.25.)

3. Optionally, enter a date and a time after which the system log is displayed. Then press Read system log. Read the log. Much of the data in the log is difficult to interpret, but it can point to unexpected causes of errors.

Installing a Printer in R/3

The complete details of installing a printer is beyond the scope of this text. First install the printer in your operating system and then in your local area network, if required. Make sure that you allot a page size (number of lines and columns) in your operating system that is equal to or greater than the page size

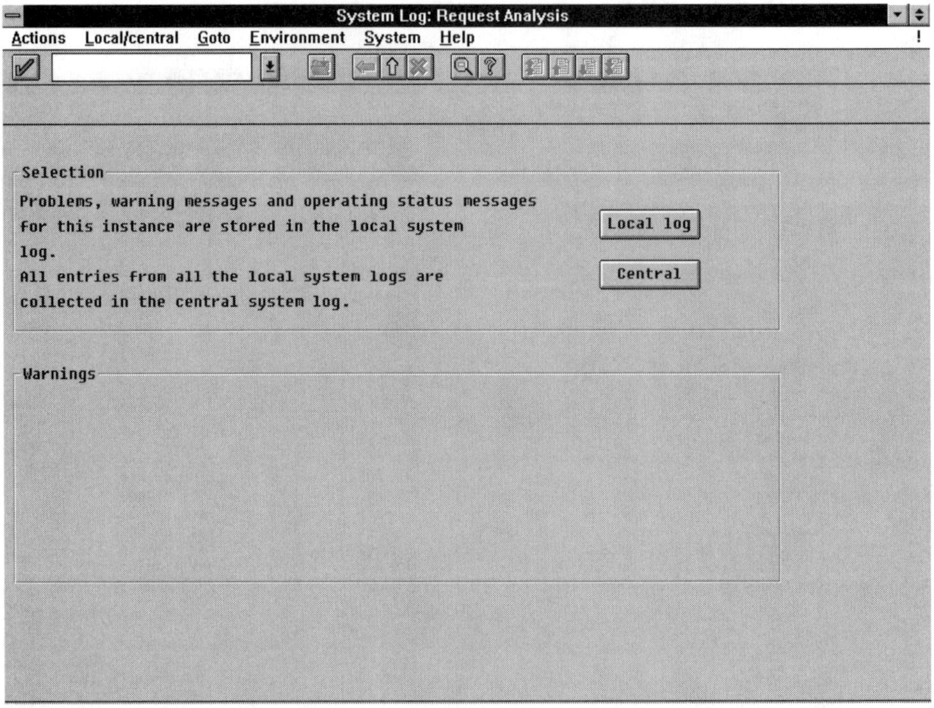

Exhibit 5.24   System Log: Request Analysis

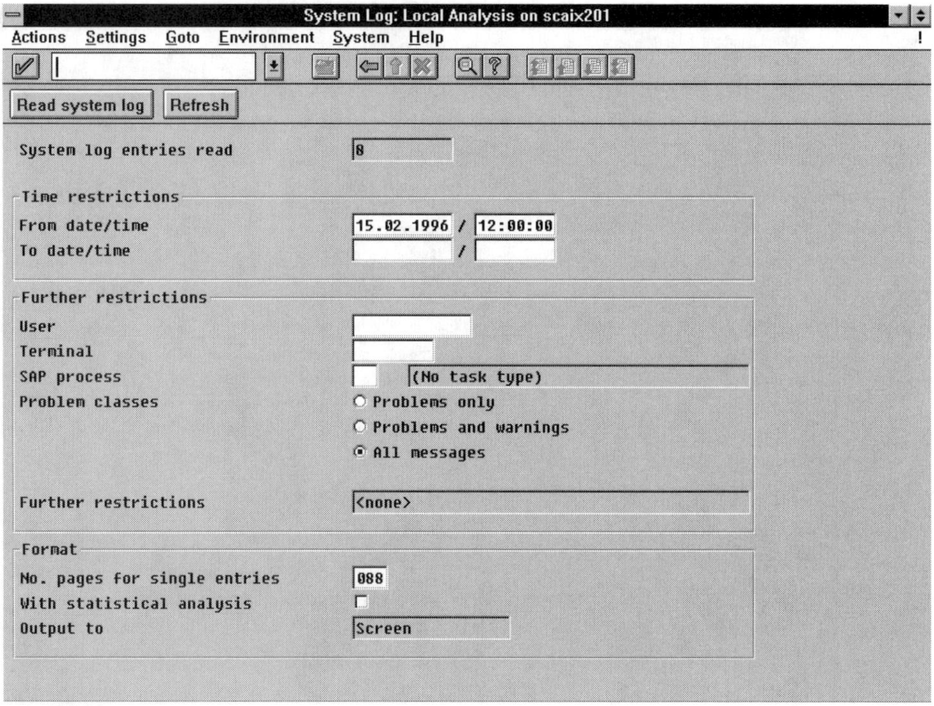

Exhibit 5.25 System Log: Local Analysis

in R/3. After this, install your printer under R/3, from the System Administration menu, select Spool ➤ Spool administration.

Finding Out Which Version You Have

To find out which R/3 version you are using, select System ➤ Status. Look in the SAP release field for the version number (1, 2, 3, etc.) and release (A, B, C, etc.). (See Exhibit 5.26.)

Updating All Tables after a Power Crash

If your electricity is cut or you have a new installation, you may have to update certain R/3 tables directly from the memory buffers. To do this, put your cursor in the command box and enter **/nSYNC.**

Other Useful Functions

You can also use the following functions to administer your system:

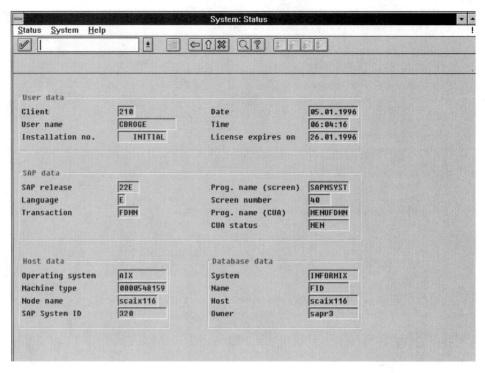

Exhibit 5.26   System Status

Function	SAP Transaction Code
Read the terminology	SE64
Read the documentation	SE61
Maintain text (translations in programs)	SE63
Read customizing documentation	SAPE
Read batch documentation	SBTU
Ping from application server to database and presentation servers	OS01
Display operating system parameters	OS02

Index